CAMBRIDGE HISTORY OF BRITAIN

Early Modern Britain

1450–1750

John Miller

Queen Mary, University of London

CAMBRIDGE
UNIVERSITY PRESS

CAMBRIDGE
UNIVERSITY PRESS

University Printing House, Cambridge CB2 8BS, United Kingdom

Cambridge University Press is part of the University of Cambridge.

It furthers the University's mission by disseminating knowledge in the pursuit of education, learning and research at the highest international levels of excellence.

www.cambridge.org
Information on this title: www.cambridge.org/9781107650138

First published 2017

Printed in the United Kingdom by TJ International Ltd. Padstow Cornwall

A catalogue record for this publication is available from the British Library

Library of Congress Cataloging-in-Publication data
NAMES: Miller, John, 1946 July 5– author.
TITLE: Early modern Britain : 1450–1750 / John Miller (Queen Mary, University of London).
DESCRIPTION: Cambridge, United Kingdom; : Cambridge University Press, 2017. | SERIES: Cambridge history of Britain; 3
IDENTIFIERS: LCCN 2016041646| ISBN 9781107015111 (hardback) | ISBN 9781107650138 (paperback)
SUBJECTS: LCSH: Great Britain – History – House of York, 1461–1485. | Great Britain – History – Tudors, 1485–1603. | Great Britain – History – Stuarts, 1603–1714. | Great Britain – History – 1714–1837. | BISAC: HISTORY / Europe / Great Britain.
Classification: LCC DA300 .M55 2017 | DDC 941.04/4–dc23
LC record available at https://lccn.loc.gov/2016041646

ISBN 978-1-107-01511-1 Hardback
ISBN 978-1-107-65013-8 Paperback

Additional resources for this publication at www.cambridge.org/CHOB-miller

Early Modern Britain, 1450–1750

This introductory textbook provides a wide-ranging survey of the political, social, cultural and economic history of early modern Britain, charting the gradual integration of the four kingdoms, from the Wars of the Roses to the formation of 'Britain', and the aftermath of England's unions with Wales and Scotland. The only textbook at this level to cover Britain and Ireland in depth over three centuries, it offers a fully integrated British perspective, with detailed attention given to social change throughout all chapters. Featuring source textboxes, illustrations, highlighted key terms and accompanying glossary, timelines, students' questions, and annotated further reading suggestions, including key websites and links, this textbook will be an essential resource for undergraduate courses on the history of early modern Britain. A companion website includes additional primary sources and bibliographic resources.

John Miller is Emeritus Professor of History at Queen Mary, University of London. His most recent books include *After the Civil Wars* (2000) and *Cities Divided: Politics and Religion in English Provincial Towns 1660–1722* (2007).

The Cambridge History of Britain is an innovative new textbook series covering the whole of British history from the breakdown of Roman power to the present day. The series is aimed at first-year undergraduates and above and volumes in the series will serve both as indispensable works of synthesis and as original interpretations of Britain's past. Each volume will offer an accessible survey of political, social, cultural and economic history, charting the changing shape of Britain as a result of the gradual integration of the four kingdoms and Britain's increasing interaction and exchange with Europe and the wider world. Each volume will also feature boxes, illustrations, maps, timelines and guides to further reading as well as a companion website with further primary source and illustrative materials.

VOLUMES IN THE SERIES

Contents

Figures

Tables

Maps

Boxes

Preface

The early modern period in Britain and Ireland does not have an immediately recognisable identity. There were substantial differences of language, society and culture between England, Scotland, Ireland and Wales. Whereas the medieval period can be described as 'feudal' and the nineteenth century as 'industrial', there is no obvious label for the period in between. One can think of a 'typical' late medieval English nobleman – say, Warwick the Kingmaker – and a 'typical' early eighteenth-century Whig grandee – the Duke of Newcastle – but not a 'typical' seventeenth-century peer. Late medieval noblemen mostly lived in fortified castles – the last, Kenilworth, was built early in Elizabeth's reign; eighteenth-century plutocrats built great unfortified country houses, like William Conolly's Palladian palace at Castletown. The early modern period was clearly an age of transition; the aim of this book is to analyse the nature and causes of that transition, an aspiration which may tempt the historian to treat the period as one of 'modernisation'. Modernisation implies 'progress'; both terms imply a movement from the primitive to the modern and, as such, a 'good thing'.

The search for the modern and modernity is in many ways a variation on the old theme of the Whig interpretation of history. As the victors in the partisan struggles of the late seventeenth and early eighteenth centuries, Whig historians depicted the triumph of Whig values as both desirable and inevitable. The nineteenth-century British constitution was (they said) based on religious liberty, parliamentary monarchy and the rule of law, which allowed for change without the bloodshed and upheaval experienced by less fortunate nations (like the French). God had guided the English to throw off the yoke of the Catholic Church and read and interpret the Bible for themselves. The Tudors tamed the nobility, opening the way for the rise of the gentry and ultimately the middle class. Within Parliament the House of Commons became increasingly assertive, demanding freedom of speech and using its power to grant taxation to extort concessions from the Crown. Charles I's refusal to recognise this shift of power led inevitably to the civil wars, after which the monarchy was only a shadow of its former self, like the French monarchy, restored in 1815 'in the baggage train of the Allies'. The way was open to the glories of the Victorian constitution.

The narrative is a familiar one but it is riddled with problems. First, between the sixteenth and nineteenth centuries it changes from an English to a British narrative, implying English dominance over Scotland and Ireland. But the only time the English fully conquered the other two kingdoms was in the 1650s. Scotland was joined to England in 1707 by a treaty which many, perhaps most, Scots came to see as advantageous. The Irish Parliament became notably more assertive from the 1690s and the Union of 1800 created an intractable problem for the British government for more than a century afterwards. Second, Protestants talked loudly of liberty, by which they meant the liberty to impose their understanding of religious truth not only on Catholics but also on misguided Protestants. Third, far from being generally welcomed, Protestantism had to be forced on the English people, many of whom cherished those elements of the Prayer Book which raised echoes of the Catholic past. Fourth, the Tudors tamed the nobility in the sense of destroying their capacity for autonomous military action, but the nobility (like so many European nobilities) changed from a territorial to a service nobility, dominating the government and the upper ranks of the army under the Georges. Nobility and gentry were never separate classes but formed different strata within a single landed elite. New nobles were recruited (mostly) from among the gentry; the younger sons of the peerage fell back into the gentry. As for the middle class, its most successful members were always rising. Merchants and bankers in the eighteenth century and industrialists in the nineteenth bought land and built country houses. Peers continued to play a major role in county government until the creation of county councils in the 1880s and peers continued to serve as prime ministers into the twentieth century.

This brings us to the relationship of Crown and Parliament. The Commons began to demand free speech under Elizabeth because she tried to prevent its members from discussing the matters that were most important to them: her marriage, the succession and the Church. Both James I and Charles I came to believe that the Commons were being misled by a group of 'popular' MPs who challenged the Crown's lawful authority. But the Commons were driven not by ambition but by fear that the two kings planned to dispense with Parliament and rule as absolute monarchs. The Commons tried to use the power of the purse and failed: when they refused to grant taxes Charles I raised the money in other ways. In the 1630s he extended his use of non-parliamentary taxation, meeting with little serious resistance in England. Very different revolts in Scotland and Ireland led to the English civil war. The burdens of that war and Parliament's authoritarian and intolerant rule led to a formidable Royalist backlash: when Charles II was restored Parliament enhanced his power, to enable him to deal with threats of revolution from below. In the early 1680s Charles established a quasi-absolute monarchy in both England and Scotland, but James II's insistence on promoting Catholicism led to his expulsion in 1688. In all these developments from the 1630s to the 1680s chance and luck, or particular conjunctures of events, played their part, from Charles I's decision to impose an English Prayer Book on Scotland to the 'Protestant wind' that blew William III to Brixham in 1688. Even after the Revolution of 1688–9 the end of the House of Stuart was far from inevitable: it still seemed likely that Anne would produce a Protestant heir.

Historians often warn of the dangers of teleology: to read history backwards from what happened and assume that it was bound to happen, especially if the author assumes that what happened was a good thing. In the words of the splendidly comic description of Mary I's reign in *1066 and all that*, 'Broody Mary ... was a bad thing, because England is bound to be C of E so all the executions were wasted'. One sees a similar approach in the study of intellectual history, in discussions of the 'age of reason'. Scholars devote much attention to challenges to the churches and revealed religion, while ignoring new surges of evangelical enthusiasm. The repeal of the witchcraft laws in 1736 did not mean the end of belief in witches or the supernatural. Christians, including clergymen, reconciled their faith with advances in scientific understanding by seeing them as evidence of God's omnipotence. It is a truism that history tends to be written by the victors, but that is no reason to ignore the losers. A distinguished historian dismissed Jacobites as 'political troglodytes', but they had many supporters (especially in Scotland) and came close to success in both 1715 and 1745. The British government tried to destroy the Highland clans, leaving only the empty husk of a fashion for tartan. In both Wales and Ireland Celtic societies continued to function hidden from the view and understanding of the English-speaking elite.

One of my aims in this book, then, is to consider the losers as well as the winners, to take them seriously, and so rescue them from what E.P. Thompson called 'the massive condescension of posterity'. I have three other major objectives. The first is to produce a work of genuine British (and Irish) or 'three-kingdoms' history: not just a study of England with occasional references to Scotland and Ireland. Second, the approach is predominantly thematic rather than narrative. I am not one of those who belittle narrative history: good narrative history requires a thorough grasp of detail and often an ability to weave together several stories at once. I started my career working on high politics under Charles II and James II, but teaching a course on 'English Society 1580–1720' made me increasingly interested in social history and led to a bottom-up study of government under Charles II and a book on politics and religion in provincial towns. I taught 'English Society' thematically, a process I likened to placing a series of illustrated transparent sheets one on top of the other, building up a fuller and fuller picture. I am using a similar approach in this book, enabling students to understand large changes over a long period.

My third objective is to reassess the significance of the upheavals of the mid seventeenth century. For decades the most important concern of seventeenth-century historians seemed to be to explain the origins of the civil war. Most started with a Whig political narrative based on the early Stuarts' difficulties with the English Parliament and grafted on to it an analysis based on social change, particularly the decline of the nobility and the rise of the gentry. Despite much effort and no little acrimony it proved impossible to demonstrate that these developments actually contributed to the taking of sides or the outbreak of the civil war (or indeed that the nobility and gentry were different classes). Moreover, this social analysis was confined to England, and a thorough re-examination of the politics of 1637–42 showed that events in Scotland and Ireland were crucial in bringing about civil war. Much less was written about the consequences of civil war and what there was usually rested on the assumption that such major upheavals must have had major consequences and that the regicide must have fatally undermined the monarchy. This reflected another assumption, that the English people must have supported Parliament, which stood for the interests of the people and the godly, not the king and the nobility. I taught courses on the civil war and Republic for many years and became more and more aware, first, of the extent of popular involvement in the civil war and popular awareness of the issues, and, second, that the English people were deeply divided between supporters of the two sides. In other words, there was both a radical (Whig and Nonconformist) legacy of the civil war and a conservative (Tory and Anglican) legacy, whose impact was very familiar to historians of the politics of 1660–1714. Historians were also coming to appreciate popular awareness of politics before 1640, but this awareness was much greater after 1660, reaching a peak under Anne. My final chapter highlights the importance of popular politics and the emergence of an informed and deeply partisan public as a result of the civil wars.

This book is the product of over forty years' experience of teaching students at London and Cambridge universities, ranging from first-year undergraduates to doctoral students. It particularly reflects my experience of teaching first-year and American year-abroad students, who often had little or no prior knowledge of the period but mostly proved quick learners, provided they were given the necessary basic information. Because it covers three centuries the information is often stripped down to a minimum, but supplemented by links to other material. I have tried to make the book user-friendly, divided into small sections which make it easier for students to navigate their way through it and to focus on what is useful for them. At the end of each chapter is a 'summary', a few key points designed to show the bigger picture; these summaries can be used individually or to follow themes further. Terms which may be unfamiliar are explained in the Glossary and printed in bold in the text. The volume contains other illustrative material: text in 'boxes', images, maps and tables. There will also be a website where further material can be accessed.

Acknowledgements

I should like to thank those who have helped in the production of this book, notably Rosemary Crawley and Sarah Turner, for their efficiency and patience. I should also like to thank colleagues who provided information and answered questions, and in particular Professor Jim Bolton and Dr Laura Stewart for their detailed advice on late medieval England and on sixteenth- and early seventeenth-century Scotland respectively.

Note on the Text

In the period covered by the book the official name of the Scottish royal house changed from 'Stewart' to 'Stuart', because James VI adopted a 'French' spelling. Also, choosing whether to call Northern Ireland's second city 'Derry' or 'Londonderry' can be seen as evidence of Catholic or Protestant loyalties. I have followed the practice of some Irish historians in using 'Derry' for the city and 'Londonderry' for the county, on the grounds that the county was named 'Londonderry' during the Ulster Plantation, by which time the city had been called 'Derry' for centuries.

Prologue: Kent, 1450

In early 1450 South East England was seething with discontent. English rule over large areas of France, which had endured for centuries, was unravelling at alarming speed, raising the prospect of French coastal raids and even invasion. Henry VI's government seemed to lack the competence or the will to stem the tide. Those around the King seemed more concerned to pursue personal feuds and to extort money, and the King seemed unable to restrain them. These alleged 'traitors' and extortioners were widely known and there were many calls for them to be brought to justice. As the King failed to act, people took matters into their own hands. In January 1450 Adam Moleyns, Bishop of Chichester and lord privy seal, went to Portsmouth to pay some of what was owing to seamen and soldiers. They accused him of trying to cheat them, 'fell on him and there killed him'. In April the most hated of the King's advisers, the Duke of Suffolk, was impeached by the Commons in Parliament, who accused him of extortion, embezzlement and helping the French King to reconquer Normandy. The King declared that on the last charge Suffolk had no case to answer, and that as punishment for his other alleged offences he should be banished for five years. Londoners attacked Suffolk's retinue as he left. He got safely on board a ship, but it was intercepted by another, the *Nicholas of the Tower*, whose crew seized him and brought him into Dover 'and there upon the ship's side struck off his head and after laid the body with the head upon the land and then departed again to the sea'. As a contemporary poet savagely exulted: 'Such a pain pricked him [Suffolk] he asked [for] a confessor./ Nicolas said, "I am ready thy confessor to be."/ He was holden so that he ne[ver] passed that hour.' In June another of the King's close associates, William Ayscough, Bishop of Salisbury, was dragged from the altar of the abbey church at Edington, Wiltshire, where he had been saying Mass. 'And then,' wrote a chronicler, 'they led him up unto a hill there beside, and there they slew him horribly, their father and their bishop, and spoiled him unto the naked skin and rent his bloody shirt into pieces and bore that away with them … and made boast of their wickedness.' The chronicler added that Moleyns and Ayscough 'were held [to be] wonder[fully] covetous men and evil beloved among the common people'. Together with Suffolk they were suspected of complicity in the death of the King's uncle, the Duke of Gloucester, in 1447.

Discontent was particularly rife in Kent and Sussex. They were vulnerable to French attack and Kent had suffered at the hands of Suffolk's associates, notably Lord Saye and Sele and his son-in-law, William Crowmer, an exceptionally unpopular sheriff. Crowmer's conduct was resented by the poor and those involved in the middling levels of county government, yeomen farmers and substantial craftsmen, used to shouldering the burdens of public office and likely to have some understanding of the law. Such men would know of the Commons' attempts to call Suffolk to account and of the King's abject failure to restrain his servants. They were also alarmed at rumours that, after the killing of Suffolk, the King had threatened in revenge to reduce Kent to a 'wild forest'. There had been a plan in January to march on London and present a petition to the King, with a list of those they believed should be beheaded. In the second half of May news of a similar plan spread rapidly. It attracted significant support among the landed gentry, but the prime movers were commoners of middling and lower status. They did not seek a gentleman to lead them, but elected as their captain a mysterious individual called Jack Cade. No-one knew where he came from: some said he was Irish. Sometimes he called himself John Mortimer, implying kinship with the Duke of York, whom the King saw as a possible rival for the throne. Whoever he was, Cade must have possessed charisma and at times affected the style of a gentleman and issued 'proclamations' in the King's name: the insurgents insisted that they were loyal to the King, and urged him to dismiss his 'evil counsellors', and rely on nobles currently out of favour, including the dukes of York and Norfolk and 'all the earls and barons of this land'. They concluded with specifically Kentish grievances.

The uprising spread and by 11 June the rebels were camped on Blackheath, south east of London. The King rejected their demands and planned to send a force to drive them away, but when it arrived it found that the rebels had withdrawn. The King sent some knights and gentlemen to punish them, which proved a mistake. Sir Humphrey Stafford (the 'manliest man' in England) and his brother William were ambushed and they and most of their followers were killed: Cade made a point of wearing some of Sir Humphrey's martial insignia. Meanwhile, Lords Savage and Dudley exacted reprisals, killing, burning and plundering, which strengthened fears that Kent could become a 'wild forest'. If anger at their misdeeds added to the rebels' determination, the defeat of the Staffords added to their self-confidence. They marched again on London, sending to the people of Essex to join them.

By now there was disaffection among the King's retainers. Many sympathised with the rebels' call for justice. The King, as a conciliatory gesture, sent Saye and Sele to the Tower, where he would be safe. The King's self-confidence evaporated and he left London for Kenilworth. His departure and the approach of Cade's forces met with mixed reactions in London. Some, particularly the mayor and aldermen, were deeply alarmed. However, many ordinary Londoners shared the rebels' aspirations and demands for justice. Cade and his men took up quarters in Southwark, while a large force from Essex encamped at Mile End and outside Aldgate. When some Kentish men began looting, Cade issued a 'proclamation' against this, but he could not control his men and he himself looted on a large scale: he eventually needed a barge to transport all that he had accumulated. On 3 July Cade and his followers crossed London Bridge into the City: Cade cut the ropes on the drawbridge at the City end to ensure that it could not be raised against them. His men, according to one chronicler, 'entered into the City of London as men that had been half beside their wit[s]; and in that furyness they went, as they said, for the common weal of the realm of England' and proceeded to burn, loot and kill; some Londoners joined them. They plundered Philip Malpas, a rich merchant and alderman, of 'much money, both of silver and gold, the value of a notable sum, and in special of merchandise, as of tin, wood, madder and alum, with great quantity of woollen cloth and many rich jewels', as well as feather beds and other household stuff.

Cade tried to focus on the rebels' political programme, but matters threatened to get out of hand: it did not help that he rode through the streets brandishing a drawn sword.

Before leaving London, the King had issued a commission of **oyer and terminer**, setting up a special court to hear charges against those accused of misdeeds. Most members of the commission had left London, as had most of those accused, but three members assembled at the Guildhall on 3 and 4 July. They tried to proceed in a judicial manner, but were overawed by Cade and his men. Saye and Sele was brought from the Tower. He demanded to be tried by his **peers**, 'but the Kentishmen would not suffer that'. He was examined on 'divers treasons' 'of which he acknowledged the death of … the duke of Gloucester'. Then the rebels took him from the Guildhall to Cheapside, where they cut off his head. This might seem a lawless act, but traditionally anyone who seized an outlaw was entitled to behead him and claim a reward; in the rebels' eyes Saye and Sele and his like might not formally be outlawed, but they were 'traitors', which was much the same thing. Meanwhile, Crowmer was beheaded at Mile End, without the pretence of a trial. The crowd placed their heads on poles and carried them around 'and at divers places of the City put them together causing the one to kiss the other'. Saye's body 'was drawn naked at a horse's tail upon the pavement so that the flesh cleaved to the stones'. Saye and Crowmer were at least charged with serious offences, but others were beheaded for no obvious reason: 'this captain in his tyranny slew many men without any judgment and would not suffer them to be shriven' (to make their peace with God before they died). Plundering became increasingly indiscriminate and after two days much of the citizens' goodwill towards the rebels had evaporated, especially after they broke open two gaols, releasing the prisoners. Some rich citizens paid Cade's men not to attack their houses. On the evening of 5 July the Londoners counter-attacked, attempting to seize control of London Bridge. The battle raged all night and it was said that hundreds were killed. It ended when Cade set fire to the drawbridge and withdrew. Two days later the rebels were offered a general pardon, which most accepted: even Cade took out a pardon in the name of John Mortimer, which was soon declared invalid, on the grounds that Mortimer was not his real name. A price was put on his head and he was captured, mortally wounded, and brought to London, where his corpse was dragged through the City and then decapitated and quartered. The survivors among those who had tyrannised over Kent used the law, and brute force, to punish their enemies. The programme of reform remained unfulfilled.

Cade's rising was often bracketed with the Peasants' Revolt of 1381 as terrible examples of popular fury designed to turn the social order upside-down: Charles I in 1642 invoked Cade's name together with Wat Tyler's when warning of a 'dark equal chaos of confusion'. There were similarities between the two revolts, including the gatherings at Blackheath and Mile End and eruptions of horrific violence. But there were also differences. Peasant grievances against landlords drove the rebels in 1381 and Tyler was definitely a peasant figure. Cade was socially more ambiguous, with his trappings of gentility and hints at semi-royal status: the use of the name Mortimer, the proclamations in the King's name, the attempt to enter the City preceded by a sword of state. Cade's rebels had a political programme, focused on the abuse of power under an inadequate King. This programme was widely supported by people from all levels of society: similar complaints were made – and acted on – in Parliament. 1450 could be seen as the nadir of the late medieval English monarchy, with the loss of its French lands and a major rebellion. Disturbances were not confined to the South East. The crowd which killed Bishop Ayscough went on to plunder his estates and treasure. His palace was attacked and estate records were destroyed. There were also attacks on the bishops of Wells, Lichfield and Norwich, and the Bishop of Winchester's palace was sacked. There were months of rioting at Sherborne, Dorset, where there was a long-running feud between the town and the abbey. Most of the bishops and abbots who were attacked were linked in some way with Suffolk, and some lesser clergy were murdered – in one case, by his own parishioners. And all this occurred in the South of England, supposedly the most advanced, orderly and governed region of Britain and Ireland. Clearly that order and governance were fragile.

SUGGESTIONS FOR FURTHER READING

There is a useful account of the rebellion in R.A. Griffiths, *The Reign of Henry VI* (Stroud, 1998), Chapter 21. The fullest account is by I.M.W. Harvey, *Jack Cade's Rebellion of 1450* (Oxford, 1991). See also I.M.W. Harvey, 'Was There Popular Politics in Fifteenth-Century England?', in R.H. Britnell and A.J. Pollard (eds.), *The Macfarlane Legacy* (Stroud, 1995).

1 Kings, Lords and Peoples

TIMELINE

1171	Start of Henry II's conquest of Ireland, creation of Lordship of Ireland
1263	Collapse of Norse power over Western Isles
1280s	Edward I defeats Welsh princes, establishes Principality, begins to build castles
1286	Edward I claims Scottish throne (start of wars of independence)
1314	Scots defeat English at Bannockburn
1320	Declaration of Arbroath (declaration of Scottish independence)
1357	English recognise David II as King of Scotland; end of wars of independence
1400–9	Glyn Dŵr's rebellion
1415	Agincourt
1422	Henry V succeeded by Henry VI
1452	James II murders the Earl of Douglas
1453	English driven out of France; fall of Byzantium
1469	Scots acquire Shetland from Norsemen

Introduction

The first two chapters will consider the societies and governance of England, Scotland, Ireland and Wales in about 1450. Chapter 1 will focus on the workings of power and law, with particular emphasis on kings and their more powerful subjects. Chapter 2 will consider the economy – above all the relationship between landlords and peasants – together with the lower levels of government and the functioning of communities, concluding with a discussion of 'mental worlds', above all religion and the spirit world. Both chapters emphasise diversity, which derived from ethnic and linguistic differences and the fundamental contrast between highland and lowland societies. Highland regions tended to be sparsely populated, dependent primarily on pastoral farming, with few towns and limited trade. Lowland regions focused more on arable farming, with larger villages, significant towns, and more developed manufactures and trade. In social and cultural terms the most striking contrasts were those between Celtic and what I shall very crudely describe as 'feudal' societies and governments, such as those of England and Lowland Scotland. We shall consider the development of systems of law and parliaments, which became the mechanisms through which kings could negotiate with their more powerful subjects, levy taxes and make laws. We shall also consider the ways in which 'feudalism' changed, in terms of the relationships between lord and peasant, between greater and lesser lords, and between lords and the king, concluding with a discussion of the supposedly degenerate 'bastard' feudalism found in England by the mid fifteenth century.

Ethnicity and Language

The most widespread and coherent groups of people were those of Celtic origin, ranging from Cornwall in the extreme South West of England, through Wales and Ireland to the Highlands and Islands of Scotland, with small pockets in Cumbria, in the far north-west of England, and across the 'border' in South-West Scotland. They spoke a variety of Celtic languages; Irish and Scottish Gaelic formed the largest linguistic bloc, and there were many links between Scots and Irish Gaelic families. The Celtic peoples were very conscious that they were the most ancient inhabitants of the British Isles. The Welsh referred to themselves as 'Britons', and claimed to be descended from either Brutus or the Trojans; they dismissed the English as 'Saxons' – barbarous newcomers lacking the ancient and distinguished lineage of the Welsh princes. Both Welsh and Gaelic Irish chiefs stressed their long pedigrees and claimed to derive their authority, their right to rule, in part, from their association with holy places in the landscape from which they sprang.

Although both Wales and Ireland had suffered invasions, these left relatively little lasting impression. The Romans had reached Wales, but not Ireland; the Vikings had established significant settlements in Ireland, including Dublin, but most were trading posts around the coast and the Vikings had shown little inclination to penetrate into the hills, bogs and forests of the interior. By contrast both England and Scotland underwent a series of invasions or migrations. England was invaded by the Romans, followed by a variety of Germanic and Nordic peoples, culminating in the Normans in 1066. From this mixture of linguistic influences emerged the English language, which by 1450 was spoken throughout almost all of England (apart from parts of Cornwall, plus a scattering of Welsh in the counties adjacent to Wales). However, the 'English' that was so widely spoken had many local variations and dialects, so that northerners found it difficult to make themselves understood in the South East. As for Scotland, apart from those of Celtic origin there were Norsemen in the Western and Northern Isles and parts of the West Coast, while Angles (Germanic in origin), who settled in the Lothians, brought with them a language that became Scots. This had developed in Northumbria from the seventh century and had similarities to English; in the fifteenth century Scotsmen and northern Englishmen could more or less understand one another, although there were many Scots words which were not found in English, such as 'anent' (about or concerning) and 'stent' (a tax). Despite Scotland's linguistic diversity (with Scots, Gaelic and Norse) by 1057 all the ethnic groups within Scotland (except the Norsemen) professed some sort of allegiance to the King; England had been governed as a single kingdom since well before 1066, but the coming of the Normans made French the language of the elite for centuries; it also became the language of law and government, along with Latin, which was also the language of the Church and of intellectuals throughout Europe. Legal records in England were kept in a mixture of Law French and Latin until the eighteenth century.

Celtic Societies

Although there were differences between the main Celtic societies of Wales, Gaelic Ireland and Highland Scotland, there were also strong similarities.

The Clan

Clans were not unknown in England (see Box 1.1, English Clans) but in general they were found in Celtic societies, which were formed of an agglomeration of tribal or family units, given their identity by descent from an (often mythical) common ancestor. The element of family was emphasised by their names, usually **patronymics** (meaning 'son of'). These took the form of adding an 's' to a forename in Wales (Jones, Edwards), the use of 'O' (O'Neill, O'Donnell) in Ireland, or 'Mac' in both Ireland and Scotland: thus the Scottish Macdonalds (or Clan Donald) were related to the Macdonnells of Ulster; Irishmen of English descent referred disparagingly to the 'Os and Macs'. (The use of patronymics was not confined to Celtic societies: they were found in Nordic societies and in Russia and the Normans added 'Fitz' (*fils*, or son of), as in the great Anglo-Irish family, the Fitzgeralds.) The antiquity of the lineages of the tribes (or smaller sub-tribes or **septs**) was emphasised by their identification with ancient holy places. Chiefs were inaugurated or proclaimed at holy stones (a tradition perpetuated in Scotland by placing the Stone of Scone under the throne at the King's coronation). The chiefs of the greatest of the Irish clans, the O'Neills, were traditionally inaugurated at the Stone of Tullaghoge, Co. Tyrone, a large boulder with three slabs around it, arranged to resemble a throne. In 1602, when Hugh O'Neill, Earl of Tyrone, had been defeated and was on the run, the English military commander sought to undermine his standing among his clansmen by smashing the sacred stone. (See Figure 1.1, Tullaghoge Fort and the O'Neill Inauguration Chair, by English Cartographer Richard Bartlett, 1602, and Figure 1.2, Sketch of O'Neill Inauguration, by Richard Bartlett, 1602.)

BOX 1.1: **English Clans**

Clans were found in a few areas near the Scottish border, in north Cumbria and Northumberland, notably Upper Tynedale, Redesdale and Coquetdale. In 1310 the North was repeatedly ravaged by Scottish raiders. Many inhabitants of the dales fled south with their cattle, leaving too few men to man the border. Edward III set out to repopulate the dales with 'hobilers', lightly armed horsemen, mounted on fell ponies, similar to Irish **kerne**. Many were recruited from existing families, including Milburns, Robsons and Charltons, still common Northumbrian names; they became known as the 'surnames'. As their main function was to provide armed men, they were required to divide their land between their sons. Families lived close together, migrated to summer pastures together, and defended one another. Within each surname there were several family groups, each with a 'heidsman' who stood surety for the behaviour of his followers, but might also protect them against the law. At first they supported themselves by farming – land was plentiful after the Black Death – but as the population grew and holdings were subdivided they survived by cattle **reiving**. By the sixteenth century they were seen as a lawless menace and they were suppressed when Elizabeth's government refused to protect them against the Scots.

See R. Robson, *The English Highland Clans: Tudor Responses to a Medieval Problem* (Edinburgh, 1989).

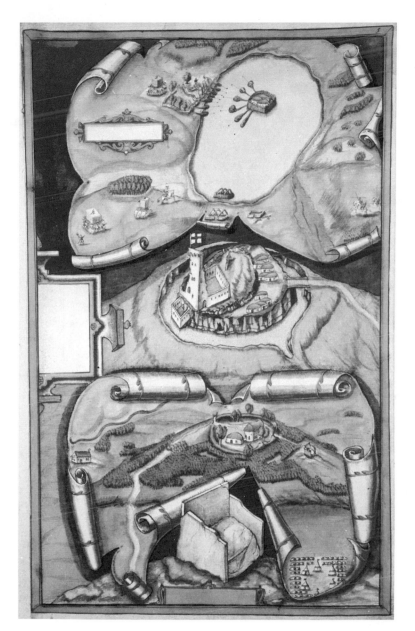

Figures 1.1 & 1.2 The chair consisted of three slabs arranged around a boulder, known as the king's stone, which was said to have been blessed by St Patrick. The pen and ink drawing of the inauguration is taken from a map of Ulster, of which one small part is occupied by the drawing, with the caption 'Tullogh oge. On this hill the Irish create their O'Neill.' In the inauguration the heads of two subaltern septs threw a shoe over the new chief's head and presented a rod of office. Mountjoy destroyed the stone in 1602. See E. FitzPatrick, 'An Tulach Tinóil: Gathering-Sites and Meeting Culture in Gaelic Lordships', *History Ireland* 9, Part 1 (2001), 23.

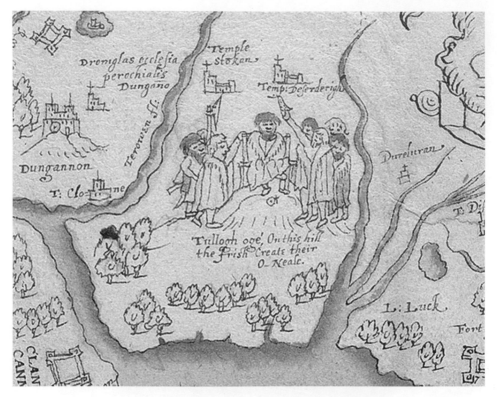

Figures 1.1 & 1.2 (Cont.)

An Oral Society

Many of these places derived their sacred character from pagan times and the clans traced their lineage back through the centuries, to long before the development of written records. Knowledge of the clan's lineage and triumphs was celebrated and transmitted by poets, known in Wales as **bards**. Oral tradition gave ample opportunities for invention, so genealogies could become longer and more fictitious. This happened in non-Celtic societies as well, but the pre-eminence of poets and oral transmission over scribes and written records gave greater opportunities for re-invention. Poets also played a key role in the transmission of historical knowledge and cultural values and were often lodged honourably in chiefs' houses: in Ireland there were specialist clans of poets. Apart from maintaining links with the past, it was the poets' task to praise the current chief, to celebrate his handsome appearance and his achievements – the battles he had won, the foes he had slain, and the booty he had taken. By the fifteenth century there were also written histories, but these tended to be simple 'annals' – bald chronological records of battles and other events, which could be embellished by the poets.

Succession

Celtic society was organised for war. If there was not a perpetual conflict of all against all, there was a constant need for military preparedness. The primary function of the chief was to lead his clansmen in war, so it was vital that he should be a militarily competent adult. In Anglo-Norman England the succession to the Crown and to landed estates was generally governed by **primogeniture**: the eldest son would inherit and his younger brothers had to find careers where they could. However, in certain regions and among poorer landholders the equal division of land among brothers was common. It was also the norm in Gaelic Ireland, which meant that peasant holdings were generally small. But among the great English landed families primogeniture was designed to secure an orderly succession and to keep the kingdom or the estate together in its entirety. It did not always work, for two reasons. First, the succession might be challenged by a younger brother or another male relative. Second, the eldest son might be a child at the time of inheritance or, worse still, an incapable adult. Royal minorities, in Scotland and England, were often a time of weak rule and factionalism, but loyalty to the monarchy was usually sufficient to keep the ruling royal house in possession. Celtic clans could not afford the luxury of a child or a weakling. The succession to an ailing chief could lead to bitter power struggles among the senior subordinate **chieftains**, often involving extreme brutality and treachery, made worse by the intervention of hostile clans and, occasionally, the English authorities in Dublin. With luck, the conflict would end with a successor tough and cunning enough to hold on to power, but often the conflict left a legacy of bitterness which destabilised the clan for many years. To reduce this risk, the greater clans often tried to arrange that a designated successor, or **tanist**, should be acknowledged in the old chief's lifetime. However, sometimes a challenger to the tanist came forward and the usual power struggle ensued.

In England the emphasis on primogeniture made the heir's legitimacy of paramount importance. **Canon law**, the law of the Church, laid down detailed rules and procedures about marriage, to maintain its sanctity and prevent fornication, incest or bigamy. Celtic attitudes towards marriage and legitimacy were more casual. Gaelic Ireland had not embraced the principle of clerical celibacy; as we shall see, there were not only married priests and bishops but even priestly dynasties. As Irish clans did not observe primogeniture, there was a limited incentive to ensure the legitimacy of a challenger for the chiefdom, provided that he was acknowledged by the old chief as his son, which would show that he was by blood a member of the clan. Perhaps the most striking example of this came when Conn O'Neill, the first of that clan to hold the earldom of Tyrone, acknowledged as his heir Matthew, later Baron of Dungannon, whose mother was the wife of a blacksmith called Kelly from Dundalk.

Internal Cohesion

At the heart of a clan's cohesion lay a powerful sense of family loyalty, at the level of the greater clan and its chief, and the subordinate septs and their chieftains. However, disputes often emerge in even the best-regulated families: more than a sense of shared lineage was needed to keep them together. The chief was expected to dispense hospitality. In the Western Highlands and Islands of Scotland much of clan life revolved around food. The peasants' task was to produce grain for the chief's granaries. In return the chief would provide great feasts which could last for days; in leaner times he was expected to ensure that his peasants did not starve. This illustrates the reciprocal obligations which, in theory, lay at the heart of the relationship between chief and clansman. This was obviously not a relationship between equals, and different clansmen performed different functions: the peasants' primary task was to cultivate the soil and raise cattle. Others had more specialised roles: priests, poets, lawyers and soldiers. At the heart of the relationship between chief and clansman was the provision of protection in return for service: the peasants needed to be able to grow food without molestation by other clans, but they also needed protection against the abuse of power by the more powerful members of their own clan. The lord, with the advice of his lawyers, was expected to act as an arbiter, to resolve disputes and provide recompense for wrongs suffered. (See below, under 'Law'.)

It is difficult to tell how far clan chiefs lived up to these ideals. Much of what happened within a clan left no trace in written records. In Gaelic Ireland there are signs of change over time. Before the first English conquest of Ireland in the twelfth century there seems to have been an element of election in the choice of chiefs; by the fifteenth century the clansmen were merely invited to endorse and acclaim decisions made, or fought out, elsewhere. Perhaps the most significant change was that, from the fourteenth century, Irish lords, instead of relying on their own peasants, built up mercenary armies. These consisted of **galloglass** and household **kerne** (as distinct from wood kerne, or bandits). Galloglass were originally recruited in Scotland or Scandinavia and had a fearsome reputation: foot soldiers who wore long mail coats and carried heavy swords or battle axes. Kerne were light horsemen, with small shields and no stirrups, used for cattle raiding and forcing lesser chieftains to pay tribute. The development of mercenary armies weakened the reciprocal ties between chief and clansmen. Galloglass and kerne were billeted on peasants, who were also required to pay a wide range of tributes in cattle, food and money, and provide for the chief's household, huntsmen and horses. **Freeholders**, peasants who owned their own land, could be forced to sign away some or all of it. The chief's traditional obligations towards their peasants seem to have given way to an assumption that the only justification for the peasants' existence was to enable their chief to live in the manner he expected. In 1600 Niall Garbh O'Donnell allegedly declared of his lands in Donegal 'the country … is mine … and I will use and govern it to my own pleasure … The people, they are my subjects. I will punish, exact, cut and hang, if I see occasion, where and when soever I list.'

There is some reason to doubt whether these alleged remarks were typical of the attitudes of Irish chiefs. They were reported by an English army officer in the latter stages of the bloody Nine Years War. But there is ample evidence of Irish chiefs imposing heavy burdens on their peasantry and of Celtic chiefs everywhere plundering the peasants of others. The peasants and lesser chieftains used various tactics to protect themselves. **Fosterage** – sending children to be brought up in a family of similar or higher status – established links which could prove useful. Those misused by their own chief could seek or buy the protection of another: chieftains built up followings, or **affinities**, based on their family, household, clients and tenants. Equals entered into compacts for mutual protection. Such arrangements offered the hope of security, but often proved unstable. Nevertheless, there is ample evidence throughout the seventeenth century and beyond that the Irish peasantry maintained a loyalty to their chiefs, which was perhaps instinctive rather than rational but remained strong. In much the same way, in Wales 'barons' – poor free tenants who claimed descent from princes – retained the respect of the peasantry because of their lineage.

Imprecision

Boundaries and rights were less clearly defined in Celtic than in Anglo-Norman society. This was partly a consequence of their reliance on oral tradition rather than written records, but it went deeper. Pastoral farming often involved seasonal migration to upland pastures, returning to the valleys in the winter. Settlements were impermanent and grazing grounds were defined roughly, if at all. Lowland arable land tended to be much more clearly marked out: not only field boundaries, but the strips within the fields. The right to own or hold land was spelled out in charters and title deeds, in which boundaries were carefully described. In Celtic societies landholding depended less on right than on power. If a chief could not defend his clan's lands, it lost them and there was usually nowhere to seek redress. The contrast between Celtic and Anglo-Norman attitudes towards land is highlighted by attitudes towards surveying. Systematic surveys within Ireland began with attempts to establish English **plantations**: surveys followed conquest. Moreover, for the English surveying meant measuring and drawing plans or maps; for the Irish the value of land was 'measured' by estimating roughly how many cattle or sheep it could support.

There was a similar imprecision in the drawing of frontiers. In Lowland England the boundaries of parish, town and county were usually carefully drawn: the first major survey, comprehensive if not complete, had been Domesday Book in 1086. In the upland regions, and especially in the **Marches** (borders) of Wales and Scotland, the terrain was worse and the frontiers more approximate, varying with the balance of military power on the ground in what were described euphemistically as the 'disputable lands'. In Ireland the well-defined boundaries of Dublin and other large towns soon gave way to poorly mapped countryside. The boundaries between English and Gaelic Ireland were constantly shifting, with continual raiding, plunder, tribute and truces on both sides.

Feudalism

Feudalism, as established in England in the eleventh century, had three main purposes – military, political and fiscal. It offered a means of enabling the king to mobilise armies; through the landowners, it helped maintain a level of law and order; and it provided both king and landowners with income. Theoretically all land belonged to the king. He granted the **tenure** of land – the right to hold it, but *not* ownership – to the great landholders (**tenants in chief**) in return for military service. They in turn granted the tenure of parcels of land to lesser landowners (mesne tenants) who became responsible for part of their lord's military service and also granted out tenure to lesser tenants. The land of all of these estates, great and small, was cultivated by peasants, most of whom were unfree (**serfs** or **villeins**). These paid rent to the lord in cash, in kind or in labour on the **demesne**, the land reserved by the lord for his own use; they would also be liable for other payments and had to grind their corn in the lord's mill. The power of lords over their tenants was reinforced by manorial courts, which a lord of the **manor** had the right to hold and which exercised jurisdiction over its inhabitants. Lords, including the king, also derived income from their tenants, partly from rent and partly from feudal '**incidents**'. These included an entry fine, or relief, when one tenant succeeded another, and also the right to the guardianship (**wardship**) if an heir succeeded when underage; he would also have the right to dispose of the heir in marriage. When a ward came of age he had to sue for **livery**, which normally cost half a year's income, in order to gain possession of his estates. In theory, the lord was acting in the heir's best interests; in practice, he often sold the rights to wardship and marriage to the heir's relatives. If a tenant in chief died without leaving an heir, or if his property was forfeited for felony or treason, his estate reverted (**escheated**) to the Crown.

Feudalism involved a pyramid of relationships, from the king at the top to the humblest serf at the bottom. In between there were relationships between greater and lesser landowners, supplemented by private agreements and indentures, but all were defined and written down and so, in theory, should have been enforceable in a court of law. Feudalism was in one sense a means of organising a society for war, but it also made for a structured, ordered society, in contrast with the informal, ill-defined relationships of Celtic societies, which often seemed to be determined by the caprices of chiefs. Feudalism seemed, therefore, to the rulers of South East England, Lowland Scotland and English Ireland to offer a means of bringing upland areas under control – to tie the chiefs in to more disciplined modes of government. This offered the prospect of reducing raiding from the wilder interior, but also the hope that with a more ordered society would develop towns, as centres of civility, manufactures and trade and, ultimately, a more peaceful and prosperous kingdom.

Attempts to extend feudalism to Highland Scotland, Gaelic Ireland and Wales enjoyed only limited success. Lords saw the advantages of introducing serfdom, in order to control or exploit the peasantry, but were less willing to submit to greater royal control. In Ireland during the century after the English conquest in 1169 more than half of the island was brought under English control and villages and manors were established on feudal lines, with small market towns. The fourteenth century saw the resurgence of the Gaelic chiefs, and the area under English control shrank dramatically. This often led to the disappearance of the manorial system and settled villages and towns: in 1500 there were no significant towns in Ulster, the most Gaelic province. The king might attempt to grant the chiefs their land and jurisdictions under feudal tenure, but often their acceptance of such grants made little practical difference: agreements made for temporary advantage were soon forgotten. Effective royal power depended on the king's ability to manage the wider nobility and, ultimately, on military force. (See p. 18.) In Wales, whatever happened in the towns, Welsh society continued to function in its own way. Only in the Scottish Highlands did the Crown slowly extend a measure of control.

 ## Law: Celtic Societies and England

Apart from **canon law**, which should in theory have been the same throughout Western Christendom, the laws provided mechanisms for resolving disputes, righting wrongs and punishing breaches of local by-laws and regulations. At first sight, it would seem that there were three major differences between law enforcement in Celtic societies and in England. First, in Celtic societies law was administered by private individuals, usually chiefs, and the right to exercise jurisdiction was a piece of property, which they could use as they wished, without answering to any overlord or king. In England judges and magistrates were appointed by the king and dispensed the king's justice in the king's courts. Second, in Celtic societies individual caprice could play a large part in the way cases were heard and in the choice of punishments. There was a recognised body of legal professionals, known in Ireland as **brehons**, who drew on an accepted corpus of law, passed down both orally and in writing. The brehons advised the chiefs or presided over their courts, but the chiefs could override them, especially when it came to punishments: offenders could be blinded, or have their hands or feet cut off. Chiefs also used their legal authority to protect their own interests: 'O'Neill shall have what his own judges shall award.' English law was based on a much wider and more elaborate body of *written* law, which in theory covered all ranks of people and all parts of the country, so was known as the common law. This corpus of law had evolved over the centuries, and was continually expanded or amended as a consequence of the decisions of judges, or Acts of Parliament. This common law was applied by legal professionals who had received their training in the Inns of Court in London. Third, in Celtic societies violent crime was seen as an offence of person against person. Chiefs and judges were concerned with restitution rather than punishment. In England violent crime was seen as an offence against the king's peace and God's peace and was punished as such.

It would seem that Celtic and English law enforcement were polar opposites, the former capricious and inconsistent, the latter professional and impartial. This was the picture put forward by English common lawyers, particularly in Ireland, where they claimed that English law and legal practices should be used to 'civilise' the Irish. In reality, however, English law enforcement was less impartial than the lawyers made out for four reasons.

First, there were many private and local courts, which for much of the time applied local custom. In Anglo-Norman England much 'public' justice was meted out by feudal lords and throughout the Middle Ages there were many areas (like the Marcher lordships) where the king's writ did not run: in other words, those who felt aggrieved could not take their cases to the king's courts. These ranged from manorial and town courts to **palatinates**, **liberties and franchises** (the largest of which were Cheshire and County Durham). There were also the Church courts, which handled a range of what might seem secular business, including defamation, marriage and the proving of wills.

Second, there was no single system of royal courts, but a variety, often with overlapping or competing jurisdictions. In the late Middle Ages kings appointed numerous ad hoc commissions to deal with particular problems of gentry violence or the misdeeds of royal officials, but by 1450 much of the routine business of law enforcement was conducted by justices of assize and gaol delivery, judges sent from London into the counties, to try those accused of **felonies** (serious offences). If the trials were conducted in the king's name, the initiative for prosecution could come from the king himself, from victims or their kin, or from the local community, through **presentments** (complaints of misdeeds of all kinds) by local **jurors**, particularly county **grand juries**. By 1450 many cases, including some felonies, could be settled by county magistrates, the **justices of the peace**. These were not professional lawyers, but local gentry who had often acquired some legal knowledge from attending the Inns of Court. To confuse matters further, the distinction between civil and criminal trials was often blurred: disputes over land often involved violent trespass and litigants

often pursued cases in more than one court, and ended up by accepting the mediation or arbitration of the king or a great lord. (Mediation tried to bring the parties
to agree through negotiation. In arbitration the king or lord laid down the terms of
agreement and required the parties to comply on pain of punishment.) (See Box 1.2,
Arbitration.)

BOX 1.2: **Arbitration**

This award by the Duke of Buckingham
in September 1455 shows the continued
importance of informal methods of dispute
resolution, at a time when the common law
courts were disrupted by the Wars of the
Roses. In the absence of effective justice from
the courts, landowners were thrown back on
their own resources (household and tenantry)
in their pursuit of disputes. This award reverts
back to an older tradition, concerned more
with restitution than with punishment. It
also shows striking similarities to the Scottish
blood feud, except that it rests solely on
the authority of the duke (or in his absence
his son) and does not involve the wider
community.

Settlement of divers controversies, strifes,
debates ... between Sir William Vernon, knight,
Roger Vernon, his brother, their men servants and
tenants on one side and Sir John Gresley, knight,
Nicholas his brother and their men servants and
tenants on the other.

First we award that the said Sir William and Sir
John shall be complete friends ... and each put
aside all grudges against the other and any rancour

of the heart. And neither of them shall vex, trouble
or pick a quarrel with any cousin, friend, servant,
tenant or wellwisher of the other concerning
past matters or quarrels ... And if any reason for
grudging occurs between them in the future the
party that finds himself aggrieved shall notify us
of the cause of his grudge if we are in the country
[county] or else our son Stafford in our absence ...

And for as much as it was previously awarded
that the said Sir William should pay to Anne,
formerly the wife of John Herte, who was killed at
Burton by the servants of the said Sir William, 20
marks for the soul of the said John and the relief of
the said Anne and her children, of which 17 marks
remains unpaid ... [this sum is to be paid to her by
1 August next]

Also we award that the said Sir John shall pay for
the benefit of Thomas Webbe of Shelley, tenant of
the said Sir William, who was maimed and injured
by the servants of the said Sir John, 13s 4d for a
severe wound to the head and for another serious
wound to the face 13s 4d and 6s 8d each for six
other wounds and for an injury to the thumb on his
left hand 100s [total £8 6s 8d].

Anthony Musson (with E. Powell),
Crime, Law and Society in the Later Middle Ages
(Manchester, 2009), pp. 201–2.

Third, common law courts did not always function impartially according to clear rules.
Titles to land were often far from clear: different documents could point in different directions. Lawyers were not unhappy about this. Litigation meant fees and lawyers successfully
resisted attempts to establish a land registry, which would make titles clearer and so reduce
the volume of legal business. The king's justice was not the only concern of those involved in
the legal process. Victims or their kin weighed the desire for punishment against the possibility of lasting resentment, and might forgo prosecution in return for compensation or an

apology. Jurors were expected to use their local knowledge in reaching their verdict. They placed considerable weight on the perceived moral worth of accuser and accused, and character evidence from respectable neighbours. They could bring the accused in guilty of a lesser offence, **misdemeanour** rather than **felony**, and so limit the possible punishment. And if some believed that the punishment handed down was unduly severe, they could appeal to the king for a reprieve or a pardon. In other words, the supposedly impersonal workings of the law were influenced by the community. There was also a concern for restitution and communal harmony similar to that found in Celtic communities.

The fourth reason why the common law was less impartial and impersonal than it seemed was that it was open to manipulation by powerful men. Effective royal control was needed to make the system work impartially and often that control was lacking, especially under Henry VI.

Scottish Law

Like its English counterpart, Scottish law was based on a mixture of custom and written documents, such as charters and parliamentary legislation. Much, in terms of content and procedure, was borrowed, or adapted, from English law. There was a network of law courts, operated by **sheriffs**, **burghs** and private individuals, usually substantial landowners, who possessed **heritable jurisdictions**. These local courts catered for the needs of local litigants and were staffed by officials rather than trained lawyers. Before the fifteenth century there was no legal profession equivalent to that of England. From the fifteenth century onwards, the most proficient lawyers were priests, trained in the canon or civil law in the new Scottish universities. Starting in the reign of James I (1394–1437) there were attempts to codify the 'Auld Lawes'; the first comprehensive digest of Scots law, James Dalrymple's *Institutions* (1681), drew upon a great deal of earlier research.

Academic writing on law developed long before its application in local courts. Whereas in England judges had heard cases in the provinces for centuries, this began in Scotland only in the later fifteenth century. Central supervision of justice was limited to the possibility of appeal to the king and his Privy Council. By the mid fifteenth century there were signs of the emergence of lay lawyers and growing demands for a national supreme court. Notaries public began to draw up legal documents, which brought greater certainty and precision to legal relationships. Nevertheless, for many the existing courts and the informal dispute resolution provided adequate justice. Arbitration was encouraged by the Church, as a means of maintaining charity between neighbours. In Scotland, it often took the form of the **bloodfeud**, which might suggest violence, but was also used in the resolution of non-violent disputes.

With royal justice rudimentary, it was usually easier and quicker to submit to the mediation or arbitration of a respected local lord and to promise to abide by his decision. The lord undertook to enforce his award and take care to ensure that the compensation and reconciliation were made as publicly as possible, involving the whole community. These rulings were accepted by the Crown as legally binding until the reign of James VI.

Parliament: 1. England

Parliament played a pivotal role in the governance of late medieval England. It was not part of the government, but helped to provide the resources and means of coercion that made government possible. It also increasingly became the forum through which subjects negotiated with their king. The king granted the right to hold land to his tenants in chief in return for service, and this land enabled them to build up the power to maintain order and enforce the law; the king could not impose his will in the provinces without the great landowners. The relationship between king and nobles was built on reciprocity: they served him, in war and in government, and expected three things in return. First, that he would treat them justly, respecting their property rights and mediating or arbitrating in their disputes. Second, they expected him to reward them for their service with lands, offices, places in the Church for younger sons or unmarried daughters, or the hand of a wealthy heiress. Third, they expected him to heed their advice, especially on matters important to them, such as war.

Under feudalism allegiance was conditional on fair treatment; although rebellion was risky, it was an option, and the king could not afford to alienate a substantial proportion of the nobility. In extreme cases nobles rebelled against the king or even deposed him. The personal bond between the king and his tenants in chief gave them a special responsibility to advise and restrain him. This led to a series of showdowns between kings and nobles, the production of documents such as Magna Carta, and the summoning of bodies of nobles, clergy, merchants and others, eventually institutionalised as Parliament. By 1450 Parliament's nature was clearly established. It was bicameral: the House of Lords consisted of **peers** (those nobles who received a summons to Parliament, plus the bishops and senior heads of monasteries), while the House of Commons was made up of elected members: two for each county and two (usually) from a wide range of towns, ranging from substantial cities (such as Norwich or Bristol) to tiny 'boroughs', such as Downton (Wiltshire) or Grampound (Cornwall) which had been granted representation despite having only a handful of electors. (London had four members.) The Commons' representative nature, however unequal by modern standards, enabled it to claim that it spoke for the common people, while the peers spoke for themselves and the bishops for the Church.

Endorsement by Parliament, or some part of it, could be seen as giving legitimacy to a deposition or handover of power.

It might seem that Parliament developed as the result of concessions forced on the Crown in times of crisis. During the fourteenth century, when the king needed large amounts of money for the Hundred Years War against France, Parliament gradually established the principle that the king could not raise taxation or make laws without its consent: **bills** changing the law or imposing taxation only became statutes (Acts of Parliament) if they had been approved by both Houses and had received the king's assent. Many bills had their origin in petitions from subjects and were shaped by the two Houses. It was also tacitly accepted, although never formally agreed, that in return for grants of taxation the king should redress the subjects' grievances. The Commons sometimes criticised the king forthrightly and tried to interfere with his most fundamental **prerogatives**. For example, although he had the right to choose his advisers, the Commons used **impeachment** to force the king to remove men like Suffolk. (See Prologue.)

Although there was sometimes acute conflict between king and Parliament, this was not the norm. Parliaments accepted the king's right to govern, but reserved the right to advise him on how to govern and to complain if he, or rather his **counsellors**, were governing badly. For the king there was also a positive side to the relationship. Because Parliament spoke for the nation, he could use it to secure consent to taxation and to new laws, so that taxes were more likely to be paid and laws more likely to be obeyed. (This was why, in most parts of Western Europe, late medieval kings encouraged the development of representative institutions.) The king's revenues, from Crown lands, feudal incidents, and the like, although substantial, were insufficient to fund a major war. The only regular taxation he received consisted of customs duties. To tax other forms of wealth – notably land – he needed the co-operation of Parliament, which expected that the war should be necessary and conducted competently. When these expectations were met, as under Henry V, Parliament responded generously. When the war effort was an abject failure, as in the 1440s, Parliament reacted angrily and brutally.

By 1450 Parliament was well established. It met frequently, often annually, and passed a wide range of legislation. Its sweeping powers made it dangerous: during the Wars of the Roses it was sometimes appropriated by one side, which used it to confiscate the lands of the other. By the end of the century it met less frequently. Henry VII found its criticism irksome and was frustrated by its failure to address his financial problems. While some Continental kings were increasing their revenue from taxation, the English Crown faced a much-reduced customs revenue, making it more dependent on the Crown lands. As the cost of war rose, the financially under-endowed English Crown would struggle to compete.

Parliament: 2. Ireland

English rule over Ireland was established following the conquest of 1169 and the Irish Parliament developed soon after that of England. Its bicameral structure was similar to its English model: in 1300 a demand for taxation towards the war in Scotland led to the first appearance of elected representatives. The Gaelic resurgence greatly reduced the area under English control and Parliament became the institution of the English. The Gaelic threat to the colony's survival led to increasing taxation and a growing willingness to criticise the Dublin administration. Parliamentary legislation was used by the beleaguered English minority to maintain its identity and to prevent settlers of English descent from marrying Irish women and 'going native'. (See below, p. 18.) Although Parliament met in various towns, it became rare for it to meet outside the **Pale**, the relatively small area around Dublin, where English control was most secure. It functioned as a high court, passing legislation and dealing with petitions. As the Anglo-Irish lords were drawn into the dynastic struggles in England, some asserted a distinctively Irish identity: in 1460 Parliament declared that English statutes were not valid in Ireland unless approved by an Irish Parliament. In 1494 the autonomy of the Irish Parliament was drastically reduced by **Poynings' Law**, which decreed that all bills to be placed before the Irish Parliament had first to be approved by the English Privy Council. This was designed less to subordinate Ireland to England than to reduce the autonomy of the lord deputy, the Earl of Kildare.

Parliament: 3. Scotland

The Scottish Parliament's origins can be found in the war of independence which began with Edward I's claim to the Scottish throne in 1286 and ended with England's recognition of David II as King in 1357. The war made necessary frequent consultations (or colloquia) between the King and his advisors (the two **estates** of clergy and nobles). Some of these meetings were described as parliaments and some authorised the King to collect taxation. Representatives of the **royal burghs** (major towns) first attended in 1326, when they were consulted about taxation, and attended regularly, as the 'third estate', from the 1350s. All three estates met in the same chamber. In the fifteenth century the king was expected to summon the estates at least once a year and this, and several royal minorities, led them to become increasingly assertive, either for or against royal policies. With independence secured, the estates argued that there was no need for taxation in peacetime and that the king should **live of his own**, from the proceeds of his lands and personal revenues. The early Stewart kings accepted this arrangement. Whereas previous kings had often granted forfeited estates to their supporters, James I and James II kept them and built up a more substantial landed base, which they managed more efficiently: between the mid 1430s and mid 1450s their landed revenue almost doubled. The old magnate families gradually died out: the last ended when James II murdered the Earl of Douglas in 1452. In 1455 the Douglas estates were declared forfeit and Parliament decreed that these and other lands should be perpetually annexed to the Crown. As the machinery of government was rudimentary and cheap the king could manage on an income about one tenth that of the English Crown, and still maintain an impressive court and regal level of display. Taxes (mostly customs) were low and elicited few protests. However, James III's attempts to develop an aggressive foreign policy were stubbornly resisted by the estates, who refused to pay for it.

Annual meetings of the estates ended abruptly after 1496. So long as the king had no need of taxation for war, or could raise money in other ways, the estates' usefulness seemed questionable. Parliament had not fully evolved. Its composition was more limited than it later became. The first two estates were similar to the English House of Lords but only the royal burghs sent representatives; the lesser burghs and the **shires** did not, nor were the lesser nobility (**lairds**) represented. The estates met sometimes as Parliament, sometimes as a great council: the distinction between the two (if any) was far from clear. In the sixteenth century a convention of **estates** was occasionally summoned instead of a Parliament. Its Acts were sometimes seen as temporary, but some conventions granted taxation which threatened to become permanent. It was also unclear whether parliamentary statutes had greater authority than ordinances of the Privy Council. The ambiguities surrounding the Scottish Parliament created opportunities for a determined and ingenious King.

Celtic Societies and Their Neighbours

The next three sections tackle the question of the relationships between Celtic societies and those who had gained the power to rule over them. In the case of Ireland and Wales English rule had been established by conquest, although in Ireland it had been greatly weakened by the Gaelic resurgence. In Scotland the relationship was more complex: Highlanders were long accepted by Lowlanders as fellow-subjects – different in some ways, but still loyal Scots. By the fifteenth century, however, Highlanders were being depicted as degenerate and dangerous.

Gael and 'Foreigner' in Ireland

With the Gaelic resurgence, some English settlers in Gaelic areas began to 'go native'. As there were few women among the settlers, Englishmen took Irish wives and mistresses. Their children were brought up by Irish servants; many learned Gaelic, and some immersed themselves in Gaelic culture. Many in the settler community deplored these developments. Successive statutes sought to maintain the distinctions between English and Irish. The Statute of Kilkenny of 1366 forbade the English to use **brehon** law and a variety of Irish customs, on the grounds that diversity of law led to diversity of allegiance. All of the English were to use the English language and English names, as well as English modes of dress, facial hair and horse riding. Such legislation was largely futile; Gaelic control over Ireland continued to spread. By the late fifteenth century the area of Ireland under English rule had shrunk to a strip along the east coast, south of Strangford Lough; the **Pale**, about fifty miles from north to south and thirty miles from east to west; and a small pocket around Wexford. The Pale was beleaguered, surrounded by a marcher area, similar to those on England's Welsh and Scottish borders, where English settlers paid '**black rent**', protection money, to Gaelic warlords. However, the Gaelic clans showed no particular hostility towards the English and were quite prepared to use them, and the Dublin administration, in their feuds with rival clans.

The English conquest of Ireland was intended to be permanent. The King took the title of Lord of Ireland rather than king, implying a feudal suzerainty rather than a title based on inheritance, but the government was a smaller version of that of England. The King appointed a viceroy, who was notional head of the civil administration and commanded a small army and a number of castles. There was a treasury in Dublin and central law courts similar to those in England. During the heyday of English rule in the thirteenth century, the Dublin government's influence was felt through much of the island. Royal judges travelled through the areas under English control. By the mid fifteenth century there was no national royal government. The royal revenue shrank almost to nothing, so the viceroy could not deploy more than a token army. It might seem that the end of English rule in Ireland was only a matter of time.

However, English rule in Ireland had hidden strengths. England was larger, richer and militarily more powerful; it was ruled by a king, rather than competing chiefs, and it had a well-developed administration, which gave its kings the potential to mount a new conquest. In the fifteenth century dynastic differences made this unlikely, but the fact that these differences extended to Ireland meant that English kings needed to keep Ireland quiet. Moreover, there was still a powerful English colonial presence. Although aspects of Gaelic life and culture aroused settlers' interest, they maintained a sense of English identity and of superiority to the Gaelic Irish. They believed that they should enjoy the rights of Englishmen, enshrined in the English common law, and that they should be bound only by laws approved by the Irish Parliament. They were proud of their lineage and of their Anglo-Norman or English surnames. Some English families retained great landed estates. Some were absentees, but others remained in Ireland, notably two branches of the Fitzgeralds (or Geraldines), headed by the earls of Kildare and Desmond, and the Butler earls of Ormond. Of the three only the earls of Kildare had the bulk of their estates in or close to the Pale, which led English kings to make use of their military power by appointing them as viceroys. This strategy had the merit of being cheap, but created the danger that the Earl of Kildare could become more 'over-mighty' than any of the English nobility.

Wales: 'Briton' and 'Saxon'

Wales was divided into two regions, the March and the Principality, as a result of two sets of incursions. Anglo-Norman warriors carved out Marcher lordships running from Chester southwards and then west across South Wales. Then in the 1280s Edward I defeated the surviving Welsh princes and established the Principality for his son, created Prince of Wales. The extent of his victory and the military nature of his regime were demonstrated by the building of massive castles, such as Caernarfon, with small towns attached. (See Figure 1.3, Caernarfon Castle, and Figure 1.4, Candleston Castle.) Through most of the Principality the English were found mainly in the castles and towns. The Welsh lived in the mountains and forests, in hamlets and farmsteads. Welsh and English lived separate lives. They were different in language and culture and followed different laws and customs. Like the Gaelic Irish, the Welsh had their hereditary poets and legal and medical practitioners. They assembled to

Figures 1.3 & 1.4 Note the huge disparity between the overwhelming strength of thirteenth-century Caernarfon and a comparatively flimsy fourteenth-century tower house.

Figures 1.3 & 1.4 (Cont.)

celebrate their ancestors and their wars against the English. In Wales, as in Ireland, landed estates were normally divided equally between sons, so landholdings tended to be small and most people remained poor. The disdain which the English showed towards the Welsh, magnified by the shame of military defeat, encouraged a hostility towards the English more intense than that found in Ireland. As they pondered on past glories, and bridled at present injustices, the Welsh found solace in prophecies that one day a messiah-like figure would overthrow the hated Saxon and establish a Welsh prince to rule all of Britain.

The separation of English and Welsh within the Principality was never complete. Englishmen married Welsh wives, ambitious Welshmen helped run the estates of English lords, and built up estates of their own. Despite the ban in many charters on Welshmen living and trading in towns, some did so, made money and bought land. But generally the English and Welsh failed to engage with one another – less a clash of civilisations than mutual incomprehension and indifference. 'The Welsh', wrote one bemused Englishman in 1296, 'are Welsh'. The Welsh in effect governed themselves, settling disputes according to their own rules, with stress on restitution and mediation. They maintained social cohesion, partly through kinship (reinforced by **fosterage**) and partly because the gentry provided protection for tenants, dependants and kin. Others not linked to them in this way could purchase their protection for a small annual sum. All of this left few traces in written records and the English were probably at best only dimly aware of what was going on.

In the Marcher lordships, the powers granted by successive kings made the lords independent princes in all but name. They had their own armies, law courts, councils and officials and there was no appeal from their courts to the king or to anyone. Their powers had originally been justified by the need to guard the borders, but now many lordships were held by English magnates who saw their lordship primarily as a source of income to be spent elsewhere. Like the Principality the lordships were mostly divided into an Englishry and a Welshry, each with its own courts and officials. English and Welsh law coexisted, with English and Welsh invoking whichever was more likely to serve their needs.

In 1400 the Welsh, led by Owain Glyn Dŵr, rose in the first major rebellion for more than a century. It was largely a response to the increasing financial demands of English landowners and lasted until 1409, with sporadic disorders until 1421. Its effect on Wales was catastrophic. The rebels targeted castles and towns, but churches and monasteries were damaged as well. The government responded to guerrilla warfare by destroying people, buildings, livestock and crops. Many communities took decades to recover; some never did. The English Parliament passed statutes forbidding the Welsh to hold property or offices in 'English' towns; there should be restrictions on bards and other 'vagabonds'; and any English person marrying a Welsh person should lose the privileges derived from being English. These laws were re-enacted repeatedly until at least the 1440s. Meanwhile, new charters to 'English' towns further restricted the rights of the Welsh, in insulting terms.

However much the Welsh resented all this, they were too battered and exhausted to rebel again. It was as much as they could do to scrape a living and repair at least some of the damage. Meanwhile the demands of the Marcher lords on their tenants continued to grow. They spent less and less time in the Marches, handing over management of their lordships to lawyers and officials, who were allowed a free hand. They were accused of extortion, feuding and plunder. Some encouraged 'buying off the sessions': lordship courts were significant sources of revenue for lords and officials, so towns were encouraged to pay money for the sessions not to be held: the lord received cash down, but if no sessions were held no justice could be done. Lords and officials were accused of protecting their followers accused of extortion or murder – and anyway such offenders could escape justice by moving to the next lordship. Some grew rich and many suffered, but not all the Welsh were victims. Some became deputies to absentee English officials, or settled and traded in towns. As agricultural production struggled to recover after the rebellion, some landlords sold up. Prices were low and astute Welshmen were among those building up estates. Meanwhile, tenants who felt oppressed could flee elsewhere and peasants refused to take on land under villein tenure. By 1450 serfdom was dead in the March and dying in the Principality, but the Welsh peasant's lot was far from happy. The rebellion and its aftermath had weakened the largely invisible system through which the Welsh were governed and undermined the loyalty of the peasantry to the gentry. However, some English landowners and officials put down roots in Wales, particularly in the South. Unlike earlier English settlers, they began to learn Welsh, to patronise poets and offer hospitality. How far their efforts were appreciated by the Welsh is uncertain: no doubt many continued to dream of the prince who was to restore Wales to its rightful place in Britain. And, surprisingly, that dream was soon, in a way, to come true.

Scotland: Lowland and Highland

Scotland's independence of England had been achieved at a heavy price, a bitter civil war. Without an effective king, Lowland landowners set up their own courts, often confirmed by the king; nobles pursued their feuds and protected their followers from justice. In the Highlands the power of the clan chiefs revived, helped by the collapse of Norse rule in the Isles. The most powerful figure was now the **Lord of the Isles**, the head of the Clan Donald, which dominated the Hebrides and the West coast and established a high level of order: their main house on Islay was unfortified. Elsewhere, however, order collapsed. Warring families, often of Lowland origin, behaved like Gaelic warlords, demanding **black rent** and sending **caterans** (masterless men) to plunder country and town. The most notorious was Alexander Stewart, the 'Wolf of Badenoch', whose caterans burned Elgin cathedral in 1390.

Before this time there was no real suggestion that Lowlands and Highlands were radically different. Anglo-Norman families and feudal modes of government had extended into the Highlands. There were differences of language – Highlanders spoke Gaelic, Lowlanders spoke Scots. But the social systems of Highlands and Lowlands were similar. Many clan chiefs had received charters empowering them to establish courts. Both Highlanders and Lowlanders had a strong sense of lineage, creating bonds reinforced by others, between lord and man and between equals, based on service and payment in return for justice and protection; **fosterage** was common. By the fifteenth century these obligations were often specified in '**bonds of manrent**', which became increasingly detailed as time went on.

By the fifteenth century, some Lowlanders claimed that Highlanders were degenerate, qualitatively different from themselves. As one wrote in the 1380s, Lowlanders were 'of domestic and civilised habits, trusty, patient and urbane, decent in their attire, affable and peaceful'. By contrast, Highlanders were 'a savage and untamed nation, rude and independent, given to rapine, ease-loving [lazy] … unsightly in dress … and exceedingly cruel'. They were, however, 'faithful and obedient to their king and country'. Such claims of Highland degeneracy were made especially by magnates charged with keeping the Highland clans in order: the Gordon earls of Huntly in the North East and the Campbell earls of Argyll in the South West had a vested interest in exaggerating the level of disorder. In the Western Highlands and Islands, raiding and plunder were at times endemic, especially after the collapse of the power of the Lords of the Isles in the 1490s. It was said (approvingly) of the chief of the Mackenzies of Kintail that: 'he was a very active man, he burnt and harried Sleat [on Skye] for his pleasure'. As late as 1689 one observer wrote: 'Once or twice a year great numbers of 'em get together and make a descent into the Lowlands, where they plunder the inhabitants ... and this they are apt to do on a kind of principle and in conformity to the prejudice they continually have to the Lowlanders, whom they generally take for so many enemies.' But the Lowlands were not without their disorders and in parts of the Highlands, especially in the centre and the North East, chiefs made great efforts to keep the peace. In the fifteenth century the more competent kings used the clan system to maintain order, pressing chiefs to take responsibility for the conduct of their clansmen. Similarly, they expected Lowland nobles to keep their dependants under control and to arbitrate in disputes.

The Decline of Feudalism

We saw earlier that feudalism involved various relationships: at the top, between the king and his tenants in chief, and at the bottom between manorial lords and their unfree peasants. By 1450 the latter had been transformed. Serfdom was effectively dead throughout Britain and Ireland. The Black Death of 1348–9 had reduced the population to a level where servile obligations and labour services were unenforceable: if lords demanded more services tenants would go elsewhere, to a lord prepared to pay for their labour (see Chapter 2). The relationship between the king and his great subjects also changed radically, but the process was more protracted and more complex.

Military Service and Fiscal Feudalism: England

As a means of military organisation feudalism proved inadequate. Nobles came to expect to be paid for military service, but their forces proved insufficient for Edward I's armies, which had to be paid for by taxation. As taxes on land could be granted only by Parliament, the king needed to win the support of a political elite wider than the great nobles. Many members of the Commons came from the **gentry**, who played an increasingly important role in county government and had definite views on taxation and the conduct of war. While it was accepted that the people should support the king in wartime, there was room to differ on how much taxation should be raised. Under Henry V the Commons made unprecedented efforts to grant money for the war in France, but under his son they sometimes refused to vote anything, arguing that the war should be paid for by the King's French territories.

The political usefulness of feudalism also declined, with the growth of the central administration and a nationwide system of common law courts. Order and justice were taken out of the hands of the landowners and delivered by legal professionals. Meanwhile the usefulness of feudal **incidents** (see above, p. 10) diminished, thanks to the ingenuity of lawyers. For the system to work, the pattern of landholding had to remain largely static. When a tenant in chief died his estates reverted to the king, who regranted them, usually to his heir. By the thirteenth century it was accepted that the heir had a *right* to succeed. Moreover, many tenants in chief also held land of other landowners, and there were frequent transfers of land below the level of tenants in chief, on which the king's claims to 'incidents' were difficult to enforce. But the king also found it hard to enforce his rights over his tenants in chief. To maximise his income, he wished to keep estates intact and to ensure that everything passed to the eldest son. But landlords often wanted to sell part of their land, to make provision for younger sons or daughters, or pay off debts. A father's wishes could not bind his son after he died. Feudalism as a tangle of reciprocal relationships had become impossibly complicated by the fourteenth century, but it remained the basis of land law. The lawyers developed **enfeoffment to uses**, whereby a landlord appointed family or friends to act as **feoffees** (trustees), to whom he granted his lands on specified conditions. This required a licence from the king, which was often granted. The lawyers also developed **entail**, whereby an heir had only a life interest in his lands, so that he could not dispose of them. This meant that if the direct male line failed the estates could pass to a collateral heir; if an estate was entailed 'in tail male', instead of falling to an heiress it would pass to the nearest male heir. Again, a tenant in chief wishing to entail needed a royal licence, but under Edward III this was often granted.

It is difficult to overstate the importance of these developments. After the Conquest the king had granted tenure of land to an individual for life and regranted it on his death. Now the nobility gained more and more complete control over their property and its transmission and could add to their estates through marriage or inheritance. The king lost the power to regulate the transmission of the lands of tenants in chief, who for most practical purposes now owned their land, subject to the possible burden of feudal incidents. This enabled them to build up larger and larger estates, which, together with dynastic marriages, gave some the power to defy the king – a major shift in the balance of power between the king and the landed elite. The Crown often acquiesced in these changes, presumably for reasons of political calculation. To fight major wars they needed the goodwill of the aristocracy and Parliament. This was one way of buying support; another was to ensure that his military objectives and strategy were acceptable to the landed elite. But this acquiescence meant a significant loss of income. Lands held by feoffees or in tail did not technically belong to the current occupant, so were not liable to feudal incidents when he died. Allowing alienations also added further to the complexity of landholding: many landholders were both landlords and tenants, holding land by various tenures. Disentangling these complexities was diffi-cult and kings did not rigorously pursue what was due to them. Either they judged it was not worth the effort or else they preferred not to antagonise powerful landowners, many of whom sat in Parliament. By the mid fifteenth century, the Crown was either forced or chose to work with Parliament. It seemed that the strategy of trying to work with the great landowners and treating them generously had not resolved the prob-lems created by fighting a major war. In some ways, notably by reducing the opportu-nities of raising money from feudal incidents, it had made them worse.

Military Service and Fiscal Feudalism: Scotland

In Scotland feudalism played a limited part in the raising of armies. The Scottish **host** was raised by summoning all able-bodied men between 16 and 60, who were obliged to defend the kingdom, at their own expense, for forty days. By the fifteenth century it was normally commanded by regional magnates and consisted mainly of infantry. The small cavalry component was provided mostly by Border lords. After independence the Scots saw little need for an army for defence and Parliament was unsympathetic to royal proposals for foreign expeditions. Scottish kings claimed var-ious feudal rights, including wardship, which they began to exploit more vigorously in the fifteenth century, encouraged by the estates: the more the king raised from 'his own' the less he would need taxes. In an Act of 1458 Parliament also encouraged the king to **feu** his lands. When a landlord granted land in **feu-farm** the tenant, in return for an increased (often much increased) rent, gained the right to pass it on to his heir; the rent was fixed in perpetuity, so he became, in effect, a freeholder paying an annual rent which fell in value as prices rose. Feuing royal estates enabled the king to make a short-term profit at the expense of long-term income; he also lost direct lordship over his tenants. This probably explains why, despite Parliament's encouragement, the feuing of royal lands was not common until the sixteenth century.

Bastard Feudalism

There is one final aspect of feudalism, which concerns relationships, not between kings and great lords, or between manorial lords and peasants, but among those in the intermediate levels of society. It is often described as 'bastard feudalism', a term coined by a Victorian historian to describe relationships based on money rather than land, seen as degenerate and disruptive, cutting across the allegiance that each sub-ject owed to his king. We have seen that classical feudalism as a social and political system was dead by the mid fifteenth century, but the term 'bastard feudalism' is still widely used of that time.

The relationship between king and landed elite was reciprocal. As the king lacked coercive power in the localities he needed the power over men which members of the elite exercised through agreements with tenants, lesser landowners, and household men, especially lawyers. These agreements were often formalised through a written **indenture**, reinforced by the payment of a fee by the lord; the payment of the fee (or retainer) led the followers of a lord to be known as his **retainers**. Apart from the fee, it was expected that the lord would be a 'good lord' to his men, just as the noble expected the king to be a 'good lord' to him. This would include protection (siding with them in their disputes, provided that this did not contravene the king's justice) and acting as arbiter and mediator. The retainers' service could be military, honorific (waiting on the lord and wearing his **livery** or badge on public occasions), or legal, including service on juries.

Conclusion

'Bastard feudalism' has often been seen as a problem, a symptom of the abuse of power by 'over-mighty subjects' during the Wars of the Roses. However, contemporaries distinguished between different types of retaining. From the 1390s Parliament passed numerous Acts to limit retaining, but not to abolish it. It was acceptable for lords to fee their household servants and legal advisers and many indentures specified that a retainer's service to his lord should not compromise his allegiance to the king. Men were linked by (often informal) reciprocal personal bonds, based on reward (or protection) and service and lubricated by favours, courtesies and gifts. This culture of reciprocity extended beyond landed society. Parliamentary boroughs needed powerful friends to promote their interests, while noblemen sought seats in the Commons for their sons. A nobleman would give venison or contribute to local charities; the corporation offered hospitality and deference, turning out in their civic regalia to welcome the noble to their humble town. The reciprocal relationship between lord and retainer operated within limits: lords were wary of embracing their retainers' quarrels too fully. For much of the time, royal justice functioned adequately and there was no need to try to influence it unduly: indeed any such attempt could prove counter-productive. When royal governance and justice failed, bonds already in place within society could be strengthened as nobles, their followers and lesser landholders sought to secure themselves against the abuse of power. Bastard feudal ties, as such, were a force neither for order nor for disorder; they were simply the means through which power operated. By the mid fifteenth century retaining probably posed less of a threat to public order than in the past. Retinues were generally smaller, and Lowland England was becoming safer and more orderly. Castles were designed more for comfort and show than for defence, and few could hold out against a sustained siege. The potential for serious disorder remained, but it would take an exceptional level of royal misgovernment to make it happen. Cade's rising showed that that level had been reached in 1450.

SUGGESTIONS FOR FURTHER READING

As a starting point, R.R. Davies, 'The Peoples of Britain, 1100–1400', *Transactions of the Royal Historical Society*, 6th series, 4–7 (1994–7) puts Britain's peoples in a broad context. • Useful introductions to Gaelic Ireland include K.W. Nicholls, *Gaelic and Gaelicised Ireland in the Middle Ages* (Dublin, 1972) (informative, concise and clear) and K. Simms, *From Kings to Warlords: the Changing Political Structure of Gaelic Ireland in the Late Middle Ages* (Woodbridge, 1987). • On Wales, see the excellent introductory chapters of R.R. Davies, *The Revolt of Owain Glyn Dŵr* (Oxford, 1997) and G. Williams, *Renewal and Reformation: Wales c.1415–1642* (Oxford, 1992). • See especially Chapter 1 in T.C. Smout, *A History of the Scottish People, 1560–1830* (London, 1972), for a wide-ranging introduction to Scotland, worthy of a book of exceptional range and depth. • For Scotland more generally, see A. Grant, *Independence and Nationhood: Scotland 1306–1469* (Edinburgh, 1991), A. Cathcart, *Kinship and Clientage: Highland Clanship 1451–1609* (Leiden, 2006), J. Brown (ed.), *Scottish Society in the Fifteenth Century* (London, 1977), especially Brown on 'the exercise of power' and J.J. Robertson on the development of Scottish law. • On English law, see A. Musson (with E. Powell), *Crime, Law and Society in the Later Middle Ages* (Manchester, 2009). • For England generally, see M.H. Keen, *England in the Later Middle Ages: a Political History* (2nd edn, London, 2003) and G. Harriss, *Shaping the Nation: England 1360–1461* (Oxford, 2005). • On the decline of feudalism, the standard work (not an easy read) is J.M.W. Bean, *The Decline of English Feudalism 1215–1540* (Manchester, 1968). • When considering the reappraisal of 'bastard feudalism' and the relationship between king and nobility, the point of departure is K.B. Macfarlane, *The Nobility of Later Medieval England* (Oxford, 1973). See also R.H. Britnell and A.J. Pollard (eds.), *The Macfarlane Legacy* (Stroud, 1995). The most thorough recent study of 'bastard feudalism' is M. Hicks, *Bastard Feudalism* (Harlow, 1995). See also C. Carpenter, *The Wars of the Roses: Politics and the Constitution in England 1437–1509* (Cambridge, 1997), chapters 1–3; A.J. Pollard, *The Wars of the Roses* (Basingstoke, 2001).

SUMMARY

- Celtic societies were qualitatively different from English society, in terms of language, social organisation and attitudes towards such matters as ownership, inheritance, measurement and justice.
- Feudalism as a form of social and military organisation was more or less defunct in England, Scotland and Wales by the mid fifteenth century; it survived only in the form of feudal

incidents, financial exactions which had largely lost touch with social reality. It had never been fully established in Gaelic Ireland.

- While Highland Scotland had strong similarities to Gaelic Ireland, Lowland Scotland was more akin to lowland England, thanks in part to a common Anglo-Norman influence on their systems of law and administration (which nevertheless remained very different). The Scottish language, while in many ways different from English, contained many similarities and the two tended to converge, to a point that by the later eighteenth century conscious efforts were made to preserve the Scots language.
- In the fifteenth century effective royal government depended on a competent adult king. In England, Scotland, Ireland and Wales there were wild regions (or lawless zones) dominated by warlords who paid little heed to royal commands. An essential precondition for a more ordered and prosperous society was to bring the warlords under control.

QUESTIONS FOR STUDENTS

1. Assess the advantages and disadvantages of English and Celtic legal systems.
2. Why were the English in Ireland driven back by the Irish in the fourteenth and fifteenth centuries?
3. Was bastard feudalism a force for order or disorder?
4. Which was the stronger in the fifteenth century – the English or the Scottish Parliament?
5. Assess the impact of English rule on the people of Wales.

2

The Lives of the People

TIMELINE

1315–18	Famine
1348–9	First outbreak of Black Death
1349	Parliament attempts to limit wages
1378–1417	Great Schism
1381	Peasants' Revolt
1453	End of Hundred Years War

Introduction

The approach of this second chapter considering Britain and Ireland around 1450 is bottom-up rather than top-down. It has three main themes. First, it discusses the economy – agriculture, trade and manufactures – and the extent to which the balance of economic power was transformed by the Black Death. Second, it looks at the communities in which people lived and the way in which they were governed. It shows that, although the better-off wielded more power than the poor, there was a significant growth in participation and self-government, as seen in the treatment of the poor. The third theme is religion – the Church's organisation and teachings, and popular belief and spirituality. It argues that, while many popular beliefs and practices did not fully reflect the Church's teachings, a substantial proportion of the people were deeply attached to the Church and its liturgy.

Making a Living: Agriculture

The great majority of the people of Britain and Ireland made their living wholly or partly from agriculture. Some rented farms from landowners, on which they were able to produce enough (more or less) to support their families. Others held little or no land and depended on selling their labour, either in agriculture or rural industry; they might also be able to gather firewood and foodstuffs from woodland. Many rural families lived close to the margins of subsistence, at the mercy of crop failure and disease. Their diet was limited and monotonous, with a heavy dependence on grain, or, in pastoral areas, dairy produce. There was as yet no staple crop (like the potato) to enable people to feed a family from a small plot of land. Those living near the sea might be able to catch fish, but meat was a rarity: those who reared cattle often did so to sell, not for their own consumption. The right to catch wild animals and river fish was jealously guarded by the landowners.

Climate and Soil

The economic opportunities open to rural people were limited by the unequal distribution of land between landowners and peasants and by the constraints imposed by climate and soil. These varied considerably between uplands and lowlands. (See Map 2.1, Highland and Lowland – England and Wales, and Map 2.2, Highland and Lowland – Scotland.) The uplands generally had poorer soils, heavier rainfall and lower temperatures. Arable farming was inhibited by steep rocky terrain and poor drainage; often rocks had to be cleared before the land could be ploughed and some could be

Map 2.1 Highland and Lowland – England and Wales

cultivated only with spades. In Scotland the clearing of the forests had impoverished the soil: nutrients were leached out, topsoil was washed away, water levels rose and potentially fertile land became bog. In the Scottish and Welsh uplands maintaining the fertility of the soil was a constant struggle, made possible only by the availability of dung and, in places, seaweed. In this way it was possible to grow cereals, notably oats: oatcakes and porridge formed the staple diet of Scottish Highlanders. Ireland was

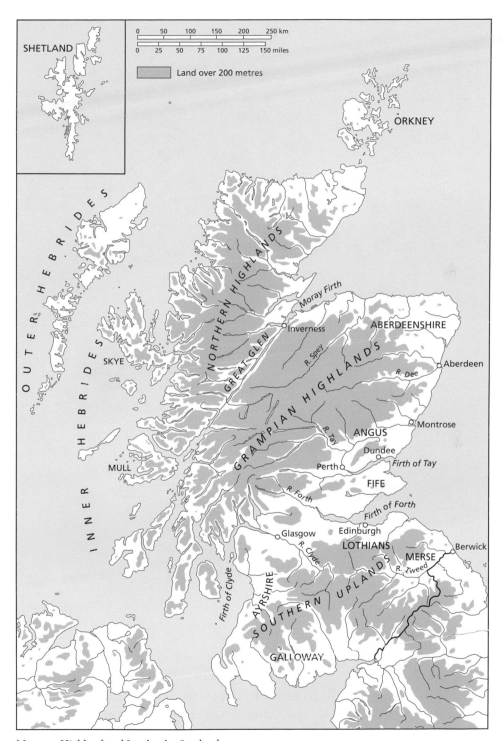

Map 2.2 Highland and Lowland – Scotland

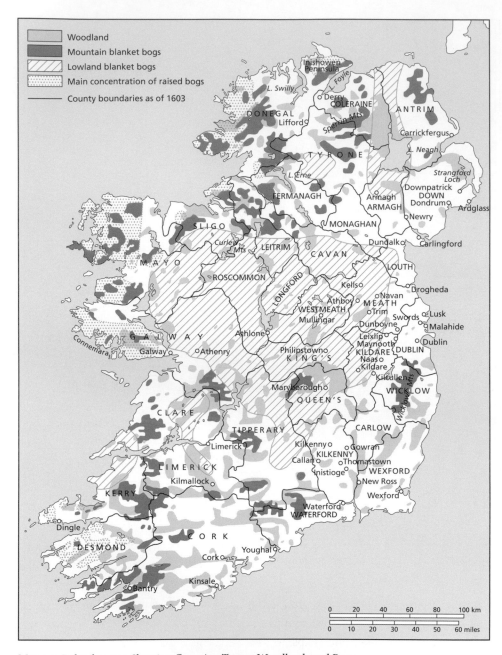

Map 2.3 Ireland *c.*1600 Showing Counties, Towns, Woodlands and Bogs

less mountainous but much was covered by forest and bog, limiting the possibilities of arable farming (see Map 2.3, Ireland *c.*1600). On the other hand, the uplands often provided good summer grazing, as did some areas of marshland. Hay was harvested to feed livestock through the winter. Limited fertility meant that the uplands could

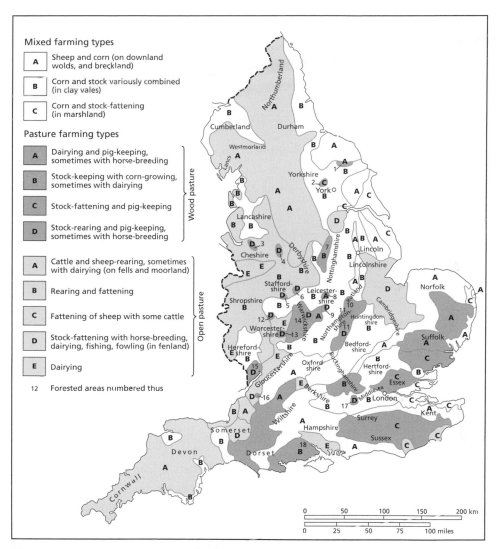

Map 2.4 Main Farming Regions in England, c.1500–1640

support only a sparse population, grouped in small farmsteads or hamlets rather than villages. Farmsteads were farmed communally, by groups of families, who cultivated the arable infield (divided into strips, to give everyone a share of the better soil) and grazed their animals on the rougher outfield. People and animals huddled together through the winter.

In lowland arable communities there was more fertile soil and more labour needed to cultivate it. Houses were grouped in nucleated villages, often around a parish church. Most villages had two to four open fields, divided into strips. As in Scotland, to some extent farming had to be regulated communally. To get the best out of the fields, crops had to be rotated, to reduce the risk of diseases or exhausting the soil; it was normal to leave one field fallow (uncultivated) each year to allow the soil to recover its 'heart'. This system could work only if all the strips in each field followed the same rotation. Where the soil was fertile enough the main crops were grains – wheat and barley, made into bread and beer. The rotation might also include peas and beans, which could either be eaten by people or fed to cattle. These cattle, or sheep or pigs, were kept on the village's common grazing land which, like the open fields, was carefully regulated, to prevent its being over-grazed and to prevent animals from straying and damaging crops. Many villagers, even landless labourers, might also have a garden in which they could grow vegetables and keep chickens. (See Map 2.4, Main Farming Regions in England.)

The Limits of Medieval Agriculture

In terms of soil fertility and climate, living in the lowlands had considerable advantages over the uplands and they were able to support a much larger population, but the productivity of agriculture was limited in three significant ways.

First, there were substantial areas within even the more fertile lowlands which were unsuitable for arable farming. There were large areas of forest, some (like the New Forest) set aside for hunting. There was heathland, often sandy and stony, covered with gorse and scrub, which could be used for grazing or managed as rabbit warrens. The soil of the fens of eastern England, from Bedfordshire to Yorkshire, was extremely fertile, but subject to flooding. They were later to be drained, using techniques pioneered in the Netherlands, but for the moment they provided rich summer grazing, abundant fish and wildfowl and reeds for thatching.

Second, peasants were often not allowed to till their fields in peace. Disturbance came not from their landlords but from rustlers and plunderers. Scottish Highlanders routinely raided the Lowlands, raiding was endemic along the Anglo-Scottish border and feuding Gaelic chiefs in Scotland and Ireland plundered one another's clansmen and burned their crops. Sometimes the raids were on a massive scale, notably those led into Ireland and northern England in the 1310s by the Scot Edward Bruce. In Gaelic Ireland many landowners ceased to farm their **demesne** lands because of the risk of their crops being destroyed. Arable farming continued, but on a smaller, peasant scale. Landlords needed peasants to grow grain to provide their households with bread and beer. They shared the risks by providing seed corn and sometimes stock, and demanded payment in the form of food and labour.

The third, and most intractable, problem facing arable farmers was that growing cereals took nutrients from the soil; if these were not replaced its fertility would decline. Nowadays farmers use a variety of fertilisers, but few were available in the fifteenth century. Of these, the most important was dung, human and animal. Lowland farmers were unable to keep enough cattle through the winter to manure their fields. In the uplands, cattle were reared in greater numbers and produced more dung for a smaller

Figure 2.1 Reconstructed from excavations of a deserted village, this cottage consisted of two rooms, which contained an open hearth and an oven. It was probably built in the thirteenth century, as cultivation expanded, and abandoned after the Black Death.

arable area; grassland was plentiful and grass could be preserved as hay. In the lowlands, grazing land and hay meadows were less extensive, because the best soil was used for growing crops. Nowadays cattle are fed in winter on fodder crops, especially roots like turnips, or manufactured cattle foods. In the fifteenth century many animals were slaughtered in the autumn. Their meat provided food during the winter, but in the spring the depleted herds had to be built up again. If the population rose there was a temptation to extend cultivation into the common grazing or less fertile land. This meant that the number of animals that could be kept would diminish and so would the amount of dung to manure the fields. Fertility would decline and eventually grain production would reach a peak and fall back, bringing dearth and famine. (See Figure 2.1, Medieval Cottage from Hangleton, Sussex.) The problem of maintaining soil fertility limited the number of people that agriculture could support.

Peasants and Landlords

The dire effects of over-population were shown in the early fourteenth century when the population of England and Wales rose to five or even six million. Thousands died of famine and disease after successive harvest failures in 1315–18, made worse by raids.

In Wales the damage done during the Glyndŵr rebellion lasted for generations: many villages were never resettled. It seemed as if the condition of the peasantry was doomed to deteriorate further and further, until the Black Death.

The Impact of the Black Death

The Black Death changed the balance of power between landlords and peasants. From the later thirteenth century landowners had exploited the rising demand for land, increasing rents, evicting farmers who fell into arrears and lumping small farms into more commercially viable units. Others, eager to profit from high food prices, exploited their **demesnes**, demanding increased labour services from their tenants. These tenants were often **serfs**, or **villeins**, and had little choice but to comply. Wool prices rose and some landlords, including monasteries, built up large sheep flocks and evicted farmers, converting arable to sheep pasture. Evicted farmers joined the swollen ranks of those who depended on selling their labour, so landlords and employers could get away with paying low wages. For those who died in the famine of 1315–18, lack of money was probably as much of a problem as shortage of food.

The first outbreak of plague, in 1348–9, was the most virulent. It may have killed 40 or even 50 per cent of England's population and spread as far as the west of Ireland. Later outbreaks were less severe but prevented any significant recovery. For those who survived, economic conditions improved. The rising demand for food had pushed cultivation into marginal land, which was now abandoned as farmers concentrated on the better soils. Rents fell and wages rose: tenant farmers and labourers were in short supply. In 1349 the English Parliament attempted to fix wage rates, but many landowners and farmers ignored the law and paid what was demanded. In the early fourteenth century many lowland landowners had rented their land out in small parcels and demanded part of farmers' rent in the form of labour on their demesnes. Now some refused, while others bought their freedom. Many who legally remained serfs were emancipated by economics: serfdom was no longer enforceable. This phenomenon was seen throughout the British Isles. In Wales when the owners of 'bond villages', where serfdom was established, tried to exact labour services, the peasants simply left. The attempts to enforce these obligations contributed to the Peasants' Revolt of 1381, in which manor court rolls, containing details of peasants' obligations, were destroyed. The Revolt showed the peasants' strength, making them more assertive and lords more conciliatory. Good tenants were hard to find and landlords made an effort to keep them. Unable to find the labour to cultivate their demesnes, landlords largely abandoned direct farming and leased the land out, adding to the amount available to rent, reducing rents further. In the first half of the fifteenth century, English landlord incomes fell by around 20 per cent in the South and Midlands, and significantly more in the North East.

Trade and Manufactures

In Wales, Ireland and Scotland the main exports were the products of agriculture and basic extractive industries: live animals, animal products, coal, salt and slate. These were traded mainly for foreign luxuries. By comparison England's economy was complex and prosperous. Traditionally the main export commodities were wool, which was much in demand on the Continent, and woollen cloth: cloth exports overtook wool exports in the fifteenth century. Other exports included Cornish tin, Derbyshire lead and Tyneside coal. England's trade links were extensive, but mainly within Europe. Companies, like the London Merchant Adventurers, attempted to establish monopolies on trades such as cloth exports to the Low Countries, concentrating on trades that they knew rather than looking further afield. They had yet to develop a substantial Mediterranean trade, so much of England's trade was handled by merchants from Italy or the Baltic. Craftsmen came from the Rhineland and the Netherlands, particularly to London. These '**aliens**' (foreigners) were not popular with English craftsmen but there was a lively demand for their products. Regulations restricting the activities of aliens were largely ignored, but occasionally resentment exploded in violence against foreigners.

The complexity of England's economy was reflected in towns with sophisticated governments. Larger towns boasted a growing range of shops and trades. A few shops offered a variety of imported commodities: grocers, for example. However, most shops remained family concerns, using local raw materials to produce a limited range of goods for a limited market. They made goods in the back room and displayed them on a shutter that folded down to make a counter. By the fifteenth century the key division within towns was between freemen and the rest. The main way to acquire freedom was by apprenticeship, usually of seven years, but it was also possible to gain freedom through patrimony (for sons of freemen) or by purchase. Freemen had the right to practise a trade and sell retail, and sought to protect it. Guilds developed initially as convivial associations, providing for members who fell on hard times, but they came to regulate either all the town's trades, or particular trades: the more complex a town's economy, the more guilds it would have. In large towns a distinction emerged within guilds between the **livery**, the entrepreneurs and employers, and the working craftsmen, or **yeomanry**. As their economic interests diverged, they developed their own forms of sociability: lavish feasts for the livery, humbler 'drinkings' for the craftsmen. In smaller towns, with fewer and smaller trades, this separation was less likely; masters and **journeymen** worked in the same workplace.

It might seem that by trying to limit competition, restricting the number of apprentices masters could take, and fixing prices, craft guilds protected the interests of the producer rather than the consumer. The guilds argued that in smaller towns demand was limited and each freeman needed to get his share. They claimed to maintain standards:

each apprentice had to produce a 'master piece' and guilds often checked on quality of workmanship and the dimensions of cloth. Conventional wisdom – and the Church – encouraged people to be satisfied with a modest sufficiency and a fair profit. Towns tried to regulate the marketing of basic foodstuffs, to ensure that the poor could buy at reasonable prices. Craft guilds embodied a way of thinking in which stability and fairness were socially preferable to the unfettered operation of market forces. But market forces were powerful. Guild regulations were never easy to enforce – even in London they applied only within the City, not the suburbs – and as the Black Death reduced urban populations labour became so scarce in some towns that women were admitted to crafts hitherto practised only by men and **journeymen** were able to demand better wages. Meanwhile guilds were making other contributions to urban life. Many developed a religious dimension, often attached to a particular parish or saint, and new, specifically religious, guilds or fraternities contributed to the town's spiritual life, in daily worship, pageants and plays.

The guild system was appropriate to an economy of small masters and workshops, like that of fifteenth-century England. There was effectively no factory industry: shipyards and coal mines were small family businesses, with a few journeymen and apprentices. Manufacturing was organised on a larger scale by combining domestic units. The basic stages of cloth manufacture took place in the home, often in the countryside: agricultural work was seasonal and farm workers made ends meet by part-time cloth-working. **Clothiers** (entrepreneurs) took wool from the farmer to the spinner, the yarn from the spinner to the weaver and the rough cloth to be dyed and finished, usually in a town and often abroad. The fifteenth century saw mixed fortunes for textile towns. Increased export duties on wool gave English manufacturers a cost advantage in foreign markets, which stimulated manufacturing in some regions. Encouraged by the government, wool and cloth exports were increasingly channelled through London, which by 1450 handled two-thirds of the nation's overseas trade. Many towns in the South prospered, thanks to their access to London and Exeter. However, war and famine disrupted markets in northern Europe and cloth production in the North and Midlands declined dramatically. While old centres like York and Coventry suffered population decline, new cloth towns appeared in East Anglia and the Cotswolds. The handsome churches and houses of Long Melford and Lavenham testify to their wealth, civic pride and self-confidence.

A Golden Age?

The period between the outbreak of the Black Death and the late fifteenth century has been described as a golden age for peasant farmers and labourers compared with what came before and after, when landlords exploited the opportunities created by a growing population. Falling rents enabled tenants to rent more land and many labourers became tenants: it has been estimated that the proportion of wage-earners in England fell from a half to a third between 1300 and the 1520s. The conditions of tenure were increasingly determined not by custom but by negotiation, and spelled out in written leases. The leases were entered into the manor court rolls and the tenant was given a copy; **copyhold** tenure came to be enforced in the courts. Security of tenure encouraged tenants to rent or buy more land. While many peasant farmers were content to provide a better diet, better clothing and a few more home comforts, some acquired land on a substantial scale. Bartholomew Bolde, from the small Welsh town of Conwy, accumulated 1,800 acres over more than thirty years. Middling landowners and successful farmers built substantial houses, with a variety of furniture and fittings. There was a growing gulf between the stone farmhouses of the South of England and the hovels of the poorest Scottish or Irish peasants, ramshackle timber structures roofed with turf, which could be constructed in a day and quickly rebuilt if destroyed by raiders. In the new English farmhouses, people and animals no longer lived in close proximity, as happened in the homes of even the better-off Scottish farmers.

The position of peasant farmers probably improved most in Lowland England, less likely to be disturbed by war or brigandage than Gaelic Ireland or Scotland. Peasants in the Welsh Border lordships faced the predatory demands of absentee lords. In the North of England lords still required tenants to perform military service, but by the custom of '**tenant right**' their rents were fixed and they were free to sell land or pass it on to their heirs. In Scotland leases were very short, but where tenants enjoyed 'kindly tenure', it was expected that they would be renewed. Scottish lords did not usually retain a **demesne**, for which they needed their tenants to perform labour services. In the long term the biggest change in the relationship of landlord and tenant came from **feuing**, which became common only in the sixteenth century. Landlords traded a one-off increase for, in effect, converting tenants into freeholders, with fixed rents. Tenants were not keen on this in the fifteenth century, because it meant an increase in rent, but in the sixteenth, as prices rose, they found it more and more attractive as the real value of their rents was eaten away by inflation. Many feus went to lesser tenants, who scraped together the money to pay the higher rent. In the fifteenth century, there was little feuing, but tenants were in short supply and leases were usually renewed on the same or more favourable terms.

In both England and Scotland the lord's courts could offer some protection to tenants. In England peasants could bring actions against their lord in his manorial court and juries could interpret customary arrangements to favour tenants. In Scotland the landlord's 'baron court' normally favoured his interests, but could provide redress in disputes between tenants. Relations between landlord and tenant seem to have been less adversarial in Scotland than in England. In the Highlands and to some extent in the Lowlands (and the far north of England) the needs of war and the traditional mutual loyalties of lord and man meant that many lords preferred to keep a numerous body of tenants, to treat them fairly and provide generous hospitality. In the fifteenth century, as incomes fell, many English landlords realised that they could no longer afford this. However, while the pressure of population on resources remained low, landlords were in a weak position and farmers and even labourers could prosper. In the sixteenth century the population rose, the pressure of population on resources grew and the balance of economic power swung once more in favour of the landlords. For the majority of farmers and labourers, the golden age was over.

Communities: 1. Towns

Self-government was most apparent in towns, which varied from large villages which had been granted a market to complex and sophisticated administrations in the larger towns. Material conditions in the mid fifteenth century depended in large part on the nature of the community people lived in. Many country people made limited use of markets or money, subsisting on what they produced or exchanging with neighbours. They had simple needs and bought their few consumer goods from pedlars or on infrequent visits to a market town.

England

England had fewer great cities than the Low Countries and Italy. Only London, with maybe 80,000 people in 1300, could compare with the greatest Continental towns and of the rest it is likely that only Norwich and Bristol had populations exceeding 10,000; Dublin's may have reached 20,000. (See Figure 2.2, Plan of Hull in the Late Eighteenth Century and Figure 2.3, View of Norwich in 1558.) Nevertheless both the number of towns in England and the urban population grew rapidly in the thirteenth century, reaching a peak in about 1300. This should not be taken as unqualified evidence of prosperity. Although many merchants prospered, a large proportion of town-dwellers were impoverished immigrants unable to find work in the countryside who formed a pool of cheap and irregularly employed labour. The towns were hit harder than the countryside by the Black Death, as plague spread quickly through overcrowded tenements and shacks. Some small towns disappeared and larger towns suffered population decrease. As labour was scarce wages rose, creating a broader prosperity, without the earlier extremes of wealth and poverty. Moreover, as we have seen, if some towns declined visibly in the fifteenth century others grew rapidly.

Even small towns had features which differentiated them from villages. They had specialist functions. Some were centres of government – ecclesiastical in the case of cathedral towns. Larger towns were venues of county meetings and law courts. Towns were centres of trade and manufactures – most had markets and offered a larger range

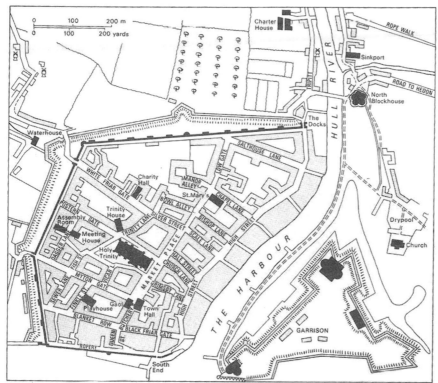

Hull before the first dock

Figures 2.2 & 2.3 A contrast in urban layout. Hull, with a population in excess of 5,000, was confined to a small area inside the medieval walls. The area within the Norwich walls was much larger, accommodating a population of over 12,000 with plenty of room for open spaces and gardens.

of shops and goods than villages. They often began when a lord secured the privilege of holding a market, in order to profit from its tolls. Many such towns remained very small and partly agricultural, but even substantial towns like Leicester retained extensive common fields for grazing and gardening. Many towns were granted **charters**, usually by the king, which gave them the right to hold and manage land, to sue and be sued, and to hold courts to deal with disorder and disputes. They also gained the right to form their own government, or corporation, which usually consisted of a mayor (or equivalent) and a one- or two-tier council. The mayor and council were often 'elected', but elections were usually indirect, with a restricted electorate. Most town governments dealt with economic matters, regulating markets, weights and measures and labour issues – apprenticeship, wages, disputes between workman and employer. Larger towns faced specifically urban problems: sanitation and sewage, maintaining and cleansing the streets (made more difficult by the presence of pigs and butchers' offal, noxious trades and the risk of fire). Householders were responsible for cleaning, lighting and repairing the street outside their homes, and the streets were ill-lit, full of potholes, dirty, noxious and often positively dangerous, especially at night.

Apart from the right to work at a trade and sell retail, freemen also gained the right to vote in civic elections and hold the more prestigious offices. (Humbler offices, like parish constable, watchman or scavenger, were not usually held by freemen.) The wealthier freemen dominated town government and managed town properties and charities. Despite fears that they might use their power for their own profit, their right to rule was rarely challenged. They were better equipped to rule than their poorer neighbours. They had more experience of government; they had the local standing to act as mediators; and as established businessmen, they had more time to devote to (unpaid) administration. But they were expected to use their power for the common good. Many towns had stringent regulations about handling public money. Town rulers lived among those they ruled, mingling with them in the market place, the tavern and the street. They had few means of coercion: the constables and the watch hardly amounted to a police force, so they were vulnerable to riot and disorder. On many issues their views coincided with those of their neighbours. They tried to keep the streets clean, lit and repaired, without spending too much. They tried to enforce market regulations designed to enable the poor to buy grain at reasonable prices and fixed the price of bread and ale. They upheld the town's economic interests and tried to clamp down on brothels, disorderly alehouses, and anti-social behaviour, which offended the respectable poor as much as the rich. If they did not always succeed, townspeople at least appreciated that they had tried.

Wales and Ireland

Here towns were alien intrusions into societies for whom urban living did not come naturally. In Ireland Viking settlements were extended by Anglo-Norman invaders; in Wales towns were English creations, whose inhabitants tried to prevent Welsh people from settling or buying property. Most Welsh towns were small market and administrative centres, often huddled around a castle. Only a few, like Carmarthen, became social centres and meeting places for county business. Craftsmen often doubled as farmers. Manufactures, such as cloth and leather, were mainly for local consumption and concentrated in poor rural areas. Towns enjoyed trading and manufacturing privileges, but those with the greatest economic influence in Wales – Chester, Bristol, Shrewsbury – were in England.

In Ireland towns were larger and better established: Irish ports traded more extensively than Welsh ports. Like Wales, most exports were agricultural in origin. The rich fisheries off the south and west coasts were often exploited by foreign ships, because local lords had granted the right to fish in return for tolls. With the Gaelic resurgence some towns virtually ceased to exist, but those of the Pale and the larger ports of the south and west, such as Cork, Limerick and Galway, continued to thrive. Dublin, much the largest town and the centre of government, was on a different scale to the rest, but by 1500 its population had fallen to between 5,000 and 10,000. It had a sophisticated administration, originally modelled on Bristol. But corporations developed elsewhere in the later Middle Ages, with systems, offices and record-keeping similar to those of English boroughs. In smaller towns, as in Wales, many craftsmen were also part-time farmers and both the government provided and the records kept appear to have been rudimentary.

Scotland

Scotland had not suffered an enforced intrusion of English urban organisation although there were attempts to imitate Norman models. As elsewhere, lords saw towns as a potential source of profit, but they operated within a primitive economy. Many transactions were based on barter; by 1450 money was more widely used for wages and taxes, but many rents were still paid in kind. Manufactures were limited: the cloth produced was rough and coarse. Most towns were situated in the Central Lowlands and the main ports were on the east coast, trading mainly with the Low Countries and the Baltic. Glasgow, the largest town on the west coast, was still comparatively small. Edinburgh, the national capital, was Scotland's largest trading centre, responsible for 60 per cent of the customs in 1500. By 1560 it had a population of maybe 10,000.

Scottish towns were of two kinds: some 200 **burghs by barony** and 60 to 70 **royal burghs**. The former had generally been built by a lord who maintained a tight control in order to maximise his profits. Many were very small, containing a market place or toll-booth and a single street. Forbidden to trade abroad, they depended on a hinterland which was often small and impoverished. Royal burghs could trade overseas, and had a monopoly of trade within their hinterland. They enjoyed a measure of self-government and sent representatives (burgesses) to Parliament, where they came to form the third estate (after the nobles and clergy). Their systems of government were more uniform than those of English boroughs. Four leading burghs (originally Roxburgh,

Berwick, Edinburgh and Stirling) had enacted a series of laws which applied in all the royal burghs. Many were small, often a single street. Often their only fortifications were a dyke or palisade, which left them vulnerable to plunder by the English. As in England there was a fundamental distinction between those who could trade by retail (burgesses) and mere craftsmen. From 1469 Parliament decreed that in new corporations craftsmen were to have no say in elections; they responded by forming guilds, leading to legislation against '**combinations**' to increase wages. The merchants controlled burgh councils, leading to accusations that they granted contracts and leases to friends and kin, and embezzled town funds.

Communities: 2. Villages

When considering government in communities smaller than towns the picture is obscure. Celtic societies generated few written records. Even in England and Lowland Scotland, where Norman habits of record-keeping had developed, village records are sparse before the sixteenth century. Unlike town corporations, which needed to keep records of property ownership and management, villages lacked corporate bodies. The most important record-keeping institution was the manor: the lord needed to keep records to show his title to land, the rights that he enjoyed over his peasants and the obligations that they owed to him. Yet even in the thirteenth century, when serfdom was still strong, there are signs of peasants participating more in the running of the village, as well as working together to pursue legal disputes with their lord. In 1381 peasant organisation was often based on the village – indeed, one reason for the revolt was a perceived threat, from manorial lords, to village self-government. As serfdom withered after the Black Death villagers took on more and more responsibility for the functioning of the village.

The institution which first involved villagers in government was the manorial court, the records of which become quite numerous from the thirteenth century. Reeves, who managed lords' estates, tried to involve villagers in matters of common interest. Manorial courts issued ordinances, at the request of or with the consent of the tenants, for the regulation of the harvest and the fraught question of **gleaning**: who, among the village poor, should be allowed to pick up fallen grains of corn, and when. Where village fields were divided into strips, co-operation was needed to maintain the boundaries between strips and ensure that everyone followed the same crop rotation. There was a common interest in maintaining hedges, so animals did not stray into arable fields, and scouring drainage ditches, so that they did not overflow. Some manorial courts were **courts leet** (like many town courts). These could deal with non-manorial business: minor criminal matters, breaches of the peace and interpersonal disputes. Leet jurors not only heard cases but also 'presented' things which were amiss: dangerous bridges, obstructions in the roads and nuisances, such as offensive dunghills or overflowing privies. The king's government also encouraged villager participation. Royal taxes (notably the subsidy first raised in 1334) needed to be apportioned and collected at the village level and in wartime villages were required to provide a quota of soldiers.

With the Black Death many lords found it increasingly difficult to enforce their seigneurial rights over the peasantry. Without serf labour, lords could not farm their demesne lands and so many manorial courts declined. But village self-government continued to develop, often through ad hoc meetings. Apart from assessing and collecting taxes and raising soldiers, villagers often rented demesne land as a group, so needed to apportion the land between them. Where the manor court had leet jurisdiction, villagers extended their competence to deal with misbehaviour of various kinds (hedge-breaking, drunkenness, scolding and the like), imposing fines and appointing officials to collect them. Where manor courts decayed or disappeared informal groups of wealthier villagers seem to have performed similar functions, regardless of whether they had any legal right to do so. Kingsthorpe, Nottinghamshire, had a non-manorial assembly in the early thirteenth century that was still functioning in the sixteenth. The village community leased the whole manor, including its jurisdiction. Some villages, like town governments, fixed ale prices, and passed by-laws which the villagers were supposed to observe on pain of a fine or a spell in the stocks. Wymeswold, Leicestershire, drew up comprehensive village by-laws in 1425 and by-laws were common by 1460. Some villages had a **cucking stool**, where scolds (usually women, sometimes men) could be exposed to public humiliation. Village officials also brought cases before the hundred or church courts. In all this it seems that the 'better sort' took the lead. The richer farmers and craftsmen were the natural leaders of the community; they were also more likely than their poorer neighbours to be able to draft documents and keep accounts. There is little sign that their leadership was resented – often they were elected – or that their values were not widely shared: scolds, alehouse keepers who gave short measure, and farmers who let their animals stray into the corn, were not likely to be popular.

Communities: 3. Parishes

Self-government, and the responsibility of office-holders to the community, can be seen more fully in the parish; many **churchwardens**' accounts survive from the fifteenth century. Parishes were not always co-extensive with villages, although they often were. Towns might be a single parish or many: Winchester at one stage had fifty-four. Within a parish, the laity were responsible for maintaining the **nave** of the church, where the people sat; the priest maintained the **chancel**, containing the altar. In time, the laity extended their involvement. Regular attendance at Mass was believed to be essential for salvation. If the priest failed to say Mass regularly, the laity, who maintained him with their **tithes**, could withhold their money. This did not imply hostility to the clergy, or lack of religious belief. On the contrary, because they took their religious duties seriously they insisted that the priest should do what was required of him.

Individual laypeople showed their devotion by bequeathing funds, in money or kind, to beautify the church or provide candles. These resources belonged to the community, not to the priest, and they were administered by elected churchwardens. They were responsible to the community, giving in accounts each year, to parish assemblies. They were chosen from among the 'better sort', because of the need to keep records and draw up accounts. Although their responsibilities focused mainly on the church, they included secular elements. In some parishes an elected council, or **vestry**, enforced payments due to the parish, mediated in disputes and punished misbehaviour. Money left to the parish for the maintenance of roads, bridges, dykes and sluices was managed by the churchwardens. In the fifteenth century religious guilds and fraternities gave money to embellish the church, endowed **chantries** (where priests said masses for the souls of the dead), relieved the deserving poor and edified the people with processions and plays. These were legally not corporations but acted as if they were and, in time, their authority was recognised by the courts. In Wisbech, Cambridgeshire, a fraternity became the de facto town government.

In many parishes churchwardens raised significantly larger sums than either royal taxation or payments to the Church. Guilds and fraternities also raised and spent significant sums. Laypeople contributed to the church (and the poor) through bequests and regular gifts, often promised in front of the congregation after Sunday service. This might suggest an element of moral blackmail, but by promising publicly they demonstrated their wealth and piety. The 'better sort' would also rent places in the most conspicuous and prestigious pews and give generously to beautify the church fabric, taking care that their generosity was recorded. The wealthiest paid to be buried in the church, rather than in the churchyard alongside the poor. Poorer people made smaller gifts, which would also be recorded. People of all ranks contributed through **church ales**, in which beer was sold, so people could enjoy a convivial evening with the neighbours. Some church ales lasted for days, with players, wrestlers and morris dancing. Some villages held several each year which raised substantial sums: Yatton, in Somerset, raised enough to build a handsome new nave. By 1450 churchwardens were building church halls, or 'parish houses', often with facilities for brewing and baking. Many parish churches were improved or enlarged and new churches were built, often through the collective endeavours of the parishioners.

The growth in the amounts raised and spent by churchwardens and fraternities, and the building and rebuilding of churches, parish houses, and the like, testify to the capacity of laypeople to manage their own affairs. Government was not imposed from above, but something which people embraced and shaped according to their own needs and values. The allocation of powers and responsibilities might not be coherent, and sometimes several bodies performed similar functions, but those involved did what seemed necessary for good order, and the higher authorities in Church and state let them get on with it. Nor did the people complain: villages and parishes were intensively governed because their inhabitants wanted them to be. The dominant elites sometimes expressed fear of the poor. The Peasants' Revolt and Cade's rebellion suggest they had reason to do so, but villagers and townspeople generally showed respect for the law and were intolerant of anti-social or deviant behaviour. Whereas leaders of the Peasants' Revolt had talked of levelling and overturning, the leaders of Cade's revolt talked of law and order and echoed grievances expressed by the House of Commons. The English were law-abiding, but not docile. Their participation in government and law enforcement gave them expectations of how the law should be enforced, which could lead them to complain and even revolt.

The Poor

Any discussion of the lives of the people requires some consideration of the poor; the treatment of the poor also casts light on the capacity of ordinary villagers to tackle practical problems. Poverty was inevitable given low levels of productivity and the unequal distribution of wealth, and could be made worse by harvest failure, war and plundering. All were present across most of Britain and Ireland in the early fourteenth century, leading to widespread starvation. Those without enough food depended on the charity of others. In Celtic societies chiefs were obliged to relieve their clansmen in difficult times; there is little evidence to show how far they did so. In English Ireland, Lowland Scotland and England there is rather more evidence. In hard times many migrated from countryside to town, in the hope of finding work or charity. Townspeople already had their resident poor to deal with. They generally distinguished between the deserving 'impotent' poor, too old, young or sick to support themselves, and the undeserving, the able-bodied unemployed, often seen as shiftless and idle. The deserving poor might receive relief or be allowed to beg: in Scotland those with licences were called 'the king's beggars'. The undeserving might be whipped and driven away. People on the move were seen as a threat, as they had no master or employer to vouch for them and they might carry the plague.

With the coming of the Black Death the condition of survivors improved. The able-bodied were more likely to find work, but the problem of the impotent poor remained. These were dependent on others, combining what small earnings they might have with help from kin and friends, or charitable gifts. This help might take the form of money, clothing, shelter, food or fuel. They might also be able to secure small loans or exercise customary perquisites, like gleaning. By combining little bits of help in money or kind (making shift) they might just manage to survive.

Attitudes to the poor were shaped by the concept of 'a just price' for every commodity, including food and labour; asking too much led to avarice, which was a sin. Market regulations attempted to ensure that the poor were not overcharged for food; Parliament forbade labourers to demand higher wages when labour was scarce. The Church's teachings were ambivalent. On the one hand, it disapproved of wilful idleness: sloth was another of the Seven Deadly Sins. On the other, it taught that relieving the poor was a Christian duty: most of the seven 'works of mercy' (see p. 54) included charity to the poor, such as providing hospitality for strangers, including poor vagrants: some regularly took them in, even setting a room aside for them. The Church taught that poverty could be holy. Some believed that the prayers of the poor were more efficacious than those of the rich. The Church's emphasis on the importance of good works for salvation meant that those who gave to the poor would receive spiritual benefits; the prayers of the grateful poor could shorten the time that souls spent in **Purgatory**, which helps explain the many bequests to the poor.

Apart from attempts to regulate food prices, most provision for the poor was either institutional or individual. The main institutions catering for the poor were hospitals and almshouses. Both provided accommodation for selected poor people. Hospitals might provide meals and some basic care; few treated the chronically ill. The inhabitants of almshouses were expected to provide their own meals and some were expected to beg to pay for their keep. Most almshouses had fewer than ten inmates, some only two or three. Selection was largely a matter of personal favour. Often inmates were respectable folk down on their luck; they were rarely chosen from the very poor. In those set up by guilds and fraternities places usually went to their own members. Inmates were expected to conform to certain rules of behaviour and could be disciplined or expelled if they did not.

People were required by law to punish vagrants and encouraged by the Church to show Christian charity towards the poor. Vagrants were often severely treated in towns, where they posed a potential threat to public order. Villagers apparently had a more relaxed attitude, perhaps because few vagrants appeared and it was easier to judge whether they deserved relief. Parliament forbade all begging, even by those unable to work, but people seem to have accepted that those in need could seek alms privately (going from door to door) but not publicly. Normally, however, those who gave alms specified that they should go only to members of their own community. Help from neighbours was important in 'making shift': 'the most needy are our neighbours'. Some donors were more indiscriminate, providing cash doles for all who attended their funeral. Some left modest sums to be distributed among the poorest of the parish or to help them pay the king's taxes. Long before Parliament required every parish to have a poor box, money for the poor was often kept in a 'common box', along with money raised through church ales. If subsidy collectors collected more than was needed they might give the surplus to the poor. Some churchwardens made more or less compulsory collections for the poor after Sunday service and handed out small quantities of money, food or drink; the recipients might clean the church or do other work in return.

Although there was no national system of poor relief, some parishes developed their own systems. Some money was paid voluntarily, especially through bequests, but there was also an element of compulsion: churchwardens could use the apportionments for the subsidy to assess what each person could contribute. Although some payments, like funeral doles, were indiscriminate, others related payment to need and perceived moral worth: in small communities people knew one another well. Not all relief was in money or kind: towns provided training for pauper children. Girls were fitted to go into service, but boys were taught only the most rudimentary skills. By 1450 the treatment of the poor could be sophisticated and complex. Some giving was self-regarding and indiscriminate, but there was also considerable discrimination between the deserving and the undeserving. There was a strong sense that people's charitable efforts should be focused primarily on their neighbours, which implied a recognition (also apparent in by-laws) that communities were responsible for their own poor. And in some communities the better-off were compelled to contribute to poor relief in proportion to their means.

The Church

The churches of England, Scotland, Ireland and Wales formed part of the Catholic Church, a huge multinational organisation; archbishops and bishops governed national and regional churches. **Canon law** was developed to regulate the behaviour of priests and people, with hierarchies of courts to enforce it. Rich laymen, encouraged to give to the Church, built churches, cathedrals and monasteries. The Church claimed that pious and ascetic individuals could bring spiritual benefits to society. New orders of monks and nuns were founded, whose duty was to work, study and pray. Laymen rushed to endow these orders, which built palatial monasteries and acquired large estates; the Church became an enormously wealthy business corporation. In England it owned about one third of the land; in Scotland the Church's income was considerably larger than the king's.

The growth of the Church as a legal and business organisation was difficult to reconcile with the saving of souls. Laypeople expected the Church to provide the sacraments and spiritual guidance through which they could achieve salvation. As the Church became richer many clergy concentrated on maximising profits. The acquisitiveness of clergymen – grasping court officials and monastic landlords, parish priests demanding increased tithes – created ill-feeling, but seems not to have undermined people's faith in priests' spiritual authority. Similarly the papacy could be seen as morally tarnished. Papal elections were fought out between rival Italian families; the papal **curia** (court) was a by-word for corruption; and the idea of the Pope as supreme head of the Church was undermined by the Great Schism (1378–1417) during which a rival pope was established at Avignon. But the Pope's position as supreme spiritual authority remained resilient: people were able to distinguish between the office and the man.

The vast power of the Church led to conflicts with secular rulers about their respective authority. In theory, kings were responsible for secular matters and the popes for spiritual, but in practice the boundary between secular and spiritual was blurred. The Church claimed privileges and exemptions, including the right to enforce its own law in Church courts. Lawyers in the secular courts also sought to extend their competence (and business), leading to clashes between the two systems. Sanctuary, whereby alleged malefactors could take refuge from the king's officials, was contentious, as were ecclesiastical appointments. If there was friction between king and pope, the king would want the bishops and clergy to take his side. Moreover, as few laymen were literate, most royal administrators were priests. A king needed to be sure that their first loyalty was to him.

The Church's wealth attracted the attention of powerful laymen, who sought to install younger sons in rich church livings and find places in nunneries for their surplus daughters. Bishoprics and headships of great monasteries brought power as well as wealth: the Bishop of Durham had his own law courts and administration, independent of the king's. A bishopric could be an important asset in regional politics, part of a great family's power strategy. Bishops also assisted their families by granting favourable leases on episcopal lands; monasteries offered even richer pickings. By the fifteenth century most had lost their spiritual momentum: the ideals of asceticism had decayed, and a few well-fed monks lived comfortably on a substantial income. Poets praised some Welsh abbots for their lavish hospitality. For landowners whose incomes had fallen since the Black Death, monasteries were an appetising prey. Some became monastic stewards, others installed their sons as abbots. The monasteries' wealth was gradually siphoned off – but there was still plenty left.

This picture of spiritual decay and aristocratic exploitation holds true throughout Britain and Ireland: the largest Welsh monastery had only thirteen monks in 1536. There were also differences. The Irish Church had developed largely independently of Continental Europe until the twelfth century. Clerical celibacy, the Church's official teaching from 1139, was slow to be accepted in Ireland, Wales and Scotland; Celtic chiefs placed a strong emphasis on lineage (and, in Ireland, had a casual attitude towards marriage). It seemed natural to them that priests or abbots should be succeeded by their sons. Irish poets celebrated the genealogies of priestly dynasties. In Wales under Henry VIII Robert ap Rhys acquired several benefices and fathered sixteen children, of whom three became abbots. Cathal Óg McManus Maguire, dean of Lough Erne (died 1498), fathered at least twelve children, one of whom (a priest) married a bishop's daughter. He (Cathal Óg) was described by an annalist as a paragon of purity and chastity. In Ireland some priests and abbots dressed like laymen and behaved like warlords. Often they were not in holy orders, but had obtained grants of their benefices from Rome.

When bishops tried to enforce celibacy, sons were authorised by Rome to succeed their fathers. Similarly, in Scotland attempts by the Crown to exclude unsuitable candidates from benefices could be undermined by appeals to Rome. Some of those installed by the Crown were equally unsuitable, including royal bastards.

In English Ireland ecclesiastical discipline was better observed but the Church was hampered by the weakness of royal power. The primate, archbishop of the strongly Gaelic diocese of Armagh, was always English and lived in the Pale; his dean and chapter were Irish and lived in Armagh. However, English and Irish were conscious of belonging to the same Church and English bishops were accepted by the Irish as the successors of St Patrick. In Wales a high proportion of bishops were English; most could not speak Welsh and many spent as little time in their dioceses as possible. In Scotland kings sought to make bishops more effective, to strengthen their control over the Church. They were resisted both by Rome and by many of the clergy, but by the end of the fifteenth century they had secured two archbishops, of St Andrews and Glasgow.

The Church's weaknesses were conspicuous: the decay of the monastic ideal, the malign interference of aristocrats, kings and the papal curia. But what mattered to laypeople was their own spiritual lives. Parishes suffered from similar neglect and predatory interference. Their tithes and endowments had often been transferred to cathedrals, monasteries and universities. Where parish benefices carried a good stipend, the patronage system usually ensured that they went to well-connected young men. These rarely wanted to minister to grubby peasants, and secured positions in cathedral chapters or universities, paying a curate to look after their flocks. So, despite the Church's wealth, throughout Britain very many parish priests were paid pitifully small stipends, unlikely to attract well-educated men. In Scotland 86 per cent of parish revenues were 'appropriated' to other institutions and some parish churches lacked windows or roofs. In Wales two-thirds of parishes were worth less than £10 a year. In Ireland many parish churches were ramshackle and decrepit. Yet not all was decay. If monastic piety was in terminal decline, the friars – evangelistic preachers, supported by the alms of the faithful – were growing rapidly in numbers and popularity. Many parish churches were rebuilt or embellished, often by the parishioners. In England, Wales, Scotland and English Ireland this was linked to the growth of religious guilds and fraternities. Only in Gaelic Ireland, with its emphasis on kin rather than community, was there little sign of such activity. To produce a rounded picture, we need to try to reconstruct what the Church, and religion, meant to ordinary people.

Religion and the People

The primary focus of lay religious life was the parish church. The building and its contents, including the priest's robes, were a source of collective pride. It was normally the largest building in the parish and its solid fabric contrasted with the homes of most parishioners. Its windows offered light and colour, which people lacked at home, while its height helped to draw people's thoughts heavenwards. All churches were built with the main door to the west and the altar to the east. Moving from the door one passed into space that was progressively more sacred, through the nave, where the people sat, to the chancel, reserved for the clergy and the choir, and finally to the altar. Above the arch separating nave from chancel was the **rood screen**, with a large picture of Christ on the cross, together with the Virgin Mary. Above or behind was a tableau of Judgment Day, when Christ, his wounds prominently displayed, would call everyone to account. (See Figure 2.4, Rood Screen at St Peter's Church, Wenhaston, Suffolk, and Figure 2.5, Rood Screen at St Ellyw's Church, Llanelieu, Powys.) The screen was pierced so that, as the congregation looked towards the altar, these images of suffering and judgment would always be before them. In time more images were added, notably saints, enhancing the importance of Christ's sacrifice.

Not all parish churches were stoutly constructed or richly decorated. Many parishes, especially in upland areas, were wretchedly poor. Churches were plundered in war or border raids. In sparsely populated upland parishes people found it difficult to get to church, especially in winter. But all parish churches served similar spiritual and social functions. In church the key rites of passage – birth, marriage and death – were solemnised, in baptism, wedding and funeral. The church and its services fostered a sense of community. At the end of the service the members of the congregation kissed an object (often containing a relic or picture) known as the pax or paxbred – a collective kiss of peace. Those not at peace with their neighbours were not allowed to kiss it, or to receive the **Eucharist**, which gave the clergy some leverage when trying to resolve quarrels. The Church provided the community's calendars: the complex Christian calendar, with its fixed and moveable feasts, and the simpler calendar of the farming year, with prayers at seedtime and thanksgiving at harvest. The Church's teachings provided the moral code that the community was expected to live by. It warned of the punishments for sin, highlighted by the Judgment on the rood screen, and urged the spiritual benefits of good works: not only pious acts and gifts to the Church but also living in charity with one's neighbours and relieving the poor. Everyone was expected to observe the Church's moral teachings; those who did not came under pressure to change their ways.

Central to the Church's teachings was original sin, the legacy of Adam and Eve. Humans could not overcome their tendency to sin, but they could keep it within bounds and make amends when they sinned, by gifts to the Church, offerings at shrines, extra prayers and masses, pilgrimages and helping the needy. The Church listed seven 'works of mercy': giving food to the hungry and drink to the thirsty, clothing the naked, visiting and comforting prisoners and the sick, providing hospitality and shelter for strangers, and burying the dead. These acts of charity could be prescribed by the priest, who was responsible for the spiritual welfare of all his flock. Before anyone could receive the Eucharist, in which the consecrated bread and wine were believed to become the

Figures 2.4 & 2.5 The Wenhaston screen was whitewashed and its original form was discovered only in 1892. It features an elaborate Day of Judgment; the crucifixion was originally positioned in the centre at the top. The decoration of the Llanelieu screen was limited to a simple cross and patterned decoration.

body and blood of Christ, they had to be in a fit spiritual state, confessing their sins and expressing due penitence. The priest then prescribed a penance which, while not wiping away the guilt of their sin, mitigated its effects and allowed them access to the sacraments. Sinners who refused to show penitence or do penance could be excommunicated: excluded from the sacraments, and so from the means of salvation. If they remained excommunicated, their souls would be consigned to hell.

The Church taught of the horrors of hell, but suggested that only the most hardened sinners would end there: it served as an awful warning, not a likely destination. However, few who avoided hell would go directly to heaven. The guilt of sin was too great for people to atone for in their lifetime, so they did so after their death in **Purgatory**, where souls could be cleansed of the guilt for lesser sins, and undergo punishment for greater, until they were fit to be admitted to heaven. Some believed that there were also preliminary torments before one reached Purgatory. It was generally accepted that cleansing involved suffering and some features earlier ascribed to hell were now used of Purgatory, including being tormented by demons, the devil's minions. God and the devil could fight for an individual's soul, especially on their deathbed. The dying person needed to confess their sins and be absolved (shriven) by the priest and then to receive the Eucharist. It was believed that deathbed acts of piety could reduce the dying person's time in Purgatory.

BOX 2.1: **The Lyke-wake Dirge**

This traditional Yorkshire ballad was first written down in 1686 but clearly dates back to before the Reformation. It is a mourning song sung during a vigil over a corpse, lit by fire and candlelight. It tells of the travails a soul must pass through before reaching Purgatory and stresses the importance of good works for salvation.

The refrain, given in italics in the first verse, is repeated in each verse. 'Ae' means one; 'fire and fleet' was a term used in wills ('flet' is house-room); 'whin' means gorse or any prickly shrub.

This ae nighte, this ae nighte.
Every nighte and alle,
Fire and fleet and candle-lighte,
And Christe receive thy saule.

When thou from hence away art past
To Whinny-muir thou com'st at last

If ever thou gavest hosen and shoon,
Sit thee down and put them on;

If hosen and shoon thou ne'er gav'st nane
The whinnes shall prick thee to the bare bane.

From Whinny-muir when thou may'st pass.
To Brig o' Dread thou com'st at last;

*If ivver thoo gav o' thy siller an' gowd,
At t' Brig o' Dread thoo'll find foothold,

*But if siller an' gowd thoo nivver gav nane,
Thoo'll doan, doon tum'le towards Hell fleames.

From Brig o' Dread when thou may'st pass,
To Purgatory fire thou com'st at last;

If ever thou gav'st meat or drink
The fire shall never make thee shrink;

If meat or drink thou ne'er gav'st nane
The fire will burn thee to the bare bane;

This ae night, this ae night,
Every nighte and alle,
Fire and fleet and candle-lighte,
And Christe receive thy saule.

The bulk of the text is taken from C. Ricks (ed.), *The Oxford Book of English Verse* (Oxford, 1999), pp. 13–14, where it is ascribed to the fifteenth century. The two verses with asterisks are from a variant text, with different spellings, but they seem to fit naturally in this version. For a different, apparently Scottish, version of these two verses, see www.musicanet.org/robokopp/scottish/lykewake.htm (accessed 16 January 2015).

Many made provision in their wills for bequests to the Church and for prayers and masses for their souls. The Mass, with its constant reminders of Christ's sacrifice and the miraculous transformation of bread and wine, was at the heart of popular devotion. Most laypeople took communion only once a year, at Easter. Often only the priest received the Eucharist, having consecrated the bread and wine at the altar, in Latin; only priests received the wine, which emphasised their spiritual status. However, laypeople frequently attended services in which Mass was said. **Hosts**, the consecrated wafers consumed in the Mass, were displayed prominently in church, surrounded by lights, and people believed that donating candles, venerating the host or simply looking as it was consecrated protected them against dying without being shriven. At the Feast of Corpus Christi the host was carried in state through town streets; people flocked to gaze at it and guilds in the procession jostled to be near it. Sermons emphasised its magical properties. Many involved Jews, who had been expelled from England in 1290, but were still demonised. It was said that when Jews tried to destroy consecrated hosts, they could not do so. A Jew was said to have converted to Christianity when he gave a host to his dog, which refused to eat it.

As the spiritual power of the host was so great, saying masses for the souls of the dead was a powerful form of intercession. Those who could afford it hired priests and special altars were established in **chantries**. The masses kept the memory of the deceased alive, as could giving communion vessels or other artefacts to the church, engraved with their names. People of all ranks arranged for gifts of money, clothing and food to those who attended their funeral, obliging them to keep them in their thoughts. The very wealthy could arrange for elaborate tombs, brasses or other memorials, or founded schools, hospitals or almshouses that bore their names. Humbler people could be remembered too: small legacies were recorded in the parish **bede-roll**, which was read, once a year, in a service known as an **obit**. The parish community included both the living and the dead.

At this point we need to ask an important question. The Church's teachings were set out in the decrees of popes and councils, the instructions of bishops, and officially approved works of prayer and devotion. But how far were these teachings understood, accepted and actively observed by the laity? Literacy levels seem low: few laypeople were able to write. Before the development of printing in the later fifteenth century, devotional works were handwritten and expensive. Parish priests were poorly paid and often poorly educated. In Wales and parts of Ireland bishops and some parish priests could not speak the language of most of the people. But there is evidence of a vigorous lay piety in the fifteenth century, especially in Lowland England. Devotional literature flourished, in manuscript and later in print, which would suggest that more people could read than write. Those who could not read might have access to the written word: reading aloud was common. Evidence of lay piety can be found in books of devotion, commonplace books and correspondence. It can be seen in bede-rolls and accounts recording myriad gifts to the Church, great and small, in improvements to parish churches and the multiplication of chantries, guilds and fraternities. These provided a form of insurance against misfortune and an opportunity to socialise, but their primary purpose was religious, especially providing masses and prayers for the dead and performing miracle plays, designed to entertain and instruct.

Guilds and fraternities were especially common in Lowland England, Lowland Scotland and English Ireland where towns were comparatively numerous. However, there is also evidence of church-building and improvement, often organised by fraternities, in Wales, where towns were few and small; this was apparent even in solidly Welsh communities. By the late fifteenth century popular devotion was flourishing in Wales, seen in improvements to parish churches and bustling pilgrimage sites. Much of the initiative for this came from the laity, but was this devotion without understanding? Did the laity believe that certain actions (like prayers and pilgrimages) had a mechanical effect, irrespective of the spirit in which they were performed? Could they buy salvation by giving money and having masses said for their souls? Reformers, Catholic and Protestant, later argued that the laity did indeed believe this. The Church placed great emphasis on miracles, the devil and the intervention of evil spirits in the material world, so it was not surprising that laypeople sought to make use of 'Church magic'. They lived in a dangerous world, at the mercy of forces which they could neither understand nor control: diseases, of people, crops and animals; the weather; fire; and predators, animal and human. There were often folk remedies or explanations for such hazards, but people also sought protection from the Church.

Officially the Church taught that its rituals should be used only for spiritual purposes, but these were often subtle distinctions and simple priests and simple people tended to blur them. Saints were pious exemplars, who had often suffered horribly for their faith. They could intercede for sinners on Judgment Day, but they themselves could not confer spiritual or material benefits. However, people believed that they could. Individual saints became associated with particular groups. St Erasmus, who had been disembowelled, was believed to offer relief for those with intestinal problems. St Katherine of Alexandria, who suffered numerous tortures, including having her breasts torn off, was believed to protect women in childbirth. Originally saints' relics were the main objects of veneration, but this later extended to their images. The Virgin Mary was especially popular; because of her gentleness and compassion, her intercession was believed to be particularly effective. Many people believed that saints could protect them against misfortune; the clergy did not discourage such beliefs, especially if their church contained a popular shrine. Similarly, if the Church encouraged the use of holy water for blessing and protection, how could it prevent people from using it for other purposes? The ambivalence of 'church-magic' was highlighted in Rogation-tide processions. These walked the parish boundaries with banners and bells, to fix them in the villagers' collective memory. They were expressions of community, ending with parishioners eating and drinking together. But they were also intended to drive out evil spirits, which might otherwise spread discord and bring sickness, and to bring good weather and abundant crops. Some said they gave rise to rowdiness and disorder, others that it was uncharitable to drive their evil spirits into the next parish. Belief in evil spirits was widespread and the Church did not discourage it.

The central features of popular religion could be found across Britain and Ireland. There was the consciousness of sin, and the belief that its effects could be offset by acts of piety, either in one's lifetime or after one's death. The saints were believed to intercede for sinners and offer protection, as did objects and rituals blessed by the Church, such as sprinkling with holy water. There was always a danger that the subtle interplay between the individual and Christ and the saints could become contractual and mechanical; aids to devotion could be seen as having material effects. Priests were expected to prevent such misunderstandings. From 1281 the English clergy were ordered to preach four times a year, in English, expounding and explaining the Creed, the ten commandments, Christ's teaching on loving one's neighbour, the seven works of mercy, the seven virtues, the seven deadly sins and the seven sacraments. How far they did so and what impact their instruction had on their flocks is impossible to tell. What is clear is that they explained the central importance of the crucifixion and the Mass and encouraged the people to meditate upon Christ's suffering and wounds. The outcome was a lay piety that was probably, by the late fifteenth century, richer and more vigorous than ever before. It combined the power of tradition and habit with the ability to evolve. If the Church as a legal and business organisation was vulnerable to criticism, as a spiritual force it was woven ever more deeply into the fabric of social life. Its failure to distinguish clearly between the spiritual and the secular was perhaps a source of strength, as the laity appropriated religious practices for secular purposes. It was certainly not on the verge of collapse in the late fifteenth century.

Conclusion

In the century before 1450 the lives of working people in much of Britain and Ireland were transformed as serfdom disintegrated in the wake of the Black Death. Hitherto the relations between peasant and lord had been shaped by a mixture of servile obligations and market forces. Now market forces predominated, tempered only by subtle social expectations. Landlords were expected to uphold gentlemanly and paternalistic values of hospitality and benevolence; employers were expected to show similar kindness to their workmen, especially as they lived and worked in close proximity. These were moral, not legal, obligations and they could not be enforced, except (possibly) by mockery or the threat of riot or strike. In time, as great landowners came to manage their estates through stewards or land agents, and the scale of manufacturing grew, landlords and manufacturers became more remote from their tenants and workers and some felt fewer constraints in their pursuit of profit. For the moment the predominance of market forces favoured tenants and labourers: it has been suggested that the purchasing power of wages reached a peak in 1450–75 that was not exceeded until the late nineteenth century. But as the population grew in the sixteenth century the balance of economic power swung back in favour of landlords and employers and real wages fell.

The consequences of the end of serfdom were not only economic. Freedom and economic power gave men the self-confidence to bargain with their landlords and employers and to play a more active part in the running of their communities. Manorial courts, which had formerly served the interests of the landlord, now served those of the community. Villages drew up by-laws and even constitutions. Towns, villages and parishes developed more effective ways of dealing with their poor: only at the end of the sixteenth century was a national system of poor relief established by Parliament. One can also detect a similar freedom and inventiveness in religious life, particularly in the multiplication of religious guilds and fraternities. The Church showed a relaxed attitude towards new devotions and accommodated practices which did not run counter to its teaching. Such flexibility was soon to end. Henry VIII prohibited a wide range of popular practices, particularly those connected with saints, and the new Protestant national church (and particularly its more radical members) tried to root out anything which smacked of 'popery'. Their efforts met with strong opposition – church ales remained popular – but parish spiritual life became plainer and more stereotyped and lost much of the richness and inventiveness it had shown in the fifteenth century.

SUGGESTIONS FOR FURTHER READING

There is a rich literature on the late medieval economy, including J.L. Bolton, *The Medieval English Economy 1150–1500* (London, 1980), R.H. Britnell, *Britain and Ireland 1050–1530: Economy and Society* (Oxford, 2004) and C. Dyer, *Making a Living in the Middle Ages: the People of Britain 850–1530* (London, 2003). • On towns, see S. Reynolds, *An Introduction to the History of English Medieval Towns* (Oxford, 1977), R. Holt and G. Rosser (eds.), *The Medieval Town: A Reader in English Urban History 1200–1540* (Harlow, 1990) and D.M. Palliser (ed.), *The Cambridge Urban History of Britain, vol. I: 600–1540* (Cambridge, 2000). • The literature on village governance and popular politics is more scattered: W.O. Ault, 'Village Assemblies in Medieval England', in *Album Helen M. Cam* (Louvain, 1960), C. Dyer, 'The Political Life of the Fifteenth-Century English Village', in L. Clark and C. Carpenter (eds.), *Political Culture in Medieval Britain,* The Fifteenth Century, IV (Woodbridge, 2004), R.B. Goheen, 'Peasant Politics? Village Community and the Crown in Fifteenth-Century England', *American Historical Review*, 96 (1991) and I.M.W. Harvey, 'Was there Popular Politics in Fifteenth-Century England?', in R.H. Britnell and A.J. Pollard (eds.), *The Macfarlane Legacy* (Stroud, 1995). • It can be argued that the growing concern with governance and by-laws within villages is evidence of the growing tensions and a weakening of communal ties which became more apparent in the sixteenth century: C. Dyer, 'The English Medieval Village Community and its Decline', *Journal of British Studies*, 33 (1994). • On the parish, see B. Kümin, *The Shaping of a Community: the Rise and Reformation of the English Parish c.1400–1560* (Aldershot, 1996) and K.L. French, G.G. Gibbs and B. Kümin (eds.), *The Parish in English Life 1400–1600* (Manchester, 1997). • On the treatment of the poor, the key works are by M.K. McIntosh: *Controlling Misbehaviour in England, 1370–1600* (Cambridge, 1998) and *Poor Relief in England, 1350–1600* (Cambridge, 2011); there is also a useful survey by C. Dyer, 'Poverty and its Treatment in Late Medieval England', *Past and Present*, 216 (2012). • Finally, on the Church and religion the prevailing historiography, based on claims that the people were hostile to the clergy and dissatisfied with the Church's teachings and worship, has been comprehensively challenged by E. Duffy, *The Stripping of the Altars: Traditional Religion in England 1400–1580* (New Haven, 1992) – essential reading for anyone interested in the English Reformation. For the most persuasive (and elegant) exposition of the traditional interpretation, see A.G. Dickens, *The English Reformation* (London, 1964). For other discussions of the pre-Reformation Church see J.J. Scarisbrick, *The English People and the English Reformation* (Oxford, 1985) and G.W. Bernard, *The Late Medieval Church* (New Haven, 2013).

SUMMARY

- In the first half of the fourteenth century England was over-populated. Farmers struggled to produce enough food and a glut of labour enabled employers to keep wages low. The situation was transformed by the Black Death: a dearth of people strengthened the bargaining position of tenants and labourers.
- In the fifteenth century the demand for English wool and woollen cloth boomed, bringing prosperity to areas suitable for grazing sheep.
- In the fifteenth century there is evidence of strong lay piety, seen in the embellishment of parish churches and the multiplication of religious guilds and chantries. There are also signs that lay expectations of the clergy were rising.

QUESTIONS FOR STUDENTS

1. Why did serfdom collapse in the later Middle Ages?
2. Was the period 1350 to 1450 a 'golden age' for the peasantry?
3. Assess the extent of popular participation in the government of either towns or villages in late medieval England.
4. Assess the importance of the Church in the lives of townsmen and peasants in late medieval England.

3 Monarchies and Their Problems 1450–1536

TIMELINE

1450	Cade's rising
1453	Loss of French territories; Henry VI's son born; Henry VI's mental breakdown
1455	Battle of St Albans; Henry VI recovers from illness
1460	York claims Crown, killed at Battle of Wakefield
1461	Yorkist victory at Towton; Henry VI flees to Scotland; Edward IV seizes Crown
1470	Edward IV flees into exile; Henry VI again proclaimed King ('Readeption')
1471	Edward IV defeats Queen Margaret; Henry VI killed
1483	Edward IV dies; Richard III seizes the throne
1485	Richard III killed at Bosworth; Henry VII proclaimed King
1487	Lambert Simnel defeated at Stoke
1497	Cornish rising suppressed; Perkin Warbeck surrenders to Henry VII
1502	Henry VII's son Arthur dies
1509	Henry VIII succeeds his father

1513	English defeat Scots at Flodden; James IV killed
1525	'Amicable Grant'
1529	Wolsey falls from power; Reformation Parliament (1529–36) assembles
1536	Union between England and Wales; Acts against Liberties and Franchises; Statute of Uses; Pilgrimage of Grace

Introduction

1450 marked one of the lowest points of the medieval English monarchy, with Cade's rebellion and the lynching of several of the King's leading servants. Henry VI was not a tyrant but his simplicity was abused by men who behaved tyrannously and by his strong-minded queen. His refusal to heed good counsel created deep divisions among the nobility, which led to civil war; the battles were often small, but followed by brutal murders of the defeated. Earlier usurpations had created uncertainty about the rightful succession, opening the way for Yorkists to claim the Crown. Civil war led to the breakdown of order in many areas and a need for stable and effective government to restore the rule of law. Yorkist rule ended with the death of Richard III, but the first two Tudors showed strong signs of dynastic insecurity. The English monarchy was underfunded compared with the great Continental powers. Henry VIII's French wars made his financial problems worse and his breach with Rome increased the danger of foreign invasion. All of this made it urgent to tackle the 'lawless zones': the Anglo-Scottish borderlands, Wales and the Welsh Marches and Ireland. The Scottish kings were free of dynastic uncertainties: Stewart rule was not challenged. However, royal minorities created problems and the Stewarts faced the problems of 'lawless zones' and the weakness of royal justice outside the major towns. They began to undermine magnate power, starting with the **lordship of the Isles**, but bringing order to the Highlands and Islands would be a long, slow process.

Scotland

The greatest threat to medieval Scotland was English military aggression. The war of independence placed huge strains on Scotland and was followed by bloody civil wars. In the fifteenth century, as the military threat from England waned, the Stewarts consolidated their power, crushing the lawless and violent in both the Highlands and the Lowlands. With less prospect of war, the Scottish Parliament saw little need to grant taxes and encouraged the kings to build up their landed estates and **live of their own**, which they were generally willing to do. Parliament would grant money only for a necessary war: a defensive war against England was seen as acceptable, but James III's schemes for Continental expeditions were not. As the Scots army was unpaid and poorly equipped it was no match for a well-resourced English army. When James IV began an ill-advised war in alliance with the King of France, his army was crushed at Flodden (1513), and James himself was killed.

Crown and Nobility

The Scottish kings of the fifteenth century came to identify themselves culturally and politically with the Lowlands: James IV (1488–1513) was the last to speak Gaelic. Loyalty to the monarchy was deeply engrained, underpinned by the belief that it dated back to the third century BC. The emphasis on ancient lineage appealed particularly to Gaelic Scotland and helped unite all ethnic groups behind the Crown. Despite several minorities, the only attempt to usurp the throne failed. When James I was assassinated in 1437 his assassins were quickly hunted down and punished. When James III was killed by rebels in 1488 the Crown passed at once to his young son. The threat from the great magnate families ended when James II murdered the eighth Earl of Douglas. Most of the old earldoms and provincial lordships had passed to the Crown and new leading families, like the Gordons and Campbells, owed their rise, at least in part, to state service. By the 1450s the Scottish nobles were less likely than their English counterparts to quarrel with one another, particularly over titles to land. There was also less danger of peasant revolts in Scotland than in England. In the late fifteenth century some nobles felt secure enough to build tower houses rather than castles.

With the bulk of the nobility loyal, kings could target individuals. They began to tackle the problem of the Hebrides and adjacent mainland, helped by divisions among the Macdonalds. In 1493 the King confiscated the **lordship of the Isles** and undermined the autonomy of other Gaelic chiefs, making them answerable for their clansmen's conduct. Kings could deprive individual nobles of life or property without due process of law, but they could not afford to antagonise a wide section of the nobility, and did not do so. The nobles' loyalty and willingness to take responsibility for governing also enabled the monarchy to survive a series of incompetent or underage kings.

The English Crown in the 1450s

In Scotland, kings' oldest sons succeeded their fathers without challenge. In England, primogeniture provided for an orderly succession in theory, but the deposition and killing of 'tyrannous' kings led to succession disputes. After Richard II, whose father was the oldest son of Edward III, was killed in 1399, the Crown was seized by Henry

IV, the son of Edward's third son, John of Gaunt, Duke of Lancaster. The second son left no male heirs, but his daughter married Edmund Mortimer, Earl of March. The Mortimers died out in the male line in 1425, but left a daughter whose son Richard (1411–60) became Duke of York. The question arose as to who had the stronger claim: the House of Lancaster, descended in the direct male line from Edward III's third son, or the House of York, descended from the second son, but through two women. There was no mechanism to resolve such a question: ultimately, as in a Scottish or Irish clan, it was a matter of who was stronger. Initially it did not seem an insuperable problem. Henry IV faced a difficult reign, but survived, and Henry V proved exceptionally forceful and capable; his son was neither.

The Problem of Henry VI

Henry succeeded his father as an infant in 1422. A regency council provided relatively stable government until he was deemed to have come of age in 1436 or 1437. He liked the idea of governing, but lacked the intelligence or strength of character to do so effectively. Unlike earlier kings he did not create an **affinity** of loyal nobles and knights to enforce his will. His French wife, Margaret of Anjou, harboured grudges and dealt forcefully with her enemies. Henry was too weak to perform more than a ceremonial role. He was deeply pious and was widely seen as a saint. His confessor wrote that 'he was more given to God and to devout prayer than to handling worldly or temporal things or practising vain sports and pursuits' – the antithesis of a virile, martial king. He was prim and censorious, condemning his courtiers' preoccupation with fashion (he dressed like a peasant), and their proneness to swearing and promiscuity. He was neither malicious nor vindictive, but succumbed to the malice and vindictiveness of others. He became embroiled in his favourites' scams and vendettas and protected them. His government was dominated by an inner circle, including Suffolk, Ayscough and Moleyns, while many of the great nobility, his 'natural counsellors', were denied access to his person. Cade's manifestos showed that Henry's weakness was well known: people called him a 'natural fool' or 'child', recklessly generous with grants and pardons. In 1453–4 he fell into a catatonic state, unable to move or speak, but he recovered to a point where he seemed rational, if uninterested in government. In 1453 his queen bore him a son, Edward, whose interests she defended fiercely. There was no prospect that Henry himself could resolve the problems that his inadequacy created.

The French War

Henry VI was uninterested in war and never commanded an army. He lived in the shadow of his father, whose victories (notably Agincourt) reflected both his military skills and exceptional French weakness. France had a larger population and superior resources:

its kings had been hampered by internal dissensions but Charles VII was overcoming his problems and a French victory was probably only a matter of time. However, it was surprising that English resistance collapsed so quickly and completely after the ending of a five-year truce in 1449. The decision to renew the war was made mainly by Suffolk and the Duke of Somerset; popular hatred of Suffolk's tyranny was compounded by military failure. By the time of Cade's rising Normandy was lost and the French were raiding the English coast. The enormity and speed of the defeat led to allegations of treachery.

The Misgovernment of the Duke of Suffolk

In East Anglia Suffolk used royal officials and institutions to pursue his own interests. As with Lord Saye in Kent, Suffolk's cronies Lord Moleyns, Thomas Tuddenham and John Heydon did his dirty work and pursued their own claims to land and goods. Moleyns and Heydon organised an armed attack on John Paston's house at Gresham, Norfolk, and plundered many of his goods. It was alleged that Suffolk's followers used force to prevent coroners holding inquests into violent deaths. Sheriffs selected packed juries which exonerated genuine miscreants and convicted their victims. If any wrongdoers were in danger of being convicted, the King transferred their cases to King's Bench, in London, or pardoned them. Petitions to the King or council were ineffectual. (See Box 3.1, Suffolk, Moleyns and East Anglia.) Favoured nobles pursued their feuds with impunity. The wealthy Sir John Fastolf dared not offer a legal challenge to Heydon's seizure of four Norfolk manors and negotiated a deal through Suffolk. A man who claimed one of the Pastons' manors boasted that he would succeed because he had Suffolk's 'good lordship and he would be his good lord in this matter'.

 BOX 3.1: **Suffolk, Moleyns and East Anglia**

The Attack on Gresham 1449

Barrow and Hegon and all the Lord Moleyns' men that were at Gresham when ye departed hence been there still … I conceived well by them that they were weary of that they hadden done. Barrow swore to me by his troth that you would liefer than 40s. and 40 that his lord had not commanded him to come to Gresham and that he was right sorry … of that that was done. I said to him that he should have compassion on you, and other that were disseised [dispossessed] of their livel[ih]ode, inasmuch as he had been disseised himself. And he said he was so, and told me that he had sued to my Lord of Suffolk divers times, and would don till he may get his good again. I said to him that ye had sued to my Lord Moleyns divers times for the manor of Gresham sith ye were disseised and ye could never get no reasonable answer of him … he said he should never blame my Lord of Suffolk for the entry in his livelode, for he said my said lord was set thereupon by the information of a false shrew; and I said to him in like wise is the matter betwixt the Lord Moleyns and you … ['Shrew' is a malevolent person, male or female]

The Lord Moleyns hath a company of brothel [worthless fellows] with him that reck not what they don, and such are most for to dread. They that been at Gresham sayn that they have not done so much hurt to you as they were commanded to don ...

Margaret Paston to John Paston, 15 February 1449, in N. Davis (ed.), *The Paston Letters* (Oxford World's Classics, 1983), pp. 16–19.

The King Protects Moleyns and his Men

[The sheriff of Norfolk] said he would do for you that he may, except for the acquittal of Lord Moleyns's men, insomuch that the King hath writ to him for to show favour to the Lord Moleyns and his men. And as he saith, the indictment longeth to the king and not to you, and the Lord Moleyns a great lord. Also, as he saith, now late the Lord Moleyns hath sent him a letter ... for to show favour in these indictments. He dare not abide the jeopardy of that that he should offend the king's commandment. He know not how the king may be informed of and what shall be said to him ...

[Paston offered the sheriff a 'surety' to 'save him harmless'] he said he might none surety take that passed £100; and the Lord Moleyns is a great lord, he might soon cause him to lose that and much mo ... [The writer concludes that he thinks the sheriff 'looketh after a great bribe'] ...

John Osbern to John Paston, 27 May 1451, *The Paston Letters*, pp. 29–31.

The language of goodlordship reminds us that, although the scale of retaining had diminished by 1450, the infrastructure of relationships was still there and could be reactivated. Unable to secure justice from the King, lords were thrown back on their own resources. However, the fact that the Commons focused on Suffolk suggests that he was seen as the greatest grievance: if he were removed, lesser miscreants might be punishable by law. But Henry showed no inclination to change his way of governing. Many of those dismissed for extortion and violence in 1450 were reinstated. Suffolk's dukedom was restored to his young son. It became apparent that the kingdom's ills could be remedied only by force.

Richard of York

Critics of Suffolk's misgovernment tried to persuade Henry to take counsel from the senior nobility, including Richard, Duke of York. Henry, however, saw Richard as a threat. Apart from his royal blood, he held very extensive lands in England, Wales and the Marches and Ireland. Until Henry's son was born in 1453 York seemed his obvious heir. In the 1430s he played a prominent part in the French war, but was superseded by Somerset and was not repaid much of what he had spent. Henry continued to rely on the Beaufort dukes of Somerset. To get York out of the way, he was made lord lieutenant of Ireland. Somerset returned to London in August 1450; soon after, York arrived from Ireland with 4,000 soldiers. He may have feared that the Beauforts threatened his claim to the throne. Like Henry, the Beauforts were descended from John of Gaunt, but by his third wife, whom he had married only after their children were born. They were thus illegitimate, and Henry IV had confirmed that they were debarred from the throne, but some feared that Henry VI might legitimise them. York posed as an advocate of reform, cleansing Henry's government of corrupt office-holders and clawing back land grants through **Acts of Resumption**. He appeared before the King at Dartford in 1452, with an armed following, but failed to trigger a rebellion and withdrew.

Percies and Nevilles

The debacle at Dartford showed that to force his way into the King's counsels York needed an ally in the North, the most militarised region of England. There, especially near the border, lords granted land in return for military service. Lineage counted and the mutual loyalty of lord and man could outweigh the loyalty of subject to king. The importance of the border was shown by the salaries of the Wardens of the East and West Marches: the former could reach £5,000 a year in wartime – more than the landed income of most peers. (Even in peacetime the salary was £2,500.) These salaries allowed the border magnates to fee retainers on a very large scale, over and above the service they received from their tenants. The earls of Northumberland spent up to 40 per cent of their estate income on retaining: one retained a total of eighty-four lords, knights and esquires: many lowland lords retained a handful and recruited most of their retainers from their households and tenants. The great border lords wielded military power far greater than any southern noble – or the Duke of York.

In the 1450s the great northern families, the Percies and Nevilles, held the wardenships of the East and West March respectively. The Percies were dominant in Northumberland and had extensive estates in the North West and Yorkshire. The Nevilles were even more formidable in Yorkshire and had been built up by Henry IV and V to rival the Percies in Cumbria. The head of the family, Richard Earl of Salisbury, procured offices, lands and castles for his numerous brothers and their clients and retainers. As well as the wardenships, the Nevilles and Percies controlled **liberties and franchises**, which they ruled independently of the King: they enforced the King's law, but the King's officers had no authority there. From 1438 to 1457 Salisbury's brother Robert was Bishop of Durham, the greatest liberty of all, and promoted his family's interests. William Percy performed a similar role as Bishop of Carlisle (1452–62). As their contest for followers escalated both sides mobilised thousands of armed men. Here were two ready-made armies, either of which could enable York to promote his claims. The decision was made when Salisbury's ruthless and ambitious son, Richard, Earl of Warwick, quarrelled with Somerset, which gave him some common ground with York. At this point Henry suffered his first breakdown; a great council was established to oversee the government and York was the natural choice as regent or 'protector'.

The Wars of the Roses 1455–1461

At the end of 1454 Henry recovered his sanity. His old counsellors reassembled, headed by Somerset. Lesser fry regained their offices. York ceased to act as protector and his allies were removed from office. Somerset summoned a great council at Leicester, to which York and his allies were not invited. As Henry and Somerset travelled north, they were intercepted by York and Warwick at St Albans. There was a skirmish, after which Somerset and Northumberland were killed, probably by Warwick. This 'battle' started a series of tit-for-tat killings, usually after battles. It marked the beginning of the 'Wars of the Roses', between the red of Lancaster and the white of York. These badges were among several used by Lancastrians and Yorkists, but they were not given any prominence until the reign of Henry VII.

As yet, York did not claim the throne. Henry, in his simplicity, seemed willing to work with him, but the Queen prepared for war. In 1459 a packed Parliament at Coventry passed acts of **attainder** against York, Salisbury, Warwick and others. They were declared guilty of treason, their property forfeit and their noble titles extinguished. Their persons were safe – York was in Ireland, Salisbury and Warwick at Calais – but parts of their estates were seized. The attainder threatened the property rights of landowners in general, creating a backlash that increased Yorkist support. York returned from Ireland in October 1460 and, to widespread surprise and disapproval, claimed the Crown. His claim was approved by a 'great council', consisting of three bishops, three temporal peers and two knights. York then demanded that the peers in Parliament recognise him as King. The lords conceded that he had a strong hereditary claim, but were reluctant to renege on their allegiance to Henry. A bizarre compromise was reached, whereby York was recognised as the rightful King, but Henry was to rule for the rest of his life. Soon after, York was killed, attacking a superior force at Wakefield.

Early in 1461, a number of Yorkist and other peers agreed to support the claim to the throne of York's son, Edward, Earl of March. They argued that he was not bound by his father's agreement to allow Henry to remain King. They needed a lawful king to authorise their continued resistance to the Queen and her supporters; if they were defeated, they would be shown no mercy. Given the Queen's implacable hostility, they could regain control of the government only by deposing Henry. Experience showed that Henry was unfit to rule, not because he was evil but because he was incapable. Since Wakefield the Queen controlled his person and militarily held the upper hand, but on 29 March 1461 the Yorkists defeated her army at Towton, Yorkshire. This was a major battle, with at least 20,000 on each side: most other 'battles' involved a few hundred or even a few score. As usual, prisoners were killed, but this time the killing was more extensive, decimating the northern nobility and gentry. Henry and his Queen escaped to Scotland; Edward returned to London to be recognised as King by the Commons.

The events of 1450–61 showed the fragility of England's government under a weak King like Henry VI. Courtiers and officials manipulated the legal system to make money and harass their enemies. Their local henchmen seized property and used force to overcome resistance or deter people from complaining. Others responded in kind, knowing that they would get no protection from the King. This happened even in the South East and East Anglia. During the 1450s there were, in effect, local civil wars, not only in the North, the Welsh Marches and East Anglia, but also in the South West, Derbyshire, Staffordshire and elsewhere. Some areas suffered something approaching anarchy, as rival forces pillaged, burned and murdered. Others experienced smaller-scale but alarming intimidation, extortion and plunder.

But, overall, order did not collapse. Many lords lacked the power to fight their oppressors, or refused to put themselves legally in the wrong. Some, like Fastolf, saw damage limitation as a wiser option than resistance. Reticence and restraint were also apparent in Cade's rebellion, particularly its early stages. After the rebels were driven out of London they thankfully accepted pardons. At no stage did they threaten the King's person, or question his right to rule: they simply called on him to rule justly. Nobles critical of misgovernment and appalled by the losses in France sought to persuade Henry to choose better counsellors. Whatever York's private ambitions, his stated aim was to take his 'natural' place in the King's council. If he hoped to claim the throne, the birth of Henry's son was a major setback. When the Queen's intransigence left the Yorkists no choice but to resist, most nobles still hoped for a compromise, even after York claimed the throne. The arrangement reached was unsatisfactory: if Henry had only a life-interest in the Crown, there was an obvious incentive to kill him. In the event, Henry escaped to Scotland and York claimed that he was not bound by the deal. Even so, many had severe qualms about Edward's seizing the throne.

Edward IV: 1. 1461–1471

In his first decade Edward faced two major problems. The first was that Henry was still alive. He enjoyed limited support within England, but the kings of Scotland and France supported his cause. Margaret handed over Berwick to the Scots, who helped her secure three castles in Northumberland. Edward's forces captured the castles in 1464 and Henry was imprisoned. There was no point in Edward's killing him while his wife and son were safe in France. The second problem was Edward's most prominent supporter, Warwick, 'the kingmaker', a greedy and ambitious man. He had been well rewarded for his support: the Earl of Northumberland, killed at Towton, was attainted, and most of his estates were granted to Warwick's brother, John, making the Nevilles the greatest landowners in the North. But Warwick expected Edward, fourteen years younger, to be guided by his greater experience. Concerning his marriage and foreign policy Edward refused to be guided. In 1464 Edward married Elizabeth Woodville. Her mother was a Princess of Luxembourg, whose first husband was Henry V's brother, but her second was a commoner until Henry VI made him a baron; Edward created him Earl Rivers. Elizabeth's first husband was a mere knight, Sir John Grey. For Edward's subjects it was scandalous that he should marry so far beneath him. Elizabeth also brought a large tribe of needy relations. Edward did not give them over-lavish grants of land, but they secured the hands of many eligible heirs and heiresses, including the young Duke of Buckingham. Warwick had difficulty finding suitable husbands for his two daughters, who were to inherit his vast estates. Conflict also arose over foreign affairs. In the struggle between the kings of France and the dukes of Burgundy, who also ruled the Low Countries, Warwick urged the King to side with France; Edward, mindful of England's commercial interests, preferred Burgundy. In 1468 Edward signed a treaty, under which the Duke, Charles the Bold, was to marry his sister.

Warwick responded by marrying his daughter to Edward's wayward brother, the Duke of Clarence. Like York in the 1450s, Warwick was determined to force himself into the King's counsels, but not sure how. In 1469 there were disorders in the North, including a rising of Warwick's retainers, led by 'Robin of Redesdale'. When Edward marched against the rebels, Warwick and Clarence denounced his 'evil counsellors' and launched the first of four invasions in two years, landing in Kent and entering London. 'Robin' defeated Edward's supporter, the Earl of Pembroke, near Banbury. Edward surrendered and Pembroke, Rivers and Elizabeth's brother John were executed. Edward was imprisoned in Warwick's castle at Middleham. Without him government broke down and Warwick felt constrained to release him. Once in London, Edward rebuilt his authority and Warwick fled to France. There he was reconciled to Margaret: their alliance was sealed by the marriage of Warwick's other daughter to Prince Edward, Henry's son. Margaret secured French backing for an invasion, which landed in Devon and proclaimed Henry VI as King. John Neville and other lords joined them. Edward fled to the Netherlands.

After Edward's flight, Henry was released from the Tower and proclaimed King. He was a confused figurehead; real power was exercised by the Nevilles. Charles the Bold was eventually persuaded to give Edward ships and money to invade England. He landed near the Humber, with fewer than 2,000 men. He found little support in Yorkshire – memories of the slaughter after Towton remained strong – but fared better in the Midlands, thanks to the loyal Lord Hastings. Together they marched to confront Warwick; the fickle Clarence came over to his brother. Edward defeated and killed Warwick and his brother John at Barnet. Meanwhile, the Queen had organised another invasion from France. She landed in Dorset and her army headed towards the Lancastrian strongholds of Wales and Lancashire. Edward intercepted and defeated them at Tewkesbury: Prince Edward was among the many killed; his mother was taken prisoner. When Edward returned to London on 20 May 1471 Henry was killed, almost certainly on Edward's orders.

Edward IV: 2. 1471–1483

With the deaths of Warwick, Prince Edward and Henry VI, the main threats to Edward IV had been removed. Like most usurpers he had limited support among the nobility and people. His surrendering in 1469, and flight in 1470, showed that he was aware of this. He had seemed an ineffective King, dominated by Warwick, with an unsuitable wife and an unreliable brother. However, after 1471 there was no strong rival claimant. The nearest was Henry Tudor, Earl of Richmond, whose claim derived from his mother, Margaret Beaufort. Henry's claim was weakened by the fact that the Beaufort branch of the royal family was generally seen as illegitimate. Henry's position seemed weak and at times he sought reconciliation with Edward and an end to his exile in Brittany. Nevertheless, Edward realised that he needed broader support: his surviving the crisis of 1469–71 had owed much to his skill and determination, but also much to luck: the Battle of Barnet was fought in thick fog.

Edward mostly used conventional methods to strengthen his regime. He combined majesty with affability and good fellowship. He improved his financial position, avoiding costly foreign war: when he declared war on France, he allowed himself to be bought off. He did much to restore the integrity of the legal system, while occasionally acting arbitrarily against dangerous individuals. He alienated some of the great peerage families (notably the Herberts and Mowbrays) by providing for his two sons at their expense; he also enabled the Woodvilles to make choice marriages. He relied on a trusted group of kinsmen and friends to control particular regions, building up their power so that they were almost autonomous. After Pembroke's death, the key figure in Wales and the Marches was the second Earl Rivers. In North Wales and Lancashire he relied, perhaps unwisely, on Thomas Lord Stanley, who had served Henry VI. There were similar doubts about the reliability of Clarence in the South West, but none about the loyalty of Hastings in the Midlands. (Clarence turned against Edward and was executed in 1477. His place was taken by Elizabeth's son, Thomas Grey, Marquis of Dorset.)

Among Edward's supporters one stood out, his brother, Richard, Duke of Gloucester, who became his viceroy in the North. He had married one of Warwick's daughters and acquired the extensive estates of the Nevilles of Middleham, along with Warwick's affinity. In 1483 an Act of Parliament, passed at Edward's behest, granted Richard and his heirs the Wardenship of the West March, Carlisle and most of the King's rights and revenues in Cumbria. It also licensed him to create a **palatinate** in South West Scotland – in effect, an independent hereditary principality; the only snag was that he had to conquer it. Unlike Clarence, Gloucester had always been impeccably loyal to his brother and he ensured that the most dangerous region of England remained relatively quiet. After the upheavals of 1469–71 the remainder of Edward's reign passed in comparative peace. Those trusted by Edward with regional power occasionally abused it, but only Clarence turned against him, and the people enjoyed a measure of peace and justice. Then, suddenly, on 9 April 1483 Edward IV died and the Yorkist regime was plunged into crisis.

Richard III

Edward had survived as King, with one interruption, and secured the succession, leaving two sons. The elder, Edward V, was twelve, old enough to be crowned King, but for a few years he would need a regency council, of which Richard was the obvious president. Gloucester's ambitions seemed focused on the North and the prospect of his principality. Edward named him as protector in his will, so when Elizabeth claimed the protectorship the council chose Richard instead. The Woodvilles were in a strong position: the young King was with Rivers in Shropshire and other family members controlled the Tower and the fleet. But Richard secured Edward, Rivers and others and began preparations for Edward's coronation and a Parliament. Then he changed his mind. He accused Hastings of treason and had him killed without trial, ordered the execution of several others, including Rivers, and pressured the Queen to hand over her younger son, who joined his brother in the Tower; he then recalled the writs for Parliament and claimed the throne, alleging that Edward and his brother were illegitimate. His claim was endorsed by a group of London citizens and members of Parliament and he took the throne on 26 June.

His actions alienated most of Edward IV's affinity and household men. The Woodvilles were implacable, Hastings was dead and the Stanleys, as so often, refused to commit themselves. Richard had support in the North and won over John Howard, a rising star in East Anglia, with the dukedom of Norfolk. He also initially had the support of the Duke of Buckingham, but in October the Duke rose in arms against him. His motives were uncertain: he claimed that Richard had had the young princes killed and that Henry Tudor was the rightful King. Buckingham was supported by the Woodvilles and former members of Edward IV's household. The rising failed, and Buckingham paid the penalty, but it forged an alliance between Woodvilles, Tudors and some old Lancastrians, including Lady Margaret Beaufort: Henry had started to make his way over from Brittany. At the heart of the alliance was a plan that Henry should marry Edward IV's daughter, Elizabeth, recreating the broad spectrum that had supported Edward IV. Richard's support was reduced by suspicions that he had had the princes killed. They were probably dead by the end of 1483 when some of their lands were granted to Richard's supporters. If they had been alive, the best way to quash the rumours would have been to produce them. On the other hand, there is no hard evidence of who killed them or how. Without their bodies Richard could not prove that they were dead, leading to rumours that they were alive; but if he produced the bodies, he would have to explain how they had died.

As Richard's support shrank he relied more and more on his trusted northern affinity. He appointed northerners to offices and granted them lands, including those of Buckingham's followers, to the annoyance of southerners. In August 1485 Henry, encouraged by reports of disaffection, landed at Milford Haven, in Wales, with 3,000 French soldiers – a larger force than Edward IV had had in 1471. He marched through Wales and confronted Richard at Bosworth, Leicestershire. Richard's army was significantly larger, although only a few peers, notably Norfolk, supported him unequivocally. Other possible supporters were cagey: Northumberland, who brought a significant force, remained aloof and the Stanleys, who had refrained from joining Henry in Wales, now took his side. The outcome of the battle owed much to luck, particularly the fact that Richard was killed, the last English King to die in battle (and the first since Richard I). The crown was allegedly placed on Henry's head, on the battlefield, by Sir William Stanley.

The Tudor Dynasty Secured

Henry VII's accession signalled the fifth change of dynasty in less than a century. Each new ruler needed to retain the throne long enough to be succeeded by his son, preferably an adult. Henry IV had managed this, despite some alarums. Henry V's title was barely contested and his son's minority was a time of relative peace and stability. Edward IV left a son who was almost of age, but was overthrown by his uncle. Henry VII had a weaker claim than Henry IV or Edward IV. The Lancastrian affinity had dwindled, but Richard's coup gave Henry the support of much of Edward's household and noble affinity. This made his promised marriage to Elizabeth of York crucial, but Henry realised that his support came mainly from dislike of Richard. An outsider and exile, he had little knowledge of the English nobility. He had few significant relatives, apart from his formidable mother and his uncle, Jasper Tudor: he placed great trust in both of them. He was less willing to trust the English nobility, given the behaviour of Northumberland and Stanley at Bosworth. To secure his dynasty, he would have to rely on his own resources.

Among possible rival claimants to the throne, most were too young, female or prisoners. Instead, Henry had to contend with **pretenders**, with support from France, Burgundy, Scotland or Ireland. Foreign assistance, and continuing Yorkist sentiment within England, meant that the pretenders posed a significant threat. Lambert Simnel claimed to be Clarence's son, Warwick; he was defeated in 1487 and given a menial job in the royal kitchens. Perkin Warbeck claimed to be Edward V's younger brother and won support from the dowager Duchess of Burgundy, Edward IV's sister, and James IV of Scotland. After first stating his claim in 1491 he organised a series of conspiracies and invasions. In 1495 Sir William Stanley was executed, for allegedly conspiring with him. In 1497 Warbeck hoped to exploit a tax rebellion in Cornwall, but arrived too late, surrendered and confessed his imposture. After yet another plot Warbeck and Warwick were executed in 1499, showing that Henry still felt insecure. His eldest son, Arthur, died in 1502. His brother Henry was underage, having been born in 1491. It was touch and go whether Henry VII would survive long enough to see him inherit the throne as an adult. In the meantime, Henry's dealings with the English nobility were driven by anxiety and suspicion.

When Henry VIII succeeded his father in 1509 he concealed the death for two days, fearful of a possible challenge. He was a large, extrovert young man, highly intelligent and eager to make his mark on the European stage. But despite his outward self-confidence, the Wars of the Roses preyed upon his mind and he remained anxious about his dynasty's future, especially when his first wife, Catherine of Aragon, gave birth to only one surviving child, Mary. (Henry had an illegitimate son, Henry Fitzroy, Duke of Richmond, but does not seem to have considered making him his heir.) The search for a male heir was a major factor in Henry's quest for a new and (hopefully) more fecund queen. His insecurity also drove him to strike at possible rival claimants to the throne. The major Yorkists were dead but others could claim descent from the sons of Edward III. These included Edward Stafford, third Duke of Buckingham, whose father had rebelled in 1483. In 1521 Buckingham was accused of adding royal insignia to his coat of arms, in effect claiming royal blood; he allegedly talked of prophecies that he would become king. He was tried for treason and executed. Even after the birth of his long-awaited son Henry's anxieties continued. In 1538, faced with a Franco-Spanish alliance, he ordered the arrest of those with any sort of claim to the throne. These included Henry Courtenay, Marquis of Exeter, son of Edward IV's younger daughter, and Henry Pole, brother of Cardinal Reginald Pole and grandson of Clarence. They were convicted of treason and executed. The Poles' mother, Margaret, Countess of Salisbury, now in her sixties, was interrogated for some months and executed in 1541.

While Buckingham, Exeter and the Poles could perhaps be seen as a potential threat, the Countess posed no threat to anybody. Her execution showed the early Tudors' ongoing dynastic insecurity. Their fears were probably exaggerated, but they help explain their eagerness to strengthen the powers of the Crown, to enable them to deal with any challenge. They sought to bring the nobility under tighter control and devoted particular attention to the borderlands which, by 1536, with England separated from Rome, seemed to threaten the regime's stability and even survival.

The Revival of Monarchy 1471–1536: 1. Resources

Effective monarchy required resources – money and men – to wage war abroad and maintain order at home. Compared with the major Continental powers, England was a small under-resourced kingdom. Since Agincourt the European state system had changed radically. In the 1420s the French King exercised authority over the Ile de France and a few scattered territories; others were held as fiefs by nobles. After conquering the English provinces, the French kings established their authority over others, including Burgundy, Brittany and Provence; the outline of France now resembled what it is today. The marriage of Ferdinand of Aragon and Isabella of Castile in 1479 led to the establishment of a dual monarchy which ruled all of modern Spain. Meanwhile, in 1477 Charles the Bold, ruler of Burgundy and the Netherlands, died; his heiress married Maximilian, heir to the Habsburg lands in Austria and the title of Holy Roman Emperor: this gave them extensive influence within the many German states. In 1519 Maximilian died and his lands and imperial title passed to his grandson, Charles I of Spain, who became the Emperor Charles V. By the 1530s the lands of the English Crown were dwarfed by the territories of Charles V and Francis I of France. In 1500, the population of England and Wales was about two and a half million, that of Spain (not including the Austrian lands and the Netherlands) was seven million, and that of France sixteen. By the 1520s both Charles V and Francis I enjoyed revenues about ten times that of Henry VIII.

This disparity in population and resources might suggest that England's king should not try to compete with his Continental counterparts. Edward IV and Henry VII avoided foreign wars, but Henry VIII wanted to make his mark in Europe. But much had changed since the 1410s. Henry V had won at Agincourt with about 9,000 men, against a French monarchy which was pitifully weak compared with that of Francis I. His key weapons were longbows and heavy cavalry. In the Franco-Spanish wars in Italy, starting in 1494, armies were much larger. The growing use of firearms and long pikes required highly trained infantry, professional mercenaries rather than feudal levies. War had become much more expensive. Francis I could raise taxes without consent; Henry VIII could not. The English Parliament might grant taxes for a successful war, but not for one going badly. If taxpayers felt taxation was excessive, they might refuse to pay. A French observer wrote in 1512: 'You [Henry VIII] are not obeyed in the same way as the king of France … [you] are so insignificant that your subjects can do as they please, to the extent that you are their servant and can only be their king by observing their wishes.'

This underestimated the English monarchy's effectiveness. The English polity functioned differently, and more cheaply, than that of France. But the Tudor monarchy was financially too weak to embark on large-scale military adventures without serious strains. Continental monarchies were moving from 'domain states', where most revenue came from royal lands and feudal rights, to 'tax states', where most came from taxation, but England increasingly became a 'domain state'. Since 1399 the English Crown lands had grown substantially. Henry IV brought to the Crown the lands of the Duchy of Lancaster, to which were added the proceeds of **attainders** and forfeitures.

Edward IV and Richard III granted many of these to their supporters, but Henry VII tended to keep them. His was the largest landholding since William I's; the income from Crown lands rose from about £8,000 a year in 1433 to £40,000 in 1504.

Fiscal Feudalism

Part of this increase came from more intensive exploitation of feudal **incidents**. The Lancastrians and (usually) Edward IV feared that increasing this revenue would provoke opposition. Henry VII did not challenge the legality of **uses**, but imposed heavy fines for technical infringements of his feudal rights. His lawyers developed the concept of the royal **prerogative**, a reservoir of powers not strictly defined by law, which could enable him to enforce his feudal rights.

The conduct of Henry's agents provoked great resentment; Henry VIII quickly sacrificed two of the most hated, Empson and Dudley. But by the 1520s he was very short of money, despite heavier taxes, and his lawyers sought ways to undermine uses. In 1532 the Commons rejected a bill to secure for the King one third of what was due for **wardship**; Henry angrily threatened to 'search out the extremity of the law'. His advisers canvassed judges and promoted test cases in the courts, in which uses were declared illegal. The judges were then summoned to debate the issue before Lord Chancellor Sir Thomas More and Thomas Cromwell, the King's Secretary of State and most influential adviser. The King promised the judges 'his good thanks' if they accepted his arguments. It seems that they did, unanimously; when a bill abolishing uses was brought into Parliament in 1536, the Houses had little choice but to pass it. This should have enabled the King to expand his revenue and a Court of Wards was established in 1540. By then, however, a Statute of Wills had passed, allowing landowners to bequeath two-thirds of their lands, leaving one third liable to pay dues to the King. Why the King backed down is unclear. It may be connected to Cromwell's fall from power, or landowners' strong opposition to the Statute of Uses, or the dissolution of the monasteries may have offered an opportunity of resolving his financial problems that landowners would welcome.

The Limits of Taxation

Whatever Henry's reasons, feudal incidents could make only a limited contribution to his revenue, partly because uses and entail were well established in law, partly because challenging them provoked opposition from a powerful segment of opinion. Taxes, by contrast, could tap into various forms of wealth and economic activity. Their potential yield could be expanded far more than Crown lands and feudal rights, which Henry VII had stretched to the limit. But one development in the later Middle Ages made it harder to rely on taxes. The long-term shift in exports from raw wool to finished cloth greatly reduced customs revenue. This reached a peak of about £110,000 a year in the

1330s; it then fell to around £72,000 in the 1370s and £21,000 in the 1470s, from which it recovered to maybe £35,000 in the 1520s.

Henry urgently needed more effective ways to tax land and other property. The basic property tax, the royal aid or **fifteenth and tenth**, was based on assessments of each town and village made in 1334, which became increasingly outdated. Edward IV was wary of asking for taxation; he promised Parliament that he would '**live of his own**' and ask for taxes only for war. Henry VII made more extensive demands, and tried to assess taxpayers individually for the royal aid. This led to the Cornish rebellion of 1497, in which the rebels marched on London. Thereafter Henry called only one Parliament, in 1504; he secured a grant of taxation, and declared that he would not call another Parliament. Henry VIII revived and extended individual assessment, with the **subsidy**, the basis of parliamentary taxation for over a century. Henry's income from taxation returned to the yields of Henry V's reign, but without the sweetener of military success. The first subsidy, in 1513, taxed incomes of less than £1 a year in wages: far more people than before became subject to taxation. But the subsidy did not bring in enough and in 1522–3 the King raised a forced loan of £250,000, which was not repaid, from his wealthier subjects: his revenue from direct taxation between 1513 and 1527 was £413,000. In 1525 Henry's chief minister, Cardinal Wolsey, demanded that everyone should give a proportion of their wealth to the King. This grotesquely misnamed 'Amicable Grant' was based on wealth, not income: wealthy laypeople would pay about one sixth, the clergy one third. There was some violent resistance, notably in the South East; and very widespread refusal to pay. Henry backed down, claiming implausibly that he had not known how much Wolsey was demanding. To continue his wars he would have to raise money elsewhere.

Henry VIII discovered that there were limits to the yield of both parliamentary and non-parliamentary taxation. With limited revenue he could not afford a standing army or a more effective local government. In an age of growing professional armies, Henry still recruited landowners' servants and dependants, with equipment and training inferior to Continental mercenaries. Similarly, medieval kings had extended their influence into the localities without a large salaried bureaucracy. Professional judges were assisted by unpaid local gentlemen. Sheriffs collected fines, served writs and selected juries; justices of the peace (JPs) took increasing responsibility for law enforcement and administration. The Crown needed the co-operation of the nobility and gentry, but also needed to control those responsible for local government. Kings needed to discipline the unruly and resolve disputes, but during the Wars of the Roses kings themselves misused their power: defeated lords were slaughtered in cold blood, fugitives were killed far from the battlefield, powerful men were put to death without due process of law. Henry VII and Henry VIII observed the outward forms of law, but sometimes had people condemned on flimsy evidence. Edward IV, Henry VII and Henry VIII demanded forced loans or forced gifts. Arbitrary punishments and exactions might make their government more effective, but set a bad example and could be used only occasionally. For government and law enforcement to work effectively, more central control was needed.

The Revival of Monarchy 1471–1536: 2. Control

Henry VII

Late medieval kings exercised power over men mainly through an **affinity**, granting lands and offices to trusted magnates or household men, and retaining knights and gentry. This required a detailed knowledge of the provincial gentry. Edward IV could win men over with charm and bonhomie, but had a good memory and was skilled in judging ability and character. However, in the final analysis he preferred to trust those he knew best: his and the Queen's families and a few others such as Hastings and the Stanleys. His judgment was not infallible, as the Stanleys showed. Edward's household men did what he asked of them and proved loyal to his legacy, turning against Richard III. Edward's major mistake was to cultivate few of the great nobles and reward others at their expense. He showed that a narrow basis of support could be a disadvantage but not a disaster. Many nobles wanted to avoid commitment and acquiesced in his rule. Richard III stepped beyond the bounds of acceptability by his usurpation, but still amassed enough support to have stood a reasonable chance at Bosworth.

Henry VII took distrust of the nobility to a new level. No noble outside a small family group was given any real trust. He created only one new peer: Jasper, Duke of Bedford. The peerage shrank from fifty-five to forty-two as titles died out in the male line. He received the submission of some who begged forgiveness, like the Earl of Northumberland, but did not trust them. Whereas Edward usually fully reversed **attainders** if he thought contrition was genuine, Henry reversed them slowly, a little at a time. Thomas Howard, son of the Duke of Norfolk who was killed at Bosworth, was imprisoned in 1485, but recovered his title of Earl of Surrey in 1489, after suppressing a rising in Yorkshire. He became the King's leading man in the North and lord treasurer, but was still on probation and did not regain his father's ducal title until the next reign. Other nobles had to be content with a pardon and the gradual restoration of estates and titles. Henry relied more on his household men and lawyers; part of their task was to watch for signs of disaffection among the nobility. Henry ordered JPs to restrict retaining and prevent perversions of justice. His Privy Council, consisting of lawyers and administrators rather than nobles, imposed a new degree of central supervision on the localities.

Henry's management of the political elite was based on surveillance and control. 'The pleasure and mind of the king's grace', wrote Dudley, 'was much set to have many persons in his danger at his pleasure.' He made extensive use of **bonds and recognisances**. In the 1490s, eleven peers were forced to enter into bonds for good behaviour; if (in the King's opinion) they misbehaved, they would forfeit a large sum of money. After Arthur's death the number under bonds increased considerably. An offshoot of the council, the council learned in the law, was used to enforce the King's financial rights and to impose fines for breaches of statutes, for example illegal retaining. Lord Bergavenny was fined £70,000: he was able to pay only a small fraction, so remained at the King's mercy. Other offshoots of the council included the **Star Chamber**, in which the council heard complaints and resolved disputes. How far the King's aim was to raise money and how far to keep the powerful at his mercy is unclear. Many complained that the King's agents stretched the law to make money for the King and themselves.

Henry VII is often seen as stabilising the monarchy and its finances. He managed his money carefully and did not die in debt, but at great political cost: resentment of his exactions became widespread. The financial road he followed was a dead end. He grasped the need to overhaul parliamentary taxation, but backed down in the face of opposition and after 1504 abandoned parliaments altogether. His huge landed estates and a relatively unthreatening international situation made this feasible, but England could not avoid war indefinitely and war was becoming more and more expensive: the future lay with the tax state. Moreover, it was unwise to marginalise the nobility, who commanded respect and loyalty and had much to contribute to government. Resentment of predatory officials and the misuse of law ran through all levels of society. Henry VII realised this: his will acknowledged that some of the wrongs he had done might have imperilled his soul.

Henry VIII

Henry VIII constructed a very large **affinity**. It included favoured nobles, but at its heart were the great officers of state, councillors and those closest to the King, the gentlemen of the privy chamber: young men of great families who waited on the King and gained private access to his person. Other members of the affinity were tied to the court by offices and wages. County landowners sought access to the King and his ministers and could be consulted, or influenced, by them. Courtiers were appointed to county offices and 'men of power and worship' in the counties were encouraged to come to court. Their names were entered in books, arranged by counties for easy consultation: the knowledge which Edward IV kept in his head was bureaucratised. Under Henry, the king's court grew in size and magnificence and became the centre of politics and patronage.

Henry VIII did not distrust the nobles as such, just those he saw as a threat. He valued aristocrats for adding to the lustre of his court and some were his personal friends.

He valued the military service that they traditionally gave, but also created an administrative nobility. Hitherto great office-holders were priests, rewarded with bishoprics. From Henry's reign, the majority were laymen, sometimes of already powerful families; they were rewarded for their services with peerages. Administrative and military service were not incompatible: Surrey was a successful general and lord treasurer. But as the new peerage families built up landed estates their influence rested on government office rather than military might.

Central supervision of local government was strengthened by two remarkable men from outside the landed elite, Thomas Wolsey and Thomas Cromwell. Wolsey pursued the traditional path of advancement through the Church and became spectacularly rich: his income was estimated at £35,000 a year, about six times as much as the richest lay peer. (See Figure 3.1, Hampton Court Palace.) He accumulated ecclesiastical benefices, including the archbishopric of York. He was an immensely capable administrator, managing the complex logistics of shipping large armies to France. As Lord Chancellor he developed the court of **chancery** which proved quicker and more flexible than the

Figure 3.1 Hampton Court is perhaps the Tudor equivalent of Castletown. Both Wolsey and Conolly came from outside the traditional ruling elite and made their fortunes serving the government, but Wolsey did so through the Church and Conolly through the financial administration. Wolsey was forced to hand over Hampton Court to the King, but when Conolly died he was praised as an Irish patriot.

common law courts. He encouraged victims of miscarriages of justice or unlawful violence to appeal to the Privy Council. He drew up instructions for sheriffs and scrutinised the conduct of JPs, removing those he saw as lax or partial; they were replaced with men from the centre, often lawyers or clergy. His aim was not to exclude the landowning elite from local office, but to ensure that they fulfilled their responsibilities.

Wolsey fell from power in 1529; he was replaced at the centre of government by his former servant Thomas Cromwell. Despite limited formal education, Cromwell was unusually well travelled and cultivated; he spoke Italian and French and many found him a charming host. Whereas Wolsey devoted enormous energy to making traditional government work better, Cromwell pursued administrative efficiency as part of a wider vision. He promoted the Statute of Uses, to increase the King's revenue and make the landed elite less able to oppose the Crown. This vision included shifting power and resources from the Church to the state, which would become the main engine of spiritual and social improvement. This required more intensive control of local government. It meant an end to local abuses of power, lawless zones and **liberties and franchises**. Two of the greatest – the Palatinate of Chester and the Duchy of Lancaster – were in the King's hands; in the Palatinate of Durham the bishop increasingly acted as the King's agent. Others, in the North and the Welsh Marches, obstructed the working of justice. In 1536, an Act of Parliament substantially curtailed liberties and franchises in England; the King's judges, sheriffs and JPs were now to be admitted. Many ecclesiastical liberties were also dismantled. The King's writ now ran through almost all of England.

This growing centralisation did not mean the end of local self-government. Wolsey and Cromwell possessed exceptional ability and energy. They created mechanisms for supervising local officials, and intruded some outsiders into offices, but sustaining that level of supervision would be difficult. Monarchs and ministers still needed men with local standing and knowledge to make government work. As the workload of local government increased, ministers lacked the time and resources to supervise it. With towns and urban problems growing, the Crown granted more powers to town corporations. The growth of effective government in Tudor England involved *both* the development of central government *and* devolving out greater powers to the localities. The French critic of Henry VIII's regime would not have understood this; but in many ways it worked.

Borderlands: 1. The North of England

The far North was a frontier zone, with a distinct social organisation and attitudes. Loyalty of tenant to lord transcended that of subject to king. The king was remote and his authority penetrated only fitfully. Well over half of Northumberland and Yorkshire consisted of **liberties and franchises**. In Northumberland, Marcher law was more effective than the king's law; as in the Scottish **bloodfeud** this was based on arbitration and restitution rather than punishment. The relationship between families on the two sides of the border was complex. There was much cross-border raiding, some of it very brutal, but some families, like the Armstrongs, had branches on both sides, who sheltered and supported their kinsmen. Although much of the frontier was clearly defined, some was not: 'debatable lands' were ravaged by both sides until they were virtually deserted. Raiding and **reiving** were a way of life, with their own rules; outsiders were not supposed to interfere.

The borderers were vital for defence against the Scots, but were difficult to manage: long-established great families like the Percies proved most effective in doing so. Other families could build themselves up with the help of the Crown, but they needed time and had to embrace the border ethos. The Cumbrian Fiennes family, whose members were admitted to the peerage as Barons Dacre, were ancient, but relatively poor. They set out to attract loyal tenants to defend their lands, so charged low rents and embraced **tenant right**; in return, leases included an obligation of military service. By the 1520s Lord Dacre could mobilise four thousand men and the lords Dacre became virtually hereditary wardens of the West March.

In the 1450s the two great northern families were the Percies and the Nevilles and their feud destabilised the kingdom. The fall of Warwick the Kingmaker left the Percies dominant, but Edward IV was reluctant to trust them. Instead he built up the power of his brother Richard, who dominated the North; the Percies gained revenge by staying neutral at Bosworth.

Henry VII was not inclined to trust Northumberland; he appointed him Warden of the East March, but only temporarily. He was killed trying to put down a tax revolt in 1489, leaving an underage son. Henry tentatively put his trust in Surrey, who had no local connections, assisted by councillors and household men, notably Richard Fox, Bishop of Durham. Investigations into feudal dues caused resentment, but the northern lords supported the King against Warbeck and the Scots, who in 1502 finally abandoned their claim to Berwick. In the West March the Percies were dominant, so Henry kept the wardenship in his own hand, with the third Lord Dacre as his deputy. He exacted **bonds and recognisances** and relied on his councillors, rather than local men, to keep the region quiet; the Council of the North ceased to function. The effectiveness of this regime was not tested until James IV renewed the war in 1513; raids and feuds proliferated and order collapsed. By the 1520s there was no sheriff in Cumberland and too few JPs to make up a quorum; law enforcement and administration effectively ceased.

Dacre was not greatly concerned at the decline of governance: he claimed that he alone could restore order, if given the necessary powers and resources. Henry reluctantly accepted this argument and Dacre eventually became warden of all three Marches, but order did not improve. In 1525 Dacre was imprisoned and charged with maladministration, but the disorder became worse. In 1527 the King conceded defeat: William, fourth Lord Dacre, became warden of the West March and Northumberland warden of the East and Middle Marches. The restoration of Dacre and Northumberland did not bring any improvement in government: both encouraged the **surnames** to raid and pillage. Changes in the Church made the disorders all the more dangerous. Cromwell and others in London blamed them on the natural unruliness of northerners, especially the surnames. The only remedy was to bring the civility of southern England to the North by appointing councillors and household men in place of the local magnates. In 1534 Dacre was charged with treason and, although acquitted on the main charge (a rare event under Henry VIII), he was removed from the Wardenship of the West March. Two years later a major rebellion in the North made possible a more thorough overhaul of the government, but the power of the great lords remained formidable. It took several generations to establish southern standards of law enforcement and administration in the North.

Borderlands: 2. Wales and the Marches

Wales and the Marches suffered from similar problems to the far North – extensive liberties and franchises, weak law and order – plus absentee lords and ethnic hostility. The absentee lords (unlike the magnates in the North) often took no responsibility for law and order. At a time of falling land revenues the lords demanded as much rent as before from the peasantry. Great lords, like York and Buckingham, had extensive estates in the Marches and plunder, killing and destruction spread there from England in the 1450s. Welsh gentlemen in the service of magnates built up estates, married well and acquired offices. The Herberts built a great castle at Raglan, Monmouthshire, which became a major centre of bardic poetry, with prophecies that the Welsh would again rule over Wales; the young Henry Tudor was educated in this household. Edward IV made William Herbert Earl of Pembroke; his son married a sister of Edward's Queen. Edward entrusted him with much of the government of Wales until he was killed, on Warwick's orders, after the Battle of Edgcote in 1469.

In 1471 the attainder of Henry's son brought Edward his lands as Prince of Wales, to add to those of Warwick, York and the Duchy of Lancaster, making Edward lord of most of the Marches. He set up a Council there similar to that in the North; its members were mostly English. After Richard III's usurpation Henry Tudor became the main hope of disgruntled Yorkists. Henry stressed his Welshness and promised to be a good lord to the Welsh, but he attracted limited support in Wales in 1485. As King he dealt with the Marches as he dealt with the North, using bonds and recognisances to rein in Marcher lords and their stewards. Henry IV's laws against the Welsh remained in force, but more Welshmen were granted **denizen** status and the rights of Englishmen were extended more widely; in some lordships inhabitants could hold offices and buy and bequeath land according to English law.

Neither Henry VII nor Henry VIII saw any need for a proactive approach in Wales until the breach with Rome convinced Cromwell and Henry that radical change was needed. Henry twice visited the Marches and sent Bishop Rowland Lee to head the Council there. Lee ensured that the laws were enforced, hanging thieves and murderers. An Act of 1536 divided Wales into counties, as in England; it aimed to 'extirpate all and singular the sinister uses and customs' of the Welsh. Other acts abolished liberties and franchises: laws were to be administered as in England. As the King held the majority of Marcher lordships, there was little resistance. Welsh landowners and townsmen saw advantages in English law: they could hold offices, buy land and pass their entire estates to their eldest sons. More sought to become English denizens and Welsh inheritance customs declined, at least among the better-off.

These acts, and their aftermath, constituted a legal and political union between England and Wales, on terms laid down by the English, but welcomed by many. Wales gained representation in the English Parliament and became liable to parliamentary taxation. Welshmen could lobby for offices and favours and their voice could be heard at Westminster and at court. Although the adoption of English law threatened Welsh customs, and legal proceedings were to be in English, the Acts did not discriminate against the Welsh language, in contrast to earlier legislation against Irish Gaelic and Welsh. Those with ambitions needed to speak English, but the peasantry continued to speak Welsh and follow traditional customs. Great landowners of Welsh extraction continued to speak Welsh with their tenants but ceased their patronage of poets. When Daniel Defoe visited Wales in the early eighteenth century, he found that the Welsh 'value themselves much on … the ancient race of their houses and families … and above all on their heroes'. The experience of Gaelic in Ireland and Scotland suggested that Welsh might eventually have declined, but it did not because it became the language of religion. Over much of Wales Welsh remains very widely spoken.

Whereas attempts to impose southern English institutions and social mores on the North met dogged resistance, the union of England and Wales provoked little opposition. The great northern lords fought to preserve their power and were willing to let the region degenerate into chaos. The nobility and gentry of Wales generally embraced the union because of the advantages it offered. The people of the hills and valleys may not have liked the changes that were happening, but they did little to affect their way of life. They had long lived separate from the English and continued to do so; if they felt aggrieved they could do little to make their voices heard. In the Welsh borderlands the 1530s brought lasting changes, unlike in the North – or Ireland.

Borderlands: 3. Ireland

The term 'frontier' is most difficult to apply to Ireland. The Anglo-Scottish border was mostly clearly defined, as was the distinction between 'Welshry' and 'Englishry'. The frontiers between Gaelic and English Ireland were uncertain, subject to local agreements and shifts in the balance of military power. Uncertain frontiers created 'debatable lands' where few farmers dared settle. The Dublin government was underfunded – its revenue was small and it received little from England. The lord lieutenant had limited powers and was usually an absentee. The government lacked coercive power; even in the Pale good government depended on the nobles and the towns, which, as in Wales, were outposts of English civility. By the mid fifteenth century the English in Ireland felt beleaguered – abandoned by the English Crown and worried that many of their fellow-settlers were going native. They were also concerned about the many Irish, mostly poor, living in the Pale: an Act of Parliament ordered them to wear English dress and adopt English surnames.

The dominant family in the Pale were the Fitzgerald earls of Kildare, who ruled a palatinate similar to that planned for Richard of Gloucester. From the 1470s they were appointed lord lieutenant or lord deputy. Like the magnates of the North they saw their lands as a source of men rather than rent. They established networks of castles and tower houses to protect key routes connecting the Pale to English settlements in the South and South West. Although Kildare power could be used to defend the Pale as a whole, their first priority was their own lands. Some levied tribute on neighbouring Gaelic chiefs, but they also married their sisters into leading Gaelic families. The earls mostly married English wives, to foster connections among the English nobility to give them influence at court. English kings built up their power, as vital for English rule in Ireland, but they were also wary of them, especially if they became embroiled in conflicts within England. The eighth earl supported the claims of both Simnel and Warbeck and had Simnel crowned in Dublin as 'Edward VI'.

In the 1530s Henry feared that hostile powers might stir up trouble in Ireland. He twice dismissed the ninth earl, appointing the Earl of Ormond lord lieutenant in his stead, but Ormond had insufficient military power in the Pale. Kildare's kinsmen and servants fomented disruption to show the King that he alone was capable of governing. His case was pressed at court by his kinsmen by marriage, the Duke of Norfolk and Thomas Boleyn. The King was persuaded that restoring Kildare as lord deputy was the least bad option, but Cromwell was determined to destroy him, and began to gather evidence. In May 1534 Kildare and Dacre were charged with treason. Kildare died in prison in September, but his son 'Silken Thomas' had remained in Ireland. He denounced Henry's religious changes and demanded that the Irish take an oath of allegiance to the Pope, Charles V and himself. Thomas raised a substantial army, which besieged Dublin castle and gained control over most of English Ireland. Henry had been warned by Surrey that only a substantial army could secure Ireland, but he had been reluctant to spend the money. In 1534 Henry sent over 2,500 experienced men and a strong train of artillery. The English gentry in Ireland had taken up arms against the King reluctantly and most deserted Kildare, leaving him with a mainly Irish army. His castle at Maynooth was captured after a short siege and he withdrew into Irish territory, from which he launched raids into the Pale. But Kildare was not comfortable about being in rebellion, and was persuaded to surrender on the King's promise that his life would be spared; he was executed in 1537.

For the first time the Crown's resources had been deployed in Ireland, but even experienced soldiers found it hard to cope with guerrilla raids by lightly armed horsemen. The destruction of Kildare led to a power vacuum in which feuds flourished. Henry now appointed English viceroys but was still reluctant to provide sufficient resources. Gradually he accepted that only an English army could prevent Ireland from posing a threat to England or serving as a base for France or Spain. The later 1530s saw the appearance in Ireland of **servitors** – soldiers and lawyers, imbued with a sense of English superiority and strong Protestantism, who saw it as their mission to bring to Ireland the blessings of English civility and efficiency. The Irish lacked firepower and were at a disadvantage in pitched battles or sieges, but were skilled in raids, skirmishes and ambushes. The English treated civilians as complicit in Irish raids; reprisal bred reprisal, atrocity bred atrocity. The assault of Henry and Cromwell on the borderlands had different outcomes. In Wales and the Marches it worked. In the North the King was able to break individuals but not to destroy the magnates' power; however, the magnates continued to defend the border against the Scots. In Ireland the destruction of Kildare led to war, intermittent but bloody, which lasted until 1603.

 Conclusion

Sir Thomas More described the Wars of the Roses as 'kings' games, as it were stage plays, and for the more part played on scaffolds, in which poor men be but the lookers on'. This was true in the sense that most of the battles were small and the meaningful killing of important men occurred afterwards. But the collateral damage from the wars, the local breakdown of order, the plunder and destruction, affected poor as well as rich. The restoration of law and order required the rebuilding of the monarchy. Henry VII and Henry VIII both attempted this in their own way; Wolsey and Cromwell tried to strengthen the Crown's control over the localities, especially the borderlands. Starting in Henry VIII's reign, Parliament passed extensive social legislation and royal officials tried to ensure that it was implemented. They were hampered by the absence of an effective bureaucracy in the provinces; they had to rely on (or win) the co-operation of local men, who expected to use their own judgment when implementing the law. This was formalised in towns by new charters, which gave corporations more extensive powers. An even more fundamental weakness was a lack of revenue: state building required money. Edward IV and Henry VII increased the Crown's landed revenues and made limited use of Parliament. Henry VIII tried, and failed, to fund his wars with parliamentary taxation, and instead hugely increased the Crown's landed estate at the expense of the Church, a policy continued by Edward VI and Elizabeth. They also sold off Crown lands on a large scale, sacrificing future revenue for present needs. It was only in the 1640s that Parliament radically restructured the nation's finances, without consulting the King, and laid the foundations of a modern fiscal system and a more powerful state.

SUGGESTIONS FOR FURTHER READING

For general overviews see S.G. Ellis (with C. Maginn), *The Making of the British Isles: The State of Britain and Ireland 1450–1660* (Harlow, 2007), R.H. Britnell, *The Closing of the Middle Ages? England 1471–1529* (Oxford, 1997), C.S.L. Davies, *Peace, Print and Protestantism 1450–1558* (St Alban's, 1977) and J. Guy, *Tudor England* (Oxford, 1988). • On the Wars of the Roses, see R.L. Storey, *The End of the House of Lancaster* (Gloucester, 1986), R.A. Griffiths, *The Reign of Henry VI* (London, 1981), C. Carpenter, *The Wars of the Roses* (Cambridge, 1997), A.J. Pollard, *The Wars of the Roses* (Basingstoke, 2001) and D. Grummitt, *A Short History of the Wars of the Roses* (London, 2013). • For the leading protagonists, see C. Ross, *Edward IV* (London, 1974), C. Ross, *Richard III* (London, 1981) and S.B. Chrimes, *Henry VII* (London, 1972). See also H. Kleinecke, *Edward IV* (Abingdon, 2009). • For the workings of Tudor Government, see P. Williams, *The Tudor Regime* (Oxford, 1979). • On the court, see D. Starkey (ed.), *The English Court from the Wars of the Roses to the Civil War* (London, 1987) and Guy, *Tudor England*. D. Starkey, *The Reign of Henry VIII: Personalities and Politics* (London, 1985) is perhaps overstated, but helped to establish the political centrality of the court and stimulated a lively debate. • On the borderlands, an essential point of departure is S.G. Ellis, *Tudor Frontiers and Noble Power: the Making of the British State* (Oxford, 1995). • On the North, see A.J. Pollard, *North-Eastern England during the Wars of the Roses* (Oxford, 1990), M. James, *Family, Lineage and Civil Society: Society, Politics and Mentality in the Durham Region, 1500–1640* (Oxford, 1974) and M. James, *Society, Politics and Culture: Studies in Early Modern England* (Cambridge, 1986). • For Wales, see G. Williams, *Renewal and Reformation: Wales c.1415–1642* (Oxford, 1992). • On Ireland, see S.G. Ellis, *Ireland in the Age of the Tudors 1447–1603* (London, 1998) and S.J. Connolly, *Contested Island: Ireland 1460–1630* (Oxford, 2007). • Finally J. Wormald, *Court, Kirk and Community: Scotland 1470–1625* (Edinburgh, 1991) packs a great deal of analysis into a limited space and deserves to be read with care.

SUMMARY

- The main cause of the Wars of the Roses was the inadequacy of Henry VI. Unable to secure justice and fair dealing from the King, great nobles were forced to rely on their own resources, while those favoured by the King abused their power, confident that they would not be called to account.
- Although the number of soldiers involved in battles was often small, the growing practice of killing prisoners after the battle embittered the contest and increased the scale of military involvement.
- In the fifteenth century the Crown lands reached their fullest extent since the Norman Conquest, encouraging kings (especially Henry VII) to rely more on their lands and feudal rights and less on parliamentary taxation. As a result the English Crown fell further and further behind the French and Spanish monarchies in terms of financial resources.
- Henry VIII's government made a serious attempt to increase the Crown's revenues and to centralise government, bringing about the union of England and Wales, but it failed to overcome the problems posed by unruly borderlands.

QUESTIONS FOR STUDENTS

1. How far did the Wars of the Roses demonstrate the weakness of the English monarchy?

2. Why did Richard III fail where Edward IV succeeded?

3. How far did Henry VII solve the Crown's financial problems?

4. Why did the nobles of the Anglo-Scottish borders pose such intractable problems for the English monarchy?

5. How far did English government become centralised under Henry VIII?

4 Henry VIII's Reformation

TIMELINE

1516	Princess Mary born
1517	Luther's Ninety-five Theses
1525	Peasants' War in Germany
1529	Wolsey and Campeggio hear divorce; fall of Wolsey; Reformation Parliament (1529–36) assembles
1533	Henry marries Anne Boleyn; Act of Appeals
1534–5	Anabaptist regime at Münster
1536	Dissolution of smaller monasteries starts; Pilgrimage of Grace; Cromwell's first injunctions
1537	Suppression of larger monasteries begins; Prince Edward born
1538	Cromwell's second set of injunctions
1539	Act of Six Articles
1540	Cromwell dismissed and executed
1543	Act limiting the right to read the Bible
1545 (–1563)	Council of Trent
1547	Henry dies; succeeded by Edward VI

Introduction

In the first decade of the sixteenth century Western Europe still seemed overwhelmingly Roman Catholic. The Church had its critics and had faced numerous heresies, most of which had been suppressed or driven underground. Twenty years later there was a bewildering religious diversity, with challenges to the Church's teachings and practice and demands for reform. The unity of Western Christendom was shattered and various Protestant churches were established. The impetus for this process came partly from below, from townsmen and peasants, and partly from above, from princes. Where Protestantism became established historians depicted it as popular, an expression of the spirit of the people. English Protestant historiography saw Protestantism as a liberating force: laypeople used the Bible to free themselves from the tutelage of priests and popes. Catholicism bred servitude and ignorance, Protestantism thrived on the freedom to which freeborn Englishmen were accustomed, thanks to parliaments and trial by jury. In this historiography the English Protestant Reformation was inevitable: by overthrowing the power of the Pope, Henry VIII unleashed popular anti-Catholicism, anti-papalism and anticlericalism. Protestant historians focused on Protestant writers and martyrs, without asking how typical they were of contemporary opinion. The picture offered in this chapter, however, is of a nation still conservative in religion in which Protestants were a minority. The Reformation was shaped mainly by Henry VIII, who forced through the breach with Rome (essential to secure his divorce from Catherine of Aragon) and a limited hybrid reformation in the localities. Some traditional practices were forbidden, especially pilgrimages and the cult of the saints, and the monasteries were dissolved, but the Mass and the Church's teachings on salvation remained largely unchanged.

Religion in the 1520s

The Lollards

England's contribution to late medieval heresy originated with John Wyclif, Master of Balliol College, Oxford, an intense, uncompromising theological scholar. From reading St Augustine he came to believe in **predestination**, that God determined from the start of time who would be saved and who damned. If true, this confined salvation to a chosen few and condemned everyone else to irrevocable damnation. It rejected the Church's inclusive view of salvation, whereby through good works and cleansing in Purgatory all but the most hardened sinners avoided hell. It undermined the sacraments and rendered the acts of men, whether priests or laymen, ineffectual. For Wyclif, **transubstantiation** was nonsense: the bread and wine in the Mass remained bread and wine. Priests had no special powers or authority over laypeople. God granted such authority only to His **elect**, who formed the only true church and alone could expound the Word of God. Scripture contained all that was necessary for salvation, without human inventions and 'traditions'. The English Church decreed that the Bible should be read in Latin, but Wyclif demanded that it should be available to all in English.

Wyclif's critique of the Church struck at the roots of ecclesiastical and priestly authority. It was denounced by bishops and peers, but won some support among the lower clergy and laymen. Many in authority argued, especially after the Peasants' Revolt, that elevating the elite of the spirit above the existing social hierarchy threatened the social order. After Wyclif's death in 1384 his works circulated in manuscript, including an English Bible (1397) of which over 200 copies survive. His followers, called Lollards (mutterers) by their enemies, carried his message around the country. Elite support for his teachings collapsed after a Lollard revolt in 1414. Only two Lollards had hitherto been executed as heretics, but now magistrates were required to hunt them down and hand them over to the Church courts. Lollardy was driven underground; it never developed an organisation and Lollards attended their parish churches and met secretly to read the Bible. Without intellectual leadership from the universities or clergy, their beliefs became simpler, centred on Scriptural assurances of salvation. The ecclesiastical authorities continued to hunt them down, but Lollard beliefs continued into the sixteenth century and were given fresh impetus by Protestant ideas, which in many ways Wyclif anticipated.

Evangelicals

Wyclif's greatest impact was not in England but in Bohemia, where the growth of the Hussites (followers of Jan Hus of Prague) forced the Pope to concede variations from normal Catholic practice. Wyclif and Hus appealed to those who yearned for access to the Bible in their own language, so that they could understand and apply it in their everyday lives. Such people are generally referred to as **evangelicals**. Demands for access to the Bible in the vernacular were found most often among those later identified as Protestants, but they were also found among those remaining within the Catholic Church, particularly intellectuals. A striking expression of evangelical ideals came in 1516 from Erasmus of Rotterdam, who wished that everyone – even women and the Irish – should make the Bible the rule of their daily lives. (See Box 4.1, Evangelicalism without Protestantism: Erasmus.) In England the ecclesiastical authorities' stubborn opposition to translating the Bible meant that evangelicals were found mainly among those inclined to Protestantism.

BOX 4.1: Evangelicalism without Protestantism: Erasmus

The following extracts are taken from 'The Paraclesis', published as a preface to an edition of the Greek New Testament, with Latin translation, published in 1516, the year before Luther produced his Ninety-five Theses. It is a powerful plea to make the Bible available in the vernacular and includes a justification of lay preaching, a concept too radical for Luther or Calvin, who adhered firmly to the principle of a learned ministry. Although Erasmus was frequently at odds with the Catholic establishment, he rejected Protestant theology and remained a highly individual Catholic.

I disagree very much with those who are unwilling that Holy Scripture, translated into the vulgar tongue, be read by the uneducated, as if Christ taught such intricate doctrines that they could scarce be understood by very few theologians, or as if the strength of the Christian religion consisted in men's ignorance of it ... Christ wishes his mysteries published as openly as possible. I would that even the lowliest women read the Gospels and the Pauline Epistles. And I would that they were translated into all languages so that they could be read and understood not only by Scots and Irish but also by Turks and Saracens. Surely the first step is to understand in one way or another. It may be that many may ridicule, but some may be taken captive. Would that, as a result, the farmer sing some portion of them at the plough, the weaver hum some parts of them to the movement of his shuttle, the traveller lighten the weariness of the journey with stories of this kind! Let the conversations of every Christian be drawn from this source ...

Erasmus argued that a true theologian was not one who developed subtle, intricate arguments but one whose demeanour and life were expressions of Christian principles.

... the Christian should not put his trust in the supports of this world but must rely entirely on heaven ... And if anyone under the inspiration of the spirit of Christ preaches this kind of doctrine, inculcates it, exhorts, incites and encourages men to it, he indeed is truly a theologian, even if he should be a common labourer or weaver ...

J.C. Olin (ed.), *Christian Humanism and the Reformation: Selected Writings of Erasmus* (New York, 1975), pp. 96–7, 98.

Protestants

Martin Luther drew on the ideas of Wyclif, Hus and many others in his challenge to the Church, sparking unprecedented theological debate across much of Europe. Princes of the Holy Roman Empire adopted his ideas because they believed in them or saw them as advantageous; urban rulers in the Empire and the Low Countries were forced by popular pressure to cleanse town churches of images and change the form of worship. Many towns had strong traditions of popular participation in government and high levels of literacy, making them open to a religion of the Word. They were centres of trade and industry and many had universities: teachers and students played a substantial role in the urban reformation. Beyond the princes and towns lay a more radical reformation. In 1525 peasants in South Germany rebelled against their landlords, encouraged by Luther's criticisms of the rich. They were brutally suppressed by their lords and Luther dissociated himself from the 'murderous thieving hordes'. Meanwhile, small groups claimed direct inspiration from God, enabling them to speak in tongues and perform miracles: one cut off his brother's head in order to raise him from the dead. To show the Holy Spirit working within, they baptised themselves; their enemies called them **Anabaptists**. Many tried to withdraw from the world, but a group of radicals established a reign of terror at Münster in 1534–5: their leader introduced polygamy and decapitated his critics in the main square. They were eventually overcome by an army of Catholic and Protestant princes. Respectable Protestants dissociated themselves from the Anabaptists: English governments watched them warily for more than a century.

There was no single dominant thinker in the Protestant Reformation. Luther sparked an international debate, but became more conservative after the Peasants' War; his directions to Lutheran churches became rigid and dictatorial, forbidding the clergy to deviate from the wording of his catechism. Luther's influence in England was outweighed by Huldreich Zwingli, from Zurich, and John Calvin, at Geneva, who became the most potent Continental influence on the English and Scottish Reformations. The three disagreed on many points of detail, but agreed on certain central issues.

First, God's will was found only in Scripture: not the Latin Vulgate Bible, which was full of mistranslations, but the original texts – Hebrew, for the Old Testament, Greek, for the New. They rejected the traditions of the Church, the writings of the early Fathers, and the pronouncements of popes, which together overlaid the purity of God's Word with a suffocating tangle of human inventions.

Second, they denied the claims to authority of popes and priests. The popes' alleged power rested partly on forged documents, such as the Donation of Constantine, in which the Emperor had allegedly granted the papacy full authority over Western Christendom. By the sixteenth century every pope was Italian and used his power to enrich himself and his family. The clergy claimed supernatural attributes which gave them power over the people. Starting with the consecration of the bread and wine in the Mass, they controlled access to the sacraments, heard confession, imposed penance and absolved sinners. The Reformers agreed on the importance of the Eucharist – highlighted by the Biblical account of the Last Supper – but disagreed as to what happened to the bread and wine. Zwingli insisted that it was purely a commemoration, Luther argued for some subtle spiritual presence and Calvin was somewhere in between (although many of his followers sided with Zwingli). If no miracle occurred in the Mass, the clergy had no claim to a superior spiritual status, emphasised in the Catholic Church by their vestments and tonsure; they did not marry and alone received the wine in the Eucharist. Protestants played down the spiritual differences between clergy and laity: their clergy's authority came from knowledge of Scripture, not supernatural powers.

A third point on which the founding fathers of Protestantism agreed was that good works played no part in salvation. Luther argued that people were justified (saved) by faith alone, which led to arguments about how far people could acquire faith and how far it was a unilateral gift from God. Zwingli and Calvin inclined to the latter, developing a view of predestination similar to that of Wyclif.

Finally, since God's Word was the sole source of authority, expounding Scripture should be the focus of the service. Zwingli and Calvin stressed the need to help people understand the Bible's relevance to their daily lives. The remainder of the service should be short, not tied to set formulae – here they differed from Luther – but in the minister's own words. They aimed to return to the **primitive Church** of the New Testament, with no ceremonies or practices not authorised by Scripture. The church interior should be plain, without images which distracted the people from the sermon and risked becoming objects of worship.

Although there were medieval precedents for most elements of Protestantism, the movements which emerged in the sixteenth century were on a different scale – and were often successful. Unlike Wyclif, the Continental Reformation won over princes and town elites, adding the power of secular government to the preachers' spiritual authority. Zwingli and Calvin established organisations which were widely replicated elsewhere, building self-governing churches from below. This happened in Scotland and parts of Ireland; there were moves, resisted by monarchs, to do the same in England. In much of Continental Europe, political power was fragmented. In England it was more centralised and the Crown tried to control and channel the Reformation. It was helped in this by the relative dearth of large towns and universities (England had only two). The English Reformation followed a distinctive path, because it was first and foremost a royal reformation.

The Catholic Response

The picture given so far of the English Catholic Church might suggest that it was conservative, popular and monolithic. It was certainly conservative: most of the clergy (and laity) were suspicious of change, and their suspicions were heightened by the Peasants' War and Münster. However, to see the Church as a monolithic organisation controlled by the papacy and clergy would be misleading. Lay piety had a momentum of its own but laypeople did not necessarily question traditional practices. Popular commitment to chantries, pilgrimages and remembering the dead remained strong in the early sixteenth century, but there was growing criticism of the clergy. Across Europe in the fifteenth century laypeople built or beautified churches and complained of the clergy's inadequacies. Some grievances, such as their demanding more in tithes and fees, had nothing to do with the clergy as pastors, but they were also accused of pastoral failings. Lazy priests and greedy monks were compared unfavourably with diligent priests and friars who preached among the people. People criticised the Church because they loved it; and their criticisms became more urgent with the spread of Protestantism. Some acknowledged that certain Catholic practices were difficult to justify. Pagan rituals had been adopted and vaguely Christianised and the cult of the saints had degenerated into saint worship. Selling indulgences, giving reduced time in Purgatory, and granting bishoprics to small children were unacceptable. To meet the challenge of Protestantism the Church needed to reform.

Despite many obstacles, the Church tackled many of its problems in the Council of Trent, between 1545 and 1563. Rather than changing to meet Reformers' criticisms it chose to restate and clarify its traditional teachings and practices. This disappointed those who urged the Church to bring the Bible to the people, but was not necessarily unwise. The Reformers had become worried by popular responses to preaching the Gospel. Some people came up with strange ideas; many more found long sermons confusing and boring. The Counter-Reformation built on the Church's strengths. First, it reinforced its use of images and rituals, dramatic processions and baroque art and architecture to dazzle and excite the emotions. Second, it intensified priests' control over their laity. They concentrated on teaching the basics through catechisms, using simple questions and answers. Third, they intensified individual spiritual direction through more systematic use of confession. Far from being negative, this could be seen as a triumphant reassertion of traditional Catholicism. It reinvigorated Catholicism in countries where Protestantism had become the state religion, including England, Scotland and Ireland. The triumph of Protestantism was not inevitable, in England or anywhere else. From the 1560s the balance of power between the two religions shifted steadily in favour of Catholicism. Where Protestantism became established, and survived, was largely a matter of political contingency.

The King and His Court

Henry VIII is the English King who has most captured the imagination of subsequent generations. Physically massive and, when young, a considerable athlete, he was an impressive figure. Highly educated and confident of his ability to rule, he was capable of profound insights but lacked the patience to master complex detail. Power and decision-making were concentrated in the court, a political jungle, red in tooth and claw. At its heart was the King: strong-willed, shrewd, capable of being moved to fits of generosity and enthusiasm, but also to savage anger. As a young man he was determined to enjoy being King and to outshine his contemporaries. As he passed his prime he became suspicious, capricious, devious and sometimes cruel. Physically and intellectually his powers diminished and he faced more intractable problems.

It is not easy to read Henry's mind or to study the politics of his court. He seldom committed his thoughts to paper: sometimes he began to make notes only to abandon the exercise. Court politics were essentially oral. Often the only guidance comes in the comments of outsiders, particularly foreign ambassadors, with limited knowledge or understanding. Briefing or position papers are often undated and shed more light on those who drafted them than on the King's response. Some may have tried to use their mastery of technical detail to manipulate him, but he could be led only so far. Wolsey and Cromwell knew that the King had raised them and could break them. Wolsey fell from power in 1529, Cromwell in 1540. Cromwell was executed, and Wolsey would have been had he not died first. Despite their huge administrative abilities and powers of persuasion, Henry would not tolerate failure: Wolsey failed to deliver the divorce, while Cromwell's religious reforms were seen as politically dangerous, at home and abroad.

In the 1530s Cromwell was the pivotal figure in court politics. He delivered Henry's divorce and carried through the breach with Rome and the royal supremacy. Henry believed that much in the Church needed reforming. To some extent he was open to persuasion as to what needed to be changed, and how. Cromwell sought to build up the power of the Crown to make it an effective engine of reform. Henry welcomed this, provided reform did not provoke opposition. He did not fully share Cromwell's evangelical vision of a society based on the application of Biblical principles in everyday life and harboured grave reservations about encouraging his subjects to interpret Scripture for themselves. Henry's religious views contained strong prejudices against monasticism and pilgrimages and retained a deep attachment to transubstantiation. Sometimes his views were idiosyncratic: in annotating the Bishops' Book of 1537, he refused to condemn women who dressed immodestly or excessive sleep, and tried to rewrite the tenth commandment as 'thou shalt not covet another man's wife without due recompense'. Cromwell was constrained by the need to carry the King with him: he once remarked that for all practical purposes he had to believe as the King, his master, believed. His many enemies despised him as an upstart and deplored his moving beyond the breach with Rome to destroy much of traditional religion. This provoked rebellion at home and raised the spectre of invasion, which greatly worried Henry, especially as the succession was far from secure. In 1539 he returned to Catholic orthodoxy, in the Act of Six Articles. In 1540 Cromwell fell and Henry, to appease disgruntled landowners, abandoned the Statute of Uses.

The struggle between conservatives and evangelicals did not end with Cromwell's fall. As Henry's health declined, it became unlikely that he would see his son, Edward, come of age, so a regency would be needed. Henry shared the conservatives' distaste for further theological change and the momentum of reform slowed. But he also feared that the conservatives would reverse the breach with Rome, which he could not tolerate. The English Church remained partially reformed: independent of Rome, and with some traditional practices forbidden, but with others (including the Mass) still in place. Its hybrid nature reflected the conflicts within Henry's own mind. The Church that his son inherited in 1547 was Henry's Church.

The Breach with Rome

Experience since 1399 showed the fragility of the succession. England had no equivalent of Salic law in France, which stated that no woman could succeed to the throne, but it was assumed that a kingdom needed a male ruler to lead his people in war; a female heir would be dominated by her husband, leading to faction and civil war. Henry VIII, therefore, needed a son, but Catherine of Aragon bore him only one child who survived, a daughter, Mary. By 1525 Catherine was forty and unlikely to conceive again. Henry had an illegitimate son, which showed that he could father a boy, and came to explain Catherine's 'barrenness' as God's punishment for his marrying his brother's widow. He found a text in Leviticus: 'if a man shall take his brother's wife, it is an impurity; he hath uncovered his brother's nakedness; they shall be childless'. The Catholic Church did not allow divorce, but sometimes annulled a marriage on the grounds that it should never have been allowed. In royal marriages the partners were often more closely related than canon law allowed, so a papal dispensation was needed. The papal **curia** often issued dispensations or annulled marriages for minor irregularities. Henry expected that this could be arranged for him, but it was unlikely. First, his text was contradicted by another from Deuteronomy, that a man was obliged to marry his brother's widow. Second, the curia was willing to annul marriages on technical grounds, but Henry claimed that the papacy did not possess the power to dispense in this case; papal lawyers would not tolerate a layman defining papal power. Third, Catherine's nephew, Charles V, the most powerful figure in Italy, pressed the Pope not to concede to Henry's demands. Finally, Henry's case was weakened by his infatuation with Anne Boleyn, a strong evangelical.

That said, the Pope did not want to offend Henry, who had written a book against Luther, for which the Pope granted him the title 'defender of the faith' (*fidei defensor*, which still appears on British coins as F.D.). He agreed to send a **legate**, Campeggio, to hear the case in England, with secret instructions not to reach a final verdict. In June 1529 Campeggio and Wolsey started to hear the case. The Italian took every opportunity for delay; Catherine appealed to have her case heard in Rome and Campeggio adjourned proceedings for the summer. Henry assumed he would not secure a favourable verdict in Rome and claimed that the case should, by right, be resolved in England. His agents threatened that, if the Pope did not recognise this right, Henry would settle the case without him, and began to develop the concept of a royal supremacy over the English Church.

Henry advanced such claims because his scope for action was limited. He had no power in Italy and could do little to hurt the Pope. Papal revenues from England were small and the Pope exercised little effective power there: the Pope 'appointed' bishops but the King chose them. But for Henry to renounce the Pope's authority over England would be dangerous. If he could not have his divorce with the Pope's approval, he would have to have it without. But the Pope claimed the power to depose 'heretical' monarchs and absolve their subjects from their allegiance. He could also excommunicate the King, so that no Christian should have anything to do with him. Deposition or **excommunication** would give foreign powers a pretext to invade England. Henry's subjects showed little enthusiasm for the divorce: two carefully selected assemblies refused to acknowledge that Henry could settle the question in England. Catherine was far more popular than Anne Boleyn. Moreover, if he was deposed or excommunicated his people might rise against him. There were also practical legal problems. Cases of marriage were heard by Church courts. If the King convened a tribunal to consider the divorce, would it be legal? The obvious choice as president, William Warham, Archbishop of Canterbury, was firmly opposed to the divorce. It was most unlikely that he would do the King's bidding.

To defuse opposition to his divorce, Henry used a mixture of persuasion and intimidation. He claimed that the Pope's jurisdiction within sovereign kingdoms was limited. He conceded that the Pope was supreme in matters of faith and doctrine, but ordered his agents to find out if the Pope had jurisdiction 'in any other matter than heresy'. This implied that legal cases could be divided into spiritual and temporal; the latter should be determined in the country where they arose. If the King's courts were independent of any foreign authority, and no English subject could be forced to appear in a foreign court. This raised familiar issues about the demarcation between royal and papal authority. The Statute of **Praemunire**, 1393, stated that the English Crown had no superior on earth and was 'immediately subject to God in all things touching the regality of the said crown'. The Church claimed that marriage was a spiritual matter, because it was one of the Church's sacraments and raised questions of morality and the nature of the family. The King now claimed that it was a temporal matter over which the papacy had usurped jurisdiction. His claim to imperial authority within his realm received some support from medieval historians, notably Geoffrey of Monmouth, who claimed that England had been converted to Christianity in the first century; only in the sixth century, with the coming of St Augustine of Canterbury, did papal authority come to England.

While Henry's persuasion was aimed partly at an international audience, his intimidation was directed at his subjects. He regarded seditious words as tantamount to treason, but the existing treason law required proof of an overt act against the King. An Act of 1534 made it treason to call the King a heretic, schismatic or tyrant. Most of Henry's intimidation focused on the clergy, the group most likely to uphold papal authority. In 1531, the clergy of England were charged under Praemunire with exercising a foreign jurisdiction. The **Convocation** of the province of Canterbury begged for pardon, which was granted, in return for a fine of £100,000; Henry graciously granted them permission to hold Church courts in future, which established (to his satisfaction) that they derived their jurisdiction from him. He also demanded that they should recognise him as supreme head of the English Church, which they did 'in so far as the law of Christ allows', with which Henry seemed satisfied. The Supplication against the Ordinaries, a long list of complaints against Church courts, largely drafted by Cromwell, was brought into the Commons. It complained that the clergy made laws (in Convocation) without the King's consent, raising the issue of Praemunire again. The King insisted that future **canons** required the royal assent and that existing canons should be vetted by a royal commission; in other words, he claimed the right to approve the content of the laws enforced by the Church courts. When Convocation showed signs of resisting, Henry told the Commons that the clergy were 'but half our subjects, yea, and scarce our subjects', because their primary allegiance was to the Pope. Eventually Convocation submitted, but the submission was signed by only three bishops.

In August 1532 Warham died, enabling Henry to nominate a compliant successor. His nominee, Thomas Cranmer, a Cambridge academic, later became a prominent evangelical, but at this stage his position was ambivalent. The Pope, eager to please Henry for once, approved the appointment. Meanwhile, Anne Boleyn was pregnant. Henry, convinced that in the sight of God he was never married to Catherine, married Anne on 25 January 1533. In May Cranmer declared Henry's first marriage null and void. To prevent Catherine appealing against this, the Act in Restraint of Appeals, drafted by Cromwell, was pushed through Parliament. This stated that 'this realm of England is an empire … governed by one supreme head and king'. Its people, lay and clerical, formed one body politic owing allegiance to the King, who was endowed by God with 'plenary, whole and entire power, pre-eminence, authority, prerogative and jurisdiction' to render justice to all. There could be no appeal to any foreign jurisdiction, except in cases of heresy. The authority for these assertions was vague – 'divers, sundry, old authentic histories and chronicles' – but it prevented Catherine from appealing against the annulment; the divorce was as secure as English law could make it.

Further legislation drew out the implications of the supremacy, regulating the succession and confirming the King's authority over the Church's legal system. For Henry the breach with Rome was irrevocable: he now believed wholeheartedly in his supremacy and deeply resented papal 'usurpation' of his authority. Many of his subjects hoped that the breach could be healed. The Pope was slow to excommunicate Henry, leaving the way open for reconciliation. Many suspected that Henry's real aim was to make the Pope concede more extensive royal power over the Church. When the clergy were ordered to erase the Pope's name from their service books, the Abbot of Woburn told his monks not to obey, saying 'it will come again one day'. This reluctance to believe that the breach was irrevocable helps explain the relative lack of resistance, but there were other reasons. For most people the Pope's authority was an abstraction, of little relevance to their spiritual lives. Church worship remained largely unchanged, which made the courage of the few who died rather than renounce the papal supremacy all the more striking. As for the divorce, Anne remained unpopular and many felt that Catherine had been unfairly treated, but the Commons had little choice but to pass the Act of Appeals. If they had refused, Catherine's appeal could have gone ahead and Henry would have been left with a dubiously legal marriage and a dubiously legal divorce. The safest option was to comply with the King's wishes and hope for the best.

The Beginnings of Reformation

Having asserted his authority over the English Church Henry had the opportunity to reform it. This reform would not necessarily be Protestant: many Catholics wanted to cleanse the Church of quasi-pagan superstitions or complained of the clergy's failure to teach the people, but this did not necessarily imply dissatisfaction with the Church's teachings. Complaints about the clergy could reflect either a belief that they were not doing their job properly, or resentment of their behaviour as landlords and their demands for tithes or fees. In 1530, during a property dispute, an angry crowd marched on Lytham priory, in Lancashire. They were rebuffed when two monks marched out holding consecrated wafers above their heads; the crowd fell back, fearful of what might happen if they damaged the host. Protestant ideas began to penetrate England in the 1520s, winning converts among gentry and townspeople, in the universities, in London and some port towns in the East and South East; Kent, under Cranmer, became a centre of evangelical preaching. But even in Kent the evangelicals faced fierce opposition, and in some regions the impact of the new religion was minimal; no record survives of evangelicals in Lancashire under Henry VIII.

Reformation from below was unlikely in England. There were few large towns and royal authority was effective, centralised and strengthened by the royal supremacy. A reformation from above was possible, but would require commitment and determination from the King. Popular piety might be theologically unsophisticated but derived strength from custom and tradition in a conservative, predominantly rural society. Reform would have to start by destroying the objects – images, lights, rood screens, relics – on which age-old practices depended, clearing the way for preaching the Gospel. Many priests, laypeople and magistrates ignored commands to remove images and 'lights', and continued to visit pilgrimage sites. Reformation required sustained and detailed effort and the wholehearted backing of the King, which was not always forthcoming. He accepted that there were too many saints' days, which encouraged idleness, and that the cult of the saints often degenerated into saint-worship. Images became objects of worship rather than aids to devotion and shrines and relics could be used to exploit the gullible. Pruning these practices did not threaten the Catholic Church's central teachings about salvation or the sacraments. Although Henry gradually lost his belief in Purgatory, he would not accept justification by faith and provided in his will for masses to be said for his soul; his belief in transubstantiation never seems to have wavered. Cromwell's position was strengthened in 1535 when the King made him his **vicegerent** in spirituals, or vicar general, but the last word in religious policy remained with Henry, whose attitude could be influenced by opposition at home or threats from abroad. More fundamentally, Henry became committed in principle to a balance between old and new, to 'the mean indifferent true and virtuous way'.

Before the breach with Rome Henry was deeply hostile to heresy and a number of heretics were burned. After the breach those who asserted the royal supremacy most wholeheartedly were evangelicals. Cromwell recruited radical preachers who both upheld the King's authority and attacked traditional practices. Preachers like Hugh Latimer provoked a storm of opposition, enabling evangelicals to depict religious conservatism as opposition to royal authority. Despite his abrasive style and radical views, Henry appointed Latimer Bishop of Worcester. Other protégés of Cromwell produced essentially Protestant books of devotion; some claimed to be printed with royal approval. Cromwell also established a network of correspondents to inform him of 'seditious' remarks by priests. In 1535, as vicegerent, he organised a visitation of the smaller monasteries. In many discipline was lax and there were too few monks to sustain a religious community. Cromwell saw the monastic lands as an underused resource and resented the encouragement monasteries gave to traditional spirituality. Henry came to share these views, denouncing the 'slothful and ungodly life' of monks and nuns. The visitors were required to investigate monastic shrines and pilgrimage sites and evangelical preachers mocked bogus relics and miracles. The dissolution of the smaller monasteries, and the confiscation of their property, began in 1536.

Also in 1536, Latimer preached the opening sermon of **Convocation**, a wide-ranging attack on traditional piety. Convocation responded with ten articles, later endorsed by the King, which defended traditional practices, including veneration of images and the cult of the saints, as aids to devotion rather than efficacious in themselves. The articles denied that particular saints could offer specific benefits and rejected the concept of Purgatory: prayers could assist the souls of the dead, but they had no mechanical efficacy. They defended holy water and 'laudable' rites and ceremonies, with the caveat that the people should be told that 'none of these ceremonies have power to remit sin, but only to stir and lift up our minds to God'. On saints' days Convocation drafted an Act, issued by the King, which drastically reduced their number, sweeping away many popular feast days. It was bitterly unpopular. At Beverley, when the priest announced that the King forbade the celebration of St Wilfrid's day there was uproar; the people 'said that they would have their holy days bid and kept as before'. Many priests and parishioners continued to observe the old fast and feast days.

To add fuel to the flames, in August 1536 Cromwell issued a set of injunctions to the clergy, in the King's name. (See Box 4.2, The Injunctions of 1536.) He urged the clergy to become first and foremost teachers, barely mentioning the sacramental aspects of priesthood. There was nothing explicitly Protestant about the content of what the clergy were required to teach. Since 1281 priests had been repeatedly ordered to explain the Ten Commandments and other key texts. What was new was the systematic nature of the teaching and the emphasis on *understanding*: fostering an active, thinking piety which would inform people's daily lives. The condemnation of idleness was not new – sloth was one of the Seven Deadly Sins – but its juxtaposition to the Act against 'superfluous' holy days gave it a different significance. The injunctions' teaching on poverty was conventional. Charity to the poor lay at the heart of the Seven Works of Mercy, but the injunctions stressed that some poverty was due to moral failings, compounded by parents' failure to educate their children properly. These statements on poverty should be linked to proposed legislation in 1535–6 designed to relieve the deserving poor, which was strongly opposed in the Commons. The injunctions were designed to change religious life at the parish level. Following the other changes earlier in the year, they helped to provoke the most serious rebellion of Henry's reign.

BOX 4.2: **The Injunctions of 1536**

Here Cromwell, on the King's behalf, orders that the Ten Articles be implemented and sets out what he sees as their wider spiritual and social purpose.

4. ... to the intent that all superstition and hypocrisy, crept into divers men's hearts, may vanish away, [the clergy] shall not set forth or extol any images, relics or miracles for any superstition or lucre, nor allure the people by any enticements to the pilgrimage of any saint, other than is permitted in the [Ten Articles] ... seeing all goodness, health and grace ought to be both asked and looked for only of God ... [The clergy should exhort the people] to the keeping of God's commandments and the fulfilling of his works of charity, persuading them that they shall please God more by the true exercising of their bodily labour ... and providing for their families, than if they went about to the said pilgrimages; and that it shall profit more their soul's health if they do bestow that on the poor and needy which they would have bestowed upon the said images or relics.

5. Also [the clergy] shall diligently admonish the fathers and mothers, masters and governors of youth ... to teach ... their children and servants ... [the Lord's Prayer, the Apostles' Creed] and the Ten Commandments in their mother tongue; and ... shall cause the said youth oft to repeat and understand; and to the intent that this may be the more easily done [they] shall in their sermons deliberately and plainly recite oft [the Lord's Prayer etc.] one clause or article one day and another another day, till the whole be taught and learned by little ... [Parents and employers should ensure that their children or servants were brought up] either to learning or some honest exercise, occupation or husbandry ... [and] that the said youth be in no manner wise kept or brought up in idleness, lest at any time afterward they be driven, for lack of some [trade] or occupation to live by, to fall to begging, stealing or some other unthriftyness; forasmuch we may daily see through sloth and idleness divers valiant men fall, some to begging and some to theft and murder ...

G. Bray (ed.), *Documents of the English Reformation* (Cambridge, 1994), pp. 176–7.

The Pilgrimage of Grace

In autumn 1536 rumours spread across the North that the King would suppress many parish churches and confiscate the treasures of the remainder, especially processional crosses and chalices; he would tax marriages, baptisms and burials. In Lincolnshire commissioners were collecting a subsidy (the first to be demanded when there was no prospect of war), suppressing some smaller monasteries, investigating the parish clergy, and enforcing Cromwell's injunctions. These threats to traditional religion, and rumours of more, led peasants and craftsmen, priests and gentlemen to occupy Lincoln and draw up a series of demands, including an end to the suppression of monasteries and the dismissal of Cromwell and other 'heretics'. The King responded by sending an army, on which the rebels dispersed. News of the rising triggered much larger disorders in Yorkshire. York and Pontefract were taken and the rebels, led by Robert Aske, set up a council to formulate their demands. Some members of the King's Council of the North, notably Lord Darcy, surrendered and then participated in the rebels' council with the aim, they claimed, of restraining them. Henry, taken aback, sent an army under the Duke of Norfolk. Unsure of the reliability of his men Norfolk was unwilling to risk a battle against much larger forces, granted the rebels a free pardon and promised to forward their demands to the King. (See Box 4.3, The Pontefract Articles,

BOX 4.3: **The Pontefract Articles, December 1536**

The following show the comprehensive conservatism of the Pilgrims' demands. The items reflect the interests of various social groups but only number 13 deals with an obviously peasant grievance.

1. [To have the 'heresies' of Luther, Wyclif and others 'annulled and destroyed'.]
2. To have the supreme head of the church touching [cure of souls] to be reserved unto the see of Rome, as before it was accustomed to be …
3. We humbly beseech our most dread sovereign lord that the Lady Mary may be made legitimate …
4. To have the abbeys suppressed to be restored unto their houses, land and goods …

7. To have the heretics, bishops and temporal, and their sect to have condign punishment by fire or such other, or else to try their quarrels with us and our part takers in battle …
13. [The] statute for enclosures and intakes to be put in execution and that all intakes and enclosures since [1489] to be pulled down except mountains, forest and parks …
15. To have the parliament in a convenient place at Nottingham or York and the same shortly summoned.
16. That the statute of the declaration of the crown by will [may be repealed] …
20–21. [The Statute of Uses and the Treason Act to be repealed.]

A. Fletcher and D. MacCulloch, *Tudor Rebellions* (5th edn, Harlow, 2004), pp. 147–9.

December 1536.) Norfolk agreed to halt the dissolution of monasteries and the confiscation of their property until Parliament convened at York. Confident that they had secured real concessions, the rebels returned home. However, Norfolk wrote to Henry, 'I beseech you to take in good part whatsoever promise I shall make unto the rebels, for surely I shall observe no part thereof.'

Henry regarded the rebels' demands as impertinent and unreasonable. He had been reluctant to grant a free pardon and had to be dissuaded by his council from ordering Norfolk to execute the ringleaders. He was particularly angry at the rebels' call to reverse the dissolution of the monasteries. He strongly suspected that abbots and monks were behind the rising and ordered the Earl of Derby to 'take the said abbot and monks [of Sawley, Lancashire] with their assistants forth with violence and … in their monks' apparel cause them to be hanged up as right arrant traitors and movers of insurrection and sedition …' Henry received some rebels, notably Aske, with apparent courtesy, but inwardly seethed with rage at their impudence in demanding a Parliament in the North – would they not trust his word as King? – and at the way in which their demands escalated. Even so, in January 1537 he still declared publicly that he would pardon all of his subjects in the North, but a small rebellion led by Sir Francis Bigod gave him a pretext to cancel the pardons and order the trial and punishment of the ringleaders: 178 were executed.

The Pilgrimage reflected the alienation and resentment of the North. This was partly due to heavy-handed treatment of the great noble families. Landowners resented the Statute of Uses. The main thrust of the rebel demands was against 'heretics' in high office, changes in parish worship and the dissolution: the rebels suspected that the larger monasteries would soon follow the smaller. Through the rumours of new taxes, the confiscation of parish treasures and the dissolution ran the connecting theme of courtiers and heretics from the South plundering the North. If the northerners could not claim ownership of the monasteries' wealth, their shrines and pilgrimage sites played an important part in their spiritual lives; parish treasures belonged to parishioners, not to the King and his hangers-on. The rebels saw their action as a demonstration against changes foisted on the King by the misinformation of evil counsellors. They aimed to open the King's eyes to what was really happening. They stood for 'the preservation of the king's person, his issue and the purifying of the nobility and to expulse all villein blood and evil councillors against the common wealth of the same'. They wanted to preserve traditional religion, with its saints' days, pilgrimages, images and prayers for the dead. Some of the northern clergy claimed that 'by the laws of the church, general councils … and the consent of Christian people the pope of Rome hath been taken for the head of the Church and vicar of Christ and so ought to be taken'; by the law of God no layman could be head of the Church. The rebels called themselves 'Pilgrims' and marched behind a banner of the five wounds of Christ. (See Figure 4.1, Banner of the Five Wounds of Christ, 1536.) Their oath required them 'to take before you the cross of Christ and your heart's faith to the restitution of his church and the suppression

Figure 4.1 This banner of the Five Wounds of Christ was carried in the Pilgrimage of Grace by Thomas Constable of Everingham, Yorkshire, a clear indication of the Pilgrims' commitment to the restoration of Catholicism. The Constables remained Catholic after the Reformation.

of heretics' opinions'. Their bitterness, anger and willingness to risk their lives contrast sharply with the general acquiescence in the breach with Rome. It showed how much royal policy towards the Church had changed since 1533.

The Pilgrimage made Henry determined to press ahead with the changes he had started. He had only contempt for peasants, describing the Lincolnshire rebels as 'the rude commons of one shire, and that one of the most brute and beastly of the whole realm'. His councillors and military commanders repeatedly urged conciliation, but Henry demanded exemplary punishment. His anger was no doubt sharpened by fear: if the rebels had marched on London his forces would have been hard pressed to stop them. But they had no intention of marching on London. They put their trust in the King's justice and the righteousness of their cause and that trust proved cruelly misplaced. They may have been encouraged by the sympathy of some local landowners and by Norfolk's apparent moderation. Henry assumed that behind the scenes the real organisers of the rising must be nobles and gentlemen, but most were reluctant to get involved. Darcy, the only nobleman to join the rebels, was executed and Henry continued to undermine the great northern families. Convinced that the monasteries had encouraged the rising, Henry became more determined to eliminate them. But in other ways, the Pilgrimage made him more wary, leaving the advocates of reformation less room for manoeuvre.

The Limits to Reformation

The area of reformation which continued strongly was the assault on the monasteries, seen as centres of superstition and opposition to the royal supremacy; seizing their lands would enhance the King's revenue without asking Parliament for taxation. Officially the smaller monasteries were dissolved because they were decayed; the larger houses were praised for their good order and piety. After the Pilgrimage Henry decided that they should be dissolved as well. No justification was offered: it was simply stated that the abbots had surrendered their possessions to the King. (Some had to be hanged to encourage the others.) In the first dissolution redundant monks were encouraged to transfer to the surviving houses; now they were pensioned off. The dissolution's impact was mixed. Around one sixth of the land in England and Wales was confiscated. The lands might have made possible a financial refoundation of the Crown but Henry needed money for his armed forces and sold off a significant proportion. Some of those involved in the process of confiscation and sale snapped up bargains: the Russells bought Covent (Convent) Garden and Bloomsbury in London. Other rights were sold with the lands: **advowsons** (the right to nominate incumbents to parishes) and **impropriated tithes**. As a result much control over the Church's personnel and income passed to laymen.

The dissolution's non-economic impact was probably limited. The monastic ideal had long been declining. Laypeople were taking responsibility for their own spiritual lives, and bequests to the Church went to parish churches, guilds and chantries rather than monasteries. The monks' parochial contribution had been limited, except in upland areas, where they said Mass in chapels too poor to support a priest. Upland monasteries provided hospitality for travellers and some charity for the poor. What laypeople probably valued most about the monasteries had been their shrines, which were now generally suppressed. Overall, the impact on popular religion of the dissolution was probably less than that of changes in cathedrals and parish churches.

The battle within the Church continued after the Pilgrimage. The bishops tried to clarify ambiguities in the Ten Articles in the Bishops' Book, but much was still ambivalent or open to argument. Divisions continued in the localities. The dismantling of shrines continued: 'pilgrimage saints go down apace'. Evangelicals disrupted services by reading the Bible out loud. The constable of Ealing, near London, told one: 'This must be left, for I am sent for to warn you by the honest men of the parish for to leave your reading, for you cause other to hear you: it were better that they prayed on their beads than to come about you.' To strengthen the reformers' hand, Cromwell issued a second set of injunctions in 1538. These included an order that every parish should have a Bible in English, paid for half by the priest, half by the parishioners. All people should be encouraged to read it, 'as … the very lively Word of God, that every Christian man is bound to embrace, believe and follow if he look to be saved'. The injunctions strongly condemned pilgrimages and the abuse of images, while accepting that images could serve a useful (if limited) purpose in instructing the illiterate. (See Box 4.4, The Injunctions of 1538.)

BOX 4.4: The Injunctions of 1538

More strongly worded and thorough-going than the 1536 articles, these increased the emphasis on the instruction of the laity, took a firmer line against pilgrimages and images, and drastically reduced the number of 'lights' in churches. However, they stopped short of a total ban on lights and acknowledged that images could serve a valid (if limited) purpose.

2. [The clergy are to provide] the whole Bible of the largest volume in English and the same set up in some convenient place in [the parish church] whereas your parishioners may most commodiously resort to the same and read it …

5. … you shall … examine every person that comes to confession to you whether they can recite [the Creed and Lord's Prayer] in English … if they be not perfect you shall declare to the same that every Christian person ought to know the same … and monish them to learn the same more perfectly by the next year following or else … they ought not to presume to come to God's board without perfect knowledge of the same …

6. [The clergy are to preach at least four sermons a year, in which they shall] declare the very gospel of Christ and … exhort your hearers to works of charity, mercy and faith … commanded in Scripture, and not to repose their trust … in any other works devised by men's fantasies … as in wandering to pilgrimages, offering of money, candles or tapers to images or relics, or kissing or licking the same, saying over a number of beads, not understood or minded on, … for the doing whereof you not only have no promise of reward in Scripture, but … great threats and maledictions of God, as things tending to idolatry and superstition, which of all other offences God Almighty does most detest and abhor …

7. [The clergy are to take down any images] abused with pilgrimages or offerings … [and] suffer from henceforth no candles, tapers or images of wax to be set before

any image or picture [with the exception of the lights before the rood loft, sacrament of the altar and sepulchre] which for the adorning of the church and divine service you shall suffer to remain; still admonishing your parishioners that images serve for none other purpose but as to be books of unlearned men that cannot know letters, whereby they might be otherwise admonished of the lives and conversation of them that the said images do represent …

Bray (ed.), *Documents of the English Reformation*, pp. 179–81.

Cromwell's 1538 injunctions aimed to transform English lay spirituality, but events conspired against him. Charles V and Francis I agreed a ten-year truce and persuaded the Pope to promulgate the much delayed excommunication, which declared Henry deposed and his subjects absolved from their allegiance. Faced with threats of invasion and rebellion, Henry partly returned to orthodoxy. In November 1538 he condemned 'superstitions and abuses' which misled his 'true simple and unlearned loving subjects', but also Anabaptists and **sacramentaries** (who denied the real presence in the Mass, 'the very body and blood of our lord, Jesus Christ'). He prohibited seditious books and attacks on 'laudable ceremonies'. In 1539 the Act of Six Articles reaffirmed traditional Catholic teaching, including transubstantiation and clerical celibacy. Two leading evangelical bishops, Latimer and Shaxton, resigned; Cranmer sent away his wife. Henry worried that unrestricted Bible reading led to 'murmur, malice and malignancy'. He believed that reformation had gone far enough. In 1540 Cromwell was executed following allegations (almost certainly untrue) that he was a sacramentary. Henry's last years saw few changes in the Church. Cranmer retained the King's favour. In 1541 Henry again ordered the removal of shrines and images. An Act of Parliament of 1543 severely limited Bible reading: no women could read it except noble- and gentlewomen, and then only in private. In 1545 he told Parliament that they should use the Bible to 'inform your own conscience and to instruct your children and family' but not for 'railing' or 'taunting'.

Conclusion

In Henry's last years conservatives and evangelicals struggled to impose their views at the parish level. The calendar of fasts and feasts had been severely pruned, but some observed those which had been forbidden and some relics and shrines were venerated in private. Sometimes images attached to shrines were renamed: at Ashford, Becket's archbishop's cross was replaced by a comb and he became St Blaise, patron saint of cloth-workers. The Ten Articles and Bishops' Book endorsed the cult of the saints, the use of images and prayers for the dead, with qualifications about their significance.

These qualifications might make sense to theologically sophisticated priests, but not to those laypeople who believed that saints could cure illnesses or prevent misfortune. Lights were still placed before images. There were still prayers and masses for the dead; new chantries were founded. The Mass was celebrated much as before, with the laity receiving only the bread. Only the power of the Crown could force change on the localities and Henry showed little inclination to do so. He was old and tired, and had his supremacy and the sort of Church he wanted: with a traditional understanding of the Mass and salvation and some 'superstitious' practices removed. He was not greatly concerned that much was shrouded in ambiguity. He had learned that reform could unleash unexpected dangers, from angry conservatives or upstart plebeians who found radical messages in the Bible. But Henry could not live for ever, and the reign of his son was to bring sweeping changes.

SUGGESTIONS FOR FURTHER READING

The finest exposition of traditional Protestant historiography is A.G. Dickens, *The English Reformation* (London, 1964). • J.J. Scarisbrick, *Henry VIII* (Harmondsworth, 1968) questions the significance of anti-papalism and C. Haigh, 'Anticlericalism in the English Reformation', *History*, 48 (1983) suggests that it focused on financial and legal discontents rather than on the Church's teachings and worship. Haigh's article is reprinted in a very useful collection, C. Haigh (ed.), *The English Reformation Revised* (Cambridge, 1987). Haigh develops his ideas more fully in *English Reformations: Religion, Politics and Society under the Tudors* (Oxford, 1993). He had earlier shown that some parts of England were unaffected by evangelical ideas under Henry VIII: *Reformation and Resistance in Tudor Lancashire* (Cambridge, 1975). • Others arguing for the strength of traditional beliefs are J.J. Scarisbrick, *The English People and the English Reformation* (Oxford, 1985) and E. Duffy, *The Stripping of the Altars* (New Haven, 1992). Duffy emphasises the limited nature of Henry's reformation, as do G.W. Bernard, *The King's Reformation* (New Haven, 2005) and Scarisbrick, *Henry VIII*, which, although almost fifty years old, wears remarkably well. D. MacCulloch, 'Henry VIII and the Reform of the Church', in MacCulloch (ed.), *The Reign of Henry VIII: Politics, Policy and Piety* (Basingstoke, 1995), is a concise and very perceptive account of the development of Henry's religious views. • For a useful recent survey which gives more weight to popular Protestantism see E. Ives, *The Reformation Experience* (Oxford, 2012). • There is a lucid analysis of the Pilgrimage of Grace in Fletcher and MacCulloch, *Tudor Rebellions* and a lengthier discussion in Bernard, *The King's Reformation*. • For local responses to the Reformation see Duffy, *Stripping of the Altars*, D.M. Palliser, 'Popular Reactions to the Reformation during the Years of Uncertainty, 1530–70', in Haigh (ed.), *English Reformation Revised*, R. Hutton, 'The Local Impact of the Tudor Reformation', in Haigh (ed.), *English Reformation Revised* and R. Whiting, 'Local Responses to the Henrician Reformation', in MacCulloch (ed.), *Reign of Henry VIII*.

SUMMARY

- Both the Protestant and the Catholic Reformation can be seen as attempts to reform late medieval Christianity, but the Catholic Church was much more concerned to retain what it saw as edifying and valuable in the old Church, whereas Protestants were more inclined to return to the **primitive Church**. Even so, more moderate Protestants accepted that some aspects of the old Church's governance and practice were worth keeping, leading to arguments about ceremonies and the balance between worship and instruction.

- Henry VIII's religious views were in some ways ill-defined and confusing. He believed that, as a scholar-king, he was well able to reform his Church, but he combined a deep hostility to some aspects of medieval practice (like the cult of the saints) with a deeply traditional view of the Mass. He also developed a hearty loathing for the papacy, which he believed had usurped authority over kings in the Middle Ages, and he regarded the rejection of his arguments for a divorce as wholly unreasonable.

- Few of Henry's subjects felt strongly enough about the Pope's authority to risk life and limb trying to defend it. Far more opposed the changes in their religious lives, including the removal of some images from parish churches and the banning of pilgrimages and the cult of the saints. The result, by the end of Henry's reign, was a pared-down version of traditional practice, with theologically peripheral (but widely loved) practices forbidden but the core elements, including the Latin service and the traditional celebration of the Mass, remaining.

QUESTIONS FOR STUDENTS

1. Consider the view that Henry VIII's divorce strategy was deeply flawed and bound to fail.
2. Why was Henry VIII so determined to dissolve the monasteries?
3. When and why did Henry abandon any thoughts of a fuller Reformation?
4. How Protestant was the English Church when Henry died?

5 The Growth of Protestantism to 1625

TIMELINE

1547	Accession of Edward VI; chantries dissolved
1549	First Prayer Book; Western rebellion
1552	Second Prayer Book
1553	Edward VI dies; accession of Mary I; Catholic liturgy restored
1554	Mary marries Philip II; papal supremacy restored
1558	Mary and Cardinal Pole die; accession of Elizabeth I
1559	(1560 in Ireland) Acts of Supremacy and Uniformity
1560	Treaty of Edinburgh; First Book of Discipline
1563	Thirty-Nine Articles
1566	James VI born
1567	Mary Queen of Scots deposed (1568 flees to England)
1570	Pope excommunicates Elizabeth
1577	Archbishop Grindal suspended
1584	Association; Black Acts

1585	Philip II declares war on England
1587	Mary Queen of Scots executed
1588	First Spanish armada
1592	Trinity College Dublin founded
1603	Elizabeth dies; James VI succeeds as James I of England
1606	Oath of allegiance (following Gunpowder Plot, 1605)
1615	104 Articles (Ireland)
1618	Synod of Dort
1621	Five Articles of Perth
1625	James VI and I dies

Introduction

In 1547 the churches of England and Scotland were not yet Protestant; by 1625 they were different, but definitely Protestant; both forms of Protestantism could also be found in Ireland, but there the majority of the population remained Catholic. This chapter considers three main themes in the growth of Protestantism.

First, it was shaped more by Continental than indigenous influences. English and Scottish clergymen encountered Protestantism in cities like Frankfurt, Zurich and Geneva (none of them Lutheran). Continental theologians came to British universities and 'Stranger' (foreign) churches were established in England. Theologically Calvin became the most potent influence: there was no British or Irish scholar of remotely comparable stature. Calvin's Geneva also provided a **Presbyterian** model of church government followed in Scotland; some hoped to establish it in England.

Second, destruction was more apparent than construction. To eradicate superstitions the objects on which they depended were destroyed. This process began under Henry VIII, with reference to shrines and images, but some images were still permitted. For committed Protestants, everything that was not commanded by scripture had to be eradicated. The lumber of centuries had to be swept away before the **primitive Church** could be recreated, based solely on the Bible. This required learned preachers, but it took decades to train enough.

Third, the spread of Protestantism was contested. Elizabeth and James VI saw the preachers' demands for a thorough reformation as dangerous, likely to alienate their conservative subjects and undermine the monarchy. Catholicism remained strong in remoter areas of England, Wales and Scotland and was the majority religion in Ireland. Many who conformed to the Church of England clung to those aspects which echoed Catholic practice and resented the efforts of the godly to suppress allegedly unruly or immoral behaviour. Pre-Reformation worship had brought the people of the parish together. The godly, with their distinction between the virtuous few and the sinful many, tended to divide them.

Edward VI: The Zenith of the Tudor Reformation 1547–1553

Henry VIII's will sought to resolve potential conflicts over the succession by declaring that his children should succeed as if they had the same mother: first the son, Edward, then the daughters: Mary and Elizabeth. Henry attempted to establish a regency council, but Edward's uncle, Edward Seymour, Earl of Somerset, set himself up as protector. The young King was a precocious scholar and convinced Protestant, and the government moved towards a more Protestant form of worship with the 1549 Prayer Book. The basic elements continued, but the rituals were simplified, the service was in English and the laity received the wine as well as the bread (now ordinary bread, not consecrated wafers). Chantries and religious guilds were suppressed; much of their property was sold off but some was used to endow the many King Edward VI grammar schools.

These changes were a greater shock than those of Henry's reign. Waves of commissioners travelled the country with orders to confiscate, deface and destroy. Often they interpreted their instructions over-zealously; they were ordered to inventory the plate, vestments and the like of parish churches, leading to fears of confiscation. Parish officials hid their treasures, or swore that they had destroyed them. The new Prayer Book led to the Western rising in Devon and Cornwall. The rebels resolved not to march on London and besieged Exeter. Somerset delayed sending troops, giving priority to widespread disorders nearer London. When Lord Russell's army eventually arrived, they killed as many as 4,000 rebels.

The government was convinced that the rebellion was religious. There were other grievances, such as a new tax on sheep and woollen cloth, but the rebel manifestos comprehensively condemned religious change. 'We will have the sacrament hang over the high altar,' they declared, 'and there to be worshipped as it was wont to be, and they that will not thereto consent, we will have them die like heretics against the holy Catholic faith.' They demanded the restoration of the old services, in Latin, adding that the Cornish 'utterly refuse this new English', and called for Cardinal Pole, being 'of the king's blood', to be summoned from Rome 'to be first or second of the king's council'. (Reginald Pole was grandson of Edward IV's brother Clarence; he had been a cardinal since 1536.)

This rebellion, and that of Ket (see Chapter 6), undermined Somerset's credibility and he was replaced as protector by John Dudley, Earl of Northumberland, who accelerated religious reform. John Hooper and other radicals complained that the 1549 Prayer Book retained distinctions between clergy and laity. True, priests were allowed to marry and their distinctive robes reduced to a white gown or **surplice**, which was abolished in a second Prayer Book (1552); but communion could still be celebrated at the altar and the people could kneel to receive. The radicals argued that communion should be a simple commemoration, celebrated at a table in the nave, with the people receiving seated, like friends around a supper table. Altars were abolished in 1550, leaving people free to focus on the pulpit and the Word of God.

Hooper and his allies did not always get their way – they were consistently opposed by Cranmer – but Edward VI's reign marked the high-water mark of Protestant and Continental influences. The plundering of the Church intensified. There were proposals to sell the lands of bishops and cathedrals, and the plate, vestments and bells of parish churches. The proposals, justified by the admission that the King 'had need presently of a mass of money', were acted upon in April 1553, but meanwhile many helped themselves. Bishop Godwin of Llandaff sold many episcopal farms and let the rest out on very long leases. The dean and two canons of Chester were imprisoned for stealing lead from the cathedral roof.

The injunctions and Prayer Books of 1549 and 1552 completed the transformation of parish churches, with whitewashed walls (apart from texts and the royal arms); where statues could not be removed they were defaced. Appeals to the senses and popular participation were drastically reduced; the people were expected to sit and listen. Outside service time many spiritual, charitable and convivial activities were swept away. In some towns, plays and processions continued. In Norwich the annual procession featuring St George (with dragon) now celebrated the installation of the new mayor and survived into the eighteenth century. The Godiva procession in Coventry continued even longer. But godly Protestants controlled many towns and had no time for processions; in rural parishes church ales fell into disuse. The rich tapestry of spiritual and social life had been replaced by dull fustian. People submitted, but acquiescence did not imply willing assent. In 1549 Lord Paget warned Somerset: 'the use of the old religion is forbidden by a law, and the use of the new is not yet printed in the stomachs of the eleven of twelve parts in the realm, what countenance soever men make outwardly to please them in whom they see the power resteth'. There is firm evidence of Protestant enthusiasm in London, the South East and the universities; but in much of the country Protestants seem to have been few. How far England had become Protestant became apparent when Edward was succeeded by Mary in 1553.

⚜ Catholic Reaction? The Reign of Mary I 1553–1558

Mary's life was scarred by her mother's divorce; declared illegitimate, she had had no prospect of marriage. When Edward died Northumberland had Lady Jane Grey, his daughter-in-law, proclaimed Queen. Her reign lasted nine days. Mary resolutely asserted her right to the throne and the people of Suffolk and London rallied to her: loyalty to the Tudors counted for more than religion. Seeing her accession as evidence of God's favour, Mary set out to do His will, restoring Catholicism and papal authority. However, many of her people cared far more about traditional parish worship than papal authority. In 1536 the Pilgrims demanded that the cure of souls should be restored to the Pope; he was not mentioned in the strongly Catholic articles drawn up by the Western rebels in 1549. Parliament agreed to re-establish papal authority, but only after Mary promised that purchasers of monastic lands could keep them; it rejected a bill to confiscate the lands of Protestant exiles.

More contentious were Mary's efforts to restore Catholic worship. In traditional Protestant histories her strategy centred on burning 'heretics'. This view owed much to John Foxe's *Acts and Monuments,* of which the first edition appeared in 1563. (See Figure 5.1, The Burning of Archbishop Thomas Cranmer, 1556.) Foxe published extensive documents and fitted the burnings into a history of persecution, going back to the earliest Christians. He portrayed the martyrs as innocent victims of wilful cruelty, but for Mary and her bishops, burning was a last resort, after milder methods had failed. Stubborn heretics were a small minority. Most of those accused of heresy were seen as simple people, who had been led astray. This attitude was patronising rather than cruel; given the low levels of popular literacy and theological understanding, it was not unreasonable. Priests were instructed to identify early signs of heresy, such as failure to take communion at Easter or show reverence to the host. The aim was to redeem rather than punish, to lead people back to obedience. Some tried to make recantation easy. One asked a woman to affirm her belief 'in the faith of Christ's church', adding 'but to ask of thee what Christ's church is, or where it is, I let it pass'. The threat of burning was intended to persuade waverers to conform. The majority of those burned had recanted and then changed their minds. Shown the light they had chosen darkness; for their soul's sake they needed to be saved from themselves.

Popular responses to the burnings were mixed: strong expressions of sympathy were confined to a few towns, notably London and Colchester; spectators could be openly hostile to the victims. Sometimes the initiative for prosecution came from fellow villagers. John Bland, vicar of Adisham, Kent, was denounced by one of his churchwardens, who brought in another priest when Bland continued to use the 1552 Prayer Book. When Bland insisted on preaching, his parishioners pulled him from the pulpit and told him: 'You know that you took down the tabernacle or ceiling wherein the rood did

Figure 5.1 Cranmer had at one time recanted his faith and then changed his mind. He is said to have thrust the hand with which he had signed the recantation into the flames.

hang, and such other things … For the queen's proceedings are, as you know, that such must up again.' Bland was imprisoned, tried and burned.

Bland's case shows opposition to Edwardian innovations even in Kent. There is much evidence of spontaneous restoration. In August 1553 Mary declared that she would allow both the old and the new religion until further order. By early September 'there was very few parish churches in Yorkshire but Mass was sung or said in Latin … Holy bread and holy water was given, altars was re-edified, pictures or images set up, the cross with the crucifix thereon ready to be borne in procession … [and all] without compulsion of any act, statute, proclamation or law'. Injunctions and visitation articles specified the vestments, books and utensils that each parish should acquire, including a stone altar. This was not easy: destruction was easier than rebuilding and it cost money to replace what had been lost. But parishes did their best, helped by the return of items that had been hidden, or by gifts of money or loans. By 1557–8 most had a rood and some had images and lights. In Kent, by 1557 almost all had a stone altar, some vestments and the books needed for the service; most had a processional cross, though some were rather battered. Hard-up parishes improvised: some kept holy water in a wooden bucket.

Cost and time limited what could be restored. Without the chantries there were far fewer priests. The range of images was now much narrower, often only the rood; the Virgin Mary appeared only as weeping for her son on the cross. There were processions, lights and the elevation of the host, but this was the slimmed-down traditional religion of Henry VIII's last years, with the calendar shorn of many saints' days. Mary could not restore monasteries or chantries without their endowments. Lay participation in worship remained significantly reduced.

Did Mary's Church offer only a limited return to old ways, or something more? When Cardinal Pole arrived in England, he brought the thinking of advanced reformist circles in Italy. The Council of Trent promoted seminaries to train young men for the priesthood; Pole planned to establish one in each cathedral town. He and his colleagues also tried to improve the instruction of the laity. An English (Catholic) translation of the New Testament was started in 1555. For Pole a priest's duties consisted 'chiefly … in the preaching of God's Word'. The clergy were to preach weekly on the creed, the commandments, the seven sacraments, the deadly sins and the works of mercy. Before their sermons they were to recite and teach the Lord's Prayer, the commandments and creed, in English; parents were exhorted to teach their children. This emphasis on instruction was reminiscent of Cromwell's injunctions, and instructions to the parish clergy since the thirteenth century. Bishop Bonner's catechism, *Profitable Doctrine*, was based on the King's Book of 1543. Like Cranmer, Mary's bishops realised that not all priests were capable of preaching, so provided **homilies**.

Mary and her bishops aimed to restore traditional rituals and objects, and underpin them with greater understanding. They avoided polemic, as generating more heat than light; they preferred to familiarise the people gradually with the basic concepts through catechism and repetition. Slow processes take time and Mary did not have time. Her reign had its traumas – the opposition to her marriage with Philip II of Spain, the loss of Calais and (closest to her heart) her failure to produce a child. But it left a lasting legacy. She chose bishops who, unusually, were theologians rather than lawyers or administrators; with one exception, they refused to serve under Elizabeth. Academics who studied under Mary later went into exile and laid the foundations of the Catholic mission to England. As for popular piety, many felt a deep attachment to the Mass, but lacked a sense of theological identity, which could not be developed in a few short years.

The Reign of Elizabeth: the Making of Policy

Mary's reign lasted five years, Elizabeth's forty-five (1558–1603), during which time England and Wales became identifiably Protestant. Had Elizabeth's reign been as short as Mary's – she nearly died of smallpox in 1562 – they might well have remained Catholic. Elizabeth occupies a special place in English history, as 'the Virgin queen', attracted to several men, but refusing to marry because she was 'married to her people'. Her gender created problems in a male political world, but she was not inclined to defer to anyone, and used her femininity to manage her ministers and appeal to her subjects.

Elizabeth was highly educated, speaking several languages. She trusted her own judgment and could be determined and stubborn. At times she fought alone against pressure from her ministers and Parliament. Her court was far less factious and brutal than her father's. She chose her ministers shrewdly and, despite occasional disapproval, supported and trusted them. They served her well, but also worked well together; when they judged that her service and the national interest required it, they pressed her to do what they advised. They collaborated with Parliament, which expressed the concerns of the wider public. In 1584 ministers promoted the **Association**: nobles and gentlemen undertook that, if Elizabeth was killed by Catholics, they would prevent Mary Queen of Scots from becoming Queen.

Elizabeth lived in dangerous times. Initially Protestantism made extensive gains across Europe, but from the 1560s the Catholics hit back. The Spanish regime in the Netherlands subjugated the southern provinces. Protestants were driven into the northern provinces and struggled for decades against the greatest military power in Europe. In France the rapid advance of Protestantism was halted by the Massacre of St Bartholomew in 1572, in which many of the **Huguenot** nobility were murdered. Only the rivalry between France and Spain prevented the Protestants' plight from becoming even worse. For Elizabeth, Spain was a greater threat than France. Militarily it was more powerful, and Philip II claimed the English throne on the grounds that Elizabeth was illegitimate and excommunicated. Elizabeth (reluctantly) offered help to the Dutch rebels; in 1585, Philip declared war on England and encouraged Irish Catholics to rebel against English rule. In 1588 a massive Spanish armada was defeated by a mixture of skilled seamanship and bad weather. Subsequent armadas were also dispersed by storms, leading Protestants to claim that England was under God's special protection.

Elizabeth's ministers and Protestant subjects were eager for her to marry. Men assumed that women were intellectually and morally inferior to men, and that a Queen's first duty was to produce an heir. Elizabeth was not in principle against marriage; the problem was to find an acceptable husband. If she married an Englishman it could provoke faction. If a foreigner, she might subordinate England's interests to her husband's, as many believed Mary I had done. Elizabeth's choice of Englishmen was not always wise. Initially her favourite was Robert Dudley, Earl of Leicester, a trusted and responsible counsellor, but his credentials were tarnished by the almost too convenient accidental death of his wife. Leicester was a strong Protestant and led a military expedition to the Netherlands, where he behaved too independently for the Queen's liking. There was no other English favourite until the 1590s, when she was long past child-bearing. The Earl of Essex was dashing, but petulant: after a disastrous campaign in Ireland, he rebelled and was executed. Elizabeth's foreign suitors were mostly Catholic; for a while they even included Philip II.

While Elizabeth remained unmarried, Mary Queen of Scots was the obvious heir: as the granddaughter of Henry VIII's sister, she had much the strongest claim. Mary came to England in 1568 after being driven out of Scotland. Elizabeth kept her under house arrest, but she became the focus of Catholic plotting. Elizabeth's ministers argued that either the succession should be changed, or Mary should be executed for conspiring against Elizabeth's life. Elizabeth opposed both because she believed they threatened her position as Queen; she refused to consider what would happen after her death. Her ministers were frustrated and perplexed: even Henry VIII had provided for an orderly succession. Their frustration found expression in the Association and repeated attempts to convict Mary of treason. In 1587 they succeeded and Elizabeth was persuaded to sign the death warrant. Thereafter England faced wars against Spain and in Ireland, but anxiety about the succession receded. Though never formally recognised, the strongest claimant was Mary's son, James VI, who was male, of age and Protestant.

The Queen's Religion

The making of religious policy was influenced by international power politics and the succession question. Elizabeth was often at odds with her advisers. She was undeniably Protestant: as Anne Boleyn's daughter, she embodied the Breach with Rome. However, in England under Edward and in exile under Mary the radical wing of English Protestantism became stronger and the moderate wing weaker. Elizabeth's Protestantism was more moderate than Cranmer's – so moderate that it had few adherents. She had a small crucifix and candles on the altar (not communion table) of the chapel royal. She was determined to maintain royal control over the Church. She blamed preachers for Calvinist rebellions in France, Scotland and the Netherlands and feared that radical changes in worship would confuse and disorient the people, leading to disaffection. The Protestant radicals wished to inspire people to an active thinking piety. Elizabeth wished the people to remain passive; the Church should teach them to be good citizens and obedient subjects.

Elizabeth's version of Protestantism was initially too Protestant for most conservatives, but not Protestant enough for radicals. Most of Elizabeth's bishops were returning exiles, who (like her ministers) wanted to complete the Reformation (although they disagreed about how a 'complete' Reformation would look). Having seen Edward's Reformation undone by Mary, they wished to ensure that this could not happen again. Elizabeth saw religious conservatives as less dangerous than radical Protestants. As ministers and bishops set out again to confiscate or destroy the objects used in Catholic worship some conservatives stayed away from their parish churches; the

Pope excommunicated the Queen; and missionary priests came from the Continent. Ministers and bishops urged a tougher line against them, but Elizabeth feared provoking revolt and reprisals from foreign Catholic powers.

Religious policy was shaped by the interaction between the Queen and her bishops and advisers. Sometimes she backed down, grudgingly agreeing to new measures against Catholics, but generally she held firm. She refused to change the Church's government, which remained essentially Catholic (without the Pope), governed by bishops appointed by the Queen. Church courts enforced canon law. Forms of service became fixed in the early 1560s, then remained largely unchanged. Ministers complained, bishops pleaded and preachers raged, but they had to comply: resistance was not an option. Until 1587 the future of Protestantism depended on Elizabeth's survival; after 1587, Queen and people were united by the threat from Spain.

Was Elizabeth's impact on religious policy wholly negative? In the longer run, the answer must be 'no'. The 1559 Prayer Book came to command loyalty and affection. Similarities with the Catholic past, denounced by radical Protestants, became familiar and loved. They made it easier for conservatives to remain within their parish congregation. A new generation grew up who actively supported the Church's liturgy. Elizabeth was probably not conscious of this, but her stubbornness made possible the growth of a 'middle way', which had few adherents in 1558, but was later seen as 'Anglican'.

The Elizabethan Church Settlement

Elizabeth's hopes of a Church settlement embracing conservatives and Protestants were thwarted in 1559 by the opposition of conservative peers and bishops. After some bishops were imprisoned, the Acts of Supremacy and Uniformity passed, with difficulty. The first re-established the supremacy, with Elizabeth as supreme governor, not supreme head, to placate those opposed to having a woman as head of the Church; she would still be unacceptable to Catholics, however. The second required everyone to attend their parish church on pain of a small weekly fine and required the clergy to use a liturgy somewhere between the Prayer Books of 1549 and 1552; on vestments and the nature of communion it included elements from both Prayer Books. In 1563, moves in Convocation to ban holy days, organ music and kneeling at communion were narrowly defeated.

Even by 1563 the Church of England was clearly odd: its government and legal system were essentially Catholic, but its doctrine was Protestant. The Thirty-Nine Articles (see Box 5.1) included a clear statement of **predestination**. Strong Protestants generally had no quarrel with the articles' doctrine and no strong feelings about Church government. Most thought that episcopacy was neither good nor bad in itself: what mattered was the nature of parish worship. Communion tables had replaced altars in 1550 but

BOX 5.1: **The Thirty-Nine Articles (1563)**

The attitude of strong Protestants to the articles, the official statement of the belief and practice of the Church of England, was ambivalent. In general they welcomed those dealing with doctrine, but had reservations (or worse) about those dealing with the conduct of services. For the godly the sermon was the focal point of the service – homilies were an inadequate substitute – and they did not accept the validity of any ceremony not expressly commanded in Scripture.

Doctrine

Good works, which are the fruits of faith, and follow after Justification, cannot put away our sins, or endure the severity of God's Judgment; yet are they pleasing and acceptable to God in Christ and do spring out necessarily of a true and lively faith.

Article XII

Predestination to life is the everlasting purpose of God whereby (before the foundations of the world were laid) He hath constantly decreed, by his counsel secret to us, to deliver from curse and damnation those whom he hath chosen in Christ out

of mankind, and to bring them by Christ to everlasting salvation.

Article XVII

Worship

It is not necessary that Traditions and Ceremonies be in all places one, or utterly alike; for at all times they have been divers, and may be changed according to the diversities of countries, times and men's manners, so [provided] that nothing be ordained against God's Word … Every particular or national church hath authority to ordain, change and abolish ceremonies or rites of the Church ordained only by man's authority, so that all things be done for edification.

Article XXXIV

The second Book of Homilies … doth contain a godly and wholesome doctrine, and necessary for these times … and therefore we judge them to be read in Churches by the ministers, diligently and distinctly, that they may be understanded by the people.

Article XXXV

Appended to The Book of Common Prayer

in 1563 royal injunctions decreed that the table should be placed altar-wise during the week and brought into the nave for Sunday service – a clumsy compromise. The questions of kneeling and what happened in communion were left ambiguous. Arguments about ceremonies called in question the Church's authority to impose **adiaphora**, things indifferent – not strictly necessary for salvation, but contributing to devotion. The Thirty-Nine Articles declared them acceptable unless they were clearly contrary to the Word of God: if not, the Church (or the supreme head) could decide whether they were desirable.

The Survival of English Catholicism

Early in Elizabeth's reign it seemed possible that English Catholicism would wither away. Most Catholic-minded people attended their parish churches; only in the late 1560s did the Pope state clearly that Catholics should not attend Protestant worship. Some priests resigned their benefices, but were reluctant to break the law by saying Mass. Catholic laymen were forbidden to educate their sons as Catholics, but the need for Catholic education was met by English seminaries established on the Continent, starting with William Allen's college at Douai. These provided the intellectual foci of English Catholicism and training for priests who then returned to England as missionaries. The majority were **seculars** – the equivalent of parish priests – but others were members of religious orders, including the Jesuits.

The first 'seminary priests' arrived in England in 1570. Their task was unfamiliar – to win converts and strengthen the faith of waverers. They had no established church or machinery of discipline to support them, nor did they have parishes or income from tithes. They depended on hospitality and gifts from laypeople. In much of the country, they were dependent on Catholic peers and gentry, for whom the priest's first duty was to minister to the family, household and tenants; some doubled as tutors. This pattern was reinforced as the laws against Catholicism became more severe. Gentlemen who harboured priests faced harsh penalties and some provided hiding places for priests within their houses. (See Figure 5.2, Priest's Hole at Oxburgh Hall, Norfolk.) It became hard for priests to extend their ministry beyond their hosts' homes. In upland regions, however, notably the North, landed gentry were few. Priests travelled from one hamlet or farmstead to another, saying Mass and receiving hospitality. This was risky, but magistrates (and Protestant ministers) were few and far between: some JPs, especially in Lancashire, were Catholics or Catholic sympathisers. Priests also enjoyed some freedom in the densely populated and cosmopolitan suburbs of London.

The coming of the missionary priests, and the opportunities for Catholic education, prevented Catholicism from withering away. The year they arrived, 1570, the Pope excommunicated Elizabeth and absolved her subjects from their allegiance. For Protestants, every Catholic was now a potential traitor. Most English Catholics claimed that they were loyal subjects, but a few publicly asserted that Catholics had a duty to resist a heretical ruler. Catholics who had reservations about the papal deposing power were reluctant to say so in the terms required by the state. The oath of allegiance of 1606 referred to it as 'impious, damnable and heretical', terms which loyal Catholics hesitated to use. The government treated all Catholics, especially priests, as potential traitors and prosecuted them for treason, for refusing to renounce the deposing power. Nearly 200 Catholics were executed under Elizabeth.

Figure 5.2 Priest's Hole at Oxburgh Hall, Norfolk.

In the 1570s and 1580s Parliamentary legislation criminalised every aspect of Catholic life. Catholics had to attend their parish churches, on pain of a fine of first one shilling a week and later £20 a month for their refusal (or **recusancy**). It was made treason for a priest to enter England, or to convert someone to Catholicism, and there were heavy penalties for saying Mass and harbouring priests. It was illegal to receive a Catholic education, or to possess Catholic books or devotional objects, such as rosary beads. If Catholics repeatedly refused to take the oath of allegiance they could forfeit all their property and be imprisoned for life. Had these laws been rigorously enforced Catholicism would have been destroyed, but they were not. Very few recusants were fined £20 a month or paid the full penalty for refusing the oath of allegiance. Magistrates and government ministers focused on priests: lay Catholics were imprisoned in times of crisis, but soon released. A few Catholic noblemen enjoyed virtual immunity from the laws. Others were linked to Protestant magistrates by ties of kinship and neighbourhood. By the 1590s Elizabeth's ministers recognised that most Catholic laypeople were loyal and tried to drive a wedge between this majority and the minority who posed a threat to the state.

The Catholic mission started too late to reconvert England; its aim was limited to preventing Catholicism from disappearing. In the seventeenth century Catholics formed 1 or 2 per cent of the population, but a disproportionately large number were peers and gentry. Until their exclusion in 1678, Catholics comprised up to 20 per cent of lay peers in the Lords. They were also influential at court. The first four Stuart kings had Catholic queens, with Catholic chapels, priests and servants. Charles I favoured a degree of rapprochement with Rome: in the 1630s the dominant faction in the Church of England seemed closer to Catholicism than to evangelical Protestantism, leading some Catholics to hope for a reunion of the churches.

The Church of England: 'Puritan' and 'Anglican'

Elizabeth's liturgical conservatism put her at odds with strong Protestants, who became known as 'precisians' or puritans. The term **puritan** is widely used, but not easy to define. Two useful definitions are, first, 'the hotter sort of Protestants' and, second, those who thought that the Church of England was insufficiently Protestant. The former emphasises zeal and commitment, the latter the desire for further reform, which could range from more preaching and fewer ceremonies to (less often) a radical reconstruction of the Church's governance. Although most Puritans were to some extent Calvinists, they were defined less by theology than by their determination to make the Bible the rule of their daily lives. Puritanism was more a mindset than a clearly defined programme, but the 'puritan' became a familiar, sometimes comic, figure, like Malvolio in *Twelfth Night*.

Debates about the Church initially covered familiar issues, such as vestments and the nature of communion, but later broadened out. Puritans attacked the Prayer Book, 'an unperfect book, culled and picked out of that popish dunghill, the mass book, full of all abominations'. They condemned set forms of service, which encouraged unthinking repetition. They complained about Elizabeth's restricting the number of licensed preachers and her preference for **homilies**: she hoped to control what was said in the pulpit. In attacking those articles which empowered the Church to impose ceremonies they challenged the authority of the supreme governor and her bishops. Elizabeth's bishops often sympathised with the Puritans' aspirations. Some made little effort to make ministers use the Prayer Book. Elizabeth suspended her Archbishop of Canterbury, Edmund Grindal, for refusing to suppress prophesyings, in which clergymen publicly discussed doctrine and morals. Grindal thought that they edified both clergy and laity, Elizabeth that they encouraged laypeople to think too much.

Grindal's successor, John Whitgift, took a firmer line, demanding that all clergymen declare that the Prayer Book 'containeth nothing ... contrary to the Word of God'. Many were reluctant to do so and some called for the abolition of episcopacy; a bill was introduced in Parliament to introduce Presbyterianism, which was already established in Scotland. Elizabeth made it clear that she would not allow it to pass, so ministers, who had begun to meet in **presbyteries**, set out to build a Presbyterian system from the bottom up. The attack on the bishops was taken further in the scurrilous 'Martin

Marprelate' tracts. The search for the tracts' authors revealed the extent of clandestine Presbyterian organisation. Some of those involved were tried before Star Chamber and Parliament passed a draconian Act against **conventicles**. The Puritan war against episcopacy ended in ignominious defeat.

Presbyterians were always a minority among Puritans. Ministers' main concerns were preaching the Gospel and worshipping without 'popish' ceremonies. They found their ministry hard going: some embraced their teaching but many remained stubbornly resistant, which 'cannot be imputed to the want of good preaching but rather to the want of good listening'. Their sermons were too intellectual, aimed at the godly few; the illiterate or semi-literate majority became bored and restless. Many also found the ministers' message unpalatable. **Predestination** divided people irrevocably into the elect and the reprobate. Rejecting Catholic teaching on the efficacy of good works, Calvinists denied any direct connection between behaviour and salvation. God alone knew who was saved, but ministers taught that those who lived virtuous lives were probably among the chosen and that God punished communities for the sins of their weaker members. In 1613 lightning struck Dorchester parish church and fire destroyed much of the town. The minister seized on this sign of God's wrath and mounted a campaign against drunkenness and fornication.

Although some of the godly were deeply anxious about salvation, others found predestination reassuring. For the less godly it seemed bleak, consigning the majority to eternal torment. It contradicted Christ's command to love one's neighbour as oneself, a central theme of the Prayer Book. Many still believed in salvation through works, though stripped of popular superstitions and masses for the dead. (See Box 5.2, A Disappointed Minister, 1602.) It was a view of salvation and conduct based on reciprocity and neighbourliness; the Puritan view of good works consisted of the godly imposing wholesome discipline on the ungodly.

Many parishioners derived benefits from the Prayer Book services. They became familiar with the Bible: the Old Testament was to be read once a year, the New Testament three times. The whole congregation was expected to recite the Lord's Prayer and the Creed and everyone could join in singing psalms. Rote and repetition, which Puritans deplored, enabled the illiterate to participate. Ceremonies added dignity and a sense of holiness. One should not exaggerate the effectiveness of religious instruction. Some, especially in upland parishes, learned very little. (See Box 5.3, The Dark Corners of the Land.) In the lowlands, the picture was more positive. Images had gone, but church buildings could still inspire awe and a sense of the sacred. The appeal to the senses, which Puritans deplored, could edify and inspire. With time the Prayer Book services became a valued part of many people's mental and spiritual lives. Attachment to the Prayer Book created a mentality which could be described as 'parish Anglicanism'. It was mainly a lay phenomenon, directed against Puritan ministers. Congregations cited ministers before

BOX 5.2: A Disappointed Minister, 1602

Josias Nichols was one of many Puritan ministers who complained that his flock was unresponsive. He may have pitched his demands too high: he wanted to examine each family each week on their minister's sermon and was said to 'offend all the congregations where he cometh'. However, his picture is confirmed in one of the best-selling works of devotion, Arthur Dent's *Plain Man's Pathway to Heaven*: 'If a man say his Lord's Prayer, his Ten Commandments and his Belief, and keep them, and say nobody harm, nor do nobody no harm and do as he would be done to, have a good faith to God-ward … no doubt he shall be saved without all this running to sermons and prattling of the Scriptures.'

I have been in a parish of 400 communicants, and marvelling that my preaching was so little regarded I took upon me to confer with every man and woman before they received the communion. And I asked them of Christ, what he was in his person: what his office; how sin came into the world; what punishment for sin; what becomes of our bodies being rotten in the graves: and, lastly, whether it were possible for a man to live so uprightly that by well doing he might win heaven. In all the former questions I scarce found ten in the hundred to have any knowledge, but in the last question scarce one but did affirm that a man might be saved by his own well doing, and that he trusted that he did so live, that by God's grace he should obtain everlasting life by serving of God and good prayers.

J. Nichols, *The Plea of the Innocent*
(Middelburg (?), 1602), pp. 219–20.

BOX 5.3: The Dark Corners of the Land

There can be little doubt that the Church of England provided more effective instruction than its Catholic predecessor. However, this anecdote from a Presbyterian minister shows that it had its failures, especially in more remote upland areas.

On November 4 1681, as I travelled towards Wakefield, about Hardger Moor I met with a boy, who would needs be talking. I begun to ask him some questions about the principles of religion; he could not tell me how many gods there be, nor persons in the godhead, nor who made the world, nor anything about Jesus Christ, or heaven or hell, or eternity after this life, nor for what end he came into this life, nor what condition he was born in. I asked him whether he thought he was a sinner, he told me he hoped not, yet this was a witty boy and

could talk of any worldly things skilfully enough … he is ten years of age, cannot read and scarce ever goes to church, his name is Thomas Brook, his parents died when he was a child.

Oh my soul, reflect on the black and barbarous ignorance of many precious and immortal souls in England … yea, in those places where gospel-light hath broken out in meridian splendour, some are willingly yea wilfully ignorant, others are lazy and careless, others brought up in ignorance, and slip into profaneness and know no better, preachers catechise not, parents and masters mind not their own souls or the souls of such as are under their charge …

O. Heywood, *Autobiography, Diaries, Anecdote and Event Books*, ed. J. Horsfall Turner (4 vols., Brighouse and Bingley, 1882–5), IV, pp. 24–5.

the Church courts for failing to use the Prayer Book. Many parishes saw running battles between the godly and the rest over **church ales** and Sabbath observance.

In the 1580s a reaction against Calvinism appeared. This was essentially clerical and theological, but its influence was substantial, thanks to the clergy's access to pulpit and press. It expressed a sense that the Reformation had destroyed much that was valuable in the old Church, notably priestly authority and the mystery of the Eucharist. Clergymen argued that the bread and wine were transformed by consecration, not physically but spiritually. This led to a theology of salvation in which the sacraments played a major part. As the clergy decided who was fit to take communion, they became judges of people's moral worth and actions, opening the way for a renewed emphasis on good works. Their critics called such clergymen **Arminians**, after Arminius, a Dutch theologian. His ideas were condemned by an international Calvinist synod in the Dutch town of Dort, to which James I sent a delegation. James's bishops were a mixture of moderate Calvinists, whose theology he shared, and Arminians, who shared his views on monarchy. Under James, divisions in the Church grew, but neither party gained the upper hand. His son handed power over the Church to the Arminians.

Wales

The Welsh reacted to the Reformation with incomprehension and hostility. They remained loyal to traditional ways, part Christian, part pagan. Welsh parishes were often wretchedly poor and attracted poorly educated clergy, including Englishmen, who spoke little or no Welsh. There was little opposition to the royal supremacy, but deep resentment of Henry VIII's attack on shrines. Attempts to impose the 1549 Prayer Book provoked claims that much of the population did not understand English. The people did not expect clear exposition from their priests and were content if they mumbled their way through the liturgy as they had in the past. The confiscation of chantry lands and parish treasures, however, created a sense of violation and plunder. Under Elizabeth they conformed to Protestantism, apparently unaware that it was significantly different. Even in the comparatively English town of Abergavenny 'the greatest part even of those who in their judgements and convictions had before been Catholics did not well discern any great fault, novelty or difference from the former religion … save only for the choice of language … in the which difference they conceived nothing of substance or essence to be'.

In fact the language was crucially important. Whereas under Henry VIII some bishops tried to insist that services in English-speaking areas should be conducted in English, it became accepted that key texts should be made available in Welsh. The first printed book in Welsh contained the Creed, the commandments and the Lord's Prayer; a Welsh New Testament and Prayer Book followed in 1567 and a complete Welsh Bible in 1588. This concern to make Welsh a language of religion reflected a change in the episcopate: thirteen of the sixteen bishops appointed to Welsh bishoprics under Elizabeth were Welsh. There remained the linked problems of poor benefices and ill-educated clergy, but standards may have improved, with more graduates. People still went on pilgrimage and venerated saints; priests elevated the host and used traditional burial rituals; bishops found it difficult to supervise remote parishes. Changing engrained habits would take generations. The Catholic mission to Wales made little impact: educated Catholics regarded many popular practices as pagan. Puritanism, with its English mindset, made little impact either. With Welsh as the language of religion the people became (in their way) loyal to the Church of England: they had a Celtic Church again. Under James I, the Welsh Church showed signs of vigour, with more preachers and more religious works published. The Welsh language no longer depended on the patronage or leadership of the landed elite. Patronage of bards was dead by the mid seventeenth century; by the early eighteenth, most landowners in South Wales no longer spoke Welsh; but Welsh literature and culture remained vibrant.

The Scottish Reformation: the Revolt of 1559–1560

Signs of Protestantism were apparent from the 1520s and by the 1550s the major influences were the Swiss Reformers. Convinced Protestants were few and were rarely harassed; most met in domestic congregations, or privy kirks. Initially small meetings for Bible-reading and prayer, these took on characteristics of parish worship, including communion; some elected elders and deacons. The hosts were usually merchants, but craftsmen, **journeymen** and apprentices attended. By the later 1550s Protestantism was becoming a popular movement. Mary of Guise, mother of, and regent for, Mary Stewart, conciliated Scottish reformers. In 1558, however, she married Mary to Francis, the French King's heir, creating fears that Scotland would come under French rule, which came a step nearer when he succeeded his father. The Regent brought over French troops and made Leith a wellnigh impregnable stronghold. Protestants became angry; in Perth and elsewhere images were broken and monasteries and friaries destroyed. Protestants seized Edinburgh late in 1559 and temporarily deposed the Regent, who died the next year. They could not maintain momentum, however, and their followers drifted away. The Reformers appealed for English support; troops arrived in March 1560, leading to the Treaty of Edinburgh, under which both French and English troops were to withdraw from Scotland.

The Nature of the Scottish Reformation

The arrival of English forces encouraged the reformers to proceed. Parliament, which met in July, approved a Reformed confession of faith, abrogated papal authority and abolished the Mass. The developments of the next few years highlighted two problems: first, uncertainty, legal and theological, and second, limited resources.

Uncertainty

The English Reformation was driven by Henry and his ministers, who had clear objectives, centred on the royal supremacy. Parliament consented to legislation on behalf of the people, ensuring that changes were legally enforceable. In Scotland there was a temporary vacuum of royal power. When Mary returned after her husband's death there was a titular Queen and later an underage King. The 1560 Parliament was attended by an unprecedented number of lairds, which shifted the balance of power; it had also not been normal for Parliament to legislate on religion. Mary never assented to the legislation of 1560, but agreed not to overturn it. Although papal authority was abolished it was unclear if any ecclesiastical authority remained in being. Much of the Scottish Reformation was shaped by bodies whose authority was questionable. Uncertainty surrounded the respective powers of parliaments and conventions of estates. Early in 1560 a group of lords commissioned some ministers to draw up a Book of Reformation. The First Book of Discipline, based on this Book, was approved by a thinly attended convention of nobles. This envisaged a national Church, but did not state that it would be overseen by any central body. The most plausible was the national synod, which developed into the **General Assembly**. Initially this consisted entirely of clergy, but in time some nobles and lairds attended too; its relationship to Parliament was unclear.

As for the Church's theology, most statements on the new order referred to preaching the pure Gospel of Christ and maintaining moral discipline. The confession of faith combined elements from several theologians. From 1562 the clergy were required to use the Genevan Book of Common Order, but until 1573 there was no attempt to weed out those who did not. Ministers were allowed some discretion and some used more than they were allowed: the Book contained no burial service, so ministers used services from elsewhere. Calvin's catechism, bound with the Book of Common Order but not formally imposed, did more than anything to make Scottish Protestantism Calvinist.

Limited Resources

Reformation depended on regeneration in the parishes. This required money, but most parish endowments were **impropriated**. The Book of Discipline proposed transferring all ecclesiastical endowments to universities, schools and hospitals and increasing the incomes of the parish clergy. This proposal was rejected by the convention of nobles, many of whom owned Church lands. The only concession to the parishes came when it was agreed that one third of existing parish revenues (a relatively small amount) should be shared equally between the new Church and the Crown.

There was also a shortage of qualified clergymen. Few were university graduates and these were often converts from Catholicism, including monks still living in monasteries, which decayed as the monks died off. Faced with inadequately trained clergy, the Church established two orders: ministers, able to preach and administer communion, and readers, who could read prayers, catechise and officiate at baptisms and marriages. In 1574 there were about 250 ministers and 750 readers: in the majority of parishes instruction centred on the catechism. The abler clergy tended to gravitate to the burghs, but these often had fewer ministers than they needed: in Edinburgh two ministers served a congregation of 7,500 adults.

As its resources were limited the Church tended to leave parishes to their own devices. The decade after 1562 was turbulent. Mary was deposed in 1567 and left for England in 1568, after which there was civil war until 1572. The Church depended on nobles and lairds to secure compliance in the parishes, or left ministers and parishioners to do as they saw fit. Parishes were urged to establish **kirk sessions** but did not have to follow a prescribed pattern; despite repeated requests Parliament never defined kirk sessions' authority. The first, established in 1559, followed the Genevan model, with a minister, elders and deacons. The parishes were supervised by a motley body of 'super-intendents', a mixture of parish ministers and former Catholic bishops. In disordered times they could do little to maintain clerical standards.

These difficulties made an effective Reformation unlikely, but by the late 1570s much had been achieved. Calvin's catechism helped make the Scottish Church Calvinist. Kirk sessions, although not established nationwide, brought a new level of parish governance and lay participation. The General Assembly began to provide central direction, and its representations were heeded by government and Parliament. The Assembly hoped to use the King's authority to promote reformation. It accepted that bishops could serve a useful purpose, but did not clearly state what that might be. In 1572 it agreed that the King should nominate suitable men to fill vacant bishoprics; initially, these were to be answerable to the Assembly. James VI was still a small child, but in time he would raise questions about the extent of his authority and the relationship between spiritual and temporal. Meanwhile some clergymen developed very different ideas about this relationship and Church government: some came to condemn bishops, once seen as useful, as unscriptural. This led to a bitter struggle which shaped the **Kirk**.

Presbyterianism: Andrew Melville

The vagueness of the early Scottish Reformation meant that it led to surprisingly little conflict. Few priests or members of burgh councils were removed for nonconformity. In the civil wars Protestants and Catholics were found on both sides. Parish religion did not change greatly and many of the old clergy continued in place. There were few confiscations of devotional objects, partly because many parishes had little worth confiscating. This relative internal peace broke down in the later 1570s as opposed visions of the Church provoked bitter conflict. The first was clericalist and Presbyterian, promoted by Andrew Melville. The second was **erastian** and episcopal, partly modelled on England, developed by James VI.

Melville was an academic and teacher. He never served as a minister but was a widely respected and repeatedly elected moderator of the General Assembly. He returned from Geneva in 1574 and in 1580 became head of St Mary's College at St Andrew's, which became a seminary for radical clergy. Melville's ideal church was based on the parity of ministers, with no bishops or superintendents, only presbyteries and the General Assembly, composed of equals. He believed that the Church should be separate from the state. He reluctantly accepted that nobles and lairds could sit in the General Assembly, but insisted that only 'ecclesiastical persons' could vote, by which he meant ministers, 'doctors' (academics) and elders. All **teinds** (tithes) should go to the Church, along with the income from alienated Church property. **Lay patronage** of benefices should be abolished. 'Ecclesiastical persons' should not concern themselves with secular matters or hold secular offices.

Melville's sharp separation of spiritual and secular might suggest that neither should interfere with the other. He certainly believed that the Church should be governed by 'ecclesiastical persons', without lay interference. Christ was the head of the Church, and the General Assembly, imbued with His spirit, was the supreme ecclesiastical authority. But Melville would not allow a similar autonomy in the temporal sphere. James was eight when Melville returned to Scotland, but there was a danger that as he grew he might seek to extend his authority. To prevent this, Melville set out to destroy bishops, through whom the King might govern the Kirk. In 1575 the General Assembly voted to establish a Presbyterian system of Church government; this was not endorsed by Parliament, but a number of presbyteries were established.

The Presbyterian System

Presbyterianism was hierarchical, with, at the bottom, the parish and **kirk session**. This consisted of the minister, who was to preach and exhort the people, assisted (in maintaining moral discipline) by **elders**, while **deacons** relieved the poor, who became the responsibility of kirk sessions. Elders and deacons were elected annually, but in the seventeenth century some served for life. The second level was the **presbytery**, made up of ministers and elders, overseeing a group of parishes. It dealt with appeals from kirk sessions, visited parishes, appointed delegates to the General Assembly and examined candidates for the ministry. The third level consisted of synods of ministers, which oversaw the work of the presbyteries and heard appeals against their decisions. Finally, the General Assembly heard appeals, resolved disputes and formed the governing body of the Church; in the late sixteenth century it was a predominantly clerical body.

Presbyterianism might seem democratic. Parishioners elected elders, kirk sessions sent representatives to the presbyteries, which sent representatives to the General Assembly. However, referring appeals and queries upwards meant that the final decision lay with the General Assembly, which expected its rulings to be obeyed. Although it claimed to represent all of Scotland, it contained a disproportionate number of delegates from the Lothians and Fife, where support for Melville was strong. The clergy, however, were concerned with truth, not majorities: John Knox could not agree 'that our religion ... shall be subject to the voting of men ... for the most part of men has ever been against God and His truth'. The General Assembly demanded that the King follow its guidance in secular, as well as spiritual, matters, if they had a spiritual dimension. As it claimed to determine what constituted a spiritual dimension, it effectively demanded the final say in temporal matters. James argued that the Assembly claimed the same powers as the Pope, but overstated his case. The Kirk did not claim the power to make law, or to interfere in government or judicial decisions. The Assembly sent its resolutions to Parliament, which was requested to make them the basis for legislation. It saw the spiritual and secular authorities as co-operating in a government based on Christian values.

James VI

James VI was a scholar and intellectual, who wrote on such diverse topics as witchcraft, tobacco and kingly and papal power. He claimed his authority came from God, comparing himself to King David, 'nursing father' of the Church and protector of the Protestants of Europe. As he grew up he became adept at managing individuals and playing the long game. In his teens, nobles and clergy worried that he might be developing an 'opinion of **absolute power**'.

In 1584, James persuaded Parliament to pass the 'Black Acts', which asserted the Crown's authority over all its subjects, spiritual and temporal, and stated that all Church assemblies (including presbyteries) had to be licensed by the King. Bishops and commissioners should answer to the King, not the General Assembly, which he hoped to eliminate. Melville was summoned before the council, charged with seditious words; rather than appear, he and others fled to England. James soon realised that he had gone too far and needed to make concessions: caution and guile were necessary. The exiles returned, the 'Golden Act' of 1592 confirmed the existence of presbyteries and James agreed that the General Assembly should meet at least once a year. He saw that he needed to manipulate, not suppress, the Assembly, and establish the authority of Crown, Parliament and Privy Council over the Church.

From the 1590s James pursued two goals: the restoration of bishops and the introduction of an English-style liturgy; he became King of England in 1603 and thought that these would reassure the Church of England and facilitate a political union. Between 1596 and 1610 episcopacy was gradually restored. He undermined Melvillian influence in the General Assembly by summoning meetings outside Edinburgh. The General Assembly was required by law to meet yearly, but the King decided on the date and place; there was no provision for it to meet without his summons. From 1597 to 1602 James attended every General Assembly, lobbying and intimidating delegates. In 1605 he prorogued the Assembly without setting a date for its next meeting. Nineteen ministers assembled anyway: Melville and others were summoned to London and forbidden to return to Scotland. Melville was imprisoned and then exiled. Bishops were appointed 'constant moderators' of presbyteries and synods. Their lands, authority and jurisdiction were restored: three were consecrated by their English brethren; James claimed that their authority was derived from the Crown. In 1600 they were re-introduced into Parliament. The General Assembly met less often, and not at all after 1618.

The Kirk under James VI

James had played his hand skilfully. He assumed that the Scottish clergy would oppose a political union with England, so excluded them from the negotiations, which many felt were one-sided: 'we must yield all to them … they will not yield anything at all to us'. Despite bad feeling, the majority of ministers and influential laypeople acquiesced. Most would be satisfied with decent Sunday worship, the communal celebration of rites of passage, and firm action against popery. Kirk sessions promoted neighbourliness and conventional morality and provided for bastards and orphans. Despite hard-liners' criticism, the bishops' contribution to presbyteries and synods was often positive, facilitating the Church's pastoral and administrative work. They helped extend the Church's mission into the 'dark corners of the land': there were no ministers in the Hebrides before 1609. The bishops were generally careful not to upset Presbyterian sensibilities: there was no suggestion that they should re-ordain ministers. The response to James's liturgical plans was much more hostile. They centred on the Five Articles of Perth, which included the requirement to kneel at communion. Only seven ministers were deprived for refusing to comply. James pushed the articles through both the General Assembly and Parliament between 1618 and 1621, but with difficulty: he promised that he would introduce no more novelties, and kept his word. When he died in 1625, the Church of Scotland had bishops, but its government was largely Presbyterian. By reaching an accommodation with the moderate majority he marginalised the radicals. Two-thirds of parishes had a qualified minister. Ministers were now better paid and enjoyed status and privileges. Parish government improved, thanks largely to kirk sessions. The Kirk's preoccupation with sexual offences might seem obsessive, but for the respectable, discipline was necessary: Parliament banned the celebration of Christmas, claiming that it was 'popish' and encouraged drunkenness and excess.

It was not only a matter of maintaining the co-operation of the clergy. The nobility and lairds had always played a significant role in the Church. Some served on the

General Assembly, others acted as elders. Presbyterians looked to them as a counter-weight to the King. James did not threaten the interests or outrage the principles of the nobles or clergy; he had reached the limit of what could realistically be achieved. His less skilful son united nobles and clergy in formidable opposition.

A minority of Presbyterians, inspired by the Melvillian message and **millenarian** expectations, criticised the General Assembly, the nobles and civic leaders for not opposing liturgical innovation. Some sought communion in other congregations if their minister failed to take a stand. Ministers, and some laymen, went into exile, in France, the Netherlands and Ulster. There were '**conventicles**' in some of the bigger towns and in the South West, which became the centre of religious radicalism. Scottish Protestants had long believed that their Church was the most perfect in Europe: Knox wrote 'there is no realm this day upon the face of the earth that hath them [doctrine and the administration of the sacraments] in greater purity'. Disillusioned with their own Church and disenchanted with those they found abroad they sought perfection in self-constituted churches of the godly.

Scottish Catholics

The other potentially dissident group was the Catholics. Under Mary 'Catholic' could mean vague social and religious conservatism rather than opposition to Protestantism: nostalgia and habit were only slowly converted into a sense of Catholic identity. Catholic dynasties, like the Gordon earls of Huntly, were prepared to accept offices; their local influence was too valuable for the King to forgo. James repeatedly avoided complying with demands that he deal firmly with Huntly, who resisted all efforts to persuade him to convert. By 1600, Catholicism in Lowland Scotland was found mainly around the homes of Catholic nobles; in 1605 there was said to be only one priest in Scotland – and he was old and frail. From 1600, priests began to arrive from Scottish colleges on the Continent; later some came from Ireland. They focused on the Highlands and Islands, where the old priests died out and the new Church made little headway: very few ministers spoke Gaelic. The number of Catholics increased during the seventeenth century, even after the fall of James VII in 1688: at least six of the fifty major clans were Catholic in the eighteenth century. But in 1625 Scottish Catholicism, outside the Highlands and Islands, was a pale and sickly survival, hardly justifying Protestants' fears of 'popery'.

Ireland: Reformation

In the 1530s the King's main concern was to prevent opposition in Ireland to the breach with Rome and the royal supremacy. There was less concern to promote Protestantism, which found limited support within the Pale and very little in Gaelic Ireland. Irish

Protestantism was created mainly by newcomers: English soldiers and officials under Elizabeth, English and Scots settlers under James I. As the Dublin government extended its influence Protestant influence spread, making Catholic nonconformity more difficult and exposing the weaknesses of the fledgling Protestant Church of Ireland.

The Irish Act of Supremacy passed with some opposition from the clergy but little from the laity; the King attempted to consolidate his authority by assuming the title of King of Ireland in 1541. Between 1537 and 1540 the monasteries and friaries were dissolved. The remaining tithes and **advowsons** belonging to monasteries were also sold off, leaving the established Church even more impoverished. Many tithes were collected by lay **impropriators**, who had long used the Church's assets to support their favourite cults and shrines, and endow chantry priests. Now they controlled larger assets; alienated from the official religion, they worshipped in private houses and supported **recusant** priests. Guilds and chantries continued to play an active part in religious life, even in the 1590s. Participation in this 'shadow church' meant that the conformity of much of the elite was a sham.

At first the government and bishops made little effort to change the Church's doctrine and worship. Some images and shrines were suppressed, but pilgrimages to holy wells continued, as did mystery plays and **obits**. Attempts to impose the English Prayer Book of 1549 received limited support even from English officials. In 1560 the Dublin Parliament passed Acts of Supremacy and Uniformity. The former required office-holders to take the oath of supremacy. The latter stipulated that the English Prayer Book of 1559 should be used in all churches; everyone had to attend, on pain of a one shilling a week fine. It proved impossible to impose the Prayer Book even in the Pale. Many clergymen used it selectively, some ignored it. In Gaelic Ireland it was used only in a few towns. Most benefices were too poor to attract an educated priest: some in Gaelic areas were worth less than £1 a year. Many churches were ruinous and became more so. Educational opportunities were limited – there was as yet no university in Ireland. In 1576, of 224 clergy in the diocese of Meath only fifteen were found to be both fit to preach and adequately paid. The majority of incumbents could read the service, but not explain it to the people. Many were 'converts' whose commitment to the new religion was minimal and who reverted to their old ways when they could.

By the 1580s the Dublin government's relaxed attitude towards conformity had hardened. The '**Old English**' – Catholics of English descent – traditionally stressed their Englishness and loyalty to the Crown, but in the 1570s some were implicated in conspiracies and revolts. Their claims to Englishness were trumped by 'New English' soldiers and officials, mostly hard-line Protestants. The Old English claimed to be Englishmen who happened to be born in Ireland, and looked down on the Gaelic Irish as 'uncivilised'; the 'New English' said they were almost as backward and degenerate as the Irish. The New English took the lead in reprisals after the risings, often using **martial law**, which the Old English claimed was illegal. Some who had

THE GROWTH OF PROTESTANTISM TO 1625

attended Protestant services now stayed away and sent their sons to Continental rather than English universities. When the rebels of the 1590s portrayed theirs as a war of religion, and Spain became involved, many could no longer reconcile Englishness and Catholicism. Some continued to worship secretly as Catholics, but Protestant bishops and officials took a tougher line on church attendance. Catholic activists, especially bishops appointed by the Pope, were hunted down and sometimes executed. Recusants were removed from offices, even if they had taken the oath of supremacy. Protestant bishops argued that the first priority was to break the habit of nonconformity. Once they learned to conform they could be converted by the law and the sword. The New English believed that evangelism was pointless, because the Irish and Old English were too ignorant to understand Protestantism.

In the 1590s most Church of Ireland bishops and clergy were Irish-born. A few kept a foot in both camps. In 1570 the Pope appointed Miler Magrath to the (Catholic) archbishopric of Cashel, which he held until his death in 1622. He also held a variety of Church of Ireland bishoprics, from which he provided lavishly for his extensive family while allowing churches to decay. He was said to have done the government good service; he was 'a powerful man among the Irish of Ulster and able to do much hurt by underground practices'. In the wars of the 1590s the military extended the power of government and Church into much of Gaelic Ireland. The bishops removed unqualified, non-resident or crypto-Catholic clergymen from the parishes and, where possible, replaced them with orthodox graduates, including some from Trinity College, Dublin, founded in 1592. By 1615 about 30 per cent of resident ministers were graduates; by 1633 over 50 per cent. In Ulster many graduates were recruited from Scotland, including Melvillians, who found Ulster relatively congenial. Parishes were well endowed, thanks to the plantation (see Chapter 7). Episcopal government was weak, and the composition of the episcopate was changing. Most new bishops were English or Scottish-born: in 1625 only three out of twenty-three had been born in Ireland; five were Scots. Many English and Scots ministers were Calvinists in theology and Puritans by temperament. In 1615 the Irish Convocation approved the 104 articles, significantly more Calvinist than the Thirty-Nine Articles. The Church of Ireland was moving away from the ambivalent centre ground which could, at a pinch, accommodate Church Papists and lukewarm Protestants.

These changes brought the Church of Ireland into line with the Church of Scotland and substantial parts of the Church of England. Indigenous Irish Protestantism, however, was weak. There were sincere converts from Catholicism, but the Church's main support was among settlers. Irish peasants abhorred its religious practices and resented paying tithes to Protestant ministers, while also supporting their priests. The Church of Ireland appeared alien. Its authority was more effective than in the past, but weakened at the parish level by lack of money, suitable ministers and sympathetic magistrates. Moreover, it had to contend with a Catholic Church that was increasingly organised and militant. The Church of Ireland had state power on its side; the Catholics had numbers, and it was far from pre-ordained which would triumph.

Ireland: Counter-Reformation

Early sixteenth-century Irish Catholic piety was enthusiastic and often disorderly: it included pilgrimages to shrines and holy wells, exuberant burials and wakes, with much drinking and bawdy games. Religious rituals were used for secular purposes: relics provided protection in battle, while fasting could harm an enemy. Rome had a relaxed attitude to such practices; Ireland was remote. Organisationally, the Church was a mixture. In the South and East parishes were small: a single priest could minister adequately to his flock. In the North and West parishes were large, with a parish church and numerous chapels, often without resident chaplains. The income from tithe was inadequate and pluralism common. The upper clergy were often concerned more with enriching their families than with their spiritual duties.

As a Protestant Church developed, the papacy tried to create a rival establishment. The Catholic Church's main weaknesses were poor organisation and an unlearned priesthood; its great strength was the intensity of popular piety. The Council of Trent aimed to create a system of dioceses and parishes with a properly trained priesthood, supervised by bishops. Faced with government hostility, such changes were necessarily clandestine. The new ideas were carried to Ireland by students from the Irish colleges on the Continent, which numbered twelve by 1611. The Pope appointed new bishops who tried to introduce Tridentine methods. In the 1580s and 1590s some were executed, others died and most of the rest were driven out of Ireland. However, from 1618 the Pope again appointed new bishops; by 1630 there were seventeen and about 1,100 priests. Synods laid the foundations of diocesan administration; by the 1630s a system of dioceses and parishes was in place. Among the laity the Church sought to replace collective and often rowdy devotions with individual piety. Priests used Counter-Reformation methods (centred on confession and penance) to instruct and discipline the laity. They lacked money and church buildings: existing churches had been taken over by the Church of Ireland, so Mass was said in private houses and cabins, or outdoors. Only a minority of priests had been trained abroad; the remainder had often merely served an apprenticeship with an older priest. The less conscientious were castigated by the bishop of Waterford in 1631: 'most of our clergy are idle, contenting themselves to say Mass in the morning, and until midnight to continue either playing or drinking or vagabonding; and as most of them are unlearned, they make a trade of being ecclesiasticals, thereby to live idle … And alas very few spend one hour in a twelvemonth to teach the Christian doctrine, or instruct young children.' However, many of the clergy had embraced the Counter Reformation, which enabled them to assume the leadership of the Irish Catholics in the 1640s.

Conclusion

The introduction to this chapter suggested three themes through which to approach the growth of Protestantism up to 1625: the primacy of Continental influences; destruction; and the opposition to thoroughgoing reformation. 'Protestantism' meant different things to different people and 'Protestants' became divided among themselves. Let us consider each theme in turn.

First, Protestantism had a constant tendency towards fragmentation, seen in the failure of Luther and Zwingli to agree on the Eucharist in 1529. Given the Protestant stress on individual interpretation of the Bible, fragmentation was probably inevitable. To maintain any sort of unity, an authority was needed to limit permissible interpretations: these included the Pope and/or general councils in the Catholic Church, general assemblies in Calvinist churches. Competing theological influences were exported to Britain and Ireland, but Calvinism proved much the strongest. Many leading theologians, such as Knox and Melville, built upon Calvinist foundations. In 1625 Scottish Presbyterianism was somewhat battered, but remained united in its Calvinism. The Church of Ireland seemed to be moving towards a Calvinist consensus. Only in England was Calvinism seriously challenged.

Second, the physical destruction which accompanied the Protestant Reformation provoked deep resentment, but people came to terms with it. Church interiors were whitewashed but remained sacred spaces. The 1559 Prayer Book simplified church services, but the spiritual essence remained, as did the element of inclusiveness: this was the Book of *Common* Prayer. Participation now centred on words (spoken or sung) rather than actions, but those words were in English (or Welsh), making for greater understanding.

Third, contention and contestation owed less to theological differences than to attempts by monarchs to control their churches. Elizabeth stubbornly opposed further reform. James VI set out to break the power of the General Assembly, which he saw as challenging his authority as King. When he became King of England he (like Elizabeth) saw puritans as a political threat, which led him to favour Arminians, whose political views he found congenial.

The most obviously divided church in 1625 was the Church of England. There was conflict in the parishes between puritans and anti-puritans, centred on forms of worship, Sabbath observance and popular recreations. However, Elizabeth had defeated puritan attempts to drive through further reformation. There were also theological conflicts involving the clergy and the more informed laity, which were to be given greater intensity by anti-popery. These were potentially deeply divisive, but James maintained a rough balance between the two sides. In Scotland, James had apparently defeated the General Assembly, brought the liturgy closer to that of England and re-established bishops, who presided over a Presbyterian system of church government. There was grumbling but only a minority found these changes intolerable. By 1625 in England and Scotland the challenges from radical Protestants seemed to have been defeated. Charles I was to revive them and make them more radical.

SUGGESTIONS FOR FURTHER READING

Useful starting points are D. MacCulloch, *The Later Reformation in England 1547–1603* (London, 1990) and Ives, *The Reformation Experience.* • On Edward VI and Mary, A.G. Dickens, *The English Reformation* is old but well worth reading. Eamon Duffy offers a powerful revisionist case in *The Stripping of the Altars* and the more recent *Fires of Faith: Catholic England under Mary Tudor* (New Haven, 2009). • On Elizabethan and Jacobean Protestantism, see the important works by P. Collinson, *The Elizabethan Puritan Movement* (London, 1967) and *The Religion of Protestants: the Church in English Society 1559–1625* (Oxford, 1982). • Also valuable are Haigh, *English Reformations*, J. Maltby, *Prayer Book and People in Elizabethan and Early Stuart England* (Cambridge, 1998), C. Haigh, 'The Taming of Reformation: Preachers, Pastors and Parishioners in Elizabethan and Early Stuart England', *History,* 85 (2000), N. Tyacke, 'Puritanism, Arminianism and Counter-Revolution', in C. Russell (ed.), *The Origins of the English Civil War* (London, 1973), N. Tyacke, *Anti-Calvinists* (Oxford, 1987) and K. Fincham (ed.), *The Early Stuart Church* (Basingstoke, 1993). • For Puritanism and anti-Puritanism see D. Underdown, *Revel, Riot and Rebellion: Popular Politics and Culture in England 1603–60* (Oxford, 1987), R. Hutton, *The Rise and Fall of Merry England* (Oxford, 1994) and P. Lake, 'Anti-Puritanism: the Structure of a Prejudice', in K. Fincham and P. Lake (eds.), *Religious Politics in Post-Reformation England* (Woodbridge, 2006). • On Catholics, see J. Bossy's magisterial *The English Catholic Community, 1570–1870* (London, 1975) and M.C. Questier, *Catholicism and Community in Early Modern England* (Cambridge, 2006). • There are two first-class introductions to the Scottish Reformation: G. Donaldson, *Scotland: James V to James VII* (Edinburgh, 1965) and Wormald, *Court, Kirk and Community: Scotland 1470–1625.* J. Goodare, *State and Society in Early Modern Scotland* (Oxford, 1999) is more narrowly focused than the title would suggest, but contains a useful discussion of James VI and the Kirk. • See also M. Lynch, 'Calvinism in Scotland, 1559–1638', in M. Prestwich (ed.), *International Calvinism* (Oxford, 1985), and A.R. Macdonald, 'James VI and the General Assembly, 1586–1618', in J. Goodare and M. Lynch (eds.), *The Reign of James VI* (East Linton, 2000). • For Wales, see G. Williams, *Renewal and Reformation.* • For Ireland, there are excellent introductions in S. Connolly, *Contested Island: Ireland 1460–1630* (Oxford, 2007) and C. Lennon, *Sixteenth-Century Ireland* (Dublin, 2005).

SUMMARY

• Edward VI's regime was determined to carry the Reformation substantially further than Henry VIII's. By suppressing the chantries it severed the link, central to medieval Christianity, between the living and the dead, as well as making church interiors and worship even plainer and simpler. Mary's regime tried to restore the Church to the way it had been in Henry's last years, preserving the core (the Mass) but without ancillary practices like the cult of the saints. In other words, it tried to bring the English Church into line with Counter-Reformation Catholicism.

- In the early part of Elizabeth's reign not all that many people in England were Protestants, but most of them were considerably more Protestant than the Queen: there was little support for (and much hostility to) her desire to create some sort of middle way between the old religion and the new. That middle way was embodied in the Book of Common Prayer, which preserved the communal emphasis of traditional worship and elements of ritual. Condemned by godly clergymen it helped to create what is sometimes known as 'parish Anglicanism': many found puritan preaching too intellectually and psychologically demanding.

- The dominant influence in the Scottish Reformation was Calvinism; pastors who had lived in Geneva wished to establish its Presbyterian form of church organisation in Scotland. This brought them into conflict with James VI, who saw Presbyterianism as incompatible with monarchy and hoped to control the Church through a revitalised episcopacy.

- In Ireland, the great majority of the population remained Catholic. The main Protestant churches were the Church of Ireland (which emerged as a rather more Calvinist version of the Church of England) and Presbyterianism, found mainly among Scots settlers in Ulster. Under Elizabeth and James VI and I, members of the Church of Ireland and Presbyterians had much in common, but it was not to last.

QUESTIONS FOR STUDENTS

1. Was Mary's religious strategy 'entirely negative and backward-looking'?

2. Why did Protestants find so much to criticise in the Elizabethan Church settlement?

3. Account for the failure to establish Presbyterianism in England.

4. Why did James VI attempt to suppress Presbyterianism in Scotland and how far did he succeed?

5. Did James I manage the English Church more effectively than Elizabeth?

6. Why did Catholicism survive in England?

6 State and Society 1536–1625 1: England and Wales

TIMELINE

1536	Pilgrimage of Grace
1549	Agrarian risings
1563	Witchcraft Act
1569	Rising of the northern earls
1589	Cottages Act
1594–7	Consecutive bad harvests
1598, 1601	Poor Laws
1604	Witchcraft Act (pact with the devil)
1607	Midland rising

Introduction

During this period the population rose substantially. The demand for food and land grew faster than the demand for labour, so food prices and rents grew faster than wages. While small farmers struggled, those who produced a significant surplus profited from rising food prices. Landlords could profit, but only if they could increase their tenants' rents; many began to manage their estates commercially, driving out unprofitable tenants. A growing gulf appeared between rich tenant farmers and their poorer neighbours, many of them now dependent on wages. The plight of the poor led to protests and petty crime. The threat of disorder led central and local government to intensify their control of the poor. They clamped down on theft and disorder, but also sought to relieve the worst effects of poverty. These developments were most apparent in England, in towns and arable areas, of which there were relatively few in Wales. The responses to poverty, developed in large towns and in villages where self-government (by the 'better sort') was strong, were eventually applied nationwide.

Population and Prices

Population

Sixteenth-century Englishmen worried that England was over-populated. Thomas Malthus later argued, in *An Essay on the Principle of Population* (1798), that population always tended to rise faster than food production, until it was cut back by famine, disease or war. (Contraception was not in general use.) He was vague about the relationship between these three scourges. Famine could clearly be linked to population growth and/or harvest failure. Disease was sometimes linked to hunger and malnutrition, but not always: epidemic diseases like 'sweating sickness' (probably a severe form of influenza), smallpox and the plague often struck when food prices were low. War's impact on population could be devastating, but it was rarely a response to population growth. The link between population growth and famine seems clear in the early fourteenth century, but then recurrent visitations of the Black Death reduced the population to well below what the land could support.

Population figures for this period contain an element of guesswork: the first reliable national census was in 1831. The quantity and quality of data available improved after the introduction of parish registers in 1536. These contain information on births, marriages and deaths, making it possible to produce statistics on age at first marriage and family size. They cannot provide overall population figures, but indicate trends which, linked to other data, produce more accurate estimates than for earlier periods. Figures for the impact of the Black Death are conjectural: England's population may have fallen from six million in 1300 to two million or less, remaining low in the fifteenth century.

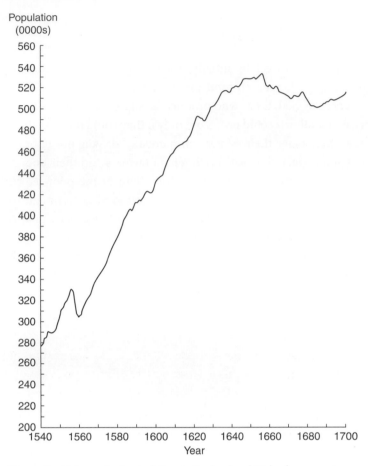

Figure 6.1 This graph of population in England and Wales from 1541 to 1701 shows an almost continuous upward trend until the mid seventeenth century (apart from a severe setback caused by an influenza epidemic in the 1550s). From around 1660 growth stops and the trend is, if anything, slightly downwards.

By the 1540s it has been estimated at nearly three million, reaching four million in the 1600s and five million in the 1640s. Between the 1540s and the 1640s it increased by almost 80 per cent. (See Figure 6.1, Graph Showing Population Trends, 1541–1701.)

According to Malthus this growth should have led to famine or disease. There is plenty of evidence of hunger and suffering: in 1623, not a particularly bad year, many were starving in Lincolnshire. (See Box 6.1, Rural Hunger.) People died of hunger in Newcastle and upland areas like Cumbria, but the death rate from the 1570s to the 1630s was much lower than in the 1680s, when food prices were low but there were several killer epidemics: shortage of food or work did not necessarily lead to mass starvation. The 'Malthusian trap', which had snapped shut in the 1310s, did not do so in the century before 1640. The most important reason for this was the relatively late age of marriage. It was assumed that young people needed to be able to support themselves

BOX 6.1: **Rural Hunger: Lincolnshire, April 1623**

A country gentleman, William Pelham, writes to his brother-in-law: note that the main problem is lack of work, and so of money, rather than shortage of food.

I am now here ... to settle some country affair, and my own private, which were never so burdensome unto me as now. For many insufficient tenants have given up their farms and sheepwalks, so as I am forced to take them into my own hands and borrow money upon use [at interest] to stock them ... Our country was never in that want that now it is, and more of money than corn, for there are many thousands in these parts who have sold all they have even to their bedstraw and cannot get work to earn any money. Dog's flesh is a dainty dish and found upon search in many houses, also such horse flesh as has lain long in a dyke for hounds. And the other day one stole a sheep who for mere hunger tore a leg out and did eat it raw. All this is most certain true and yet the great time of scarcity [before the next harvest] not yet come.

J. Thirsk and J.P. Cooper (eds.),
Seventeenth-Century Economic Documents
(Oxford, 1972), p. 24.

before they could marry. To take on a small farm or set up as an artisan shopkeeper, a young man needed to acquire the necessary skills, tools and capital. Those unable to support themselves were discouraged from marrying. (See Box 6.4, Article 20.) In the late sixteenth century the average age of first marriage was 27 or 28 for men and 24 to 26 for women; in the early fourteenth century girls often married in their late teens. By marrying later, women reduced the potential size of their families. From the 1620s a significant proportion remained unmarried in their early forties – up to 25 per cent in the late seventeenth century.

The late age of first marriage reduced the rate at which population might outstrip resources, but there were other factors. Cultivation was extended into land which had either never been cultivated or fallen out of use. Much was marginal but still viable; some was potentially very productive. The problem of maintaining the goodness of the soil without sufficient manure continued; crop rotations still included a year of fallow. But there were smaller improvements, such as experiments with other types of fertiliser and the use of water meadows to enrich grazing. Grain marketing became more efficient, so that areas which produced little could buy in from elsewhere and there were measures for the relief of the poor. Like those in Lincolnshire who had to sell their bed straw, many suffered from hunger, sickness and cold, but most survived.

Prices

Measuring prices is more difficult than measuring population. Different towns used different weights and measures and most records of purchases come from institutions (such as Oxbridge colleges and hospitals) rather than families. Drawing up a 'shopping

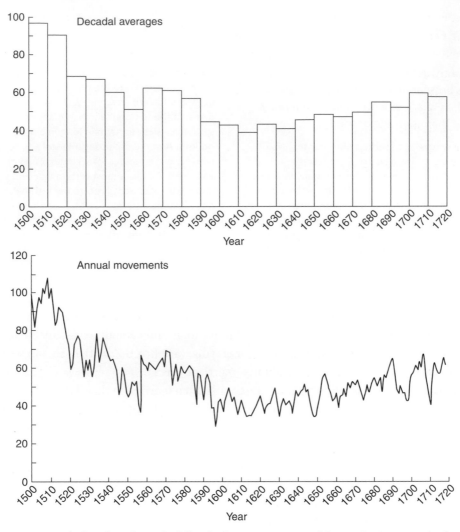

Figure 6.2 The bar chart shows the fall and subsequent recovery of the purchasing power, by decade, of builders' wages between 1500 and 1719. Between 1500 and the 1610s it fell by more than half, rising again from the 1650s but remaining much lower than at the start of the sixteenth century. The graph is based on the same data but presented year by year, and emphasises the great annual variation of food prices.

basket' of the food, fuel and consumer goods used by a 'typical' family is highly speculative. The best statistics available suggest that prices had risen 50 per cent from the 1450–75 level by the 1530s and threefold by the 1550s. With consecutive bad harvests in 1594–7, prices shot up to five times the 1450–75 level. There followed a period of relative stability into the 1640s. What mattered for poor families were not national annual averages but short-term changes in their local market. The prices of goods rose at different rates. Food prices rose more than those of manufactured items and the prices of poorer bread grains (oats, barley and rye) rose more than wheat or meat, which the poor could not afford. Finally, one can assess the significance of price levels only if they are related to wage levels, which again can be found mainly in institutional records. In the 1520s the wages of an average building worker would buy about one third less than those of his forebears in 1450–75. By the 1590s the figure had fallen to less than half and in the 1610s to under two-fifths. (One should add that many building workers commanded high wages: Oxford and Cambridge saw a building boom in this period.) Moreover wage *rates* can be misleading at a time when many labourers worked more and more irregularly. For very many families, necessities became much more expensive and family earnings purchased less and less. (See Figure 6.2, Bar Chart and Graph Showing the Fall and Rise in the Purchasing Power of Wages, 1500–1719.)

Landlord and Tenant

Rural society consisted of three groups of people. At the top there were wealthy landowners, peers, knights and gentry. These did not work with their hands and shared common values, based on status, lineage and honour and ideals of hospitality and charity. With labour scarce after the Black Death, many landowners leased out their **demesne** lands, rather than farming them with serf or wage labour. Their landed income now depended primarily on rents and the balance of power between landlord and tenant shifted in favour of the tenant: landlords cherished good tenants. Second, there were tenant farmers. A minority of wealthy yeomen produced a significant surplus for sale. They acquired additional tenancies and plots of freehold land and in the fifteenth century built houses and affected a lifestyle similar to the gentry. At the other end of the spectrum were husbandmen, whose farms never produced a significant surplus and in bad years could not feed their families. To bridge the gap, they worked as farm labourers or in industry. During the fifteenth century rents were low and most husbandmen survived, but they were vulnerable. Finally, labourers depended on whatever farm or other work they could get. They might have a small garden or access to the village common; where wood was plentiful they collected fallen timber for firewood. In the fifteenth century work was relatively plentiful, but this was to change.

In the sixteenth century need or greed drove landowners to manage their estates more commercially. They faced problems, notably inflation, but there were also opportunities. First, English cloth exports flourished, reaching a peak in the 1550s. Landowners built up massive sheep flocks – the Townshends of Raynham, Norfolk, had 18,000 in 1516. To graze their flocks they enclosed arable and the common lands on which poorer villagers depended: there was talk of sheep 'eating up men'. Second, competition for land enabled landlords to play potential tenants off against one another and push up rents: a few yeomen with substantial farms paid better than many poor husbandmen. They evicted poorer farmers (or refused to renew their leases) and aggregated their farms into large units. Some tenants faced substantial rent increases. Those with rents fixed by custom were not necessarily secure. When a lease was renewed the tenant paid an entry fine; if this was not fixed the landlord could push it up to an impossibly high level. In many arable villages small farmers were replaced by a few very substantial yeomen and a growing number of landless labourers. In Chippenham, near Newmarket, after 1544, two inhabitants had landholdings of over 90 acres, twenty-nine had between 20 and 90 (a 20-acre farm was just about viable), twenty-four had under 20 acres and twenty-one held no land at all. By 1712, three farmers held 250 acres each, four held between 90 and 250, two held between 20 and 90 and thirty-one held none, so the majority of villagers were dependent on wage labour and the number of families in the village had fallen significantly. While the national population had almost doubled, the number of families in Chippenham had fallen from 66 to 49. Many villagers had left, unable to find work.

Not all landlords behaved in this way. Some believed they were morally obliged to treat their tenants well. A Cheshire gentleman told his son in 1636 that they had been 'planted under you not to be tyrannised over but to be protected, not to be ruined but to be fostered by you'. Others were unable to maximise their profits because the peasants enjoyed security of tenure and strong common rights. In Willingham, in the Cambridgeshire fen, one tenant held more than ninety acres in 1575, fifty-seven held less than twenty and at least thirty-eight none at all. But the villagers enjoyed extensive common rights, including fen grazing and fishing; arable was secondary. The lord of the manor failed to overturn their common rights and Willingham continued to be a village of small landholders: only eight held more than twenty acres in the 1720s. The villagers could afford to hire a schoolmaster, with 100 contributing £1 each per year. Wigston Magna, now a suburb of Leicester, was a large village, with two lords of the manor, neither of whom could increase rents or entry fines. They sold more than half the village to the farmers, who managed the common land and other assets, including charities providing corn and coal for the poor. Most farms were small – twenty to forty acres or less – and initially there was land to accommodate incomers. Like Willingham, Wigston Magna remained a relatively egalitarian community of small farmers. The same was true of many forest or upland villages. Pressure from lowland landowners led Parliament to pass an Act in 1589 against building cottages with less than six acres of land. In forest and upland villages settlers were more welcome. There was waste and scrub to be cleared and woodland crafts offered a modest living; the forest also offered building materials, food and firewood. At Myddle, Shropshire, the lord of the manor allowed settlers in for a small rent, but as at Wigston, the pressure of settlers told in the later seventeenth century.

Peers and Gentry

Commercial pressures on landlords even affected the North. Border lords traditionally charged modest rents for small farms and granted tenancies to successive generations of the same families. The Tudors viewed them with suspicion: some were Catholics. The establishment of a friendly regime in Edinburgh in the 1560s made the magnates' military services less necessary. Henry VII, Henry VIII and Elizabeth all set out to undermine the great Border lords, relying instead on outsiders, but none could command the same loyalty. In the end the lords' power over men was eroded less by royal action than by economics. They began to aggregate small farms into larger ones, to push up rents and entry fines, and to evict unprofitable tenants, fatally weakening the loyalty to lineage on which their power had rested. In 1569 there were signs that the tenants' loyalty to the seventh Earl of Northumberland had diminished, but they shared his Catholicism. In 1642, when the tenth Earl summoned his tenants to follow him, they blockaded him in Alnwick Castle. Where once the Percies had protected the **surnames**, or turned a blind eye to their **reiving**, now they did not. Elizabeth granted many of the lands they occupied to English landlords, who demanded high rents and fines (as did the Earl of Northumberland). The surnames were finally evicted in 1622; some who remained were bound to virtual serfdom by the new landlords.

The Percies' experience illustrates the changing position of the landed nobility. Most were not ruined by inflation: they adapted their estate management and remained the greatest landowners, but lost their regional influence and military-based powers of coercion. Noble rebellions were no longer a realistic proposition: the northern earls took up arms more in fear than hope in 1569. The nobles' military resources still seemed useful in an emergency: Elizabeth summoned her peers in 1588, as did Charles I in 1640 and 1642. But their skills lagged behind those of professional armies on the Continent and the routine watching of the coasts and the suppression of minor disorders were better left to the **militia**. Most lords lieutenant, who commanded the militia, were nobles, but their powers came from the Crown, as did those of their deputies, drawn from the leading gentry. Lords lieutenant acted as de facto governors of their counties; monarchs and ministers sought their advice, but did not feel obliged to follow it. Within his county a lord lieutenant was first among equals. Deputy lieutenants and justices of the peace helped him to get things done and would turn out in his following, even wear his livery, but in return they expected him to heed their advice and to secure favours from the Crown.

In the early seventeenth century the peers remained at the apex of the landed elite and commanded respect, as the King's greatest subjects and natural counsellors. They were not a separate caste and had fewer privileges than Continental nobilities; younger sons did not inherit noble status. The peerage remained relatively small, with a continual turnover of personnel as titles became extinct in the male line. New peers were recruited from the gentry, while peers' younger sons fell back into the gentry. Since the days of bastard feudalism the balance of power between nobles and gentry had shifted in favour of the gentry, who had grown collectively in numbers and wealth, but individually the nobles were still, on average, wealthier, more powerful and more prominent in the Crown's service. They no longer had the power to challenge the Crown, but the eighteenth century would see a new type of noble power, based on control over Parliament and the machinery of central government.

Manufactures

Manufacturing retained the same features as in the fifteenth century. It was small-scale and handicraft-based, processing (mostly) local raw materials for a market limited in size and purchasing power. Family businesses combined manufacture and retail and produced a limited range of goods. Although style and fashion influenced the luxury end of the market, most people could not afford to buy things they did not need. Furniture and household goods were utilitarian: people chose what would last, not what looked good. Bad harvests meant higher food prices and depressed the demand for clothing. Cloth workers were laid off, so did not have enough money to buy food. With no capital tied up in factories it was easy for employers to lay workers off in response to falling demand, and with so many seeking work they could pay low wages. Many people needed a variety of employments, in agriculture and manufacturing, in order to survive: 'making shift' became even more difficult.

Cloth manufacturing, England's main export industry, enjoyed mixed fortunes. Initially it was buoyant, with a boom in exports that ended with a spectacular crash in 1552. The boom created problems in the countryside, with arable converted to sheep pasture. The crash exposed the industry's inherent weakness. Technically it lagged behind the major European cloth-producing areas, the Low Countries and North Italy. England produced mainly heavy broadcloths, not suitable for warmer climates; their quality was unreliable and much had to be sent abroad for dyeing and finishing. From the 1560s England's major markets, the Low Countries and France, were disrupted by war and some rulers imposed punitive tariffs on English cloth. For some, however, these wars brought opportunities. Protestant cloth workers from the southern Low Countries, facing persecution from their Spanish Catholic rulers, fled to England. Some towns set out to attract them. In 1570 Norwich expelled inhabitants with no visible means of support, while welcoming 'French' and 'Dutch' (Walloon and Flemish) cloth workers. The corporation was explicit that it wanted only cloth workers: reluctantly it agreed that the '**strangers**' could have a few bakers and 'aqua vita' (gin or brandy) makers to supply their needs. It made the 'strangers' responsible for checking the quality of all cloth produced in the city, which had to be inspected and sealed at the French or Dutch Hall. (The same happened in the Dutch Hall in Colchester.) Several thousand strangers settled in Norwich, making up a quarter to a third of the population. Revitalised, the industry remained the key to the city's prosperity for a century and more.

The success of Norwich and Colchester was not matched elsewhere. The French Protestant refugees who poured into Canterbury and Sandwich did not possess cloth-working skills, although some who came to London were skilled metal workers. Skilled settlers could impose their own terms: those who came to Halstead, Essex, moved out when the local cloth-workers would not allow them control over quality. Over much of England the cloth industry, and manufacturing generally, struggled in the late sixteenth and early seventeenth centuries. A few industries grew, such as Tyneside coal, but this started from a low base and remained small. The spectacular success of Drake's buccaneering voyages should not mislead us into believing that overseas trade was buoyant; England's American colonies grew slowly. English trade and manufactures did not expand enough to employ those who could not make a living in agriculture, many of whom moved to towns, where they joined the ranks of unemployed or underemployed. (See Box 6.2, Urban Poverty.) While a fortunate or shrewd minority were getting richer, a very large cross-section of the population was getting poorer, which created hardship and resentment and posed a potential threat to public order.

 BOX 6.2: **Urban Poverty: Sheffield 1616**

The following relates to a census carried out by twenty-four substantial inhabitants. Sheffield was a manufacturing town, producing metal wares, especially knives. A few of the wealthier artisans had plots of land.

... it appeareth that there are in the town of Sheffield 2207 people; of which there are 725 which are not able to live without the charity of their neighbours. These are all begging poor. 100 householders, which relieve others. These (though the best sort) are but poor artificers; among them

is not one which can keep a [plough] team on his own land, and not above ten who have grounds of their own that will keep a cow. 160 householders not able to relieve others. These are such (though they beg not) as are not able to abide the storm of one fortnight's sickness but would be thereby driven to beggary. 1222 children and servants of the said householders; the greatest part of which are such as live of small wages, and are constrained to work sore to provide them necessaries.

S. and B. Webb,
English Poor Law History: Part I,
The Old Poor Law (1927), pp. 82–3.

§ Rebellion

Conventional views of the social order emphasised hierarchy and harmony. Each order of men had their allotted role in society. The poor were to obey their betters, work hard, stay put and keep quiet. The better-off were to use their authority and economic power responsibly. Magistrates were to enforce the law justly; landlords should respect the customary rights of their tenants and charge fair rents and fines; farmers should not inflate prices in times of dearth; and workmen should not exploit labour short-ages to demand unduly high wages. In the sixteenth century the balance of economic and political power shifted in favour of landlords and substantial farmers, but ideals of the 'just price', fair dealing and responsible landlordism remained strong and were endorsed at times by magistrates and the Crown. 'Commonwealth's men' – writers, courtiers, civil servants – condemned the covetousness of landowners. Parliament, encouraged by Henry VIII and his ministers, passed laws against 'depopulating' enclo-sure. Protector Somerset launched a vigorous investigation into enclosures in the South and Midlands. At first he appointed commissions consisting mainly of landowners, but later he included tenant farmers. He practised what he preached, abandoning some of his rights after complaints that they were oppressive, granting pardons to rioters and ensuring that they were legally watertight. His actions reinforced the belief of the vic-tims of enclosure that their complaints were just.

Somerset and the 'Commonwealth's men' expected the common people to wait pas-sively while they remedied their grievances. Better-off tenant farmers, however, were often active in local government and litigation and had proved capable of organising substantial demonstrations and even rebellions. They did not challenge royal authority, but responded indignantly to the King's failure to protect them. Their leaders tried to maintain the moral high ground by keeping order among their followers, but did not always succeed.

The Peasant Rebellions of 1549

The summer of 1549 saw popular protests across most of Lowland England. They had two main causes, religion and economics. Religious issues were dominant in Devon, Cornwall and parts of the Midlands. Here the main theme was opposition to changes in the Church and the destruction of 'superstitious' objects. In East Anglia the new religious order seems to have been welcomed, with demands that the clergy should preach more. The major complaints were economic: rapacious landowners confronted an assertive and litigious peasantry. Some built up great sheep-flocks; others built deer parks or extended rabbit warrens, playing havoc with local farming; many ratcheted up rents and entry fines; and a few, like the dukes of Norfolk, tried to reintroduce serfdom, to provide cheap labour for their demesnes: hence the demand that 'all bond men may be made free'.

The protesters were encouraged by Somerset's declarations against enclosure. On 1 July 1549 he summoned leading landowners to Windsor, which was widely seen as an endorsement of the commons' complaints and an opportunity to hasten the righting of wrongs; a new enclosure commission, with more sweeping powers, reinforced the impression that he was on the peasants' side. Disorder spread like wildfire. Unlike the Pilgrims of 1536 or the Western rebels, the peasants did not seek noble or gentry leadership, but gathered in at least eighteen camps, where they drew up petitions and manifestos. The camps were not necessarily warlike – some had a festive air – but they raised echoes of Cade's men on Blackheath and made the gentry and government nervous. How they turned out depended on the reaction of the authorities. The largest was on Mousehold Heath, just outside Norwich, said to contain 20,000 people – more than the city's population. The Mousehold rebels' leader was Robert Ket, a minor landowner initially targeted by the rebels. He and his followers saw Somerset as their (perhaps unexpected) ally against their local oppressors. Somerset's attitude towards religious protest was implacable: protesters were urged to go home and obey the government, or be punished as rebels. He was more sympathetic towards agrarian protesters. He used gentlemen trusted by the commons to assure them that they would be fairly treated. Almost everywhere this policy worked and the protests ended peacefully. Only at Norwich did the mutual distrust of landlords and peasants lead to bloodshed.

Like Cade, Ket and his leading followers sought to maintain discipline within the camp. They established a council, which dispensed justice under the 'Oak of Reformation', tried to ensure that provisions were paid for and issued warrants in the King's name. The articles drawn up by the council showed legal knowledge and reiterated items from Somerset's declarations. (See Box 6.3, Demands of Ket's Rebels, 1549.) But the leaders could not always control their followers. As in 1450 the rebels claimed that their enemies intended to starve them to death and destroy their villages. Wild, ragged young men came looking for trouble and plunder. Houses were looted, sheep, deer and rabbits killed and eaten. Landowners and their bailiffs were set in the stocks, a punishment reserved for the disorderly poor. After an uneasy stand-off, the mayor and corporation of Norwich closed the gates and the rebels broke in to the city. Gentlemen were imprisoned and their homes attacked. Somerset sent a herald to offer a pardon if they dispersed, but many cried out that it was a trick. A youth turned his back on the herald, dropped his trousers and 'did a filthy act', whereupon a gentleman shot him. An army of foreign mercenaries, with some Norfolk landowners, was sent to Norwich. The rebels refused to surrender and as many as 3,000 were slaughtered.

BOX 6.3: **Demands of Ket's Rebels, 1549**

These articles read as if they were put together during discussions at the camp at Mousehold. There follow two groups, dealing with landlords and the clergy.

3. We pray ... that no lord of no manor shall common upon the commons ...

11. We pray that all freeholders and copy holders may take the profits of all commons, and there to common, and the lords not common nor take profits of the same ...

14. We pray that copyhold lands that is unreasonably rented may go as it did in the first year of King Henry VII and that at the death of a tenant or of a sale the same lands [to be] charged with an easy fine as a capon or a reasonable ... sum of money for a remembrance. [There are similar demands concerning meadows and marshes.] ...

16. We pray that all bond men may be made free for God made all free with his precious blood shedding ...

23. [We pray that no man under] the degree of an esquire shall keep any coneys [rabbits] upon any of his own freehold or copyhold unless he pale [fence] them in so that it shall not be to the commons' nuisance ...

8. We pray that [any priest] ... that be not able to preach and set forth the word of God to his parishioners may be clearly put from his benefice, and the parishioners there to choose another or else the patron or lord of the town ...

15. We pray that a priest [shall not be a chaplain] nor no other officer to any man of honour or worship, but only to be resident upon the benefices whereby their parishioners may be instructed with the laws of God ...

20. We pray that every [parish clergyman] having a benefice of £10 or more by year shall either by themselves or by some other person teach poor men's children ... the catechism and the primer.

Fletcher and MacCulloch,
Tudor Rebellions, pp. 156–9.

The events at Norwich dominated memories of the 'Commonwealth' disorders of 1548–9, but they were atypical. The gathering at Mousehold became known as 'Ket's rebellion', which allegedly aimed to kill and plunder the gentry: the anniversary of its bloody suppression was celebrated locally for over a century. But to emphasise violence on either side misrepresents the much wider agrarian protests. Human casualties were few. In Seamer, East Yorkshire, four Protestant gentlemen were killed and their bodies left naked in the fields. A nobleman, Lord Sheffield, was murdered in Norwich, as was an Italian mercenary captain who was also stripped of his fine clothing. The Western rebels killed a gentleman who urged them to remain peaceable and some threatened to 'kill all the gentlemen'. But most violence involved shaming or mockery rather than bloodshed, because Somerset and the government were seen as sympathetic. Only at Norwich did Somerset's conciliatory approach fail.

Tudor Rebellions: a Brief Overview

The Pilgrimage of Grace (see Chapter 4) and the rebellions of 1549 seriously threatened the Tudor regime. In 1536, the King's forces were too small to risk battle with the Pilgrims; in 1549 they could not cope with both the Western rising and the disorders in the South and Midlands. However, the rebellions posed no threat to the King's person, but urged him to assert himself and do them justice. Henry VIII had no intention of complying with the Pilgrims' wishes, nor did Somerset consider meeting the grievances of the Western rebels, but their faith was not totally misplaced. Somerset tried sincerely to remedy agrarian grievances – and fell from power as a result. Unlike Cade in 1450 or the Cornish in 1497 the rebels of 1536 and 1549 did not march on London. The instability of the fifteenth century had owed much to dynastic uncertainty and a militarily strong nobility. From Henry VIII's death in 1547 until Mary Stuart's execution in 1587 there was again dynastic uncertainty, as each monarch faced a potential rival of the opposite religion. A toxic mix of dynastic rivalry and religious upheaval, compounded by high taxation and agrarian conflict, might seem a recipe for civil war, but it did not happen. The Wars of the Roses had been played out among a small number of noble families. By the 1540s the military power of the nobility was waning, even in the North; in 1536 the sixth Earl of Northumberland, distrusted by the King and on bad terms with his family, took the extraordinary step of making the King his heir.

After the 1490s the dynastic element in Tudor rebellions was limited. Henry VIII ruthlessly eliminated potential rivals: the only ones he could not reach were his sister Margaret's family in Scotland. The Tudors constantly stressed that their subjects' first allegiance was to the Crown, and most Catholics and godly Protestants accepted that in temporal matters they should obey the monarch. The leaders of Wyatt's rebellion in 1554 appealed for support against a foreign king, but kept quiet about their plans to replace Mary with Elizabeth (and promote Protestantism). The northern earls in 1569 claimed to take up arms for the Catholic religion: to advance Mary Stuart's claims would have been counter-productive. This loyalty to the Tudors was in striking contrast to the changes of dynasty in the previous century. Despite its problems, the mid-Tudor regime had achieved a fundamental stability which would have seemed improbable under Henry VII.

Riot

Ket's rebellion revealed economic and social divisions reminiscent of 1381. Whereas the 'traitors' identified by Cade's rebels were royal servants, now they were 'the gentlemen'. As in 1450 the protests were led by yeomen whose interests were later to diverge from those of poorer farmers, depriving them of their natural leaders. The 'better sort' now used their authority and offices to keep the 'poorer sort' under control, especially in Lowland England. Economic and social protests became riots rather than rebellions – smaller-scale and more limited in scope. They were still taken seriously by those in authority, who often addressed their grievances, either because they feared disorder or because they believed the rioters had a case. Rioters still couched their demands in legal terms and aped those in authority, but there was substantially less violence than in 1450 and 1549. Anti-gentry rhetoric was largely abandoned. In 1596, an Oxfordshire man called on the people to rise up against the local gentry; only three men joined him.

There were three main types of 'economic' riot.

Food Riots

Usually these attempted to prevent grain being transported, to London or abroad, in times of dearth. Women and children were prominent: sometimes they simply stood in front of a convoy of wagons. Town authorities generally agreed that it was wrong to send away grain that was needed locally. Royal **Books of Orders** blamed high food prices on hoarding and speculation and ordered magistrates to search for hoarded grain and have it brought to market and sold at reasonable prices. Town governors appealed to the Privy Council to prohibit grain exports, alleging that hungry people might riot. The council was unsympathetic, especially once the Crown started selling export licences. Grain riots were rarely violent; if rioters were prosecuted, they were rarely severely punished. In only one, or perhaps two, cases in the seventeenth century were grain rioters executed.

Enclosure Riots

Long-term threats to people's livelihoods led to more serious disorders, with violence directed mainly against fences and animals. Rioters claimed similar legitimation to food rioters, as royal statements repeatedly condemned enclosure. In the 'Midland Rising' of 1607, covering several counties, the rioters' leader, 'Captain Pouch', claimed that, if the King were informed of their grievances, he would redress them, on which the rioters would disperse. 'The cause of their rising was no undutiful mind to his majesty but only for reformation of those late enclosures which made them of the poorest sort ready to pine for want.' After the rising had been bloodily put down by the local landowners, the King wrote that, having punished the rioters, the government should now punish the enclosers. The Privy Council ordered lords lieutenant to send up to London those who had caused the most serious depopulation 'to receive the censure of the laws for their offences'.

Rioters generally showed respect for the law. Legally a riot was a gathering of three or more people to commit an illegal act, so rioters often divided into groups of two.

Often rioters marched in a military manner, like the militia; in festive mood, families took food and beer, danced around bonfires and drank the King's health. But sometimes the mood became uglier. Landowners pursuing property disputes hired men to pull down fences and occupy contested land. At Cranbrook, Kent, there was a long-running dispute between clothiers and ironworkers competing for timber. Along the River Lea, north-east of London, bargemen and badgers (carters) competed to transport malt and barley to London. The bargemen damaged bridges and weirs, the badgers impeded navigation by smashing locks. In each case both sides had supporters among the magistrates.

Forests and Fens

Still more acrimonious were disputes caused by the development of potentially profitable land largely untouched by agriculture. Charles I used his influence to ensure that the developers' opponents had no chance of legal redress and that rioters would be punished severely. Forest areas in the West Country were granted to courtiers, landowners or London merchants, who cleared the land for grazing, dividing it between large tenant farmers. Smallholders, artisans and those who had enjoyed free grazing lost out. In the Forest of Dean miners had long dug coal for free or in return for a nominal payment. Now the mining rights were granted to patentees, who charged far more. Such assaults on traditional common rights were obnoxious at every level. Long continuance had made them seem inviolable. Those who cleared and enclosed the forests were outsiders seeking a quick profit. When artisans and miners sought to defend their rights they were driven off by hired thugs and then they, not the thugs, were prosecuted.

A similar scenario was seen in the richest untapped resource, the fens of Eastern England. Draining them required capital and expertise and the common rights of the fenmen were legally well established. Epworth, Nottinghamshire, had a medieval charter which guaranteed their right to the fen in perpetuity. To break the fenmen's opposition the drainers and the King bent the law even more unscrupulously than in the forests. When fenmen refused to abandon their rights, the Attorney General brought an action claiming that they had no legal title to them which would be upheld by the courts. Alternatively, commissions of sewers, who supervised drainage ditches, would be packed with Crown appointees, who found that extensive new drainage works were needed and imposed a heavy rate to pay for them. When the commoners refused to pay, the contract would be awarded to drainers, who were awarded a large amount of land as payment. The drainage engineers, and their workmen, were generally Dutch or Flemish. Most spoke no English, so violence was the only language they would understand. Fenland communities were used to acting together and were fighting for their livelihood: for once the 'better sort' made common cause with their poorer neighbours. Crowds of over 100 were common and the largest was 600. There was more violence than usual, but some was symbolic, such as burning drainers in effigy, and the worst came from strong-arm men brought in by the drainers. At the most, two people may have been killed by rioters during the seventeenth century. Rioters were brought before Star Chamber or King's Bench in London, without a local jury. Conviction was a near certainty: those tried in Star Chamber were sentenced to a fine or imprisonment, but let off if they abandoned their common rights. If the drainers' henchmen were charged with assault or murder, they were acquitted by King's Bench.

Comparing fenland riots with Cade's or Ket's risings the level of violence and destruction was low: the first recourse of village communities was to the law. If they resorted to riot, it was often restrained and even festive. This restraint is striking, given how blatantly government and law were manipulated against them. The state, it would seem, had tamed 'the people'. They no longer protested about politics or religion, only about threats to their livelihood. And when their protests were defeated, they submitted meekly. Only in London were people more turbulent. In more than half the years between 1603 and 1640, apprentices pulled down brothels or theatres on Shrove Tuesday. The Spanish embassy was besieged in 1618 by a crowd of several thousand after rumours that the ambassador's coach had run over a child. In 1628 the Duke of Buckingham's astrologer was lynched in the street, because he had allegedly enabled the Duke to bewitch the King. The Duke's assassination later in the year was greeted by wild celebrations. The capacity of ordinary English people for autonomous violent action was dormant, not dead. It revived with a vengeance from 1640.

The Concern for Order

Competition for resources sometimes led to violence, but more often to litigation: between 1590 and 1640 more cases came to court than ever before. The courts were accessible to those of modest means (though not the poor) and often ruled in favour of tenants against landlords. Star Chamber fined landlords who unlawfully evicted tenants, insisted that entry fines should be 'reasonable' and upheld claims to common rights. Litigants asked JPs to bind over their opponents to keep the peace. The law was an accessible resource, offering an alternative to violent self-help, but did not always resolve disputes. Sometimes an adverse verdict left lasting resentment or litigants refused to accept arbitrators' decisions.

Those with most to lose were most concerned about disorder. Landowners feared the landless poor; town governors feared that the unemployed, who came looking for work which was not there, would resort to begging, prostitution or crime. Parish officials feared incomers putting pressure on stretched resources. Vagrants were a particular concern: without visible means of support or a master to answer for them, they were seen as rootless, lawless and possibly criminal. Some of them were, and a 'rogue literature' described marauding bands roaming the countryside. The better-off feared the multitude, the 'many-headed monster', which they saw as brutish and dangerous. They knew that the forces of law and order were puny. The only police forces were the town watch and the parish constable, both quite incapable of dealing with serious disorder. There was no standing army and many believed that the **militia** was as likely to join a riot as to suppress it.

To compensate for the weak machinery of law enforcement the courts and JPs imposed severe punishments. From the 1550s the 'loose, idle and disorderly' poor could be sent to the Bridewell, or **house of correction**, where they would be whipped and put to hard labour; from 1610 every county had to provide at least one. Other punishments were more public. Both men and women were stripped to the waist and whipped until their backs were bloody, sometimes in the market place on market day. Some offences were punished by branding: vagrants were marked on the thumb with a 'V', so carried their criminal record with them. Moral offences also carried corporal or shame punishments: mothers of bastard children were whipped, adulterous couples paraded round the town riding backwards on a horse, prostitutes exposed to public ridicule in the 'cage', scolds ducked or made to wear a bridle. The drunk and disorderly were put in the stocks. The pillory, for more serious offences, could be dangerous: the victim could be pelted with dirt or stones; some were injured or killed. The ultimate deterrent was death. A hanging was a spectacle, in which the victim was expected to exhort those present to learn from his example. These punishments were not designed to redeem offenders but to deter others.

The government and Parliament enlarged the powers of JPs and parish officials. Small groups or individual JPs could punish minor offences, or misdemeanours, without a trial or jury. A JP could summon alleged wrongdoers, interrogate them informally and hand down punishments. JPs began to hold **petty sessions** – smaller meetings to supplement the regular quarter sessions. This summary justice deprived the poor of much of the protection offered by the courts: there was little prospect of challenging a commitment to the house of correction or a binding to the peace. Sometimes people acquitted of felony by a jury could be bound to the peace and then sent to the house of correction if they could not find sureties.

Severe punishments showed the anxieties of the propertied and respectable. It could easily be argued that these were exaggerated. The hungry poor were desperate rather than dangerous. Ket's was the last peasant rebellion to wreak revenge on landowners. Later riots were more restrained and limited in focus. Complaints against individuals did not lead to attacks on landowners in general. There was an increase in prosecutions for property offences in the 1580s and 1590s, mainly thefts of food or easily-sold goods; officers searched houses for stolen goods and watched for **nightwalkers** – people out at night for no good reason. Many who brought prosecutions were far from wealthy, vulnerable to opportunist thefts of chickens or linen. Few prosecutions related to offences committed specifically against the gentry, such as deer stealing. Nevertheless, the poor were widely seen as posing a threat to the better sort.

Criminal behaviour had for centuries been seen as evidence of moral failure: idleness, drunkenness and gambling led to promiscuity and crime. It followed that it was necessary, for the public good, to suppress disorderly alehouses and rowdy popular celebrations. Puritan advocacy of moral reformation was a more rigorous assertion of widely held concerns. It required the punishment of drunkenness, gambling, profane swearing, fornication and the profanation of the Sabbath by work or play. Traditionally communities tolerated pre-marital sex, provided the couple intended to marry. Puritans insisted wives who were pregnant when they married should be whipped for fornication. As Church courts did not take these offences sufficiently seriously, Parliament made some moral offences the responsibility of secular magistrates. Alongside 'real' crimes, with obvious victims, such as homicide or theft, there was a growing range of offences with no victim other than the community, or God. To the divisions between rich and poor were added divisions between the godly and the less godly, with the former eager to impose their vision of moral control.

The Making and Enforcement of Social Policy

Sometimes social policy originated with kings or ministers. Thomas Cromwell promoted economic and social legislation and he persuaded Henry VIII to urge the Commons to pass it. Protector Somerset had a clear 'Commonwealth' agenda. Monarchs also issued proclamations commanding magistrates to address particular problems and enforce particular laws, and **books of orders** with more detailed instructions. Further tasks for local officials were added by Acts of Parliament: William Lambarde, a Kentish JP under Elizabeth, complained of being weighed down by 'stacks of statutes'. From 1598 petty constables were questioned on how they fulfilled their ever-growing responsibilities.

Tudor and Stuart legislation did not usually originate with the government. Monarchs saw Parliament primarily as a source of revenue and rarely saw any need to legislate, except when pushing through the breach with Rome or establishing Protestantism. The initiative came instead from Parliament, particularly the Commons. Parliament, like the monarch, received many petitions and MPs often received instructions from their towns or counties. Acts of Parliament were essential for levying money or creating new powers or offences. Some were 'public', affecting the whole realm, others 'private', relating to particular people and places. As Parliament met irregularly for short periods only a small proportion of the **bills** promoted by MPs and peers ever passed.

For the monarch, some bills were unwelcome. These bills might be lost in the Lords, or vetoed (a last resort), or the monarch might feel constrained to pass them in return for taxation. Much social legislation reflected the views of MPs, such as a bill Elizabeth vetoed in 1598, which criminalised gleaning, stealing from gardens and hedge-breaking (taking wood from hedges for fuel). (When the bill was reintroduced in 1601 she gave her assent.) Such bills reflected the experience of the localities and wider knowledge than the monarch or council possessed. The Poor Laws of 1598 and 1601 built not only on earlier legislation, and the experience of trying to enforce it, but also on local experiments and expedients. Local initiatives helped shape legislation and local magistrates and officials exercised discretion when enforcing it. Acts of Parliament stated that vagrants should be arrested, whipped and sent back to their home parishes, but usually this did not happen. Travellers were mostly young single people looking for work; magistrates did not usually allow them to settle but gave them a little money or food and let them go on their way. Those who begged, settled without permission or seemed criminally inclined were punished as the law directed.

Witchcraft, Society and the Law

Witchcraft prosecutions bring together several issues from this chapter: competition for resources, the creation of new criminal offences and the extent to which the legal position of the poor became weaker. Witchcraft cases reached a peak in the hungry 1580s and 1590s, when people were less able to help their neighbours. Parliament brought witchcraft within the criminal law by creating new felonies: **maleficium** (harming a person by occult means) in 1563 and making a pact with the devil in 1604. But although the legal position of the poor was weakened in minor offences, in felony cases the protection offered by common law procedures and the jury system remained largely intact. Although sleep deprivation and psychological pressure were sometimes used in interrogations, particularly in the 1640s, torture was not routinely used in England as it was in witch-hunts in Scotland and on the Continent.

Witchcraft was a crime with victims, who believed they had suffered injury to themselves, their families, their livestock and foodstuffs. The punishment for those found guilty was the same as for other felonies – hanging. But it raised peculiar problems of proof. The only unquestionable proof was if the accused confessed to a pact with the devil. Unlike other felonies involving injury it was usually impossible to *prove* that the accused had caused the injury, by occult means. The prosecution had to build up a case by linking suspicions and circumstantial evidence, which made it likely that the evidence would be discussed in court in some detail.

A typical scenario would begin with a poor person, often an old single woman or widow, asking a neighbour for milk or food. The neighbour refused and the old woman went away muttering. Later a child fell ill or the butter would not churn and the neighbour wondered if the woman had cursed them. If such incidents recurred, suspicion might build up that she was a witch. If she lived with an animal, particularly a cat,

Figure 6.3 Hopkins, the self-styled witch-finder general, was by far the leading English witch-hunter, who secured convictions by putting pressure on the accused to confess to having made a pact with the devil. These two old women are depicted with their familiars.

this could add to the suspicion. For centuries English people had believed that a witch derived her powers from a familiar, an animal who gave them to her in return for blood. (See Figure 6.3, Frontispiece to Matthew Hopkins, *The Discovery of Witches*.) If villagers accused her of witchcraft, she might deny it or hint that she had magical powers, hoping that this might make them more charitable. Witchcraft suspicions could give power to the powerless, but to play along with them was dangerous. Victims might take their suspicions to a magistrate, who would interrogate the woman and, if persuaded, appoint a group of married women to search her for the 'witch's mark', a growth from which her familiar could suck her blood. If they found a wart, particularly in her groin, it was likely that she would be brought to trial.

The great majority of those accused of witchcraft were women, who were seen as intellectually and morally inferior to men: more easily moved by their passions and more easily tempted. The law treated women as less responsible for their actions and assumed that they should be subject to their husbands or, if single, their employers. A woman's property was subsumed into that of her husband and the law accepted that he could use 'reasonable' force to discipline his wife. Given this mindset, one could see witch-beliefs as a device to keep women in order, but to see witch-beliefs as a cynical male ploy to maintain women in subjection strains credulity. For a start, it projects backwards the modern assumption that no rational person could believe in witchcraft. But many highly educated people did believe in it, and in a whole spirit world that existed alongside the physical world, and interacted with it. Those who could tap into the power of the spirit world could influence the physical world, for good or ill.

Belief in the occult was widespread and strong, but did not ascribe greater powers to women than to men; there were cunning men as well as cunning women. To find why more women than men were accused we need to consider the position of older single women, on the margins of village society, in difficult times. Older single men were more likely to find work. We also need to explain why the majority of witchcraft accusations were made by women. The neighbour who refused charity was probably the wife, because the husband was out at work. Household provisions and preparing food were the wife's responsibility, as were children: often accusations started after a child fell ill. Women discussed domestic matters with other women, washing clothes in the stream or attending a neighbour in childbed. Through discussions among women suspicions built up: often wives were the main witnesses, with husbands corroborating their evidence.

Accusations of witchcraft were the start of a legal process fraught with uncertainty. Prosecutors tried to prove their case by accumulating circumstantial evidence, but standards of proof became progressively more demanding. James I, while King of Scotland, believed that witches had tried to kill him by sinking his ship and wrote a book against witchcraft, but he insisted that no-one should be convicted without adequate proof. Witnesses might fail to persuade the jury and judges became increasingly sceptical. That said, some of those accused convicted themselves, confessing in open court to a pact with the devil. As time went on some confessions included accounts of witches' Sabbaths. These, unlike familiars, were not part of traditional English witch-beliefs, but were developed by Continental demonologists. They may have been suggested during interrogation, and were then publicised in printed accounts of trials. Shunned by her neighbours and with little to live for, being identified as a witch made a poor old woman the centre of attention. In general, however, apart from the peak in the 1580s and 1590s, the number of convictions was low and gradually fell. In five counties around London 474 people were indicted of witchcraft between 1560 and 1701, almost

60 per cent of them in Essex. Of these, 104 (22 per cent) were hanged. People still believed in witches and the spirit world but demanded evidence more compelling than hearsay and supposition. Many innocent people were executed for witchcraft but the procedures of the criminal law ensured that many others survived.

The Poor

As the population increased in the sixteenth century, traditional methods of relieving the poor seemed inadequate; some disappeared at the Reformation. The Church still played a prominent role, but that of Parliament became notably more important. Family and kin were still expected to take primary responsibility for those unable to support themselves. One traditional resource was closed (in theory) when begging was forbidden in 1598. It was generally agreed that the impotent poor, the old, the sick and children had to be relieved, but attitudes towards the able-bodied became more nuanced, with a growing awareness that many who tried to find work could not earn enough to support their families. The government considered various expedients, including temporary payments in difficult times or providing work materials and setting them on work. The latter was rarely successful. It made economic sense only if the goods made could be sold, but people could not afford to buy them. Often the work was provided in a house of correction, which made people see it as a punishment.

Poor Relief: the Parish Context

Legislation and contemporary comment give the impression that if people were poor it was their own fault, but this view was far from universal. In rural areas there were few vagrants and people often gave them hospitality. Power and discretion lay with the 'better sort', who applied statutes as they judged appropriate. A constitution drawn up for the village of Swallowfield in 1596 offers a rare insight into the thinking of parish governors. The 'chief inhabitants' formed a 'meeting' to deal with village affairs and control the behaviour of their poorer neighbours. (See Box 6.4, The Swallowfield Articles.)

The Poor Laws of 1598 and 1601

Legislation extended common practice, encouraging voluntary contributions and establishing poor boxes. Parish officials were ordered to identify the deserving poor and ensure that they were relieved. By 1570, some larger towns were making censuses of the poor, to distinguish locals from incomers; they began assessing the better-off and requiring them to give to the poor. Many, however, still saw idleness as the problem and Acts of 1572 and 1576 strengthened the penalties for vagrancy (death for a second

BOX 6.4: The Swallowfield Articles

On 4 December 1596 the self-styled 'chief inhabitants' of the scattered village of Swallowfield, most of which was in Berkshire, but some in Wiltshire, approved a constitution. 'For that the Justices are far off, this we have done to the end we may the better and more quietly live together in good love and amity to the praise of God and for the better serving of Her Majesty when we meet together about any … business of Her Majesty's whatsoever or any other matter … concerning the Church, the poor or the parish.' This group arrogated to itself to act in the name of the community, detecting and reporting unacceptable behaviour. Any member of the meeting who refused to accept the meeting's decisions 'shall not be accounted one of our company'. While stressing the need for solidarity among themselves, they showed little sense of accountability to the wider community; the meeting's proceedings were kept secret. The articles distinguished between the deserving and undeserving poor, but did not mention those who, despite their best efforts, could not earn enough to support their families.

15. … everyone promiseth … to end all strifes … between neighbour and neighbour be they poor or rich. And that such as be poor and will malapertly compare with their betters and set them at naught shall be warned to live and behave themselves as becometh them. If such amend not then no man to make any other account of them [but] of common disturbers of peace and quietness and the Justice of the shire to be made privy of such misdemeanours that ... such persons may be reformed by the severity of the law …

18. … all shall do their best to suppress pilferers, backbiters, hedge breakers and mischievous persons and all such as be proud dissentious and arrogant persons

19. … all shall do their best to help the honest poor, the blind, the sick, the lame and diseased persons

20. … all of us have an especial care to speak to the minister to stay the marriage of such as would marry before they have a convenient house to live in according to their calling. That thereby the parish shall not be troubled with such inmates. [Preventing marriage in this way was in fact illegal.]

8. … whosoever doth take into his house either wife or other woman with child and suffer her to be brought a bed in his house that thereby the parish shall be charged with a child or children there born. Everyone upon knowledge thereof shall give warning to the constable that thereby some present order may be taken and due presentment made by the churchwardens

13. … if any … unmarried woman shall be … gotten with child, then presently to find out the father and force him by the help of the Justice to put in good surety for the discharge of the parish, if she be a town born child, if not to banish her the parish

22. … and for the better observation to see that the Sabbath day with more reverence and less profaning thereof, then shall be appointed two of us to see that all the tipplers shall after the second ring of the bell … shut in their doors and so come to the church

S. Hindle, 'Hierarchy and Community in the Elizabethan Parish: the Swallowfield Articles of 1596', *Historical Journal*, 42 (1999), pp. 835–51 (articles on pp. 848–51).

offence) and ordered that the poor be set on work. Parishes were allowed to assess and collect compulsory poor rates. Begging was still often permitted and there were complaints of crowds of beggars around churches at service time.

After the Acts of 1572 and 1576 some parishes still raised money through church ales, but more relied on formal assessments; some payments were voluntary but many were compulsory. Most collectors were nominated by the minister and churchwardens but some were elected by the whole parish. There was no clear demarcation between the roles of the secular and ecclesiastical authorities. Confusions, uncertainties and the practical difficulty of enforcing payment were highlighted by the bad harvests of 1594–7, a time of high taxation and a surge in prosecutions for property crime. Parliament's response was the Poor Laws of 1598 and 1601. These banned almost all begging by individuals, even in their own parishes. The hybrid of voluntary and compulsory contributions was replaced by a compulsory system; to ensure that the money was properly managed, churchwardens and **overseers of the poor** (who replaced collectors and were appointed and supervised by the JPs) had to keep full records, and produce accounts. Overseers and churchwardens were to assess people in proportion to their means; those refusing to pay faced fines or imprisonment. They were to relieve the impotent and set the able-bodied on work. Those refusing to work would be sent to the house of correction or gaol.

After these Acts, payment of poor rates was compulsory, but churchwardens and overseers decided whether they needed to raise a rate, and if so how much. In some counties they began to raise rates only in the 1630s. In the North doles (money payments) were seen as a last resort and the impotent poor were allowed to beg. Drastic rural poverty was most associated with arable villages of the South and East, where the labouring poor were most dependent on wages; some JPs and parish officials condoned begging, especially if it kept the poor rate down. Alternatively, they tried to transfer the responsibility for the impotent poor to kin and neighbours. 'Making shift' remained the key to survival for many of the rural poor. In forest areas the Cottages Act was widely ignored and settlers were allowed to move in. As difficult times continued, attitudes towards outsiders, lodgers and cottagers hardened. Whether they were allowed to settle depended, not on JPs, but on parish officials or village elites. Although there was no formal process for gaining 'settlement' until 1662, it was becoming accepted that each parish was responsible for its own poor.

❦ Conclusion

The English Poor Laws were an enormous achievement, the only national welfare system in Europe. If many parishes were slow to comply with legislation, others did more than was demanded by law. The national government sometimes complained of their relative lack of compliance, but JPs were generally content to let parish officials do as they thought fit. They had the local knowledge and influence to secure compliance, and were more sensitive than outsiders to the mood of their neighbours. Officials would raise as much money, and deal as severely with the disorderly, as the 'better sort' thought necessary. The ability to grant or withhold relief gave parish officials power, which many used to punish those they judged morally undeserving. Doles were often paid out after church services, so those who did not attend lost their money. Puritan ministers, JPs and parish officials tried to suppress Sunday recreations (despite James I's issuing a book listing sports that he judged suitable for the Lord's Day), along with disorderly alehouses and church ales, prenuptial pregnancy and bastardy: by the 1630s both the fathers and mothers of bastards were whipped – but only the mothers were sent to the house of correction. In this tightening of moral discipline, discretion in the allocation of poor relief provided one instrument among many. It led to further polarisation between the 'better sort' and the unruly poor, between the self-styled godly and those they labelled ungodly. At its heart lay a clash between two cultures. On one hand there was a 'culture of sociability', a rough and ready approach to personal relationships, based on good fellowship, conviviality and traditional communal celebrations. In this culture a man who could enjoy his drink and use his fists would be respected by his neighbours as a 'stout fellow'. In the other, a 'culture of order' or culture of discipline, such attitudes were seen as rough and uncouth, an affront to Christian morality and to God. By the 1630s this clash of cultures divided many villages and parishes; those divisions were to become even more marked in the 1640s and 1650s.

 ## SUGGESTIONS FOR FURTHER READING

There are several good studies of England's economy and society in this period, including C.G.A. Clay, *Economic Expansion and Social Change: England 1500–1700* (2 vols., Cambridge, 1984), K. Wrightson, *Earthly Necessities: Economic Lives in Early Modern Britain, 1470–1750* (London, 2002), K. Wrightson, *English Society, 1580–1680* (revised edn, London, 2003), J.A. Sharpe, *Early Modern England: a Social History* (2nd edn, London, 2003), J. Thirsk (ed.), *The Agrarian History of England and Wales IV 1500–1640* (Cambridge, 1967) and D.M. Palliser, '"Tawney's Century": Brave New World or Malthusian Trap?', *Economic History Review*, 2nd series, 35 (1982). • On Chippenham and Willingham, see M. Spufford, *Contrasting Communities: English Villagers in the Sixteenth and Seventeenth Centuries* (Cambridge, 1974); on Wigston Magna see W.G. Hoskins, *The Midland Peasant* (London, 1957). • S. Hindle, *The State and Social Change in Early Modern England 1550–1640* (Basingstoke, 2002) brings together several of the major themes of this chapter. • Data on population, wages and prices can be found in E.A. Wrigley and R.S. Schofield, *Population History of England and Wales* (Cambridge, 1989) and E.H. Phelps Brown and S.V. Hopkins, 'Seven Centuries of Building Wages', in E.M. Carus-Wilson (ed.), *Essays in Economic*

History, II (London, 1962). • On the nobility, see L. Stone, *The Crisis of the Aristocracy 1558–1640* (Oxford, 1965), James, *Family, Lineage and Civil Society: Durham 1500–1640*, M. James, *Family, Politics and Culture: Studies in Early Modern England* (Cambridge, 1986) and (most original of all) J.H. Hexter, *Reappraisals in History* (London, 1961), chapters 2, 5 and 6. • A useful introduction to questions of order and disorder is A. Wall, *Power and Protest in England, 1525–1640* (London, 2000). The classic overview of rebellion is Fletcher and MacCulloch, *Tudor Rebellions*. The most important recent addition to the literature is A. Wood, *The 1549 Rebellions and the Making of Early Modern England* (Cambridge, 2007). • The best introduction to riot, apart from Wall, is J. Walter, *Crowds and Popular Politics in Early Modern England* (Manchester, 2006). J. Walter and K. Wrightson's classic article, 'Dearth and the Social Order in Early Modern England', *Past and Present*, 71 (1976), has not been superseded. • The best study of the fens is K. Lindley, *Fenland Riots and the English Revolution* (London, 1982). • On London, see K. Lindley, 'Riot Prevention and Control in Early Stuart London', *Transactions of the Royal Historical Society*, 5th series, 33 (1983). • The best study of witchcraft and the criminal law is J.A. Sharpe, *Instruments of Darkness: Witchcraft in England 1550–1750* (London, 1996). • On the question of proof see M. Gaskill, 'Witchcraft and Evidence in Early Modern England', *Past and Present*, 198 (2008). • On village governance see Hindle, *State and Social Change*, Hindle, 'Hierarchy and Community in the Elizabethan Parish' and K. Wrightson, 'The Politics of the Parish in Early Modern England', in P. Griffiths, A. Fox and S. Hindle (eds.), *The Experience of Authority in Early Modern England* (Basingstoke, 1996). • Among many good works on the Poor Laws are Hindle, *State and Social Change*, S. Hindle, *On the Parish? The Micro-Politics of Poor Relief in Rural England, c. 1550–1700* (Oxford, 2004), M.K. McIntosh, *Poor Relief in England 1350–1600* (Cambridge, 2012) and P. Slack, *Poverty and Policy in Tudor and Stuart England* (London, 1988).

SUMMARY

- Population increase transformed the balance of power between landlord and tenant and between employer and employee. Food production grew more slowly than population, pushing up prices. As people had to pay more for food they had less money to spend on manufactured goods, so industrial workers were laid off or put on short time. The result was a decline in manufacturing. With more people looking for work employers paid lower wages. The result was a growth of hardship and poverty and a growing anxiety, among the better-off, about the perceived threat from the unemployed and vagrant poor.

- Rising prices forced landowners, especially the nobility, to manage their estates more efficiently and commercially. Old loyalties of landlord to tenant and vice versa were eroded by the landlord's need to increase his income. This undermined the nobles' longstanding power over men, particularly in the North, and with it their military power (which was also being rendered obsolete by changes in warfare).

- Concerns about the threat from the hungry poor were exaggerated. There was no agrarian rebellion under Elizabeth to compare with those of 1549 and riots generally involved little violence and displayed considerable discipline. There was rather more violence under James I and Charles I, partly because the rioters' livelihoods were threatened by predatory entrepreneurs who were supported by the Crown.

- The fear of disorder underlay the great Poor Laws of 1598 and 1601, which were concerned with discipline (or punishment) as much as relief.

QUESTIONS FOR STUDENTS

1. How far did Tudor rebellions pose a threat to the Crown?

2. How far did the nature and power of the peerage change in this period?

3. How far were the values expressed by rioters shared by their rulers?

4. Why were far more women than men accused of witchcraft?

5. How novel was the approach to poverty in the Poor Laws of 1598 and 1601?

7

State and Society 1536–1625 2: Scotland and Ireland

TIMELINE

1541	Henry VIII becomes King (rather than lord) of Ireland
1556	Attempted plantation in King's and Queen's County
1569	Munster rebellion
1579–83	Desmond rebellion; start of Munster Plantation
1580	Massacre at Smerwick
1585	Spain declares war on England
1598	Act forbidding feuding (Scotland); Tyrone's victory at Yellow Ford; Munster Plantation destroyed
1601	Spanish army arrives in Ireland; Tyrone defeated at Kinsale
1603	Tyrone surrenders to Mountjoy
1607	Flight of the earls (Tyrone and Tyrconnell); way open for Ulster Plantation
1625	Death of James VI and I

Introduction

The experiences of Scotland and Ireland differed greatly from each other and from those of England and Wales. Scotland faced similar economic problems, but the major theme (apart from the Reformation) was the gradual growth of central government and the establishment of order on lines similar to earlier developments in England. In Ireland any economic problems were outweighed by the impact of escalating violence, as the English regime tried in vain to deter resistance, finally embarking on a full-scale conquest, which left the country exhausted. This conquest led to a massive confiscation of Irish Catholics' lands, which were used to establish English and Scottish **plantations**, which further complicated Ireland's ethnic and religious divisions.

Scotland's Economic Problems

In the fifteenth century Scottish peasants enjoyed relative prosperity. Their diet was likely to include some meat, chicken, fish and dairy produce, as well as oatmeal. As the population rose in the sixteenth century people could no longer afford beef: cattle had to be sold to pay rent. Faced with possible harvest failure peasants concentrated on oats, which had lower yields but were less risky than barley or wheat. But sometimes the oats failed too, leading to widespread famine. The effects of population growth were felt more slowly than in England. There were strong social expectations that leases would be renewed, that sons should succeed fathers and that kin should be given precedence over strangers. However, if landlords were inhibited from evicting tenants, they did increase rents. When famine came its impact was devastating: death from starvation was common, in the 1580s, 1590s and early 1620s. One response was large-scale emigration: in the early seventeenth century about 20 per cent of young men left Scotland for the Continent, where many served in the Thirty Years War.

The Scottish Poor Law

As in England, concern for the impotent poor was mingled with fear of vagrants and idle beggars. In 1574 an Act of Parliament made each parish responsible for its own poor. Only the 'crooked', 'impotent' and weak were allowed to beg. Others taken begging – minstrels, jugglers, fortune tellers, 'vagabond scholars of the universities' – should be punished. Each parish was to list its deserving resident poor and the inhabitants were to be assessed for a poor rate. The Act emphasised punishment rather than relief and the first resort of the impotent poor was to be begging. Opposition to a compulsory parish poor rate was strong: only two or three had been established by 1700. In 1592 Parliament admitted that legislation had proved ineffective by acknowledging **kirk sessions**' responsibility for the poor. The money was raised from legacies, fines and collections; much was given to beggars, who were very numerous, often had no identifiable parish and were allegedly prone to drunkenness and debauchery. The secular authorities rarely intervened, but in the famine year of 1623 the Privy Council ordered a temporary poor rate. It was strongly opposed in wealthy East Lothian, where the local elite complained that it 'smells of a taxation'. A county meeting in Midlothian declared that the poor were too weak from illness and hunger to travel and there were no officials to relieve or punish them, so each landowner should relieve the poor on his estate. Some poor relief systems, also funded by legacies, voluntary contributions and fines, were established in towns, some of which had almshouses or houses of correction. Kirk sessions were concerned that relief should be restricted to the morally deserving who went to church. Although the ethos of poor relief was similar in England and Scotland, the introduction of compulsory poor rates in England made possible a much more effective system.

The Problem of Minorities

Royal minorities always tended to weaken the monarchy; magnates competed to act as regent and used grants of royal lands to reward their clients. When a young king attained his majority he needed to claw back what had been taken from him and seize lands forfeited for rebellion or treason. The sixteenth-century House of Stewart suffered consecutive long minorities. James V was a year old when his father was killed at Flodden in 1513. He himself died, apparently of shock, at his army's defeat at Solway Moss in 1542; his infant daughter, Mary, became the first Queen to rule Scotland in her own right. James VI was a year old when his mother was forced to abdicate in 1567. To complicate matters further, in Mary and James's reigns Scotland was deeply divided in religion. Small wonder that the authority and resources of the Crown suffered badly.

When James V reached his majority his income was half that of his father. As Parliament would grant taxation only for war he looked elsewhere. The Pope authorised a tax of £10,000 (Scots) per year, eventually ratified by Parliament, to fund a 'college of justice'. James also sought a wife with a rich dowry. Madeleine, daughter of Francis I, died less than two months after arriving in Scotland, so he married another Frenchwoman, Mary of Guise, who chose him in preference to Henry VIII. Both brought a substantial dowry, but tied him closely to France. His final plan was to take a tough line against disorder, punishing malefactors with forfeitures and fines and paying off scores against those who had wronged him during his minority, particularly the Earl of Angus and his family: Angus's sister, Lady Glamis, was burned for allegedly conspiring against the

King. He issued an Act of revocation in 1537, endorsed by Parliament three years later (which suggests serious reservations about it). The Act was designed to force its victims to **compound** – to offer a lesser (but still considerable) payment over a period of years, leaving them at the King's mercy if they defaulted. Such methods, reminiscent of Henry VII's, kept the nobility cowed (and resentful) but did not provide any means of tapping the kingdom's wealth through taxation.

When James V died the formidable Mary of Guise acted as regent. She arranged her daughter's marriage to the Dauphin, which led to her brief period as Queen of France. Mary Stewart's gender made it difficult for her to rule effectively once she came of age: many Scots, like John Knox, believed that the 'monstrous regiment' (rule) of men by women was unnatural. Mary's political errors added to her problems. As with Elizabeth, her subjects expected her to marry, but were likely to disapprove of any choice she made; her marriages to first Lord Darnley and then the Earl of Bothwell, and her complicity in Darnley's murder, lost her the support of both subjects and foreign allies. By fleeing to England in 1568 she abandoned her many supporters and triggered a period of civil war.

The Resources of the Scottish Crown

As James VI approached his majority he faced three major problems. The first, and oldest, was the threat from the great nobility, who retained a sense that loyalty to the Crown was conditional. Second, the emergence of the Kirk brought a theory of monarchy, similar to that developed during the French wars of religion, but given a Scottish twist by Knox and James's tutor, George Buchanan. French Protestant writers sought to justify actively resisting their lawful (Catholic) King. Reluctant to allow a right of resistance to the people in general, they claimed that it lay with the 'inferior magistrates', who had a duty to oppose a tyrant. These magistrates were generally nobles, the rulers of regions and provinces. Buchanan justified the deposition of Mary Queen of Scots with accounts of the deposition of mythical medieval kings. The growth of hard-line Presbyterianism gave the Kirk a central role in bringing errant kings to account.

The third problem facing the monarchy was dwindling resources. In the fifteenth century kings increasingly relied financially on their landed estates. In 1575, when James VI was eight, Parliament passed an Act revoking all grants of Crown lands since the death of James IV. It proved unenforceable and it became clear that the Crown could not subsist on its landed income: thanks to **feuing**, rents could not be increased and crown tenants could not be evicted. The young King was therefore faced by a powerful nobility, an ideological challenge to kingly power, and revenues falling in real terms. He responded to these challenges with determination and ingenuity.

James responded to Buchanan's ideological challenge in *The Trew Law of Free Monarchies* and *Basilikon Doron*. The books were published in 1598–9, in the later stages of his battle with the Melvillians, but the ideas were developed earlier. They centred on the 'divine right of kings'. Royal power was created by God and kings were answerable only to God. A king should consult his counsellors and consider his subjects' petitions, but he should not avoid the responsibility of making decisions. Active resistance by subjects could never be justified: in resisting the king they resisted God. A king was obliged to observe the law – he became a tyrant if he did not – but he could not be forced to do so, nor did he have to take the advice of lawyers if it seemed to him contrary to common sense and natural justice. He admitted that a king might abuse his power, but if he did only God could punish him; subjects' only recourse was to prayers and tears. James's was a Christian view of kingship, with echoes of the traditional obligation to do justice and to protect the weak. Neither clergymen nor nobles could tell the king what to do: the only limits on his conduct were imposed by his own reason and conscience.

This view of monarchy diverged from traditional noble attitudes and the Kirk's claims to be the keeper of the king's conscience. It relied on the king's high opinion of his own integrity, which others sometimes found difficult to share. Often his conduct seemed duplicitous, indeed treacherous, but his vision of monarchy found wide acceptance. It was based on peace abroad and order at home, with a legal system which functioned according to known rules. This required a central government with effective powers of coercion, but James took care to win the support of the key sections of society. If he committed occasional acts of injustice, he treated most of his people fairly; he was careful to maintain cordial relations with the nobility, and respect their interests. This personal contact became more difficult when he succeeded to the English Crown in 1603, but access to the greater resources of the English Crown increased the patronage available for his Scottish friends.

James VI and Parliament

James began to strengthen the Crown in the 1580s, exploiting ambiguities and uncertainties about the powers of Parliament and related assemblies. He could call a 'convention of estates' (a hand-picked assembly to approve taxes) instead of a full Parliament. This enabled him to raise taxes in peacetime from 1581, including the first taxes on land – traditionally the only direct taxes were on exports. The new taxes were unpopular with the landed elite and difficult to collect, so James extended the range to include taxes on imports, rents, annuities and interest payments on loans. Parliament also passed a series of Acts to curb the misuse of noble power, culminating in the prohibition of feuding in 1598.

To push through his taxes and legislation, James strengthened his control over Parliament. Traditionally it consisted of three estates – nobles, clergy and representatives of the royal burghs. **Lairds** could attend as well and sometimes turned out in force, but often few appeared. James sought to ensure a substantial attendance of lairds to counterbalance the nobility; in 1597 Parliament passed an act providing for the election of two representatives from every shire. As the clerical estate had dwindled almost to nothing, James reintroduced bishops into Parliament, starting with three in 1600. Bishops were among the reliable supporters he installed in the **Lords of the Articles**, which decided which petitions should go before Parliament and so provide possible subjects for legislation. The Articles included representatives of the shires and burghs but from 1621 these were nominated by the nobles and bishops, giving the King effective control: Parliament would not be able to pass legislation unacceptable to the King, but could still reject bills placed before it. James's attempts to manipulate Parliament caused resentment, but often succeeded. After 1603 he made less use of Parliament and, when he did, he sometimes provoked serious opposition, but the legislative achievement of the 1580s and 1590s was considerable. James now had an income sufficient to fund the government and a small royal guard, even if he could not afford a permanent army. And he had the resources he needed to manage the nobility.

Taming the Scottish Nobility

In the sixteenth century the feud was a major obstacle to Scotland's governance and prosperity; nobles used kinship, clientage and **bonds of manrent** to mobilise armed men. Although some claimed feuding was a sign of manliness, it often involved treachery and killing women and children. It was especially prevalent in the Highlands and the Borders. Some Wardens of the West March, responsible for keeping the peace, burned and plundered the houses of rival families. In 1592, Andrew Forrester, several times provost of Stirling, in the Lowlands, was accused of gathering a thousand retainers to prevent the Privy Council from investigating a property dispute. Merchants and traders complained that feuding interrupted commerce, Lowland landowners that it hindered cattle droving, encouraged banditry and made it even more difficult for peasants to scratch a living. The Kirk condemned lawlessness and violence on principle. Feuding was banned by the Act of 1598, after which bonds of manrent withered away. Edinburgh lawyers, eager to increase their incomes, extended their criticisms from the feud to the **bloodfeud**, which offered quicker and more effective justice than the King's courts. The lawyers, however, argued that the bloodfeud depended on magnates' whims and favouritism and that those accused of violence should be summoned to the Edinburgh courts, where consistent rules were applied and justice was seen to be done.

BOX 7.1: James VI's Advice to His Son

James wrote *Basilikon Doron* (published 1599) as advice to his elder son Henry (1594–1612). Here he sets out his views on the nobility, the law and the Highlands.

The Nobility

… virtue followeth oftest noble blood. The worthiness of their antecessors craveth a reverent regard to be had unto them; honour them therefore that are obedient to the law among them as peers and fathers of your land. The frequentlier that your court can be garnished with them, think it the more your honour, acquainting and employing them in all your greatest affairs, sen [since] it is they must be your arms and executers of your laws … [However, heritable sheriffdoms and regalities in the hands of great men] wracketh the whole country, for which I know no present remedy but by taking the sharper account of them in their offices …

The Law

Press to draw all your laws and processes to be as short and plain as you can; assure yourself the longsomeness both of rights and processes breedeth their unsure looseness and obscurity, the shortest being ever both the surest and plainest form and the longsomeness serveth only for the enriching of the advocates and clerks with the spoil of the whole country …

The Highlands

As for the Highlands I shortly comprehend them all in two sorts of people: the one that dwelleth in our mainland that are barbarous for the most part and yet mixed with some show of civility; the other that dwelleth in the Isles and are all utterly barbarous, without any sort or show of civility. For the first sort put straitly to execution the laws made already by me against their overlords and the chiefs of their clans and it will be no difficulty to dantone [tame] them. As for the other sort, think no other of them all than as of wolves and wild boars. And therefore follow forth the course that I have begun of planting colonies among them of answerable in-lands subjects that within short time may root them out and plant civility in their rooms.

James VI, *Basilikon Doron* (1599: facsimile edn, Menston, 1969), pp. 56–8, 108–9, 42–3. Reprinted (from a slightly later edition) in James VI and I, *Political Writings*, ed. J.P. Sommerville (Cambridge, 1994), pp. 29, 45, 24. The later version replaces the last two sentences as follows: 'As for the other sort, follow forth the course that I have intended in planting colonies among them of answerable in-lands subjects, that within short time may reform and civilise the best inclined among them, rooting out or transporting the barbarous and stubborn sort and planting civility in their rooms.'

James VI's attitude towards the nobility was ambivalent. (See Box 7.1, James VI's Advice to His Son.) He knew from his own minority that noble power could threaten the King and that noble lawlessness could get out of hand. He believed that the King should provide justice through his courts, but also that the nobles were the 'arms and executers' of the law. He prevented lawyers from gaining control of civil disputes and cases of murder on both sides, hitherto dealt with by bloodfeud: only with murder on one side did the lawyers get their way. James believed that the way to prevent nobles from behaving irresponsibly was to manage them sensibly, not strip them of their remaining power. He was a shrewd judge of character, adept at dealing with people face to face. He treated the nobles courteously, encouraged them to come to court and rewarded them with pensions and offices.

Another reason for James's reluctance to abolish the bloodfeud was his suspicion, even dislike, of lawyers. He resented being told that only those with a thorough training and long experience could fully understand the law and believed that the lawyers were concerned more for their own profits than for the public good. (See Box 7.1, James VI's Advice to His Son.) Nevertheless, the lawyers gradually took control of admission to their profession. In 1605 stringent criteria were laid down for the appointment of judges: candidates had to analyse a legal text (in Latin) and hear a case, discuss the legal issues that it raised, and give a judgment. This marked the culmination of the lawyers' emergence as a professional caste, linked by kinship and a common training. The system of central courts became more elaborate and judges brought the King's justice into the provinces.

James VI's reign saw a transformation of the Scottish nobility similar to that of the English nobility under the Tudors. Their traditional military role became irrelevant as peace with England left Scotland without natural enemies, but their influence and **heritable jurisdictions** could facilitate law enforcement and tax collection. By 1603 Scotland's government was becoming more formal and regular and there was a growing demand for offices. As the administration grew, the King and his council held it together. He was the source of patronage, so those seeking offices or rewards mobilised their friends at court. The Privy Council, like its English counterpart, contained both great nobles and officers of state. James believed it was necessary to involve the nobles, but needed the administrators' expertise. A few nobles held high offices, but most civil servants were lairds or lawyers. Other nobles became courtiers, which gave them access to the King and to the patronage they needed to maintain their clients: government was held together partly by the operation of its formal structures, partly by the informal mechanisms of lordship and clientage.

After 1603 James's approach to governing Scotland became more authoritarian and less effective, particularly when he tried to make Scotland more like England. Effective government in Scotland required a resident king, to listen, argue and persuade. His reign after 1603 was not a disaster: he had enough experience, and innate caution, to know when he had reached the limits of the possible. Much of what he had set in motion continued, especially the extension of the court system and the taming of the Borders. Even so, his rule was less effective after 1603 than before.

Lawless Zones: the Borders

Medieval Scottish kings were more concerned about the Borders than about the Highlands. They could not control the Highlands so did not try. The Borders mattered more because of the proximity of England. From the early sixteenth century they developed two strategies for curbing disorders. First, lords were made financially responsible for the misdeeds of their tenants and followers by means of the **general band**. Second, the Crown demanded hostages from suspect families, as a pledge that they would keep the peace and seize criminals. However, as long as miscreants could escape into England disorder continued. The ending of hostilities with England made cross-border co-operation possible, but only after 1603 did it become effective, with punitive raids and the execution without trial of 'broken men' with no lord to answer for them. The Border lords came to accept responsibility for keeping the peace and their tenants mostly gave up cattle raiding. By 1625 the problem of the Borders had largely been solved.

Lawless Zones: the Highlands

James VI regarded the Highlanders, and especially the chiefs, as 'barbarous', and encouraged Parliament to pass laws designed to 'civilise' them. (See Box 7.1, James VI's Advice to His Son.) Chiefs were made responsible for their followers (and even those passing through their lands); this was later formalised through an equivalent of the **general band**, and the giving of hostages. Lists were to be made of members of delinquent clans, so that their lord could be made to find cautions for them; this led some lords to compel their followers to give cautions to keep the peace. This was more difficult than in the Borders: much of the Highlands lacked any machinery of local government or justice. Some areas were plagued by **caterans**, who extorted protection money, stole cattle and hired themselves out as enforcers. Plantations would be hard to establish in such lawless conditions, so rougher methods were needed. An Act of 1581 allowed victims of theft to kill the thief or any member of his extended family and the King issued commissions empowering the victims of crime to seek revenge with fire and sword. Highland legal cases were transferred to Lowland courts or the Privy Council, which claimed jurisdiction over cases of riot. However, Parliament would not grant the money for a permanent force in the Highlands, so the best that James could manage was the occasional punitive expedition. From 1609 he increasingly handed over responsibility for these raids to 'loyal' chiefs, notably the Campbell Earl of Argyll, who was given a commission to root out the MacGregors 'without mercy'.

James's policy towards the Highlands went beyond his policy in the Borders in two ways. First, he hoped to bring the more amenable chiefs to heel, but for the irredeemable the only remedy was to challenge their title to their lands. An Act of 1597 required chiefs to produce written proof of title and pay all moneys due to the Crown. Where these dues had fallen into disuse, they were renegotiated. James claimed that, since the forfeiture of the Lordship of the Isles in 1493, much land held by clans rightfully belonged to the Crown, which had leased the lands out; the rents had been paid sporadically at best and the clans came to see them as their own property. Now James demanded rent and some clans were expelled from their lands: the MacDonalds lost Kintyre and Islay. The King's annual income from Islay rose from occasional small payments in the 1590s to £6,000 (Scots) in 1615. His second distinctive policy was to expose the Highlands to the civilising influence of the Lowlands. The Statutes of Iona of 1609 aimed to reduce the scale of chiefs' hospitality and the number of unproductive men in their households; the surplus grain formerly consumed in feasts was to be sold. Members of the **fine** were given privileges – they alone could bear arms – but also responsibilities: some were to act as sureties for their chief. Chiefs were to give an annual account of their conduct to the Privy Council; to succeed them their sons had to learn English. Plantations of Lowlanders were less successful: settlers on Lewis were twice driven out by hostile islanders. James's limited military resources meant that he could never subjugate the Highlands. He did, however, establish successful Scottish plantations in Ireland, where the English government had far greater military force at its disposal.

Ireland: After the Kildare Rebellion

The Kildare rebellion ended English attempts to rule Ireland through a single Anglo-Irish family. The Fitzgeralds' landed wealth, clientele and agreements with Gaelic lords gave them greater influence than the small, underfunded English administration in Dublin. The London government had worked through Kildare as the cheapest way of managing Ireland. In the years after 1536 the English government had two key objectives in Ireland. The first was to defend the Pale against raids by Gaelic lords. Beyond the Pale lay the wider lordship of Ireland, over which the Dublin government exercised a precarious influence, thanks to powerful but independently minded Anglo-Irish families. The lordship stretched to the south and west of the Pale and comprised much of Leinster and Munster. It contained many Gaelic lords, some only a few miles from Dublin. The defence of the Pale, therefore, shaded into a second objective, minimising the threat posed to English Ireland by the Gaelic lords: the Pale could never be secure so long as that threat continued.

The English government could pursue two possible strategies towards the Gaelic lords, based on force or negotiation. First, it could either increase the military resources of the Dublin government, or build up other Anglo-Irish lords, such as the Butler earls of Ormond, or both; but the London government had no intention of pouring money into Ireland or creating another Kildare. An alternative was to reach bilateral agreements with Gaelic lords through **surrender and regrant**. The lords promised to keep the peace, embrace English ways of dress and agriculture, and speak English; they would also serve in local government and (in some cases) the House of Lords. In return they received a secure title to their lands under English law, for which they paid a small annual rent to the Crown. To facilitate this, the Irish Parliament passed an Act in 1541 recognising Henry VIII as King, rather than lord, of Ireland. The Act stressed that he wanted no distinctions between his subjects: 'diversity … in tongue, language, order and habit' should cease: in other words, the Irish should become like the English. Many Gaelic lords took advantage of surrender and regrant: those granted peerages by the King attended the Lords, where Ormond explained to them, in Irish, what was going on.

Surrender and regrant might seem a realistic alternative to a strategy based on force. Waging war in Ireland was expensive and difficult. Soldiers had to find their way through forests and bogs; roads were few and rudimentary, difficult for men and horses and well-nigh impossible for carts and artillery. English soldiers were trained for sieges and pitched battles, but Irish warfare was based on ambushes and skirmishes; if defeated they withdrew and regrouped. But the biggest problem of English commanders was that their armies were far too small to accomplish the military tasks set for them. Sir William Skeffington and Lord Grey tried to terrorise the enemy into submission by a policy of atrocity, killing prisoners taken in battle. At Maynooth Skeffington, after trying members of the garrison by **court martial**, ordered the killing of some whose surrender he had earlier accepted. (See Box 7.3, Massacres.) Such tactics proved counter-productive; the Irish responded with equal brutality. Gaelic lords sometimes beheaded or maimed defeated enemies; hosts sometimes murdered their guests. But the level of English violence and treachery appalled the Irish. Those killed in struggles to control a clan were usually protagonists rather than followers. Prisoners were generally ransomed rather than killed. The Irish regarded it as dishonourable to kill 'churls' (peasants) who anyway were economically valuable. Few Irishmen could match the cruelty or perfidy of Henry VIII, who executed 'Silken Thomas' and two of his uncles after pardoning them.

Plantation and the Alternatives 1556–1579

This lack of mutual trust undermined surrender and regrant. Those who took advantage of it gained a legal title to their lands, but what if the Crown challenged that title? Those who entered into agreements did not necessarily abide by them; some were overthrown by rivals, and sons often did not feel bound by their father's undertakings. Promises to keep the peace and embrace English ways were easily forgotten. Many English soldiers and administrators became convinced that paper agreements would never bring stability. They saw Ireland as potentially prosperous, but held back by predatory and parasitic lords and priests, who gave the peasants no incentive to work hard. The mistaken belief that Irish peasants longed to be freed from the tyranny of their lords continued throughout the sixteenth and seventeenth centuries. Edmund Spenser was one of many who argued that Gaelic Ireland would have to be totally destroyed in order to build a new, civilised and anglicised Ireland; English **plantations**, like those soon to be established in North America, could provide a model for the indigenous population to follow. (See Box 7.2, Edmund Spenser on the Irish.)

BOX 7.2: Edmund Spenser on the Irish

Spenser was both a major poet (note his scornful dismissal of Irish poetry) and a serious analyst of Irish society and the problems of establishing English rule over Ireland.

All the rebellions which ... from time to time happen in Ireland are not begun by the common people but by the lords and captains of countries upon pride or wilful obstinacy against the government, which whensoever they will enter into they draw with them all their people and followers, who think themselves bound to go with them because they have booked them [listed them as members of the clan] and undertaken for them ... you have few such bad occasions here in England by reason that the noblemen ... have no command at all over the commonalty, though dwelling under them, because every man standeth upon himself, and buildeth his fortunes upon his own faith and firm assurance ... (p. 147)

... there is one general inconvenience that reigneth almost throughout all Ireland, and that is of the lords of lands and freeholders, who do not there use to set out their lands to farm or for term of years to their tenants, but only from year to year, and some during pleasure; neither indeed will the Irish tenant or husband otherwise take his land than for so long as he list himself. The reason hereof in the tenant is for that the landlords there use most shamefully to rack their tenants, laying on him **coign** and livery at pleasure, ... so that the poor husbandman ... dare not bind himself for a longer time ... (p. 81)

There is amongst the Irish a certain kind of people called the bards, which are to them instead of poets, whose profession is to set forth the praises and dispraises of men in their poems or rhymes and which are had in so high regard and estimation amongst them that none dare displease them, for fear ... to be made infamous in the mouths of men ... they seldom use to choose unto themselves the doing[s] of good men for the ornaments of their poems, but whomsoever they find to be most licentious of life, ... most dangerous and desperate in all parts of disobedience and rebellious disposition, ... him they praise to the people and to young men make an example to follow ... (pp. 72, 73)

E. Spenser, *A View of the Present State of Ireland*, ed. W.L. Renwick (Oxford, 1970).

The main advocates of plantation were '**servitors**' – civil servants, lawyers and soldiers. The Irish claimed that they lacked the lineage claimed by the Irish lords. In fact some came from distinguished families, often younger sons looking to make their fortunes. They included men of learning, such as Sir Henry Sidney, Sir Walter Raleigh and Edmund Spenser, who used as a model Imperial Rome, which settled soldier-farmers to secure its frontiers. Spenser suggested establishing garrisons to 'drive' the 'enemy' and devastate the country, preferably in winter, to starve Ulster into submission. Those who submitted should be transplanted to the lands of the O'Byrnes and O'Tooles, whose followers would be sent to Ulster. Disbanded soldiers should be settled to keep order among them. Wide paths should be cut through the woods and bridges built over rivers in place of fords. Roads should be fenced on both sides, to make travel safer, and **provost marshals** should punish idle vagrants under martial law. Above all, towns should be established 'for nothing doth sooner cause civility in any country than many market towns, by reason that people repairing often thither for their needs will daily see and learn civil manners'.

Military conquest was the essential precondition for the changes advocated by Spenser. Only force could break the power of the Irish lords. Although Spenser stressed that only common law could create a truly ordered society, he argued that trial by jury could never work because Irish jurors would always favour their lords. Initially, therefore, army officers should punish disorder using **martial law**; common law should be used to invalidate Irish land titles. Despite surrender and regrant, many Irish landowners could not produce documentary proof of ownership, so their title could be challenged in the courts, making significant amounts of land forfeit to the King, available for servitors by grant or purchase. However, a viable plantation would require larger-scale forfeitures, which could come only after a rebellion, which servitors were eager to provoke.

The servitors pressed on further and faster than the London government wished to go. It feared that their programme would cost too much and that a rebellion would invite foreign intervention: Spain's relations with England worsened in the 1570s, leading to war in 1585. Conscious of the financial argument, military commanders tried to finance their raids and expeditions by non-parliamentary means, billeting troops on private houses and demanding food for the army either below market rates or with no payment at all. Spenser was scathing about the soldiers' conduct, 'placing themselves at their pleasures, exacting meat and drink far more than competent and commonly money for them, their boys, women and followers'. One told the mayor and townspeople of Cork, 'You are but beggars, rascals and traitors, and I am a soldier and a gentleman.' Spenser acknowledged that the soldiers' conduct 'breedeth great hatred to our nation, and not without cause'.

For two decades from 1546 the English sought to subjugate the Irish lords. The number of regular troops grew from 900 to 2,200, supported by auxiliaries from the Pale, followers of Ormond and Desmond and compliant Gaelic lords. They were better armed than Gaelic forces. Military expeditions, although depicted as counter-insurgency measures, often involved pre-emptive strikes and scorched-earth tactics. In 1557 (in Mary's reign) a commander was authorised to 'plague, punish and prosecute with sword and fire … all Irishmen and their countries' who gave shelter or assistance to dispossessed rebel lords. It was left to him and his officers to decide what constituted 'shelter and assistance'. Military commanders issued commissions of martial law, some empowering junior officers to kill 'suspected enemies', for which the officer would receive one third of the deceased's possessions. This was an invitation to wage war on the local population and many exceeded the powers in their commissions. They aimed to destroy the peasants' subsistence so that they would no longer obey their lords or lodge their soldiers. In 1558 the Church of Ireland Archbishop of Armagh wrote that it was possible to ride for thirty miles in South Ulster and see no sign of life. In 1566 Armagh was burned, except for the houses of the Archbishop and Dean. (See Figure 7.1, Armagh City, Still in Ruins, in 1602, by Richard Bartlett.) Some commanders killed almost for sport: Sidney remarked that he had killed so many 'varlets' that he had lost count.

Figure 7.1 Armagh is shown almost totally in ruins, apart from the cathedral, which suggests that little has changed since its destruction in 1566.

The military were also empowered to punish 'idle vagrants', which was interpreted to include peasants travelling to and from summer pastures. This responsibility fell to seneschals, each responsible for a district and a band of soldiers, for whom they hoped to provide farms. One particularly turbulent region was Laois and Offaly, renamed King's and Queen's Counties, where the first plantation was attempted in 1556. Lands were to be let only to English tenants, who were to keep weapons to defend themselves; they were not to sublet to Irishmen. The local clans, who traditionally hated each other, joined in fierce resistance. Government forces responded with burning and killing. The chiefs at first killed only men, but soon responded to the killing of their own women and children. At Shillelagh in 1568 the men abandoned the town, assuming that the women and children would not be harmed; they were all killed.

The clans' resistance prevented the establishment of a viable plantation. In 1566 Elizabeth ordered the lord deputy to 'cleanse' the area of 'disordered persons', but her government did not provide sufficient money. Meanwhile the English extended their destructive raids elsewhere, particularly into Ulster, where they harassed the greatest of the Ulster chiefs, Conn Bacach O'Neill, first Earl of Tyrone, hitherto loyal to the Crown. O'Neill's men wrought havoc in the English Marches and even the Pale; other Irish lords followed his example. The government's strategy of conquest fostered a sense of Irish national identity, over-riding clan and provincial loyalties, fuelled by hatred of the English and, increasingly, by Counter-Reformation Catholicism.

Although the servitors favoured conquest and plantation, an alternative system was established in Connacht, which saw no attempt at colonisation under Elizabeth. Financial and military resources were transferred from local lords to a president, with an army, who was responsible for defence and order and to whom lesser lords and freeholders paid an annual rent. Counties were established on the English model. This arrangement potentially benefited most of society. Great lords no longer needed to keep expensive armies and their position within their clan could be strengthened by office and the president's support. Lesser lords and peasants paid less than before and everyone enjoyed greater security. In the south of the province the major families, the O'Brien earls of Thomond and the Burke earls of Clanricard, remained loyal to the Crown and made the system work. In the North it was disrupted by family succession disputes. In County Sligo the Binghams used a mixture of legal chicanery, martial law and brute force to amass lands, wealth and power, showing how much servitors could get away with under lax (or non-existent) supervision. Most of the other provinces probably resembled north rather than south Connacht. The experience of Connacht is unlikely to have persuaded servitors that there was an alternative to plantation.

The Dilemmas of the Old English

The Reformation transformed the relationship between the English Crown and Ireland. Most of the Irish outwardly accepted the royal supremacy. The attempts to impose Protestantism under Edward VI and Elizabeth had a limited impact but with the coming of Protestantism they were open to allegations that their first loyalty was to the Pope. Like many English Catholics they tried to distinguish between spiritual and secular: on questions relating to faith and morals they obeyed the Pope, but their secular allegiance was to the Crown. As time went on their Catholicism distanced them further from the political establishment. Alienated by persecution and killings many were driven into **recusancy**, abandoning their partial conformity to the Church of Ireland. Servitors extended their condemnation of Irish Catholics to include the Old English; Spenser claimed that they 'are now much more lawless and licentious than the very wild Irish'. He was writing in the later 1590s, when some of the Old English were in rebellion, but allegations that the Old English were hostile to English rule can be found much earlier. It turned them against the English regime and drove some into conspiracy and revolt. The servitors were unable to keep them out of Parliament, where the Commons, which still had a Catholic majority in 1585–6, denounced the servitors' use of martial law and non-parliamentary taxation as illegal. (The majority of the Old English lived in Leinster, which paid the lion's share of these taxes.) They also prevented the draconian English penal laws against Catholics being extended to Ireland. In some ways, this was a Pyrrhic victory: Parliament was not summoned again in Elizabeth's reign. For the moment, however, they hoped that their predominance in the Commons would enable them to influence government policy. Their friends and kinsmen at the English court argued that the servitors' conduct was likely to provoke rebellion and played on Elizabeth's fears of having to spend vast sums in Ireland. The Spanish war, however, enabled the servitors to stress the danger of Spanish intervention in Ireland and to argue that the Irish had to be subjugated so that they could not assist an invader. Elizabeth was unconvinced, but events played into the servitors' hands. A series of conspiracies and rebellions enabled them to promote the policy of plantation on a larger and larger scale.

The Munster Plantation

From 1565 the Connacht presidency had a counterpart in Munster, with an English president, a council and a small army, paid for by taxes levied by the president and council. The scheme was designed to undermine the great lords and involve independent freeholders in local government. It met with considerable support, but faced two great problems. The first was the dominance and rivalry of the earls of Ormond and Desmond: if one supported the scheme, the other would oppose it, and their affinities followed them. The second problem was that the scheme was linked to plans for a plantation. It was suggested that the necessary land could be found from former monastic estates and lands forfeited to the Crown, but strong fears of English land grabbers led to a rebellion in 1569. A new president, Sir John Perrot, had hundreds convicted of treason and felony; by 1573 he claimed to have hanged 800 people. He banned **Brehon** law, native dress and bardic poetry and had lists drawn up of the recognised followers of lords; 'masterless men' could be executed.

BOX 7.3: **Massacres**

It was normal practice in sieges that defenders who resisted the besiegers could be killed, but that those who had surrendered and been taken prisoner should be spared. In both these cases, prisoners were killed a significant time after their capture. At Maynooth their heads were set on spikes around the castle and elsewhere; it was also alleged that some defenders were killed in their beds and that others were domestic servants. The executions were calculated to intimidate and deter the remnants of Kildare's following.

Maynooth 1535

Lord Deputy Skeffington wrote to the King that Maynooth was the most strongly fortified castle ever seen in Ireland, but it was stormed after a seven-day bombardment and about sixty of the defenders were killed, as against seven attackers. Thirty-seven were:

taken prisoners and their lives preserved by appointment until they should be presented to me … and then to be ordered as I and your council though good. And considering the high enterprise and presumption attempted by them against your grace's crown and majesty, and also that if, by any mean, they should escape, the most of them being gunners, at some other time would semblably elsewhere aid your traitors and be an example and mean to others to do likewise, we all thought expedient and requisite that they should be put to execution, for the dread and example of others.

[Two days later they were examined and depositions taken and then they were] arraigned before the provost marshal and captains [in a court martial] and there, upon their own confessions, adjudged to die, and immediately twenty-five of them before the gate of the castle [be]headed and one hanged …

State Papers published under the Authority of His Majesty's Commission (10 vols., London, 1830–52), II (Henry VIII, part III), pp. 236–7. See also D. Edwards, 'The Escalation of Violence in Sixteenth Century Ireland', in D. Edwards, P. Lenihan and C. Tait (eds.), *Age of Atrocity* (Dublin, 2007), pp. 55–7.

Smerwick 1580

Lord Deputy Grey's account of the killing of Italian prisoners, stripped of their arms and armour.

I sent straight certain gentlemen in to see their weapons and armours laid down and to guard the munition and victual there left for spoil. Then put I in certain bands who fell straight to execution. There were 600 slain; munition and victual great store, though much wasted through the disorder of the soldier, which in that fury could not be helped.

Captain [Walter] Raleigh … who had the ward of that day, entered into the castle and made a great slaughter, many or the most part of them being put to the sword.

National Archives, SP 63/78/29, Grey to Elizabeth, 12 November 1580, quoted in V.P. Carey, 'Atrocity and History: Grey, Spenser and the Slaughter at Smerwick (1580)', in Edwards, Lenihan and Tait (eds.), *Age of Atrocity*, pp. 90, 84–5.

The rebellion led to the break-up of the Desmond lordship, but some of Desmond's kinsmen, together with the Pope, organised an invasion. An Italian force landed at Smerwick, County Kerry, which encouraged Desmond to join the rebellion. Ormond and the lord deputy, Lord Grey of Wilton, led the suppression of the revolt. When the Italians offered to surrender, Grey accepted unconditionally, and then had all 600 of them killed; Walter Raleigh, that paragon of English chivalry, played a leading part in the killing. (See Box 7.3, Massacres.) In a bruising guerrilla war both sides destroyed food and killed sheep and cattle; people died in their thousands, or tens of thousands. Munster, a 'rich and plentiful country', was reduced to a wasteland, where people fed on recently buried corpses.

The rebellion continued until late 1583, when Desmond was killed. The forfeiture of his lands offered the prospect of a substantial plantation, with rich pickings for servitors. Before it could proceed the lands had to be surveyed and those whose lands were forfeit had to be attainted, which is why Parliament was summoned in 1585: an Act of **attainder** was much quicker, and more certain, than lengthy proceedings in the courts. It was estimated that 300,000 acres of land would be available for servitors or undertakers who could bring over settlers from England. The aim was to plant English farmers and English farming; they were to be allowed to take Old English tenants, but not Gaelic Irish, a rare recognition that they were different. The plantation soon faced problems. The survey had been rushed; lands which had not been forfeited were mixed up with those that had. Many who had paid rent to Desmond claimed that they were freeholders, forced to pay tribute. Others claimed to have been pardoned, or to hold land on mortgages. Often their claims were upheld, to the servitors' annoyance. These legal uncertainties slowed the establishment of the plantation, but it became much the largest in Elizabeth's dominions. It was destroyed in two weeks in 1598.

Tyrone's Rebellion

By the late 1580s the English regime in Ireland exercised some semblance of control over three of the four provinces. Leinster, apart from Gaelic areas in Wicklow, was the most governable, despite excessive taxes. In the southern part of Connacht the presidency system proved reasonably effective. In Munster the Desmond lordship had been broken up, Ormond was conspicuously loyal and the plantation offered hope for a more ordered and prosperous future. Ulster was the most Gaelic and disorderly province, with forbidding mountains and treacherous bogs; moving troops and artillery was even more difficult than elsewhere. Ulstermen were renowned as fierce fighters and recruited 'redshanks' (mercenaries) from Scotland. However, Ulster contained good grazing, and arable land which was capable of being improved: landowners brought in labourers from the Pale and advisers from the Netherlands. The O'Neill lands produced a significant food surplus; they could afford to hire mercenaries, leaving their peasants to concentrate on farming. Hugh O'Neill's annual income was £80,000, far larger than that of any English lord.

Ulster had many clans, but three predominated. The greatest were the O'Neills, fragmented into many septs, but with their heartlands in Tyrone. Their chiefs were cunning and ruthless and brought in foreign soldiers to train their followers in modern warfare. They knew that Elizabeth's government would prefer to manage them peacefully, so held out hopes of co-operation, while seeking English assistance in their power struggles. Some were masters of theatre: in 1562 Shane O'Neill appeared before Elizabeth in full Irish dress, prostrated himself and confessed, in Irish, that he had been a rebel. He also established close relations with the powerful Earl of Leicester. The O'Donnells, lords of Tyrconnell, were a smaller clan, but the government often supported them against the O'Neills. The third clan, the Macdonnells, became the dominant influence along the Antrim coast, recruiting and supplying redshanks, often their Macdonald kinsmen. All three clans were slippery negotiators, who reneged on or reinterpreted agreements, and stubborn and treacherous fighters.

In Ulster warfare the advantage lay with the locals; if forced to accept terms, they might not observe them, even if they had given hostages; alliances held only until a better one came along. Dissident O'Neills allied with rival clans or the English, who tried various tactics. Garrisons along the borders were isolated and difficult to defend. A scheme to colonise the North East came to nothing, mainly because the relevant lands had yet to be conquered. In the 1580s the English established four new counties in Ulster and tried to undermine the lords' authority, but lacked the necessary military power. Nevertheless, the Ulster lords felt threatened. The chief of the O'Neills resigned the headship to Hugh, second Earl of Tyrone, a wily politician. He mounted small-scale operations to disrupt the extension of English influence, usually followed by submission and negotiations, only for Hugh to embark on similar actions. He tested Elizabeth's patience, without driving her to an expensive military response. He moved into open defiance in 1595. His stated intention was to secure recognition of his lordship in Ulster and the withdrawal of sheriffs from Tyrone and Armagh; he did not try to exploit unrest elsewhere in Ireland but did enter into an alliance with Spain. His army of 2,500 was well trained and armed, ready to intervene outside Ulster.

His opportunity came in August 1598, with an ill-planned military expedition. Tyrone resoundingly defeated the English at the Yellow Ford, just south of Lough Neagh; over 800 were killed. His victory raised his standing, triggered revolts across the country and made a Spanish invasion much more likely. In Munster, English settlers were driven out of the plantation lands, which were reclaimed by their former owners. Elizabeth sent the second Earl of Essex to reassert her authority. His army numbered 17,000, enormous by Irish standards; he dispersed much of it in garrisons, while the remainder failed to secure Munster. When he eventually challenged Tyrone, his army was outnumbered and he negotiated a disadvantageous truce. Tyrone moved out of Ulster, gathering contingents from several parts of Ireland. He issued a manifesto, centred on the restoration of Catholicism and the political rights of the Irish.

Early in 1600 Elizabeth appointed a far more capable commander, Lord Mountjoy. He used his army more effectively and won over disaffected lords and commanders. His main priority was Ulster, establishing garrisons near Derry in the west and at Mountnorris and Blackwater in the east. In September 1601 the long anticipated Spanish army arrived at Kinsale. It numbered only 3,400 men and when Tyrone tried to join forces Mountjoy drove him back with heavy losses; the Spaniards were later allowed to surrender and return home. Tyrone's confederate army broke up and he sued for peace. Mountjoy tightened the military pressure on Ulster, adding more forts so that cavalry raids could reach almost all parts of the province, and broke the stone at Tullaghoge where the O'Neill chief was traditionally inaugurated. Tyrone took to the woods for over a year, while English commanders burned homes and crops and slaughtered men, women and children, arguing that peasants grew grain and women milked cows, thus enabling the fighting men to fight. Mountjoy was no bigot, but thought the killing 'necessary', adding 'even the very best of the Irish people were, in their nature, little better than devils'. Continual raids allowed the people no respite and thousands died of hunger. But by now the war in Ireland was costing four-fifths of the Crown's normal revenue. Chief minister Robert Cecil wrote, 'in short time the sword cannot end the war, and in long time the state of England cannot well endure it'. Early in 1603 Elizabeth authorised Mountjoy to offer Tyrone 'life, liberty and pardon' if he surrendered, which he did on 30 March. Mountjoy knew, but Tyrone did not, that Elizabeth had died six days earlier.

The Plantation of Ulster

Tyrone's pardon was generous, restoring almost all the lands he had held before his rebellion. Rory O'Donnell, who had fought alongside Tyrone, and surrendered in 1602, was regranted the O'Donnell lands and created Earl of Tyrconnell. Mountjoy presented the two earls to James I. As military force had failed to undermine the loyalty of their followers, James and Mountjoy hoped to use the earls to discipline their clansmen, much as James tried to manage the Highland clans through Argyll and Huntly. The servitors were appalled by the earls' reinstatement, especially as their proprietorship and lordship now had the full sanction of English law. Without the expected bonanza of forfeitures, there was comparatively little land left for them. There now seemed no prospect of a plantation in West Ulster unless the earls forfeited their lands. Lord deputy Sir Arthur Chichester and Attorney General Sir John Davies set out to undermine the terms granted in 1603, through a commission for defective titles. Like surrender and regrant, this gave lords an opportunity to gain secure titles, but now the aim was to compel those without title to surrender their lands and receive a modest proportion back, the rest going to the Crown. The earls came under pressure to surrender lands claimed by the Church, and to grant freehold estates earlier promised to lesser lords. Tyrconnell, under pressure from other O'Donnells, agreed to create some freeholds; when the lands were granted out, part was reserved for the Crown. Convinced that he would lose his lands Tyrconnell arranged to enter the Spanish service and fled abroad in September 1607. To the surprise of many, Tyrone, whose position seemed much more secure, went with him. He had been summoned to London for a hearing of the dispute about freeholds and he may have feared imprisonment or assassination.

The flight of the two earls opened the way for plantation. Their estates, 'imaginatively interpreted', were declared forfeit. Soon most of the rest of Ulster, except for Church lands, was also declared forfeit after a revolt led by Sir Cahir O'Doherty. The only counties not forfeited were Antrim and Down, already being settled by Scots, and Monaghan, where surrender and regrant had been established. Despite the failed plantation of Lewis, James believed that plantation was the best way to bring order to Ireland. Chichester welcomed settlers from Scotland, who spoke a similar language and professed a similar religion to the English. He had no wish to evict Irish peasants, whose labour would be needed, and accepted the need to provide for some of the lesser Irish lords, who otherwise might make trouble. Even so, the plantation was intended to change Ulster's social order radically.

The plantation scheme centred on undertakers, who were to be granted land on which to install an agreed number of farmers and craftsmen, and to build forts and towns: Chichester built Belfast virtually from scratch. The most basic fortification was a **bawn**, an enclosure surrounding a tower house or farmstead, with corner towers and protected gateways: sufficient to guard against cattle thieves, but not serious military assault. The scheme aimed to promote trade, manufactures and towns. The servitors had not wanted such a wide-ranging or expensive scheme: they had wanted a change of landlords but not much else. Many undertakers promised more investment than they were able or willing to make; some London livery companies invested under duress. Their involvement led to the renaming of Derry as Londonderry; Protestants still tend to say Londonderry and Catholics Derry. Many undertakers, however, were private individuals. The original allocation covered some 442,000 acres. The largest share was earmarked for private undertakers (36 per cent), followed by 21 per cent for 'natives' (Irish) (of which about one third went to O'Neills, opponents of Tyrone), 17 per cent for the Church (and Trinity College, Dublin), 12 per cent for servitors and 10 per cent for the London companies. (See Map 7.1, Official Allocation of Lands in the Ulster Plantation, c.1610.) All who received land were required to use English agricultural methods; in addition, Irish undertakers should match English standards of manners, dress and civility.

Map 7.1 Official Allocation of Lands in the Ulster Plantation, c.1610

The plantation fell short of its promoters' hopes. The survey was rushed and the Irish measured land by the number of cattle or sheep it would support. The building of forts and towns was hindered by a shortage of craftsmen and materials. English undertakers brought over too few tenants and many tenants sublet to Irishmen, who were prepared to pay higher rents. The Scots brought over more settlers, but little money; they diligently fortified their settlements, but were less inclined to build towns. Overall, 152 bawns were built between 1610 and 1622. Many planters gave up, and those who remained gravitated to the better land, leaving the less fertile for the Irish. A particularly large influx from both England and Scotland between 1614 and 1620, a time of hunger, drove out many Irish. Where the English were strong they established manors and parishes, English courts, forms of governance and rudimentary law and order.

⚮ Conclusion

In both Scotland and Ireland the threat posed to the Crown by over-mighty nobles had greatly diminished by 1625, but not (as time would show) disappeared. Clan loyalties proved remarkably resilient and were reinforced by Catholicism. But James's rule over his three kingdoms faced different threats from dissident Protestants, often humble people driven by a fierce faith. The Ulster Plantation brought new divisions to Ireland. Some parts of Ulster became almost wholly British, others almost wholly Irish, separated by religion and language. The Irish tended to live in the Highlands, the English and Scots in the Lowlands. But there were also concentrations of English and Scots, distinct in dialect and religion. Across northern Ulster (especially in Down and Antrim) most British settlers were Scots. Parts of mid and south Ulster, and County Londonderry, were predominantly English. The segregation of British and Irish, English and Scots, was a testimony to the profound changes wrought by the plantation. In Leinster and Munster a thin layer of English landlords was superimposed on essentially Irish communities. In Ulster, English and Scots communities developed with a profound sense of difference: that of the Scots would soon be sharpened by a strong Presbyterian organisation, which fostered a mindset of a beleaguered godly remnant in a hostile land.

⚮ SUGGESTIONS FOR FURTHER READING

The best starting point for Scotland in this period is Wormald, *Court, Kirk and Community*. See also Donaldson, *Scotland: James V to James VII.* • J. Goodare, *State and Society in Early Modern Scotland* (Oxford, 1999) has a very useful chapter on the Highlands and Borders. On the Highlands, see also the early part of A.I. Macinnes, *Clanship, Commerce and the House of Stuart 1603–1788* (East Linton, 1996). • J. Wormald, 'James VI and I: Two Kings or One?', *History*, 68 (1983) is a groundbreaking comparison of James's kingship in Scotland and England. • The literature on Ireland in this period is extremely rich. Four surveys stand out: S.J. Connolly, *Contested Island: Ireland 1460–1630* (Oxford, 2007), C. Lennon, *Sixteenth-Century Ireland* (Dublin, 2006), S.G. Ellis, *Ireland in the Age of the Tudors* (Harlow, 1998) and R. Gillespie, *Seventeenth-Century Ireland* (Dublin, 2006). • They can be supplemented by the multi-author *A New History of Ireland volume 3: Early Modern Ireland*, ed. T.W. Moody, F.X. Martin and F.J. Byrne (Oxford, 1976), still very useful despite its age. • S.G. Ellis, *Tudor Frontiers and Noble Power: the Making of the British State* (Oxford, 1995) compares Kildare rule in Ireland and the power of the English Border nobility. • N. Canny, *Making Ireland British, 1580–1650* (Oxford, 2001) is a massive work of scholarship, essential reading for any student of this period. • The increasing violence and brutality of the English in Ireland is discussed in an important collection of essays: Edwards, Lenihan and Tait (eds.), *Age of Atrocity*; Edwards's own essay, 'The Escalation of Violence in Sixteenth-Century Ireland', is particularly useful. • The plantations of James I's reign are discussed at length by Canny in *Making Ireland British* and P. Robinson, *The Plantation of Ulster* (Dublin, 1984).

SUMMARY

- James VI used a mixture of parliamentary legislation and limited military force to establish some control over the Scottish nobility, but he lacked the financial and military resources to complete the process. Attempts to establish Scottish plantations, notably on the Isle of Lewis, were unsuccessful.
- The first English attempts at plantation in Ireland, in Leix and Offaly, were frustrated by the determined opposition of the local Gaelic clans. English commanders tried to deter opposition by acts of calculated brutality, which proved counter-productive: reprisals provoked further reprisals. Increasingly the main English strategy was to lay the country waste, destroy food supplies and starve the Irish into submission.
- Spain's declaration of war against England in 1585 introduced a new dimension into the conflicts in Ireland. Initially, Spain's strategy centred on seaborne expeditions against England, which failed, and it was not until 1601 that a Spanish force landed at Kinsale. By then the Earl of Tyrone's rebellion had gathered momentum but his forces were defeated at Kinsale and he became a fugitive, surrendering to Mountjoy in 1603.
- Tyrone (and the Earl of Tyrconnell) surrendered on generous terms: the cost of English military operations in Ireland was crippling and Elizabeth was desperate to end the war. With the two earls confirmed in possession of their lands the amount available for plantation was much reduced. Once they had been 'persuaded' to flee abroad the Plantation of Ulster could begin.

QUESTIONS FOR STUDENTS

1. How far did James VI tame the Scottish nobility?
2. Why did the Dublin government fail to establish control over the Gaelic chiefs between 1536 and 1579?
3. What problems faced the 'Old English' under Elizabeth?

4. Why did the military conquest of Ireland finally succeed at the end of Elizabeth's reign and how far was it incomplete?
5. What were the aims of the Ulster Plantation and how far were they achieved?

8 The Coming of War in Three Kingdoms 1625–1642

TIMELINE

1625	Charles I's accession; Commons refuse to vote customs for life
1626	Impeachment of Buckingham; forced loan
1628	Petition of Right; Buckingham assassinated; the Graces offered in Ireland
1629	Parliament dissolved; start of Personal Rule
1633	Laud Archbishop of Canterbury; Wentworth to Ireland
1636	Punishment of Prynne, Burton and Bastwick
1637	Hampden case; Prayer Book rebellion
1638	Covenant promulgated; King summons Parliament and General Assembly in Scotland; start of Covenanter Revolution
1640	Laud besieged at Lambeth; Charles defeated at Newburn; Long Parliament convenes
1641	May: army plot; Strafford executed; Commons approve Protestation
1641	August: King to Scotland
1641	October: the 'Incident'

1641	November: news of Irish rising; Commons vote to print Grand Remonstrance; King returns to London
1642	Attempt on Five Members; King leaves London; Parliament increasingly takes over King's powers; King raises standard at Nottingham

Introduction

In this period developments in the three kingdoms were intertwined: one cannot understand why civil war broke out in England without understanding why war had first broken out in Scotland and Ireland. The need for a 'three-kingdoms' approach makes it futile to explain the English civil wars in terms of changes in *English* society. Moreover, war broke out within two polities, Scotland and England, which had become more orderly. In England, civil war would seem more likely in the mid-sixteenth century than in the mid-seventeenth because the succession was questionable. Under Charles I the Stuart succession was unchallenged and secure. And yet the civil war happened, and much of the blame for this lay with Charles I.

The English Legacy of James I

James had been an unusually successful King of Scotland, apparently taming both nobility and kirk. In England he has received a more hostile press, especially regarding his later years. His infatuation with male favourites, especially George Villiers, Duke of Buckingham, attracted much criticism; sodomy was a capital offence. In the early 1620s Buckingham seemed to control key areas of policy-making, including foreign policy, and developed dubious money-making schemes to fund his expensive tastes. James was tired and disillusioned. He had hoped to bring Scots and English together after centuries of conflict, but the English dismissed the Scots as beggarly and verminous. He found governing England tedious; its government was larger and more complex than Scotland's and involved far more paperwork. English lawyers claimed that England's law was more ancient and sophisticated than Scotland's and urged him to follow their guidance. Finally, there were money problems. England was a richer country, but (as in Scotland) there never seemed to be enough revenue for his needs.

Many blamed James's money problems on his generosity to friends and favourites: James Hay, Earl of Carlisle, received rewards (including Barbados) worth £400,000.

James had little sense of the value of money, but the Crown's fundamental financial problem was that it was underendowed. Under Elizabeth the yield of the **subsidy** fell substantially in real terms because of inflation. Subsidy commissioners appointed by the Commons allowed friends and neighbours to underassess themselves grossly: Lord Treasurer Burghley returned his net income as £133 a year, on which he built Burghley House. When the Commons granted two, four or six subsidies, underassessment became even more blatant. Between the 1590s and 1628, a time of substantial inflation, the yield of a single subsidy fell from £150,000 to £65,000. Nevertheless, for much of her reign Elizabeth lived within her means. When absolutely necessary (as with the fortification of Berwick) she spent heavily, but she eschewed vanity projects and military adventures. As most monastic land had been sold Elizabeth plundered the Church on a smaller scale, keeping bishoprics vacant and collecting their revenues. With the war against Spain and the Nine Years War in Ireland expenditure escalated. She disliked borrowing, so raised money by selling Crown lands, which produced ready cash at the expense of future income. Her successors continued the sales so that by 1640 the net revenue from Crown lands, the main source of Henry VII's income, was only a few thousand pounds a year.

Where possible Elizabeth cut expenditure, but maintaining the support of the political elite cost money. Much of James's Scottish income went to nobles and courtiers. England's political elite was much larger. Those who toiled unpaid in local government expected some recognition, as did civil servants and courtiers. If the Queen could not reward them herself she allowed them to reward themselves, by granting **patents** to perform certain tasks of government, for which they charged fees. Some tasks were ostensibly useful, such as road or river improvements, but often the patentees performed the work shoddily or not at all. The Queen also granted **monopolies** on particular commodities to favoured courtiers. In 1601, faced with an exceptionally hostile Commons, Elizabeth withdrew most of the monopolies and patents; they were soon to return.

There were two possible ways to increase the Crown's revenue. One was to persuade Parliament that it was insufficient to pay for the government his people expected. However, James feared that if he allowed Parliament to investigate what he regarded as his private affairs MPs would seize gleefully on evidence of extravagance and complain about the Scots. James's second alternative was to raise money using his **prerogative**: powers traditionally exercised by the King (for example, in an emergency) for the general good of his people. Used in ways that were widely seen as acceptable, they were uncontroversial. In Scotland, James often stretched the letter of the law. When he behaved similarly in England, Parliament and lawyers attempted to define the prerogative more precisely.

Parliament granted two major forms of revenue. **Subsidies** were occasional land taxes, voted for war, to prepare for war, or to make good the cost afterwards. The customs were granted for life at the accession of each monarch since Richard III, but any increase in the rates charged had to be approved by Parliament; they remained unchanged throughout Elizabeth's reign. In 1606 a legal case gave James the opportunity to establish the legality of **impositions** – additional import duties exacted by the King without Parliament's approval. A merchant called Bate refused to pay a duty on currants, claiming that it was illegal. The judges agreed that it would be illegal if it was designed to raise revenue, but tariffs could also be used to make imports more expensive and so protect English merchants and manufacturers. James claimed that his motives were protectionist rather than fiscal, but many did not believe him. Further impositions followed Bate's case and MPs expressed fears that he intended to introduce French-style **absolute monarchy**, overturning traditional English liberties, which depended on parliaments and juries. French kings were believed to tax and legislate on their own authority, and imprison people and confiscate property without due process of law. As the courts no longer seemed to protect Englishmen's liberty and property, some invoked the concept of '**fundamental laws**', which the King was expected to respect.

Parliament's fears might seem exaggerated, but Bate's case showed that the law offered insufficient protection against ingenious lawyers. James, however, believed that he had a legal right to raise impositions. He feared that those who questioned his powers had an ulterior motive and by the end of the Parliament of 1610 accused trouble-makers in the Commons of 'popularity', appealing to the turbulent multitude in an effort to undermine the Crown's authority. Therefore, between 1610 and 1621 he summoned only one short-lived Parliament: MPs' fears were apparently becoming a reality. Suspicion and mistrust were growing on both sides. When Parliament next met the situation had changed in two important ways.

First, the Duke of Buckingham's rise to power and favour provoked distaste and resentment. James called him his 'sweet child and wife' and himself Buckingham's 'dear dad and husband'. His craving for physical contact may have stemmed from loneliness but was widely seen as evidence of a homosexual relationship. Behind Buckingham's handsome face lay a cunning and ruthless mind. As his power grew so did his ambition. He was recklessly extravagant and had an extensive family and clientele to provide for. He sold peerages, which offended peers and demeaned the nobility. He revived monopolies and patents in a more extreme form; his City cronies managed them or gave him a share of the profits. Under a licensing patent, alehouse keepers had to buy licences from the patentees; if they did not their premises were wrecked, but the patentees did nothing to ensure that alehouses became more orderly. Perhaps the most cynical was the patent for a lighthouse on the dangerous headland of Dungeness; patentees were empowered to collect tolls from ships, and in return set up a single candle. By 1621 James's court was seen as harbouring essentially criminal enterprises.

The second development was the outbreak of the Thirty Years War in 1618, triggered by Frederick, James's son-in-law, accepting the Crown of Bohemia. Frederick was driven out of both Bohemia and his own princedom, the Palatinate. James was urged to lead the Protestant side in what was seen as a religious war. He feared that if there was a war, 'popular' MPs would use their financial power to reduce him to a figurehead. He sought to resolve the conflict peacefully, by marrying his son, Charles, to a Spanish infanta (princess). For English Protestants, Spain was the great Catholic enemy, seeking 'universal monarchy' in Europe and the Americas. Charles and Buckingham travelled to Madrid (in false beards) to woo the infanta. The Spaniards gradually increased their demands until Buckingham realised that there was no prospect of agreement; they returned determined on war with Spain – and suddenly popular.

In 1621 Parliament gave vent to ten years of pent-up grievances, starting with monopolies and patents. The Commons revived impeachment, last used in 1459. Two patentees, Mompesson and Mitchell, were convicted, as was Lord Keeper Bacon, who had sealed their patents. Buckingham then arranged the impeachment of Lord Treasurer Cranfield, who had warned the King against Buckingham's reckless expenditure; James dismissed Cranfield, supinely remarking that all good lord treasurers were unpopular. With England at war with Spain, James feared that Parliament would gain in power, but Buckingham was confident that he could manage it. When James died in 1625 Charles was soon on a collision course with Parliament.

'The Crisis of Parliaments' 1625–1629

James I had been articulate and intelligent; Charles was diffident (he stammered) and intellectually simplistic, thinking in terms of good and bad, right and wrong. Whereas James had debated skilfully and exploited ambiguities, Charles demanded to be obeyed and saw any attempt to argue as disobedience. Initially he was under Buckingham's spell: swept along by the Duke's boundless self-confidence, he supported him uncritically. Most saw Buckingham as criminally incompetent, and some ascribed the King's infatuation to witchcraft. Charles's mixture of weakness and authoritarianism, and Buckingham's recklessness, greed and vindictiveness, led to a rapid and dangerous escalation of distrust.

James and Charles both came to believe that the Commons wished to usurp the king's right to govern. Traditionally, the king was responsible for major appointments and religious, domestic and foreign policy. Parliament could offer advice and inform the king of subjects' grievances, which the king could choose to remedy or ignore. If the king wanted new taxes or laws, Parliament's assent was essential. Taxation was the more important: the Crown often had little need to legislate, but its need for taxation potentially gave Parliament some influence on policy: only a foolish monarch would go to war without parliamentary support. Moreover, government worked better if the monarch heeded the views of the people.

In the 1620s many felt threatened by an increasingly authoritarian monarchy: Sir Benjamin Rudyerd MP declared in 1628: 'This is the crisis of Parliaments: we shall know by this if Parliaments live or die.' Conversely, James and Charles believed that the Commons threatened their legitimate authority. Most members were 'dutiful subjects … it being some few vipers amongst them that did cast this mist of undutifulness over most of their eyes'. King and Commons each saw the other as behaving unreasonably. In 1625 the Commons refused to grant Charles the regular customs for life. Their aim was probably to negotiate a deal on impositions; convinced that he had a right to the customs, Charles collected them anyway. In 1626, the Commons agreed in principle to raise subsidies for the war against Spain, but delayed completing the necessary bills while they impeached Buckingham; Charles, convinced that he was morally entitled to this money, ordered the raising of a similar sum through a **forced loan**. Many refused to pay: some were imprisoned and there was talk of conscripting others into the army.

The Commons' anxiety and anger were compounded by Buckingham's mismanagement of the war. One bungled expedition followed another. The nadir was an expedition to the Ile de Ré which, Buckingham believed, would bring France into the war. The ladders brought to scale the citadel walls were far too short and the soldiers retreated along a narrow causeway, picked off with ease by French snipers. France declared war, but against England, which now faced the two greatest powers in Europe. Buckingham blamed everyone except himself and kept up the army over the winter of 1627–8, leading to rumours of a military coup. His career ended abruptly when he was stabbed by John Felton, a disgruntled army officer. The King was prostrated with grief; Londoners danced in the streets.

Charles's refusal to heed criticism of Buckingham, and his authoritarian style, worried many of his ministers. A royal spokesman warned the Commons of the terrible consequences of forcing the King to follow 'new counsels'. (See Box 8.1, 'New Counsels'.) The King told members that he would not threaten them, as he scorned to threaten anyone but his equals. Details of council discussions were widely leaked, so MPs knew that some councillors gave the King good advice, but that he chose instead to follow Buckingham. MPs were reduced to tears by their inability to get through to him. They believed they had succeeded in 1628 when he accepted the **Petition of Right**. Approved by both Houses, this claimed to restate existing law, but made novel claims that **martial law** was illegal and that the council had no right to commit people to gaol without showing cause. The common law courts did not recognise martial law, but it was tacitly accepted that **courts martial** were necessary to maintain military discipline in wartime. Similarly, the council had committed people to gaol without showing cause in treason cases, like the Gunpowder Plot, but now did so to prevent

BOX 8.1: 'New Counsels'

In a speech to the Commons on 12 May 1626 Sir Dudley Carleton warned against provoking the King.

... I beseech you, gentlemen, move not his Majesty with trenching upon his prerogatives, lest you bring him out of love with Parliaments ... [he has often told you] that if there were not correspondency between him and you he should be enforced to use new counsels. Now I pray you consider what these new counsels are and may be ... In all Christian kingdoms you know that Parliaments were in use anciently, by which their kingdoms were governed in a most flourishing manner, until the monarchs began to know their own strength and, seeing the turbulent spirit of their Parliaments, at length they little by little began to stand upon their prerogatives and at last overthrew the parliaments throughout Christendom, except here only with us.

And indeed you would count it a great misery if you knew the subjects in foreign countries as well as myself, to see them look not like our nation, with store of flesh on their backs, but like so many ghosts, and not men, being nothing but skin and bones, with some thin cover to their nakedness, and wearing only wooden shoes on their feet, so that they cannot eat meat or wear good clothes but they must pay and be taxed unto the king for it. There is a misery beyond expression and that which yet we are free from. Let us be careful, then, to preserve the king's good opinion of parliaments ...

J.P. Kenyon, *The Stuart Constitution* (2nd edn, Cambridge, 1986), p. 45.

forced loan refusers from challenging the loan's legality. Seeing the Petition as further evidence of the Commons' determination to undermine his powers, Charles did not feel bound by its terms, especially when the Commons endorsed a remonstrance, setting out Buckingham's misdeeds; a copy was found in Felton's pocket. Charles had always believed that complaints against the Duke were unfounded; now he blamed the Commons for his murder.

Buckingham's killing added another twist to the spiral of distrust between King and Parliament. For Charles, the Commons' refusal to grant the customs for life had denied him the money he needed to fight the war which they had demanded. Their impeachment of Buckingham forced him to levy the forced loan. The Petition of Right undermined his prerogatives. Threats of 'new counsels' added to his subjects' anxieties, as did his preference for 'Arminian' clergy, who stressed the divine origins of kingly power and the subject's duty of obedience. There was one final twist to this spiral when Parliament reconvened early in 1629. After a short, ill-tempered session the King ordered the Speaker of the Commons to adjourn proceedings so that the Houses could be dissolved. Two burly MPs held the Speaker down, while the House agreed resolutions condemning Arminianism and the collection of customs duties without Parliament's consent. This was a gross violation of the House's procedures, which showed (the King later claimed) that they aimed 'to erect a universal, overswaying power to themselves, which belongs only to us and not to them'. He announced that he would call no more parliaments for the foreseeable future.

The Personal Rule in England 1629–1637

Charles did not blame himself for his disputes with Parliament. He believed that a few years of his wise, benevolent government would show that he had been misrepresented. The ending of the wars reduced tension and financial pressure. His **ordinary revenues** were still inadequate. He bought the magnificent art collection of the Duke of Mantua and was a patron of Rubens and van Dyck. His building projects included the completion of the Queen's House at Greenwich and the construction of the Banqueting House at Whitehall. Unwilling to adapt his spending to fit his means, he needed more revenue. He was still collecting both the regular customs and impositions without Parliament's consent, but after the subsidies granted in 1628, he received no tax on land. Like Henry VII he would have to make more from his feudal rights and prerogative.

Under Elizabeth and James the most significant feudal source of income was **wardship**, but its yield could not be greatly increased, as those who paid it were powerful landowners. Other feudal rights had fallen into disuse. The royal forests, set aside by William I for hunting, were subject to forest laws, which forbade building, agriculture or mining, which damaged the deer's habitat. While investigating forgotten Crown rights, lawyers discovered that the forests had once been much more extensive; those who unknowingly lived in areas of encroachment could be fined. Local juries were bullied into recognising the King's 'rights'. The circumference of Rockingham Forest was extended from six miles to sixty. Three peers who owned land there were fined between £12,000 and £20,000. Although they were able to **compound** for smaller sums, the memory rankled. Another forgotten device was **distraint of knighthood**: anyone holding land worth more than £5 a year was obliged to be knighted or pay a fine. This was intended to provide knights for the King's armies, but warfare had changed and the value of £5 had greatly diminished. Those summoned to be knighted were often given insufficient notice, and fined for default. Landowners who had enclosed land contrary to law were fined under Tudor legislation; they were not required to reverse the enclosures, so in a few years could be fined again.

The Act of 1624 against monopolies had made an exception for corporations charged with maintaining standards of workmanship, such as craft guilds. Corporations were now created which made a show of quality control. A monopoly on soap anticipated modern marketing by demonstrating to peeresses and laundresses that monopolists' soap washed whiter. Other schemes smacked of extortion. The City of London was prosecuted in 1637 for failing to fulfil its obligations in Ulster. It had brought over too few English colonists, renting land to Irishmen instead, but Crown claims that it had made enormous profits were completely unfounded. The City was fined £70,000 and publicly accused of incompetence and fraud. Civil servants were threatened with an end to treating offices as private property, with holders remunerated by fees rather than salaries. The civil servants presented a substantial sum to the King, and the proposals were dropped.

The proceedings against the City, like those for opposing the Crown's fen drainage schemes, were heard in **Star Chamber**. This did not follow the procedures used in common-law courts or use of juries. Its proceedings were quick and cheap, but the simplicity which was an asset in proceedings between subjects offered no protection against the Crown. Many prosecutions were for disobeying proclamations, rather than offences against common or statute law; Star Chamber also claimed jurisdiction in cases of riot. It was used to enforce press censorship, which rested on the royal prerogative. Although it could not punish in life or limb, it could impose mutilation, as in the cases of William Prynne, Henry Burton and John Bastwick – a lawyer, a clergyman and a doctor – sentenced to lose their ears for publishing libels against bishops. It was not normal to inflict corporal punishment on gentlemen or professionals, and they were widely seen as martyrs. (See Figure 8.1, Archbishop Laud and Henry Burton, After Laud's Fall from Power, *c.*1645.)

The King's advisers used Star Chamber because there they could be confident of securing the desired verdict, but for one fiscal device they needed the judges' approval. **Ship Money**, used by Elizabeth among others, required coastal counties to provide ships to oppose a possible invasion – a maritime equivalent of the militia rate. Charles levied it without protest in 1627, but it was revived in 1634 and, from 1635, it became an annual levy and was extended to inland counties. Some refused to pay, hoping to challenge its legality in court. In 1637 John Hampden, one of the richest commoners in England, got his chance before all twelve judges. Prosecution and defence argued across one another. The King's lawyers said that there were ample precedents for raising Ship Money to defend the realm in an emergency; it was up to him to decide what constituted an emergency. (It might be argued that an annual emergency was a strange concept, and that taxpayers were given five months to pay.) Hampden's counsel argued that Ship Money was a tax (their opponents claimed it was a rate, like the militia rate) and that taxes could be granted only by Parliament. The judges ruled seven to five in favour of the Crown (although three found for Hampden only on a technicality).

Hampden's case seemed to show that Ship Money was legal; it was also efficient. Unlike subsidies, in which taxpayers were assessed individually, each county and town had a quota; if one quota was reduced, another had to be increased. High yields, often well over 90 per cent, became the norm. Although it was assessed at a modest level, it could in theory be increased repeatedly. We need to consider, therefore, since the principle of parliamentary approval for taxation was well established, why the judges decided in the King's favour. They may have feared dismissal, but Charles did not subject them to undue pressure, unlike James II in 1686–8. The judges were probably more comfortable with precedents and technicalities than with arguments based on

Figure 8.1 Laud has earlier been instrumental in Burton's being sentenced to have his ears cropped for seditious publishing, but now he has been sentenced to death for treason and vomits up canons (of which Convocation passed a new batch in 1640), Star Chamber decrees and orders against the full observance of the Sabbath.

common sense, and were wary of questioning the King's integrity: if he said there was an emergency, they had to believe him. Above all, the judges had already been asked, in Exchequer Chamber, if the King would be justified in extending Ship Money to inland counties if he judged that the emergency threatened the whole country. They decided that he would, so when a legal challenge came, he could be confident of winning. This raised the prospect that Parliament's law-making functions could be taken over by the judges: in Ireland English judges were drastically rewriting Irish land law in the financial interests of the Crown.

Charles's policy towards the Church also provoked anxiety and anger. His father had maintained a balance between Calvinist and **Arminian**; Charles favoured the Arminians. He saw Puritans as hostile to monarchy, and found their worship unedifying. He believed the laity should go quietly to church to learn to obey God and the King, and stressed the importance of 'the beauty of holiness'. He found a kindred spirit in William Laud, created Bishop of London in 1628 and Archbishop of Canterbury in 1633. Laud was obsessively tidy: he tried to make the students of his Oxford college wear their hair short and stay out of alehouses. He tried to bring Oxford's liturgical standards to all parish churches: they were to have all the prescribed books, altar furnishings and priestly vestments. It was no longer acceptable that communion wine should be served in an alehouse tankard or that babies should be baptised in a bucket.

Laud's meddling was irritating, and cost parishioners money, but the resentment went deeper. Laud shared the King's ideal of a passive laity. He distrusted preaching, preferring that the priest read **homilies**, which taught obedience and wholesome doctrine. He hoped to restore the spiritual authority of priest over people which had been lost at the Reformation. At the heart of that authority was the priest's role in communion. Under Elizabeth, communion was generally dispensed from a table in the nave, and the people received the bread and wine seated, a commemoration of the Last Supper. Laud wanted to reintroduce spiritual mystery into communion, by moving the consecration of the bread and wine to an altar at the east end of the church, railed to keep off the congregation's dogs and create a sacred space which only the priest could enter. The people should come to the altar and receive communion kneeling. Laud also wanted to beautify church interiors, with images to aid devotion and understanding.

Puritans were naturally outraged by this return to 'popery'. As Laud tightened his grip, good sermons became hard to find and many Puritans went 'gadding', spending Sunday in another parish. There they mixed with Puritans from other parishes, forming their own godly gatherings. By the late 1630s many were emigrating to the Netherlands or North America. Laud's attempted counter-reformation also angered many 'parish Anglicans'. They had grown up with the Prayer Book services and they resented 'popish' changes to *their* ceremonies and *their* church interiors. Much divided these 'parish Anglicans' from Puritans, but they shared a common loathing of Laud, who by 1640 was the most hated man in England. In 1637, however, that hatred had no way to find expression. The few who dared criticise the government or the bishops were punished by Star Chamber. Hampden's case established the legality of Ship Money and the City of London was resentful but cowed. The country seemed to enjoy a profound peace.

English Rule in Ireland 1625–1639

James I consistently supported plantation and the promotion of the English (and Scottish) interest in Ireland. He had profound contempt for the Gaelic Irish, but was prepared to listen to the Old English, whose titles to land were rarely challenged. Charles was less consistent. In the late 1620s, in return for money, he offered concessions known as Graces. He offered to confirm the titles of New English undertakers in Ulster, even if they had not fulfilled their contracts. To the Old English he offered various concessions, most notably the extension to Ireland of a recent English Act, whereby possession for a period of years provided a secure title to land without the need for documentary proof. The Old English also wanted to use the militia to defend Ireland against Spanish attack; the New English argued that they could not be trusted and urged the King to rely on his (Protestant) army. The Old English paid the money they promised, but Charles failed to confirm the Graces.

In 1633 a new lord deputy, Sir Thomas Wentworth, brought a radical and brutal coherence to English government in Ireland. (See Figure 8.2, Thomas Wentworth, Later Earl of Strafford, by Studio of Anthony van Dyck, 1636.) Wentworth and Laud advocated a policy of 'thorough', imposing the King's will, without fear, favour, or pussy-footing qualms about legality. Like the New English, Wentworth claimed that, as a conquered country, Ireland should be remoulded – but according to the King's wishes, not the settlers'. The King's prerogative in Ireland, long ineffectual, should be extended, along with English law and courts, particularly **Castle Chamber**, the equivalent of Star Chamber. English standards of order should be established and all land seized that was not ultimately held of the King. The revenue and army should be increased and Old and New English, Scots and Irish, subjected to the Crown. His eventual aim was to seize all land in Catholic hands for the King, starting in Connacht, which had hitherto escaped plantation. Some landowners had surrendered their lands, in order to have them regranted, but the surrenders had never been formally enrolled and so made effective. Once the King's wealth and power were secured, the people could be converted to his brand of Protestantism. He could re-endow the Church, clawing back monastic lands sold under the Tudors, and create a well-trained, mostly English, clergy. The Catholic clergy could be expelled and Catholicism rooted out. In 1634 Castle Chamber seized church lands from both Catholics and Protestants. From being more Calvinist than the Church of England, the Irish Church was to be forced into line with it. The 104 articles of the Church of Ireland were replaced by the Thirty-Nine Articles of the Church of England.

Figure 8.2 Wentworth is presented as an essentially military figure, a contrast to the lawyers and clergymen who made up most of Charles I's advisers.

Wentworth's programme was ambitious and guaranteed to alienate every major interest group in Ireland; understandably, he kept it to himself. When he called a Parliament in 1634 it granted the King subsidies. Wentworth encouraged the Old English to hope for confirmation of the Graces, but he would not agree to a statute of limitations or to confirm the titles of landowners in Connacht: plantation would be extended to the lands of the Old English. In Connacht, Wentworth ordered that county juries investigate the King's title to land. He presided over the enquiries, intimidating the jurors with 'stern looks'. The juries found in the King's favour, but in Galway the jury, predominantly Old English, refused to find that all land in the county was the King's. It was summoned to appear before Castle Chamber but a delegation went to put its case at the English court. Wentworth ensured that they were dismissed and, on returning to Ireland, they were fined and imprisoned. After months in gaol the jurors acknowledged the King's title; they were released and their fines reduced. A new Galway jury found for the King.

However, no plantation ensued in Connacht, thanks largely to Charles's problems in Scotland. The King ordered Wentworth to raise an army to suppress the rebellious Scots. The army, much of it Catholic and poorly disciplined, was quartered in Ulster, where Scots were most numerous. Wentworth tried to prevent Presbyterian ministers from returning to Scotland and imposed an oath on those who remained, dissociating themselves from the Covenanters. With his energies taken up by the Scottish problem, Wentworth's grand design for Ireland faded into the background. He returned to England in 1639 to head the King's war effort. His conduct in Ireland had caused much alarm: many feared it offered a blueprint for Charles's regime in England.

Charles I and Scotland: the Covenanter Revolution

Born in Scotland, Charles grew up in England and did not return until his coronation in 1633. He had no experience of Scotland, its institutions and people, but developed a high view of his prerogative and made it clear that he would not tolerate criticism. Shocked by the lack of 'decency' in the Kirk's worship, he insisted on using the English liturgy for his coronation, with a crucifix and candles. He issued new canons for the Church, which extended the bishops' powers and provided for moving communion tables to the east end of the church and placing them as if they were altars, but did not mention presbyteries. In 1637, after consulting the few Scottish bishops who favoured liturgical change, he issued a Prayer Book for Scotland, similar to Common Prayer in England.

The Prayer Book attempted to introduce a set liturgy into the Kirk: the Book of Common Order had provided guidance to ministers to develop their own liturgies. Charles apparently assumed that he was the supreme governor of the Scottish Church, which he was not, and that he had no need to consult with Parliament, or the Privy Council. In England or Ireland such a book would have been considered by Convocation; the nearest Scottish equivalent was the General Assembly, in abeyance since 1618. Charles took to heart his father's rhetoric about the absolute authority of kings. As King he was right, so his subjects must obey him. But the traditional values of the Scottish nobility and the teachings of the Kirk saw allegiance as conditional upon the King's behaving justly and obeying the laws of God. When the Prayer Book was first used there was a major riot in St Giles's, Edinburgh, and many disturbances elsewhere. At Brechin its introduction passed off quietly only because the bishop carried two loaded pistols into the pulpit.

Charles refused to withdraw the Book, making his opponents more determined. Petitions and 'supplications' (one signed by 400 nobles and lairds) denounced all ecclesiastical innovations since 1603. Nobles, lairds, burgesses and ministers, the four 'estates' in Parliament, were each known as a 'Table'; they formed an executive council, the Fifth Table, which from February 1638 became Scotland's unofficial government. Its programme centred on the **Covenant**, a compact, or rather two compacts, between God, king and people to maintain God's truth and the king's person and authority. The compact between the people and God was unconditional – the people had to obey God – but that between the people and the king was conditional: the people were obliged to obey him only so long as he upheld the pure teaching of God's Word, the pure worship of the Kirk, and the laws and liberties of the Scots. This implied that Parliament, as the people's representative, was supreme under God; if the King failed to obey the law of God or threatened to become a tyrant he could be resisted. (See Box 8.2, The Covenant, 27 February 1638.)

Much about the Covenant was vague. Those who framed it avoided statements that could be construed as treasonable. Some features of the Kirk condemned as corrupt or popish had been introduced by parliaments and general assemblies: references to 'free and lawful' parliaments and assemblies implied that some had been neither. The assertion of a right of resistance echoed French Calvinist writings, but the Covenant dealt with the peculiarly Scottish problem of a legitimate but absentee king: the Scots, like the English,

BOX 8.2: **The Covenant, 27 February 1638**

Much of the Covenant was taken up with the Scottish Confession of the Faith and the many Acts of Parliament expounding and confirming the doctrine and practice of the Kirk. The collective promise came near the end.

We noblemen, barons, gentlemen, burgesses, ministers and commons under subscribing, considering ... especially at this time, the danger of the true reformed religion, of the king's honour, and of the public peace of the kingdom, by the manifold innovations and evils generally contained and particularly mentioned, in our late supplications, complaints and protestations, do hereby ... resolve all the days of our life constantly to adhere unto and defend the aforesaid true religion ...

... we declare before God and men that we have no intention or desire to attempt anything that may turn to the dishonour of God or to the diminution

of the king's greatness and authority; but on the contrary we promise and swear that we shall to the utmost of our power ... stand to the defence of our dread sovereign the king's majesty, his person and authority, in the defence and preservation of the aforesaid true religion, liberties and laws of the kingdom ...

Neither do we fear the foul aspersions of rebellion, combination or what else our adversaries from their craft and malice would put upon us, seeing what we do is so well warranted, and ariseth from an unfeigned desire to maintain the true worship of God, the majesty of our king and the peace of our kingdom, for the common happiness of ourselves and posterity.

S.R. Gardiner (ed.), *Constitutional Documents of the Puritan Revolution 1625–60*
(3rd edn, Oxford, 1951), pp. 132–3.

developed the concept of **fundamental laws**. The Covenant related to James's reign as well as Charles's and encouraged passive disobedience, which would leave the King unable to impose his will. All who held public offices were required to subscribe it and many who held no office were encouraged to swear to do so. Many communities obtained copies and carefully preserved them; the names of those subscribing or swearing were noted. It was seen as a founding document: the day when it was first subscribed in Greyfriars kirk was later described as 'the most glorious marriage day of our kingdom with God'. Usually only men subscribed or swore, but sometimes women and even children did so. Some subscribed only under pressure and others refused, especially in Aberdeen and the North East, but subscribers far outnumbered refusers and the Covenant was a truly national document. It gave coherence to the resistance to Charles I and enabled the Scots to avoid the fragmentation suffered by English Puritanism in the 1640s.

The Covenant was not a comprehensive manifesto, still less a declaration of independence: Charles was seen as a misguided King of Scotland, not as an English King. The Covenanters saw it as a basis for negotiation, but Charles was not prepared to negotiate. Late in 1638, in an effort to defuse opposition, he summoned a General Assembly and a Parliament. The Assembly abolished episcopacy and liturgical innovations, returning to the Presbyterian system of government, as it existed in the 1590s; it also declared that the Kirk, not the King, should summon the Assembly once a year. Parliament set up shire war committees to raise, equip and train troops, paid for by a tax on rents. Charles refused to accept the abolition of episcopacy and raised armies in England and Ireland to reassert his authority. War was inevitable and the Covenanters were the better prepared: many who had served in foreign armies returned to train the county levies.

By early 1639 the Covenanters' confrontation with the King had become a 'British' dispute requiring a 'British' solution. They claimed that England and Scotland's grievances were similar, and proposed a union that would go further than the personal union of 1603, but not as far as the union of parliaments and peoples that James initially hoped for. This had alarmed both nations, especially the lawyers and clergy. In the churches James was probably aiming for greater congruence rather than a full union: he valued preaching more than Elizabeth did, and thought Scotland could benefit from England's 'decency' of worship. Charles believed he had nothing to learn from Scotland. The Covenanters called for a federal union of parliaments and churches, within two sovereign nations.

During 1639 the Covenanters prepared for war, but neither side was eager to fight; after gathering a makeshift army Charles came to terms in the Pacification of Berwick, but the two parties differed as to what had been agreed: Charles often reinterpreted agreements. Unable to trust him, the Covenanters set out to reduce his power so that he would be unable to harm them and sought support within England, insisting that their quarrel was not with the English but with a 'Canterburian faction': in June 1640 an angry crowd besieged Laud in Lambeth Palace. (See Figure 8.3, Archbishop Laud Besieged at Lambeth Palace, 1640.) The Scottish Parliament assembled without the

Figure 8.3 One of the earliest and most startling outbursts of popular violence in 1640–2 was an attempt by a crowd to storm Lambeth Palace, the Archbishop of Canterbury's London residence. The illustration is taken from a volume celebrating parliamentary 'triumphs', including Strafford's execution.

King's summons and stripped him of effective power. They expelled the bishops and increased the lairds' representation. All office holders had to subscribe the Covenant, or face dismissal. A Triennial Act declared that Parliament should meet at least every three years, with or without the King's summons. The **Lords of the Articles**, through which James had controlled legislation, were abolished. Outside parliamentary sessions executive power was to be exercised by a committee of estates, half of which was to remain in Edinburgh and half with the armies.

The legislation of 1640 vested effective power in Parliament, the committees of estates and the General Assembly; the King could undo these changes only by armed force. He began to raise an army, but found even less enthusiasm for his cause than in 1639; many English people saw the Scots as liberators rather than enemies and some Catholic officers were killed by their men. Charles summoned the English Parliament, then rejected its demands as unreasonable. Summoned to attend him at York, the peers sent excuses or urged him to come to terms. Charles was adamant, so his disorganised forces confronted a well-trained Scottish army. The Battle of Newburn, near Newcastle, was not a huge military defeat, but the Scots occupied Northumberland and Durham and threatened to march south if they did not receive £850 a day for their subsistence. The King did not have the money and the City refused to lend: he could raise the money only through Parliament. In the 1620s he had dissolved parliaments and raised money without consent, but he no longer had that option; Ship Money yields plummeted as tax-payers refused to pay. So long as the Scots remained in the North he would have to keep this Parliament and the Scots insisted that Parliament should be included in their negotiations with him. It seemed that he would have to make meaningful concessions.

The Long Parliament and the Scots 1640–1641

Parliament needed the Scots to ensure its survival and put pressure on the king, and some of the Scots' demands related to England. They stipulated that both parliaments should meet every two or three years; an English Triennial Act was followed by an Act stating that this Parliament could not be dissolved without its own consent. Neither kingdom should make war on the other without its Parliament's consent, and the Prince of Wales was not to marry without the consent of both parliaments. The kingdoms were to have a single confession of faith and episcopacy was to be abolished. The Scots assumed that Charles was incorrigible and that his position of exceptional weakness would not last: England could normally impose its will on Scotland. The Covenanters therefore planned to export their revolution to England, building up the power of the Parliament at the expense of the King. To prevent Charles from bringing the Kirk into line with the English Church they sought to bring the English Church into line with the Kirk.

This was not to be an 'incorporating' union, whereby two polities became one, but a confederation of two sovereign kingdoms.

If the Scots thought in British terms, the English Parliament did not. Most members wished to remedy specific grievances and punish 'evil counsellors', but then revert to traditional ways. But Charles was unwilling to admit he was wrong and made concessions with bad grace. The major issue in the first six months of what became known as the Long Parliament was the impeachment of Wentworth, now Earl of Strafford. The Scots hated Strafford because of his ill-treatment of the Ulster Scots, and, like shrewder English politicians, believed that Strafford was the only adviser who would urge Charles to resort to force. He was investigating potentially treasonable contacts between English and Scots in 1639–40, so many powerful men wanted to silence him. Strafford was accused of advising Charles to bring over his 'Irish popish' army to subjugate 'this kingdom': probably Scotland, but many feared he meant England. He allegedly told Charles that he was 'loose and absolved from all rules of government; being reduced to extreme necessity everything is to be done that power might admit'. He was charged with treason, not for an overt act against the King, but for placing him in danger by alienating his people. When the impeachment became bogged down, the Commons switched to a bill of **attainder**, which stated that Strafford was guilty of treason and should die. As the proceedings reached their climax, the King moved additional soldiers into the Tower, provoking fears of a military coup. Londoners thronged the streets in their thousands, terrified that their homes would be pounded to rubble. Amid extreme tension the bill passed the Lords; fearing for the Queen's safety, Charles gave his assent and signed the death warrant. On 11 May a crowd said to number 200,000 watched Strafford's execution.

Strafford's death eased the tension for the moment. Parliament passed Acts against Ship Money and other fiscal devices and abolished Star Chamber. But a lasting settlement was no nearer. Charles bitterly resented what he saw as Strafford's judicial murder and wanted the heads of those responsible. He still hoped to regain his power by force and was implicated in a plot to turn disgruntled army officers against Parliament. He was encouraged by divisions among his opponents. Many were worried by the growing popular involvement in politics, much of it violent. The calling of the Long Parliament raised hopes that all grievances would be redressed. Many resorted to self-help, pulling down enclosures, burning manorial records, ripping out altar rails and plundering deer parks. Those glad to see Strafford dead included many uneasy about the role played by the London crowds and the Commons' Protestation, which urged the people to defend Parliament and the Protestant religion against the Papists. (See Box 8.3, The Commons' Protestation, 3 May 1641.)

A second cause of division was religion. Some MPs called for the removal of altars and altar rails and in September the Commons voted to 'cleanse' church interiors of 'superstitious' items. The House's committee for scandalous ministers encouraged

BOX 8.3: The Commons' Protestation, 3 May 1641

Modelled on the Covenant, this claimed that there had recently been a design to overthrow the fundamental laws and the Protestant religion and establish 'an arbitrary and tyrannical government'. The Commons had drawn up a protestation to declare 'our united affections and resolutions'; other well-affected people were encouraged to subscribe.

I ... promise, vow and protest to maintain and defend, as far as lawfully I may, with my life power and estate, the true reformed religion, expressed in the doctrine of the Church of England, against all popery and popish innovation within this realm, contrary to the said doctrine and according to the duty of my allegiance to his Majesty's royal person, honour and estate; as also the power and privilege of Parliament, [and] the lawful rights and liberties of the subjects.

Here the Commons gave their endorsement to the allegation that the political crisis of May 1641 was the product of popish plotting and urged Protestants to defend Protestantism and parliaments against popery. In other words, there was a straightforward conflict between good and evil in which Protestants were urged to identify themselves. Note that:

1. Protestantism was defined in terms of the *doctrine* of the Church of England, not its worship and government.
2. Those who subscribed promised to defend the King's 'person, honour and estate', but not his powers and prerogatives. The Covenant had included a promise to defend his 'authority'.
3. On the other hand, they promised to defend the 'power and privilege' of Parliament.

Kenyon, *Stuart Constitution*, pp. 200–1.

parishioners to denounce their pastors and to install **lecturers** in the place of those who failed to preach. Ministers who failed to wear a surplice or use the Prayer Book went unpunished. Laudian clergy were summoned before the committee and harassed by puritan parishioners. In many parishes a puritan reformation was imposed by a 'godly' minority, not warranted by law and widely unpopular. Religion also divided English and Scots. The Scots wanted to abolish episcopacy 'root and branch'. They helped promote a massive petition for abolition in late 1640 but no bill was introduced until June 1641, after the Lords refused to expel the bishops from their House; it failed to pass the Commons. The Scots had become increasingly unpopular, because of their interference in English affairs and the cost and ill-discipline of their army. Their English allies promised much and delivered little, and the Scots were increasingly prepared to leave contentious issues to be settled later. They agreed the Treaty of London with King and Parliament in August; it did not mention abolishing episcopacy.

Charles left for Scotland soon after. He had earlier agreed to disband his English army, but had hopes of the Scots army, which remained in England. His prospects were badly damaged by 'the Incident', a botched attempt to kidnap three leading lords; it was not certain that Charles was implicated, but most assumed that he was. He was forced to concede that henceforth in Scotland Parliament should approve his choice of ministers, a concession noted in London. His hopes of setting Scots against English were finally destroyed in late October by news of a bloody rebellion in Ireland.

The Irish Rising of 1641

The calling of the Long Parliament and Strafford's impeachment encouraged all elements of Irish society to hope for the redress of grievances. A mixed delegation, Protestant and Catholic, travelled to London to offer evidence against Strafford and seek a return to government under the 'municipal and fundamental laws of England'. Wentworth had united all groups against him, but religion soon divided them again. The King talked of confirming the Graces, but lacked the power to deliver. The Catholic delegates returned fearful that the English and Scots would strip the King of his power and destroy Catholicism in all three kingdoms. It was rumoured that English Catholics were ready to rise in defence of the King and Queen. A pre-emptive strike could be seen as self-defence and as preserving the King's lawful authority. Whereas the English and Scots believed their safety depended on reducing the King's power, the safety of the Irish depended on maintaining it. Once the rising started, other groups joined in, with agendas of their own.

It started among Gaelic landowners in Ulster, who had lost, or feared losing, their lands. They aimed to seize key forts and wring concessions from the Dublin government; instead they triggered a major popular revolt. One of their leaders, Sir Phelim O'Neill, claimed to have a commission from the King to take up arms on his behalf. This was just a legal document with the Great Seal attached, but it was seen as legitimising the rising, including attacks on English settlers and their property.

The Ulster rising was initiated by the main losers in the plantation. In Leinster the Old English were far more numerous: most still had their estates but risked losing them if plantation continued. They usually stressed their loyalty to the Crown and respect for the law, but many joined the rising, for two reasons. First, as the popular revolt spread from Ulster, armed bands plundered settlers' goods and cattle, and Old English landowners feared their tenants might do the same unless they joined the rising. Second, the Dublin government responded to a failed attempt to seize the city with random and brutal reprisals against Catholics; it rejected pleas from some of the Old English for arms to defend themselves. Similarly, the Catholic gentry of Munster were driven to take up arms by pre-emptive reprisals by the president. By doing so they kept control over the peasantry, so Munster saw relatively little popular violence.

The Ulster insurgency triggered a wide-ranging movement to reverse and avenge a century of conquest, expropriation and atrocity. It involved both Gaelic Irish and Old English: 'distrust, aversion, force and fear united the two parties which, since the [twelfth-century] conquest, had always been the most opposite'. It offered the dispossessed an opportunity to recover their lands and debtors a chance to cancel their debts. It also offered an opportunity for revenge. Over much of the country the English were few and isolated, so their homes could be plundered and burned with impunity; some were tortured, to make them reveal where their valuables were hidden. But the resentment went deeper: the Irish hated English arrogance and contempt for Irish culture. They took revenge through humiliation, stripping men and women of their clothing (a mark of ethnic allegiance and social status) and turning them naked into a hostile countryside in winter. Recently buried corpses were dug up and thrown in ditches, or reburied face down: the Irish believed this would ensure that their souls ended up in hell. Encouraged by their priests, the people desecrated Protestant bibles, prayer books and pulpits – revenge for the destruction of shrines, images and pilgrimage centres. Ministers were maltreated and humiliated.

The rising saw very extensive violence against English Protestants, but not against English Catholics or Scots. There were a number of massacres, mostly by drowning or burning rather than the killing of individuals: the victims were driven into rivers or herded into barns. The largest drowning, at Portadown, was of about 100 people. It is impossible to estimate how many died overall: many must have died of exposure. It seems clear that deliberate killings involved fewer victims than those of the Elizabethan conquest – Smerwick for example – and there was no equivalent of the devastation and mass starvation in Ulster in 1601–2. It seems also that the clergy restrained the people – there were few recorded cases of rape – and urged them to concentrate on symbolic violence. Nevertheless, reports of wholesale murder and torture quickly spread to England and Scotland: some estimates of the numbers killed exceeded the total English Protestant population in Ireland. (See Figure 8.4, Alleged Atrocities Against the English in the Irish Rising.) The Dublin government insisted that the entire Catholic population was implicated in the rising. The most influential account, published in 1646 by Sir John Temple, claimed that the Old English had been planning the rising for years and aimed to kill the entire English population; in fact, many refused to join the rising and others did so reluctantly. Like Elizabethan servitors, Temple impugned the loyalty of the Old English, hoping to make their lands available for English settlers.

News of the rising led to panic in England. Rumours spread that the Irish had landed and were slaughtering men, women and children. For the King it was a disaster. He had tried to separate the English and Scottish parliaments, but the rising brought them together to defend the Protestant interest. In London the Commons had just rejected a proposal that Parliament should have a veto on the King's choice of ministers. After news of the rising arrived, the House resolved that, if the King refused to remove 'evil counsellors', it would provide for Ireland without him. It also approved the Grand Remonstrance, a comprehensive denunciation of the King's misgovernment, and voted (narrowly) to print it – an appeal to the people against the King. On 3 December came news of O'Neill's alleged commission; four days later a militia bill to transfer the King's control over the armed forces to Parliament was brought into the Commons. The rising and O'Neill's commission forced MPs to consider whether they could trust the King with an army: the majority decided that they could not.

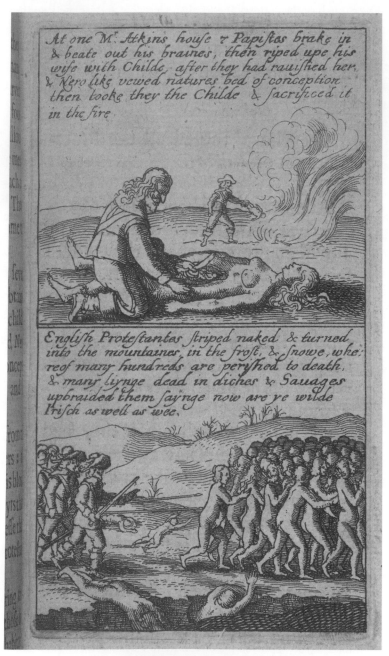

Figure 8.4 This was one of numerous accounts of the atrocities, real or invented, against the English during the Irish rising. They were designed to reinforce English preconceptions about the savagery and perfidy of Irish Catholics and the need for the complete subjugation of Ireland.

The Coming of Civil War in England 1641–1642

In 1640 the King was too isolated politically to fight a civil war. By the autumn of 1641 he had disbanded the army raised in 1640, and failed to win the Scots' support. But in the summer of 1642 he was able to fight with some prospect of success, despite repeatedly showing that he did not honour agreements and wished to re-establish his authority by force. The army plot in May 1641 was followed by another in the autumn, together with the 'Incident'. Charles returned to London on 25 November accompanied by aggressive army officers, or 'cavaliers', who picked fights with citizens and apprentices. By the end of the year a temporary barracks, big enough for 500 soldiers, had been erected outside Whitehall Palace. In January 1642 Charles, with several hundred soldiers, tried unsuccessfully to arrest five leading MPs in the Commons; he left amid cries of 'privilege of Parliament'.

All of this would suggest that Charles could not be trusted to rule responsibly but for many fears of a military coup were offset by fears of revolution from below. Most MPs had hoped for a return to responsible monarchy and moderate Protestantism. Instead, a new spiral of distrust drove the King to use force and his opponents to dismantle the Crown's powers. His right to choose his ministers and command the armed forces was challenged, as was his supremacy over the Church. The Commons encouraged a radical reformation in the parishes, although they had no authority to do so: the Lords pointedly ordered that parish worship should continue unchanged. The Commons' leaders sought popular support. The Protestation invited popular subscription – echoes of the Covenant. The Grand Remonstrance denounced Charles's misgovernment and put forward a programme of radical reforms. (See Box 8.4, The Grand Remonstrance, 1641.) The Commons welcomed petitions, especially against innovations in the Church. Nearly a thousand were received, some accompanied by threatening crowds. Many were printed, encouraging others to petition as well. The collapse of press censorship, unenforceable without Star Chamber, meant that news of riots, rumours and iconoclasm, and disparaging stories about Laudian clergymen, were widely disseminated. Politics and politicians were subjected to unprecedented public scrutiny and political and religious issues were debated with a new freedom. Although radical ideas were developed, conservative opinions also found a voice: in 1642 there were numerous petitions against puritan disruption of parish life.

This dissemination of news was not new, but the scale and intensity of reporting were, as was the extent that it led to disorder. The crowds that poured into London's streets while the King considered his response to Strafford's attainder bill were matched on the night the Commons debated printing the Grand Remonstrance: a thousand armed young men gathered at Westminster and it was said that, if printing had been rejected, they would have stormed the House. Later, in an effort to end the stalemate between the Houses, crowds prevented the bishops from taking their seats in the Lords. The King's

BOX 8.4: **The Grand Remonstrance, 1641**

This was a comprehensive condemnation, by the Commons, of the King's misgovernment, again couched in terms of a popish plot, now (allegedly) proved by the Irish rising. Approved by only one House it had no legal force. It offered a series of remedies for grievances, which would have stripped the King of most of his prerogatives: here the Commons claimed a right to veto his choice of ministers or officials on the most flimsy and subjective grounds – for example, accusing someone of being 'a known favourer of papists'.

That his Majesty be humbly petitioned by both Houses to employ such councillors, ambassadors and other ministers ... as the parliament may have cause to confide in, without which we cannot give his Majesty such supplies for support of his own estate, nor such assistance to the Protestant party beyond the sea, as is desired.

It may often fall out that the Commons may have just cause to take exceptions at some men for being councillors, and yet not charge those men with crimes, for there be grounds of difference which lie not in proof [and] there are others which, though they may be proved, yet are not legally criminal [for example] to be a known favourer of Papists, or to have been very forward in defending or countenancing some great offenders questioned in Parliament ... we may have great reason to be earnest with his Majesty not to put his great affairs into such hands though we may be unwilling to proceed against them in any legal ways of charge or impeachment.

Kenyon, *Stuart Constitution*, pp. 216–17.

attempt to arrest the Five Members was followed by a *coup d'état* in London, in which a 'committee of safety' took over the City's government and militia. Fearing he was no longer safe, Charles left London. The two Houses passed the militia bill and seized key towns, notably Hull; they claimed that their militia 'ordinance' had the authority of a statute, even though it had not received the royal assent. As the King toured the provinces looking for support, Parliament controlled the central administration and took control of the navy. Each side blamed the other for the political breakdown. Parliament claimed the Irish rising was proof of a popish plot, and the O'Neill commission proof of Charles's complicity. The King's supporters, it claimed, were mostly courtiers, papists or Arminians. The Royalists appealed to personal loyalty to the Crown and stressed the danger of revolution from below. Conservative gentlemen were suddenly conscious of the fragility of order and Charles's advisers tapped in to their anxieties. A royal declaration of June 1642 stressed the benefits of England's mixed and balanced constitution and argued that its balance had been upset by Parliament's appeal to the people. It would only be a matter of time, the King declared, until the people, realising their own strength, would turn against Parliament, led by a Jack Cade or a Wat Tyler, 'destroy all rights and proprieties [properties], all distinctions of families and merit, and by this means this splendid and excellently distinguished form of government end in a dark, equal chaos of confusion'. These fears, shared by many lower down the social scale, enabled the King to embark on a civil war. He raised his standard at Nottingham on 22 August 1642.

Conclusion

The complex interaction between the three kingdoms in this period can be summed up as follows.

In England there was widespread dissatisfaction with Charles's fiscal and religious policies, but it rarely took the form of open defiance or resistance. Nobles no longer had private armies, peasant riots were suppressed and criticism of the bishops was punished. Taxes were paid – indeed, Ship Money yields were exceptionally high. In 1637 England was calm: there was no hint yet of the wave of popular violence that erupted in 1640.

Until 1637 Scotland was deceptively calm. James VI had done much to bring the nobles under control, but they were still militarily more formidable than their English counterparts. Outrage at the introduction of the Prayer Book gave a focus for dissatisfaction and Presbyterianism offered a means of organisation that English dissidents lacked; Charles then played into the Covenanters' hands by summoning Parliament and the General Assembly. The shire committees provided a military organisation and the many returning soldiers ensured that the Covenanters' army was more effective (and motivated) than Charles's militia-based rabble. In 1639–40 the military balance within Britain for once favoured Scotland and, even more unusually, many English people saw the Scots as liberators.

Irish Catholic resistance to English Protestant rule had apparently been broken by military conquest and plantation. The rising of 1641 was a desperate response to the imminent collapse of royal power and the growing threat of an Anglo-Scottish drive to root out Catholicism. The English authorities responded with a mixture of military weakness and random but brutal reprisals and the outbreak of civil war in England prevented any serious attempt to suppress the rebels.

SUGGESTIONS FOR FURTHER READING

The literature on this period is substantial and complex, partly because it has been exhaustively researched, partly because many writers integrate material on England, Scotland and Ireland. This is true of S.R. Gardiner, *History of England 1603–42* (10 vols., London, 1883–4), a monumental work far ahead of its time. More recent overviews include two by C. Russell: one narrative, *The Fall of the British Monarchies 1637–42* (Oxford, 1991), and one thematic, *The Causes of the English Civil War* (Oxford, 1990); and T. Harris, *Rebellion: England's First Stuart Kings* (Oxford, 2014). Shorter studies include A.I. Macinnes, *The British Revolution 1629–60* (Basingstoke, 2005), which stresses the crucial impact of the Covenanter revolution. • On the politics of 1625–9, two works stand out: C. Russell, *Parliaments and English Politics 1621–9* (Oxford, 1979) and R. Cust, *The Forced Loan and English Politics*

1626–8 (Oxford, 1987) (of wider significance than the title might suggest). Cust has also written the best biography of *Charles I* (Harlow, 2005). • On the Personal Rule of 1629–40, Russell offers a concise and lucid discussion in *The Crisis of Parliaments, 1509–1660* (Oxford, 1971). There is a much fuller account in K. Sharpe, *The Personal Rule of Charles I* (New Haven, 1992), which is based on massive research and is unusually sympathetic to the King. • On the judges and the law, see W.J. Jones, *Politics and the Bench: the Judges and the English Civil War* (London, 1979). • On Scotland in the 1630s, apart from the works by Russell, Harris and Macinnes cited above, see J.S. Morrill (ed.), *The Scottish National Covenant in its British Context* (Edinburgh, 1990), L.A.M. Stewart, 'Authority, Agency and the Reception of the Scottish National Covenant of 1638', in R. Armstrong and T. Ó Hannracháin (eds.), *Insular Christianity: Alternative Models of the Church in Britain and Ireland c.1570–c.1700* (Manchester, 2012), and A.I. Macinnes, 'The "Scottish Moment", 1638–45', in J. Adamson (ed.), *The English Civil War* (Basingstoke, 2009). • For Ireland, a useful starting point is T.W. Moody, F.X. Martin and F.J. Byrne, *A New History of Ireland vol. III (1530–1685)* (Oxford, 1976). There are first-rate recent textbooks by R. Gillespie, *Seventeenth-Century Ireland* (Dublin, 2006) and S.J. Connolly, *Divided Kingdom: Ireland 1630–1800* (Oxford, 2008). A. Clarke, *The Old English in Ireland 1625–42* (Dublin, 1966) was a pioneering work. • On the 1641 rising, see the long chapter in N. Canny, *Making Ireland British*, several chapters in Edwards, Lenihan and Tait (eds.), *Age of Atrocity* and E. Darcy, *The Irish Rebellion of 1641 and the Wars of the Three Kingdoms* (Woodbridge, 2013). • The literature on England in 1640–2 is extraordinarily rich. Gardiner, *History of England*, IX and X, offers an excellent starting point. Key works include Russell, *Fall of the British Monarchies*, A. Fletcher, *The Outbreak of the English Civil War* (London, 1981), J. Adamson, *The Noble Revolt: the Overthrow of Charles I* (London, 2007), D. Cressy, *England on Edge: Crisis and Revolution 1640–2* (Oxford, 2006) and J. Walter, *Understanding Popular Violence in the English Revolution: the Colchester Plunderers* (Cambridge, 1999).

SUMMARY

- Charles I was not a man to avoid confrontation if he believed he was in the right. Convinced that 'popular' MPs were undermining his rightful authority, he asserted his authority and threatened them with the full weight of his wrath. The threats, far from cowing opposition, intensified it. The men who impeached Buckingham or pushed through the Petition of Right were angry, frightened and frustrated that they could not engage in dialogue with the King; in a political system which depended on give and take, Charles's stubborn belief that he was right and his critics were wrong was dangerous.
- Between 1629 and 1637 Charles I's regime showed how far it was possible to stretch the letter of the law with the approval of the judges. In the Ship Money case the judges acknowledged that the King had the right to act as he saw fit if he judged that there was an emergency; they did not feel it was their role to consider whether there really was an emergency or if the King's response to it was appropriate. As a result the judges endorsed what were effectively changes in the law, usurping the legislative role of Parliament.

- Of all the fateful decisions made by Charles I, the most disastrous was his insistence on imposing an English-style Prayer Book on Scotland. Quite apart from the Book's content, Charles assumed that he possessed a royal supremacy over the Church of Scotland, which he did not: if there was any supreme authority in the Kirk it was the General Assembly. Having stirred up fierce resistance Charles summoned the Convention of Estates and the General Assembly, ensuring that the Covenanter revolution was carried through by legitimate authorities.

- One persistent theme of Charles I's reign was his refusal to make concessions; when he did, he did so with visible reluctance. Throughout 1641 he cherished hopes of reasserting his authority by force. He hoped to use the English army raised in 1640 to expel Parliament and planned a military coup to enable him to save Strafford. He returned to London late in 1641 accompanied by a large body of 'Cavaliers', many of them quartered in a barracks outside Whitehall Palace. His obvious refusal to negotiate in good faith drove his opponents to demand further restrictions on his powers.

QUESTIONS FOR STUDENTS

1. Account for the growth of mistrust between Charles I and the English Parliament between 1625 and 1629.

2. Why was there so little opposition to the Personal Rule in England between 1629 and 1637?

3. Why was Wentworth's rule in Ireland so unpopular?

4. Why did the Covenanters develop and implement such a radical programme?

5. Why did the execution of Strafford not lead to a political settlement?

6. What was the Irish rising of 1641 trying to achieve?

9 British Wars, English Conquests 1642–1660

TIMELINE

1642	Formation of Confederation of Kilkenny; King raises standard at Nottingham
1643	Parliament establishes assessment and excise; Solemn League and Covenant
1644	Marston Moor
1644–5	Self-Denying Ordinance; establishment of New Model Army
1645	Naseby
1646	King surrenders to Scots
1647	Commons agree Declaration of Dislike; army organises (sets up General Council) and takes political stance (especially in Declaration of 14 June). Showdown with Parliament, army marches into London; divisions within army lead to Putney debates; King agrees Engagement with Scots
1648	Second civil war; Scots invade England, defeated at Preston; army again marches into London; Pride's Purge (6 December)
1649	Commons set up high court of justice which condemns King to death: executed 30 January; monarchy and House of Lords abolished, England declared a Commonwealth or Free State (alias 'the Rump'); Cromwell to Ireland: massacres of Drogheda and Wexford

1649–52	New Model conquers Ireland
1650–1	Charles II in Scotland; invades England, defeated at Worcester
1652	Rump passes Act for punitive land settlement in Ireland
1652–4	First Anglo-Dutch war
1653	Rump dissolved; Nominated Parliament summoned and dissolved; Instrument of Government adopted, Cromwell appointed Lord Protector: beginning of Protectorate
1654	First Protectorate Parliament
1655	Major Generals established
1656	Second Protectorate Parliament; draws up Humble Petition and Advice, including offer of Crown
1657	Cromwell refuses the Crown, accepts the rest of the Humble Petition
1658	Oliver dies; succeeded by son Richard who summons Parliament
1659	Army forces Richard to dissolve Parliament; army summons, then dismisses, Rump; December army recalls Rump again in the face of Monk's invasion from Scotland; 'Old Protestant' coup in Ireland
1660	Monk's army enters England; survivors among MPs excluded at Pride's Purge readmitted to Commons, who agree to take steps to bring Long Parliament to an end and hold elections for a Convention; Convention invites Charles II to return

Introduction

Events in Scotland and Ireland continued to exercise a major influence on England in the 1640s, helped by England's deep, complex internal divisions. Both Parliament and King hoped to bring the Scots army into the English civil war. The Scots initially plumped for Parliament, only to be disillusioned again by its failure to deliver on its promises. In 1647 a section of the Scots nobility signed an agreement with Charles, which fatally divided the Covenanters. Parliament had no intention of wooing the Irish Confederate Catholics, but at times Charles was desperate enough to do so, doing himself great political harm: the prospect of an Irish invasion of England in 1649 helped bring about his execution.

The divisions within England were ultimately contained by the New Model, which defeated the Royalists and pushed through Pride's Purge and the King's execution. The New Model was not popular, which it saw as confirmation of its own rectitude: in its own eyes it was a despised minority, raised up by God to overcome the ungodly. Its self-confidence was increased by its conquests of Ireland and Scotland. Both were inspired by the threat from Charles II, proclaimed in both kingdoms on the news of his father's execution. Having conquered them, the English government and army set out to remould them. In Scotland the process was relatively limited: the Kirk and the Scottish legal profession were too deeply entrenched to be significantly changed, but the power of the nobility was undermined and continuing disorder made an English military presence necessary. In Ireland a bloody conquest was followed by a programme of land confiscation and ethnic cleansing, designed to clear some areas of Catholics altogether and to separate Catholic landowners from their tenants.

War in Three Kingdoms 1642–1646: Ireland

In early 1642 the Scottish and English parliaments prepared to send armies to Ireland and the English Parliament passed the Adventurers Act, encouraging people to invest in the reconquest of Ireland, with a prospect of forfeited 'rebel' lands. The Irish Catholics had numbers, but needed a nationwide organisation, which only the clergy could provide, reinforced by spiritual authority over the laity. The Confederation of Kilkenny, created in June 1642, had a General Assembly, elected on the basis of parliamentary constituencies, but by Catholics only. This elected an executive body, a supreme council of twenty-four. There was to be no distinction between provinces or between Irish and Old English. All Catholics were to take an oath of association, swearing allegiance to the King, and promising to obey the supreme council and to respect the King's prerogatives and the privileges of the Irish Parliament.

The oath, with its emphasis on constitutional monarchy and English law, showed Old English influence. Many Old English would have been satisfied with clandestine worship, but the clergy insisted on freedom of worship and many wanted to retain parish churches seized from the Protestants. War aims differed. Some aimed to avoid defeat in Ireland and use Irish resources to re-establish Charles in England. Others hoped for complete victory in Ireland and the full restoration of Catholicism. These were largely, but not entirely, divisions between Old English and Irish, and between laity and clergy. They became deeper when a papal nuncio, Giovanni Battista Rinuccini, demanded complete freedom of worship for Catholics and the full re-establishment of the Church. In 1646, as the King faced defeat in England, the General Council agreed to a truce. Rinuccini summoned a council of bishops, which declared that Catholics need not obey the council, and nominated a council of his own.

Between 1642 and 1646 the war in Ireland was inconclusive; much of the fighting was localised and small-scale. The Catholics lacked experienced commanders. The Protestants were divided, with the Dublin government's forces commanded by the Royalist Marquis of Ormond, a Scottish army in Ulster, and a token force sent by the English Parliament, not to mention various local commanders and warlords. Ireland's economy was disrupted by war and plague, and coin was in short supply. Short of weapons and especially artillery, both sides avoided pitched battles, concentrating on sieges and raids. There was much plundering and brigandage; scorched-earth tactics were widely used.

The Confederates did not aim to create an independent Ireland, which would require the support of France or Spain, currently at war; without foreign help a military victory in Ireland was unlikely. Charles was reluctant to buy support with concessions that would alienate his English subjects. In 1643, when the Scots promised the English Parliament military assistance, Charles and the Confederates agreed a truce and Irish soldiers, most if not all Protestants, were sent to England; Parliament claimed they were all Catholics. As Charles's fortunes waned in 1644–5 he promised to repeal the laws against Catholic worship and office-holding, to readmit Catholic bishops to Parliament and to appoint a Catholic lord lieutenant. His agent, the Earl of Glamorgan, promised more and the Queen more still. Charles never secured the troops he wanted and his war effort collapsed. Documents showing his dealings with the Confederates were published under the title *The King's Cabinet Opened*. (See Figure 9.1, *The King's Cabinet Opened*, 1645.) His dealings with the Confederates brought him little military benefit and enormous political harm.

War in Three Kingdoms 1642–1646: England and Scotland

The first civil war was much the largest that England had ever seen. Few areas were totally free of fighting and some were fought over continually. Estimates suggest that one third of adult males were in arms at some time, and at least one tenth at any given time; 80,000 were killed in fighting and 100,000 died of disease and other war-related causes, which suggests that a higher percentage of the English population died in the civil wars than in the First World War. (The figures for Ireland and Scotland were much higher.) The scale of the fighting brought suffering and destruction to many areas and exposed much of the population to the reasons why the war was fought: the explosion of news continued. Issues and principles influenced the taking of sides. Many farmers, craftsmen and labourers made up their own minds rather than following their landlords or masters. Each side developed an identity in opposition to a

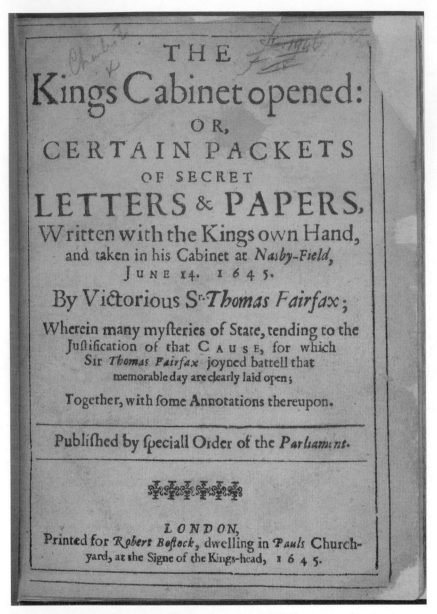

Figure 9.1 After the Battle of Naseby, the army seized many documents showing the extent of the King's dealings with the Confederate Catholics. Parliament gleefully ordered their publication.

hostile 'other'. Parliamentarians portrayed Royalists as vain, drunken and immoral, a menace to any decent woman. Royalists saw Roundheads as hypocrites, whose masks of godliness concealed greed, contempt for lawful authority and a determination to make their neighbours' lives miserable. (See Figure 9.2, Caricatures of Cavalier and Roundhead, 1642.) Years of conflict over church ales and Sunday observance underlay

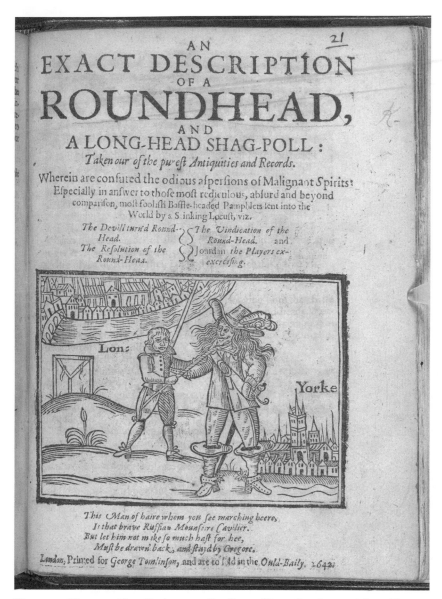

Figure 9.2 The mutual hostility between Cavalier and Roundhead was reinforced by caricatures like this. The Royalist is flashily dressed, with large boots and a broad-brimmed hat (with a feather), a beard and moustache and of course long hair. The Roundhead has short hair, no beard or moustache and is simply dressed. Royalists were accused of drunkenness and lechery, Roundheads were allegedly hypocrites.

the mutual hatred of Royalist and Roundhead. Popular Royalism originated not in the bovine obedience of unthinking peasants but in resentment of the banning of traditional pastimes and the suppression of fun and was reinforced by the King's identification with traditional values.

Initially both sides lacked experience of warfare: Oliver Cromwell started soldiering in his forties. Some experienced soldiers returned from the Continent, but military training took time. In geographical terms, Parliament's main strength lay in London, the South East and East Anglia, while the King was strongest in the North, and Wales; other areas were contested. The first major battle, Edgehill, in October 1642 was inconclusive, but the King's army marched on London and was stopped by the City militia at Turnham Green, near Chiswick. Parliament controlled the central government and probably had greater public support, but after Edgehill it was clear that there would be no quick victory and 1643 saw numerous inconclusive engagements. Parliament raised its forces on a county basis, using the militia, but county officials placed local defence before national considerations. The King granted commissions to raise forces to individuals, which did not make for a co-ordinated war effort. The two sides seemed evenly matched.

In 1643 Parliament addressed the problem of funding the war. Initially reluctant to raise taxes without the King's assent, it created the **assessment** and the **excise**, which would transform Parliament's ability to raise money and make possible a much more powerful state. (See below, Chapter 12.) In the short term Parliament needed an immediate accession of military strength. The Covenanters' army was the most effective in Britain. Negotiations began before Edgehill, to facilitate closer political co-operation while maintaining the kingdoms' separate legal and constitutional identities, endeavouring to bring the Church of England into line with the Kirk. The Solemn League and Covenant included a promise to preserve the King's 'just power and greatness', which might imply that unjust use of power could be resisted. At its heart lay a commitment to reform religion in England and Ireland 'in doctrine, worship, discipline and government, according to the Word of God and the example of the best reformed churches'. Both parties promised to root out popery, '**prelacy**', heresy and schism and to punish 'malignants' and 'incendiaries' (Royalists). Although the commitment to abolish episcopacy was clear, there was no explicit promise to establish Presbyterianism. The Scots undertook to send an army of 20,000 into England and Parliament promised £30,000 a month to pay for it. Experience should perhaps have made the Scots sceptical: much of the £300,000 promised by Parliament in 1640–1 had never been paid.

A Scots minister wrote, 'The English were for a civil league, we for a religious Covenant.' Parliament had no intention of establishing Presbyterianism in a form acceptable to the Scots. It abolished bishops, forbade the use of the Prayer Book and traditional festivals, including Christmas, but refused to set up a systematic parish-based system of church discipline or the hierarchical organisation needed to make it effective. Parishes could elect **elders** and groups of parishes could send representatives to '**classes**', or synods, but there was no provision for presbyteries and coercive discipline. The Scots became concerned at the growth in England of '**gathered churches**', which opted out of the national Church and operated their own forms of discipline. Some adopted practices which the Scots regarded as heretical, such as adult baptism and lay preaching. (See below, Chapter 15.) Although these radicals were not very numerous, they were conspicuous in London and some units of the army.

Apart from Parliament's stance on religion the Scots felt their military contribution was undervalued, despite their capturing Newcastle and tipping the balance at Marston Moor in 1644. They were starved of resources, forcing them to live on **free quarter** and plunder. When Parliamentarian commanders failed to follow up Marston Moor, mainly because their men were sick and exhausted, they were accused of half-heartedness or treachery. The more radical MPs called for a collective act of self-sacrifice, whereby aristocratic commanders (notably the earls of Essex and Manchester) would resign their commissions and new officers would be appointed on merit. Despite fierce opposition the Self-Denying Ordinance passed and the officer corps was substantially remodelled. Alongside regional armies in the North and West the Ordinance made possible the creation of a national ('New Model') army. This developed a reputation for religious radicalism, which led many to transfer from other armies or join as volunteers. Some regiments became 'gathered churches', with long prayer meetings and lay preaching. It became the most generously resourced and disciplined army and won a crucial victory at Naseby in June 1645.

The creation of the New Model increased the Scots' marginalisation; there were calls to drive them back over the border. Parliament had agreed that the English and Scots should co-operate in imposing a settlement on Ireland, but when it presented the Newcastle Propositions to the King the Scots were not consulted or mentioned. By the end of 1645 they saw Parliament and army as hostile to the federal union of England and Scotland; Charles, as King of both kingdoms, stood for union and now seemed to the Scots a lesser evil than Parliament – and much less dangerous. For his part, Charles saw the Scots as less dangerous than Parliament. When he suffered his final defeat he surrendered to the Scots.

Reactions to the English Civil War 1642–1646

In 1642 Parliament probably enjoyed much wider popular support than the King, but it was soon seen as acting more illegally than the King. It acted on the principle that those not active for Parliament should be treated as enemies. Many accused of 'malignancy' were interrogated by parliamentary committees and committed to gaol, often on the basis of hearsay evidence; many had lands confiscated without due process of law. To mobilise men and money Parliament established **county committees**, chosen for their zeal for the cause, real or pretended; some were from established county families, but most were humbler men, with no tradition of service. They were accused of arbitrary imprisonment, embezzlement and extortion. Rival committees waged war on each other, with accusations of maltreatment and even torture.

The county committees oversaw the assessment and collection of taxation, which gave them opportunities for profit and victimisation. Taxation in some counties was more than twelve times higher than before the civil war. But money came in too slowly to meet the armies' needs, so soldiers resorted to **free quarter**, demanding what they wanted and giving promises to pay that might (or might not) be honoured by Parliament. Often, soldiers simply took what they wanted. (See Box 9.1, The Burden of Soldiers.) They had weapons and civilians did not; men who normally lived in poverty ate and drank well, helping themselves to their hosts' possessions, with the occasional bonus of sacking a town after a siege: 'plunder' entered the English language in 1642. Apart from quartering soldiers, civilians faced demands from county committees and garrison commanders for food, horses and work on fortifications. Reluctance was interpreted as 'malignancy': a garrison commander in Warwickshire demanded the work 'upon pain of imprisonment and plundering'. Populations seen as hostile suffered plunder and destruction; officers and ministers encouraged the vandalising of churches.

If Parliamentarians behaved badly, Royalists were little better. Initially, the King's men sought some form of consent to the taxes they levied, but the worst atrocities were committed by Royalists. Military convention indicated that, if a besieged town

BOX 9.1: **The Burden of Soldiers**

These extracts are from the return of the parish of East Barnet, Hertfordshire, to the county sub-committee of accounts in December 1644. Hertfordshire was strongly Parliamentarian and saw little fighting; there is no suggestion that the parish was being punished for Royalist 'disaffection'.

It also appeareth daily and is notorious amongst us that divers pretending to be soldiers and other loose persons come to the inhabitants' houses in a bold and terrifying way, craving relief, both in meat and money, which the inhabitants have been, for fear in a manner inferred, to yield them, and that charge having continued for a long time hath been and is an extreme burden unto them.

Also during the time of quartering soldiers amongst us, divers sheep, swine and poultry have been taken away by the soldiers, some in the presence of the owners, some by stealth to the very great burden of the inhabitants. Also during the said time divers gates in the several grounds of the inhabitants as also their hedges and fences have been commonly broken, spoiled and carried away by the soldiers and some more corn ... hath been taken and given to horses and spoiled.

And what is as grievous as any, the houses and lands of the inhabitants in these times some cannot be let at all, [some can be let only at much reduced rents] and few tenants are able to pay those rents they take grounds at, whereby the inhabitants are impoverished extremely.

A. Thomson (ed.),
The Impact of the First Civil War on Hertfordshire 1642–7 (Hertford, 2007), p. 118.

did not surrender before the walls were breached, the besiegers could sack it and kill the garrison, although the latter was rare. Parliamentarians slaughtered the garrison of Basing House, but a newspaper wrote: 'You must remember … they were most of them Papists.' Some women in the garrison were killed, others were treated 'somewhat coarsely', but left with some clothes. (Rape seems to have been rare.) After Charles's truce with the Confederates, Parliament decreed that any Irish Catholic taken in arms should be killed. Some Irish soldiers and camp followers were killed; Prince Rupert retaliated by killing English prisoners, remarking that both English and Irish were the King's subjects. Rupert also ordered the sack of Bolton, where between 1,200 and 1,500 were killed, including at least 700 civilians.

In time the burden on civilians became unbearable and the war itself became the enemy. **Clubmen** appeared in many counties: farmers and craftsmen who appeared, armed, to protest against the soldiers. Sometimes they complained of one side, often they condemned both. They generally demanded a return to the days 'before the civil wars', when counties were governed by established gentry, not upstart committee men, taxes were low and disputes were settled by due process of law. By 1646 there were also complaints about religious changes and the banning of Christmas. With the war over, Parliament was urged to end wartime taxation, disband the armies and, above all, reach a settlement with the King. Parliament, however, insisted on stringent safeguards against future misrule and confirmation of the abolition of episcopacy. As the taxation and armies continued, popular impatience grew and there were calls to settle with the King on almost any terms: defeated and powerless he posed no threat, while Parliament's behaviour was increasingly seen as tyrannical. Aware that opinion was shifting in his favour, Charles waited for his enemies to fall out among themselves.

The Rise of the New Model Army 1646–1647

The key to the complex politics of 1646–9 was the King's refusal to make meaningful concessions. In 1642–6 Parliament sought a settlement based on the traditional constitution, with safeguards against the King's abusing his power. At first it hoped that, if it avoided defeat, he could be persuaded to agree reasonable terms. Failure to reach agreement showed that they would have to defeat and impose terms on him, but Charles did not accept any obligation to make concessions. He saw his powers as God-given, not his to trade away for political advantage. This kernel of conviction was obscured by his often devious behaviour. He offered concessions less substantial than they seemed and reinterpreted what his opponents thought he had agreed. He offered to concede control over the **militia** and choice of ministers for a period or for his lifetime, but not in perpetuity. To other key demands – agreeing to the abolition of bishops and punitive measures against Royalists – he returned (more or less) consistent negatives. When the Queen urged him to agree to abolish episcopacy, Charles replied bluntly that his conscience would not allow it.

Despite his defeat Charles believed his bargaining position was strong, because he was indispensable for a viable settlement. Parliament's proposals assumed that England would remain a monarchy with Charles as King. There were few calls to depose him or abolish the monarchy. Charles's stubbornness left his opponents with two logical alternatives: to settle the kingdom on his terms, or to settle it without him. The first was unthinkable after four years of civil war; the second was simply unthinkable. Until somebody was prepared to think the unthinkable, there was no option but to continue negotiating, hoping something would turn up. The failure to reach a settlement created tension within Parliament and between Parliament and army.

In 1642–6 parties, labelled Presbyterians and Independents, appeared in Parliament. They lacked the organisation of modern political parties and consisted of a core of consistent supporters with less committed followers. The balance of power between them changed with circumstances. After the failure to follow up Marston Moor the initiative passed to the Independents. By 1646 it had swung back to the Presbyterians, led by Denzil Holles and William Prynne. Apart from a settlement with the King, they had two major objectives. First, they wanted to maintain the Church as it was – national, parish-based, with a learned clergy and orthodox Calvinist doctrine, with neither bishops nor presbyteries. The Independents championed liberty for the godly, but not for Catholics or Prayer-Book Anglicans. Their second objective was to disband the armies, especially the New Model. The army treated Parliament with outward respect, addressing it in petitions and complying with most of its commands, but ignored its prohibitions of lay preaching.

Early in 1647 the Presbyterians planned to disband the New Model and send the soldiers to Ireland. Some regiments drew up petitions to their commander in chief, Sir Thomas Fairfax, which presupposed that the army would disband, but demanded full arrears of pay, and provision for widows, orphans and maimed soldiers. Some demanded an indemnity for actions 'in time and place of war', on and off the battlefield: soldiers were being prosecuted for debt or the maltreatment of civilians. Soldiers feared magistrates and jurors would favour complainants, and that, once disbanded, they would be at civilians' mercy. When the Presbyterians heard of these petitions, Holles rushed a 'Declaration of Dislike' through a sparsely attended Commons. It described the petitioning as tantamount to mutiny, imposing conditions on Parliament and obstructing the relief of Ireland. If the petitioners persisted they would be 'looked upon as enemies of the state and opposers of the public peace'.

Faced with what they saw as an affront to their honour, officers and men debated their next move, seeking God's guidance in prayer meetings; some regiments chose 'agitators' (agents) to speak for their fellow soldiers. Officers often encouraged this, conscious of the need to maintain unity. The agitators called for a general rendezvous

BOX 9.2: **The Army's Declaration of 14 June 1647**

In this declaration, approved at a general rendezvous, the New Model asserted its right and duty to bring about a political settlement. It stresses that its proposals are warranted by Parliament's own Declarations and asserts the principle *salus populi est suprema lex* – the people's safety is the supreme law.

... we shall before disbanding proceed in our own and the kingdom's behalf to propound and plead for some provision for our and the kingdom's satisfaction and future security ... especially considering that we were not a mere mercenary army, hired to serve any arbitrary power of a state, but called forth and conjured by the several Declarations of Parliament to the defence of our own and the people's just rights and liberties. And

so we took up arms in judgment and conscience to those ends, and have so continued them, and are resolved, according to your ... Declarations, and such principles as we have received from your frequent informations, and our own common sense concerning those our fundamental rights and liberties, to assert and vindicate the just power and rights of this kingdom in Parliament, for those common ends premised against all arbitrary power, violence and oppression, and against all particular parties or interest whatsoever. The said Declarations still directing us to the equitable sense of all laws and constitutions, as dispensing with the very letter of the same, and being supreme to it when the safety and preservation of all is concerned ...

J.P. Kenyon, *The Stuart Constitution* (2nd edn, Cambridge, 1986), p. 264.

---

of the army, which agreed a Solemn Engagement not to disband until Parliament rescinded the Declaration of Dislike and guaranteed a full indemnity. It also set up a **General Council**, made up of two officers and two soldiers from every regiment, plus fifteen of the general staff; until January 1648 this was the army's decision-making body. Meanwhile, a junior officer invited the King, under house arrest in Northamptonshire, to accompany him to the army. The King, apparently, went willingly, encouraging hopes of a negotiated settlement. On 14 June the army agreed a 'declaration or representation'. (See Box 9.2, The Army's Declaration of 14 June 1647.) This demanded that Parliament should be purged of 'corrupt' and 'delinquent' members; that it should arrange for its dissolution; that future parliaments should be 'freely, equally and successively chosen' and last for only three years; and that once the misdeeds of those handling public monies had been investigated and punished, there should be a general act of oblivion.

The Declaration was followed by 'the Heads of the Proposals', presented to Charles in July. This stated that parliaments should last for two years and that as constituencies varied enormously in size, seats should be redistributed on the basis of taxation. After limiting Parliament, the Heads turned to the King. His negative voice (veto) would be limited. He would share executive power with a council of state, chosen by Parliament, which would control the armed forces for ten years. Parliament could veto his appointments to office for ten years, with a partial veto thereafter. Finally, most forms of Protestantism would be tolerated, including Common Prayer; the national Church could have bishops, but with no power over those outside the parish system.

These terms were the best Charles was offered in 1646–8, allowing him to restore the Prayer Book and bishops and gradually recover many of his powers, but he rejected them, following a riot in London. To prevent Parliament capitulating to the army, citizens and apprentices marched to Westminster. The apprentices invaded Parliament and 'carried' a resolution to invite the King to London. Members of both Houses fled to the army. Others stayed away from Westminster, leaving the Presbyterians dominant, but their resistance collapsed when the army entered London. The Commons agreed to expel the eleven Presbyterians most obnoxious to the army, which ordered the destruction of the City's fortifications. After its show of force it hoped that Parliament would prove more co-operative.

It did not. The Commons were slow to grant the army's pay. Officers and soldiers became impatient, calling for the expulsion of many more Presbyterians. There were links between the army and the Levellers, civilian radicals who, earlier in the year, had developed ideas on political reform similar to the army's. Militant soldiers and Levellers referred to their leaders as **Grandees**, remote from ordinary soldiers' concerns. By October the Grandees, worried by the extent of disaffection within the army, summoned the General Council to meet at Putney, where it discussed the Levellers' Agreement of the People. (See Box 9.3, The Agreement of the People, 28 October 1647.) The Grandees agreed that the Agreement merited serious consideration, but General Henry Ireton steered discussion onto the franchise: should numbers or wealth determine who was represented? This gave rise to a passionate debate. 'I think it's clear,' said one senior officer, 'that every man that is to live under a government ought first by his own consent to put himself under that government; and I do think that the poorest man in England is not at all bound … to that government that he hath not had a voice to put himself under.' The debate set back the Grandees' attempt to move towards consensus and they became increasingly annoyed by the Levellers' attempts to undermine their authority and portray Leveller views as the general sense of the army. The agitators were sent back to their regiments and Fairfax, much respected by his men, promised that their grievances would be remedied and that there would be free and equal elections. Most accepted his assurances, and the officers restored discipline. Parliament agreed to reduce the army by almost half, removing those with Presbyterian or Leveller sympathies. The Levellers remained influential in London, but no longer threatened the high command.

From Engagement to Purge 1647–1648

The army had restored its unity and discipline, but had few supporters outside London, and even there they were in a minority. The wider public became angry and frustrated. There were riots against the banning of Christmas, and attacks on county committees. Petitions to Parliament called for the redress of grievances and a settlement with the

BOX 9.3: The Agreement of the People, 28 October 1647

This was presented to the General Council of the Army, which resolved to consider how far its demands were compatible with the army's engagements, notably the Declaration of 14 June (see above) and the Heads of the Proposals. It asserted the legislative *and executive* supremacy of the House of Commons (by implication against King and Lords, although this was not spelt out); Parliament had increasingly assumed an executive role since 1642. Experience showed that the Commons could abuse their power so needed to be made more answerable to the people (through frequent elections and electoral reform) and by laying down 'fundamentals' (or **fundamental laws**) that Parliament could not touch. It did not call for the deposition of the King or the abolition of the monarchy, but deplored that the people 'are yet made to depend for the settlement of our peace and freedom upon him that intended our bondage and brought a cruel war upon us'. It declared:

> That the people of England being at this day very unequally distributed by counties, cities and boroughs for the election of their deputies [n.b.] in Parliament, ought to be more indifferently proportioned according to the number of the inhabitants …
>
> That the power of this and all future representatives of this nation is inferior only to theirs who choose them, and doth extend, without the consent or concurrence of any other person or persons, to the enacting, altering and repealing of laws, to the erecting and abolishing of offices and courts, to the appointing, removing and calling to account magistrates and officers of all degrees, to the making war and peace, to the treating with foreign states, and generally to whatsoever is not expressly or implicitly reserved by the represented to themselves.

Gardiner (ed.), *Constitutional Documents of the Puritan Revolution*, pp. 333–5.

King. One, from Surrey, was accompanied by 3,000 people; in a confrontation with the military, ten petitioners were killed. Parliament passed an ordinance against 'tumultuous petitioning'; in 1640–2 its leaders had welcomed such petitions as expressions of popular feeling. Several thousand regular troops were needed to keep order in London, which faced a tax strike. There were bonfires on the anniversary of the coronation; a riot forced the lord mayor to take refuge in the Tower. Parliament co-operated with the army only under duress and its behaviour became increasingly defiant.

Although a prisoner on the Isle of Wight, Charles negotiated a deal with a group of lords, who hoped, with his help, to regain power in Scotland. Under the **Engagement** the Scots undertook to restore the King's control over the militia, his veto over legislation and his right to choose his advisers in England. There would be Scots on the English Privy Council and vice versa. Charles agreed to suppress the sects and to establish Presbyterianism in England for three years. Scottish Presbyterians saw these provisions as inadequate and impractical. In England, many opposed bringing Scottish armies back into the country and establishing Presbyterianism even temporarily. For the army the Engagement showed that Charles refused to recognise his defeat as God's verdict against him. A few had talked at Putney of the need to depose or execute the King; now anger within the army spread more widely. In January 1648 the Commons voted to make no further addresses to him; the Lords concurred, but only under pressure from the army. In April civil war resumed with a Royalist rising in South Wales. For many in the army this was final proof of Charles's blasphemy and blood guilt. On the 29th a prayer meeting at Windsor vowed to bring 'Charles Stuart, that man of blood' to account for the blood that he had shed.

The second civil war was on a smaller scale. The Royalists planned local risings to divide the army and open the way for a Scottish invasion; above all they hoped to seize London. To some extent the strategy worked: the army committed 8,000 men to the siege of Pembroke, but the rest of the Welsh rising had been suppressed before a short-lived rising in Kent and the siege of Colchester. The Scots, delayed by poor organisation and political divisions, found little support and were slowed down by unseasonably bad weather. On 17 August they were resoundingly defeated by Cromwell at Preston. The Commons defiantly resolved to revoke the vote of no addresses and agreed in principle to a Presbyterian Church settlement; the eleven MPs expelled in 1647 returned. Cromwell wrote to the Speaker ascribing victory to 'the hand of God' and urging the Houses to do God's work 'and not hate His people, who are as the apple of His eye, and for whom even kings shall be reproved'. They should cherish those who live peaceably 'and they that are incapable and will not leave troubling the land may speedily be destroyed out of the land'. His meaning was clear: there should be no further negotiations. The Commons ignored him, resolving on 15 November that Charles should be restored to a position of lawful power and allowed to come to London.

In response to these resolutions a meeting of officers approved a remonstrance to Parliament. Soldiers called for direct action against Parliament and London; at least thirty petitions from regiments and garrisons supported a recent Leveller petition to Parliament. Some Grandees, led by Ireton, sought an understanding with the Levellers: the army needed all the allies it could get. When the remonstrance was presented on 20 November the Commons resolved to postpone considering it for a week, which was tantamount to a rejection. The remonstrance proposed an electorate far narrower than implied in the Agreement of the People: only those who subscribed the Agreement should be eligible to vote; later the Levellers resolved to restrict the franchise to male house-holders assessed for the poor rate, who were not servants, wage-earners or Royalists. The most striking provisions of the remonstrance related to the King. It stated that it was pointless negotiating with him as he would not keep his word. He had broken his covenant with his people and was responsible for the bloodshed of the civil wars. His popularity was another reason not to negotiate with him: the army had never valued popular opinion and the Levellers were coming to agree with them. Finally the remonstrance called for the King's trial and condemnation (but not necessarily his execution).

As Parliament insisted on continuing negotiations, the army marched on London; Fairfax declared that they would quarter in the City until all assessment arrears had been paid. As an affront to the City and Anglican sensibilities cavalry were quartered in St Paul's cathedral; there was some looting. The officers had no clear plan and seem to have hoped that Parliament would purge itself of 'corrupt' members. Their dilemma was resolved on 5 December; after an all-night debate the Commons voted that the King's latest answer was a sufficient basis for a settlement. The army's allies in Parliament drew up a list of those who had supported this vote. On the 6th Colonel Thomas Pride stood at the door with the list, arresting forty-five MPs and excluding ninety-eight. The number excluded eventually rose to 186, after some refused to make a declaration required by the army. Others stayed away in protest.

From Purge to Regicide 1648–1649

After Pride's Purge neither army nor Parliament seemed inclined to put the King on trial. New demands were drawn up, to be presented to the King by the Earl of Denbigh; on 25 December a meeting of officers resolved by an overwhelming majority that if Charles accepted them his life would be spared. He rejected them and on 1 January 1649 the Commons voted that it alone represented the people and resolved to set up a 'high court of justice', which convened on the 20th. Westminster Hall was decked out to emphasise the solemnity of the proceedings, but only about half of the 135 judges appeared. Charles refused to plead, claiming that the court had no authority to try anyone: 'if power without law may make laws' nobody's liberty or property would be safe. Most of the judges had hoped that the King would be found guilty of some token charges, reprimanded and deposed, or replaced by one of his sons. His refusal to plead made it impossible to proceed in the normal way and deprived the court of its freedom to determine his punishment: under common law, refusal to plead carried the death penalty. The court repeatedly urged him to plead, but he refused. On the 26th the court found that he was a 'tyrant, traitor and murderer' and sentenced him to be beheaded. When he tried to respond he was hurried out. Even now, the judges begged him to plead, but he refused. On 30 January he was taken to the Banqueting House, whose ceiling, painted by Rubens, showed his father being received into heaven. (See Figure 9.3, The Banqueting House, Whitehall, 'Apotheosis of James I' by Rubens.) When he tried to speak the soldiers tried to drown him out, but he was heard to say that the people had a right to have their lives and property secured by law, but not to play a part in government: 'a subject and a sovereign are clear different things'. He was said to have lost his usual stammer. When the executioner held up his head the soldiers cheered and the crowd groaned. On 6 and 7 February the monarchy and the House of Lords were abolished.

Figure 9.3 The Banqueting House is all that survives of the old Whitehall Palace. It was built as a venue for royal display and its crowning glory was Rubens's ceiling showing James I being received into heaven. It was chosen as the place for the King's execution to emphasise the overthrow of the monarchy.

For most in Parliament these outcomes were neither anticipated nor desired. They believed they had to take away the King's power to resume the war. The Confederate Catholics were making common cause with Irish Parliamentarians and on 17 January 1649 they agreed a truce with Ormond and the Royalists; Rinuccini left in February. As the Confederates now had a fleet they might be able to launch an invasion, in conjunction with the Dutch; hope of Irish assistance may have led Charles to turn down the Denbigh proposals. Although Charles's supporters agreed on the need to curb his power they could not agree how. They were under pressure from all sides, notably the Dutch and Scots: Charles's son-in-law William II, Prince of Orange, was eager to support him, and the Scots resented the English putting their King on trial. Some English Royalists suggested that he abdicate in favour of one of his sons. But Charles was not prepared to compromise: he believed that would be morally wrong and as early as 1642 was prepared to die for the monarchy: 'either I will be a glorious king or a patient martyr'. Those who hoped to frighten, bully or persuade him did not understand this. At his trial he played out his role with a dignity based on total conviction.

The English Republic

The regicide and abolition of the monarchy were carried through by Englishmen, unconcerned by reactions in Scotland and Ireland. In the 1640s most Covenanters and the more moderate Confederates thought in terms of the three kingdoms ruled by one King. Now a minority of Englishmen constructed a polity dominated by England, with Scotland and Ireland subordinate; they generally spoke of 'England', not 'Great Britain'. (See Chapter 14.) The driving forces in Britain and Ireland were the English government and army. England enjoyed internal peace and stability under administratively efficient regimes, with high standards of professionalism. The law courts functioned, taxes were paid. County committees were wound up, local government returned to near-normality. These regimes were outwardly parliamentary, which might imply that they were based on consent, but they were not, for four reasons.

First, they lacked legitimacy. They were established after the army purged Parliament and one House of Parliament set up a 'high court of justice' which tried and executed the King. His defeat in the civil war and his comportment at his trial provoked popular sympathy, compounded by the publication soon after his execution of *Eikon Basilike*, supposedly a collection of his devotional writings. Even more potent than the text was the frontispiece, showing the King kneeling, his earthly crown on the ground, a crown of thorns in his hand, and his eyes fixed on a heavenly crown. (See Figure 9.4, *Eikon Basilike*.) It vividly expressed the divine right of kings, established Charles as 'the royal martyr' and undermined attempts by the regimes of the 1650s to claim legitimacy.

Figure 9.4 *Eikon Basilike* was probably the most influential image of the seventeenth century, with its depiction of Charles I as a martyr for the monarchy and the Church of England. Its message was reinforced by an Act of Parliament marking the anniversary of his execution with a day of fasting and humiliation.

The second reason for the regimes' unpopularity was that they were supported mainly by the 'godly' minority. Cromwell's 'toleration' applied only to the gathered churches – Independents, Baptists and Quakers. The government tried to ensure that the parish clergy were of adequate learning and good character, which made their ministry acceptable to Presbyterians, but not to Prayer-Book Anglicans; there was much clandestine Prayer-Book worship. The assault on drunkenness, promiscuity, Sabbath-breaking and 'disorderly' popular pastimes intensified. Attempts to impose godliness were reinforced by fears of Royalist conspiracy: alehouses, hunts and race meetings could serve as covers for plotting. After an abortive rebellion in 1655 local government was put under the control of eleven major-generals, who strove to establish a more godly moral order and tighter surveillance of Royalists. The surveillance proved effective, but moral order

proved elusive; the prohibition of Christmas continued to cause ill-feeling. The restoration of the monarchy was marked by an outbreak of maypoles and morris-dancing.

A third reason was that the regimes were also politically narrow. The Parliament
purged in 1648 was entirely Parliamentarian: any remaining Royalists had been
expelled in 1642 and replaced in 'recruiter' elections. Pride's Purge removed a majority
of the Commons. Those who remained were nicknamed 'the Rump': boys cried 'kiss
my Parliament'. Although some of those excluded in the purge later returned, the Rump
did not represent the majority of Parliamentarians. Presbyterians deplored the regicide
and hated the sects (and the army). The restoration of traditional local government
partially reconciled them, but they would still have preferred a (limited) monarchy.

The final reason was that ultimately the regimes depended on the army, the driving force behind the purge and regicide. The army remained self-consciously separate
from, and (in its own eyes) superior to, the civilian population: God's chosen. It did not
aim to set up a military dictatorship, although the major-generals came close. It saw
itself as the servant of civilian government, with a duty to remonstrate if that government fell short of expectations. In a crisis it would intervene to secure the gains of the
civil war: religious liberty and government without a king. For many soldiers the army
had become a career and they resented civilian interference. The army did not determine policy, but set limits to what the government could do: politicians always needed
to consider its possible reaction.

Oliver Cromwell

The man who tried hardest to reconcile soldiers and civilians was Cromwell. An obscure
backbencher with no military experience, he became lieutenant general of cavalry in
the Eastern Association: he was one of the few to straddle Parliament and army. Despite
Leveller criticism he retained the loyalty of his men and looked after their material
well-being; he was also a firm disciplinarian and shared the army's strong belief in
Providence. He saw the army's successes and his own rise to pre-eminence as evidence
of divine approval. He did not assume that whatever the army thought fit must be the
will of God, but his all-pervading belief in Providence made it difficult to cope with failure. Cromwell believed that God's purposes were so vast and inscrutable that mortals
could never fully understand them, and preferred to wait until God made His wishes
clear, through events, before taking action: he agreed to the army's march on London
in 1647 only after the apprentices invaded Parliament and the Speakers fled to the army.

Cromwell was not the dominant figure in the army in 1649: Fairfax was commander
in chief and Ireton was the main political strategist. But Fairfax resigned, Ireton died
in 1651 and Cromwell found himself the most powerful man in the land; he had not
consciously sought power, so concluded God had work for him to do. Until 1652 he

was busy suppressing the remaining resistance in the three kingdoms, but thereafter he devoted much attention to the central conundrum of how to satisfy the conflicting aspirations of civilians and army.

The Rump Parliament 1649–1653

The Rump's members mostly believed that change had gone far enough. Survival was the main priority: as a republic in a world of monarchies it had many enemies. The young Charles II had taken refuge first in The Hague and then in France, but the French government was suffering its own civil wars. Spain was still preoccupied with its ongoing war against France, while other powers were exhausted by the Thirty Years War, which ended in 1648. Until the death of William II in 1650 the main threat came from the Dutch, in conjunction with the Confederates. Initially a major priority was building up the navy, to guard against attack by the Dutch; trade rivalry and **Orangist** support for the Stuarts led to an Anglo-Dutch war in 1652–4, in which the English held their own against Europe's greatest maritime power. The Rump worked hard to provide resources for both navy and army, but the army demanded reform at home, including law reform and the abolition of **tithes**; it also urged the Rump to arrange for its dissolution and organise a general election under a more equitable electoral system. The Rump had no wish to alienate the legal profession and the clergy, and feared fresh elections would produce a Royalist Parliament. In April 1653 Cromwell, probably acting on misinformation, ordered a file of musketeers to expel the Rump, the last vestige of the Long Parliament.

The Nominated Parliament and the Instrument of Government 1653

In dissolving the Rump Cromwell acted suddenly, believing that God had made His will clear. He summoned a 'godly' assembly, which (he hoped) God would guide to produce godly measures. Members were nominated by gathered churches or godly preachers and their reform programme was similar to the army's. Cromwell became increasingly impatient at their failure to address practical issues and was glad when the majority resigned; the remainder were expelled by soldiers.

Cromwell later blamed the Parliament's failure on his own 'ignorance and folly'. He now promoted a balanced constitution, the Instrument of Government, drafted by his second-in-command, John Lambert. A single-person executive, the Lord Protector, was to govern with an elected Parliament and a council of state, elected by Parliament. Elections to Parliament were based on fewer and larger constituencies, each electing several MPs; voters had to satisfy high property qualifications and those elected could be excluded by the council of state if judged morally or politically unsuitable. The Instrument aimed to win over Presbyterians, and to some extent it worked: many stood for election and engaged in the political process, but only in order to change the regime from within. The Instrument stretched, but did not destroy, the army's loyalty to Cromwell. No constitution could alter the fact that the aims of army and Presbyterians were incompatible. The army wished to preserve religious liberty, the republic and its own existence. The Presbyterians wished to establish an intolerant Puritan national church, re-establish the monarchy and get rid of the army. Cromwell could never satisfy both: 'I am as much for government by consent as any man, but where shall we find that consent?'

 ## The Protectorate

Cromwell's first elected Parliament in 1654 ended with little progress towards consensus. In the second, in 1656, experience of the major-generals made members eager to make the regime more civilian; the Humble Petition and Advice centred on Cromwell's being offered the Crown. Other provisions included tax cuts, an end to the exclusion of members by the council of state, and the denial of religious freedom to Quakers and other radicals. There was to be an upper (or 'other') House, in effect a House of Lords. Cromwell accepted most of the provisions, but refused the title of king. (See Box 9.4, Cromwell, Providence and Kingship.)

BOX 9.4: **Cromwell, Providence and Kingship**

In a speech to the parliamentary committee on 13 April 1657, Cromwell sets out his reasons for refusing the Crown.

I am a man standing in the place I am in, which place I undertook not so much out of the hope of doing any good, as out of a desire to prevent mischief and evil, which I did see was imminent upon the nation. I saw we were running headlong into confusion and disorder ... I think from my very heart that in your settling of the peace and liberties of this nation ... you should labour for somewhat that may beget a consistency, otherwise this nation will fall to pieces. And in that, as far as I can, I am ready to serve not as a king, but as a constable ... [whose duty is] to keep the peace of the parish ...

[He then talks at length of the contribution of God's providence and godly soldiers to the army's success and stresses that he has a duty not to agree to anything that might disturb their consciences.]

... it is the providence of God that does lead men in darkness. I must needs say I have had a great deal of experience of providence, and ... truly the providence of God has laid this title [king] aside ... God ... hath not only dealt so with the persons and the family, but he hath blasted the title ... I would not seek to set up that that providence has destroyed and laid in the dust and I would not build Jericho again ...

O. Cromwell, *Speeches*, ed. I. Roots (London, 1989), pp. 132–3, 136–7.

Cromwell had tried hard to accommodate the Presbyterians but his troubles were not over. He nominated many of his supporters to the Other House; when Parliament reconvened early in 1658 those excluded by the council of state took their seats. A mixture of strong Presbyterians and zealous adherents of the Rump made so much trouble that Cromwell dissolved the Parliament with the words 'Let God judge between you and me.' All his efforts to win consent seemed to have ended in failure. The army was deeply hostile to the Humble Petition, even without the title of king: Lambert resigned rather than accept it. In accepting it, Cromwell made concessions that he did not intend to observe, notably the commitment to persecute sectaries. The tax cuts added to the regime's already serious financial problems. Government spending (mostly on the army and navy) was now financed mainly by borrowing; sooner or later bankers and financiers would refuse to lend any more. Cromwell seemed old and tired and had no obvious successor. Under the Humble Petition he could nominate his heir. The more capable of his sons was Henry, who had done much to reconcile the ruling Scottish and Irish elites to the Cromwellian regime, marginalising the sects and reducing the army's influence. Perhaps for this reason Cromwell chose his other son, Richard, who had no military experience and was widely seen as an amiable nonentity: the restored monarchy left him unmolested.

Oliver died on 3 September 1658, the anniversary of his victories at Dunbar and Worcester. Richard summoned a Parliament, chosen under the old electoral system, which was aggressively Presbyterian and urged Richard to purge the army of radicals. Richard faced Oliver's problem of retaining the co-operation of both Presbyterians and army, but unlike his father he had no strong bond of mutual loyalty with the army. In April 1659 the council of officers forced Richard to dissolve Parliament; he then resigned, rather than become a powerless figurehead. The army needed a civilian regime to cover the nakedness of military rule, and preferably one that could grant taxes. The least bad option seemed the Rump, the only constitutional link with the Long Parliament. Despite their difficult past relationship they now needed each other. The regime remained fragile, dependent above all on the army remaining united. Towards the end of 1659, however, there were signs of a major split.

The Conquest of Ireland

The King's trial and execution led to agreements between Ormond, the Confederates and the Ulster Scots, creating a serious military threat to the new republic. In August 1649 Cromwell led an expedition to Ireland, well provided with men (12,000), artillery, munitions and cash, so his soldiers could pay for their provisions; if they stole they would be punished. He believed that 1641 had seen acts of unparalleled barbarity, but did not blame the peasants: if they were brutes, they had been made so. (See Box 9.5,

BOX 9.5: Cromwell's 'Declaration for the Undeceiving of Deluded and Seduced People', January 1650

This was a response to a Declaration by the Irish Catholic bishops and clergy, meeting at Clonmacnoise. He accused the clergy of misleading and exploiting the laity and claimed that the Catholic Church had never been lawfully established in Ireland.

Your Covenant is with death and hell ... God is not with you ... You had generally equal benefit of the protection of England with them [the English settlers]; and equal justice from the laws ... You, unprovoked, put the English to the most unheard-of and most barbarous massacre (without respect of sex or age) that ever the sun beheld ... You are a part of Antichrist, whose kingdom the Scripture so expressly speaks should be laid in blood, yea in the blood of the saints. You have shed great store of that already; and ere it be long you must all of you have blood to drink: even the dregs of the cup of the fury and the wrath of God, which will be poured out unto you.

O. Cromwell, *Writings and Speeches*, ed. W.C. Abbott (4 vols., Cambridge, Mass., 1937–47), II, pp. 197–8, 199.

Cromwell's 'Declaration for the Undeceiving of Deluded and Seduced People', January 1650.) He assured them that, if they refused to follow their clergy and chiefs and lived peaceably, they would not be harmed. His men generally paid for their provisions and some were hanged for pillaging.

His efforts to reassure the Irish were undone by the massacres at Drogheda and Wexford. Drogheda had never been in Confederate hands and much of the garrison was English, including one Protestant regiment. The garrison decided to resist, but the wall was breached and Cromwell ordered that the defenders should be killed, including officers taken prisoner. Those killed numbered about 3,500, including at least 2,800 soldiers (which implied that some civilians were killed as well); the governor, an English Catholic, was allegedly beaten to death with his wooden leg. Cromwell's losses numbered 150. After the massacre he headed for Wexford. The town and castle had different commanders; the castle's governor surrendered, the town rushed to surrender and was quickly overrun; a few soldiers made a stand, which was made a pretext to kill much of the garrison. Cromwell estimated that 2,000 were killed; priests were hacked down as they tried to protect themselves with crucifixes. Cromwell acknowledged that the town was about to surrender. He gave no order to kill the inhabitants, but did not rebuke those who did so.

Cromwell justified the killings at Drogheda and Wexford in three ways. First, as God's 'unexpected providence', and 'righteous justice' – punishment for 1641. Second, he claimed they would 'discourage others from making opposition': 'I believe this bitterness will prevent much effusion of blood.' Third, he argued that they were justified under the rules of war. To the first, one can only say that interpretations of providence were subjective. Concerning the second, if that was the intention, it failed: garrisons fought on, rather than risk being slaughtered. After failing to take Duncannon and Waterford, Cromwell began to offer generous terms (and observe them). As for the third, contemporaries believed that if defenders had not surrendered before a breach was made, they could be killed, but this rarely happened in England or Scotland. At Drogheda every officer in the garrison was killed except Richard Talbot, who was left for dead; at Colchester, after one of the bitterest English sieges, only three defenders were killed out of 300.

When Cromwell returned to England in May 1650, Ireton moved from one slow siege to another; garrisons resisted, fearing the consequences of surrender, and he had to raise the siege of Galway. He restrained his officers from acts of vengeance, allowed Irish soldiers to enter foreign service and even enlisted Irish soldiers in his army when casualties mounted. At his death in November 1651 the major strongholds outside Connacht had been taken and Protestant Royalist resistance had dwindled, but 'independent bands' of brigands and guerrillas remained. Their knowledge of the terrain and the sympathy of the population made it hard for local commanders to seek them out, so they resorted to systematic brutality, burning crops and killing cattle. Some used martial law, others killed indiscriminately: one observer wrote: 'You may ride twenty miles and scarce discern any … object but dead men hanging on trees and gibbets.' Famine and plague stalked the land. Major General Fleetwood's commission in 1652 authorised him to execute martial law against the enemy 'and them to pursue, … kill and destroy by all ways and means whatsoever'; he would decide who constituted 'the enemy'. Cromwell acknowledged the massacres at Drogheda and Wexford and tried to justify them. The later stages of the conquest saw unrecorded and indiscriminate killings, very different atrocities in a different kind of war. The governor of Wexford was accused of killing 4,000 people in four days.

The Irish Land Settlement

Although the struggle against the 'independent bands' lasted until 1655, by 1652 the conquest was complete enough to begin the process of settlement. The English forces in Ireland now numbered almost 35,000. The wars had taken a terrible toll: the population is estimated to have fallen by 40 per cent since 1641. In 1652 the English Parliament passed an Act of Settlement, which excluded many people from pardon (for rebellion). 104 individuals were excluded by name, including Ormond and other Protestants. Those Catholics who had not been in rebellion but had failed to show 'constant good affection' to the Commonwealth were to lose between one fifth and two-thirds of their land, and to exchange the rest for land elsewhere. As many as 80,000 men (approximately half the adult male population) were liable to be executed and to forfeit all their lands. Together with the many who would forfeit a part, this would create a huge reservoir of land to complete the policy of plantation. Some 35,000 were sent abroad, to serve in foreign armies or to work on Caribbean plantations.

It is not known how many of those excluded from pardon were executed. Sir Phelim O'Neill had claimed to have a commission from the King. The Dublin authorities wanted evidence of Charles's complicity in the rebellion, but O'Neill now denied that Charles had been complicit and was executed. Commanders in the provinces convened military 'high courts of justice', which probably executed hundreds, rather than thousands. Meanwhile nobody had any idea how much land there was or how much had been forfeited. In planning the plantation the London government's priorities were paying for the conquest and ensuring that Irish Catholics posed no future threat. The conquest had cost nearly £5,000,000. To raise this amount all Catholics' and Royalists' lands would have to be confiscated, but it was acknowledged that some Catholics were 'innocent' of rebellion; others were covered by surrender articles; and some Protestant Royalists **compounded**. To remove the Catholic threat Ireland was divided into three zones: first, an area in the South East, including Dublin; second, Connacht; and third, the area in between. It was ordered that *all* Catholics, including tenant farmers, labourers and servants, should be cleared from the South East. Catholics who retained some land were to be transported to Connacht, where they would receive land allegedly equivalent to what they had left. Hemmed in between the Shannon and the sea they would be separated from their former tenants and labourers, and policed by soldiers settled in Connacht or along the Shannon. Other soldiers would settle in the central zone and replicate the role played by soldier settlers in the Roman Empire. (See Map 9.1, The Cromwellian Land Confiscation Scheme in Ireland, *c.*1652–3.)

This ambitious scheme of ethnic cleansing was not fully carried out. English landlords in the South East needed Catholic tenants and labourers. Only about 1,900 of the 3,000 Catholics designated for transplantation to Connacht actually went. Even so, the Catholic lords were greatly weakened by the loss of their land and the erosion of their power over men. There were to be no more great Catholic regional lords like Clanricard or Antrim. Catholics were also driven out of many towns; some now had a Protestant majority for the first time. The Protestant population increased by much less than the settlement's promoters hoped. Englishmen who invested in Irish land had no obligation to bring over settlers. Soldiers had received much of their pay in credit notes which could be redeemed for land. Many sold them at a heavy discount, receiving as little as 20 per cent of their value. Much forfeited and soldiers' land was bought relatively cheaply by 'Old Protestants', pre-1641 Protestant settlers, who were richer and more numerous than the settlers of the 1650s. civilian settlers numbered about 8,000 (the London government had hoped for 36,000) together with 7,500 soldiers. The shift in economic power from Catholic to Protestant was enormous: between 1640 and 1660 the Catholic share of the land fell from about 60 per cent to 9 per cent. As for the peasants, as one Irish historian put it, their condition was 'possibly not markedly more wretched than it had been before'.

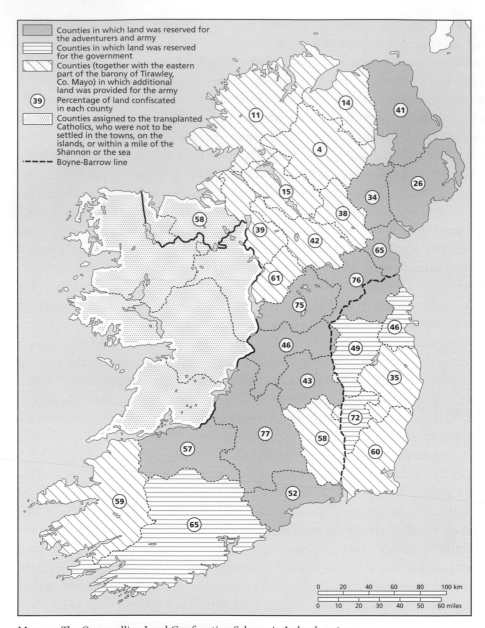

Map 9.1 The Cromwellian Land Confiscation Scheme in Ireland, *c.*1652–3

Cromwellian Ireland

In 1652–5 the English regime in Ireland was dominated by the military, who favoured the new settlers rather than the pre-1641 Protestants, whom they regarded as insufficiently godly. From 1654 'Irish' MPs sat in the Westminster Parliament, but too few to wield significant influence. The military rulers promoted radical religion. Use of the Prayer Book was forbidden; episcopacy, church courts and tithes were abolished. The structures of the established Church collapsed but in strongly Protestant areas Church of Ireland worship continued clandestinely. The Ulster Presbyterians had begun to build their own organisation from the bottom up in the 1640s; by 1660 the system was complete and was to offer serious competition to the restored Church of Ireland. (See Chapter 15.) The military rulers tried to disrupt Presbyterian worship, so many met in **conventicles** in private houses or fields. The Baptists made little headway and the Quakers not much more. Catholic worship and organisation were, predictably, badly disrupted: by the late 1650s there were about half as many priests in Ireland as in 1622. The regime made little effort to evangelise the natives and there were few conversions. After 1655, under Henry Cromwell, the regime's military element was reduced (although the army was still needed) and it made more effort to work with the pre-1641 settlers. The law courts, JPs and the old machinery of local government were gradually re-established. Although army radicals enjoyed a final brief period in power in 1659 the English regime in Ireland was learning to work with those who now held the bulk of the land and the power.

Scotland: Presbyterian Divisions

The Covenanters intervened in English in 1643 to secure Presbyterianism and the Scottish constitution of 1641. The more radical elements, led by the Earl of Argyll, increasingly controlled Church and state. Noble influence diminished, while that of the hard-line clergy increased. Successive purges removed those whose theology or morals were suspect, leading to an increasingly narrow oligarchy. The burdens of war imposed severe strains on Scotland, which led to bitter political and religious divisions. Relatively few troops were left in Scotland, which offered opportunities to Royalists and Catholics, who exploited discontent among the Highland clans: Argyll's rapacious accumulation of land had made him many enemies. After Montrose's striking victories, the civil war in Scotland degenerated into brutal devastation by both sides, especially in Argyllshire, where Argyll received no rent between 1644 and 1647.

As discontent grew, the Duke of Hamilton emerged as the leader of a motley collection of moderates and Royalists, alarmed at the radicals' extremism and concerned for the King's safety; they sought to wrest back the initiative with the **Engagement**. The clergy were outraged, but Parliament endorsed it by a large majority; the General Assembly also approved it, showing that the radicals did not speak for the Kirk. There was fierce opposition to recruiting for the army in the South West, the heartland of radical Covenanters, who formed their own **conventicles**, or 'privy kirks'. Known as '**Whiggamores**', they formed a 'Western association' to prevent intervention in England. After Preston a 'Whiggamore raid' ousted the Engagers from power and

Cromwell came to Edinburgh to demand a thorough purge of Engagers. On 23 January 1649 Parliament passed the Act of **Classes**, which gave the Kirk a veto over civil and military appointments, putting orthodoxy before competence. The Kirk, united since the adoption of the Covenant in 1638, faced a deepening schism. (See Chapter 15.)

Although radical Covenanters condemned the Engagement, they believed firmly in the monarchy and the House of Stuart, proclaiming Charles II King of Great Britain and Ireland – not just Scotland – and hoping to mould him into a Covenanted King. Initially, Charles pinned his hopes on the Irish; only after Cromwell's campaign in Ireland did he heed overtures from the Scots. Hearing Charles was going to Scotland the government sent Cromwell north. His stunning victory at Dunbar, against considerable odds, but helped by the purge of the army, gave him control of much of southern Scotland. Charles was crowned at Scone in January 1651, and the Act of Classes was repealed. Despite the English presence and divisions among the Scots, Charles and a Scottish army were able to enter England, only to be crushed at Worcester on 3 September. After a series of picaresque adventures, he escaped to France. His defeat did not end Scottish resistance. Guerrilla warfare, by Royalists and Whiggamores, continued until 1655. Some military commanders responded by burning and killing, but on a smaller scale than in Ireland. For Cromwell the Catholic clergy of Ireland were 'a part of Antichrist', whereas Scottish Presbyterians were misguided fellow-Protestants: he wrote to the General Assembly, 'I beseech you in the bowels of Christ to think it possible that you may be mistaken.'

Scotland: Occupation and Union

Endemic disorder forced the English to occupy Scotland, with 10,000 soldiers and a string of fortresses. Scotland had been conquered but, instead of annexing it, the Rump drew up a 'tender of incorporation' and sent commissioners to purge its government of 'malignants' and propagate the Gospel. Fewer than half the shires and burghs fully subscribed the incorporation, but only a handful totally rejected it. A deputation was sent to negotiate the terms of Scottish representation at Westminster. It persuaded the government not to replace Scots law with English law, but the union's legal status remained unclear, receiving parliamentary sanction only in 1657. Scotland became a subordinate province, allotted thirty seats in Parliament, of which at least half were taken by Englishmen. Initially taxation was unbearably high, but the government came to accept that the army in Scotland, as in Ireland, had to be paid partly from the English revenue.

In tackling disorder in the Highlands the authorities initially relied on force, but then attempted to use the authority of clan chiefs and the **fine**, who were required to enter into bands, and give sureties, for their and their followers' good conduct. In return, they were granted an indemnity and some relief from taxes and debts, so it was not in their interest to collaborate with Royalists. In time more positions of power went to Scots, partly because unpaid magistrates were cheaper than English soldiers. Like Henry Cromwell in Ireland, Lord Broghill, president of the council of state, sought to involve more of the aristocracy in government. Another parallel with Ireland was an attempt to free the peasantry from noble 'tyranny'. **Heritable jurisdictions** were abolished, in theory, but proved too varied and complex to unravel; many landowners negotiated deals to preserve them. **Caterans** were enlisted for military service or sent abroad. The McGregors, one of the more unruly clans, undertook to prevent raiding into the Lowlands. The abolition of many private courts made it difficult for landlords to avoid paying debts, which undermined their power, enabling lairds to exercise greater influence. The regime undermined the Kirk: freedom of worship was granted to everyone except Catholics and Episcopalians. Attempts to promote English sects were even less successful than in Ireland. Presbyterianism remained vigorous in the parishes and Church courts functioned as before. The futility of introducing English ways was seen in the central law courts. An attempt to introduce English common law failed; instead English judges administered Scottish law.

English attempts to transform Scotland were more pragmatic than the changes imposed on Ireland, for several reasons: hostility towards the Scots was less intense; the majority of the population could practise their religion unmolested; the government focused on security rather than transformation; and Scotland, unlike Ireland, was not seen as offering real economic opportunities: no proposals survive for plantations in Scotland at this time. Last but not least, forfeitures by Royalists or Catholics were more limited than in Ireland or even England. Even those seen as seriously disaffected could often **compound** or do deals with the government. By late 1659 English control over Scotland was secure enough for the army commander, General George Monk, to march most of his forces into England. And it is to Monk and his army that we now turn.

Monk and the Restoration

Unusually among Cromwell's generals Monk was no religious radical, but a career soldier and former Royalist. Cromwell put him in charge of Scotland because he trusted him. He maintained firm discipline and his men respected him because he was fair and ensured that they were paid as regularly as possible. He knew his officers and weeded out those he could not trust. Contemporaries found him difficult to read – 'He is a black Monk and I cannot see through him', one wrote – and he kept his own counsel, helped by a strong head for drink. He believed in order in Church and state, in 'ministry and magistracy', and was perturbed by the disorders following Richard's fall. He believed the military should be subject to the civil power and was concerned when the army ended the Protectorate and expelled the Rump (again) in October. He demanded the Rump's reinstatement and prepared to march into England, taking care to ensure good order in his absence. On 7 January 1660 he issued a declaration that he was preparing to move on behalf of 'the nation of Scotland' so that its people 'may enjoy an equality with the nation of England'.

Monk's stand-off with the army emboldened its enemies. In Ireland there was a power struggle between radicals and moderates. On 13 December 1659 the moderates staged a coup. Theophilus Jones seized Dublin Castle, Broghill secured Munster and Sir Charles Coote Connacht. A council of officers agreed to summon a **Convention** (a Parliament not summoned by the King) to raise funds for the army and secure the interests of Protestant settlers, old and new, in the event of the King's return. The Convention met on 7 February 1660: it contained some Royalists and Ulster Scots, but 98 of 138 members were 'Old Protestants'. The King was proclaimed in Ireland on 14 May, after he was proclaimed in England. The Convention invited him to return, and urged him to call a Protestant Parliament and restore the Church of Ireland.

These events were followed with interest in England. In London citizens and apprentices taunted the soldiers, who became disoriented and demoralised. One regiment threatened to lay down their arms unless they were told for what or for whom they were fighting. The high command capitulated to popular pressure, recalling the Rump on 26 December: the commander in chief declared that God had spat in his face. As Monk moved south he was bombarded by petitions for a free Parliament, which many believed, but no-one admitted, would bring back the King. Monk's public stance was of obedience to the Rump, which made it over-confident. On 8 February the London **common council** resolved to pay no taxes until the City's MPs were restored. The Rump ordered Monk to take down the City's gates and, when he demurred, resolved that the army should be governed by five commissioners, so Monk could be outvoted. Monk now demanded elections, with all Parliamentarians eligible to vote; the Rump insisted on excluding all but those committed to a government without a 'single person' or House of Lords. On 21 February those excluded in Pride's Purge took their seats, guarded by soldiers. Monk commanded this restored House of Commons to dissolve itself and hold elections for a Convention. The Presbyterians tried to debar Royalists from voting, but the elections produced a House equally divided between Royalists and Parliamentarians. By now it was clear that the King would be restored; the Presbyterians tried in vain to impose preconditions. On 8 May he was proclaimed, amid wild rejoicing. When Charles and his brothers came to London on 29 May cheering crowds lined the road for thirty miles; in the City every window and balcony was crammed with people. The King charmed the spectators with his affable manner and the rejoicing seemed to know no bounds. After the death, misery and upheaval of civil war, the rightful King was restored without bloodshed, amid the acclamations of his people. As the diarist John Evelyn wrote: 'I stood in the Strand, and beheld it, and blessed God.'

Conclusion

The outcomes of the civil wars were radically different from what most participants had expected or wanted. Most English Royalists and Parliamentarians had hoped to retain the traditional constitution, revised to guard against misrule by Charles I. Instead they found themselves with the republic and Protectorate, both dependent on the army, determined to maintain government without a king and religious liberty – for the godly. Only when the army split in 1659 did its lack of civilian support become a fatal weakness, allowing the return of Charles II. In Scotland the Covenanters had hoped to extend their vision of godly reformation to England and Ireland. They failed in England but enjoyed success among Scottish settlers in Ireland. Divisions among Scottish Presbyterians weakened their bargaining position at the Restoration. In Ireland the Confederates' hopes of securing freedom of worship were crushed by the New Model. The real winners were the pre-1641 Protestant settlers, who bought up much of the confiscated land and seized power in 1659–60, so that Charles II had little option but to work with them.

In the long term what happened in the 1640s and 1650s brought radical changes to the three kingdoms, which are considered thematically in the next seven chapters. For decades historians explained the English civil wars in terms of social change within England, but in many ways little changed. Politically, economically and socially the landed elite remained pre-eminent. The trading, financial and manufacturing sectors of the economy grew, but successful merchants, bankers and industrialists imitated, rather than challenged, the landed elite, buying country estates and building country houses. England (and to a lesser extent Ireland and Scotland) became more prosperous thanks to the growth of trade and empire, although prosperity was unevenly distributed. Charles II inherited a modernised fiscal system, used after 1689 to raise a larger revenue than ever before. He also inherited a much enlarged navy, which continued to expand, along with a standing army. The state's financial and military resources made possible England's (later Britain's) emergence as an imperial and world power.

But the legacy of the civil wars was also divisive. Bitter disputes about the nature of the monarchy and the relationship between King and Parliament continued long after 1660; Charles I's 'martyrdom' strengthened popular support for divine-right monarchy. The fragmentation of Protestantism in all three kingdoms led to fierce conflict, between High and Low Church, Church and Dissent, and among Dissenters. These disputes raged through all levels of society. The dissemination of news and opinion which reached a peak in the 1640s was reined in somewhat in the following decades but gained new momentum from the 1690s. Parliamentary elections became more frequent and hard-fought and society was divided on party lines. Finally, the inter-relationship between the three kingdoms remained fraught, leading to the Union between England and Scotland and an often awkward relationship between the Anglo-Irish elite and the London government.

SUGGESTIONS FOR FURTHER READING

The literature on this period is enormous. There are large overviews by A. Woolrych, *Britain in Revolution 1625–60* (Oxford, 2002) and M. Braddick, *God's Fury, England's Fire: a New History of the English Civil Wars* (2008) and shorter studies by D. Scott, *Politics and War in the Three Stuart Kingdoms 1637–49* (Basingstoke, 2004) and J. Miller, *A Brief History of the English Civil Wars* (London, 2009). • Many of the most important articles and essays from the 1970s to the 1990s can be found in R. Cust and A. Hughes (eds.), *The English Civil War* (1997). • On the first civil war, and the taking of sides, see D. Underdown, *Revel, Riot and Rebellion: Popular Politics and Culture in England 1603–60* (Oxford, 1985), J.S. Morrill, *Revolt in the Provinces 1603–48: the English People and the Tragedies of War* (Harlow, 1999), J.S. Morrill, *The Nature of the English Revolution* (Harlow, 1993), M. Stoyle, *Loyalty and Locality: Popular Allegiance in Devon in the English Civil War* (Exeter, 1994) and R. Hutton, *The Royalist War Effort 1642–6* (Harlow, 1982). • On Scotland see A.I. Macinnes, *The British Revolution 1629–60* (Basingstoke, 2005) and K.M. Brown, *Kingdom or Province? Scotland and the Regal Union 1603–1715* (Basingstoke, 1992). • For Ireland see Connolly, *Divided Kingdom*, Gillespie, *Seventeenth-Century Ireland* and Moody, Martin and Byrne (eds.), *New History of Ireland*, vol. III. For the Confederates see M. Ó Siochrú, *Confederate Ireland 1642–9* (Dublin, 1999). • The fullest study of the New Model is I. Gentles, *The New Model Army in England, Scotland and Ireland 1645–53* (Oxford, 1992); for a recent re-think see Gentles, 'The Politics of Fairfax's Army, 1645–9', in J. Adamson (ed.), *The English Civil War* (Basingstoke, 2009). See also M. Kishlansky, *The Rise of the New Model Army* (Cambridge, 1979). For the army in 1646–8 see R. Ashton, *Counter-Revolution: the Second Civil War and its Origins* (New Haven, 1994) and A. Woolrych, *Soldiers and Statesmen: the General Council of the Army 1647–8* (Oxford, 1987). • On reactions to the wars see three volumes edited by J.S. Morrill: *Reactions to the English Civil War* (Basingstoke, 1982), *The Impact of the English Civil War* and *Revolt in the Provinces*. See also B. Donagan, *War in England 1642–9* (Oxford, 2008), A. Thomson, *The Impact of the First Civil War on Hertfordshire* (Hertfordshire Record Society, 2007) and I. Roy, '"England turned Germany?" The Aftermath of the Civil War in its European Context', *Transactions of the Royal Historical Society*, 5th series, 28 (1978). • On Pride's Purge and the regicide see D. Underdown, *Pride's Purge* (Oxford, 1971), J. Peacey (ed.), *The Regicides and the Execution of Charles I* (Basingstoke, 2001) and S. Kelsey, 'The Trial of Charles I', *English Historical Review*, 116 (2003). • For the Commonwealth and Protectorate see B. Worden, *The Rump Parliament* (Cambridge, 1974), A. Woolrych,

Commonwealth into Protectorate (Oxford, 1982) and C. Durston, *Cromwell's Major Generals* (Manchester, 2001). • There are many biographies of Cromwell but the best introduction is a collection of essays: J.S. Morrill (ed.), *Oliver Cromwell and the English Revolution* (Harlow, 1990). • On the conquest and land settlement in Ireland, see Gentles, *New Model Army* and M. Ó Siochrú, *God's Executioner: Oliver Cromwell and the Conquest of Ireland* (London, 2008) (less hostile to Cromwell than the title would suggest). P.J. Corish, 'The Cromwellian Regime', in Moody, Martin and Byrne (eds.), *New History of Ireland,* gives a clear account of the land settlement.

SUMMARY

- In the first civil war Parliament won the military battle but lost the battle for hearts and minds. The arrogance, heavy-handedness and (allegedly) corruption of many of its agents in the localities created enormous resentment, as did the depredations of soldiers. While Parliament and the New Model insisted that Charles had to make concessions, to guard against another Personal Rule, the public mood increasingly favoured settling with the King on almost any terms.
- The emergence into politics of the New Model came as a surprise to everyone, including the soldiers themselves. They felt driven to petition Parliament about their grievances as soldiers and were outraged to be described as enemies of the state. Their conduct made the army even more unpopular than it already was, but the soldiers were not concerned about majority opinions because they believed that they were in the right.
- The trial and execution of the King and the establishment of the republic were foreseen, and desired, by a relatively small minority. Charles I in effect forced the Rump and army to try and condemn him, as if he was bent on martyrdom. His execution was exploited by the Royalist press, which portrayed him as a martyr for the Church of England and the monarchy, adding a new dimension and force to belief in the divine right of kings.
- The Cromwellian confiscations in Ireland did not complete the transfer of land from Catholic to Protestant, but they ensured that Protestants now held well over half the land. The majority of the population remained Catholic but the greater part of the land, wealth and power was now in Protestant hands.

QUESTIONS FOR STUDENTS

1. Why was Parliament's victory in the first civil war not followed by a political settlement?
2. When and why did the New Model emerge as a political force?
3. Why was the English Parliament so hostile to the army during the second civil war?
4. Why was Charles I tried and executed?
5. Was Cromwell's conduct at Drogheda and Wexford 'indefensible'?
6. Why did Oliver Cromwell not achieve a lasting political settlement?
7. Why was there so little opposition to the Restoration?

10 Empire

TIMELINE

1585	Abortive English settlement at Roanoke
1599	Foundation of English East India Company
1602	Dutch East India Company formed from earlier companies
1607	Jamestown: first lasting English settlement in North America
1620	Voyage of the *Mayflower*
1620s	Barbados founded
1632	Maryland charter granted to Lord Baltimore
1655	English capture Jamaica from Spain
1663	Foundation of South Carolina and the Royal African Company
1664	New York granted to James Duke of York
1675	Bacon's rebellion in Virginia
1675–6	King Philip's War in New England
1681	Establishment of Pennsylvania

1682	French lay claim to 'Louisiana'
1723	Foundation of Georgia
1750s	Britain conquers 'New France' (Canada); East India Company gains control of Bengal

Introduction: the Nature of Empire

This chapter and the next will consider empire and trade which, like power and profit, were closely linked. Traditionally 'empire' was understood in terms of control over territory, and the resources that it contained, predominantly but not exclusively within Europe: the Roman Empire was the greatest example. In the Middle Ages and beyond the main 'empire' within Europe was the Holy Roman Empire, in which the Habsburg emperors ruled a variety of territories, including Austria and Hungary, and exercised a looser authority over very many more, mostly in what became Germany. Further west the Normans and Angevins ruled an Anglo-French empire: kings of England ruled a considerable part of France until the 1450s.

From the late fifteenth century a new meaning of 'empire' developed. It was used mainly of lands outside Europe and focused on the acquisition of highly profitable commodities of three types.

First, precious metals. The Spanish conquests in South America opened Europeans' eyes to the enormous profits that could be made from plunder and mining in a continent rich in gold and silver. Many of the early English colonists in North America hoped to make their fortune in this way but were doomed to disappointment.

Second, staple crops, particularly sugar and tobacco, for which a strong demand quickly developed in Europe. There was a strong incentive to grow these on a large scale, on plantations, in order to maximise production and profits. Production on such a scale developed first in the Portuguese sugar plantations in Brazil, but the Spaniards followed their example where conditions were suitable, notably in the Caribbean; so, later, did the English.

Third, spices and other very high-value commodities. This trade, mostly with Asia, had begun long before the sixteenth century but competition intensified as European demand increased. European traders vied with one another to secure the best deals from local growers and rulers – and to exclude their competitors. There was similar competition between the English and French for the North American fur trade.

The exploitation of precious metals and staple crops involved the subjugation of the native population (where one existed) and its use as labour in the mines and plantations. As we shall see, this did not always prove possible and so colonists became increasingly reliant on slaves from Africa. The Asian trade depended on establishing good trading relations with powerful and sophisticated regimes, which often tried to keep European traders at arm's length. All three involved the use of naval and military power to keep out European competitors as each power sought to monopolise its profitable trades.

The Workings of Empire: the Establishment of Colonies

Colonies were usually established in one of three ways.

First, by small groups, usually with some state support or recognition. This could include naval or financial backing or (in the case of England) charters establishing 'royal' colonies or empowering individuals to establish **proprietary** colonies – essentially private enterprise operations, but following rules laid down by the Crown, which expected to profit from taxes on colonial commodities.

Second, by chartered trading companies. Of these by far the most powerful was the Dutch East India Company, established in 1602 by combining several companies trading in Asia. The economic success of the Dutch in the sixteenth century was extraordinary. From a small territory, the seven northern provinces of the Netherlands, they fought an eighty-year war of independence against Spain, the greatest power in Europe. With few natural resources, they built their prosperity on fishing, trade and shipping, transporting other people's goods more economically and efficiently than they could themselves. As the Dutch grew rich they built a powerful navy, used to protect their trading fleets and deter rivals rather than to conquer territory. As a joint-stock company, whose capital consisted of shares purchased by the merchant community, the Dutch East India Company was able to build on this foundation of commercial success and developed into a formidable naval power in its own right. The English East India Company, established in 1599 in deliberate imitation of the earlier Dutch companies, failed to achieve anything like the same level of success until the eighteenth century. It had less mercantile wealth to draw on and the English navy was weaker than the Dutch until the 1650s.

Third, deliberate initiatives by the Crown. The Spanish Crown quickly began to take an active interest in South America once it realised that the flood of bullion created the potential to enhance its power in Europe. French kings, faced with the comparative sluggishness of the nation's trade, sought to encourage commercial and colonial ventures. With the beginnings of world-wide geopolitical rivalry with England, Louis XIV set out to disrupt and contain English trade and colonies in the Caribbean, North

America and India. The development of New France, in what is now Eastern Canada, was driven more by military than by economic concerns and focused on forts rather than trading posts. The English Crown usually played a less active role in establishing colonies: the most obvious exception was the Duke of York's charter for New York.

The Workings of Empire: Control

It was one thing to establish a colony, quite another to exercise control over the way it functioned. The most fundamental problem was distance. It could take weeks or months for letters to travel between Europe on one hand and America or Asia on the other (assuming that the ships carrying them did not sink en route). Aware of this, kings and ministers were often reluctant to be too prescriptive, leaving it to the men on the spot to use their judgment. When letters did arrive colonial rulers could delay replying or waste time by asking for clarification. Even if the colonial authorities obeyed the Crown's orders, they might find it difficult to secure obedience within the colony. Local officials or rogue individuals might pursue their own aims, ignoring those nominally in authority over them. On the colonial frontier, land-hungry farmers and colonial office-holders killed Indians or drove them off their lands. In Ireland army officers used sweeping powers under martial law to imprison or kill natives who they claimed were 'disaffected' and to seize lands for their own use. In India the government had no direct control over the East India Company, which in turn had only limited control over its agents in the sub-continent. The Spanish and French kings were more concerned than the English monarchs to maintain a degree of control. In the sixteenth century there is strong evidence that officials in 'New Spain' were under considerable pressure to do the bidding of Madrid. The settlements in New France were primarily military, trappers and fur traders were not particularly interested in acquiring land and military commanders did not have to contend with truculent colonial assemblies. The English Crown's ability to intervene, in America or Ireland, was weakened by its reluctance to commit men and money. The New England colonies, in particular, largely ignored the government in London. The attempt by the Duke of York, later James II, to bring them to heel ended with his loss of the Crown in 1689. Without significant financial or military support from England until the 1750s, the colonies were left to defend themselves against the French as best they could.

It will be apparent that the English colonies were subjected to relatively little direction or control from the home government. As a result they developed in various ways, often influenced more by what happened on the periphery than at the centre: there was no single narrative of colonial development. What follows is an attempt to impose some sort of order on a not very orderly story, starting with the English experience in Ireland, which in its use of extensive, indeed systematic, violence and large-scale expropriation anticipated English treatment of the native population of North America. As the Amerindians were both ill-equipped and unwilling to cultivate the lands seized by the English, landlords looked elsewhere: to impoverished workers, convicted felons and defeated soldiers from England, Scotland and Ireland and then to African slaves. We then move on to consider particular colonies or groups of colonies, in the Caribbean, North America and finally India, which suddenly in the 1750s became the most important part of the British Empire.

Ireland: a Prototype for Empire?

The first English attempt at plantation took place in Ireland. The Tudor conquest was driven by a mixture of geopolitical and economic factors. The English government feared that Spain might use it as a base from which to attack England. The economic incentives had nothing to do with precious metals but the belief that Ireland (unlike Scotland) possessed unfulfilled potential; however, its agriculture and trade could thrive only if it was 'pacified'. A small but growing number of English Protestants in Ireland argued that this could be achieved only through military conquest and the confiscation of the lands of the 'rebellious' Irish. This confiscated land would be granted to entrepreneurs, who would settle it with Englishmen and Scots. The element of profit was clearly present: land meant wealth and it was widely believed that it would be more profitable if it was farmed in the English manner. There was no prospect of introducing radically new crops to Ireland, but the aim was to manage traditional crops and traditional animals more productively. The English showed contempt for the native people in both Ireland and America. Although some felt a grudging respect for their understanding of the local terrain, their ability to find their way through bogs and forests, they were seen as lawless, bloodthirsty and treacherous. The refusal of the Irish to embrace English conceptions of order and civility meant that the only way to subjugate them was by force, including massacre and starvation. Apart from Raleigh's massacre at Smerwick, an expedition under Sir Francis Drake killed 300 to 400 Macdonnell women and children on Rathlin Island, off the Antrim coast. Many of the earliest colonists in America had served in Ireland, and brought with them a casual attitude to human life and a relish for killing.

The Elizabethans and America

The English were slow to respond to the models of empire based on plantations and trade. Men like Raleigh and Drake, John Hawkins and Sir Richard Grenville were not interested in agriculture; although Raleigh acquired a massive estate in the Munster Plantation, his interests lay elsewhere, in plunder, adventure and quick profits.

Elizabeth's government licensed such men as **privateers**, state-authorised pirates, in return for a share of the profits. In this way, it damaged Spain without, it hoped, provoking outright war. The treasure fleets which carried gold and silver to Spain were too well protected, but merchant ships trading with Spanish colonies were more vulnerable. To attack them was still risky: there was a substantial Spanish naval presence and the English had to contend with French and Dutch privateers, who did not welcome English competition. English privateering expeditions made some spectacular profits, but some ended in disaster, as when Sir Richard Grenville refused to surrender when confronted by fifty-three Spanish ships in 1591. With Grenville the reckless courage often shown by Elizabethan seafarers toppled over into near-insanity.

This same reckless (and impractical) spirit permeated the first English expedition to establish a colony in North America, at Roanoke Island, in 1585. Its objectives were confused. Promoted by Raleigh, it won government approval as a base for attacks on Spanish shipping. It also carried English plants and seeds, but few of the men had any experience of farming and most expected to find precious metals. The expedition suffered extensive losses in storms and the survivors depended on the local Amerindians to help them to grow or buy enough food to survive the winter. Raleigh urged his men not to use violence against the natives, but to 'instruct them in liberal arts and civility': his objective was 'riches with honour, conquest without blood'. This peaceable, if condescending, attitude was not shared by most members of the expedition. They made little effort to prepare the ground and plant seeds but stole food from the Amerindians and headed upriver looking for gold. Their governor, Ralph Lane, who had served in Ireland, became increasingly convinced that the natives were plotting against the English. Friction led to violence and the killing of a chief. Lane returned to London and the colony fell apart; later visitors to Roanoke found no survivors.

Amerindians

The native peoples of North America were enormously varied. Unlike the Gaelic Irish, who spoke a single language and professed one religion, the Amerindians spoke very many diverse languages and practised a wide range of non-Christian religions. Their ways of life varied with the territory they occupied, but they tended to live off the land, through agriculture, hunting and fishing. Land was plentiful: tribes would clear a stretch of forest by felling and burning, cultivate the land until it lost its fertility and then clear another area. If they had a harvest surplus, they stored grain for leaner times ahead. For building and much else they relied on timber from the forests. If the animals they hunted became scarce, they moved on. They placed little value on precious metals, but some treasured **wampum**, cowrie shells from Atlantic beaches, made into strings and used as currency.

BOX 10.1: **Jean Boyd III, a Huguenot of Scottish Descent, Describes the Torture and Killing of an Amerindian Chief in a Letter from Charleston, South Carolina, in 1691 (Translation)**

Here is the manner in which they deal with a chief taken in war. They tie him to a post around which they pile up wood and they begin by pulling out his fingernails and hair. They make incisions on his arms and his thighs, pulling out his tendons and staunching them with hot cinders to staunch the blood. He suffers thus a long time after which they remove the flesh of his cranium which they also cover with ashes. He suffers all of this without making the least grimace. On the contrary, he laughs saying 'Oh! I have done worse to your relatives.' They untie him and dance with him. Then they tie him up again and with little pieces of dry wood they grease his body all over. They cut the flesh which they grill in front of him and which they give him to eat. Finally they make him suffer until he is weary of his life and then they set fire to the wood which is around him, catching the sticks with which he was greased on fire. He first suffocates. Those who suffer the longest are the most respected in their eyes. They mourn him as a group for two days.

H.C. Leland and D.W. Ressinger (eds.), '"Ce païs tant désiré." This much longed for country', *Transactions of the Huguenot Society of South Carolina*, supplement to no. 110 (2006), p. 30.

The Amerindians' life was far from idyllic. As in Ireland, tribal warfare was endemic and vicious. There were succession disputes within tribes and conflicts over territory and access to hunting and fishing grounds. Villagers built wooden palisades to protect their homes and food stores, but these were easily set on fire and enemies could trap them inside so that they burned to death. Food and livestock could be plundered or destroyed, threatening the defeated with starvation. The men might be taken prisoner, sold into slavery or killed. It was common for prisoners to be tortured to death, either as entertainment for the victors or as revenge for earlier killings. (See Box 10.1, The Torture and Killing of an Amerindian Chief.) Some tribes practised 'mourning wars': bereaved women called on their leaders to capture prisoners who could either be tortured to death or adopted to replace the lost menfolk. Tribal membership and identity were somewhat fluid. The losers in battles within tribes, or those who had suffered crippling casualties, might be taken into another tribe to make up depleted numbers.

Amerindians and Europeans

Europeans were aware of North America by the early sixteenth century, notably the rich fishing grounds off Newfoundland. Traders and explorers arrived as the century wore on – French in the St Lawrence, Spaniards and French in Florida. In the seventeenth century the English established a string of colonies along the Atlantic seaboard, while the French consolidated around the gulf of St Lawrence and towards Hudson's Bay, as well as heading south west into the Mississippi valley. Dutch and Swedes settled in what became New York and New Jersey. In time, settlers from the English colonies penetrated westwards into the Ohio valley and towards the Mississippi. As Europeans spread further and further west, they came into contact with more and more Amerindian tribes.

Often the Amerindians welcomed the Europeans, who brought goods that they wanted, some ornamental, like copper pots or glass vessels, some useful, like hard-edged metal tools. Above all they brought firearms, ammunition and gunpowder, which was especially precious, because it had to be imported and did not keep well. In return the Amerindians could provide goods which Europeans wanted, particularly beaver and other furs. Although it might seem foolish for the Europeans to supply the Amerindians with guns and powder, they were often prepared to do so. Europeans were always looking for native allies in their conflicts with one another, so arming them could prove advantageous. If one set of Europeans refused to sell arms, the Amerindians could find another that would, and rogue elements within the colonies would sell them anything if the price was right.

Amerindians also often welcomed Europeans as powerful, if dangerous, allies in inter-tribal wars. Amerindian alliances were similar to those among the Gaelic Irish: they were useful while they lasted, but often each party had reason to complain of the perfidy of the other. Some tribes were simply too powerful to neglect, such as the Huron and their eventual nemesis, the five (later six) 'nations' of the Iroquois Confederacy, although it should be added that the 'nations' did not always speak with one voice. Among lesser tribes European firepower could help them defeat or eradicate their enemies; conversely, Europeans could use Amerindian knowledge of the terrain to root out and disperse disruptive tribes, as with the Pequot in Massachusetts. The coming of the Europeans did not lead to straightforward conflict between settlers and natives: the tribes were never as united against the settlers as the Gaelic Irish came to be against the English.

Nevertheless, the coming of the Europeans damaged the Amerindians and their way of life, for three reasons. First, the Europeans brought diseases to which Amerindians initially had little or no resistance. Disease drastically reduced the population of some tribes, but had less effect on others, perhaps because earlier contacts had helped them to develop some immunity. This is a complex subject because it worked both ways: many early English settlers on the James River in Virginia died from swamp diseases, probably malaria. African slaves brought diseases, notably yellow fever, which killed both Europeans and Amerindians, and both died in large numbers from epidemic diseases like smallpox. There seems little evidence at this stage that diseases were deliberately spread to wipe out the indigenous population.

Second, the Europeans, especially the English, showed an insatiable appetite for land which could be satisfied only at the natives' expense. As more settlers arrived the Amerindians were pushed further and further west. In Virginia and South Carolina poor settlers were granted a generous allocation of land, while frontier farmers were eager to extend their holdings at the natives' expense. As forests were cleared for tobacco planting, hunting became more difficult. If the Amerindians tried to resist they could be driven out and their villages looted and burned. For the moment there was still land for the displaced Amerindians to move into. This was a vast underpopulated continent, but the pressure on land was beginning to tell; with it came friction between tribes and between settlers and natives.

Third, Christian missionaries, French Jesuits and New England Protestants, converted many Amerindians and persuaded them to abandon their old gods and communities. They were relocated in mission villages – in New England, 'praying towns'. They developed a new Christian identity, which cut across tribal loyalties, and they learned to disparage their old values and way of life. For some Amerindians Christianity was bringing to the 'savage' Amerindians the 'civility' that Raleigh had spoken of.

Labour in the English Colonies

The English colonies were all initially agricultural, based on arable farming supplemented by livestock rearing and fishing; manufacturing developed on a significant scale only later, if at all. Agriculture required labour and knowledge of soils and climate. Many came to America voluntarily, seeking religious freedom or economic betterment. As the early English settlers in Virginia found the climate far too hot and humid, later settlers headed further north, to New England and the Middle Colonies, where the climate was more temperate and the soils more suited to their type of farming. Pennsylvania proved suitable for growing wheat, which (like barley, rye and oats) had been unknown in America: the Amerindians relied on maize. New Englanders found that the wheat they planted suffered from diseases, so grew maize instead.

Voluntary Emigrants

Those who migrated for religious reasons hoped not for great wealth but a modest sufficiency, a 'competency'. Often they came as families – whereas early Virginian settlers were usually single men – so brought their labour force with them. The strong Puritanism of New England deterred non-puritan settlers, who were attracted instead by the more diverse and tolerant middle colonies. Initially most came from England, but later, after a severe economic slump in late seventeenth-century Scotland, many came from Scotland and Ireland (especially 'Scotch-Irish', who had initially migrated to Ulster). In the mid-century there were Dutch and Swedish settlements, and many French Huguenots and German Protestant refugees. Catholics settled in Maryland, but the other colonies were strongly Protestant. The 'Great Awakening' of the 1740s, driven by charismatic preachers, made colonial American society more intensively religious but without any single dominant church.

The areas with the greatest labour shortages were the plantation colonies from Virginia southwards and the Caribbean islands, where the free white population was too small to cultivate the land and mortality from disease was high. One possible solution to this problem was to recruit indigenous peoples, but these were often hostile – non-existent in Barbados – and unfamiliar with the crops that were being grown. In many Amerindian tribes the women farmed the land while the men hunted and fished. Most grew maize, squashes and beans, for subsistence rather than profit; with no concept of money, they had no incentive to work for wages. While some tribes were docile and welcoming, hostility grew as the colonists took their lands and cut down their forests. Punitive raids and counter-raids occasionally escalated into full-blown wars. In such circumstances it became increasingly unlikely that the Amerindians would work with or for the colonists, who therefore had to bring labour in from outside.

Indentured Servants, 'Rebels' and Felons

There were two main sources of such labour, both to some extent unfree. The first were white and their loss of freedom was temporary. **Indentured servants** were free men who undertook to work for an employer, who paid for their passage, for a period of years, usually four to seven. After that time they could acquire land: free settlers were entitled to a grant of fifty acres in Virginia and 150 in South Carolina. The main problem was to survive the period of their indenture without succumbing to disease or maltreatment. From the 1650s indentured servants were joined by thousands of Irish Catholics, and smaller but substantial numbers of Scots, expelled after their defeat by the New Model. Later many felons, convicted of capital offences, had their death sentences commuted to **transportation**, usually for seven or fourteen years. In the first half of the eighteenth century the number of executions in England fell dramatically while the number transported increased. If a transported person – some were women – returned before their time was up they could be executed, but once they had served their time they were free to build a life in the New World. In the later seventeenth century the number of indentured servants fell, as employment opportunities and wages improved in England (although not in Scotland). Contemporaries tended to lump indentured servants, 'rebels' and felons together as 'white slaves'.

From the point of view of employers Irish rebels and English felons often proved poor workers. Some were too old, young or puny to cope with heavy work in a hot climate, but also many (particularly the Irish) proved intractable and undisciplined, which some planters blamed on their priests. These problems were particularly acute in the sugar colonies. Sugar required intensive labour and substantial capital. Vegetation had to be cleared and the cane tended and harvested. It was then taken to the sugar mill to be crushed, extracting the juice which had to be boiled immediately, before it fermented. This was backbreaking, unremitting work and indentured servants could not cope. English planters came up with the same solution to this problem as the Portuguese in Brazil: African slaves.

Slavery

Black slaves became the most important source of labour, initially in the Caribbean, later in the southern colonies: by 1750 they could be found in all the American colonies. The slave trade centred on the Guinea coast of West Africa and had existed for more than a century under the Portuguese and Spaniards before the English became involved in it. African traders brought slaves from the interior to ports where they were bought by European traders who shipped them across the Atlantic. By 1640, despite fierce competition from the Spanish, French and Swedes, the dominant traders were the Dutch. The English already traded with West Africa, and established several forts along the Gold Coast (now Ghana), but dealt mostly in commodities other than slaves. This changed with the establishment of the Royal African Company in 1663. Both the Company and merchants who opposed its monopoly (**interlopers**) set out to grab as much of the slave trade as they could. By 1680 England had emerged as the leading slaving power and slave labour fuelled the rapid expansion of the production of sugar in the Caribbean, tobacco in Virginia and rice in the Carolinas. African slavery was the foundation of the prosperity of the British Empire in the eighteenth century and brought great wealth to Bristol, Liverpool and Glasgow.

Initially there was little criticism of the slave trade. Although Englishmen rejoiced in being 'freeborn', in contrast to the 'slavery' of the French, they apparently saw nothing wrong with enslaving others. Black Africans, like Gaelic Irish or Amerindians, were seen as not fully human. There was little effort to convert slaves to Christianity, which was seen as intellectually beyond them. Colonies with substantial slave populations enacted 'slave codes', to subjugate them as effectively as possible, and established militias to guard against slave revolts. Employers generally wanted male slaves so there was an imbalance between the sexes. Families were often split up and the slave experience was one of disorientation: slaves came from different tribes and spoke different languages. They learned to communicate through simple pidgins or more complex creoles – types of language based on English with much simplified vocabulary and syntax. 'Creoles', blacks born in the colonies, were more likely than African-born slaves to be proficient in these languages, which they learned as children. They were often treated more favourably by their owners and became the leaders of slave society.

In time some slave owners came to see the benefits of using incentives rather than threats and punishment. Some slaves were allowed time off to tend their own plots of land, others were spared labour in the fields to act as household servants or practise a trade. But in general, severity and the misuse of power were the norm. Slaves were overworked and undernourished; owners took it for granted that they needed to purchase more each year to keep up the numbers. In white communities where women were scarce masters forced themselves on slave women. Whites were very conscious that they were heavily outnumbered by blacks and slave revolts made them nervous.

In Jamaica runaway slaves (maroons) took to the mountains and resisted all attempts to hunt them down. Slave codes gave owners the power to discipline their slaves and the normal means of discipline was whipping, often administered with what looks like sadistic cruelty. It should be added that whipping played a prominent part in the English criminal law – a woman convicted of a small theft could be publicly whipped until her back was bloody. Soldiers and sailors were sentenced to hundreds of lashes and defiant convicts were flogged until they lost consciousness. Nevertheless, in the case of slaves savage punishment was part of a general subjugation: slaves had few, if any, legal rights – killing a slave was punishable only by a fine – and most lacked any control over their daily existence.

The Crown and the Colonies

Some English settlements abroad were small trading posts or garrisons, which required little governance. As the plantations in the New World grew, they raised issues which required the Crown's attention. These included friction or open war with rival powers, privateering and piracy – Jamaica was a haven for buccaneers – and the enhancement of the royal revenue. The first of the English **Navigation Acts** was passed in 1651 and confirmed and extended by further legislation after the Restoration. It had two main aims. The first was to challenge the Dutch domination of the carrying trade. Ships carrying goods to or from English ports were to have either English crews or crews from the country of origin: in other words, Swedish iron could be carried by Swedish ships or English ships, but not Dutch ships. The second was to ensure that the colonies traded only with England and to prevent them trading with other colonies, English or foreign. By the 1680s customs and excise duties on staple crops like sugar and tobacco made up a substantial part of the royal revenue. Colonies were expected to enrich the mother country and the Crown was determined to secure its share.

Creating governments from scratch for new settlements thousands of miles away was a novel problem. Ireland could not serve as a model. Its government was a smaller replica of England's, in some respects elaborate and sophisticated, but ineffective outside the limited areas under English control. Throughout the seventeenth century the Crown took it for granted that these were English colonies, governed according to English models and English law, as far as this was practical. In theory, their governments derived their powers from the Crown, often through royal charters similar to those which empowered English towns to run their own affairs. Some were granted to companies, including Virginia, Massachusetts Bay and Hudson's Bay. Neither of the first two worked well. The settlers in Virginia were factious and lawless: James I cancelled the charter and Charles I tried to subject the colony to direct royal rule. Members of the colony's assembly defended their role in its government, taking their stand (like the Old

English in Ireland) on the claim that they still enjoyed the full rights of Englishmen. The Massachusetts Bay settlers took their charter with them and established their own system of government without reference to king or charter. It was unclear by what authority other colonies, such as Connecticut and Rhode Island, were established in New England.

Disillusioned with chartered companies, Charles I established the first **proprietary** colony in 1625, granting 'the Caribbean islands' to the Earl of Carlisle. Unfortunately he granted the same islands to the Earl of Pembroke in 1628, which led to several years of bloody conflict before the King confirmed the grant to Carlisle. To prevent such confusion, the charter to Lord Baltimore for Maryland in 1632 was more carefully drafted. Baltimore was granted sweeping powers similar to those of the Bishop in the **Palatinate** of Durham: he could grant lands with manorial rights (the owners could hold their own courts), incorporate towns and raise revenue on his own authority. He was to exercise these powers with the advice and consent of the free men of the colony, but the preponderance of power lay with the proprietor. This proprietary model was followed for South Carolina (1663), New York (1664) and Pennsylvania (1681).

The 1650s saw another attempt at direct rule. The Protectorate lacked the authority which the Crown had possessed in the colonies, many of which remained neutral in the civil wars. When the English took Jamaica they installed a garrison and used it as a base from which to attack Spanish trade and colonies. The restored monarchy reverted to establishing proprietary colonies and set up the Royal African Company to build up England's share of the slave trade. James Duke of York's charter for New York concentrated power in the Duke, who was reluctant to agree to an elected assembly and restricted its powers. The New Yorkers resented this and demanded the sort of participatory government established in Massachusetts. As the colonies' population and wealth grew Charles II's government sought ways to establish greater control over their government and trade. In the 1680s York (who became James II in 1685) saw the northern and middle colonies as nests of political and religious radicals and set up the Dominion of New England (which also included New York) to bring them under tighter control.

The English in the Caribbean

Although the earliest English colonies were on the American mainland, for much of the seventeenth century the most economically important were in the Caribbean. The Spaniards in South America and Mexico expanded into the Caribbean because the larger islands were often very fertile and offered ports from which trade with Spain could be protected. Spain secured Havana (Cuba), Hispaniola (now Haiti and the Dominican Republic), San Domingo (Jamaica) and Puerto Rico. As the Spaniards and

Portuguese effectively kept other European powers out of the mainland these powers concentrated on privateering and plundering. In the 1620s and 1630s they seized some of the smaller islands which Spain had not secured because they had few obvious assets.

For England the most important acquisition was initially Barbados. Modest-sized, unclaimed and uninhabited, it proved well suited for producing sugar, of which Brazil was currently the largest producer. As there were no indigenous people on the island, labour had to be brought in, first indentured servants and then African slaves. With sugar fetching high prices in Europe the planters became rich, plantations grew larger and wealth was concentrated in fewer hands; the most successful planters returned to England where they became extremely influential in Parliament and at Whitehall.

The other sugar islands in the Caribbean were mostly small and often contested: Nevis was divided between England and France and changed hands several times. Such insecurity did not encourage investment; in addition the terrain tended to be less suitable than in Barbados and the indigenous Carib people, the Kalinagos, were turbulent and hostile. The one exception to this picture was the much larger island of Jamaica, acquired almost as consolation for the failure to take Hispaniola in 1655. Jamaica became important as a sugar producer, especially as sugar prices fell and the fertility of the Barbados plantations declined. But Jamaica had a much more diverse agriculture than Barbados, which had focused on sugar to a point where it had to import much of its food.

The Caribbean, especially its sugar islands, played a vital role in the economy of the English Atlantic in the second half of the seventeenth century. The islands supplied mainland colonies with sugar and molasses (for rum) and imported grain and other foodstuffs, ships, timber and an increasing range of manufactured goods, especially textiles. For those on the mainland, especially in New England, the Caribbean offered a richer market than yet existed in North America.

 ## England's North American Colonies

The South

The first successful colony was Virginia, which started in 1607 with a settlement at Jamestown, on the James River shortly before it flowed into Chesapeake Bay. The settlers were ill-prepared for the conditions they found there, but the project was saved by the discovery that high-quality tobacco would grow well. After suffering heavy mortality in the early years the settlers moved upriver, where conditions were better, but where they came more into conflict with Amerindian tribes, leading to war with the Powhatan in 1609–14. The population grew slowly, partly because of high mortality, partly because most would-be settlers were single men. Even in 1620 the population numbered less than 1,000, the profits from tobacco were still disappointingly small and only the hope that they would increase kept the colony going.

The Virginians continually quarrelled with their governors, and clashed with the Amerindians. After a series of Indian wars a settler revolt broke out in 1675, led by Nathaniel Bacon, a disreputable and unruly Suffolk gentleman. It started in the lawless frontier zone and was driven by anger that Governor Berkeley was trying to prevent the frontiersmen from seizing as much land as they could. Despite the governor's efforts, they were supplying friendly Indians with firearms, in the hope of wiping out those opposing the settlers. In the event, Bacon's followers killed many of his Indian allies (but few of his enemies) and burned Jamestown before the revolt was ended by Bacon's unexpected death.

Charles II was sufficiently concerned by Bacon's rebellion to send over a thousand soldiers, but by the time they arrived the rebellion had petered out. What most worried the King was that the revolt seriously interrupted tobacco exports and his revenue from customs duties. Virginia might be unruly, but power lay with the great landowners and the colonists were loyal to the Crown. The same was true of North and South Carolina, founded in the reign of Charles II. The proprietors of South Carolina granted extensive powers of self-government through an elected assembly with the sole right to tax the colonists. Power lay with the great estate owners. While the Indians were relatively docile, South Carolina was troubled by raids from Spanish Florida. The need to defend the southern frontier was one reason for the founding of Georgia in 1732, but its main aim was religious and philanthropic, to provide opportunities for England's 'worthy poor' to make good and perhaps convert the local Amerindians. The trustees who initially ran the colony were not allowed to profit from it, and after twenty-one years it was to revert to the Crown. Georgia, like Virginia and the Carolinas, was a plantation colony with great landed estates and a labour force consisting predominantly of slaves. Their social and ethnic composition made them very different from the northern and middle Colonies.

New England

The New England colonies were founded by Puritan dissidents fleeing the 'corruption' of the Church of England. They likened themselves to Old Testament Jews, driven by God's displeasure into a 'howling wilderness', where they would suffer hardship but be free to live and worship in their own way. From small beginnings the population grew rapidly with the 'Great Migration' of the 1630s, when Laud tightened his grip on the Church. They struggled to survive the first winters, but, fortuitously, most of the local Amerindian tribes had recently been almost wiped out by disease, for which the settlers thanked God; as one minister put it, the 'woods were almost cleared of those pernicious creatures to make room for a better growth'. They continued the process in the Pequot wars in 1637, in which several hundred women, children and old men were massacred at Mystic River and many men were enslaved or executed. The settlers paid no heed to the King's authority. As soon as the *Mayflower* arrived in 1620, the free adult male passengers agreed to set up their own government and to obey laws drawn up by their elected representatives. Land was to be divided up, much of it into modest freehold family farms: farmers were not to be beholden to a landlord. In Massachusetts and Plymouth churches were organised on congregational lines, bound together by a founding covenant; town governments agreed with their people to live in harmony. These covenants were not always obeyed and, even when they were, churches and towns often differed from one another, but in both Church and state government rested in theory upon consent.

Not all settlers were godly, but church attendance and subjection to the churches' moral discipline were compulsory for everyone. In Massachusetts full political rights were confined to Church members, who could persuade existing members that they had undergone a conversion experience. Often their claims were rejected, even though they were children of members, so Church members became fewer and fewer and town governments (which also oversaw the allocation of land) were dominated by small groups of the godly. The churches, so vociferous in their denunciations of the Church of England, showed little tolerance of divergent opinions among their fellow-settlers. Quarrels about theology and Church discipline led to secessions and the creation of new colonies – Connecticut, New Hampshire and Rhode Island. The last was founded by the combative Roger Williams and embraced the principle of full religious toleration while also excluding the ungodly. (Williams also argued that the Crown could not grant Indian lands to settlers.) Rhode Island formed a loose association of churches and communities, whose members often disagreed with one another. What they had in common, apart from a commitment to toleration, was a stern puritan morality.

By 1650 immigration to New England had almost ceased, but the population grew from 23,000 in 1650 to 90,000 in 1700, due to natural increase: New Englanders tended to marry young and have large families. A growing population required more land, which led to renewed friction with the Amerindians, culminating in the most destructive of all Indian wars, 'King Philip's War' of 1675–6. The Indians destroyed a dozen towns and the military seemed unable to contain them, so the settlers destroyed the Indians' food, starving them into submission. King Philip was assassinated and many Indians were, as before, executed or sold into slavery. Indian resistance was effectively ended, which the settlers interpreted as evidence of God's favour. The colonies also survived an attempt to destroy their autonomy by subjecting it to direct royal rule. This was defeated by the Glorious Revolution in England which led to severe, but short-lived, upheavals in America. Thereafter New England enjoyed peace and a modest prosperity. Travellers might complain of drab towns, squalid lodgings and dangerous roads and bridges but the New Englanders apparently were unconcerned.

They had their self-sufficiency and their status as God's chosen people. The problem of shrinking Church membership was partially resolved by granting provisional (or 'half-way') membership to the sons of members until they could demonstrate their conversion. In the eighteenth century the contagion of Protestant diversity spread even to New England. More and more people worshipped outside the official Congregational Church and the ideal that Church and community were one became untenable. But in other ways the distinctive character of New England was maintained.

The Middle Colonies

Between Virginia and Maryland to the south and New England to the north the English made no purposeful effort to establish colonies until 1664. Into this vacuum moved others: a few English, Huguenots, Swedes, Africans and above all Dutch. They concentrated their settlements in the valleys of the Delaware and Hudson, through which they could trade with the Indians of the Great Lakes region and the French. On the Hudson the Dutch established New Amsterdam, near the mouth, and the trading post of Fort Orange, upriver. Unlike their counterparts in the South and New England the settlers usually managed to remain at peace with the Indians in the later seventeenth century, thanks to a series of complex peace treaties, notably the 'Covenant Chain' with the Five Nations. Discord arrived when an English sea-captain captured New Amsterdam and renamed it New York, after Charles II's brother, the Duke of York, who was granted a large stretch of territory east of the Hudson as a proprietary colony. He claimed the right to issue laws and control trade and refused to grant a genuinely elected assembly. Soon he hived off a substantial section along the seaboard, which became two proprietary colonies, East and West New Jersey. The Dutch briefly retook New York in 1673, after which James tried to tighten his grip on his colony; Fort Orange was renamed Albany, after his Scottish dukedom.

The Middle Colonies were much more diverse than New England or the South. The Dutch presence was strong, especially in New York City and Albany. In East New Jersey, Scots established a compact settlement of large landed estates, while in West Jersey Quakers established settlements, mostly of modest family farms. This was followed by William Penn's better-known settlement in Pennsylvania, again including many small farms, together with a bustling port at Philadelphia, which played a central role in trade with the Caribbean colonies. Diversity, ethnic and religious, bred division and unruly popular politics. The Dutch resented the English taking their colony and where there were large landed estates (for example in New York and East New Jersey) the political power wielded by the proprietors provoked much resentment, as did James's authoritarian attitude and his 'Dominion of New England'. Penn was less authoritarian, but he sought to maintain a measure of control over his colony in order to resolve his serious financial problems. After the Glorious Revolution there were a series of risings, notably in New York, where Dutch and English clashed violently. The Dominion was abolished and an elected assembly established, which helped to perpetuate factionalism. New York and Philadelphia became notoriously volatile and unruly cities and were to play a prominent role in the revolt against British rule later in the eighteenth century.

The Origins of British Canada

Between 1689 and 1815 France was England's (later Britain's) main military, commercial and colonial rival. In North America the French established forts along the St Lawrence, in the Great Lakes, and down the Mississippi to 'Louisiana' – a vast tract of land claimed by France since 1682. Although there was a hiatus in hostilities in Europe between 1713 and 1744 this did not extend to America. Unlike the British, the French did not establish densely populated settlements. The French presence was sparse – in 1687 English colonists outnumbered French by almost ten to one – but from the 1690s the French compensated for this with a substantial regular army. They also had powerful Amerindian allies, skilled in guerrilla warfare (which the British were not). The French were forced to cede Nova Scotia and Newfoundland to Britain in 1713, together with a large and mostly uninhabited area around Hudson's Bay, but they retained New France (Acadie), comprising both banks of the St Lawrence (including Quebec), and the Great Lakes, home to powerful Amerindian tribes.

Amerindian allies offer one explanation for the relative lack of British military success – and as survival was the main aim of the French, British lack of success was tantamount to a French victory. Another was that the French had unified command: the governor general of New France did not have to answer to elected assemblies. The British government gave only fitful military and naval aid to the colonies until the 1740s, so the colonists had to rely on their own resources. Some colonies felt little threat from the French and their allies, while the South was more concerned with the threat from Florida. The main burden of defending the British colonies fell on New England and New York. As they were fighting with their own 'militia' colonial assemblies made the key decisions about raising and paying troops and frequently became mired in disputes. In the war of 1744–8 the colonists (with British naval help) took Louisbourg, a key fort on the St Lawrence, but failed to take Quebec. In the Seven Years War (1756–63) the British colonists received far more military assistance from home, but the French did not: Louis XV's government had decided that New France could not be saved. The French put up stubborn resistance in a series of bloody battles, but could not prevent the British from taking Quebec and Montreal. After the war

France ceded New France (now known as Quebec) to Britain, as well as all the land east of the Mississippi down to the Gulf of Mexico and all the northern part of North America, now called Canada. This vastly increased the area under notional British rule, although much was sparsely populated. It also opened the way for English settlement to expand westwards, across the St Lawrence, into the Great Lakes and towards the Mississippi.

The British in India

In Asia the British had to contend with much more sophisticated societies than in America, with administrative structures and weaponry at least equal to Europeans. Conquest was not an option and access could be difficult: the British were excluded from Japan and could trade with China only through Canton. The Chinese trade grew in the eighteenth century, as imports of tea and porcelain increased, but by far the most important trade was with India. Initially this consisted of pepper and spices but in the seventeenth century the great majority of English imports from India were textiles: light, brightly coloured cloths, which were re-exported in large quantities to Africa and the Americas. They became so popular at home that, following loud complaints from English textile manufacturers, Parliament banned the import of calicoes in 1722; women who wore them risked having them ripped from their backs. As there were few English commodities that Asian consumers wanted, most imports from Asia were paid for with bullion.

England's trade with India was conducted by the East India Company. It was high-value and high-risk: voyages lasted many months and were subject to many hazards, notably the Dutch East India Company. The English Company had a chequered history in the seventeenth century – for a while, there were two rival companies which merged in 1709. The Company handled the trade between Britain and India, China and elsewhere in Asia. It had forts in several Indian cities (Surat, Madras and Calcutta) where the role of its agents was essentially commercial: for textiles and agricultural products like coffee they dealt with many small producers, so getting together the items to make up a cargo took time and local knowledge. In the early eighteenth century it as yet played no political or governmental role. That was to change quite suddenly in mid-century.

Apart from the commodities sent to Britain in Company ships, Company employees traded on their own account, between different Asian states and within India; this was known as 'the country trade'. In doing so they dealt with Indian merchants and officials, especially tax collectors, which involved them in Indian government and politics. When there were trade or succession disputes within Indian principalities Company employees might be drawn by their financial interests to support one party. From 1746 disputes became bound up with military conflict in India between Britain and France, both of whom had Indian allies. In 1756 the Nawab of Bengal seized Calcutta, vital for the Company's trade. The Nawab's forces were defeated by Robert Clive at Plassey and Bengal became a client state, not of Britain, but of the Company. Although the Company had a small British force of its own, two-thirds of Clive's army at Plassey consisted of sepoys, Indian soldiers in British service; at the Battle of Buxar in 1764 the proportion of sepoys was almost 90 per cent. Through their Indian contacts the Company's servants were able to assemble a significant army, which was answerable to Company agents in India, not the directors in London and certainly not the British government. In taking over the government of Bengal the Company exercised rule over twenty million people – very much more than the population of the North American colonies or Britain – and in the decades that followed the Company, and later the British government, came to rule over more and more of India. In terms of wealth and population, the centre of gravity of the Empire shifted from the Atlantic to India.

Conclusion

The British Empire – the term was first used in 1773 – was not the product of any plan or vision. The English were slow to get involved in the Americas or Africa and, although English merchants had long traded with Asia, in establishing an East India Company the English, as so often, imitated the Dutch. The government of the Dutch Republic was for much of the time dominated by merchants. In England merchants, privateers and colonial promoters had to contend with greedy courtiers and a timid and underfunded monarchy, which responded to the initiatives of others. England's American and Caribbean colonies were shaped by men and events on the ground and by conflict with indigenous peoples and European rivals. From the 1640s the English state became increasingly strong, with an increased revenue, navy and army, but much of that strength was used to make war in Europe rather than aid the colonies. From the 1650s the London government tried harder to influence the colonies but it was hampered by distance. Only in the Seven Years War did the British government give full military support to the American colonists and the East India Company gained control of Bengal without the assistance (or knowledge) of the British government. Nevertheless revenue from the colonial trades helped strengthen the state and the state came to use the navy and army to foster trade and protect the colonies. In addition, the ever-growing Empire created new strategic and geopolitical concerns which required the deployment of military and naval force. The growth of empire also had a significant impact at home. It increased British self-confidence – or arrogance – but it also had a significant impact on the economy and the quality of life within Britain, which will be the subject of the next chapter.

SUGGESTIONS FOR FURTHER READING

An excellent starting point is the multi-author *Oxford History of the British Empire*, of which the first two volumes are N. Canny (ed.), *The Origins of Empire* and P.J. Marshall (ed.), *The Eighteenth Century* (both Oxford, 1998). Both volumes offer a mixture of studies of particular colonies and broader themes. • Another multi-author work, but with a strongly thematic approach, is D. Armitage and M.J. Braddick (eds.), *The British Atlantic World 1500–1800* (2nd edn, Basingstoke, 2009). See also K.R. Andrews, N. Canny and P.E.H. Hair (eds.), *The Westward Enterprise: English Activities in Ireland, the Atlantic and America, 1480–1650* (Liverpool, 1978). • Two very different works focus on military aspects of empire: B.P. Lenman, *England's Colonial Wars 1500–1688: Conflicts, Empire and National Identity* (Harlow, 2001) robustly debunks the idea that the origins of empire can be found in English national consciousness under Elizabeth and to this end he devotes considerable attention to Ireland; and I.K. Steele, *Warpaths: Invasions of North America* (New York, 1994) considers colonisation from an Amerindian perspective. • On the Caribbean, see R.S. Dunn, *Sugar and Slaves: the Rise of the Planter Class in the English West Indies* (Chapel Hill, NC, 1972). • Finally, see J. Keay, *The Honourable Company: a History of the East India Company* (London, 1991).

SUMMARY

- England was much slower than the Portuguese and Spanish to establish colonies in the Americas and lagged behind the Dutch in setting up trading posts in Asia and the East Indies. Under Elizabeth English ambitions focused on privateering and plunder; their attempts at plantation were mostly limited to Ireland. Interest in the Caribbean and North America became more apparent in the early seventeenth century and was given a major boost by the massive expansion of the navy in the 1640s and 1650s.
- English colonies in the Americas fell into two broad types: those producing staple crops, such as tobacco and sugar, using indentured or slave labour; and those founded by religious exiles, mostly Puritans, seeking to escape persecution in England. The former were found mostly in the South and the Caribbean, the latter in New England. The middle colonies fell somewhere between the two.
- England's world-wide rivalry with France and the threat it posed to New England led to attempts to conquer Canada, which were hampered by limited support from the British government and the quarrels of the colonists.
- The extension of British involvement in India was due to the activities of the agents of the East India Company, often acting and trading on their own account, independently of either the Company in London or the British government. In the 1750s agents of the Company gained control of Bengal, with a population far larger than Britain.

QUESTIONS FOR STUDENTS

1. In what ways did England's New England colonies differ from those in the South?

2. Why did slaves become so important for the Caribbean colonies?

3. In what ways did the British presence in India differ from that in the Americas?

4. Why did it take the British so long to defeat the French in Canada?

11 Prosperity and Poverty, 1660–1750

TIMELINE

1651	Navigation Act
1662	Act of Settlement
1673	First Corn Law (restrictions on imports, bounties on exports)
1690s	War and bad harvests; food riots and corporations of the poor (England); agricultural depression and emigration (Scotland)
1697	Act for badging paupers
1709	Severe harvest failure
1722	Act prohibiting import of Indian calicoes
1723	Black Act; Workhouse Act (making possible 'unions' of villages)

Introduction

The century after 1660 can easily be seen as a period of prosperity and elegance. Many English people enjoyed a seemingly endless choice of delightful objects from around the world. But many did not share in this prosperity. Agricultural wages were low and Scotland (and to a lesser extent England) suffered disastrous harvest failures and famines in the 1690s and 1709. Ireland was again ravaged by war in 1689–91 and there remained a huge gulf between the palaces of the Anglo-Irish elite and the hovels of the Catholic peasantry and crumbling tenements of Dublin. As England's trade became global, manufacturers tried to reduce costs in order to compete, especially with Indian textiles. Faced with wage cuts workers organised in **combinations** (trade unions) and went on strike; violence against employers and their property was common. Parliament passed legislation against combinations and protected the interests of the landed elite. This led to occasional agrarian violence and sometimes virtual warfare between smugglers or deer poachers and the agents of the state.

This chapter will examine both sides of this growing divide. On one hand, there was a growing range of goods (including food and drink) available to those with money. There were attempts to make towns more attractive and pleasant. This was the first great period of London squares and the capital's architectural styles, and entertainments, were increasingly imitated in the provinces. Consumer demand led to developments in manufacturing, which generated a broader prosperity as well as creating tensions between employers and workers. The problem of poverty grew and the poor relief system initiated under Elizabeth came under considerable strain. The chapter will conclude with an attempt to assess the extent to which the landed elite abused their economic power to the detriment of the poor and the extent to which the poor could show their resentment.

Population and Prices

In the century before 1640 England experienced substantial population growth and rising prices. From the 1640s to 1750 the pattern changed. The population of England and Wales dipped below five million in the 1680s and 1690s but otherwise remained between five and six million. While in most decades the birth rate remained similar to the century before 1640, the death rate was often higher, notably in the 1680s, 1730s and 1740s. Emigration rates were highest between the 1640s and early 1660s; in Scotland and Ireland they were often very much higher. Food prices, which had tended to rise before 1640, stabilised and at times, notably in the 1680s, 1730s and 1740s, fell significantly. As wages in some industries tended to rise, many wage-earners had a surplus to spend on better food, leisure or consumer goods.

It should be stressed that, while population figures are based on a variety of substantial sources, those for wages and prices are more conjectural. A rather different picture can be found in 'A Scheme of the Income and Expense of the Several Families of England, 1688, by Gregory King' (see Table 11.1). King was a pioneer of 'political arithmetic', applying mathematics to economic and social issues, but his approach was coloured by his belief that William III's government was bankrupting the country. King divided the population into those increasing and decreasing the wealth of the kingdom; the latter, who could not subsist without poor relief, were the more numerous. They included labouring people, paupers and vagrants. Whereas historians have tended to focus on the emergence of a 'consumer society', King and others were well aware of the problem of poverty. Daniel Defoe, an astute social commentator, drew up a succinct description of the social order in 1709:

1. The Great, who live profusely.
2. The Rich, who live plentifully.
3. The Middle Sort, who live well.
4. The Working Trade, who labour hard but feel no want.
5. The Country People, Farmers etc. who fare indifferently.
6. The Poor, that fare hard.
7. The Miserable, that really pinch and suffer want.

Like Defoe's, King's emphasis on the problem of poverty was born of personal observation. He had conducted a detailed survey of the large, overcrowded forest parish of Eccleshall, Staffordshire. Many of the inhabitants had come from elsewhere and scratched a living as best they could, often from more than one occupation. Some made their living as farmers (see Defoe's comment); rather more were craftsmen (especially leather and wood workers) and retailers, who in turn were outnumbered by labourers and widows, 'cottagers' and 'encroachers' (those who had encroached on the forest). Many were described as 'poor', who survived by 'making shift' and would at times need relief from the poor rate. The poorest man to leave a will (many had virtually nothing worth leaving) was John Croft, who left goods worth £2 1s. He had two bedsteads, four blankets and two sheets, a chest and coffer, two cupboards and his tools. His only clothes were two coats, a waistcoat and a pair of breeches. He was not described as poor, but lived in danger of sliding into poverty· one of those 'that fare hard'. Sometimes workers who were normally well above the margin of subsistence were driven to desperation. Norwich's textile trade was badly hit by imports of calicoes and in the 1720s it was reported that many cloth-workers, unable to support their families, had run away, leaving them to be maintained by the poor rate.

Table 11.1 A Scheme of the Income and Expense of the Several Families of England Calculated for the Year 1688, by Gregory King.

This is a complex mathematical exercise, designed to delineate the various elements in the social order, but also to demonstrate the extent of poverty (which King had seen at first hand in Eccleshall). Slightly more than half of the population are described as 'decreasing the wealth of the kingdom' – in other words, spending more than they earn, which in many cases meant receiving poor relief.

Number of Families	Ranks, Degrees, Titles and Qualifications	Heads per Family	Number of Persons	Yearly Income per Family		Total of the Estates or Income	Yearly Income per Head		Expense per Head			Increase per Head			Total Increase per Annum
				£	s.	£	£	s.	£	s.	d.	£	s.	d.	£
160	Temporal Lords	40	6,400	2,800	0	448,000	70	0	60	0	0	10	0	0	64,000
26	Spiritual Lords	20	520	1,300	0	33,800	65	0	55	0	0	10	0	0	5,200
800	Baronets	16	12,800	880	0	704,000	55	0	51	0	0	14	0	0	51,200
600	Knights	13	7,800	650	0	390,000	50	0	46	0	0	4	0	0	31,200
3,000	Esquires	10	30,000	450	0	1,200,000	45	0	42	0	0	3	0	0	90,000
12,000	Gentlemen	8	96,000	280	0	2,880,000	35	0	32	10	0	2	10	0	240,000
5,000	Persons in offices	8	40,000	240	0	1,200,000	30	0	27	0	0	3	0	0	120,000
5,000	Persons in offices	6	30,000	120	0	600,000	20	0	18	0	0	2	0	0	60,000
2,000	Merchants and traders be sea	8	16,000	400	0	800,000	50	0	40	0	0	10	0	0	160,000
8,000	Merchants and traders be sea	6	48,000	200	0	1,600,000	33	0	28	0	0	5	0	0	240,000
10,000	Persons in the law	7	70,000	140	0	1,400,000	20	0	17	0	0	3	0	0	210,000
2,000	Clergymen	6	12,000	60	0	120,000	10	0	9	0	0	1	0	0	12,000
8,000	Clergymen	5	40,000	45	0	360,000	9	0	8	0	0	1	0	0	40,000
40,000	Freeholders	7	280,000	84	0	3,360,000	12	0	11	0	0	1	0	0	280,000
140,000	Freeholders	5	700,000	50	0	7,000,000	10	0	9	10	0		10	0	350,000
150,000	Farmers	5	750,000	44	0	6,600,000	8	15	8	10	0		5	0	187,000
16,000	Persons in sciences and liberal arts	5	80,000	60	0	960,000	12	0	11	10	0	1	10	0	40,000
40,000	Shopkeepers and tradesmen	4½	180,000	45	0	1,800,000	10	0	9	10	0		10	0	90,000
60,000	Artisans and handicrafts	4	240,000	40	0	2,400,000	10	0	9	10	0		10	0	120,000
5,000	Naval officers	4	20,000	80	0	400,000	20	0	18	0	0	2	0	0	40,000
4,000	Military officers	4	16,000	60	0	240,000	15	0	14	0	0	1	0	0	16,000
511,586 Fam.		5¼	2,675,520	67	0	34,495,800	12	18	12	0	0		18	0	2,447,100

			Decrease	£ s.	£	£ s.	£ s. d.	£ s. d.	£
50,000	Common seamen	3	150,000	20 0	1,000,000	7 0	7 10 0	10 0	75,000
364,000	Labouring people and outservants	3½	1,275,000	15 0	5,460,000	4 10	4 12 0	2 0	127,500
400,000	Cottagers and paupers	3¼	1,300,000	6 10	2,000,000	2 0	2 5 0	5 0	325,000
35,000	Common soldiers	2	70,000	14 0	490,000	7 0	7 10 0	10 0	35,000
849,000 Fams.		3¼	2,795,000	10 10	8,950,000	3 5	3 9 0	4 0	562,000
	Vagrants		30,000		60,000	2 0	3 0 0	1 0 0	60,000
				£ s.	£	£ s.	£ s. d.	s. d.	£
849,000		3¼	2,825,000	10 10	9,010,000	3 3	3 7 6	4 6	622,000

So the General Account is.

				£ s.	£	£ s.	£ s. d.	s. d.	£
511,586 Fam.	increasing the wealth of the kingdcm	5¼	2,675,520	67 0	34,495,800	12 18	12 0 0	18 0	2,447,100
849,000 Fam.	decreasing the wealth of the kingdcm	3¼	2,825,000	10 10	9,010,000	3 3	3 7 6	4 6	622,000
1,360,586 Fam	Neat totals	4 1/20	5,500,520	32 0	43,505,800	7 18	7 11 3	6 9	1,825,100

⚬⚬ Landlords, Tenants and Labourers

In the century before 1640 landowners had developed an increasingly commercial approach to estate management, leasing out land in larger units which could be farmed at a good profit. Subsistence farmers were forced out of business and joined the swelling ranks of landless labourers. This transition from a rural order based on landlords with numerous small tenant farmers to one based on landlords, relatively few substantial tenant farmers and many landless labourers continued after 1660. Farmers, too, became more commercially minded. As food prices fell they needed to develop new techniques and crop rotations in order to increase productivity. Fodder crops enabled them to keep more cattle over the winter, which meant more manure to keep arable fields fertile. In years of really low prices farmers struggled; landlords often decided that it made economic sense to help them through difficult times, waiving arrears of rent and encouraging them to adopt new techniques. Landlords also became interested in stock breeding and calculating crop yields. Improvements in productivity could be spectacular. In the sixteenth and early seventeenth centuries yields were often as low as three or four pounds of grain for one pound of seed, from which one pound of seed corn for the next year had to be deducted; when Arthur Young toured Britain and Ireland in the later eighteenth century he found yields of eight or nine to one, or more. This increased productivity meant that a relatively small agricultural sector could feed the nation, freeing up people to work elsewhere in the economy.

If increased productivity was good for landlords and farmers, it was less good for labourers. (See Figure 11.1, Labourer's Cottage from Washington, Sussex.) To keep costs down farmers paid their labourers as little as possible. A gulf of economic interest opened up between labourers and farmers, whose interests increasingly coincided with those of the landlords. Both saw common land, which provided labourers with grazing for cows or pigs, as unproductive. Common rights usually rested on long usage, but this could be over-ridden by Acts of Parliament. Both Houses were dominated by landowners, who used legislation to advance their economic interests. From 1673 Parliament passed 'Corn Laws' to protect the interests of grain producers, with a bounty on exports and a ban on imports until prices rose above a certain level. Both provisions were designed to keep grain prices up. Before 1640 the government normally tried to keep prices down and banned exports when prices were high. After 1660 Parliament agreed to temporary bans on exports when prices were exceptionally high, but reluctantly and for a short time. Town governments, faced with angry consumers, were sometimes forced to intervene in the grain market. In the 1690s crowds reacted violently to merchants buying up grain for export. At Northampton women came to market armed with knives 'to force corn at their own rates'. In 1709 400 Kingswood colliers appeared at Bristol market in a menacing manner 'under pretence

Figure 11.1 This was probably the home of a landless labourer, built around the middle of the seventeenth century on the edge of the village common. It had two storeys but virtually no windows and a single fireplace in a smoke bay, a primitive form of chimney.

of demanding bread'. After they had broken open several warehouses, the corporation agreed to sell grain at low prices.

By the 1690s consumers of food could no longer trust the government to protect their interests; town governments were caught between the townspeople and the central authorities. Those defending customary rights showed increasing distrust of the King's government and Parliament. They looked back longingly to a time when the Crown defended the people against greedy grain dealers. Parliament inexorably extended landowners' property rights. New game laws restricted the right to hunt to men of a certain wealth and status: poorer landowners could not legally hunt on their own land. **Gleaning**, a traditional perquisite of the poor, was made a criminal offence. A series of raids on deer parks led to the Black Act in 1723, so called because many of the raiders wore masks or blacked their faces. The Act created some fifty new capital offences. It was rarely enforced, but showed the alarm of landowners, faced with violence against horses, cattle and buildings. More important than the Black Act was a long series of enclosure acts, which empowered the owners of manors to confiscate common lands and to reallocate the land between the landlord, the farmers and the parson. Landless labourers lost their last vestiges of economic independence and became wholly reliant on wages.

✂ Trade and Manufactures

The mid seventeenth century marked a watershed in English trade and manufactures. Hitherto England had produced a relatively narrow range of goods – mainly raw materials and woollen cloths – for which demand was limited, because of widespread poverty at home and competition and protectionism abroad. Now more English consumers had money to spend and the growth of colonial populations created new markets and units of production which the English hoped to monopolise by means of the **Navigation Acts**. The restored Stuarts inherited a much enlarged navy with which to enforce the Acts, but never entirely succeeded in keeping out European competitors, and in time the American colonies became competitors in their own right. However, the dual stimulus to demand, at home and in the colonies, encouraged a rapid growth of English manufactures. This did not amount to an 'industrial revolution'. The typical unit of production remained the home or the workshop. There was limited use of power other than human or animal muscle: hence the use of the term 'manufactures' (or 'handicrafts') rather than industry. It was not that contemporaries were incapable of producing on a large scale. The state led the way with the royal dockyards, by far the largest enterprises in the first half of the eighteenth century, but most merchant ships were built in small yards, with a master shipwright, his apprentices and journeymen. Other large-scale enterprises included London breweries, where a large market made economies of scale worthwhile, and a few mills, where the use of water power necessitated a concentration of production. Extractive industries were concentrated where the minerals could be found. Some, like the Yorkshire alum industry, with a lengthy production process and complex transport requirements, needed substantial capital. (See Box 11.1, The Yorkshire Alum Industry.) But in general English manufacturers produced a wide range of increasingly sophisticated and attractive goods without radical reorganisation of the means of production. In 1500 England had been well behind other European countries in terms of techniques and styles but by 1750 it surpassed most of them. There were many small but significant innovations in technology and design, often assisted by craftsmen from the Continent, where the study of design played a greater part in the training of apprentices. As consumers became familiar with exotic goods, such as Chinese porcelain and Venetian glass, English manufacturers tried hard to imitate them: Josiah Wedgwood spent decades trying to discover the secret of making top-quality china.

The growth of England's empire and overseas trade led to a substantial growth in merchant shipping. This in turn created many skilled, well-paid jobs in ship-building and ship-repairing. The growth of imports created a demand for docks and warehouses, around which new industries arose, such as syrup- and treacle-making. As the range of products increased a specialist retail sector developed. In place of the artisan shopkeeper, with his folded-down shutter and narrow range of goods, there were

BOX 11.1: The Yorkshire Alum Industry

Alum was a term used to describe a variety of complex compounds based on aluminium sulphate. It was used in many industries, most importantly in the textile industry where it was used to fix dyes, so that colours did not fade with time. Techniques for its extraction spread from the Eastern Mediterranean via the Papal States to Western Europe; alum production became significant in England in the seventeenth century. It was a slow, complex process, made viable only by the high prices that alum could command.

Alum was mined in the form of shale in various regions, including North Yorkshire. The shale was burned very slowly in large heaps, ten metres or more in height, covered with a thick layer of rock and soil. The heap was built on brushwood, which was set on fire. Once combustion was complete the shale, now crumbly in texture, was transferred from one large pit full of water to another, every few days, until impurities had been removed, leaving an alum liquor. This was transferred by pipes to an alum house, with lead or copper pans up to three metres across, in which it was repeatedly boiled over a coal fire, so that it became concentrated. An alkali was then added (either human urine or seaweed); as the hot liquor cooled, it crystallised. It was then washed and broken up into manageable pieces and transported in barrels or bags.

This was a complicated set of processes and English producers took a long time to learn them. It required large amounts of capital, and manpower, to hew and carry the shale

to the heaps, to build conduits to carry the liquid to the pits and then to the pans, and to build the alum house. Coal was brought from Sunderland, urine from London and seaweed from Scotland. Ships came into Whitby harbour or were run up on the beach and their cargoes carried up the cliffs, in wheelbarrows or by pack-horses; Sandsend, near Whitby, has the highest cliff in England. On top of the initial outlay the protracted production process – the shale could burn for up to a year – meant that manufacturers saw no return on their outlay for many months or even years, until the finished alum could be sold. Initially the industry was protected, but also exploited, by monopolies granted by the Crown, but by the 1680s it was funded by landowners seeking to profit from their estates' mineral resources, with whatever backing they could get from investors in London. The alum industry shows that English entrepreneurs were capable of developing large-scale high-capital industries, with long production processes, outside large towns – alum was a rural industry – and relying on human muscle rather than machines. If few alum manufacturers made spectacular profits, the industry was the making of Whitby's merchant shipping fleet, which by 1702 was the sixth largest in England.

See D. Pybus and J. Rushton, 'Alum', in D.B. Lewis (ed.), *The Yorkshire Coast* (Beverley, 1991), and R. Barker, *The Rise of an Early Modern Shipping Industry: Whitby's Golden Fleet 1660–1750* (Woodbridge, 2011), www.wovepaper.co.uk/alumessay2.html (accessed 12/11/2014).

shops with glass windows, mirrors and shop assistants. Whereas in the past furniture and other household items had been functional, built to last, now they were designed to delight the eye. New beverages created new forms of sociability: the coffee-house for men, the tea-party for ladies; the latter created the need for china tea sets. People bought ornaments for their houses, not because they needed them but because they liked looking at them, which encouraged the fashion for larger windows. Furniture became lighter and more slender, with flowing lines, delicate decoration and inlays of exotic woods. Fabrics were more colourful and eye-catching. Fashion became a major concern in buying clothes and manufacturers brought out cheaper versions of popular fashions, so that it became difficult to distinguish a lady from her maid. For centuries clothing had been an indicator of status and Parliament had passed sumptuary laws, which tried to limit high-status items to members of the social elite. The last English sumptuary acts were passed in Elizabeth's reign: by the end of the seventeenth century efforts to restrict people's right to dress as they pleased were defeated by market forces.

The developments in consumption and shopping after 1660 have been described as a 'consumer revolution'. Clearly there were major changes, both qualitative and quantitative. The choice of artefacts, food and drink and leisure facilities grew substantially, while the growth of the retail sector, together with advertising and merchandising, made consumers far more aware of what was available. Manufacturing became increasingly driven by consumer demand and taste, and by the wholesalers who supplied the shops. Workshops produced clothes and household items to order; craftsmen now had less control over what they produced. But there is a danger of seeing the glittering shops of London as the norm and forgetting the wider picture. This prosperity and growth of consumerism were initially confined mainly to England. The Navigation Acts were designed to keep Scottish and Irish merchants from trading with the empire and the London Parliament banned imports of Irish cattle and Irish woollen cloth in order to protect English farmers and manufacturers. After the Union of England and Scotland some Scottish merchants, notably those of Glasgow, eventually profited handsomely from the American and slave trades. However, Scottish agriculture suffered a severe depression in the 1690s and many Scots emigrated. While Edinburgh and some larger towns flourished, over most of Scotland there were few signs of prosperity and the colonial trade made little impact. In South Wales the gentry, few of whom now spoke Welsh, looked not to Cardiff and Swansea but to Bristol and London. English towns enjoyed mixed fortunes. Some had shops, but many did not. Small towns could not compete with larger centres and those who lived in small towns and villages – the great majority – had to make do with what was on offer locally or brought by pedlars: small items, such as ribbons, trinkets and cheap print. A 'consumer revolution' required choice, but the inhabitants of small communities had little choice, because they had limited access to consumer goods and could not afford them. Others seem to have chosen not to buy such goods. The inventories attached to wills show that some had accumulated a wide range of goods but others had very little. Instead they had invested in urban property or loaned money to their neighbours and kin. This was especially true of Quakers and other Nonconformists, who believed that it was wrong to overvalue the things of this world.

Urban Growth

Although England was more urbanised than Scotland, Ireland or Wales, in 1700 less than 20 per cent of the population lived in towns of more than 2,500 people – and of these more than half lived in London. Between 1520 and 1670 London grew from a little over 50,000 to almost 500,000, but provincial towns grew slowly, if at all. In 1670 the largest were Norwich and Bristol, each with about 20,000; only two others – York and Newcastle – had over 10,000. By 1750 nineteen provincial towns had populations of 10,000 or more, and these included major industrial centres such as Birmingham, Manchester and Leeds, as well as two dockyard towns, Chatham and Portsmouth. London, meanwhile, had continued to grow, to around 675,000, but some provincial towns had grown substantially faster: Bristol from 20,000 to 50,000 and Birmingham from 6,000 to 24,000. (See Table 11.2, Urban Populations in England, c.1520–1801.) Other towns declined, including the once prosperous ports of Rye and Sandwich, whose harbours had silted up.

Whether or not a town grew depended in large part on economics, but towns made their livings in different ways; often they had more than one source of wealth. Some were older industrial centres, such as Norwich, Exeter and Newcastle. These were all administrative centres as well, but some specialised in that role. Winchester was the county town of Hampshire and had no real rival as a centre of county business, shopping and gentry sociability: Portsmouth was a rough working town, Southampton was a decayed port and Basingstoke was too small. In addition, Winchester had the cathedral, with its array of genteel clergymen and their wives, and the school, which many gentlemen's sons attended. For some towns a spa offered a way to prosperity, but it was essential to attract people of wealth and fashion, and some failed or quickly became outmoded. There was no sure route to success. Bath had been a spa town since at least the time of the Romans and became the most elegantly built town in England in the eighteenth century. Tunbridge Wells had not existed until a spring was found in a field in 1606. A century later it had lodging houses, a market, a church and shaded gravelled walks where ladies and gentlemen could stroll and be seen. It also acquired a unique form of government: decisions about the well-being of the town were taken by 'the company resorting to the wells' for the time being, who also elected the town's officers. (See Figure 11.2, The Pantiles, Tunbridge Wells, 1748.)

In order to prosper, provincial towns usually needed places where wealthy people from the countryside could find quality shopping and entertainment and mingle with people of similar interests. Traditionally, provincial towns had not been much concerned about aesthetics. People beautified the interiors of their homes and corporations took pride in their town halls, but public outdoor space had been treated as functional. Animal dung lay in the streets, which were rutted by the wheels of heavy carts. Market places stank, especially in the summer, with the detritus of butchers' and fishmongers' stalls. Privies

Table 11.2 Urban Populations in England (Thousands), c.1520–1801.

Figures for town populations before the nineteenth century tend to be unreliable, but certain developments are clear. First, the proportion of English people living in significant towns grew substantially. This is not simply a reflection of national population growth: between 1660 and c.1700 the population stagnated or fell. Second, the number of towns over 5,000 increased substantially. Third, while some successful medieval towns (such as Bristol, Norwich, York and Newcastle) continued to prosper, they were joined or overtaken by industrial centres like Birmingham and Manchester.

c.1520	c.1600	c.1670	c.1700	c.1750	c.1801
London 55	London 200	London 475	London 575	London 675	London 959
Norwich 12	Norwich 15	Norwich 20	Norwich 30	Bristol 50	Manchester 89[a]
Bristol 10	York 12	Bristol 20	Bristol 21	Norwich 36	Liverpool 83
York 8	Bristol 12	York 12	Newcastle 16	Newcastle 29	Birmingham 74
Salisbury 8	Newcastle 10	Newcastle 12	Exeter 14	Birmingham 24	Bristol 60
Exeter 8	Exeter 9	Colchester 9	York 12	Liverpool 22	Leeds 53
Colchester 7	Plymouth 8	Exeter 9	Gt Yarmouth 10	Manchester 18	Sheffield 46
Coventry 7	Salisbury 6	Chester 8	Birmingham ⎫	Leeds 16	Plymouth 43[b]
Newcastle 5	King's Lynn 6	Ipswich 8	Chester ⎪	Exeter 16	Newcastle 42[c]
Canterbury 5	Gloucester 6	Gt Yarmouth 8	Colchester ⎪	Plymouth 15	Norwich 36
	Chester 6	Plymouth 8	Ipswich ⎬ 8–9	Chester 13	Portsmouth 33
	Coventry 6	Worcester 8	Manchester ⎪	Coventry 13	Bath 33
	Hull 6	Coventry 7	Plymouth ⎪	Nottingham 12	Hull 30
	Gt Yarmouth 5	King's Lynn 7	Worcester ⎭	Sheffield 12	Nottingham 29
	Ipswich 5	Manchester 6	Bury St Edmunds ⎫	York 11	Sunderland 26
	Cambridge 5	Canterbury 6	Cambridge ⎪	Chatham 10	Stoke 23[d]
	Worcester 5	Leeds 6	Canterbury ⎪	Gt Yarmouth 10	Chatham 23[e]
	Cambridge 5	Birmingham 6	Chatham ⎪	Portsmouth 10	Wolverhampton 21[f]
	Oxford 5	Cambridge 6	Coventry ⎪	Sunderland 10	Bolton 17
	Colchester 5	Hull 6	Gloucester ⎪	Worcester 10	Exeter 17
		Salisbury 6	Hull ⎪		Leicester 17
		Bury St Edmunds 5	King's Lynn ⎪		Great Yarmouth 17
		Leicester 5	Leeds ⎬ 5–7		Stockport 17
		Oxford 5	Leicester ⎪		York 16
		Shrewsbury 5	Liverpool ⎪		Coventry 16
		Gloucester 5	Nottingham ⎪		Chester 16
			Oxford ⎪		Shrewsbury 15
			Portsmouth ⎪		
			Salisbury ⎪		
			Shrewsbury ⎪		
			Sunderland ⎪		
			Tiverton ⎭		

Notes:
a Including Salford
b Including Devonport
c Including Gateshead
d Stoke and Burslem
e The Medway towns: Chatham, Rochester and Gillingham
f Wolverhampton, Willenhall, Bilston and Wednesfield

Figure 11.2 Daniel Defoe wrote of Tunbridge Wells: 'Tunbridge wants [lacks] nothing that can add to the felicities of life, or that can make a man or woman completely happy, always provided they have money.'

overflowed into the streets, pigs often wandered at will. Rich and poor lived in close proximity, with larger houses on the main thoroughfares and small tenements and shacks in back alleys and courts. Not all of the well-to-do were content with the squalor of urban living and some who had travelled abroad realised that there was another way: exclusive public squares from which the poor and insanitary could be excluded. The Place Royale in Paris (now Place des Vosges) was a symmetrical square with a large central space planted with trees; colonnades ran all the way around, where people could shop in cool shade. It was the model for the first such development in London, Covent Garden, built in the 1630s by the Earl of Bedford, with a market and a church. By 1700 the normal plan for a London square had become established with a green space in the centre and stables and mews to the rear of terraces of houses, which prevented the sort of infilling which had previously been normal. There were to be no poorer people in such squares, except servants. (See Figure 11.3, Soho Square, London, 1725.) Ideally the houses should have been built to a standard style, with symmetrical fronts, large windows and standard front doors, preferably with classical pediments. Often, however, the developers were eager to make a quick profit and leased out plots which lessees could develop as they wished. Even such upmarket developments as St James's Square, Piccadilly, contained a variety of architectural styles and building standards were so low that some houses soon began to subside or fall down; builders' rubble and offal were dumped in the middle.

Figure 11.3 Soho Square (originally King's Square, from the statue of Charles II in the middle) was laid out by Gregory King in 1681. This engraving of 1725 shows that it was in many ways a typical London square, symmetrical, with an entrance in the middle of each side and a green space in the middle. However, the engraving suggests that the trees were too few and small to provide any real shade.

After 1660 many towns tried to improve their built environment, with mixed results. New town halls and markets were built. Where there was no space for new development, householders improved their facades according to their own tastes. In the most successful developments one individual had full control, as with Bedford at Covent Garden, Lord Lowther at Workington, and the Earl of Warwick, who rebuilt Warwick after a major fire. Elsewhere the initiative came from the townspeople and corporation. Bristol's rulers did not have a great record as improvers – they opposed proposals to replace the existing water supply, even though dead cats were sometimes found in the pipes – but they made a real effort to develop the Marsh, a unique area, undeveloped because it was liable to flood. The ground level was raised and the corporation ordered that walks should be laid out and trees planted. It then proposed building a street, and eventually a square, 'and the buildings to be uniform'. The corporation did not attempt to prescribe a single architectural style, but (like the Corporation of London after the Great Fire of 1666) it insisted that facades should be of brick; it also laid down minimum heights for each storey. Many Bristolians were less than enthusiastic about the development. They were used to dumping dirt or timber on the Marsh and continued to do so, but by 1706 Queen Square was in a reasonably finished state. The people of Birmingham (which was not a corporate town) were not highly regarded by their fellows: 'Brummagem' meant shoddy or counterfeit. However, they built the Square, with symmetrical buildings, trees, and a new church, St Philip's, completed in 1725 and paid for by public subscription. Together the square and the church demonstrated that the manufacturers of Birmingham were as capable of beautifying their town as great nobles or rich merchants. (See Figure 15.5; see also Box 11.2, Contrasting Towns.)

Try as they might, urban rulers could never fully control the public space in their towns. Their hopes of cleaner, better-paved streets were thwarted by continually increasing populations and the need to get goods to market. The responsibility for cleansing and paving lay with each householder and it proved impossible to compel them to fulfil their obligations. From the 1730s commissions to cleanse, pave and light the streets were established by Acts of Parliament but their efforts often proved insufficient because of the sheer number of people. Nor could the elites isolate themselves

---

BOX 11.2: **Contrasting Towns**

Celia Fiennes, the unmarried granddaughter of a viscount, undertook a series of journeys, on her own, around England between about 1685 and 1703. She was a woman of strong opinions as these extracts make clear. (It should be noted that she was a Presbyterian, and had a low opinion of bishops.)

Nottingham (1697)

Nottingham is the neatest town I have seen, built of stone and delicate large [wide] and long streets much like London and the houses lofty and well built, the Market place is very broad, out of which runs two very large streets much like Holborn but the buildings finer and there is a piazza all along one side of the streets, with stone pillars for walking that runs the length of the street, which is a mile long; all the streets are of a good size all about the town and well pitched [paved], there are several good houses in the town, there are three or four large houses of the Duke of Newcastle's with the Castle, which is a fine thing stands very high on a hill ...

Ely (1698)

... by reason of the great rains the roads were full of water even quite to the town which you ascend a very steep hill into, but the dirtiest place I ever saw, not a bit of pitching in the streets so it's a perfect quagmire the whole city, only just about the [bishop's] palace and churches the streets are well enough for breadth but for want of pitching it seems only a harbour to breed and nest vermin in, of which there is plenty enough, so that though my chamber was near twenty steps up I had frogs and slow-worms and snails in my room – but I suppose it was brought up with the faggots ... it's true were the least care taken to pitch their streets it would make it look more properly an habitation for human beings, and not a cage or nest of unclean creatures ...

The bishop does not care to stay long in this place not being for his health; he is the Lord of all the Island [Isle of Ely], has the command and the jurisdiction: they have lost their charter and so are no corporation, but all things are directed by the bishop and it's a shame he does not see it better ordered and the buildings and streets put in better condition ...

The Journeys of Celia Fiennes, ed. C. Morris (1949), pp. 72, 155–6.

from the uncouth and insanitary poor. Private clubs and societies multiplied in the eighteenth century, but gentlemen also frequented taverns and coffee-houses, essentially public spaces. There were some spaces (London pleasure gardens or provincial assembly rooms) from which the poor could be excluded by entry fees or dress codes. On the other hand, Londoners assumed that they had a right to use the parks and pulled down the gates when the authorities tried to restrict entry. At horse races and theatres cheap and expensive seats were separated, but in the theatres the poor sat in the upper levels, from which they could spit or lob objects at the wealthy people below. In the streets and market places all ranks were equal; in the anonymity of the crowd, or the poaching gang, the poor could avenge themselves on the rich.

The Treatment of Poverty: England

It may seem strange that, amid strong evidence of growing prosperity, between the 1650s and 1696 the amount spent on poor relief increased substantially, from about £100,000 to between £400,000 and £600,000 a year. This striking increase could be explained in two ways. Either the incidence of poverty or the amounts granted to those claiming relief were increasing. It is also possible that many of the poor were becoming more exclusively dependent on wages and losing alternative means of 'making shift'.

In the early seventeenth century poor rates were seen as occasional expedients, to be levied in particularly bad years. Under the Acts of 1598 and 1601 paupers did not have a *right* to relief, but had to petition the parish authorities. Officials could reject their petitions, but also tried to deter paupers from petitioning in two ways, both used initially in towns which had developed schemes of poor relief before the national system was established. First, paupers might be required to wear a distinguishing badge or gown. This was partly to prevent them from spending their dole money on drink: if a badged pauper was found in an alehouse they could lose their dole. But the badge was also seen as a mark of humiliation and some paupers refused to wear it; if they did they forfeited their right to relief. Parliament established badging nationwide in 1697, but this did not prevent many towns and villages from introducing their own schemes. Second, paupers could be required to enter the workhouse as a condition of receiving relief. For many the workhouse was indistinguishable from the **house of correction** and they refused, in which case they again lost their dole money.

During the seventeenth century conflict developed between parish officers and county magistrates. In the 1650s the government encouraged magistrates to supervise poor relief more closely, to ensure that the money raised was properly accounted for and paid only to the deserving. This may have been intended to deny relief to the unworthy, but magistrates also began to encourage those who claimed to have been unfairly denied relief to petition for redress, which encouraged others to do the same. Parish officials complained that magistrates were too generous and pointed out that magistrates did not usually pay poor rate in parishes where they intervened. Magistrates accused parish officers of meanness and petty tyranny. In 1692, as anxiety mounted about the spiralling cost of poor relief, Parliament decreed that only the JPs could add new names to those receiving regular relief. The Commons, which contained many magistrates and few parish officers, seemed to think excessive generosity by parish officers was to blame for the rise in costs; parish officers blamed the magistrates' gullibility or laxity. They also complained that paupers were petitioning magistrates directly, rather than petitioning the parish officers first. It was also alleged that paupers saw relief as a right, an entitlement, which the parish officers denied. Paupers negotiated with parish officers about the amount due to them. In towns like Norwich the mayor and aldermen each year summoned families claiming relief to appear, with their children, to give an account of their earnings and their needs, so that the award of relief was based on full, accurate information.

These developments were made more contentious by the Act of Settlement of 1662. It had already become accepted that each parish should be responsible for its 'own' poor. The Act laid down procedures whereby magistrates should determine where a person was 'settled' and issue a settlement certificate. Settlement could be based on birth, marriage or a minimum period of residence. Settlement in a parish conferred a right to remain there. It did not confer a right to relief, although many poor people believed that it did. In the eyes of the parish officials, relief had to be petitioned for and could be granted or denied, taking into account factors such as the severity of illness or disability, or the absence of close kin. Moreover, a significant proportion of those granted relief were not settled in the parish in question. The Act has often been seen as hindering the mobility of labour, tying people to their home parish, but it is necessary to look beyond its provisions to see how it operated in practice. Migrant or seasonal workers were given certificates stating that they were settled in a parish and so should not be treated as vagrants. In Norwich far fewer people were punished for vagrancy under Charles II than under James I and in almost every case they were also charged with another offence, such as petty theft, telling fortunes or selling ballads. The Act made it difficult to find settlement in a new parish, laying down stringent conditions such as finding sureties that they would not become a burden on the poor rate. However, it seems that as long as incomers supported themselves their neighbours were unlikely to report them. Compared with Elizabeth's reign the economy was buoyant and work was relatively plentiful. Some townspeople received incomers as lodgers in return for a small rent: one woman in Bristol in 1665 was said to have forty-six. If incomers could avoid detection for long enough they could claim settlement. Establishing settlement was probably easier for men. Town authorities, and the neighbours, were suspicious of single women 'living at their own hand', who might become pregnant and a double burden on the poor rate; they were usually told to find a master or employer, or leave. In 1697 Parliament decreed that incomers could be removed only if they became chargeable.

It seems that in larger towns the administration of the poor law became relatively impersonal and impartial after 1660. In rural areas personal factors remained important: those regarded as undeserving could be denied relief and their families urged to provide for them. Women in the last stages of pregnancy might be carried over the parish border to give birth. Town authorities were more likely to abide by the rules but did what they could to instil better habits. They discouraged begging, but it continued, particularly around Christmas. The Norwich authorities dissuaded the working poor, especially the young, from wasting time and money on medicine shows (surgical operations performed live on stage, mixed with comic sketches and music) and human and animal freak shows. The Norwich grand jury demanded that the poor and young be prevented from spending their Sundays drinking and gambling 'by which we mean not such as are civil and sober, whose circumstances will allow them a refreshment, but such whose poverty bespeaks better husbandry': only those who could afford it could have a drink after Sunday service.

Anxieties about the rising cost of poor relief peaked in the 1690s. War and privateering disrupted trade and manufacturing, so work was hard to come by. Bad harvests and corn exports pushed up the price of food. There was a widespread anxiety about rising crime and declining public morals, leading to the establishment of Societies for the Reformation of Manners, which prosecuted those accused of drunkenness, gambling and prostitution. The belief that immorality and the profaning of the Lord's Day would provoke God's wrath led successive monarchs from William III to George II to issue proclamations against drunkenness, gambling and disorderly behaviour on Sundays. This mixture of financial, economic and moral concerns led to the establishment of **corporations of the poor**. The Poor Laws had always rested on the assumption that the impact of poverty could be reduced by the punishment of idleness, the provision of relief for the deserving 'impotent' poor and setting the able-bodied unemployed to work. This last had proved problematic: workhouses were expensive to establish and deeply unpopular with the poor. Corporations of the poor were established by Acts of Parliament, which allowed towns to elect guardians, or trustees, who would receive the poor rates from the parishes, seize idle persons and vagrants and incarcerate them in workhouses, where they would be set to work. The Maidstone workhouse, opened in 1720, bore the slogan 'to subject the poor to a better discipline of life'. All inmates had to work: boys were taught a trade, girls learned to spin and helped in the kitchen, old people looked after the smaller children. Moral lapses, such as drunkenness, were punished.

Corporations of the poor were established in fifteen towns, which had different problems. Norwich's textile industry suffered from overseas competition and the disruption of trade, and unemployment was high. Bristol had a large and unruly transient population, en route for Ireland or America. Hull had no serious unemployment or disorders, and used its workhouse to train pauper children. Most corporations of the poor failed to match expectations, struggling to raise the capital to equip a workhouse; it was difficult to sell the goods produced there, usually low-quality cloth, during an economic depression. Guardians often lacked the powers needed to fulfil their responsibilities. At Bristol they could not arrest vagrants or women living at their own hand, only report them to the magistrates; they refused to take responsibility for the transient 'casual poor'. Bristol's guardians enjoyed unusually strong support from the town's government and strongly Nonconformist business elite: when a theatre opened in 1706 the council was persuaded to close it. The guardians were hampered by political and religious rivalries. Most were Whigs, but many parish officers were Tories, who clung to their control of the poor rate. Eventually Bristol's guardians achieved many of their aims, helped by Whig parliaments. By 1727 it was said that Bristol had become more orderly and begging had been eliminated.

Bristol, despite its problems, was a large and wealthy city. In small decayed towns, or rural parishes like Eccleshall, the problems of poverty remained intractable. Villages could not afford to set up a corporation of the poor, or a workhouse. This latter problem was alleviated by an Act of 1723 which, apart from taking away the magistrates' control over grants of relief, authorised groups of villages to form **unions** to establish joint workhouses. They faced the same problems of start-up and running costs, and the difficulty of selling what they produced. Some workhouses were managed by entrepreneurs, who were accused of exploiting the inmates and fiddling the accounts. However, making a profit was not the main purpose of the workhouses. Their aim was to cut costs by taking away the dole of those who refused to enter them, and in this they seem to have succeeded. By 1750 there were about 600, with an average of forty to fifty inmates. Most of the poor feared the workhouse, and some were forced into it by illness or other misfortune, but there were too few workhouses for their impact to be felt by more than a small fraction of the population.

Meanwhile, conflicting complaints and allegations continued. It was alleged that working men were overpaid, that rising wages made them idle and inclined to take time off. Some claimed that the well-to-do and well-educated avoided parish offices, so that they fell to barely literate men who kept inadequate accounts or embezzled money. There were claims that the poor rates were rising sharply, or had been reduced by the establishment of workhouses. In 1748–50 a parliamentary investigation suggested that the yield of the poor rate was about £700,000, which would suggest an increase since the 1690s, but far smaller than that between the 1650s and 1690s. Attempts to assess long-term trends are probably misleading: poor rates could vary widely from year to year – bad harvests or epidemics could make an enormous difference – and from parish to parish. Moreover, the magistrates' role in supervising poor relief remained important. No doubt they varied in diligence, but it should not be assumed that magistrates always chose the path of parsimony and severity. In 1795, during the war with revolutionary France, some Berkshire magistrates responded to farmers' paying starvation wages by a resolution to subsidise wages from the poor rates. Their example was followed by others all over the country; the Old Poor Law was abolished in 1834 because it was seen as too generous.

⚇ The Treatment of Poverty: Ireland and Scotland

It is easy to exaggerate the severity of the English Poor Laws. The provisions of the many Acts of Parliament relating to the poor create an impression of harshness, indeed ferocity. But many Acts imposed punishments which were designed to deter rather than to be implemented rigorously. We find many whipped vagrants and badged paupers, but also many poor people, including the mentally ill, receiving relief and practical assistance. The fact remained that England had the only *nation-wide* system of poor relief in Europe based on a compulsory poor rate: sophisticated urban institutions for the poor, in the Low Countries or Italy or France, often contrasted with an absence of provision in the countryside. Not that the English system was universal within England and Wales: there were parts of Wales which continued to rely on traditional means of charitable provision by the better-off. The English Poor Laws were never exported to Ireland. Parish vestries sometimes used parish funds to provide for abandoned children or others of the deserving poor, or issued badges to local beggars to distinguish them from incomers. In the hungry 1690s two bills in Parliament to enable parishes to raise money for the poor did not pass. Dublin acquired a workhouse in 1706 and two substantial famines in 1726–9 and 1739–41 saw significant fund-raising to buy food. In general, provision for the poor in Ireland was far more limited than in England.

We have seen (Chapter 7) that Scotland in some ways followed England's model, but avoided compulsory rates; instead its provision rested on voluntary contributions and legacies. In times of crisis – 1623, the 1690s – the Scottish Privy Council urged the assessment of wealthier inhabitants for compulsory taxes; Parliament hinted at the same in 1649. The fact that these two different authorities issued similar commands shows uncertainty where the responsibility for poor relief really lay. Within the parishes it clearly lay with the **kirk sessions**, which administered gifts and legacies and was also responsible for the minister's salary, his manse and the parish school. But in 1623 the Privy Council had also urged **heritors** (landowners rated for parish responsibilities including the minister) to relieve the poor on their own land.

In the 1690s three developments undermined the kirk sessions' control of poor relief. First, the expulsion of many ministers from the Kirk in 1689–91 disrupted the kirk sessions. There were disputes between rival ministers: one expelled minister took the sessions register and poor box with him. Second, the Privy Council repeatedly raised the issue of assessment for compulsory rates, even if it offered little practical guidance on how to introduce them. Third, heritors came to see these calls for assessment as a threat to their interests. They began to demand a greater say in how the voluntary parish contributions were spent. If heritors were responsible for relieving the poor on their estates, they demanded their share of the parish funds to enable them to do so. From 1751, after a series of acrimonious court cases, it became established that poor law affairs and documentation should be kept separate from other parish business and that heritors were to supervise the administration of parish Poor Law funds. These developments marked a divergence between poor relief in Scotland and in England, which ironically became more apparent after the Union of 1707. In England the principle of compulsory assessment had become accepted and landowners (as magistrates) supervised the operation of the system. In Scotland landowners played an increasingly powerful role in the administration of parish funds, raised by voluntary contributions, in order to protect themselves against a compulsory poor rate. However, from the 1720s JPs (on the English model) were introduced in many Lowland shires. Some urged parishes not to give alms to vagrants and to raise funds by assessment. This led to greater co-operation between heritors and parishes, which may have enabled them to reduce the impact of the disastrous harvest of 1740.

Conclusion: a Divided Society?

In the century after 1660 there are signs that English society was becoming more divided. There were political and religious divisions, the legacy of the civil wars. There were divisions within arable villages, between a few substantial tenant farmers and many landless labourers. Within industry the face-to-face workplace was giving way to a manufacturing system dominated by the wholesaler: both masters and workmen now had to work to his specifications and deadlines. Faced with global competition employers cut wages or demanded more cloth for the same pay. Industrial disputes became more common and more acrimonious. The mine owners of the Tyne and Wear tried to cut the pay of the **keelmen** who transported the coal to the fleets of colliers which carried it to London. Landowners used Parliament to protect their own and their tenants' interests at the expense of consumers, keeping up grain prices and encouraging exports in years of dearth. Market regulations to protect poorer consumers were abandoned or bypassed. Hundreds of enclosure acts reallocated land in favour of landowners and tenants and Parliament extended definitions of property to include various types of game, and of theft to include traditional 'rights' like gleaning.

With a growing gulf between rich and poor, food riots and industrial disputes became more violent. With rising customs and excise duties, smuggling became more profitable; smugglers became more organised and ready to use force. The deer poachers whose activities led to the Black Act were not stealing because of hunger – they sold their venison to London dealers. Their notoriety and bravado attracted much public interest and support: one gang paraded several carcases from the Bishop of Winchester's park through Farnham, Hampshire, on market day. Some victims of the poachers refrained from prosecuting because they feared losing the goodwill of their neighbourhood. It might seem that the poor were showing increasing hostility to the rich: violence, damage to property, seditious words and anonymous letters seemed more common.

Violence directed against landlords and their servants developed on a large scale in Ireland in the later eighteenth century, but earlier violence against animals, fences and buildings was more common than violence against people. The same seems to be true of Scotland. In 1711–12, 'Houghers' killed thousands of sheep and cattle in several counties in the West of Ireland, apparently in an attempt to prevent the extension of stock rearing at the expense of arable farming. Similarly, in Scotland tenants of the second Duke of Argyll responded to his radical tenurial reforms by maiming his cattle. In 1724, when some landowners in Galloway evicted tenant farmers in order to create large cattle farms, groups of 'levellers' destroyed the walls of cattle enclosures at night. This seems to have been the only such protest in Lowland Scotland and the perpetrators were not seriously punished.

The poor complained that customary rights were being overturned by new legislation and called on the rich to show the paternalistic concern for the poor to which they had traditionally paid lip service. Although the concept of 'class' did not fully develop until the widespread development of factory industry in the first half of the nineteenth century, was there something akin to 'class conflict' a century earlier?

It is possible to see the landed elite using their wealth and political influence to promote their interests at the expense of both the Crown and the people. Experience of the Stuarts made this elite wary of a strong state: the army was useful for suppressing riots, but they had no wish to see a repeat of Cromwell's military rule. Their expensive lifestyles, their parks and palaces, led them to exploit their estates to the detriment of the labouring poor. The key weapon in this exploitation was Parliament. This had been used for centuries to protect the interests of landowners – note the attempts to hold down wages after the Black Death – but from 1689 Parliament met for many months each year and had time to pass much more legislation. Much of this legislation was 'public', dealing with such matters as deer poaching or bounties on grain exports. But there were also private acts, enabling individuals to reallocate their land in a few large farms, reducing small farmers to wage labourers. Some historians have also argued that the landed elite further consolidated their power in their capacity as magistrates, using the criminal law and its punishments to protect their property. This suggested that property crime against the elite could be seen as 'social crime', a form of social protest.

How convincing are claims that the misuse of power by the landed elite provoked social protest? They can be criticised in several ways. First, the concept of 'social crime' rarely seems applicable at this time. Most victims of property crime were relatively poor: the rich were better placed to protect their property. Deer poaching was one of the few property crimes where the victims were by definition rich. Moreover, landowners did not control the criminal law. Prosecutions were brought by the victims or their kin and there were various inputs into the process which led to the final verdict, from the prosecutors, grand and petty jurors, character witnesses and the presiding judge. (See Box 11.3, The Criminal Law in a Shropshire Village.) Criminal justice was relatively quick and cheap: it was in civil cases that poor litigants were at a disadvantage.

BOX 11.3: **The Criminal Law in a Shropshire Village**

The following is taken from a yeoman's history of his village, written in 1700–1. It shows several aspects of the criminal law: the fact that prosecutions originated with the victims of crime, who could choose other ways to punish the criminal; the firm steer which the judge gave to the jury; and the collusion between judge and jury to ensure that Aston – a 'silly man', which suggests that he was a bit simple – should not suffer the death penalty. In a case of felony, if the jury valued the chickens at twelve pence or more the accused might be hanged.

But I must not forget John Aston, because many in the parish have reason to remember him. He was a sort of silly fellow, very idle and much given to stealing of poultry and small things. He was many times catched in the fact, and sometimes well cudgelled by those that would trouble themselves no further with him. But at last he grew unsufferable, and made it his common practice to steal hens in the night and bring them to Shrewsbury, where he had confederates to receive them at any time of night. He was at last imprisoned and indicted for stealing twenty-four cocks and hens. The judge, seeing him a silly man, told the jury that the matter of fact was so fully proved that they must find the prisoner guilty, but they would do well to consider of the value, and thereupon the jury found him guilty of felony to the value of eleven pence, at which the judge laughed heartily and said he was glad cocks and hens were so cheap in this country [county]. This made John Aston more careful, but he left not his old trade wholly.

R. Gough, *The History of Myddle*, ed. D. Hey (Harmondsworth, 1981), pp. 145–6.

A second problem is that this is an essentially rural model, based on the relationship between landowners and peasants. The tensions between manufacturing employers and their workers were different, and more violent. Troops were used to protect clothiers or to suppress rioting keelmen (or smugglers), but rarely against rural disorder: the 'Waltham Blacks' were an exception. Moreover, whereas the sympathies of the government and Parliament were with the victims of deer poaching, in industrial disputes their response was more ambivalent. The governments of George I and George II were suspicious of **combinations**: they saw **Jacobite** plotting everywhere. But they generally dealt mildly with working men struggling to defend their livelihoods. The striking Wearside **keelmen** in 1719 got off lightly, with the exception of Richard Flower, a schoolmaster, who had drafted a 'paper of combination' for the keelmen, by which they undertook not to return to work until their wages had been increased. Ministers saw Flower as a troublemaker and argued that this was none of his business. Similarly, army officers sent to put down rioting clothworkers in the winter of 1726–7 showed distaste for the task and made it clear that they sympathised with the workers. (See Box 11.4, Responses to Weavers' Riots in Wiltshire, December 1726–January 1727.)

A third problem is that a model based on landowners and labourers has no place for the middling sorts, particularly those of the towns. These were likely to be literate and informed about events, ideas and literature. They had the income, the clothes and the social awareness to mingle with the urban elite and the gentry, in assemblies and literary and philosophical societies. They constituted an important and vocal part of 'public

BOX 11.4: Responses to Weavers' Riots in Wiltshire, December 1726–January 1727

A series of weavers' riots in Trowbridge, Bradford on Avon and other cloth towns generated a flurry of correspondence between magistrates, army officers and the King's ministers. The magistrates blamed the riots on some clothiers (wholesalers, who employed the weavers), who had changed the measures used for cloth, so that weavers had to produce more work for the same wages; it was these clothiers whose houses were attacked. The magistrates stressed, and the weavers acknowledged, that other clothiers behaved fairly; indeed, some resented being undercut by those who cut costs by oppressing their weavers and were not sorry to see them 'disciplined' by the rioters. The clothiers accused of sharp practice alleged that Jacobite plotters were responsible for the riots, which some army officers suspected, but the magistrates denied this, as did the weavers, many of whom chalked 'King George's weavers' on their hats. The clothiers asked for troops to suppress the rioters, claiming that only force could restore order, but also tried to provoke the rioters to more extreme measures. At Bradford the clothiers forced shopkeepers to undertake not to allow the weavers any credit, so that they would have to steal or starve. They also armed a 'mob' to fight the weavers and gave them strong beer.

Several magistrates, encouraged by ministers, persuaded the weavers to petition Parliament about their grievances, with supporting evidence. This raised the problem of who could draft such a document: hardly any of the weavers could write and those who could feared the clothiers' wrath. A clothier, Mr Hilson, sent two weavers involved in the petition to prison, which infuriated the rest. Following assurances from the magistrates many weavers had gone home, but now about 2,000 assembled at Bradford and resolved to march to Salisbury to free another of their brethren imprisoned there. The officers and soldiers in the town tried to dissuade them and eventually dispersed them by force: one weaver was killed and many wounded. The commanding officer, Colonel Paulet, complained that his troops had been insulted and that Frome, where he was stationed, was a Jacobite town; the weavers complained that the King had sent troops to murder them. Paulet had procured an order from the magistrates to suppress any disorder if the weavers reassembled, but he also summoned a meeting of clothiers and weavers, assuring the latter that, if the JPs could not resolve their grievances, they would petition Parliament on their behalf; the King and Lord Townshend approved of this move. Throughout, the concern of the authorities (including the military) was to give the weavers a chance to air their grievances and to resolve their disputes with the clothiers peacefully. The army used force only when the clothiers provoked the weavers to reassemble.

Compilation based on The National Archives, SP 35/63, nos. 93–95(3), SP 35/64, nos. 1–4.

opinion', held civic offices and often had votes in parliamentary elections. From their number emerged articulate and committed political radicals.

A final problem was that, even allowing for increased levels of violence, England remained an ordered society. Respect for the law remained strong, even if it was occasionally abused by the powerful. There were no longer overmighty subjects with private armies, at least in England. The limited response to the 1715 rebellion in England showed that, even in the far North, the nobility could no longer mobilise armed men. Political violence could be alarming, but it was restricted in time and place, occurring mainly on election days. The riots against Nonconformist chapels in the summer of 1715 were more serious and led to the Riot Act, which enabled George I's enlarged (and Whig) army to deal effectively with subsequent disorders. The first two Hanoverians were not popular, but the 1715 rising showed that support for a Jacobite challenge within England was limited, confined to gestures and slogans rather than serious action (see Chapter 16).

SUGGESTIONS FOR FURTHER READING

The standard work on population is E.A. Wrigley and R.S. Schofield, *The Population History of England and Wales, 1541–1871* (Cambridge, 1989). • The best survey of economic and social change (which includes Scotland) is K. Wrightson, *Earthly Necessities: Economic Lives in Early Modern Britain, 1470–1750* (London, 2002). D.C. Coleman, *Industry in Tudor and Stuart England* (London, 1975) is admirably clear and concise. T.C. Smout, *A History of the Scottish People 1560–1830* (London, 1972) is wide-ranging and very perceptive. • On Gregory King, see M. Spufford, *Poverty Portrayed: Gregory King and the Parish of Eccleshall* (Keele, 1995) and G. Holmes, 'Gregory King and the Social Structure of Pre-Industrial England', *Transactions of the Royal Historical Society*, 5th series, 27 (1977). • On changing habits of consumption, see the pioneering work by N. McKendrick, J. Brewer and J.H. Plumb, *The Birth of a Consumer Society* (London, 1982). L. Weatherill, *Consumer Behaviour and Material Culture in Britain 1660–1760* (London, 2nd edn, 1996) makes extensive use of probate inventories. • The starting point for studies of urban growth after 1660 is P. Borsay, *The English Urban Renaissance: Culture and Society in the Provincial Town 1660–1770* (Oxford, 1989), which set the agenda for subsequent works. R. Sweet, *The English Town 1680–1840: Government, Society and Culture* (Harlow, 1999) is a wide-ranging survey, which gives useful insights into the practicalities of urban government. • On London, N. Brett-James, *The Growth of Stuart London* (1934) is old, but based on an immense amount of archival knowledge. More generally, see A.L. Beier and R. Finlay (eds.), *London 1500–1700: the Making of the Metropolis* (Harlow, 1986). • J. Miller, *Cities Divided: Politics and Religion in English Provincial Towns, 1660–1722* (Oxford, 2007) contains material on various aspects of towns including growth, government, poverty and disorder. • Poverty in this period has been extremely well covered. Two books by P. Slack – *Poverty and Policy in Tudor and Stuart England* (London and Harlow, 1988) and *From Reformation to Improvement: Public Welfare in Early Modern England* (Oxford, 1999) – focus mainly on towns, especially the latter. On rural poverty, see the meticulously researched and carefully nuanced study by S. Hindle, *On the Parish? The Micro-Politics of Poor Relief in Rural England, c.1550–1750* (Oxford, 2004). On poverty in Scotland, see the classic article by R. Mitchison, 'The Making of the Old Scottish Poor Law', *Past and Present*, 63 (1974), pp. 58–93. • The most sophisticated proponent of the idea of 'Class Struggle Without Class?' was E.P. Thompson, initially in an article of that name in *Social History*, 3 (1978). A revised and enlarged version of the article, 'The Patricians and the Plebs', was later

published in a collection of Thompson's essays, *Customs in Common* (London, 1993), Chapter 2. See also Thompson's *Whigs and Hunters: the Origins of the Black Act* (London, 1977).
• For critiques of Thompson's arguments on the criminal law and the Black Act, see J.H. Langbein, 'Albion's Fatal Flaws', *Past and Present*, 98 (1983), pp. 96–120, and J. Broad, 'Whigs, Deer-Stealers and the Origins of the Black Act', *Past and Present*, 119 (1988), pp. 56–72.
• For analyses of the criminal law and its enforcement which differ substantially from Thompson's, see J.A. Sharpe, *Crime in Early Modern England, 1550–1750* (Harlow, 1984) and J.M. Beattie's magisterial *Crime and the Courts in England, 1660–1800* (Princeton, 1986).

SUMMARY

• From the mid seventeenth century the population levelled off. The pressure of people on land diminished and, thanks to more efficient farming, food prices tended to fall. With the growth of empire and the Navigation Acts, trade and manufactures grew: the colonies formed an important market for English goods. With a buoyant and diversified economy, the wages of many industrial workers grew and many more people had surplus disposable income to spend. The result was a growing demand for, and production of, consumer goods.
• The growth of consumerism was particularly visible in London and the more fashionable towns, which became centres for entertainment, leisure and shopping. More interest was shown in the built environment and in providing places where the well dressed and well heeled could see and be seen, epitomised by Bath and Tunbridge Wells.
• Alongside this conspicuous affluence there was poverty, less conspicuous but deep and enduring. Agricultural labourers were often poorly paid, but so were those producing low-value goods and working in low-skilled crafts.
• Although the language of 'class' had yet to be developed, there are growing signs of tension within society. In manufacturing, many people still worked in small workshops under a master craftsman, but he was increasingly likely to work for a middleman who commissioned items to be sold on by retailers. In the countryside, farmers became more remote from their landlords who dealt with them through a manager or land agent. Landlords also used their power, especially as legislators, to strengthen their position against their less productive farmers and the rural poor.

QUESTIONS FOR STUDENTS

1. How far did the organisation of manufacturing change in this period?

2. How far did England become a 'consumer society' in this period?

3. To what extent did this period see an 'urban Renaissance'?

4. Did the treatment of the poor become more severe in this period?

5. How convincing is the evidence of growing social division?

12 Money and Power: the Growth of the British State 1640–1750

TIMELINE

1643	Commons approve assessment and excise
1664	Commons grant £2,500,000 for war against the Dutch
1672	Stop of the Exchequer
1689	First mutiny act
1694	Bank of England established
1701	Act of Settlement
1715	Army enlarged and purged of Tories

Introduction

One of the most extraordinary developments of the seventeenth and eighteenth centuries was the emergence of England (from 1707 Britain) as a major European and world power. Under the Tudors, despite Henry VIII's posturing, England was much weaker than Spain, France or the Holy Roman Empire. At the root of this weakness lay a lack of money. The Tudors and early Stuarts failed to tax the nation's wealth effectively in the face of opposition from Parliament and people. During the first civil war Parliament for the first time faced up to the problem of raising as much money as possible as quickly as possible. It granted the assessment and the excise which together formed the basis of government revenue in the eighteenth century. They produced a substantial and *predictable* income, a secure base for government borrowing. Governments which could mobilise large sums through borrowing could fight wars on a larger scale than governments dependent on taxation alone. The wars against France between 1689 and 1713 led to a second series of increases in taxation and borrowing. Parliament agreed to these taxes, despite its deep suspicion of standing armies, because the Commons retained tight control over the funding of the army and the means of maintaining military discipline. The first two Hanoverian kings had at their disposal a much larger army, navy and fiscal apparatus than the Tudors or early Stuarts, but it was only the fiscal and military aspects of government which were centralised. Local government remained decentralised and local agencies in towns and counties extended their powers.

The impetus for these developments came primarily from England. The Scots were the first to raise money without the King during the Bishops War, and the Scots Parliament agreed to raise a substantial militia under Charles II, but between 1689 and 1707 the Scots Parliament was reluctant to raise money for England's French wars. After 1707 Scotland was taxed (many would claim over-taxed) by the British Parliament. The Irish Parliament agreed to taxes similar to those in England, including excises, but these were used mainly to support the Irish military establishment; on only one occasion were they used as security for borrowing. The English government's main concern in Ireland was to keep a military presence sufficient to guard against French or Jacobite invasion and to keep the Catholic majority quiet.

Strengths and Weaknesses of the Tudor and Early Stuart State

Strengths

The Tudors inherited an institutionally well-developed medieval monarchy, which required a strong king to make it work. The nobles were willing to serve the king provided that he treated them fairly. Henry VIII dealt severely with disaffected nobles and eliminated potential rival claimants to the throne. Popular rebellions were brutally suppressed. Wolsey and Cromwell set out to strengthen central control over the machinery of government and began to establish greater order in the northern and Welsh marches, a process completed in the North under Elizabeth. By the end of her reign any military threat from the nobility had disappeared. Henry VIII subjected the Church to the authority of the Crown and the scope and effectiveness of local government increased as Acts of Parliament extended the powers of county and parish officials. The Tudors were lucky compared to the Stewarts in Scotland, in that they faced only one royal minority (and none of their successors faced any). But the fact that the Crown passed relatively smoothly to a minor and then two queens between 1547 and 1558 showed that the Tudor regime rested on a strong foundation of popular loyalty and obedience.

Weaknesses: Money

If the regime was strong within England, on the international stage it looked weak and vulnerable. The Crown's key problem was shortage of money. France, Spain and other Continental monarchies had established taxes, which tapped the wealth of their subjects in a variety of ways: customs duties, land taxes, or taxes on consumption of (say) wine and salt. Some of these had been approved by representative assemblies, but often they rested solely on the King's authority. Medieval English monarchs relied mainly on their **domanial** revenues rather than taxes, which tended to diminish in value over time because of inadequate assessment or inflation. By the later fifteenth century, parliaments had become more assertive and the Crown relied more, not less, on its domanial resources: the Yorkists and Henry VII controlled more land than their predecessors. But domanial revenues alone could not raise enough for a major war and the Tudors had to seek grants of taxation. Parliament agreed to revise the assessment of the land tax (now called the **subsidy**). Henry VIII, faced with the Pilgrimage of Grace, did not dare to impose new taxes and hugely expanded his domanial resources by plundering the Church, a policy continued by Edward VI and Elizabeth. But the Crown's financial needs were many and pressing. In time the plundered Church lands were sold off, followed by many other Crown estates, as Elizabeth funded her wars against Spain and in Ireland by selling the royal patrimony.

Weaknesses: Navy and Army

The Tudors lacked the money to build and maintain a substantial fleet, so hired merchant ships or private warships when necessary. The defeat of the Spanish armadas owed much to luck with the weather; incompetent and corrupt naval administration under James I meant that during Charles I's wars in 1626–8 the majority of 'naval' ships were hired merchantmen. The ships for the Cadiz and La Rochelle expeditions carried victuals that were mostly unfit for human consumption and a combination of sailors binge-drinking (at Cadiz) and total military incompetence (at La Rochelle) meant that the expeditions were humiliating disasters. During the 1630s Charles used much of the revenue from Ship Money to build up the navy, but he did little to improve the quality of his land army, probably because before 1637 he saw no need to do so. The result in 1639–40 was further humiliation, as Charles dithered and many of his English subjects refused to fight for him.

The Reforms of the 1640s

By 1642 Parliament had abolished almost all Charles I's contentious revenues, including Ship Money, knighthood fines and fines for breaches of the forest laws. Essentially, the King had no revenues left other than what little remained from the Crown lands, so was dependent on whatever Parliament chose to give him. In 1642 the Commons had no intention of granting the King money, but were reluctant to grant taxes without his assent. They overcame that reluctance in 1643 and devised a system of revenue which rested on two models. First, the Scots: in 1638 Scottish Parliament set up shire war committees to raise money for an army to defend them against the King. The Covenanters offered a precedent for opposing the King and depriving him of his powers. They raised money as they saw fit, although they tried (when possible) to have their military expenditure reimbursed by the English Parliament (which rarely paid what it promised). The other model was the Dutch Republic: a small country fighting the might of Spain, the Dutch had to exploit their assets efficiently. Although poor in natural resources, the Republic was cash-rich, thanks to its trade, and Amsterdam had a Bank and a thriving money market. As trade and manufactures played such a prominent part in the economy, the Dutch developed the **excise**, on commodities produced and consumed at home, including alcohol and tobacco. It provided good security for loans and the money market meant that these were relatively easy to secure. The Stuart kings had considered introducing an excise, but decided that it would be too unpopular; Parliament had no such scruples.

Parliament's new taxes were just two of many fiscal expedients, including confiscation of Royalists' estates, but these were of lasting importance. The **assessment** was a tax on land which offered a solution to the problem of assessment, which had bedevilled previous land taxes. For the subsidy, commissioners nominated by the Commons assessed the value of each estate which, at a time of inflation, meant that the real value of the assessment fell continually. Ship Money tackled this question by fixing a quota for each county and dividing it between taxpayers. This meant that, after initial claims of over-assessment had been dealt with, the amounts charged became stable and yields became predictable – usually well over 90 per cent of the estimate. Parliament, needing large sums of money urgently, was in no mood to haggle with individual taxpayers, so adopted the Ship Money approach, but with the quotas fixed at twelve times as much, or more. The practice of voting a fixed sum for the assessment (or land tax) continued into the eighteenth century.

The **excise** was even more significant in the long run. It brought a large section of the population, who had previously paid no taxes, within the tax system. It was levied on alcohol (including imported wines and spirits, which had already paid customs duties). The main novelty was the taxing of the everyday drinks of the poor (beer, ale and cider, to which were later added coffee and tea), together with tobacco and, for a while, salt and meat. The excise initially met with strong resistance. Introducing the meat excise at the main London meat market, Smithfield, was tactless, especially as butchers were armed with knives and cleavers and had a reputation for violence. It was also unwise to collect the beer excise from customers in alehouses, so the excise men negotiated with the brewers so that the duty was included in the alehouse price. The managers of the excise tried in various ways to damp down resistance. Dealing directly with brewers, and offering a deal on ullage (beer that had become unfit to drink), was one way; another was to employ as collectors local men, who could win acquiescence, if not enthusiasm, from the community. Whereas in the first civil war many financial exactions were made by county committeemen who were widely seen as corrupt, the excise collectors were seen as officials rather than political zealots. In time, excise collection became routine: brewers would leave the key for the excisemen if they were out. After the early stages the excise attracted little violent opposition – far less than the hearth tax introduced in 1662. This was widely seen as unfair, especially as it was often collected on industrial hearths, like those of the cutlers of Sheffield. It was also resented that hearth tax collectors could demand access to people's homes to count the hearths. Many collectors were beaten up and some were killed; the tax was abolished in 1689. (See Box 12.1, Abolition of the Hearth Tax, 1689.) The excise, however, went from strength to strength: once the principle was established it could be extended to more commodities and a predominantly landed Parliament preferred new excises to an increased land tax.

 BOX 12.1: **Abolition of the Hearth Tax, 1689**

Whereas his Majesty, having been informed that the revenue of Hearth Money was grievous to the people, was pleased ... to signify his pleasure either to agree to a regulation of it or to the taking it wholly away ... [The Commons] do find that the revenue cannot be so regulated but it will occasion many difficulties and questions, and that it is in itself not only a great oppression to the poorer sort but a badge of slavery upon the whole people, exposing every man's house to be entered into and searched at pleasure by persons unknown to him ... [the Commons] do most humbly beseech your Majesty that the said revenue of hearth money may be wholly taken away and abolished ...

Statutes of the Realm, vi.61.

The Emergence of the Financial Sector

Compared with the Dutch Republic, England's financial sector was small and primitive. Commercial activity was limited by the scarcity of credit. There were no English banks, although some individuals acted as bankers, and many people borrowed small sums from family members or neighbours to tide them over short-term difficulties. Aristocratic customers expected shopkeepers to allow them credit, which was usually factored into the amount charged. The state's capacity to borrow depended on the personal credit of the king, which was usually poor. Kings mostly borrowed from those beholden to them, such as foreign bankers, the City of London (obliged to lend to protect its privileges) and customs farmers: syndicates of merchants who contracted to collect customs dues, paying some of the money in advance. The farmers' profits could be substantial, but so were their risks. But even these groups could refuse to lend, as the City did after the legal action about the Londonderry Plantation. In a world where government borrowing was increasingly essential, the fragile credit of a king was of limited value. The credit of a Parliament, especially the Long Parliament, was stronger; the credit of the Protectorate was strong so long as it met its obligations, which it did with increasing difficulty in the late 1650s. After 1660 Charles II's regime at first tried hard to improve its credit, promising that orders for payment from the Exchequer should be met in strict chronological order. This progress was undone by the Stop of the Exchequer in 1672, which ruined many bankers and Charles spent most of the rest of his reign trying to restore his credit. From 1689 it was no longer a question of the king's credit, but of Parliament's. After some difficult years under William III, the government's credit became stronger and stronger, so that by the 1730s it was borrowing at rates as low as 2 per cent. By this time it had become accepted that the National Debt was permanent, but so long as individual lenders received their interest and could demand the repayment of their capital, deficit finance flourished.

The 1650s saw an unprecedented volume of financial activity. Apart from government borrowing, many Royalists had had their lands confiscated and bought them back for a proportion of their value. To raise the necessary money they borrowed on the security of their land; others borrowed in order to buy land. Some individuals, especially goldsmiths, were already acting as bankers, receiving deposits, on which they paid interest, and making loans, on which they charged interest. The documents in which these transactions were recorded became financial instruments in their own right, and could be transferred at a discount. There was similar trade in the debentures which soldiers received for their pay, in lieu of cash. There was also trading in the shares of joint-stock companies, like the East India Company. In the half-century after 1660, there were new opportunities for investment – more joint-stock companies, like the Royal African and Hudson's Bay, and, from 1694, the Bank of England. Private bankers continued. One of the most successful, and trusted, was Sir Stephen Fox, paymaster of the forces, who received poundage on all the money that passed through his hands, which essentially underwrote his banking business. By the early eighteenth century family banks appeared alongside individual bankers; in both cases the bank's credit-worthiness depended on the personal reputation of the banker. A further addition to the financial sector was insurance: fire insurance, developed by the Dutch, was brought to England by a property developer of dubious reputation, Dr Nicholas Barbon, in 1682. Soon after, more wide-ranging forms of marine and other insurance were on offer at Lloyd's coffee house, which became Lloyd's of London.

Among the beneficiaries of the growth of the financial sector were great landowners, especially Royalists, who remortgaged their estates to pay off their debts. Henry Somerset, first Duke of Beaufort, was the grandson of the first Marquis of Worcester, the greatest landowner in England and Wales, after the King, and a Catholic. Worcester assessed his losses in the civil wars as more than £800,000. As he regarded his son as financially incompetent – he was obsessed with claiming the dukedom of Somerset and designing a steam engine – the marquis looked to his grandson. After converting to Protestantism, Henry systematically renegotiated the family's debts. He abandoned the family castle at Raglan in South Wales and moved to England, where he built Badminton House and kept a household of 200 servants. Beaufort's experience shows that those best placed to borrow had large amounts of the best security, land. Few Royalists were ruined by the civil wars, and these were usually already in financial trouble when the wars began. Despite the growth of other forms of wealth, from trade or banking, the social and political dominance of the landed elite continued. Most of the King's senior ministers were peers and many MPs were the sons or clients of peers. Peers and their kin dominated the higher echelons of the Church and the armed forces; successful bankers, like Samuel Hoare at Stourhead, built houses that emulated those of the landed elite. No merchant was raised to the peerage in the eighteenth century, and only one banker, the first Lord Carrington.

The Restoration 1660–1688

The monarchy of Charles II reaped the benefits of the state-building of 1640–60. Charles inherited a substantially enlarged navy – 106 ships had been built between 1646 and 1659 – and he continued to enlarge the navy and its manpower. In 1660, for the first time under the monarchy, the Commons calculated how much money the King would need to support his government. Their estimate of need was rather low and their calculations of the yield of taxation were optimistic, but they agreed to grant him revenues for life to support his government. They could have granted revenues for a limited period but, in a gesture of trust (or a leap of faith), they did not. They estimated the King's needs at about £1,200,000 a year. Initially, yields fell well below that, thanks in part to the Plague and Fire. But in the 1670s and 1680s trade and revenue (especially from the excise) grew considerably, helped by an increasingly professional administration. The customs benefited less, not least because the King, desperate for loans, reverted to tax farming, but by the early 1680s the revenue was about £1,500,000 – much more than Charles I's revenue in the 1630s and without any hint of illegality. In 1685 James II's Parliament confirmed his brother's revenues and added more so that his was not far short of £2,000,000.

It is clear that the royal revenue rose significantly between 1660 and 1688, but what did this mean in practical terms? Charles built up substantial debts in the 1660s and embarked on two wars against the Dutch (willingly) and one against France (unwillingly), all of which added to his financial problems. He again came under considerable pressure to take a firm stand against Louis XIV in 1682–4. It was clear that he could not consider making war without additional revenue from Parliament. Such revenue could be forthcoming – the Commons voted £2,500,000 for war against the Dutch in 1664, about six times Charles I's largest grant from Parliament. However, by the 1670s many MPs felt that they had been too generous in 1660 and should not make the same mistake again. Charles extracted some modest subsidies from France, but on the whole he depended on his own revenues, which enabled him to maintain a very much larger navy than the Tudors. He also spent significantly on building, modernising Windsor Castle and building a new palace, modelled on Versailles, at Winchester, which was not quite finished when he died.

Charles was also able, unlike his royal predecessors, to maintain a modest army, ranging from 5,000 to 10,000 men. Parliament strongly opposed the idea of a standing army, which raised echoes of Cromwell. (See Figure 12.1, *The Commonwealth Ruling with a Standing Army*, 1683, and Box 12.2, Arguments Against a Standing Army.) MPs referred to it as 'guards and garrisons', which it essentially was: for much of the reign there was a garrison of 2,000 to 3,000 in Tangier. Charles always feared that his army would prove too small if there was another civil war, and planned to bring troops from Ireland or Scotland in case of emergency. His use of the army took account of civilian fears and suspicions. Soldiers were garrisoned in the environs of London or around the coast and their commanders kept on good terms with the civilian authorities. When in 1672 a group of soldiers ransacked the town hall and insulted the magistrates of Huntingdon (Cromwell's home town) the King cashiered the officer in charge and ordered that he be tried at the assizes. James II's use of the army was very different. After the Duke of Monmouth's rising in 1685 James doubled the army's size and appointed some Catholic officers, contrary to law. He also stationed troops in towns throughout the kingdom with instructions to watch out for disaffection. Although he promised to investigate complaints against soldiers, and punish them if they had misbehaved, officers soon realised that they could escape censure if they claimed to have acted out

The Common wealth ruleing with a standing Army

The Fruits of a Common wealth.

Figure 12.1 Produced at the height of the Tory reaction, this identifies a standing army (and, by implication, the Whigs) with the Republic, trampling on Crown and Church, laws and liberties, and devouring the nation's wealth through taxes like the assessment and the excise.

BOX 12.2: Arguments Against a Standing Army

Arguments against standing armies could be found across the political spectrum. Trenchard and Moyle were radical Whigs: note the remarks about Cromwell.

Our countryman Oliver Cromwell turned out that Parliament under which he served and who had got immortal honour through the whole world by their great actions; and this he effected by the assistance of an army, which must be allowed to have had as much virtue, sobriety and public spirit as hath been known in the world since amongst that sort of men …

… King James's army joined with the Prince of Orange, now our rightful and lawful king. And what could have been expected otherwise from men of dissolute and debauched principles who call themselves soldiers of fortune? who make murder their profession, and enquire no farther into the justice of the cause than how they shall be paid; who must be false, rapacious and cruel in their own defence. For having no other profession or subsistence to depend upon they are forced to stir up the ambitions of princes, and engage them in

perpetual quarrels, that they may share of the spoils that they make …

I have purposely omitted speaking of the lesser inconveniences attending a standing army, such as frequent quarrels, murders and robberies; the destruction of all the game in the country; the quartering upon public and sometimes private houses; the influencing elections of Parliament by an artificial distribution of quarters; the rendering so many men useless to labour … together with a much greater destruction of them by taking them from a laborious way of living to a loose idle life; and besides this the insolence of the officers, and the debaucheries that are committed by them and their soldiers in all the towns they come in, to the ruin of multitudes of women, dishonour of their families, and ill example to others …

[J. Trenchard and W. Moyle],
An Argument Showing that a Standing Army is Inconsistent with a Free Government and Absolutely Destructive to the Constitution of the English Monarchy (1697), pp. 10, 28–9.

of zeal for the King's service. In 1688, as he prepared for a general election, army officers bullied and harassed civilians. By the autumn, with a Dutch invasion imminent, the army was expanded further, but it is unlikely that James could have mobilised its paper strength of 40,000. James's reign intensified English suspicions of standing armies and Parliament was determined to remove any threat of military tyranny in the future.

The Revolution of 1689–1690

Although few were inclined to recognise it, the Revolution was a military conquest. William III brought over a substantial army which put pressure on James until he fled to France. He was able to ensure that no radical new restrictions were imposed on the Crown's powers. The Bill of Rights stated that it was illegal to have a standing army in peacetime without Parliament's consent, but did not define what constituted a standing army; in practice, Parliament accepted the need for a modest force of 'guards and garrisons', but opinions on the size of that force varied. Parliament took two practical steps to remove any threat posed by an army. The first was to grant the money needed for the army for only a year at a time. The second related to the **Articles of War**, the rules of discipline issued by the King (as commander in chief) which were enforced by **courts martial**. The Articles of War made possible the punishment of mutiny and desertion, which were not punishable under common law. The legal standing of the Articles of War was established by the Mutiny Act of 1689, which was temporary, normally renewed for one year at a time. If Parliament ever felt that martial law was being misused, it could refuse to renew the Act, which would make the maintenance of military discipline within England difficult, if not impossible.

The Wars Against France 1689–1713

The second major phase in the strengthening of the English state depended, like the first, on Parliament's commitment to fighting and winning a war, which in turn rested on the perception that defeat would be a catastrophe, opening the way for the imposition of absolute monarchy and popery. James II's flight to France and William's elevation to the English throne made both the Nine Years War (1689–97) and the War of the Spanish Succession (1702–13) wars of the English succession. In the first, Louis XIV committed himself to restoring James II; when James died in 1701 Louis transferred that commitment to his son, the Old Pretender. By 1688 James had alienated almost all of his English subjects – the Whigs who had earlier tried to exclude him from the succession and the Tories who deeply resented his vindictive treatment of the Church of England. The Tories might not like William and his regime, but they saw him as a lesser evil than a Catholic Stuart re-established by a French army. A Tory Parliament secured the Protestant succession in the house of Hanover in 1701 and, although many Tories loathed the thought of a German king, they loathed the prospect of a papist even more. Both parties agreed on the need to guard against the misuse of the army, by William (who had a reputation as an authoritarian ruler) as well as James. But having done so, and despite vigorous disagreements about how best to fight the war, they worked hard to provide the resources – men, munitions, ships and above all money – needed to win.

The means used to raise money included some novelties, like lotteries and a tontine, but the main pillars – land tax, customs and excise – remained the same. The level of taxation continued to rise. James II's revenue reached a peak of £2,000,000 a year, but the average annual yield of taxation in 1689–97 was about £5,500,000 and in 1702–13 £8,500,000 – in other words, more than eight times Charles I's income in the 1630s. The King's personal power had been reduced, but he was now the ruler of a great power. In each war about two-thirds of the costs were met from taxation and one third from borrowing. Initially, interest rates were relatively high, as investors were unaccustomed to government borrowing on this scale. There was an odd mixture of old and new. In the 1690s the Treasury still recorded borrowing on tallies: willow twigs on which the sum borrowed was marked by notches and which were then split down the middle, with each party keeping one part. On the other hand, the Tonnage Act of 1694 provided for a loan of £1,200,000 at 8 per cent; the subscribers were to be incorporated as the Bank of England and empowered to deal in bills of exchange and issue bank notes. The Bank, and the great trading companies, became the intermediaries through which the state borrowed from the public. The creation of the Bank helped give confidence to lenders, but that confidence was ultimately based on the fact that the Bank and the revenues which served as security rested on Acts of Parliament, so the place of Parliament within the constitution was secure; indeed, with Parliament meeting regularly the Commons began to take a constructive interest in the practicalities of raising money. The economic problems of the 1690s and the sheer size of the sums that were needed made lenders nervous, but the money was raised, the armed forces expanded, along with the revenue, military and naval administrations. At the same time the move towards a truly professional revenue service continued, with more emphasis on appointment and promotion according to merit.

In the war of 1689–97 the pattern of naval warfare changed, from large fleet actions to smaller-scale raids on commerce. The emphasis in the English navy under Charles II had been on large, heavily armed ships, but these were of limited use for anything other than fleet actions. The navy kept its largest ships (first to fourth rates) but increased the number of small fifth and sixth rates, which were used to protect England's trade and colonies. In the early 1690s the French fleet was large enough to take on the English and Dutch fleets combined, but from the following decade the French and Dutch fleets contracted while the English fleet continued to grow. More striking was the growth of the army, which reached a peak of almost 87,000 men in 1689–97 and averaged 93,000 in 1702–13. These figures exceeded those for the New Model in the 1650s and dwarfed those of the Tudors. Moreover, the army now operated on a global scale. Cromwell's military operations outside the British Isles were confined to smallish interventions in the Caribbean and Flanders. From 1692 to 1697 there were between 21,000 and 29,000 English troops in Flanders and a further 19,000 to 27,000 foreign troops in English pay. England was the driving force in a series of anti-French alliances and English armies ranged from the Netherlands to Bavaria and Spain, as well as fighting the French in the Americas and Asia.

The Early Hanoverian State: the Standing Army

By the time the Treaty of Utrecht brought the War of the Spanish Succession to an end the British public was weary of war; most of the army was disbanded. Relations with France improved after Louis XIV died (1715) and George I's Whig ministers were eager to bring taxes down. Sir Robert Walpole was particularly concerned to reduce the land tax, to keep landowners happy, and instead made more extensive use of excises. The commitment to lower taxation meant that there was no prospect of paying off the National Debt accumulated during the wars, but low interest rates meant that the debt could be serviced relatively easily. The army of George I and George II was modest by contemporary Continental standards but significantly larger than that of Charles II. It was a British and imperial army, extending across England, Scotland and Ireland and overseas to European stations (such as Gibraltar and Minorca), the Caribbean and North America. Its peacetime strength rarely exceeded 35,000, of which around 12,000 would be in Ireland and at least 15,000 in England and Scotland. The small army which George I inherited was rapidly expanded in response to the **Jacobite** rising of 1715 and its officer corps was purged of Tories so that it became a self-consciously Whig force. Soldiers could be called upon to suppress riots or arrest smugglers, but their role was to assist the civil authorities: they were not to act on their own initiative. More generally, the soldiers were seen as guarding against the **Jacobite** threat. The army was scattered across the three kingdoms, sometimes in large garrisons, around London, Dublin, Edinburgh or Glasgow, but more often in smaller units: two or three troops of horse or companies of foot, or sometimes just a handful of men. The only barracks in England were in the London area and at Berwick-upon-Tweed, a small town which often had to lodge whole regiments en route between England and Scotland; barracks established earlier at Hull and Portsmouth seem to have fallen into disrepair. In most towns in England men were lodged in inns and public houses in close proximity to civilians. In Scotland some Lowland towns had barracks and it was legal to quarter troops in private houses, so there was less reliance on inns. In Ireland, where towns were few and small, with few inns or public houses, soldiers were generally lodged in barracks or, in bandit country, in redoubts: crudely built buildings, not unlike police stations, to house a small number of men.

George I, like James II, was determined to prevent his soldiers from fraternising too closely with civilians. Both kings aimed to create a military caste, loyal only to the Crown. Regiments were not quartered where they were recruited and moved on to new quarters after one or two years. The Irish army was supposed to consist only of English and Scots, but many Irish Protestants (and a few Catholics) served as well. Regiments were also moved frequently between England, Scotland and Ireland; an unlucky few were sent overseas, where mortality was high and regiments tended to remain for substantial periods. The regiments in Ireland were separated from civilians more easily than their counterparts elsewhere, because of the barracks and because the majority of the people spoke Gaelic. Officers might add a little gallantry to the social life of a small Irish town, but their men were likely to get bored, get drunk and get into fights. In England, too, the officers were often welcome, as were the soldiers if they behaved themselves and paid their way. Some soldiers integrated into civilian society by taking part-time jobs or, in the case of NCOs, selling liquor, usually to their soldiers. But conflict could arise, for two reasons. First, soldiers were often volatile and unstable, especially when drunk. While some seem to have signed up looking for adventure, others were rootless young men who could not settle to a trade and fell into petty crime. Some deserted – almost always claiming, if caught, that they had been drunk – only to re-enlist in another regiment, to claim the 'shilling' for signing on.

The second reason why conflict arose was the soldiers' role in the suppression of Jacobitism. When soldiers found civilians making 'seditious' remarks or singing Jacobite songs they were inclined to take matters into their own hands and to arrest, or beat up, offenders. George I's reponse to such behaviour was ambivalent. Officially he disapproved of violence by soldiers against civilians and promised to deal in person with all such cases. This made good disciplinary sense but was also politically necessary. The renewal of the Mutiny Act gave MPs frequent opportunities to complain about the misdeeds of soldiers: many Whigs, as well as the Tories, disliked any hint of military rule, so the government needed to keep such misdeeds to a minimum. When they did occur, it usually managed to keep them out of the newspapers, but ministers felt that they had to go through the motions of investigating complaints; the Secretary at War explained that if he took no action, 'I shall be speeched every day in the House of Commons.' However, it was striking how often the King found complaints to be unfounded and how willing he was to believe that complainants were 'disaffected'. This was strikingly apparent in two army riots in Bridgwater, Somerset, in 1717 and 1721. (See Box 12.3, A Military Riot in Bridgwater, 1721.)

George I's response to complaints about the military was similar to James II's, although the level of army misbehaviour was greater under James II. The disorders in Bridgwater were exceptional but not unique: soldiers were equally unruly in Oxford in 1716 or, on a smaller scale, at Gloucester in 1723. The military played a far more

BOX 12.3: A Military Riot in Bridgwater, 1721

On 10 June 1721, the Pretender's birthday, an effigy appeared in the town, adorned with white roses, horns and turnips. The soldiers swept through the town, tearing white roses from the few people who were wearing them, mostly women. A group then marched around with a **warming pan** containing a 'mommet' [rag doll] crying 'Here is your bastard, here is your Pretender, God damn you, here he is'. They met a poor washerwoman called Jane Jenkins and asked her to give the mommet 'suck'. She refused, angry words ensued, and later they grabbed her by the breast and shoulder and threw her washing in the dirt. The soldiers beat several men in their homes. Robert Headford junior raised his arm to protect himself and was slashed by a sword. A surgeon found that he had lost the 'substance' of his arm above the right wrist, 'about three inches long and almost the whole breadth of his arm'.

The soldiers' commanding officer, Lieutenant Colonel Archibald Hamilton, realised that many MPs would be appalled by the soldiers' behaviour, if they ever heard of it. He claimed that the injuries inflicted were minor – Headford's was 'a slight cut' – but nevertheless offered Headford five guineas as compensation; the surgeon said that would not cover his fees. Meanwhile, Hamilton concocted a rival version of events, in conjunction with a local customs officer, historian and Whig polemicist, John Oldmixon. In this version the soldiers had been attacked by the townspeople and conducted themselves with exemplary patience; the blame for the disorders lay with the town authorities who had failed to prevent, and even encouraged, the riot. In an earlier army riot in 1717 the corporation had prosecuted the offenders at the assizes, where they had been convicted; the King was furious that they had not referred the case to him. Now they gathered affidavits [testimonies on oath] and forwarded them to the King; Hamilton and Oldmixon sent in another set of affidavits, mostly by soldiers, which were less detailed and often inconsistent. The King found that the blame lay entirely with the town. Unlike that of 1717, the case did not make it into the public domain and was not reported in the newspapers.

Compiled from The National Archives, SP 35/27, especially nos. 52–53. Quotations from SP 35/27, no. 54, fo. 246, and no. 52, fo. 229.

prominent role in public life in peacetime under George I and George II than under Charles II or his predecessors.

Conclusion: the Extent of the 'Fiscal-Military State'

In recent years historians have used the term 'fiscal-military state' when describing the growth of English (later British) military and naval power and the expansion of the revenue and borrowing that paid for it. The creation of the fiscal-military state marked an abrupt insertion of 'modern' modes of administration into a system of government which was still largely medieval. It rested on the careful accumulation of records and systematic keeping of accounts. The concept of 'office' changed. Under the Tudors and early Stuarts, offices were treated as private property, which might be purchased or inherited; personal favour was the key to advancement. Most carried small salaries and remuneration was mainly through fees, which encouraged those dealing with officials to offer sweeteners to secure preferential treatment, with lesser sweeteners for the underlings of senior officials as a 'remembrance' 'to be the welcomer when we come next'. Accounts were often eccentrically organised and convoluted, designed to make them difficult for the uninitiated to understand. (The continued use of Roman numerals made the confusion worse.) The subsidy was chronically underassessed as commissioners treated their friends favourably, confident that they would return the favour when the roles were reversed. The customs administration was weakened by farming in which the search for maximum yield was sacrificed for short-term advantage. The problems with the customs continued in the late seventeenth century, but the excise represented a fresh start. Offices and promotions were granted on merit and officials were paid salaries: to earn more money they needed to work hard and do their job well. Self-advancement through personal favour was replaced by a concept of public service. By the 1650s a new breed of public servant was changing the ethos of administration: Samuel Pepys or Sir Joseph Williamson, with their professionalism and love of order and method, are often cited as examples, although Pepys was determined to use his office to get rich. (See Box 12.4, The Ethics of Office in the Reign of Charles II: Samuel Pepys.) This more 'modern' approach was found especially in the Treasury and other departments geared to war, such as the Admiralty, the War Office and the Ordnance Office, but it was not universal. Military commissions were obtained by favour or by purchase. George I wanted to abolish this tradition, but he failed: landed families saw buying commissions as a way of providing for younger sons. Commissions in the navy, by contrast, were granted according to ability and experience. The skills involved in captaining a ship or commanding a squadron took much longer to learn than those of an infantry captain.

The sale of army commissions, like the use of Exchequer tallies to record loans, offer reminders that the old persisted alongside the new. Even in the eighteenth century the number of professional administrators in England was very small compared to France. Most were found in London, with small groups of revenue officials in seaports and other provincial towns. Most local government, in town and county, was still carried out by unpaid amateurs, drawn from the leading members of the community. These had been loaded with extra responsibilities under the Tudors and Stuarts and had been empowered, by Parliament, to raise local rates to cover the cost of the services they provided. This continued in the eighteenth century, as

BOX 12.4: **The Ethics of Office in the Reign of Charles II: Samuel Pepys**

Pepys came from a relatively modest background, but had influential relatives, notably the Earl of Sandwich, so was able to secure employment and advancement through a mixture of patronage and talent. Sandwich told him in 1660 that 'it was not the salary of any place that did make a man rich, but the opportunities of getting money while he is in the place'. He was always on the lookout for additional income, while taking pains, in his diary, to stress that this was not incompatible with his service to the King. The following extracts show some of his dealings in 1663–4 with Mr Dering, a merchant, who offered £50 down and £200 a year 'if I would stand his friend'.

I was glad to hear both of these, but answered him no further than that as I would not in anything be bribed to be unjust in my dealings, so I was not so squeamish as not to take people's acknowledgment where I have the good fortune by my pains to do them good and just offices. And so I would not come to be at an agreement with him, but I would labour to do him this service and expect his consideration thereof afterward, as he thought fit. So I expect to hear more of it.

... I told him that I would not sell my liberty to any man. If he would give me anything by another's hand, I would endeavour to deserve it, but I will never give him himself thanks for it, not acknowledge the receiving of any – which he told me was reasonable. I did also tell him that neither this nor anything should make me to do anything that should not be for the king's service besides.

[Given £50 from Dering] for my pains in this business and which I may hereafter take for him – though there is not the least word or deed I have yet been guilty of in his behalf but what I am sure hath been to the king's advantage and the profit of the service, nor ever will I ...

S. Pepys, *Diary*, ed. R.C. Latham and W. Matthews (11 vols., 1971–83), IV, pp. 415–16, 436, V, p. 5. For the quotation from Sandwich see *Diary*, I, p. 223.

magistrates sought and were granted new powers and authorised to levy further rates. New powers were also granted to specific groups. The corporations of the poor were an early example, and they were followed by commissions for urban improvements. Paving, cleansing and lighting commissioners, who could also levy rates, took over the responsibility for maintaining the streets hitherto exercised (at least in theory) by householders. Some towns established their own waterworks, others were set up by private companies. Other improvements were on a larger scale and were more commercial in intent, particularly canal and turnpike trusts: the former enabled great landowners to exploit valuable minerals on their estates. The innovations of the fiscal-military state affected limited and specific areas of government, which by definition required central direction and control. During the eighteenth century those areas of government that were not directed from the centre grew in scale and diversity. All they needed from the centre were enabling, often local, Acts of Parliament, and they affected the people of England in an increasing variety of ways. The English medieval tradition of local self-government proved extraordinarily adaptable and effective.

SUGGESTIONS FOR FURTHER READING

The conceptual framework of this topic was laid down by J. Brewer, *The Sinews of Power: War, Money and the English State 1688–1783* (London, 1989); Brewer also coined the term 'fiscal-military state'. • His main focus was the period after 1688, but others pointed out the importance of the changes of the 1640s: see P. O'Brien and P. Hunt, 'The Rise of a Fiscal State in England, 1485–1815', *Historical Research*, 66 (1993) and two books by M.J. Braddick: *Parliamentary Taxation in Seventeenth-Century England: Local Administration and Response* (Woodbridge, 1994) and *The Nerves of State: Taxation and the Financing of the British State 1558–1714* (Manchester, 1996). • For the Restoration, see C.D. Chandman, *The English Public Revenue, 1660–88* (Oxford, 1998). Brewer and most others have built on the massive work by P.G.M. Dickson, *The Financial Revolution in England, 1688–1756* (London, 1967). A briefer and more accessible introduction can be found in H.G. Roseveare, *The Financial Revolution, 1660–1760* (Harlow, 1991). • For an attempt to argue that James II promoted a 'modern' vision of government which revolutionised the English state, see S. Pincus, *1688: The First Modern Revolution* (New Haven, 2009). • For a concise account of the growth of the navy, see M. Duffy, 'The Foundations of British Naval Power', in M. Duffy (ed.), *The Military Revolution and the State 1500–1800* (Exeter, 1980), pp. 49–85. • On the eighteenth-century army see J.A. Houlding, *Fit for Service: the Training of the British Army, 1715–95* (Oxford, 1981), whose coverage is wider than the title suggests. There is also relevant material in T. Hayter, *The Army and the Crowd in Mid-Georgian England* (1978) and J. Miller, *Cities Divided: Politics and Religion in English Provincial Towns 1660–1722* (Oxford, 2007), chapters 5, 10 and 13. • The best introduction to the civil service is G.E. Aylmer, *The Crown's Servants: Government and Civil Service under Charles II* (Oxford, 2002). This may be compared with his earlier studies *The King's Servants* (1961) and *The State's Servants* (1973), which dealt with Charles I's reign and the 1650s respectively.

SUMMARY

- The early modern period saw European nations moving away from the medieval 'domain state' to a more modern 'tax state'. In the domain state the monarch relied on income from lands and feudal rights; in the tax state revenue came from taxes – on land, transactions and goods. As a means of tapping the nation's wealth, the tax state was much the more effective. Parliament had granted taxes for centuries but with the introduction of the assessment and excise in 1643 taxation became much more broadly based.
- A second basis for a modern fiscal system was the opportunity for the state to borrow from private individuals, using its own credit and that of banks. Until the seventeenth century bankers were usually foreign, especially Italian, but English private bankers appear from the mid century. By the eighteenth century there was a range of private bankers, a few great trading companies and the Bank of England.

- The French wars of 1689–1713 saw a large increase in taxation and borrowing. Parliament agreed to fund much larger armies because they were essential for national survival. But MPs remained suspicious of standing armies and used their control over their funding and discipline to keep them in check. After 1715 the majority of MPs tended to agree with Whig ministers that the army was a necessary defence against Jacobitism. Criticism of the military remained, but the army became larger and to some extent it was used to police political disaffection.

QUESTIONS FOR STUDENTS

1. Assess the importance of the assessment and excise for the subsequent development of the English revenue.
2. Account for the growth of the financial sector and government borrowing in this period.

3. Why was Parliament willing to grant increasingly high taxes in this period?
4. Why, despite widespread suspicion of standing armies, was Parliament willing to fund a peacetime army and endorse martial law?

13 Crown and Parliament 1660–1750: 1. England

TIMELINE

1660	Declaration of Breda; election of Convention; Act of Indemnity; vote to grant Charles II ordinary revenue for life
1661	Election of Cavalier Parliament; Militia Act; Corporation Act
1664	Triennial Act; Commons vote £2,500,000 for war against Dutch
1665–7	Second Dutch War
1672–4	Third Dutch War
1673	Test Act; Duke of York marries Mary of Modena
1677	Princess Mary marries William III
1678	Popish Plot; second Test Act excludes Catholics from House of Lords; end of Cavalier Parliament
1679	Election of first and second Exclusion Parliaments
1680	Second Exclusion Parliament meets (October)
1681	Second and third Exclusion Parliaments dissolved
1685	Charles II dies, succeeded by James II; Monmouth's rebellion
1687	Declaration of Indulgence

1688	Birth of James Francis Edward; invasion of William III; James flees to France
1689	Crown offered to William and Mary; war with France; resolution against Catholic monarchs; Bill of Rights; Toleration Act
1690	Commons vote to grant ordinary revenue for limited period
1694	Triennial Act
1697	Peace of Ryswick
1701	Act of Settlement
1702	Anne succeeds William; war with France
1707	Union with Scotland
1713	Peace of Utrecht
1714	George I succeeds Anne
1715	Riot Act; Jacobite rebellion
1716	Septennial Act
1720	South Sea Bubble
1727	George II succeeds George I
1733	Excise Crisis
1745	Jacobite rebellion

Introduction

This period saw the Westminster Parliament become a permanent and regular institution. Before 1640 it had been neither. Having met almost annually in the fifteenth century, it met only once in the last decade of Henry VII's reign. Under Henry VIII it met irregularly and often briefly, except for the Reformation Parliament of 1529–36. Under Elizabeth, Parliament met on average every three years, for a few weeks, and it became more irregular under the early Stuarts: it met only once, briefly, between 1610 and 1621 and not at all between 1629 and 1640. The five parliaments that met between 1621 and

1629 were characterised by conflict and concerns about the institution's future. The **Triennial Act** of 1641 tried to address these concerns, but it was a moot point whether Charles I could be trusted to abide by it. A new Triennial Act was passed in 1664 but it lacked provisions for its effective enforcement and Charles II ruled without Parliament for almost four years at the end of his reign. Only after 1689 did Parliament meet annually for a period of months. With its existence secure it was able to extend its range of legislation and to develop as an instrument through which more and more public and private business could be done. At the same time its importance, especially in the granting of money, meant that its management became the primary concern of kings and ministers.

Parliament's rise to pre-eminence and permanence was neither inevitable nor predictable. On the Continent the autonomy and indeed existence of representative assemblies seemed threatened. France's national representative body, the Estates General, did not meet between 1614 and 1789, and the provincial estates began to grant without question the sums that the King demanded. In the 1620s anxious MPs exclaimed that England was the last country in Europe to retain its ancient liberties. The Scottish and Irish parliaments met irregularly. The Dublin Parliament did not meet between 1586 and 1613 or between 1666 and 1692 and the powers of the Scottish Parliament were ill-defined. After 1660 the English Parliament met every year except two until 1681, but in the 1680s it again seemed under threat. It did not meet between 1681 and 1685 and faced a very different threat in 1687–8 when James II attempted to manage a general election so rigorously as to destroy the representative nature of the Commons.

Parliament was saved by the Revolution of 1688–9. The key to its survival lay in the Commons' power to grant money. Under the Tudors it became customary to grant each incoming monarch the customs (tonnage and poundage) for life. In 1625 the Commons broke with this tradition, but Charles I collected them anyway. Parliament radically reformed the revenue system in the 1640s, but at the Restoration the Commons reverted to granting the King his **ordinary revenue** (intended to cover normal peacetime revenue) for life. In 1689–90 the Commons refused to grant William III his ordinary revenues for more than a limited period. With major revenues – notably the grants for the army and navy – granted annually he was forced to summon Parliament each year and the Commons could demand concessions in return for money. As the Commons were often divided on party lines the leaders of the majority party could use their control of the Commons to press the monarch to give them the policies and make the appointments to office that they wanted. Under William III and Anne the party leaders did not always get their way, but between 1714 and 1760 the Whigs' control over Parliament was rarely challenged and George I and George II presided over a regime in which effective power lay with the politicians rather than the King. The Whigs used their control over the monarch and the increasing resources of the state to manage the electoral system and the two Houses of Parliament. By the 1740s the **prerogatives** of the Crown no longer posed any threat to the liberty of the subject, but what became known as 'the **influence of the Crown**', the ability to buy support with places (offices) and pensions, enabled the Whig oligarchs to control both King and Parliament. They were not popular, but their control over the electoral system enabled them to reverse the growth of the electorate, seen through much of the seventeenth century, as a result of which general election results had increasingly reflected public opinion.

The Restoration Settlement

The restoration of the monarchy followed the disintegration of the republican regime which, under Oliver Cromwell, had been edging back towards something akin to monarchy. Oliver alone had been able to maintain the trust of both the army and civilian supporters of the regime who, by the end of 1659, were totally at odds with one another. Moreover, the New Model's morale was shattered by the defection of part of the army in Ireland and the decision of George Monk, its commander in Scotland, to demand the reinstatement of the Rump. As Monk marched south in January 1660 he was bombarded by calls for elections for a free Parliament, which would very probably recall the King. In February he ordered the Rump to readmit the members excluded from the Commons in Pride's Purge in 1648, and the enlarged Commons made provisions for the election of a **Convention** – it could not be a true Parliament as it was not summoned by a king. The outgoing Parliament tried to shape its successor by banning Royalists from voting, but this was widely ignored and the Convention was fairly evenly divided between Royalists and Presbyterians – moderate Parliamentarians, who favoured a limited monarchy. The Royalists managed to prevent the imposition of significant preconditions for the King's return, which was duly proclaimed and celebrated with wild rejoicing. When the King dissolved the Convention, elections in the spring of 1661 produced a much more Royalist body, the 'Cavalier' House of Commons.

Charles II had, on the face of it, contributed nothing to his restoration: he had watched from abroad as his people called him home. In one way, however, he significantly facilitated it. His Declaration of Breda on 4 April strove to reassure those who might fear the consequences of his return. Charles promised a 'free and general pardon' to all who sought it, excluding only those who were to be excepted by Parliament. Purchasers of Crown, Church and other lands were assured that claims to ownership would be referred to Parliament. Soldiers would receive their full arrears and be 'received into our service upon as good pay and conditions as they now enjoy'. Finally, Charles noted that 'the passion and uncharitableness of the times' had led to divisions of religion, and declared his willingness to assent to an Act of Parliament to grant 'a liberty to tender consciences and that no man shall be disquieted or called in question for differences of opinion in matters of religion which do not disturb the peace of the kingdom'.

The Declaration showed a shrewd understanding of the concerns of those who stood to lose by the Restoration and Charles did his best to deliver on his promises. Theoretically anyone who had fought against Charles I could face prosecution for treason. Charles made it clear that this would not happen and repeatedly urged both Houses in the Convention – a growing number of peers had taken their seats in the Lords – to pass a comprehensive act of indemnity (for past offences) and oblivion (to prevent the raking up of past misdeeds in future). The latter proved impossible: Royalists did not intend to forget the past and the King himself, worried by the apparent threat of rebellion, urged magistrates to watch vigilantly those suspected of rebellious principles. The issue of land sales proved too complicated for Parliament and was largely left to the law courts, which often tried to reconcile the interests of old and new proprietors. The army's arrears were indeed paid off, but the Commons had no wish to allow Charles an experienced standing army. Finally, on religion, sects like the Baptists and Quakers saw the Declaration as a promise of freedom of worship. They claimed that they were 'peaceable' – George Fox drew up the Quaker 'peace testimony' in 1661 – but neither the King nor the Commons accepted that such groups 'do not disturb the peace of the kingdom' and blamed the Baptists and Independents for the regicide. Charles did try to accommodate the Presbyterians, who had deplored the regicide and facilitated the Restoration, but was opposed by a majority of the Cavalier House of Commons.

The failure to impose conditions on the King before his return meant that the Restoration settlement was negotiated between Charles and two very different parliaments. The Convention largely liquidated the legacy of the past, especially by passing the indemnity and disbanding the army. It also resolved the question of which legislation from 1640–60 was in force by declaring that only Acts which had received the royal assent should be valid, thus annulling all but a handful of measures from the beginning of 1642 onwards. Other questions were resolved by the Cavalier Parliament and reflected ex-Royalists' anxieties and eagerness for revenge. Like the King they were fearful of revolt: it seemed inconceivable that the radicals and the army would melt quietly back into civilian society. In fact, most of them did. Many were deeply demoralised by the events of 1659–60 which severely shook their conviction that God was with them. One general went into exile commenting that the godly were now to take their turn in the wilderness. Despite all the rumours there was only one small rising in England in the 1660s in the far North West, a small rain-sodden debacle, which was easily suppressed.

The old Cavaliers blamed the upheavals of the 1640s on the Long Parliament's weakening of the monarchy. Charles I's warning in 1642 that upsetting the balance of the constitution would end in a 'dark equal chaos of confusion' seemed amply borne out by events. The Commons therefore built up the King's powers to enable him to suppress any attempt at revolution from below. The most fundamental challenges to the King's prerogatives in 1641–2 had been demands that he should share with Parliament his control over the armed forces and his choice of advisers. The Militia Act of 1661 stated that control of the armed forces had always been, and should always be, vested solely in the King, adding that 'the contrary thereof hath of late years been practised, almost to the ruin and destruction of this kingdom, and … many evil and rebellious principles have been distilled [sic] into the minds of the people'. As for the King's choosing his ministers, Charles began to do so immediately after his return. The Commons did not challenge this, so his right was restored by default.

Other legislation extended the King's powers to guard against the threat from below. Many blamed recent upheavals on the press. The pre-civil-war system of censorship had rested on the royal prerogative. Now it was given parliamentary authorisation, by the Licensing Act of 1662. Memories of the 1640s also underlay an Act against 'tumultuous petitioning', which ironically echoed the ordinance of 1648. Petitions to the King or Parliament could be presented by no more than ten people. But the most remarkable enhancement of the King's authority was made by the Convention. As many of the old royal revenues had been abolished in 1641, and the new fiscal legislation from 1643 had been declared invalid, there was clearly a need to address the question of the revenue. After estimating the annual cost of the civil and military government at £1,200,000, the Convention resolved to grant taxes calculated to raise such a sum, either for the King's lifetime or in perpetuity. If the King was to govern, as in the past, he would need the necessary resources. But it was entirely up to the Convention to decide on what terms, and for how long, to vote the money. Nothing would have been easier than to grant the money for a limited time, but instead it was voted for life, or forever.

This decision significantly reduced Parliament's bargaining power in its dealings with the King. It was an act of generosity, of trust, which some would later regard as foolhardy, surprisingly so in a body in which Royalists and Parliamentarians were evenly balanced. The Cavalier Parliament was less generous. Having reluctantly accepted that the estimates of likely yields had been over-optimistic, it voted for a tax on domestic hearths, a crude property tax which was widely seen as unfair and intrusive. Otherwise it refused to add to the ordinary revenue and showed itself wary of increasing the King's authority in other ways. The Licensing Act was only temporary, but was eventually extended until the first session of the next Parliament (which was to be in 1679). Also, while reasserting the King's control over the militia the Commons refused to grant money for raising additional forces. Like the Convention its members had had enough of standing armies. The Cavaliers' attitude may partly be explained by resentment of the King's persistent attempts to adapt the liturgy of the Church of England to accommodate Presbyterians, which the Commons rejected. They certainly resented the favour that the King showed to Presbyterian grandees like Manchester and Holles. They felt that Charles was seeking to conciliate his former enemies rather than relieving or rewarding his old friends. Historians may plausibly suggest that Charles deserved credit for refusing to wreak vengeance on his father's enemies (with the exception of some regicides and a few others); for the Cavaliers it smacked of ingratitude and betrayal.

The Restored Monarchy

Historians disagree about the strength and viability of the Restored monarchy. Some argue that it was institutionally weaker than that of Charles I: the Triennial Act reduced the King's ability to summon and dismiss parliaments and the abolition of the prerogative courts (notably Star Chamber and High Commission) meant that he could prosecute his enemies only in the common law courts, with juries. Others claim that monarchy lost its mystical, divine aura with the trial and execution of Charles I. But the revised Triennial Act proved ineffective and did not establish a minimum length for parliaments: that of March 1681 lasted only a week. The early 1680s were to show that Charles could destroy his enemies through treason trials in the common law courts. And the public response to the regicide, and especially *Eikon Basilike* and the cult of the royal martyr, strengthened rather than diminished belief in the divine right of kings. (See Chapter 16.) Although the monarchy had been restricted by the legislation of 1641 the civil war broke out because the Parliamentarians believed that these restrictions were insufficient to prevent future misrule by Charles I. Moreover, some of the changes of 1641, notably the abolition of many of the fiscal devices abused in the 1630s, turned out to be advantageous to the monarchy. Ship Money, forest fines and the like had been deeply unpopular and (with the exception of Ship Money) fiscally inefficient, falling on relatively small numbers of people. The new fiscal devices, the assessment and the excise, were both more efficient and spread over a much wider range of the population. The excise along with the customs was continued at the Restoration and formed the basis of the King's **ordinary** revenue. The assessment soon emerged as the main form of **extraordinary taxation** – one-off grants voted by Parliament either for war or to compensate for shortfalls in the ordinary revenue.

The granting of the ordinary revenue for life proved to be one of Charles II's greatest assets. It was not intended to be over-generous and initially yields fell well short of the estimate (not helped by the plague and the Great Fire). However, the upsurge in overseas trade in the 1670s and 1680s, and greater efficiency of collection, boosted the revenue from customs and excise. The Convention's estimate of the annual cost of government, £1,200,000, was a little low, but not unreasonable. In the 1660s the ordinary revenue was often well below £1,000,000, but by the end of the reign it had reached £1,500,000 – a real increase, because the inflation of the century before 1640 had stopped. In his last years Charles was able to dispense with Parliament and build himself a palace at Winchester. (See Figure 13.1, Sir Christopher Wren's Design for the King's House at Winchester.) And this revenue was legal – granted by Parliament – and so politically uncontentious. The legacy which Charles inherited from the 1640s and 1650s was in many ways advantageous. Apart from the new fiscal system he inherited a greatly enlarged navy and a modest standing army, described euphemistically as

Figure 13.1 Drawing by Sir Christopher Wren of Charles II's palace at Winchester: the influence of Versailles is very apparent. Charles was eager to move in, but died before it was finished. His successors showed no interest in it and it was allowed to decay.

'guards and garrisons': never fewer than 5,000 men and about 10,000 by the end of the reign. Charles, who harboured exaggerated fears of rebellion, thought this army was too small, but it proved more than adequate to maintain order in England. Charles I had had no standing army.

Charles II and Parliament (to 1678)

With his army and navy and his modernised fiscal system Charles II presided over a stronger state than his father. However, for much of his reign his ordinary revenue was insufficient to cover the expenses of government, for various reasons: debts inherited from the Interregnum, exacerbated by the initial shortfall of the ordinary revenue; extravagance, compounded by Royalists seeking compensation for their losses and large numbers of greedy and predatory courtiers; and the costs of war. He had to seek additional grants from Parliament, which initially was generous: in 1664 the Commons voted £2,500,000 for a war against the Dutch – about six times the largest grant received by Charles I – plus a further £1,250,000, but these unprecedented sums proved insufficient. Charles was unable to send out a fleet in 1667 and the Dutch sailed unopposed into the Medway and carried away his flagship. By the time of the third Dutch war, in 1672, Parliament was far less generous, mainly because Charles had allied with Louis XIV, who was aggressively Catholic and seen as aspiring to 'universal monarchy'. By 1678 Charles had apparently turned against France. He had married his niece, Mary, to William III, Prince of Orange, the leading figure in the Dutch Republic and the French King's inveterate enemy. In the first half of 1678 Charles prepared for war against France, raising a substantial army, but he delayed declaring war and allowed himself to be bought off with a (relatively small) French pension.

Charles's difficulties with Parliament had a variety of causes: resentment of the libertinism, extravagance and corruption of his court; the mismanagement of the second Dutch war; and mounting evidence of his duplicity and bad faith. Between 1666 and 1668 Louis XIV emerged as the most formidable monarch in Europe, with a massive army and, ominously for England, a much enlarged navy: France was now a serious commercial and colonial competitor. And yet, far from responding to this threat, Charles courted France, leading to suspicions that he was planning, with French help, to establish absolute monarchy in England. (Had they known that Charles had promised Louis, in 1670, that he would declare himself a Catholic they would have been even more alarmed, but the promise remained secret and Charles failed to act on it.) In 1671 Charles asked the Commons for money to guard against the threat from the French navy, only to join with France in attacking the Protestant Dutch in 1672.

To make matters worse there were signs that Charles's only surviving brother, James Duke of York, had become a Catholic. In 1673 Parliament passed the **Test Act** whereby all office-holders were required to take communion in an Anglican church and to declare that the bread and wine did not (as Catholics believed) turn into the body and blood of Christ. James and Lord Treasurer Clifford refused to take the test. Although he had fathered numerous bastards, Charles had no legitimate children. If he died first, James would succeed him and England would have its first Catholic monarch since Mary Tudor. James had two daughters, Mary (who married William) and Anne. Both were raised as Protestants, but in 1673 James was married a second time, to Mary Beatrice of Modena, a Catholic. If she bore him a son, he would take precedence over his half-sisters and there would be the prospect of an ongoing Catholic dynasty. Mary bore James several children, none of whom lived beyond infancy, but the possibility of a healthy prince loomed in the minds of English Protestants throughout the second half of Charles's reign.

The Exclusion Crisis

Public concerns about France, the newly raised army and the succession were brought to a head by the revelation of an alleged Popish Plot to kill the King. The chief informer, Titus Oates, had an unsavoury record, but he told his story with great self-confidence and a grasp of detail which many found persuasive. Among those he named was Edward Coleman, former secretary to the Duke of York, a busy papist who dabbled in news-writing. Coleman's letters included correspondence with Louis XIV's confessor, in which Coleman asked for money to enable the King to dissolve Parliament, claiming that this would strike a blow at Protestantism (the 'pestilent Northern heresy'). His claims were overblown, but the letters were genuine and seemed to offer independent corroboration of the Plot. They also stated that James knew of the correspondence (which he frantically denied). Coleman was arrested, tried, convicted of treason and executed. In his trial he tried to justify his conduct, but was quickly silenced by the judges. He had already done more than enough damage.

Coleman's letters removed, or silenced, doubts about the Plot. Meanwhile, Charles's former ambassador in Paris produced in the Commons letters which showed that Charles had been seeking money from Louis to enable him to make peace with France while asking Parliament for money to make war. This was yet more evidence of Charles's duplicity and suspicions about possible uses of the newly raised forces were increased when it was revealed that they included Catholic officers and soldiers. Anxieties about the threat from a possible Catholic successor mingled with suspicions about the intentions of the present King. From late 1678 until the summer of 1681 Charles was on the defensive. He sent away his brother, first to Brussels, then to Edinburgh. He dissolved the Cavalier Parliament and held three general elections in less than two years, but each House of Commons demanded a thorough investigation of the Plot, the remedying of grievances and the punishment of 'evil counsellors'. From May 1679 there were three attempts to pass bills excluding James from the succession on the grounds that, as a Catholic, he would be bound to introduce 'arbitrary government'. Only one bill came to a vote, and was rejected in the Lords. After the second election of 1679 Charles delayed meeting his new Parliament for more than a year, which led the supporters of exclusion to organise petitions asking the King to summon Parliament and to allow it to sit until all grievances had been remedied. Charles saw this, rightly, as a threat to his prerogative of summoning and dismissing parliaments and welcomed loyal addresses condemning (or abhorring) the petitions: 'petitioners' and 'abhorrers' were soon converted into '**Whigs**' and '**Tories**'.

The Tory Reaction 1681–1685

As in 1641 the extreme demands and populist tactics of the King's critics provoked a conservative backlash. For many the suspicions and resentments which had built up in the 1670s were outweighed by fears of a revolution from below, another 'Forty-one'. Unlike his father in 1641, Charles did not try to appeal to force, although he had his army ready if needed. Instead he used the legitimate powers of the Crown and the law courts. By 1681 all the judges were Tories and in most shires Tory sheriffs returned Tory juries. The King did not appoint the sheriffs of the towns, and especially in London, where elected, unashamedly Whig sheriffs returned strongly Whig juries. As one contemporary remarked: 'Tis now come to a civil war, not with the sword but law and if the king cannot make the judges speak for him he will be beaten out of the field.' Charles complained theatrically that he was the only man in his kingdom who could not get justice and set out to break the autonomy of the corporate towns. His law officers mounted legal actions claiming that rulers of corporations had breached the terms of the charters under which they governed. The key case was London; once its charter had been declared forfeit many other corporations surrendered without a fight. London's government was dissolved and it was ruled by commissioners nominated by the King. Flattering courtiers told Charles that he was now truly King of England.

In the 'Tory reaction' of 1681–5 Charles became what he had refused to be at the Restoration, a partisan King. Like the Tories he had been shaken by populist rhetoric, mass demonstrations and rowdy street politics. He was further shaken when crowds flocked to see his illegitimate son, the Duke of Monmouth, on a series of quasi-royal 'progresses' in 1682. Many saw Monmouth as a Protestant alternative to York, but he could also be seen as challenging his father. Monmouth was linked to, if not implicated in, the Rye House Plot of 1683, a plan to assassinate Charles and James en route from Newmarket to London. The Plot was a mysterious mixture of designs, some more fully formed than others, but there were indications that some of those involved had planned to kill the King. When Monmouth refused to condemn his former allies Charles banished him to Holland. Charles increasingly supported the Tories as they harassed and punished the Whigs and their allies, the Protestant Dissenters. By the time of his death, in February 1685, he had raised the Stuart monarchy to the zenith of its power. He did not wish to call Parliament, and financially he had no need to. Without Parliament he could not afford a foreign policy which might involve war, but, having pursued an adventurous foreign policy in between 1668 and 1672, he had no wish to do so again. He was happy to live out his last years in peace, unaware that the security which he had created was to be demolished at breakneck speed by his successor.

§ James II

James II was a natural Tory who, like his father, had straightforward views on authority and obedience: kings were born to rule, subjects to obey. Government was the king's business: subjects could petition the king, but he was answerable to God alone. James was convinced that sedition and republicanism were widespread in all three kingdoms and equated religious nonconformity with disaffection. In this he had much in common with English Tories and Scottish Episcopalians, with whom he co-operated closely during his brother's last years. But James had converted to Catholicism, whose dogmatic certainties and hierarchical authority he found easier to grasp than the more nuanced teachings of Protestant churches. In the 1680s the Church of England proclaimed that active resistance to the King could never be justified, with the tacit reservation that, if required to act against the law of God, Christians should refuse and passively accept the consequences. For James such reservations were unmanly equivocations. He expected Anglicans to obey him unquestioningly and accused them of betraying their principles if they did not.

James believed that he was straightforward and honourable, and in some ways he was. He declared in 1687: 'We cannot but heartily wish, as it will easily be believed, that all the people of our dominions were members of the Catholic Church.' Although he went on to say that he believed that conscience should not be coerced, in the eyes of most Protestants Catholicism could spread only through coercion. At other times his statements seemed intended to mislead. At his accession he stated: 'I know that the principles of the Church of England are for monarchy and the members of it have shown themselves good and loyal subjects; therefore I shall always take care to defend and support it.' The catch was the word 'therefore': James committed himself to support the Church only so long as he judged its members to be behaving loyally. He also promised to preserve the government as by law established, but James's understanding of the law differed from that of most of his subjects. He had no time for legal subtleties and sought to extend his powers in ways which seemed logical to him, seemingly unable to understand that by extending those powers he also transformed them. After the judges ruled in 1686 that he could dispense individuals from the penalties of particular laws 'for particular necessary reasons', James assumed that he could suspend laws, thus dispensing the whole population, without enquiring (as the judges had required) into the merits of individual cases. Nor did he have any qualms about putting pressure on the judges to endorse his view of the law, dismissing them if they refused, because he believed he was self-evidently right. (See Box 13.1, The Dispensing and Suspending Powers.)

James's main aim was to convert his kingdoms to Catholicism, not by force but through willing conversions. The truth of Catholicism seemed so obvious to him that he was sure that others could be equally persuaded provided he could remove the

BOX 13.1: **The Dispensing and Suspending Powers**

The Crown traditionally had the power to dispense individuals from the penalties of certain laws. Late in 1685 James pardoned about seventy Catholic army officers for accepting commissions without taking the Test, but found the judges divided as to whether he could dispense them from taking the Test (and the oaths of allegiance and supremacy, which Catholics also refused to take). For the moment James was content to recommission them – they would not have to take the Test for three months – while he set out to secure a ruling from the judges that the dispensing power was legal. Six were dismissed for insisting that it was not; their replacements proved more compliant. The lord chief justice summoned the twelve judges together to consider the case of *Godden vs Hales*. A Catholic officer was prosecuted for accepting a commission contrary to law: he pleaded the King's pardon. The judges resolved on 16 June 1686:

We think that ... the king may dispense in this case; and the judges go upon these grounds:

1. That the kings of England are sovereign princes.
2. That the laws of England are the king's laws.
3. That therefore 'tis an inseparable prerogative in the kings of England to dispense with penal laws in particular cases and upon particular necessary reasons.

4. That of those reasons and those necessities the king himself is sole judge ...

J.P. Kenyon, *The Stuart Constitution* (2nd edn, Cambridge, 1986), p. 404.

During the latter part of 1686 James used his dispensing power to allow congregations of Dissenters to worship freely. On 4 April 1687 he extended that freedom to the whole nation. He did not consult the judges, presumably assuming that the suspending power followed logically from the dispensing power; nevertheless he distinguished between them:

We have thought fit by virtue of our royal prerogative to issue forth this our Declaration of Indulgence, making no doubt of the concurrence of our two Houses of Parliament, when we shall think it convenient for them to meet.

We do likewise declare that it is our royal will and pleasure that from henceforth the execution of all and all manner of penal laws in matters ecclesiastical ... be immediately suspended ...

And forasmuch as we are desirous to have the benefit of the service of all our loving subjects, which by the law of nature is inseparably annexed to and inherent in our royal person ... We do further declare it to be our pleasure and intention from time to time hereafter to grant our royal dispensations under our Great Seal [from taking the oaths and Test] to all our loving subjects so to be employed, who shall not take the said oaths ...

Ibid., pp. 390–1.

obstacles that prevented Catholics from competing on equal terms: the penal laws, which forbade Catholic worship and all other aspects of Catholic life, and the Test Acts, which excluded Catholics from public offices and Parliament. The only way to remove these laws permanently was to have them repealed by a Parliament. James had high hopes of the strongly Tory House of Commons elected in 1685, but this refused to ease the restrictions on Catholics. James resolved instead to appeal to Protestant Dissenters. Like Catholics, Dissenters were subjected to penal laws and were excluded from office by the Test Acts. James hoped that in return for freedom of worship and access to office Dissenters would grant similar liberties to Catholics. However, most were strongly anti-Catholic; they were also less numerous and influential than conformists. To compensate for this James issued a Declaration of Indulgence in 1687 (reissued in 1688) whereby he used his prerogative to dispense them from the penalties of the penal laws and Test Acts and declared his intention to have this confirmed by Parliament.

The Indulgence alone could not make up for the Dissenters' lack of numbers. James's allies among the Dissenters urged him to exploit the imbalances within the electoral system. The great majority of MPs represented boroughs, often small boroughs. Dissenters were relatively strong in towns, and boroughs with small electorates were easier to manipulate. James used the powers which Charles had gained over many corporations to replace Anglicans with Dissenters. Some, particularly Baptists and Quakers, seemed prepared to comply with his wishes, but the more numerous and prosperous Presbyterians were generally hostile. James dispensed Dissenters from the need to take the oath of allegiance and the Test, but many new magistrates insisted on doing so. Frustrated, James and his agents fell back on force and fraud. A batch of new charters in 1688 not only installed new magistrates, nominated by the King, but declared that the right to elect MPs was solely in the corporation. When these new magistrates seemed disinclined to co-operate they were browbeaten and threatened by the King's agents and military commanders.

James II's campaign to pack Parliament posed a more serious threat to England's liberties than earlier periods of rule without Parliament. Had James succeeded, parliaments would have ceased to be representative in any meaningful sense. The electorate would have been even more politically restricted than in the 1650s, when former Royalists had been barred from voting, giving the illusion of popular consent without the substance. Whether or not James's design would have succeeded is a moot point: in September 1688 he announced that the promised general election would be delayed. His measures had met with hostility from across the political and religious spectrum, from Tories and Whigs, Anglicans and Dissenters. He faced the strongest opposition from High Tory squires, Oxford dons and the Anglican clergy, the great majority of whom refused to read the King's Declaration of Indulgence in their churches. Seven of the bishops refused to order them to do so and were tried for seditious libel and acquitted, amid rejoicing from both Churchmen and Dissenters.

James might be isolated politically but his regime was not on the verge of collapse, nor was there much danger of rebellion. Many of the Whig gentry had been disarmed in the early 1680s and the militia, commanded mainly by Tories, had been run down since 1685. Instead, James placed his trust in his army. Faced with a rebellion led by Monmouth in 1685 James had raised new regiments which he kept in being after the rebellion was over; he also commissioned some Catholic officers and dispensed them from taking the Test. By the end of 1685 his army numbered about 20,000, larger than Cromwell's army in England in the 1650s; he raised more regiments in the autumn of 1688. Whereas Charles II's army had been deployed mainly in London and around the coast, James's was quartered in towns across the kingdom. He tried to divorce soldiers from civilian society, stationing them away from where they were recruited and moving them around regularly. James made it clear to his officers that he expected them to suppress disaffection. If they were over-zealous and treated civilians roughly, he was inclined to accept the soldiers' version of events. The size, and loyalty, of James's army made rebellion impractical, and the same was true, after 1685, in Scotland and Ireland. James's grip on power could be challenged only by a professional army from the Continent.

William III, who was both James's nephew and son-in-law, watched events in England with anxiety. He had married Mary because it gave him a chance of succeeding to the English throne, but by 1687 he feared that James's policies might provoke a rebellion. His fears were exaggerated, based partly on the hopes of English and Scots exiles in the Dutch Republic, partly on frequent references to disaffection in James's letters. Mary was still the heir presumptive to the throne, but in the autumn of 1687 it was reported that James's Queen was pregnant. The Catholics at court were confident that God would bring him a son, convincing many Protestants that the Queen was not pregnant and that the Jesuits planned to pass another's child off as the King's son. On 10 June 1688 the Queen gave birth to a healthy boy; as was common with royal births, the bedchamber was crowded with courtiers and nobles, including some Protestants, but rumours soon spread that a 'suppositious' baby had been smuggled in, perhaps in a **warming pan**. When these rumours reached William and Mary, they stopped having prayers said for the new prince in their chapel.

The birth of James Francis Edward was a severe blow to William; Mary was relegated to second in line to the throne, after her new half-brother. William had been well aware of the widespread scepticism in England about the Queen's pregnancy and, being a shrewd and resourceful man, he had taken steps to protect Mary's claim. His aim was not so much to enhance his own power as to bring England's resources, especially its navy, into the latest round of the great struggle against Louis XIV's attempts to dominate Europe. He saw this as urgent, because he believed (like many English people) that James and Louis had formed a secret alliance against the Dutch. In fact, there was no such alliance, but some of Louis's statements implied that there was. Many of William's English contacts urged him to intervene and assured him that he would be welcomed by the great majority of people and that James's army – still mainly Protestant, despite the presence of some Catholics – would not fight. In May, before the Queen gave birth, William assured a group of English nobles that he would be ready to invade in the autumn, if he was invited. The invitation, dated 30 June, was signed by only seven men, a mixture of Whigs and Tories (including one bishop).

⚘ The Revolution of 1688

William quickly began to mobilise ships and soldiers, partly for an invasion of England, partly to guard against a possible French attack on the Dutch Republic. In the end no attack materialised and the only assistance that Louis gave to James, threats and bluster, proved counter-productive. James was slow to appreciate that an invasion was likely. After an abortive attempt, when William's fleet was driven back by storms, William's fleet sailed unopposed past the Thames estuary and south-west along the Channel; on this occasion, the easterly 'Protestant' wind favoured William. His army landed at Brixham, Devon, on 5 November, the anniversary of the Gunpowder Plot. He had placed no reliance on assurances that he would face no resistance and brought an army strong enough to defeat James's in battle. At around 20,000 it was somewhat smaller than James's, but more experienced and more highly motivated. It was multinational – as well as Dutch, English and Scots it included Danes, Huguenots and a contingent of black soldiers from Surinam. James's army included experienced men, but the new regiments raised in 1688 were incomplete and in some cases existed only on paper. There were also tensions between Catholics and Protestants, especially after James brought regiments over from Ireland, which led to a mutiny at Portsmouth.

William believed that his army could beat James's but preferred to avoid battle, because he did not wish to harm his father-in-law. As he advanced slowly towards London, he was joined by some nobles and gentlemen, but others avoided committing themselves. James appealed to the Tories, whom he had snubbed and dismissed from office, but few would bestir themselves on his behalf and those close to him urged him to make more and more extensive concessions. Tories were encouraged in their inertia by William's declaration, setting out his reasons for invading. He stressed that he was coming by invitation to rescue the English from the threat of popery and arbitrary government. There followed a list of grievances, all dating from James's reign, which appealed to Tories as well as Whigs. Whig grievances dating from the Tory reaction were not mentioned. These misdeeds were, conventionally, blamed on 'evil counsellors', not James himself. It concluded with the greatest grievance of all, the birth of the Queen's alleged son. William demanded that this should be fully investigated and made clear the outcome he expected.

James, meanwhile, was in poor psychological shape. He had become convinced that God favoured his designs for Catholicism: he had survived exile and exclusion to succeed to the throne, culminating in the birth of his son. Since then his plans had unravelled. William had successfully undertaken a major expedition during the autumn gales. The Tories exploited his predicament, trying to undo all that he had achieved since 1685. There were rebellions in the North and Midlands (his younger daughter Anne joined the Midland rebels); and when he marched to Salisbury Plain his nephew,

Lord Cornbury, and his protégé John Churchill, future Duke of Marlborough, defected to William. In fact, the majority of the army remained loyal, but if those closest to James deserted him, whom could he trust? Assailed by contradictory reports of the whereabouts of William's army and suffering from insomnia and nosebleeds, James resolved to retreat.

William continued his slow advance; there were skirmishes but no major battles. Reports multiplied of anti-Catholic riots and attacks on Catholic houses and chapels. What happened around England during November and December suggests that the Revolution was far from 'bloodless', as was sometimes claimed, albeit less bloody than in Ireland or Scotland. The disorder was reminiscent of 1641–2: the Duchess of Beaufort heard that country people were saying that there was no longer any law. James became aware of how much many of his subjects hated him and his religion. He agreed to negotiate, promised to consider William's proposals overnight and then took a boat, hoping to flee to France. When William heard the news he said nothing but looked pleased. He was less pleased when he heard that James had been captured and brought back to London. He had to be allowed to escape again, and eventually reached France on Christmas day.

The Revolution Settlement 1689–1690

With James gone there was no real alternative to making William king. His army was stationed around London, putting pressure on the capital and guarding against the threat from James's army, still loyal, which had been disbanded but not disarmed. William had the military power to impose his will, but wished, for the sake of English and foreign opinion (the Dutch were now at war with France), to be invited to assume power, just as he had earlier been invited to invade, to come to London, to summon a Convention and to take temporary charge of the government. He did not make public threats, but made his will known privately to leading politicians. He insisted on being made king in his own right: he would not agree to be a mere consort, as Philip II had been under Mary I, because if Mary died first (which she did) he would lose his authority. Initially he and Mary were joint King and Queen, but executive power was vested solely in William. He was also determined that he would not allow extensive new restrictions to the royal prerogative. The Declaration of Rights, agreed by the Commons early in 1689, contained a mixture of restatements of what most thought was existing law and new restrictions which would require fresh legislation. The latter were dropped and the former were incorporated in the Bill of Rights, to which William assented later in 1689. This declared that the suspending power, and the dispensing power 'as it hath been assumed and exercised of late', were illegal. Referring back to the disarming of Whigs in 1683–4 it declared that Protestants had the right to keep arms for their defence 'suitable to their conditions and as allowed by law': landowners could keep guns, labourers could not. There were also anodyne statements with which few could disagree: elections ought to be 'free', parliaments should be held 'frequently'. The one clear novelty was 'that the raising or keeping a standing army in time of peace, unless it be with consent of Parliament, is against law'. The Commons had claimed this in the 1670s, but the statutory position had remained that of the Act of 1661, that the king had sole command of the armed forces.

There were two main reasons for the relative lack of innovation in the Bill of Rights. First, William was determined to preserve the royal prerogative. Before becoming king, he had threatened to return to Holland with his army if his authority was insufficient, leaving the English to face a probable civil war. Once king, he could veto unpalatable legislation. Second, the political make-up of the Convention made partisan measures unlikely. The Whigs had a majority in the Commons, the Tories in the Lords. The wording of important resolutions was left ambiguous, to accommodate both parties. The Houses resolved unanimously that experience showed that it was incompatible with the safety of a Protestant kingdom to be governed by a popish prince. This view was shared by Whigs and Tories, but the reference to 'experience' justified the Tories' refusal to exclude James from the succession untried. A more convoluted composite resolution made it possible to see James as having been deposed for misgovernment, or as having abdicated and deserted his people.

There were three other major changes in the reign of William III, which could be seen as consequences of the Revolution. The first was the Toleration Act of 1689. Seeking to form a common front against James, some bishops had approached moderate Dissenters, holding out hopes of either **comprehension** – changes to the liturgy to accommodate Presbyterians – or toleration. However, in 1689, alarmed by James's expulsion and William's friendliness towards Dissenters, the Anglicans in the Commons produced a grudging measure, allowing freedom of worship for most Dissenters but excluding them from public office (see Chapter 15). Second, the failure to renew the Licensing Act in 1695 deprived the Crown of the legal power to regulate the press, but hardly anyone supported the principle of a free press. Most asserted their right to print what they wished while preventing the publication of seditious or irreligious material. Finally, the Act of Settlement of 1701 marked a major break in the succession to the Crown. The change of ruler could be seen in 1689 as a mere blip. If one ignored the Prince of Wales, as most people did, Mary and William had succeeded James during his lifetime, but that was his fault for deserting his people. As they had no children, after their deaths the Crown would pass to Anne, who seemed very likely in 1689 to produce an heir. Only when her last child died in 1700 did a more drastic jump in the succession become necessary: she was to be the last Protestant Stuart. All the nearest claimants were Catholics, excluded by the resolution of 1689. The nearest Protestant was Sophia, Electress of Hanover, daughter of Elizabeth, daughter of James I. Sophia died shortly before Anne, who was therefore succeeded by George, Elector of Hanover, as George I. The Commons made clear their distaste for the prospect of a German king by imposing restrictions on a future foreign ruler, to come into effect after Anne's death. He was forbidden to leave the three kingdoms without Parliament's permission, or to embark on wars in the interests of a foreign state (Hanover), or to appoint any foreigner to office.

Crown, Parliament and Politicians under William III and Anne

The change of ruler in 1689 and the Bill of Rights would not seem to merit the title of a 'revolution', and yet the nature of monarchy was to change dramatically. William was able to insist on being made king in his own right and to keep the Crown's prerogatives intact, but he could not make the Commons grant his ordinary revenue for life. Moreover, his accession brought England into a very expensive war against France. The Commons used the King's need for money, and occasionally legislation, to make regular annual parliaments indispensable and to strengthen their bargaining position. Remembering the generosity of their forebears in 1660 and 1685, they granted the ordinary revenue for only a limited period: 'Our greatest misery was our giving it to King James for life and not from three years to three years.' In the words of a former Speaker: 'If you give the crown too little you may add to it at any time, if once you give too much you will never have it back again.'

William complained that the Commons 'used him like a dog', but had to accept that concessions were 'the price of money'. Parliament made effective the provision against keeping a standing army in peacetime without Parliament's consent, in two ways. First, the common law did not recognise the offences of mutiny and desertion, so Parliament passed temporary, usually annual, acts empowering the King to set up courts martial to enforce martial law. If it failed to do so the King would be unable to maintain discipline. Second, as part of the large sums granted for the war, the Commons voted the army and navy estimates each year; this continued in peacetime. As the Commons granted more money, they became more concerned about how the money was spent. During the 1690s they appointed committees of accounts, which scrutinised public expenditure, looking for signs of waste, mismanagement and corruption. Government could no longer be seen as the private preserve of the King and his ministers. Similarly, having tried to keep diplomatic negotiations secret, William ended up showing treaties with foreign powers to Parliament: experience showed that the Commons were more likely to grant money if they were kept informed. He also learned the hard way that, although in theory he was free to choose his ministers, in practice he needed to appoint men who could push his measures, especially money bills, through Parliament.

In demanding the right to scrutinise royal government, the Commons under William reflected a growing public concern about the growth of government and of taxation.

As leader of an unwieldy coalition William directed a war effort which was focused on Europe and particularly the Netherlands, leading to complaints that he was pursuing Dutch rather than English interests. English trade was badly disrupted by French privateers, there were poor harvests and rising food prices. Payments to the forces in Flanders led to a lack of good coin; a recoinage in 1696 led to serious local shortages. Government borrowing soared, increasingly channelled through the Bank of England, established in 1694. The English were unused to banks and suspicious of their alleged clandestine influence on government. Many of the Bank's directors were of Huguenot or Netherlandish descent, giving rise to complaints about Dutch finance and a Dutch king. The 1690s were a time of financial innovation: stockbroking and insurance developed rapidly and money-making schemes of all sorts flourished. As City financiers grew rich, provincial taxpayers suspected sharp practice and corruption, and not without reason: a Speaker of the Commons was expelled from the House for taking bribes from one of two rival East India Companies.

In the 1690s the Commons and the public were unusually concerned about misgovernment and corruption. In 1694 William reluctantly assented to a **Triennial Act** which, unlike that of 1641, laid down not that Parliament should meet at least once every three years – it already met every year – but that no more than three years should elapse between general elections. With the government handling so much more money, and employing so many more people, there was a danger that MPs might be bribed with pensions and places it was widely believed that parliaments grew more corrupt with age. This Act was designed to ensure that MPs had to face the electors regularly. Frequent elections added to the 'rage of party' and ensured that party issues spilled over into municipal politics. Party zealots, but also independent 'Country' MPs, suspicious of politicians and London, were returned to Westminster. Both in their own way made life difficult for William. He grew weary of the carping of backbenchers and the demands of party politicians, but experience of Dutch politics enabled him to cope.

Under William many of the issues which most exercised the Commons reflected 'Country' suspicions of the corrupting effects of power. Under Anne party issues came more to the fore. The War of the Spanish Succession was even more costly than that of 1689–97, but trade was disrupted less. There were still complaints about the power of the 'moneyed interest' (see Box 13.2, The Rise of the Moneyed Interest), but the most divisive issues – the conduct of the war, Church and Dissent – set Whig against Tory. Underlying everything else was the Hanoverian succession. The Whigs cultivated Sophia and George and denounced the Tories as **Jacobites** – supporters of James II and his son, the Old Pretender. The Tories denounced the Whigs as crypto-republicans and atheists. Many Tories were deeply unhappy about the Hanoverian succession, which would bring to an end truly hereditary monarchy and the divine aura of kingship, exemplified by touching for the **King's Evil**. The best that could be said for a German

BOX 13.2: The Rise of the Moneyed Interest: Henry St John (Later Viscount Bolingbroke) to Lord Orrery 1709

St John was a brilliant if mercurial politician, a man of sharp wit who lacked the traditional Tory attachments to monarchy and the Church of England, but was deeply convinced of the moral superiority of landed wealth, which rooted landowners in their locality and fostered a sense of duty and service. Much more articulate than the average Tory, St John played on suspicions of the malign and covert power of moneyed wealth. He defected to the Pretender in 1715 but later returned and became one of Walpole's most forthright critics.

We have been twenty years engaged in the two most expensive wars that Europe ever saw. The whole burden of this charge has lain upon the landed interest during the whole time. The men of estates have, generally speaking, neither served in the fleets nor armies, nor meddled in the public funds and management of the treasure.

A new interest has been created out of their fortunes, and a new sort of property which was not known twenty years ago is now increased to be almost equal to the terra firma of our island. The consequence of all this is that the landed men are become poor and dispirited. They either abandon all thoughts of the public, turn arrant farmers and improve the estates they have left; or else they seek to repair their shattered fortunes by [en]listing at court or under the heads of parties. In the mean while those men are become their masters who formerly would with joy have been their servants. To judge therefore rightly of what turn our domestic affairs are in any respect likely to take, we must for the future only consider what the temper of the Court and of the Bank is.

G. Holmes and W.A. Speck (eds.),
The Divided Society: Parties and Politics in England 1694–1716 (1967), pp. 135–6.

Lutheran was that he was (slightly) less bad than a Catholic Stuart. Under Anne, Tories indulged in a last doomed wallow in divine right and the cult of the royal martyr. There had been relatively little debate about the civil war under Charles II, because the Whigs knew that denigrating Charles I would be unpopular. Under William and Anne they had no such inhibitions and the civil wars were fought again in press and pulpit.

Queen Anne had to contend with bitter party divisions. As a woman she could not actively lead the war effort or manage Parliament: these were left to the Duke of Marlborough and Lord Godolphin respectively, who for much of the reign managed to navigate the shoals of party. But the party leaders became increasingly demanding and vindictive. By instinct Anne leaned towards the Tories and the Church of England, but she was also determined to uphold the royal prerogative and to do what she judged best for her people. Her room for manoeuvre was limited most by decisive results in general elections. After 1708, the only clear-cut Whig victory, she was forced to grant offices to men like Lord Wharton, whom she despised as an irreligious rake. In 1710 and 1713 the Tories won overwhelmingly and pursued policies of which she disapproved, removing Marlborough from his command and concluding an over-generous peace with France.

Despite the pressures on her, Anne maintained a degree of independence, but power shifted a little further in favour of the politicians. They finally triumphed under the first two Georges.

The Creation of the Whig Supremacy 1714–1715

Under Anne Whig politicians cultivated the 'reversionary interest', her designated successor, partly because the Tories generally had the better of elections, partly because Tory politicians regarded Hanover with distaste. The Whigs relentlessly assured Sophia and George that the Tories were all Jacobites: they might pay lip service to the Protestant succession but in their hearts they favoured the Stuarts. Whig newspapers described political divisions in terms of Whigs against Jacobites: they used the word 'Tory' rarely, if at all. George was not fully persuaded: he was wary of being manipulated and some Tories defended his interests in Parliament. When the new King succeeded in August 1714 he appointed several leading Tories to offices alongside the Whigs.

The experiences of his first year in England changed his mind. On his coronation day Whig celebrations were in many places disrupted by Tory riots, which often mocked the King. Two leading Tories, Ormond and Bolingbroke, defected to the Pretender. From spring to late summer Dissenting chapels were attacked and often destroyed. The King agreed with his Whig ministers that the rioters aimed to create disorder to pave the way for a Jacobite invasion, an analysis apparently confirmed when the Pretender invaded Scotland. The King removed his remaining Tory ministers and Tories were purged from local government and the army, which was greatly increased in size and became a crucial pillar of the Hanoverian regime. The Whigs won the general election of 1715 in which they stressed the dangers from Jacobitism and popery. Having lost the two previous elections they were not confident about their prospects in the next, which was due in 1718. Claiming that it would be dangerous to hold an election while disaffection was rife, they pushed the Septennial Act through Parliament. This said that there should be a general election only every seven years, which gave them four more years to consolidate their position.

The Consolidation of the Whig Supremacy

The machinery established by the Whigs in the late 1710s was elaborated and extended in the following decades and lasted into the 1750s. The position of Whig ministers was occasionally challenged either by rival Whigs, or by Tories cultivated by a king weary of Whig tutelage, or by the 'reversionary interest': Hanoverian kings were usually on bad terms with their heirs. The supremacy rested on control of four main centres of power.

The Court

Without access to, and influence over, George I and George II the Whigs could not have remained in power. The king was still the head of government and commander in chief of the armed forces. However, he was expected to delegate the details of policy and administration to his ministers. The often-repeated claim that George I knew no English is an exaggeration, but he had limited knowledge of English government and institutions. However, administration was not part of the remit of an eighteenth-century monarch, which focused on diplomacy and war: George II was the last reigning monarch to lead a British army into battle. Both George I and George II naturally fostered the interests of Hanover, but as kings of Great Britain they had a wider role to play in European diplomacy, especially given the threat still posed to them by the Stuarts. Their court remained a significant centre of power, intrigue and lobbying, a magnet for aristocrats visiting London and a theatre where the king could display his power and grandeur. The Hanoverians, like William III, did not claim the power to cure by the 'royal touch', but they still sought to project an image of dignity and majesty. The Whig ministers, apart from the access they possessed to the king, ensured that those close to the king's person fed the king the ministerial interpretation of current events. Ministers also cultivated influential women, notably George I's two mistresses and Caroline, George II's Queen. Sir Robert Walpole, much trusted by George I and distrusted by his son, was able to survive the transition between the reigns by assiduously courting Caroline during George I's reign. When George II agreed to continue him in office Walpole remarked smugly, if rustically, that he had had the right sow by the ear.

Cabinet

Traditionally the main body advising the monarch was the Privy Council. This comprised a mixture of high office holders, senior officials of the royal court and nobles with extensive territorial power. They were summoned individually by the king and could be removed if they displeased him. Over time the council tended to become large and unwieldy and monarchs sought advice from a small inner circle, especially when secrecy was required. By Anne's reign the inner council was becoming more clearly defined and became known as the cabinet council. Under George I it provided a means by which ministers exerted collective pressure on the King. Whereas today ministers are expected not to dissent publicly from decisions agreed in cabinet, under the Hanoverians these decisions were also expected to bind the king. George I sometimes complained petulantly about appointments agreed in cabinet of which he disapproved, notably in the army. George II chafed under cabinet tutelage and at times tried to go his own way, only to be brought to heel by his ministers. (See Box 13.3, George II and His

BOX 13.3: George II and His Ministers

The first extract describes an interview between George and Lord Chancellor Hardwicke in 1744.

KING: I have done all you asked of me. I have put all power in your hands and I suppose you will make the most of it.

CHANCELLOR: The disposition of places is not enough if your Majesty takes pains to show the world that you disapprove of your own work.

KING: *My work!* I was forced: I was threatened.

CHANCELLOR: I am sorry to hear your Majesty use those expressions. I know of no force; I know of no threats. No means were used but what has been used in all times, the humble advice of your servants, supported by such reasons as convinced them that the measure was necessary for your service …

W.C. Costin and J.S. Watson (eds.), *The Law and Working of the Constitution* (1952), I, pp. 375–6.

The second extract was part of a letter received by the English envoy in Venice, who transcribed it and passed it on. It describes the King's attempt in 1746 to replace Henry Pelham and his brother Newcastle by Lord Granville, which led to a mass resignation. The King, finding Granville could not carry the Commons, was forced to take the Pelhams back and to sign what was effectively a treaty promising to follow his ministers' advice.

… finding a change had been made in a scheme of foreign politics, which they had laid before the king and for which he had thanked them; and perceiving some symptoms of an invitation to dismiss them at the end of the session; they came to a sudden resolution not to do Lord Granville's business, by carrying the supplies and then to be turned out; so on Monday morning, to the astonishment of everybody, the two secretaries of state threw up the seals; next day Mr Pelham with the Treasury … and almost all the great officers, and offices, declaring they would do the same … [The offices were granted to others.]

Thus far all went swimmingly. They had only forgot one little point, which was to secure a majority in both Houses … On the Wednesday … [Granville] went to the king and told him he had tried the House of Commons and *found it would not do.* Bounce went all the projects into shivers, like the vessels in the Alchemist, when they are on the brink of the Philosopher's Stone. The king, who had given in to all these alterations was fatigued and perplexed; shut himself up in his closet … At last he sent for Mr Winnington … and sent him to Mr Pelham to desire they would all return to their employments. Lord Granville is as jolly as ever; laughs and drinks; owns that it was mad and that he would do it again tomorrow …

E.N. Williams, *The Eighteenth-Century Constitution* (Cambridge, 1960), pp. 83–4.

Ministers.) His Lord Chancellor tried suavely to explain that what his ministers advised was always in his best interests, but George was not convinced. 'Ministers,' he observed, allegedly smiling, 'are the kings in this country.'

Patronage

For centuries patronage – the giving of rewards in return for service and the establishment of patron–client relationships – had been a key feature of government. It also played a part in the management of Parliament and, as partisan divisions grew, it became a way of solidifying support: principle and profit reinforced one another. In the 1670s the Earl of Danby, Charles II's lord treasurer, tried to bring cohesion to the old Royalists in the Cavalier Parliament. Under Anne, the Whigs tried to root Tories out of senior positions, only to be purged themselves after 1710. The purges of George I's early years were more systematic and extensive and the higher echelons of the Church, army and administration were filled with Whigs. There were numerous complaints about the predominance in Parliament of Whig bishops, Whig army officers and MPs who were awarded sinecures (jobs with no real duties, or which could be performed by a deputy). The buying of political support in this way became known as the **influence of the Crown** and it continued throughout the eighteenth century and beyond.

It was widely claimed that those who accepted places and pensions sold out to the government, but this was an exaggeration. Many saw their rewards as recognition of past services, not a commitment to toe the party line in the future. Some who usually voted with the ministry occasionally voted against. And at any given time placemen and pensioners made up only a minority of the two Houses. To carry any important vote ministers needed to win the support of independent backbenchers. One reason why Walpole remained in power as long as he did was that he was careful to pursue policies acceptable to backbenchers. If he got it wrong, as when he proposed a general excise in 1733, he quickly backed down. It should be added that George I opposed the use of certain types of places as political patronage, notably places at court and in the army, in which he took a particular interest. He believed firmly that promotions within the army should be based on military merit and tried hard, but unsuccessfully, to end the selling of army commissions.

Elections

The Whigs' greatest weakness was their unpopularity, as shown by their electoral performance under Anne. During the seventeenth century the electorate had grown. Constituencies in England were of two types: shires and boroughs. Each shire, whatever its size, chose two members on a standard franchise, set in 1422: a property qualification of freehold land worth forty shillings (£2) a year. (In practice those holding land by other tenures could often vote as well.) With inflation, more and more freeholders met the property qualification. The largest county, Yorkshire, had about 18,000 qualified voters, of whom almost 8,000 voted in 1710; the smallest, Rutland, had over 500. Borough constituencies ranged from the cities of London and Westminster to tiny West Country boroughs like Heytesbury or Grampound, where the number of resident electors could be swollen by the creation of non-resident freemen. Franchises ranged from all adult male inhabitants (Southwark), to those paying local rates to the freemen or the members of the corporation, to those owning specific properties or **burgages**. The number of electors ranged from 14,000 in Westminster, of whom over 7,200 voted in 1708, to the thirteen 'burgesses' of Buckingham. By Anne's reign it has been suggested that around one third of adult males had the right to vote, a higher percentage of the population than *after* the Great Reform Bill of 1832.

The Whigs set out to change all that. The Septennial Act gave them longer to prepare for elections and increased the value of a seat in the Commons, and so the amount that candidates were prepared to spend. Control over patronage, especially in the Church and the revenue service, created bodies of voters dependent on the government for their livelihood – and promotion. Whig magnates spent heavily to establish control over small 'pocket' boroughs. The Whig electoral machine depended on a mixture of government patronage and private money; the Union with Scotland added to the supply of small venal boroughs. Election days were notorious for eating and drinking, but the treating had often begun days or weeks before. Violence and intimidation were common. The rising cost of elections deterred many would-be candidates and those who attempted a contest often fell foul of partisan returning officers or the Commons committee of elections, which now generally opted for the narrower franchise. The Whigs never took victory for granted. They worked hard in the build-up to elections and on the day. Whig newspapers trumpeted the threat from Jacobitism. Noblewomen wooed the electors, manufacturers cajoled and threatened their employees. But after each election the outcome was much the same. The Tories had captured the majority of the counties and larger towns, but the Whigs had won enough of the small boroughs to secure a comfortable majority.

Conclusion

In the Whig historical tradition, which found its finest expression in Lord Macaulay's *History of England from the Accession of James II*, the Revolution of 1688 was depicted as saving England from the threat of royal absolutism and setting it on course for the glories of the Victorian constitution: parliamentary monarchy, religious and political liberty and a democracy in which the franchise was limited to those with sufficient property to be trusted to vote responsibly. Writing in 1848, a year of revolutions in Europe, Macaulay declared that England had not suffered a bloody revolution like that of 1789 because it had undergone a bloodless revolution in 1688. Macaulay also claimed that the 1688 Revolution contained the seeds of every good and liberal law passed in the next 150 years. We have already seen that the Revolution was not exactly bloodless in England, let alone Scotland and Ireland. Macaulay's view of Britain was profoundly anglocentric: he glorified the *English* constitution, into whose blessings the Scots and Irish were admitted in 1707 and 1800 (see Chapter 14). It is hard to see 1688 as containing the seeds of Catholic emancipation (granted in 1829), which was precisely what it was designed to prevent. It is also hard to see the electoral system as more democratic under the Georges than under Anne: indeed the opposite seems to have been the case.

In Victoria's reign, Parliament acted as a check on the Crown and became answerable to an increasingly large and independent electorate, but this was not the case under

George I or George II. The alternative to Stuart 'tyranny' turned out to be not democracy but oligarchy. The electoral methods of George I's ministers were in some ways similar to those of the Protectorate and James II. So was his use of the army, to suppress riots and disaffection. This does not mean that politics became confined to a small elite. Popular politics continued to be vigorous and often violent. Popular aspirations found less effective expression through elections, but could still make an impact. Politics under the early Georges were less a matter of fledgling democracy than of authoritarianism tempered by riot. The Duke of Newcastle, the greatest electoral fixer of his day, who took pride in having led a mob, remarked: 'If we go on despising what people think and say, we shall not have it long in our power to direct what measures shall be taken.'

SUGGESTIONS FOR FURTHER READING

The best introductions to this period are two volumes by G. Holmes, *The Making of a Great Power, 1660–1722* (Harlow, 1993) and (with D. Szechi), *The Age of Oligarchy, 1722–83* (Harlow, 1993), along with J. Hoppit, *A Land of Liberty? 1689–1727* (Oxford, 2000) and P. Langford, *A Polite and Commercial People, 1727–83* (Oxford, 1992). • On the Restoration see J. Miller, *The Restoration and the England of Charles II* (2nd edn, Harlow, 1997), T. Harris, *Restoration: Charles II and his Kingdoms 1660–85* (London, 2005), J. Miller, *After the Civil Wars: English Government and Politics in the Reign of Charles II* (Harlow, 2000) and P. Seaward, *The Cavalier Parliament and the Reconstruction of the Old Regime, 1661–7* (Cambridge, 1989). • The best study of the Exclusion Crisis is M. Knights, *Politics and Religion in Crisis, 1678–81* (Cambridge, 1994). • On James II, see J. Miller, *James II* (2000) and J. Childs, *The Army, James II and the Glorious Revolution* (Manchester, 1980). For a massively researched but controversial alternative analysis, based on political economy, which sees James trying deliberately to create an absolute monarchy, see S. Pincus, *1688: the First Modern Revolution* (New Haven, 2009). • For a discussion of 'absolutism' see J. Miller, 'The Potential for "Absolutism" in Later Stuart England', *History*, 69 (1984). • S. Sowerby, *Making Toleration: the Repealers and the Glorious Revolution* (Cambridge, Mass., 2013) reassesses the importance, and the plausibility, of attempts to secure toleration for Dissenters in 1687–8. • On the Revolution of 1688, see J. Miller, *The Glorious Revolution* (2nd edn, Harlow, 1997), T. Harris, *Revolution: the Great Crisis of the British Monarchy 1685–1720* (London, 2006), J.I. Israel (ed.), *The Anglo-Dutch Moment: Essays on the Glorious Revolution and its World Impact* (Cambridge, 1991), L.G. Schwoerer, *The Declaration of Rights, 1689* (Baltimore, 1981) and C. Roberts, 'The Constitutional Significance of the Financial Settlement of 1690', *Historical Journal*, 20 (1977). • For the wider context of the Revolution see J.R. Jones (ed.), *Liberty Secured? Britain Before and After 1688* (Stanford, 1992). • For politics under William III and Anne, see H. Horwitz, *Parliaments, Policy and Politics in the Reign of William III* (Manchester, 1977), E. Gregg, *Queen Anne* (London, 1980) and G. Holmes, *British Politics in the Age of Anne* (revised edn, London, 1987). • D.W. Hayton's 'Introductory Survey' to the *History of Parliament: the House of Commons 1690–1715* (5 vols., Cambridge, 2002), vol. I, is by far the most comprehensive study of Parliament in this period and casts a much wider light on politics in general. • The standard biography of George I is R.M. Hatton, *George I: Elector and King* (London, 1978). The best overview of early Georgian monarchy is H. Smith, *Georgian Monarchy: Politics and Culture, 1714–60* (Cambridge, 2006). • On the creation of the Whig oligarchy, see J.H. Plumb, *The Growth of Political Stability in England, 1675–1725* (London, 1967). For Tories and Jacobites, see L. Colley, *In Defiance of Oligarchy: the Tory Party 1714–60* (Cambridge, 1982), P. Monod, *Jacobitism and the English People 1688–1788* (Cambridge, 1989) – the best general study of English Jacobitism – and D. Szechi, *1715: the Great Jacobite Rebellion* (New Haven, 2006). • On Walpole, see J.H. Plumb's unfinished biography, *Sir Robert Walpole* (2 vols., London, 1956, 1960) and P. Langford, *The Excise Crisis: Society and Politics in the Age of Walpole* (Oxford, 1975). • On elections, see G. Holmes, *The Electorate and the National Will in the First Age of Party* (Lancaster, 1975). On popular politics see K. Wilson, *The Sense of the People: Politics, Culture and Imperialism in England, 1715–85* (New York, 1995), N. Rogers, *Crowds, Culture and Politics in Georgian Britain* (Oxford, 1998) and Chapter 16.

SUMMARY

- The decision of the Convention of 1660 to grant Charles II revenue sufficient to support the peacetime government marked a major turning point in the relationship between Crown and Parliament. A domain state was no longer feasible: the Crown no longer had the landed wealth or the feudal revenues to support the government. So the assessment and the excise, the foundations of the English tax state, continued under the monarchy and were extended substantially (particularly the excise) in the eighteenth century.
- In one respect the Convention continued the practice of pre-civil war parliaments. Charles II was granted his main revenues for life, just as monarchs from Richard III to James I had been granted the customs revenues at their accession. James II's Tory Parliament of 1685 did the same, but the Convention of 1689–90 deliberately granted the major revenues for a limited period, thus retaining the financial power to bring the monarch to heel. William III soon learned that he could not ignore the Commons' wishes and began to take them into his confidence.
- Under William and Anne there was no single dominant party in the Commons: the balance fluctuated according to the outcome of general elections. After 1714 there was single-party rule and Whig politicians used their control over the majority in the Commons to impose their will on the King; often persuasion was sufficient.
- As a result there was a separation between the power of the Crown and the person of the King. Increasingly the Crown's authority was exercised by ministers acting in the King's name but not necessarily at his command or even with his approval.

QUESTIONS FOR STUDENTS

1. Why did Parliament grant Charles II such extensive powers at the Restoration?
2. Why were James II's subjects so reluctant to oppose William III's invasion?
3. Assess the long-term significance of the English Parliament's revenue settlement of 1689–90.
4. What was the significance of the Act of Settlement of 1701?
5. How were the Whigs able to establish themselves in power in the decades after 1715?

14 Crown and Parliament 1660–1750: 2. Scotland and Ireland

TIMELINE

(Sc) indicates Scotland, (Ir) Ireland

1661	Act Rescissory (Sc)
1662, 1665	Acts of Settlement and Explanation (Ir)
1666	Irish Parliament votes Charles II revenue for life; does not meet again until 1692
1681	Test Act (Sc)
1684–5	Peak of 'Killing Times' (Sc)
1685	Tyrconnell disbands militia and begins to remove Protestants from army (Ir)
1687	Declarations of Indulgence (Sc)
1688–91	Jacobite Wars (Ir)
1689–97	Anglo-French war
1689	Convention of Estates agrees Claim of Right and Articles of Grievance (Sc); James II to Ireland; Dublin Parliament
1689–90	Re-establishment of Presbyterianism (Sc)

1690	Battle of the Boyne; James leaves Ireland
1691	Treaty of Limerick (Ir)
1692	Parliament asserts 'sole right' to initiate money bills (Ir)
1697–1700	Darien scheme (Sc)
1701	Act of Settlement (England)
1703	Act of Security; Act anent Peace and War (Sc)
1707	Act of Union (Sc)
1712	British Parliament grants toleration to Episcopalians and restores lay patronage (Sc)
1715	Jacobite rising
1720	Declaratory Act (Ir)
1724–5	Wood's Halfpence (Ir)
1725	Glasgow Malt Tax riots
1743	Archibald Campbell succeeds his brother as Duke of Argyll (Sc)
1745	Jacobite rising
1782	Declaratory Act repealed

Introduction

The relationship between Crown and Parliament was more irregular and complex in Scotland and Ireland than in England. The Irish Parliament did not meet for substantial periods and the Scottish Parliament ceased to exist as a separate institution in 1707. The composition of the Irish Parliament remained more or less the same, except for the Catholic Parliament of 1689, but the Scottish Parliament's composition varied, as did its powers and relationship with the Crown. The Covenanter Revolution of 1638–41 was reversed at the Restoration, substantially re-enacted in 1689 and finally laid to rest by the Act of Union of 1707. The Irish Parliament strengthened its position in the 1690s and met regularly (usually every two years) throughout the eighteenth century.

Parliaments and People

Elections

Despite its anomalies the English electoral system under Anne delivered results which broadly reflected shifts in public opinion (see Chapter 13). Alongside the pocket boroughs were many constituencies where the electorate was too large to be bribed or browbeaten. Despite the Whigs' efforts after 1714 to reduce and control the electorate some large boroughs continued to assert their independence, sometimes violently. Whig election managers could never take the outcome for granted.

Electoral franchises in Ireland were similar to those of England: forty-shilling freeholders in the counties, corporation members, freemen, burgage owners or ratepayers in the boroughs. The key difference was that there were fewer voters in Ireland because the Catholic majority was debarred from voting. The largest electorates were in Ulster, with 6,000 in County Down. Many constituencies, including some counties, were controlled by one or two great landed families. In the counties they mobilised phalanxes of tenants and dependants, in the towns they installed their clients in the corporation. By the late eighteenth century, only ten boroughs were regarded as 'open', ranging from about 500 voters in Drogheda to 4,000 in Dublin. Relatively few Nonconformists could meet the property qualifications for election to Parliament, or secure election to municipal offices (from which they were excluded after 1704 by the sacramental test; see Chapter 15). Almost all of those elected to Parliament were Church of Ireland landowners or their sons.

In Scotland's single-chamber Parliament some sat as of right (nobles and, at times, bishops), while others were elected, often indirectly. In the shires the franchise had been fixed in 1427 at 40s (Scots) freehold. Elections were dominated by landlords: the Earl of Sutherland's vassals could be relied upon to return his nominee for Sutherland. Less dominant landlords expanded their following by 'grants' of land to servants or clients. The number of qualified county voters ranged from five in Cromarty to eighty in Perthshire. It has been calculated that the total number of voters in the Scottish shires in 1707 (1,200) was smaller than the number in any English county (except Rutland). The sixty-six royal burghs each sent one 'commissioner' to Parliament, chosen by the corporation. (Edinburgh sent two.) The larger burghs were dominated by merchant oligarchies, smaller burghs were often controlled by local landowners: the Duke of Argyll nominated the corporation of Campbeltown.

In neither Ireland nor Scotland did the elected part of Parliament represent the mass of the people. The landed elite translated their economic dominance into political dominance, but parliamentary politics were not irrelevant to ordinary people. At times anger and resentment were so widespread that they influenced Parliament, and disgruntled politicians appealed to the public.

Crown and Parliament

The Nature of the Relationship

The relationship between Crown and Parliament was based on power. The king's power rested on the control of the executive, the army and sometimes the established Church. He had the right to summon and dismiss parliaments within any limits set by parliamentary legislation. Parliament's power rested on its ability to approve or reject legislation, which might extend or restrict the king's powers. For the Crown, the most important legislation was usually that granting revenue: in normal circumstances the king was expected to seek Parliament's consent for taxation. After the Irish Parliament voted Charles II's revenue in 1666 he did not call it for the remainder of his reign.

Both parties could bring to bear power from outside Parliament. The king had significant powers of coercion and persuasion. He could buy support with gifts, offices and pensions and his ministers and more powerful servants could deploy their patronage in his interest and in elections. Parliament's influence in the wider political world derived from its representative nature: it spoke for the nation. On issues which aroused deep public concern many people took to the streets to support the stand taken by Parliament and could significantly influence the outcome.

Scotland 1660–1690

The seventeenth century saw a protracted struggle for power between king and Parliament. The 'Covenanter revolution' stripped the king of his power over the Kirk and the General Assembly and his power to call and dismiss parliaments at will, thanks to the **Triennial Act**. The bishops and **Lords of the Articles** were abolished. Parliament gained the power to approve the king's choice of advisers and de facto control over the executive and the raising of revenue as it mobilised Scotland for war. Many of the Covenanters' innovations were imitated in England. From 1641 to 1660 Charles I and Charles II were unable to reassert their power. This changed abruptly at the Restoration.

Charles II and Royal Absolutism

The legislative keystone of the Restoration was the Act Rescissory of 1661, which repealed all legislation passed since 1633. This opened the way for restoring the **Lords of the Articles**, in which the bishops played a conspicuous role. Once they were re-established, the bishops chose the eight representatives of the nobility. They then elected eight bishops and the nobles and bishops together elected eight shire and eight burgh representatives. The prominent role of the bishops gave the king a large measure

BOX 14.1: The Sanquhar Declaration, 22 June 1680

At a time when many Presbyterians were being coerced into conformity with the established Church, Richard Cameron and his followers issued this striking call to arms and rejection of the King, which helped to keep Presbyterian resistance alive.

... although we be for government and governors, such as the word of God and our Covenant allows; yet we ... the representatives of the true Presbyterian kirk and Covenanted nation of Scotland ... disown Charles Stewart that has been reigning, (or rather tyrannising, as we may say) on the throne of Britain these years bygone, as having any right, title to, or interest to or in the said crown of Scotland ... as forfeited several years since by his perjury and breach of Covenant both to God and his kirk and usurpation of his crown and royal prerogatives ... For which reasons we ... do declare a war with such a tyrant and usurper, and all the men of his practices, and enemies to our Lord Jesus Christ and his cause and Covenants and against all such as have strengthened him, sided with or any wise acknowledged him in his tyranny ...

A. Browning, *English Historical Documents 1660–1714* (London, 1953), pp. 626–7.

of control over the legislative process: 'Nothing can come to the Parliament but through the Articles, and nothing can pass in the Articles but what is warranted by his majesty, so that the king is absolute master in parliament both of the negative and the affirmative.'

Charles II's restoration was greeted with enthusiasm. Many nobles and lairds wanted a strong king: they had resented the authoritarian rule of both the Covenanters and the English army of occupation. To restrict the power of the Presbyterian clergy they pressed for the restoration of bishops. Charles hesitated to commit to this, but came to see the bishops as an important instrument of his power. Presbyterian opposition to the re-establishment of episcopacy led to an Act which established the royal supremacy in Scotland. The Presbyterians' opposition to both episcopacy and the supremacy enabled their opponents to depict them as hostile to the monarchy, but only a very small minority (often called **Cameronians**) denied the King's right to rule. (See Box 14.1, The Sanquhar Declaration, 22 June 1680.) This alleged threat to monarchy led to the expansion of the army and the creation of a large militia, later supplemented by a 'Highland Host'. When the government ordered that **heritors** be required to enter into a bond that their followers would not attend **conventicles**, many in the South West refused, on which the Highland Host was sent to cow them into submission.

In 1681 Charles summoned a Parliament in Scotland and sent his brother James to preside over it. Charles aimed to show that if James was excluded from the English succession he would have support from Scotland. Parliament passed Acts asserting that Scottish kings derived their power from God alone and that all government and jurisdiction were vested in the king, who could take cognisance of any case, bypassing the regular courts and empowering anyone, including military officers, to try and punish those accused of religious and political disaffection. James promoted the **Test**, a general oath against resistance to lawful authority. Ostensibly aimed at both 'fanatics' and papists, it was to be taken by all civil and military officers, clergymen, burgh magistrates and university teachers. They were obliged to swear that it was unlawful to take up arms against the King or those commissioned by him, or to attempt any change in Church or state, and that they were in no way bound by the Covenants. Many were removed for refusing to take the Test, including some orthodox parish clergy. It was to be tendered to those voting in parliamentary elections, ensuring that future parliaments would be dominated by Episcopalians and Royalists.

The Test, and the Cameronians' killing of soldiers and ministers, led to an escalation of violence in the South West. The government treated all religious dissidents as rebels and republicans: Claverhouse, the commander of the King's forces, declared 'there were as many elephants and crocodiles in Galloway as loyal or regular persons'. Others spoke of a 'levelling fury'. Faced with guerrilla tactics and a hostile population, commanders tried to starve or bludgeon people into submission. Charles authorised the use of torture, notably thumbscrews and the '**boots**'. Commissions to 'exercise justice' were used to punish anyone seen as disaffected. More than a hundred people perished in the 'Killing Times'.

James VII

As in England, James aimed to allow Catholics freedom to worship and hold offices. He relied initially on the Episcopalians in Parliament, which recognised his 'absolute' authority, but a bill granting liberty to Catholics contained so many qualifications and caveats that he rejected it and resorted to his prerogative. His Declaration of Indulgence (12 February 1687) granted freedom of worship to Catholics and Quakers; moderate Presbyterians could worship in private houses. It annulled the Test and other restrictions on office-holding and replaced them with an oath renouncing resistance to the Crown. The laws against field **conventicles** were still enforced and 'moderate' Presbyterians had to take an oath to defend the King's 'absolute' power. Most refused to accept indulgence on these terms and continued to attend parish worship. James decided that he had to offer them the same liberty as Catholics; the ban on field conventicles continued.

Apart from the Cameronians the Presbyterians accepted. Many meeting houses were built and Presbyterians ceased to attend parish churches. Exiled or imprisoned ministers returned to their flocks. Presbyterian organisation began to function again. By the end of 1688 the Presbyterians had largely recovered their unity and self-confidence, but Episcopalians were divided and demoralised. James had destroyed the foundations of the established Church, but most of the clergy refused to renounce their allegiance. Some refused to recognise the indulgence, others tried to disrupt Presbyterian worship. The scene was set for a spectacular reversal of fortunes.

The Revolution in Scotland 1689–1690

Late 1688 and early 1689 saw extensive violence in Scotland. Claverhouse, now Viscount Dundee, defeated a Williamite army at Killiecrankie, but his death in battle robbed Jacobite resistance of its momentum. Popular violence focused on Episcopalians and Catholics; ministers were 'rabbled' out of their livings. (See Chapter 15.) While Episcopalians had more reservations than their English counterparts about removing James from the throne, Scottish Whigs and Presbyterians saw in James's flight an opportunity to reverse Charles II's restructuring of the Scottish polity. As the moves towards royal absolutism had been more extensive in Scotland than in England, a largely consensual and restorative settlement, like that in England, would be insufficient.

On 7 January 1689 William convened a meeting of Scottish peers and gentry in London and asked their advice. They invited him to take over the government for the time being and to call a **Convention of Estates** for 14 March. Rabbling continued during the elections; burgh electorates were widened to include all burgesses and many who had refused the Test were allowed to vote. The unenfranchised supported Presbyterian candidates and intimidated Episcopalians. When the Convention met it was subjected to strong pressure from the citizens of Edinburgh and the **Cameronians** provided a guard. Some Jacobite and Episcopalian members withdrew. On 4 April the Convention resolved that James had forfeited the right to the Crown, having 'invaded the fundamental constitution', by altering it from 'a legal limited monarchy' to 'an arbitrary despotic power'. A large majority agreed that the Crown was vacant and it was offered to William and Mary.

On 11 April the Convention approved the Claim of Right, setting out the terms on which the Crown was to be offered. It condemned the policies of both Charles and James and sought to redefine the Crown's powers. It excluded Catholics from the succession and called for the abolition of episcopacy. Like the English Declaration of Rights it stated that parliaments should be held frequently. The Articles of Grievances (13 April) condemned the Lords of the Articles, saying all committees should be freely chosen, and called for the repeal of the Act of Supremacy and the Act stating that all jurisdiction lay in the Crown.

As with the English Declaration of Rights there was some uncertainty as to whether the offer of the Crown was conditional on the King's accepting these documents, or whether they were for information only. William, naturally, preferred the latter interpretation, but the Convention insisted that he could not exercise full regal power until he had accepted the Grievances and taken the coronation oath. In the end William promised to redress all grievances before he took the oath; episcopacy was abolished some weeks later. William still claimed that he had promised to redress grievances only in general terms. He wished to retain the Articles in some form and to prevent the full re-establishment of Presbyterianism, but the Convention, which had declared itself a Parliament, was adamant. It abolished the royal supremacy and William was eventually forced to agree to the full establishment of Presbyterianism (see Chapter 15). The legislation of 1689–90 re-enacted much, but not all, of the Covenanter Revolution. The Act Rescissory was not repealed, so only items that were specifically re-enacted became law. In re-establishing Presbyterianism there was no reference to the Covenant or the Solemn League and Covenant. The legislation that deprived Charles I of his right to choose his ministers and command the armed forces was not re-enacted, nor was the Triennial Act. The Whigs and Presbyterians had got their way on religion but had not greatly curbed the powers of the Crown, which probably reflected William's priorities. It soon became apparent, however, that the changes he had agreed to, particularly the abolition of the Articles, would make it much more difficult to manage the Scottish Parliament, which led, in time, to the Union.

The Road to Union

The Act of Union in 1707 was a pivotal event in Scottish history. Scots have viewed it variously. It has been seen as a betrayal of nationhood, the Covenants and a thousand years of independence. **Jacobites** deplored that Scotland's ancient royal line was replaced by Germans with a tenuous hereditary claim. And it was seen as economically damaging, as Scots initially gained little from being allowed free trade with England while paying heavier taxes. All these resentments were found in the decades after 1707, but many were positive about the Union, arguing that Scotland, backward and impoverished, could gain from being joined to her richer, stronger neighbour. From the 1740s, the Scottish economy grew rapidly: Scotland industrialised even faster than England. Economic arguments did not satisfy everyone: Robert Burns complained that Scotland had been 'bought and sold for English gold'. But by the second half of the eighteenth century Scotland was a self-confident country. While England's universities stagnated Scotland's became internationally recognised leaders in philosophy, science and economics. Scots played a disproportionately prominent role in the armed forces and empire and some, like Robert Adam, made a substantial contribution to architecture and interior decoration in both England and Scotland: Scottish towns increasingly matched those of England. (See Figure 14.1, The Library at Kenwood House, Middlesex, designed by Robert Adam.) Scottish historiography in the nineteenth century revelled in Scotland's economic success and imperial role. Only in the twentieth century did attitudes change with the growth of nationalism, culminating in devolution and the hard-fought referendum of 2014.

From the union of crowns in 1603 there had been proposals for a federal or an incorporating union. The former envisaged two independent kingdoms with a degree of convergence and co-operation, for example in religion. The latter involved a full

Figure 14.1 Robert Adam was one of the many Scottish architects and interior designers who came to England to build their careers and adopted and developed the fashionable neo-classical style. For fifteen years he was employed by a distinguished lawyer, the Earl of Mansfield, to remodel Kenwood House, to which he added the library (pictured). (Mansfield was born in Scotland, but trained as a lawyer in England.)

political and economic union, but with the possibility of each nation retaining distinctive features, such as their legal systems. James VI and I's hopes of a fuller union were rudely rebuffed by the English, but in 1689 many Scottish Whigs favoured some form of union to prevent any recurrence of the regime of Charles II or the return of James VII. After the settlement of 1689–90 secured them against royal misrule, new issues emerged to sour the relationship between William's government and the Scots.

Managing the Scottish Parliament

Scotland was deeply divided, between Whigs and Jacobites, Presbyterians and Episcopalians. Parliament was dominated by a nobility riven with faction; politicians jostled for power and the rewards that went with it. A substantial 'court party' was kept more or less loyal to the King's Scottish ministers by pensions, offices and other rewards. It could not deliver a reliable majority and needed the support of leading nobles. The position of the King's ministers was further weakened by two developments. First, the abolition of the Lords of the Articles made it much harder to control parliamentary business. Second, three divisive issues enflamed emotions within Parliament: the startling deterioration of the Scottish economy; Darien; and the Act of Settlement.

The Economy

Scotland's economy was inherently weaker than England's. Its agriculture was held back by poor soils, a colder, wetter climate, and a lack of investment. Manufactures were equally primitive: exports consisted mainly of coal, salt and poor-quality linen and woollen cloth. Scottish trade was hampered by the English Navigation Acts, which excluded many Scottish goods from England and its colonies. Scottish merchants compensated to some extent by trading with the Dutch and Scandinavians and illicit trade with English colonies; English merchants were quick to seek protection against Scottish competition.

The 1690s saw perhaps the worst harvest crisis in Scottish history. There was widespread starvation and emigration. Food prices rose, and food riots became common; the demand for manufactures fell. Moreover, during the Anglo-French war of 1689–97 French privateers took a huge toll of English and Scottish merchant shipping, despite the best efforts of the Royal Navy. Scotland's navy comprised only three ships and its merchant fleet suffered greatly.

Darien

A bad situation was made worse by the Darien adventure, a project to establish a colony in Panama. It was organised by the Company of Scotland, which encouraged investment from private investors and Scotland's two recently established national banks. Its promoters talked of fruitful soil and friendly natives, but not of the unhealthy climate, rugged mountains or extremely hostile Spanish settlers. The project was as poorly organised as the first English expeditions to Virginia: one contemporary wrote of 'too many knaves, too many fools, too many lairds' bairns that think it below them to work' motivated by 'fantastic hopes' of handfuls of gold. When the expedition got into difficulties the Company expected William to help them, but Spain was England's ally and

William wished to retain its goodwill. English merchants opposed the project, fearing Scottish competition in the Americas. The colonists surrendered to the Spaniards in March 1700.

For the beleaguered Scottish economy Darien was a disaster. The expedition had cost £400,000: more than double the annual value of Scottish exports. A large proportion of the Scottish landed elite and many burgh corporations had invested and lost their money. Some realised that the scheme had been impractical and Kirk saw its failure as God's punishment for Scotland's sins. But many angrily blamed William and the English. There was a desperate shortage of coin, debtors could not pay creditors, port towns could not maintain their harbours and French privateering resumed in 1702. Many Scots argued that a union, to give Scots access to the markets of England and the colonies, was the only way out. But a union would depend on constructive dialogue and unrelated developments in 1700–1 made this unlikely.

The Act of Settlement

Most Tories had accepted the change of ruler in 1689 because James II's removal seemed to secure a Protestant Stuart succession. The death of Anne's last surviving child meant that England faced a choice, when Anne died, between a Catholic Stuart and a Lutheran with a weak hereditary claim. The predominantly Tory Commons decided in favour of Hanover, but the Scots (and Irish) were not consulted and the Scots were furious that their royal family was being set aside. To make matters worse, when Anne succeeded William in 1702 her ministers at first refused to hold a general election in Scotland, as was customary. They eventually changed their minds, following a tax strike. The election showed the depth of public anger and the new Parliament was more anti-English than the old, with an increased Jacobite presence; the London government's tenuous control collapsed. There followed a trial of strength which culminated in the Act of Union.

The Making of the Union

The relationship between Anne's ministers and the Scottish Parliament was fraught and ill-tempered. The Scots tried to use their power to give or withhold their consent to the Hanoverian succession to secure further restrictions on the monarchy's power within Scotland. To bring the Scots to negotiate about union the English threatened the economic interests of the Scottish elite and the Scottish nation. Both sides were well aware of England's superior resources and military power, especially after Marlborough's victories at Blenheim (1704) and Ramillies (1706). (Nevertheless in 1703 Parliament ordered that all Protestant adult males should muster in arms once a month and in

BOX 14.2: **Act of Security 1703**

This was designed to give the Scottish Parliament the final say in the succession and further restrict the Crown's prerogatives. Note the reference to 'English or any foreign influence'.

... upon the said death of her Majesty, without heirs of her body or a successor lawfully designed and appointed ... [the Scottish Parliament is] authorised and empowered to nominate and declare the successor to the imperial crown of this realm

[Scotland] ... the said successor ... being of the royal line of Scotland and of the true Protestant religion; providing always that the same be not successor to the crown of England ... unless that ... during her Majesty's reign there be such conditions of government settled and enacted as may secure the honour and sovereignty of this crown and kingdom, the freedom, frequency and power of Parliaments, the religion, liberty and trade of the nation from English or any foreign influence ...

Browning, *English Historical Documents*, p. 678.

1706 some Scottish Whigs dreamed of another **Whiggamore** raid like that of 1648.) In return for the suppression of the Scottish Parliament the English were prepared to grant economic concessions and placate powerful interest groups, agreeing that the Kirk and legal system should remain unchanged. Scots were to be given access to English and colonial markets but required to pay customs and excise duties at English rates. As existing Scottish duties were levied at lower rates and widely evaded the Scots complained that the burden would be too great, so it was agreed that the new rates should be phased in gradually. The English initially refused to pay compensation for Darien and the Scots refused to bear a share on the English national debt. Compromise was eventually reached, but both sides (especially the Scots) tended to believe that they were getting a bad deal.

A Legislative Trial of Strength

The new Parliament passed the Act of Security (1703), which refused to settle the succession but claimed the right to choose a successor after Anne's death. The Scots Parliament would then choose the designated successor to the throne only if measures were taken during her lifetime to curb the royal prerogative and secure frequent parliaments. In short, they wished to redress the shortcomings of the Revolution settlement (see Box 14.2, Act of Security 1703). Parliament threatened not to grant money for the war against France unless the Act passed. In the Act anent Peace and War the Scottish Parliament claimed power over these matters if the two kingdoms had a common successor. The English responded with the Aliens Act of 1705, which stated that, if negotiations for a union had not started by Christmas, all Scots not domiciled in England would be treated as aliens and there would be a total embargo on imports from Scotland and a ban on selling arms and horses to Scotland. The Act called the Scots' bluff; it hit Scottish nobles with lands in England particularly hard. Despite riots and protests, many Scots realised that in terms of power this was an uneven contest. Negotiations could secure their religious and economic interests and the English were willing to negotiate, which suggested that they preferred a peaceable resolution of differences. Experience showed that this was correct – the English repealed the Aliens Act in 1706 – but it did not prevent considerable ill-feeling.

The Treaty of Union

But who was to choose the commissioners to negotiate on Scotland's behalf? Opposition to union was widespread but divided. The Jacobites opposed it because it would exclude the Pretender. Many Scottish Whigs opposed it because they sought to curb the Crown's power. They were also deeply hostile to popery and the Pretender, as were Presbyterians, who worried that union could lead to creeping Anglicisation of the Kirk. Elements of all these could be found in the vociferous popular opposition to union. Most expected the Scottish Parliament to elect the commissioners, but it was persuaded to ask the Queen to nominate them. This can probably be explained by growing fears of disorder; also the candidates favoured by Parliament were overwhelmingly anti-union, suggesting that the Scots were not serious about reaching agreement. Asking Anne to nominate commissioners increased suspicions that the negotiations were rigged, which were compounded by allegations of bribery. Money certainly changed hands, but it was often legitimately due for services rendered. The English negotiators' attitude was constructive: they agreed that minutes of their discussions should be published and ratified by both parliaments, and that the Scots should receive an 'equivalent' for Darien which would help repay Scottish debts and boost the economy.

The treaty, as agreed, contained five main elements. First the Scottish Parliament would cease to exist. Instead there would be Scottish representatives in the British Parliament: forty-five members of the Commons and sixteen lords, elected by their peers. With the exception of Edinburgh the royal burghs were divided into groups of four or five, returning a total of fifteen members; the remainder would represent the counties. The Scots had argued that the basis for calculating representation should be population, but the English insisted that it should be wealth. The disappearance of the Scottish Parliament removed the threat of its trying to impose the Claim of Right or challenging the Hanoverian succession. Second, the Scots were to be admitted to trade in England and the empire, subject to the qualifications mentioned earlier, which were to be sweetened by the equivalent. Third, the worship, discipline and government of the Church of Scotland were to remain unchanged. Fourth, the Scots legal system was to remain independent and unchanged. And fifth, as a sweetener to the nobility, **heritable jurisdictions** were to be re-established.

There remained the problem of securing the Scottish Parliament's approval for the treaty. Pro-union members ran the gauntlet of hostile crowds and there were riots in the provinces. Scottish ministers sought assurances of military help, if needed, and there were rumours of English troops gathered at Carlisle and Carrickfergus. Having declared that the articles were non-negotiable, the English agreed to amendments. Strong hostility to taxes on malt and salt led to their being reduced, delayed or both. The assurance that the Kirk would be 'effectually and unalterably secured' were sufficient to satisfy most Presbyterians. The most difficult arguments to counter focused on Scotland's honour, liberty and independence; some were met by promises that the nation's regalia and records would remain in Scotland forever. For many the union was a price worth paying to regenerate the economy and repel the Jacobite threat. The Scottish Parliament ratified the treaty by 110 votes to 67 on 16 January 1707; having passed the English Parliament it received the royal assent on 6 March.

After the Union

When the new Parliament of Great Britain convened, the Scots soon discovered that they were too few to wield much influence at Westminster and the English government became much less accommodating. Ministers no longer needed to hide their irritation with Scottish nobles' factionalism. The abolition of the Scottish Privy Council in 1708 removed another focus for in-fighting, but also the most effective means of co-ordinating Scottish government. The London Parliament now had sole control over legislation, including the voting of taxation. Some measures (like the Malt Tax bills of 1713 and 1725) were deeply unpopular in Scotland; unable to defeat them in Parliament Scottish peers and MPs used the threat of rioting to persuade ministers not to introduce or enforce them. Often ministers paid little heed to the Scots, but after the malt-tax riots in Glasgow in 1725, Walpole proved more willing to listen.

The Scots' problems were compounded by uncertainties about where power lay in Scotland. The most obvious way to resolve this was by appointing a secretary of state for Scotland, and this was done for most of the period 1708–25 and from 1742 to 1746. But these secretaries had less power or influence than their two English counterparts, who took over responsibility for Scotland in the absence of a Scottish secretary and generally showed little understanding of, or interest in, Scottish affairs. Power within Scotland lay partly with the nobility, and partly with the judges and other lawyers. The extension of English taxes brought to Scotland boards of customs and excise, subject to the English treasury and bringing unfamiliar procedures and bureaucracy. Resistance to taxation led to an upsurge of smuggling, riots and murder: it took decades to make the Scots as accustomed as the English to paying taxes. Both judges and the Scottish people tended to sympathise with rioters; the judges (and General Wade, the army commander in Scotland) advised against undue severity.

The early years of the Union were particularly difficult for the Scots. They claimed that the government favoured English industries. The elections of 1710 and 1713 brought strong Tory majorities in the Commons, with a visceral dislike of Presbyterians and the Union. Acts of 1712 granted toleration to Scottish Episcopalians and restored **lay patronage** in the Kirk. It could be argued that neither was against the strict letter of the Treaty of Union, but they certainly contravened its spirit. In 1713, in response to the Malt Tax Act, the Scots at Westminster brought in a bill to repeal the Union, which was defeated by only four votes. Hostility to the Union helped fuel Scottish support for the Jacobite rising of 1715.

The Jacobite Rebellion of 1715

Jacobite Support

The main centre of Jacobite support was Scotland. Irish Catholics lacked the military power (and the will) to challenge the Whig regime. In England Catholics were few and lacked the military resources to trouble the government: only a few, from the far North, declared for the Pretender in 1715. Many High Churchmen and Tories loathed the Whig regime, but their exclusion from office reduced their ability to oppose it. Their resistance took the form of insults and gestures, songs and toasts. The government claimed that support for the Pretender in Scotland came mainly from Highlanders and Catholics, allegedly the backward elements in society, clansmen forced to fight by their lords. But Jacobitism was strong over much of the area north of the Tay, a mixture of Lowland and Highland, which contained more than half of Scotland's population. It was strongest in the North East, the centre of Episcopalianism; Catholics were relatively few, even in the Highlands. The clan system, used to mobilise men, was not confined to the Highlands and was also used by the Whig dukes of Argyll. By 1715 the bond between chiefs and followers was being eroded by commercial pressures; chiefs came to treat ancestral clan lands as their own property, as a source of money rather than men. On the other hand, Jacobite support in 1715 received a huge boost from disillusionment with the Union. Scottish society was still more militarised than English. England was larger and richer, but its army was much reduced after the peace of 1713 and the Whig regime doubted the loyalty of many of the officers. New regiments raised in 1715 were inexperienced and the London government's priority was defending England, not Scotland. In 1745 Scotland was dangerously denuded of troops for the war on the Continent. In both 1715 and 1745 the government was militarily vulnerable in Scotland.

The Rising

The Jacobites faced a difficult task. Seaborne expeditions were notoriously risky, as shown by the Spanish armadas. A rebellion within Britain and Ireland was unlikely without substantial foreign assistance, which was unlikely without a strong prospect of rebellion. Their most likely foreign backer, Louis XIV, died, most inopportunely, in August 1715. The best time for a rebellion would have been soon after George I's accession, before his regime could purge the administration and army. The Jacobites' most capable military commander, the second Duke of Ormond, tried twice to land in England, but his ships were driven off by first customs officers and then a storm. The Old Pretender, the notional commander in chief, fared even worse, arriving in Scotland a month after the inconclusive Battle of Sheriffmuir; he left six weeks later. In his absence, command fell to the Earl of Mar, who failed to take advantage of much superior numbers at Sheriffmuir. There was a great deal of inconclusive manoeuvring, with considerable plunder but few casualties. Many families hedged their bets, eager to ensure that one branch was on the winning side. Those on the losing side were often saved from destruction by their kinsmen. The leaders of a small rising in Northumberland hoped to link up with Mar, but were cornered and defeated at Preston. Those taken (including James II's illegitimate son, the Earl of Derwentwater) were punished more severely than Mar's followers, being executed publicly in London.

Governing Scotland after the Fifteen

The Whig regime of George I was in many ways acceptable to the Scots. It was strongly anti-Jacobite and hostile to High-Church Anglicanism (and by extension Scottish Episcopalianism); there was no more anti-Presbyterian legislation. But Whig politicians put English economic interests first and expected the Scots to pay their share of taxation: Walpole especially was determined to keep taxes down. They looked to the Scottish authorities to take a firm line against disorder and make full use of the Riot Act. They also expected them to keep the Highlands in order, without the expensive deployment of regular troops. And they expected them to ensure the election of amenable Whigs to Parliament. But power was much more widely dispersed in Scotland than in England and keeping order depended in large part on managing the nobility, who were both powerful and needy: attempts to imitate English lifestyles drove many into debt. As under James VI, keeping the nobles happy cost money and required a detailed knowledge of who needed to be rewarded, and with what. English party bosses accepted reluctantly that some rewards (offices, pensions, commissions in the army and the like) had to go to Scots, but were determined to give them as little as possible. They needed Scottish managers who were unimpeachably Whig, extremely powerful in their own right and with an extensive clientele and knowledge of the Scottish elite: an exacting series of qualifications.

They found them in successive heads of Clan Campbell. John, second Duke of Argyll, had a distinguished military record (his nickname was Red John of the Battles) and played a major part in securing the Union and defeating the Fifteen. He later fell out with Walpole on a series of issues and was dismissed from his offices. He was a cantankerous man, quick to defend Scottish interests against English indifference. His brother Archibald, Earl of Islay (and third Duke from 1743), was very different: the brothers did not speak for many years. Islay was an emollient and shrewd lawyer, notoriously unkempt, who seemed to derive intellectual satisfaction from the subtle manoeuvring of court politics. The Campbell power-base was enormous. By 1700 their lands covered over 500 square miles and their influence over subaltern clans extended even further; it was said that they could mobilise over 5,000 armed men. They held a wide range of offices: as hereditary sheriffs and lords lieutenant of Argyllshire they controlled both justice and the armed forces. They had many clients among the lawyers: by the 1730s most judges owed their appointments to a duke of Argyll and they used senior legal officers, such as the lord president, Duncan Forbes of Culloden, as their political agents. They were not always benevolent landlords. Some sold their poorer tenants into **indentured servitude** and the second duke tried to let all farms directly to the highest bidder. Islay realised that this would dangerously reduce the Campbells' military resources and reverted to the old practices and lower rents, while insisting that tenants should swear allegiance to the chief.

English ministers learned quickly that it would be impossible to control the Western Highlands without the Campbells and rather more slowly that, although Red John could be difficult, his brother was more amenable. He trod a difficult line, reminding ministers of his power and indispensability in Scotland and delivering more favourable election results than his brother. He spoke against measures likely to prove unpopular in Scotland without voting against them. In 1745 he was criticised for rushing to London rather than opposing the Pretender's forces, but it seems likely that he wanted to make it clear that he had not joined the Pretender and gain time to see how the rebellion turned out.

The 1745 Rising

By 1745 resentment of the Union had diminished, thanks to growing prosperity, but there remained a sense that Scotland's identity as a nation had been sacrificed. Charles Edward, the Young Pretender, possessed more charm and charisma than his father. After the 1715 rising the government had sought to 'modernise' the Highlands: the SSPCK (Scottish Society for the Propagation of Christian Knowledge) tried to promote

Protestantism and the English language, with limited success. There were attempts to open the region up to the British army by building forts and military roads, but the programme was soon scaled down because of cost. There was no Scottish army as such: English and Scottish regiments were stationed in various garrisons in Britain, Ireland and the colonies and moved every few years. The most distinctively Scottish regiment, the Black Watch, raised in the Highlands in 1739, had been withdrawn for service on the Continent in 1745; it is possible that the government doubted its loyalty. In 1715 the government had appointed loyal clan chiefs as lords lieutenant, responsible for defending the Highlands, but the lieutenancies were not renewed at George II's accession and both Forbes and Argyll warned in 1745 that nobody had the legal authority to raise forces against the Pretender (except Argyll, who was a hereditary lord lieutenant).

Charles Edward in 1745 showed the initiative, and enjoyed the luck, that his father had lacked, despite failing to win French support. Some clans supported him enthusiastically, others more cautiously. The reaction in the Lowlands was ambivalent: there was little overt Jacobitism but perhaps a sneaking sympathy for the ideal of a revived Scottish nation. Charles declared that the Act of Union would be repealed, but no Jacobite regime could abandon the union of crowns. He raised his standard in Inverness-shire on 19 August. The King's commander in Scotland, Sir John Cope, failed to stop his army entering the Lowlands and capturing Perth and Edinburgh. After Cope's army was routed at Prestonpans, Charles had little left to gain in Scotland. London, not Edinburgh, was the heart of government and Charles agreed to march into England. His hopes that English Jacobites would flock to his standard proved illusory, but his army continued south, reaching Derby on 6 December. London was in a panic, but news of government forces advancing from the North and Midlands led the chiefs to insist on retreating.

The army withdrew in good order, defeating George II's forces at Falkirk, but news came that his brother, the Duke of Cumberland, who had a reputation for ruthlessness, was heading north. As the retreat continued, more and more Highland levies went home. Charles was advised to take to the hills for a guerrilla war, but would not hear of it. Culloden was a one-sided battle, with the Jacobites half-starved, outnumbered and outgunned. The slaughter that followed owed something to Cumberland's approach to warfare and much to the response of his soldiers (many of them Scots) to their humiliating defeats by this 'inferior' army. In the years that followed the government set out to destroy Highland society. The SSPCK renewed its efforts and the Gaelic language and the wearing of tartan were outlawed. The population was disarmed, some chiefs were exiled and their followers transported as indentured servants. **Heritable jurisdictions** were abolished, weakening landlords' power over their tenants, but landlord power increasingly rested on economics rather than law and lineage. Landlords no longer needed the peasants' labour and military service: black cattle or sheep were more profitable. The peasantry were driven from the hills to the coast where they were encouraged to develop crofting (based on a cottage and smallholding), fishing and gathering kelp – seaweed that was much in demand as a fertiliser and in the glass industry. For a while they managed to scrape a living but then the demand for kelp collapsed. Many starved and emigration, particularly to North America, soared.

Restoration Ireland

In dealing with Ireland Charles II faced incompatible expectations. Many Catholics had served him faithfully in the 1650s and Ormond's treaty with the Confederates in 1649 included promises of toleration for Catholics and the restoration of their lands. New Protestants remained powerful in the army. Charles had been careful to reassure their English colleagues in the Declaration of Breda; in November 1660 he issued a declaration which stated that Cromwellian settlers and soldiers could keep the lands granted to them. But the people in power in Ireland in 1659–60 were the Old Protestants, who had seized Dublin and summoned the Convention; they claimed (and Charles accepted) that they had brought about the Restoration. Charles's initial instinct was to reassure all parties, but some were bound to be disappointed.

The Land Settlement

This was the most urgent – and intractable – problem. The most legally effective way to resolve it would be through parliamentary legislation, especially as the Act of Settlement of 1652 had been declared null and void (along with all other Interregnum legislation) by the English Parliament. As the Parliament elected in 1661 was wholly Protestant this would put the Catholics at a disadvantage, but under **Poynings' Law** all bills put before the Irish Parliament had to be approved by the English Privy Council. Charles was determined that, while parliamentary legislation could lay down general principles, individual cases would be decided by a court of claims, staffed by Englishmen nominated by him. Some Catholics with connections at the English court were able to regain substantial tracts of land, but others received little or nothing. There were also large grants to English courtiers, particularly the Duke of York. The former Lord Broghill, now Earl of Orrery, claimed that there was enough land to satisfy both 'innocent' Catholics and Protestants; Ormond warned (more accurately) that to satisfy all claimants would require another Ireland. The 1662 Act of Settlement rested on the assumption that Cromwellians whose lands were restored to Catholics could be compensated elsewhere; the 1665 Act of Explanation decreed that soldiers and adventurers should forfeit one third of their lands to compensate 'innocent' Catholics. Some avoided doing so and the court of claims went on hearing cases until 1669. Who gained and who lost depended largely on luck and favour. Estimates of the Catholics' share of the land differ, but it has been widely accepted that it fell from about 60 per cent in 1641 to as little as 9 per cent in 1659, rising to a little over 20 per cent in 1670.

The Financial Settlement

Under pressure from the English government the Irish Parliament of 1661–6 restructured the King's revenue on the English model. In place of a ragbag of feudal and traditional revenues it granted a range of excises and a hearth tax, together with the customs, in perpetuity. As in England, yields initially fell well short of expectations, but the economy soon revived, despite the English Parliament's ban on imports of Irish cattle. Exports of other agricultural products grew, as did trade with the colonies. Towns grew: Dublin's population tripled in size under Charles II to over 50,000, Cork's increased to 20,000. The Dublin government adopted English methods of revenue administration and the yield of customs and excise increased substantially. In the early 1660s the cost of military and civil government was about £180,000 and the revenue only £120,000. By 1683–4 the customs and excise revenue had more than doubled and Ireland was paying more taxation per head than England (whereas Scotland was paying very much less).

Protestant and Catholic

By far the greatest item of expenditure was the army. Charles had inherited the remains of the Cromwellian army, which Ormond, as lord lieutenant, reduced from 15,000 to 5,000, weeding out Nonconformists. Parliament also provided for the creation of a large Protestant militia. By the 1680s the army was increased to 8,000, to guard against the threat from the Ulster Presbyterians and to act as a reserve of force in case of rebellions in England or Scotland. Charles and Ormond were less concerned about the Catholics. The loss of their lands and the Protestants' overwhelming preponderance of military power ensured that they posed a much smaller threat to the Protestants than in 1640; those who had recovered their lands would be reluctant to risk losing them again. The poor and dispossessed had nothing to lose and some took to banditry. Outlaws, often in large bands, preyed on travellers. Some focused on the English but most also robbed the Irish poor, as well as demanding protection money or betraying one another to the authorities for money. The word **tory** appeared in the 1640s, followed by **rapparee** in 1689–91. They aroused anxiety among the Protestants, but no worse: Ormond remarked in 1679 that he had no fear of the Catholics 'beyond torying'. (See Box 14.3, Contrasting Views of Protestant Ireland in the 1670s.)

James II

In 1683–4 York expressed concern about the alleged preponderance of 'Cromwellian' officers in the Irish army and urged his brother to grant commissions to Catholics. He was encouraged in this by his long-time client, the sole survivor of the Drogheda massacre, Richard Talbot, created Earl of Tyrconnell in 1685. Like many Irish Catholics, Talbot

BOX 14.3: Contrasting Views of Protestant Ireland in the 1670s

Sir William Petty

Petty was a pioneer of 'political arithmetic', the application of mathematics to the analysis of public affairs.

... the British Protestants and Church have three quarters of all the lands, five sixths of all the housing, nine tenths of all the housing in walled towns and places of strength, two thirds of the foreign trade. That six of eight of all the Irish live in a brutish nasty condition, as in cabins with neither chimney, door, stairs nor window; feed chiefly upon milk and potatoes, whereby their spirits are not disposed for war. And although there be in Ireland eight papists for three others; yet there are far more soldiers and soldier-like men of this latter and lesser number than of the former.

... His Majesty, who formerly could do nothing for, and upon Ireland, but by the help of England hath now a revenue upon the place to maintain, if he pleases, 7,000 men in arms, besides a Protestant militia of 25,000 more, the most whereof are expert in war.

W. Petty, The Political Anatomy of Ireland (London, 1689), p. 27.

The Duke of Ormond

In a letter of 15 July 1679 the lord lieutenant explains to the Earl of Burlington his anxiety about the divisions among Irish Protestants.

All I can tell your lordship of this kingdom is that since the defeat of the rebels in Scotland [at Bothwell Brig] there seems to be a great calm. I confess before that I was not without some apprehensions of the common sort of the Scots in the North, being well assured that their false teachers held correspondence with their brethren in Scotland. The English (some few giddy and poor fanatics excepted) have no inclination to disturb the government, tho' they do not in all things acquiesce or observe the constitutions of it, and I have not any fear of the Irish, beyond torying, but [except] in case of a civil war amongst those that go under the name of Protestants or in case of an invasion.

Historical Manuscripts Commission Reports, Ormonde MSS, New series, V, p. 155.

hoped that James would restore their lands and influence. He urged James to suppress the militia and to replace Protestants with Catholics, in the army and (later) civilian and municipal offices. James believed that Ireland should remain a subordinate kingdom and feared that such changes could jeopardise his plans for England. Tyrconnell, however, was a forceful personality, skilled in emotional blackmail, and usually got his way. He also considered what would happen if James either died without a Catholic heir or was driven out of his kingdom. He suggested to French agents in London that, in such circumstances, Louis XIV might act as protector of the Irish Catholics. In the meantime, he strengthened the Catholics' grip on the army and the government.

The Jacobite Wars in Ireland 1688–1691

Tyrconnell had met with little opposition from Irish Protestants. Armed resistance seemed futile without the army and militia and many fled to England. After James's flight to France Tyrconnell recruited many more Catholic regiments and soon controlled most of Ireland, apart from Derry and Enniskillen; he appealed for help to Louis XIV, who ordered James to go to Ireland. He convened an overwhelmingly Catholic Parliament, thanks to Tyrconnell's installing Catholics in borough corporations, which elected MPs. It demanded the repeal of the Acts of Settlement and Explanation and passed an Act of **Attainder** against almost 2,400 Protestants. James opposed these measures, fearing that they would make it harder for him to regain the English throne. He is 'infatuated with this rotten principle, provoke not your Protestant subjects' grumbled an Irishman. The French and Irish were equally unimpressed by his military leadership. Irresolution plagued his attempt to capture Derry and eventually the siege of the city was lifted. But an English expeditionary force proved equally ineffective, so in the spring of 1690 William reluctantly decided that he would have to go to Ireland himself. Like Cromwell he brought a substantial army, plenty of money and a printing press. He quickly sought out James's army and they faced each other across the river Boyne, near Drogheda. William's army forced its way across the river and attacked a section of James's forces, but the rest were prevented by the terrain from coming to their aid. James's army was driven from the field and headed south towards Dublin.

James arrived ahead of them. His self-belief and sense of God's special favour towards him had been destroyed by the collapse of his cause in 1688. He barely paused in Dublin before heading towards France. William, having taken Dublin, assumed that the war was over. He also assumed, like Cromwell, that the peasants had been forced to fight by their landlords; he issued a declaration promising that if they surrendered they would be well treated. But the bond between lord and tenant remained strong: when officers were killed their men often refused to serve anyone else. (See Box 14.4, The Loyalty of the Irish Peasantry.) The Jacobite commanders, freed from James's ineffectual leadership, put up a dogged resistance. As the weather worsened William's forces suffered heavy casualties from disease and were forced to abandon the siege of Limerick. With the war destined to continue into 1691, William, desperate to move his forces to Flanders, ordered his commander, Ginkel, to negotiate the best terms he could get. Like Cromwell and Ireton, Ginkel negotiated surrenders and stood by what he had agreed, despite Anglo-Irish grumbles that the terms were too generous.

In October, Ginkel accepted the Jacobites' surrender on terms set out in the Treaty of Limerick. First, 'all persons' would be allowed to leave Ireland (if they wished) for any country other than England or Scotland, with their families and household possessions. Soldiers who wished to go to France would be transported at England's expense. Second, many categories of people, including those living in garrison towns or in arms at the time of the treaty, could have their estates and properties restored if they submitted to William. Third, the Catholics of Ireland were to enjoy privileges which they had enjoyed under Charles II or were consistent with Irish law. William and Mary undertook to call a Parliament in Ireland and try to secure measures to protect Catholics from persecution.

BOX 14.4: The Loyalty of the Irish Peasantry

William King, Bishop of Derry (later Archbishop of Dublin) tries to explain the continuing subjugation and exploitation of the Irish peasantry by their landlords. 'Coshering' means living at free quarter on dependants.

It is the humour of these people to count an estate their own still, though they have sold it on the most valuable considerations or have been turned out by the most regular proceedings of justice; so that they reckon every estate theirs that either they or their ancestors had at any time in their possession, no matter how many years ago. And by their pretended title and gentility they have such an influence on the poor tenants of their own nation and religion who live on those lands that these tenants look on them still, though out of possession of their estates, as a kind of landlords; maintain them after a fashion in idleness and entertain them in their coshering manner. These vagabonds reckoned themselves great gentlemen and that it would be a great disparagement to them to betake themselves to any calling, trade or way of industry; and therefore either supported themselves by stealing and torying, or oppressing the poor farmers, and exacting some kind of maintenance, either from their clans and septs, or from those who lived on the estates to which they pretended.

W. King, *The State of the Protestants of Ireland under the Late King James's Government* (London, 1692), p. 36.

The Jacobite wars marked the last attempt by Irish Catholics to reverse the conquest begun under Elizabeth. There was great devastation and destruction by both soldiers and **rapparees**. One officer was said to have 'robbed the whole country about Mullingar as bad as the Turks can do at Belgrade'. It has been estimated that at least 25,000 were killed in battle and many more died of disease and starvation. Substantial though these figures are, they are much lower than those from the 1640s and 1650s. The atrocity stories from the Jacobite wars are less numerous and harrowing than those from the earlier period. Anxious Protestants expected another 1641 and it had not happened: victims suffered plunder and humiliation rather than torture and death. Nevertheless, Protestants felt a sense of betrayal: the Treaty of Limerick was the work of three Dutchmen – William, his chief adviser the Earl of Portland, and Ginkel. The next Parliament could be expected to try to undermine it.

The Penal Laws

And so it transpired. When the treaty was confirmed in 1697 it was greatly weakened. The toleration of Catholics was omitted and many fewer Catholics were secured in their lands, opening the way for further forfeitures. Meanwhile, the Protestant monopoly of military power was reinforced. Catholics were forbidden to bear arms, or serve in the army, or own a horse worth more than £5. The militia had been revived in 1690 and was mobilised in emergencies thereafter. The regular army became more substantial and permanent, especially after William was forced by Parliament to reduce the English army; **Huguenot** regiments were transferred from England to Ireland. Most other regiments in Ireland were English and Scots and served there for a limited period. They were generally quartered in barracks or redoubts, so their contact with Irish civilians was limited. Penal legislation continued. In 1697 Catholic **regulars** and bishops were banished. **Secular** priests could remain if they registered with the authorities and took the **oath of abjuration**, denying the Pretender's right to the throne. There was legislation to reduce further the Catholics' share of the land. They were forbidden to purchase land or to take leases for longer than thirty-one years. The estates of Catholic landowners were to be divided equally among their heirs, but if one heir converted to Protestantism he would inherit the whole estate. Catholics owned a smaller and smaller proportion of the land, but a significant number accumulated substantial amounts of leasehold land, which they let to (mostly Irish) sub-tenants.

Together such measures removed any remaining Catholic threat to Protestant rule in Ireland. Although there is strong evidence of Catholic sympathy for the Stuart cause – especially as immediate memories of James II's inglorious stay in Ireland faded – and although the new Whig regime feared the Jacobite threat in 1715, Ireland did not see a significant Jacobite rebellion. The Jacobites' foreign backers favoured a landing in mainland Britain: a landing in Ireland was not the way to restore a Stuart regime in London.

The Irish Parliament and the British Government

Under Charles II power over Irish policy was increasingly concentrated in London. The lord lieutenant or lord deputy had a limited say except in military appointments. Apart from Ormond the lords lieutenant under Charles II were Englishmen. As the revenue grew, those seeking rewards at Charles's court looked increasingly to Ireland: the Earl of Essex, when lord lieutenant, compared Ireland to a stag's carcass, torn to pieces by hounds. With no Parliament meeting after 1666 there was no forum for expressing Irish grievances: the banning of imports of Irish cattle was just one example of Ireland's economic interests being subordinated to England's. Charles and James were under no financial pressure to summon Parliament, but William needed additional revenue to meet the costs of war. Parliament, recalled in 1692, criticised the Treaty of Limerick amid partisan recriminations about responses to James II and the conduct of the war, but its main concern was to ensure regular meetings of Parliament by exploiting the government's need for money. To get round **Poynings' Law** Parliament claimed the '**sole right**' to initiate money bills: Parliament, not the English Privy Council, should determine which revenues to grant and how much. This led to a stalemate, eventually resolved by a compromise, whereby the council preserved the formal authority to present bills, but in response to 'heads of bills' drawn up in Dublin. In return Parliament finally 'confirmed' the Treaty of Limerick.

These seemingly technical changes transformed the relationship between the Irish Parliament and the London government. Parliament began to grant taxation for two years at a time, after scrutinising the government's accounts and considering other legislation. Having gained the financial whip hand Parliament was careful not to vote too much, nor was there any attempt to follow England in using the revenue as security for extensive borrowing. Such a system would require trust, which was undermined by the English Parliament's assumption that it could legislate for Ireland, highlighted by a bill to ban Irish woollen exports. An Irish MP, William Molyneux, claimed that Ireland was a separate kingdom under the Crown and could be bound only by legislation passed by the Irish Parliament. His claim that men could be bound only by laws to which they had consented seemed to the English a dangerous expression of independence, especially when the death of the Duke of Gloucester raised the problem of the succession. The Irish Parliament did not meet in 1701; when two-yearly meetings resumed in 1703 resentment of England's undermining the Irish economy continued.

For the remainder of Anne's reign the battles between Whig and Tory loomed larger than Ireland's relationship with England. Party animosities, regular sessions and long intervals between elections encouraged the development of parliamentary management, which hitherto had had little chance to develop. Managers learned to explain complex issues to backbenchers, using not only the prospect of rewards but charm, tact and appeals to pride and honour: 'smiles, good dinners, threatenings'. Such methods could work only if the managers knew the members well and were to some extent trusted by them. Lords lieutenant increasingly left it to managers to push measures through. After 1715 all were Englishmen, who came to Ireland every two years for the session of Parliament. At other times the administration was headed by two **lords justices**, usually a bishop and a senior lawyer or revenue official. The most important was William Conolly, from a Derry Catholic family, who made a fortune from forfeited lands in the 1690s. Under George I he became Speaker of the Commons, chief commissioner of the revenue and a lord justice, and built himself a palatial country house at Castletown, County Kildare (see cover illustration). Like Islay in Scotland Conolly had the delicate task of explaining to the lords lieutenant the limits of the possible. The Irish were also touchy about the appointment of Englishmen to offices in Ireland, either because there were not enough English offices to satisfy demand, or because ministers expected Englishmen to be more politically reliable. This was especially true of bishops, who had votes in the Lords; at times (as on the sacramental test) English bishops voted one way and Irish the other.

Although Whigs dominated both the London and the Dublin governments after 1715 they did not fully control Parliament or the electoral system (although Conolly did his best in Ulster). Much of the legislation in Parliament was uncontentious, such as bills to build canals or turnpikes, or to encourage the linen industry. Every now and then an issue aroused serious anti-English feeling and usually loyal members would rebel. In 1719 a complex Irish land dispute led to an address to the King in which Parliament justified its conduct on the grounds that Ireland was 'a distinct dominion'. The English Parliament responded with the 1720 Declaratory Act, which asserted that the English Parliament could legislate for Ireland. This made the Irish Parliament wary of English encroachment and particularly attempts to impose direct taxation, which helps explain the reaction to George I's patent for coining £100,000 worth of copper halfpennies and farthings, which he granted to his mistress, who sold it on to an iron-master called William Wood. The coins raised memories of the 'brass money' coined by the Jacobites in 1689–91, and fears spread that a flood of base coins would bring economic ruin. The government's Irish allies had not been consulted and were soon swept up in the popular outcry; the revenue commissioners refused to co-operate with Wood's agents. Jonathan Swift, in *Drapier's Letters* (1724–5), argued that by the laws of God, nations and Ireland, government without the consent of the governed was 'slavery'. Grand juries refused to find a true bill against Swift and threatened to prosecute anyone trying to circulate the copper. A mixture of popular outrage and advice from Irish Whig grandees persuaded Walpole that he had to back down. In an effort to mollify Irish opinion the government built a new Parliament House in Dublin, considerably grander than the English Houses of Parliament. (See Figure 14.2, The Parliament House, Dublin.) After Wood's halfpence, English ministers were more cautious in the demands they made on Ireland and confrontation gave way to mutually beneficial deals and tactful management. Under George III the Irish saw the grievances of the American colonies as similar to their own and took advantage of the government's difficulties to secure the repeal of the Declaratory Act in 1782. The French revolution and the upheavals of the 1790s led the British to fear that Ireland might follow the Americans in throwing off British rule, so the Irish Parliament was abolished and Ireland was united with Britain in 1800.

℘ Conclusion

The Union with Scotland marked a major stage in the establishment of English power over Wales, Ireland and Scotland. The effective incorporation of Wales into England followed centuries of military occupation and the tacit threat from England's military power underlay the Union. However, in the middle of a major war against France, war with Scotland was not a practical proposition, so the Scots were invited (under some duress) to negotiate and English ministers made significant concessions. After a difficult period, in which the English reinterpreted some aspects of the treaty, English ministers

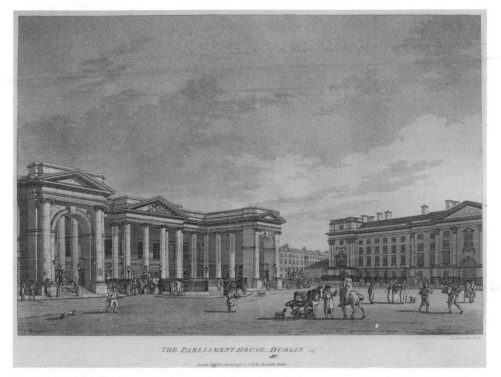

THE PARLIAMENT HOUSE, DUBLIN

Figure 14.2 After the furore over Wood's halfpence the British government was eager to placate the Irish Parliament. In the early eighteenth century it met in Chichester House in College Green, Dublin, which was badly decayed. It was rased to the ground and a new Parliament house designed by Sir Edward Lovet Pearce, in an Italianate neo-classical style, with a circular chamber for the House of Commons. It was far grander than the Palace of Westminster, home of the British Parliament.

(following Scottish advice) began to avoid measures which would provoke opposition in Scotland and the Scots began to enjoy the benefits of free trade. But although the Scots retained their legal system and their Presbyterian established Church, politically and socially they were increasingly subsumed into England. Ireland had long ceased to be an independent kingdom and, unlike Scotland's, its ruling elite consisted mainly of English settlers; the Ulster Scots were second-class citizens (see Chapter 15). In the eighteenth century the Anglo-Irish elite, like the American colonists, claimed the rights of Englishmen. In 1800 Ireland too was united with England (and Wales and Scotland) to form the United Kingdom, but the kingdoms were united on England's terms. Welshmen, Scots and Irishmen were admitted to the English Parliament and the benefits of the English constitution. Apart from the Scots they were subject to English law, and all public documents were in English. Although English hegemony over Britain and Ireland was not fully achieved by 1750 it was already far advanced.

SUGGESTIONS FOR FURTHER READING

The best overview of Britain and Ireland throughout this period is J. Smyth, *The Making of the United Kingdom 1660–1800* (Harlow, 2001). T. Harris's volumes *Restoration* and *Revolution* cover England, Scotland and Ireland from 1660 to the 1690s and are particularly strong on Scotland (and especially the Revolution settlement). • For Scotland, see R. Mitchison, *Lordship to Patronage 1603–1745* (London, 1983) and Brown, *Scotland and the Regal Union*; see also T.M. Devine and J.R. Young (eds.), *Eighteenth-Century Scotland: New Perspectives* (East Linton, 1999). • On Ireland, S. Connolly, *Divided Kingdom: Ireland 1630–1800* (Oxford, 2008) is outstanding, as is T. Barnard, *A New Anatomy of Ireland: Irish Protestants 1649–1770* (New Haven, 2003). • On Restoration Scotland, see Harris, *Restoration* and C. Jackson, *Restoration Scotland, 1660–90* (Woodbridge, 2003). • The tercentenary of the Union saw two major volumes. C. Whatley, *The Scots and the Union* (Edinburgh, 2007) places great emphasis on Scotland's dire economic plight in the 1690s, which led many Scots to embrace the Union. A. Macinnes, *Union and Empire: the Making of the United Kingdom in 1707* (Cambridge, 2007) argues that England forced the Union on Scotland because Scottish commercial competition was too successful, especially illicit trade with the American and Caribbean colonies. The interpretation given in this chapter tends to follow Whatley, partly because illicit trade cannot be quantified but more because of strong evidence that most Scottish exports were low-quality and low-value. However, Macinnes is an original and thoughtful historian and his arguments should be taken seriously. • On Scotland after the Union, see E. Cregeen, 'The Changing Role of the House of Argyll in the Scottish Highlands', in N.T. Phillipson and R. Mitchison (eds.), *Scotland in the Age of Improvement* (Edinburgh, 1970), R. Mitchison, 'The Government and the Highlands, 1707–1745', in Phillipson and Mitchison, *Scotland in the Age of Improvement,* and J.M. Simpson, 'Who Steered the Gravy Train, 1707–1766?', in Phillipson and Mitchison, *Scotland in the Age of Improvement.* See also A. Murdoch, *The People Above: Politics and Administration in Mid-Eighteenth Century Scotland* (Edinburgh, 1980) and D. Allan, *Scotland in the Eighteenth Century: Union and Enlightenment* (Harlow, 2002). • For the Jacobites and the Highlands, see M. Pittock, *The Myth of the Jacobite Clans* (2nd edn, Edinburgh, 2009), A. Macinnes, *Clanship, Commerce and the House of Stuart* (East Linton, 1996), Mitchison's essay in Phillipson and Mitchison (cited above), D. Szechi, *1715: the Great Jacobite Rebellion* (New Haven, 2006) and B. Lenman, *The Jacobite Risings in Britain 1689–1746* (London, 1980). • On James II and the Jacobite wars in Ireland, see J.G. Simms, *Jacobite Ireland 1685–91* (1969), P. Lenihan, *The Last Cavalier: Richard Talbot (1631–91)* (Dublin, 2014), J. Childs, *The Williamite Wars in Ireland 1688–91* (London, 2007) and B. Whelan (ed.), *The Last of the Great Wars* (Limerick, 1995). • For the importance of the revenue in the establishment of regular parliaments, see C.I. McGrath, *The Making of the Eighteenth-Century Irish Constitution: Government, Parliament and the Revenue, 1692–1714* (Dublin, 2000). • For Irish Jacobitism see E. Ó Ciardha, *Ireland and the Jacobite Cause, 1685–1766: a Fatal Attachment* (Dublin, 2002). • For government and politics, see D. Hayton's excellent collection of essays, *Ruling Ireland 1685–1742: Politics, Politicians and Parties* (Woodbridge,

2004), S. Connolly, *Religion, Law and Power: the Making of Protestant Ireland 1660–1760* (Oxford, 1992) and P. Walsh, *The Making of the Irish Protestant Ascendancy: the Life of William Conolly, 1662–1729* (Woodbridge, 2010).

SUMMARY

- The fortunes of the two parliaments in this period were radically different. The Scottish Parliament had imposed conditions on Charles I during the Covenanter revolution (for example, insisting that Parliament approve his choice of ministers). Under Charles II the Covenanter legislation was repealed and Parliament was subordinated to an increasingly authoritarian monarchy especially after the Test Act of 1681.
- The Convention of 1689–90 used William III's need for its support (and a strong groundswell of opinion against the regimes of Charles II and James II) to reassert its autonomy, re-enacting much (but by no means all) of the Covenanter programme. The Scots Parliament resented the indifference (if not hostility) of William's regime to Scottish interests and particularly the Act of Settlement. Under Anne it attempted to achieve greater independence of English control, only to be forced by the Aliens Act to negotiate about a Union. The terms of the Union were not ungenerous in the long run, but with the passage of the Act the Scottish Parliament ceased to exist.
- Before 1692 the Irish Parliament met infrequently and exercised limited influence. It had abandoned its financial bargaining power in 1666 by granting Charles II his revenues for life. In 1692 William's government needed Parliament's agreement to the Treaty of Limerick and Parliament used this as a lever to secure English recognition of its **Sole Right** to initiate money bills. This enabled it to regain a measure of financial leverage, which it retained by granting revenues for two years only. The London Parliament claimed the right to legislate for Ireland, passing measures to protect English economic interests. The Irish protested loudly, but to little effect. On the other hand Whig ministers came to accept that they could not push measures (like the repeal of the sacramental test) through the Irish Parliament if there was a strong majority against them.

QUESTIONS FOR STUDENTS

1. How far did the Scottish monarchy become absolute under Charles II?
2. How far did the Scottish Convention of 1689–90 succeed in re-enacting the Covenanter Revolution?
3. Why was Scottish opposition to Union so extensive and why did it eventually fail?

4. Why was Jacobitism more effective in Scotland than in Ireland?
5. Why did the Irish Parliament meet regularly in the eighteenth century?

15

The Fragmentation of Protestantism 1640–1750

1688–90	Episcopalian ministers 'rabbled' out of parishes (Sc)
1689	Toleration Act
1689–90	Presbyterianism re-established (Sc)
1696	John Aikenhead executed for blasphemy (Sc)
1701	Bevis Marks synagogue opened
1704	Sacramental test (Ir)
1710	Sacheverell trial
1711	Occasional Conformity Act
1712	British Parliament grants toleration to Episcopalians and re-establishes lay patronage (Sc)
1714	Schism Act (against Dissenting schools)
1715	Jacobite rebellion
1730s	Development of Methodism
1740s	Moderate movement develops (Sc)

Introduction

In the Reformation Catholics argued that, having rejected the Church's authority and traditions, Protestants developed competing interpretations of the will of God. Human reason, or the Holy Spirit, led some to explain divine wisdom in new and (some said) blasphemous ways. Mainstream Reformers and Protestant princes argued that university-educated theologians should define 'true doctrine' and established churches, and the secular magistrate, should impose this orthodoxy on the people. Bible-reading laypeople, however, did not always meekly submit to the clergy's guidance. Many denounced continuing 'Catholic' practices or argued about the Eucharist. On the vexed question of salvation Catholic teaching stressed good works and the sacraments and was broadly inclusive. Protestant teachings, especially predestination, claimed that God alone determined who would be saved and that these would be a select few.

The issues raised by the Reformation created differences between Catholic and Protestant and within Protestantism. First, who could claim to interpret Scripture and on what grounds: theological training, reason, the Holy Spirit? Second, what was the purpose of worship: expounding the Word, edification, or an affirmation of community? Third, what was a 'church': all the people living in a parish or nation, or a self-selected body of 'visible saints'? Fourth, how far had national churches the right to compel individual consciences? Between 1640 and 1750 these and other questions irrevocably divided the Protestants of England, Wales, Scotland and Ireland.

The Established Churches in 1640

England

Since Elizabeth's reign the Church of England had contained a spectrum of opinions about worship, theology and government. The first, worship, centred on the question of **adiaphora**: should the Church return to the practice of the **primitive Church** or could it command practices not authorised by Scripture? Should communion be celebrated in the nave or at the altar? Should the people receive it sitting or kneeling? Under Elizabeth, parishes differed, but most used a communion table rather than an altar. Many ministers followed the rubrics of the Prayer Book but others did not. Theology was initially less obviously divisive. Debates about doctrine were common, but often abstruse, and usually within the parameters of mainstream Protestantism. Church government became an issue only when puritan impatience with the bishops' imposition of ceremonies led to an abortive movement to establish a Presbyterian system. What was later called English Presbyterianism was parish-based puritanism, without bishops (or with bishops with limited powers).

Under Elizabeth and James I the Church accommodated divergent opinions and practices. This became more difficult for two reasons. First, the rise of **Arminianism** challenged the mainstream Protestant theological tradition within which most debate had taken place: the sole authority of Scripture, justification by faith alone, and a theology of the Eucharist which rejected **transubstantiation**. Second, when Arminians gained power within the Church, they set out to eradicate the earlier flexibility. They shifted the focus of the service from preaching the Word to repeating Prayer-Book rubrics and homilies, and demanded that laypeople should receive communion, kneeling, before a railed-in altar. Godly preachers were silenced, ceremonies enforced, Sunday sports tolerated. Many puritans responded by gadding to sermons or emigrating.

Scotland

By 1625 James VI seemed to have defeated the hard-line Presbyterians; some were dead or in exile, others withdrew into **conventicles**. He had re-established bishops and given them a role within the Presbyterian system. He had also brought the Kirk's worship more into line with the Church of England. Resentment of this Anglicisation exploded when Charles I tried to introduce his Prayer Book. The Covenant, while not winning universal support, united Scottish Presbyterians. By contrast, Charles's attempts to raise an army to suppress the Covenanters showed how many English sympathised with the Scots. His defeat in 1640 placed him at the mercy of his critics, Scots and English.

Ireland

The Church of Ireland was the weakest of the established churches. Catholics formed a substantial majority of the population, the Church was poorly endowed and there was a growing Scottish Presbyterian population in Ulster. Unequivocally Calvinist, the Church initially shared much common ground with the Scots, who felt little need to form separate churches. Under Charles I, the Irish Church's liturgy and theology were brought into line with England's and Wentworth planned a **Laudian** reformation. With the Prayer Book rebellion the Ulster Scots developed a strong solidarity with their brethren in Scotland. Wentworth sent troops, including many Catholics, to Ulster to deter them from rising and pressed their ministers to renounce the Covenant. By 1640 the co-existence of the Church of Ireland and the Ulster Scots had been replaced by hostility.

In 1640 the Kirk was much the strongest of the established churches. In England and Ireland a rough theological consensus and tacit divergence of practice had broken down as an atypical minority tried to enforce its vision. In Scotland, grudging acquiescence under James gave way to widespread support for the Covenant against a clearly perceived enemy: Laud and his bishops. So long as the enemy remained clearly defined, the Covenanters held together. As the picture became more complicated, cracks began to show.

England 1640–1660: the Established Church

In the 1640s the Church of Elizabeth and James was destroyed. In many parishes Puritans destroyed altar rails and altars and disfigured or whitewashed images. 'Laudian' clergymen were replaced by 'godly' preachers; the rights of Royalist patrons of livings were ignored. Parliament's committee for scandalous ministers rooted out 'ungodly' clergymen The Church's government was dismantled. The Church courts ceased to function in 1641 and bishops had lost effective power well before episcopacy was abolished in 1645. Other consequences of the Solemn League and Covenant included the banning of the Prayer Book and the abolition of the traditional Christian calendar, including the celebration of Christmas.

Amid this destruction the parish system continued, helped by the repeated rejection of calls to abolish tithes. Most people continued to worship in their parish churches, although some (not necessarily puritans) stayed away. There was no prescribed form of parish worship. Parliament set up the **Westminster Assembly of Divines**, which drew up a **Confession of Faith** but reached no agreement on liturgy or Church government. The Scottish **Directory**, which replaced the Prayer Book, contained recommendations rather than requirements; ministers devised their own forms of worship. Some used the Prayer Book more or less openly, others did so clandestinely, and some were prosecuted by their congregations for *not* using it. Successive regimes used the parish to provide basic religious instruction, while also allowing freedom to worship elsewhere. Cromwell established **triers** and **ejectors** to examine candidates for the ministry and to remove those deemed inadequate. If the 'Anglican' character of parish worship diminished, the sense of the church as the spiritual centre of the community continued.

England 1640–1660: the Rise of the Gathered Churches

Before 1640 English Protestants disagreed about the form of parish worship but very few rejected the concept of an inclusive national church. Puritans who gadded to sermons were making choices within the Church, not leaving it. Separatists were regarded with deep suspicion: under an Act of Parliament of 1593 the penalties for attending **conventicles** were forfeiture of all property and imprisonment for life.

The collapse of traditional ecclesiastical authority unleashed a surge of **millenarian** excitement and England's version of the radical Reformation of the 1520s and 1530s. Many believed that they were entering the last days, when God would overthrow earthly rulers and the martyred saints would take their place at His right hand. Men and women claiming inspiration from the Holy Spirit challenged university-educated clergymen. Some claimed that Scripture represented God's will at some point in the past, but the Holy Spirit expressed God's will now. For Puritan clergymen, such challenges to their learning were alarming. The majority remained committed to the parish system and hoped to construct some form of Presbyterian organisation. But a minority favoured congregational autonomy.

Independents and Congregationalists

These terms were often used interchangeably to describe congregations led by Calvinist ministers who opposed attempts to impose Scottish-style Presbyterianism: 'new Presbyter is but old priest writ large'. For a model they could look to New

BOX 15.1: **The Evils of Toleration**

By 1646 many conventional puritans were deeply alarmed by the effects of de facto religious freedom and believed liberty had degenerated into licence. The following, addressed to Parliament, is taken from the most famous attack on the gathered churches, published in three lengthy sections in 1646. Its author, Thomas Edwards, was a Presbyterian minister and its title, *Gangraena*, depicts the sects as a cancer, eating away at religious order and truth. See A. Hughes, *'Gangraena' and the Struggle for the English Revolution* (Oxford, 2004).

You have, most noble Senators, done worthily against Papists, and scandalous ministers, in casting down images, altars, crucifixes, throwing out ceremonies &c. but what have you done against other kinds of growing evils, heresy, schism, disorder, against **Seekers**, Anabaptists, **antinomians**, Brownists, Libertines and other sects? You have destroyed Baal and his priests, but have you been zealous against the golden calves and the priests of the lowest of the people? Are not these grown up and daily increase under you? Are any effectual means used against them? You have made a Reformation ... but with the Reformation have we not a Deformation and worse things come in upon us than ever we had before? Were

any of those monsters heard of heretofore, which are now common among us? As denying the Scriptures, pleading for a toleration of all religions and worships, yea for blasphemy and denying there is a God ... we have those who overthrow the doctrine of the Trinity, oppose the divinity of Christ, speak evil of the Virgin Mary, slight the apostles ... We have many that cast to the ground all ministers ... cast out the sacraments, baptism and the Lord's Supper ... many take away and cry down the necessary maintenance of the ministers; ... we have ... all public prayer questioned and all ministerial preaching denied ... we have all ten commandments [taken away] at once by the Antinomians; yea, all faith and the Gospel denied, as by the Seekers. The worst of the prelates ... held many sound doctrines and had many commendable practices; yea, the very Papists hold and keep to many articles of faith and truths of God ... but many of the sects and sectaries in our days deny all principles of religion, are enemies to all holy duties, order, learning, overthrowing all ... and the great opinion of an universal toleration tends to the laying all waste and dissolution of all religion and good manners.

> T. Edwards, *Gangraena: or a Catalogue and Discovery of Many of the Errors, Heresies, Blasphemies and Pernicious Practices of the Sectaries* (London, 1646), Epistle Dedicatory.

England where Congregational churches were supported by the secular authorities. Some claimed more autonomy than others and there were varying degrees of separation from the parish system. They agreed that 'private Christians' could form autonomous assemblies, without seeking permission from any authority. Some gathered around a parish minister, others set up on their own. They agreed on the need to admit only 'visible saints', to separate from the ungodly, and to be bound by their own system of discipline. They were denounced as sectaries by both Scots and English Presbyterians (see Box 15.1, The Evils of Toleration), but some recognised that although 'all sectaries are Independents ... all Independents are not properly sectaries'. While demanding liberty for themselves, they were reluctant to allow it to others, notably Baptists and Quakers.

Baptists

The first English Baptist congregation was formed in 1616. They derived their inspiration from the Mennonites, Dutch Anabaptists who remained committed to adult baptism, but exchanged their forebears' radicalism for quietism: some regarded the secular state as inherently sinful. In the 1640s their numbers grew rapidly. Their preachers were mostly artisans, who supported themselves financially and claimed to be inspired by the Holy Spirit. Some congregations allowed women to preach, but with less authority than men; acceptance into a Baptist church was marked by re-baptism. (See Figure 15.1, Frontispiece to Daniel Featley, *The Dippers Dippt*, 1645.) Baptists' confessions of faith stressed that they did not reject conventional morality or earthly authority, but from an early stage they were divided on the question of salvation. Particular Baptists remained within the Calvinist tradition, but General Baptists rejected predestination, teaching that salvation was potentially open to all who were willing to receive God's grace.

Quakers

Quakers took Baptist, particularly General Baptist, ideas to their logical conclusion: God could inspire the individual believer through the 'inner light'. In their meetings Quakers looked to the light for guidance and especially to the superior 'light' of those later known as 'weighty Friends'. Crucial to their success was the leadership of George Fox. A charismatic figure, Fox also grasped the importance of publicity, lobbying and organisation. Quakers' behaviour was designed to attract attention: they gathered accounts of their 'sufferings' and made extensive use of the press.

Early Quaker tactics centred on the 'lamb's war'. They challenged ministers in their churches or denounced people's sins in the market place or street, calling on them to repent; sometimes they went naked 'for a sign'. The response was often violent: congregations dragged Quakers into the churchyard and beat them, or ran them out of town. The Quakers would walk back through the crowd, on which they were often beaten again. (See Box 15.2, The 'Lamb's War'.) Their sufferings provoked both sympathy and hostility. Congregations resented the disruption of services, townspeople disliked being denounced as sinners. Quakers had no time for courtesy: they refused to doff their hats to magistrates and used the familiar 'thee' and 'thou' rather than 'you'. They refused to swear oaths, which were seen as essential for an ordered society and legal system. Quakers argued that swearing oaths took God's name in vain. Finally, for Quakers women were equal to men: Fox argued that the female prophets in the Bible showed that women were capable of receiving the 'light' and suffering for it. (See Figure 15.2, *The Quakers Dream*, 1655.)

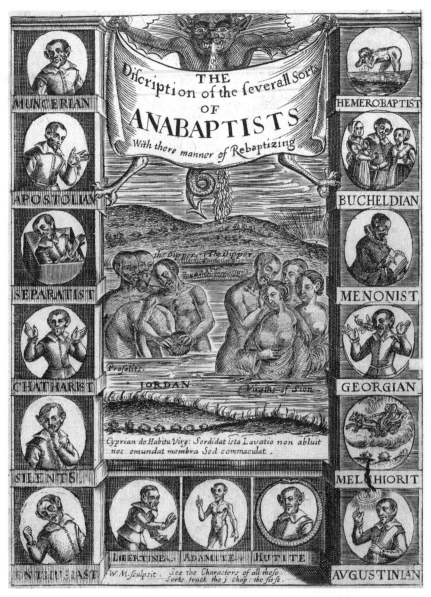

Figure 15.1 This purports to show the many varieties of Anabaptists and features a salacious image of 'virgins of Sion' being immersed by naked men.

Wales 1640–1660: the Propagation of the Gospel

Despite the translation of the Bible and Prayer Book the grass-roots impact of Protestantism was limited before 1640. Most parish clergymen were poorly paid, making pluralism an economic necessity; they made little effort to instruct the people who

BOX 15.2: The 'Lamb's War'

The phrase refers to the ten kings who will give their power to the Beast: 'they will make war on the Lamb and the Lamb will conquer them, for he is the Lord of lords and King of kings, and those with him are chosen and called and faithful' (Revelation, 17, verse 14). Here George Fox recounts his reception at Warwick in 1655: note that not all the townspeople were hostile and the distinction between the 'rude' people and the rest, whom he often describes as 'civil' (not in the sense of 'polite').

And the town rose up against us in the open street, and the rude people gathered about us and got stones and one of them took hold upon my horse bridle ... And there came another man or two to throw stones at my face; and they were stopped and made to loose the other man's hands that hung at the horse bridle. And as we rode through the streets people fell upon us with cudgels and

stones, and much abused us ... And the bailiff did not stop or so much as rebuke the rude multitude, so that it was much we were not slain in the streets among them. And when we were ridden quite right through the town I was moved of the Lord to go back again into the street to offer my life among them, and said to Friends whoever found freedom [felt themselves free to do so] might follow me, and they that did not might go on to Dunchurch. And John Crook followed me, declaring the word of life to them. So I passed up the street and people fell upon me with their cudgels, and abused me and struck me and threw my horse down, yet by the power of the Lord I passed through them, and called upon the town and shopkeepers and told them of their immodest state, how they were a shame to Christians and the profession of Christianity.

G. Fox, *Journal*, ed. J.L. Nickalls (London, 1975), pp. 226–7.

showed little interest in listening. Cults of the saints, pilgrimages and holy wells continued. The sons of the better-off emerged from university Protestants but not, as a rule, radicals. Those with rights of presentation to livings nominated moderate conformists. Puritans were relatively few, but they included William Wroth, who established a separatist church in Glamorgan in 1639.

Radical Puritanism was strengthened by the Commission for the Propagation of the Gospel in Wales, created by the Rump in 1650. The confiscation of the many **impropriated** tithes belonging to Royalists made it possible to address the problem of clerical poverty. In England such tithes were used to enhance the incomes of the parish clergy. In Wales the collection of tithes was taken over by the commissioners. They ejected the majority of the parish clergy as inadequate and used tithe revenue to fund itinerant preachers, many of them English. These preachers saw themselves as bringing light to dark corners of the land; they made a significant impact, although their appeal was limited by their radicalism and (often) inability to speak Welsh. Even those of Welsh origin tended to view the Welsh as backward and ignorant. Nevertheless, they helped shift the balance within Welsh Protestantism: Nonconformists became increasingly numerous and would soon outnumber Anglicans.

Figure 15.2 The early Quakers were notorious for shrieking, shaking and speaking in tongues, but the allegations of promiscuity were probably less well founded: going naked 'as a sign' is here presented as dancing naked.

Scotland 1640–1660: Schism among the Covenanters

The origins of the schism that developed in the 1640s lay less in theology and church polity than in politics (see Chapter 9). The Covenanters' unity held together until at least 1641. The failure to abolish bishops in England was a disappointment, but the Irish rising reinforced their sense of common danger. When civil war started in England the majority of Covenanters favoured Parliament, but a growing minority declared their loyalty to the King. Others distrusted Parliament's leaders, who had failed to deliver on Church reform or pay the money promised in 1640 to the Scots army. The alliance of ministers and noblemen came under strain as the clergy came to dominate the Covenanting movement. After securing the **Solemn League and Covenant** the Scots were disappointed (again) by the English Parliament's failure to keep its promises; in 1645 they were excluded from negotiations with the King. The King and bishops no longer posed any threat to the Kirk but the New Model was openly hostile. The ministers were alarmed at the growth of gathered churches and Scottish (and Irish) Royalists inflicted considerable damage in Scotland. Atrocities on both sides deepened the divisions between Royalist and Covenanter.

The King's defeat added to their dilemma. The Covenanters had no wish to overthrow their rightful King. The Engagement, to invade England and restore his power, finally split the Covenanters. Hardliners bitterly opposed military intervention in England and condemned the safeguards for Presbyterianism as woefully inadequate. The invasion failed ignominiously and radical **Whiggamores** seized power in Scotland, with Cromwell's help (see Chapter 9). They established a godly Presbyterian regime and abolished **lay patronage**, transferring power within the Kirk from nobles to the members of presbyteries and kirk sessions. After Worcester the hard-liners seceded from the General Assembly and became known as Protestors. Under the English occupation the General Assembly was abolished but the radicals were supported by only a minority of ministers. English attempts to encourage Baptists and Quakers made little impact.

Ireland 1640–1660: the Rise of Presbyterianism

Between 1641 and 1652 war and conquest left Ireland devastated and its population drastically reduced. Radical English military rulers distrusted the pre-1641 settlers, whether Church of Ireland or Presbyterian, as insufficiently godly, but from 1655 Henry Cromwell and Broghill worked with these **Old Protestants**, who were wealthier and more powerful than the new settlers.

In the 1640s the Confederate Catholics regained many parish churches and the Dublin authorities abolished episcopacy and banned the Prayer Book. Tithes were abolished and Church lands confiscated; bishops and Church courts ceased to function but many ministers remained in place and the hostility of the English military led many 'Old Protestants' to return to their parish churches. The Ulster Scots built a Presbyterian organisation under the protection of the Scottish army. The English military regime hoped to use confiscated Church lands to fund godly preachers (as in Wales) but there was not enough money and few suitable ministers came to Ireland; parishes and congregations chose their own. These had to be approved by **triers**, who endorsed mostly

Congregationalist, Church of Ireland or Presbyterian ministers. Baptists and Quakers made limited headway. By 1659, despite its survival at parish level, the Church of Ireland had apparently ceased to exist as an institution and the nearest thing to an established church was the Presbyterian Kirk.

England 1660–1690: Church and Dissent

In 1660 it seemed certain that the Church of England would be re-established, but in what form? Would it be narrowly 'Anglican' or the broader church of James I?

The Restoration Settlement: 1660–1663

It clearly would not include separatists, but Presbyterians hoped to be included in a comprehensive Church and Charles II seemed to favour their inclusion. Although he began to appoint bishops as soon as he returned, these were moderates rather than Laudians. Evidence on the making of the 1662 Act of Uniformity is sparse, but it was probably not the King or bishops who made the Act rigidly 'Anglican' but the 'Cavalier' House of Commons elected in 1661. Driven by revenge, or a determination to remove ministers intruded into their parishes, MPs made it as difficult as possible for Presbyterians to remain within the Church. They insisted that the clergy should give their 'unfeigned assent and consent' to everything in the Prayer Book and required them to swear that neither they nor anyone else was bound by the Solemn League and Covenant. If they wished to serve in the Church they had to seek re-ordination by a bishop.

Although some Presbyterians later suspected that Charles secretly favoured their ejection, he seems to have tried sincerely to prevent it, calculating that Presbyterians would make less trouble if they remained within the Church; he appointed several Presbyterian privy councillors. The clergy were required to declare their conformity by 24 August 1662. About one fifth of parish ministers lost their livings between 1660 and 1662, but fears that their departure would lead to serious disorder proved unfounded.

The Restoration Church of England

The exodus of Presbyterians narrowed the basis of the Church. Some remained, with the help of a sympathetic bishop or by stretching their consciences. The departures left the Church narrower but not narrow. This was not the **Laudian** Church which Charles I had sought, but something closer to the ideal of 'parish Anglicans'. Iconoclasm and whitewashing had left church interiors plain and often damaged; few altars survived. The following decades saw churches beautified and altars rebuilt, but this took time and reflected a changing popular mood. A new generation of clergy emerged from the universities, many of them High Churchmen in terms of their liturgical preferences, veneration for monarchy and attitude towards Nonconformity.

The Laws against Nonconformity

In the 1660s legislation aimed to limit the perceived threat from the Presbyterian clergy. The Five Mile Act was designed to prevent ejected ministers from coming to any corporate town or parish where they had once served. Concern about towns also underlay the **Corporation Act** of 1661, designed to exclude 'disaffected' persons from municipal office, by requiring that they subscribe several oaths and declarations (including renouncing the Covenant). Apart from an Act against Quakers, Parliament was slow to pass legislation against Dissent. The first **Conventicle** Act (1664) was only temporary. A much more severe Act – 'the quintessence of arbitrary malice' – was passed in 1670. People who allowed their houses to be used for meetings could be fined and informers who brought prosecutions could be awarded a share of any fine. The 1673 **Test Act** was aimed primarily against Catholics (it required a declaration against transubstantiation) but also required all office holders to take communion in an Anglican church, which would exclude conscientious Dissenters.

Presbyterians

The Presbyterians were in an anomalous position: believing in a national Church they found themselves outside it. The clergy felt this most keenly: the Act of Uniformity had been directed mainly against them and their conduct was closely watched. Some dutifully attended their parish churches or preached to small groups, to keep within the law. Some yearned to take communion but would not kneel. To continue their ministry they would have to defy the law, which some found painful, but a younger generation accepted separatism more easily. Presbyterian laymen faced fewer difficulties, attending their parish churches or Presbyterian or Independent meetings as opportunity offered. Presbyterians remained the most numerous Nonconformists, but, as the heirs of parish Puritans, the least inclined to organise separately. Many longed to be included within the Church, but it was not to be.

Independents, Baptists and Quakers

These denominations just wished to seek God in their own way. Faced with allegations that their nonconformity implied political disaffection they claimed to be peaceable. For the Baptists this was second nature, as they dissociated themselves from Münster. For the Independents and Quakers it was a new experience: the former regarded themselves as part of the Puritan mainstream, while the latter had seen the Inner Light as sufficient justification. Now Fox reinvented them as (still) suffering, but harmless. But the identification of disaffection with nonconformity continued. Memories of the civil wars remained raw, helped by the annual commemoration of Charles I's 'martyrdom' and growing support for High Church Anglicanism. Charles II's flirtations with toleration for Dissenters (and Catholics) created an Anglican backlash, seen in the 1670 Conventicle Act and the persecution of 1681–5. As their meetings were disrupted Presbyterians, Independents and Baptists met secretly; sheriffs' officers and informers hunted them down. Meeting houses were smashed and boarded up and they were driven to meet in barns and fields. Many preachers and worshippers ended up in gaol.

The worst sufferers were, as always, the Quakers. Refusing to compromise their witness, they met publicly at stated times and ignored orders to disperse. The sheriffs' officers were forced to drag them through the streets, which attracted a crowd. Brought before the mayor they refused to remove their hats or promise not to meet, saying that they were only seeking God and had done no wrong. Whereas earlier their conduct had annoyed bystanders, now their sufferings often elicited sympathy. Neighbours supported them and tried to protect their property. Their lack of deference still annoyed those in authority but some proved surprisingly sympathetic. The future Judge Jeffreys had Quakers released from prison. Like many Tories he regarded them as eccentric but harmless: the Church's greatest enemies were 'schismatics' (Presbyterians) and **occasional conformists**, who took communion in order to qualify for office and undermine the Church.

Persecution and Toleration 1685–1689

James II regarded all Protestants as equally wrong, but initially preferred Anglicans to Dissenters, as loyal to the monarchy. Persecution continued and many Nonconformists suffered for their involvement in Monmouth's rebellion. However, when the Tories complained of his granting army commissions to Catholic officers James rethought his position, influenced by William Penn's claim that Dissenters had been driven to disobedience by persecution. In 1687 he granted toleration to all Protestants and replaced Tories with Dissenters in local and municipal offices. The bishops countered by declaring their willingness to adapt the Church's liturgy to accommodate Presbyterians (**comprehension**) and hinted at toleration for other Dissenters. (See Chapter 13, 'James II'.)

James's flight and the installation of William and Mary embarrassed the bishops and other Tories. They had failed to oppose the ejection of a lawful King. William was cool towards Churchmen and friendly towards Nonconformists. The bishops regretted their earlier assurances. They could not renege on them altogether but were determined to concede as little as possible. Negotiations about comprehension failed. The bishops offered too little to attract the most moderate Presbyterians; many younger ministers had no wish to join the Church. For the bishops and Tories toleration was the price for avoiding comprehension: the Church would be narrower, but purer.

The Toleration Act, 1689

This was in some ways a grudging measure. Dissenting meeting houses had to be licensed by a magistrate and their doors kept open during meetings, to show that sedition was not preached inside. All preachers were to subscribe the Thirty-Nine Articles, but could omit those relating to the lawfulness of ceremonies and (for the Baptists) infant baptism. Preachers were required to take an oath of allegiance to the monarchs. However, the Act allowed de facto freedom of worship to almost all Protestants. The Quakers were accommodated after intense lobbying; the oath of allegiance was a potential stumbling block but they were usually able to affirm rather than swear. The only Protestants excluded came from the extremes of the spectrum. **Socinians** or Unitarians (who denied the Trinity) were condemned by all conventional Protestants. Non-jurors, a significant minority of the Anglican clergy, headed by six bishops, refused to swear allegiance to William and Mary. Their numbers dwindled with time, but their defiance was a constant reproach to their brethren. It was ironical that they alone were punished for holding conventicles.

Of non-Protestants, Catholics were still subject to penal laws, which were extended after 1689. Jewish worship was neither legally recognised nor forbidden. Expelled in 1290, Jews had been informally readmitted in the 1650s and lived a twilight existence. Most were Sephardic, of Spanish or Portuguese descent. Although they were legally aliens, lacking the rights of citizens, their wealth and numbers grew; many adopted English dress and manners and became integrated into polite society. Their first synagogue, Bevis Marks, was opened in London in 1701. The newspapers printed accounts of Jewish weddings and religious customs, implying a degree of curiosity. But they did not enjoy formal freedom of worship or easy access to full citizenship until the nineteenth century.

For almost all Protestants persecution ended in 1689. The clergy could no longer drive people to church, but Dissenters were still second-class citizens: freedom of worship was the price of keeping them out of positions of power. The Corporation and Test Acts imposed oaths and declarations and required office-holders to take communion in an Anglican church. These requirements were erratically enforced and many thought bread and wine a small price to pay for a job. But some scrupled to take communion and many resented being treated as disaffected or inferior. The Test and Corporation Acts continued to rankle until their repeal in 1828.

Scotland 1660–1690: from Episcopacy to Presbyterianism

At the Restoration most Protestants were Presbyterians to some extent. Presbyterian orthodoxy could perhaps be defined as follows.

First, theology: Calvinist as set out in the Westminster Confession of 1643 or an earlier authoritative confession.

Second, organisation: Defined by the Covenant and the Solemn League and Covenant, this should be Presbyterian, with kirk sessions, presbyteries, synods and a General Assembly – 'the ordinance of God, appointed by Jesus Christ, for governing his visible church'. These forms of government, their decisions and censures should be supported and enforced by the secular government.

Third, selection of ministers: Ideally they should be chosen by the congregation, either as a whole or through its leading members (elders or **heritors**).

Fourth, liturgy: The Kirk had no set liturgy: ministers devised liturgies as they judged appropriate. However, Presbyterians were firmly opposed to bowing to the altar, kneeling for communion and other 'popish' rituals.

By the 1650s the reality of Presbyterianism often did not match these ideals. Shifting political realities had forced compromises: the Covenants demanded an unequivocal commitment to introduce Presbyterianism in England but in the Engagement Charles I agreed to do so for three years only. Similarly, a dominant local landowner could demand the right to nominate the minister. Such compromises may not have unduly concerned the average kirk-goer, provided parish life functioned as before, but for diligent Covenanters they were an abomination, and ministers urged their flocks to reject them.

Church and Dissent under Charles II

Despite the efforts of James VI and Charles I episcopacy had never put down significant roots in Scotland. There remained widespread support for the Kirk's doctrine, liturgy and parish discipline. The Covenanting Revolution had weakened the Scottish monarchy and nobility, and Charles II's agents in Scotland set out to reverse this. The Act Rescissory of 1661 repealed all legislation passed since 1633, including the abolition of episcopacy and lay patronage. In 1669 an Act established the royal supremacy.

Charles aimed initially at a more limited episcopacy than his father's, but some nobles wanted bishops, to subjugate the Covenanters and preserve social order; they also wanted to restore lay patronage. However, they made no effort to create an episcopalian Church order, which they feared might give the clergy too much power. The established Church lacked **canons**, a liturgy and a **Convocation** or law-making body. The King, fearful of provoking the Presbyterians, would not let the episcopalians adopt set forms of prayer, so they found it hard to create a distinctive form of service. The Privy Council ordered that ministers settled in churches since 1649 should be dismissed unless they submitted to presentation by a lay patron and installation by a bishop. By 1663 about one third of the 950 clergy had been ejected, mostly from the West and South West (34 out of 37 in Galloway). Some of the ejected preached as itinerants or in field **conventicles**; their parishioners drove out their replacements and stayed away from church. The government responded with a mixture of limited toleration (for moderates) and armed force (against field conventicles and hardliners). For a while, despite a rebellion in 1679, such methods seemed to work, but the emergence of the 'Cameronians' (also known as '**Society People**') encouraged a new intransigence. (See Chapter 14, Box 14.1.) Some fifty ministers refused to take the **Test** and resigned their livings; some became itinerants, often with armed followers. The last years of Charles II's reign saw an escalation of violence in the South West.

The Re-establishment of Presbyterianism

William's arrival and James's flight opened the way for the restoration of Presbyterianism. From December 1688 Episcopalian ministers were rabbled out of their parishes, often violently. This was illegal, but many claimed that the laws had been dissolved by James's flight; the Society People played a prominent role. One group who expelled their minister declared 'this they did not as statesmen, nor as churchmen, but by violence and in a military way of Reformation'. Another stated that 'they would not adhere to the Prince of Orange nor the law of the kingdom, any further than the Solemn League and Covenant was fulfilled and prosecuted by both'. Rabbling continued during elections for the Scottish **Convention** and continued in Edinburgh when it met; for a while the Society People provided a guard.

The Convention's Claim of Right was more radical than the English Bill of Rights, recommending that '**prelacy**' should be abolished, as 'a great and insupportable grievance and trouble to this nation and contrary to the inclinations of the generality of the people'. The Articles of Grievances called for the repeal of the Act of Supremacy as 'inconsistent with the establishment of the Church government now desired'. In July the Convention passed bills to abolish prelacy and restore ministers ejected for refusing the Test, but neither initially received the royal assent. William's advisers, fearing an adverse reaction in England, wished to avoid the full re-establishment of Presbyterianism, but it became clear that the Presbyterians would not grant money until they got their way. When the Convention reconvened in April 1690 William was prepared to agree to abolish the royal supremacy and restore ejected ministers, but the Convention demanded that all ministers accept the Westminster Confession of 1643 and voted to restore the General Assembly, with the power to remove 'scandalous' ministers. It also abolished **lay patronage**, resolving that ministers should be elected by

heritors and elders, and passed an Act declaring that rabbled ministers had deserted their livings.

These measures re-enacted the Covenanter Revolution, but more vindictively. There had been few Episcopalian ministers under Charles I and Presbyterians had suffered far less then than under Charles II. Most Episcopalians were driven from their livings, often with no pretence of due process. The General Assembly removed those who failed to swear allegiance to William and Mary or subscribe the Westminster Confession, or were deemed 'unfit' for the ministry. Altogether 664 out of 920 ministers were ejected, the majority in 1688–90, often before the new settlement became law. This was a far higher proportion of ejections than in either England or Scotland at the Restoration. 116 conformed to the new order and a few kept their livings without conforming, supported by their congregations.

Presbyterian Reactions

Despite its claims, support for the new Presbyterian regime was far from universal: none of the General Assembly elected in 1690 came from North of the Tay and William prudently retained the right to summon it. In 1694–5 it resolved that all ministers should swear that Presbyterianism was the only valid form of Church government. In 1698 it resolved that Christ was the head of the Church and denied that it rested upon the people's approval or Acts of Parliament. It is unlikely that these resolutions commanded widespread support. Most laypeople were apparently content with the traditional liturgy, doctrine and government.

The dissatisfied were found at the extremes. As in England, **Non-jurors** were harassed, but in Scotland they were much more numerous and enjoyed greater support. The **Society People** continued to meet armed. Some joined the established Church, but others refused to accept public office, or recognise any church not explicitly founded on the Covenant, or swear allegiance to an uncovenanted king. They struggled to maintain a ministry; disagreements and schisms were frequent. The Kirk mainstream held together, but the danger of schism remained.

Ireland 1660–1690: Church and Dissent

In 1660 the Church of Ireland was in disarray. It had always been poorer and institutionally weaker than the Church of England and had suffered greater destruction during the wars. In the Convention of 1660 the majority supported a learned ministry supported by tithes. This might suggest that they favoured Presbyterianism, but they were prepared to recognise the surviving bishops. In fact, a broad Protestant Church was unlikely because Irish Presbyterianism was now far closer to its Scottish than its English counterpart. Charles II began appointing bishops in Ireland in June 1660. The Irish Parliament passed a new Act of Uniformity in 1666, designed to drive Presbyterians out, not bring them in. The clergy were to use the Prayer Book and ministers had to be ordained by bishops and renounce the Covenant: 61 out of 69 Ulster ministers refused ordination. However, there was no legislation against conventicles and older laws against nonconformist worship proved unenforceable. The **comprehension** of Presbyterians and Churchmen in a single church, always unlikely, had become impossible.

Church of Ireland

The Church recovered confiscated lands and tithes but the damage to church buildings often proved irreparable. Services were often held 'in a dirty cabin or a common alehouse', putting them on a par with many Catholic congregations. The Church's main strength was in the larger towns and the Pale. In Dublin churches were rebuilt and beautified and there was a vigorous parochial life. At first many parish clergy were Presbyterians or Independents, but these resigned in 1666. As Trinity College was small – about 340 students in the 1680s – many of their replacements were recruited from England. The bishops ranged from John Bramhall, Wentworth's chief agent for the promotion of Laudianism, to Henry Jones, brother of a Parliamentarian colonel, who remained loyal to the Church but collaborated politically with the Parliamentarian authorities.

Presbyterians

The Presbyterians were now closely identified with the Scottish Covenanters. By 1660 there were five presbyteries in Ulster which organised visitations, covering several parishes, enquiring into the minister's doctrine and the people's fitness for admission to communion. The Presbyterians built meeting houses to rival the parish churches. Their alienation from the Church was increased by the restoration of bishops in Scotland and an influx of itinerant ministers, who preached to clandestine meetings. The government, with only a hazy idea of the inner workings of Presbyterianism, feared meetings were a cover for conspiracy.

In the 1670s visitations and communion services lasted for up to a week and attracted huge crowds. In 1673 the government launched a drive against both Presbyterian and Catholic worship; attempts to suppress Presbyterian meeting houses were resisted and Ulster bishops found it difficult to govern their dioceses. The lord lieutenant thought dissident Protestants posed a greater threat than Catholics (see Box 14.3), but he doubted whether it was wise – or legal – to persecute them vigorously: there remained a residual sense that Protestants should stand together against the Catholic majority.

In 1681–5, with escalating violence in Scotland, Ulster was heavily policed and meeting houses were closed. Dissident ministers and copies of the Sanquhar Declaration made their way to Ireland. The entrenched positions of Church and Presbyterian prevented a common front against James II. During the Jacobite wars of 1688–91 the Presbyterians defended Derry and Enniskillen against James's forces and accused the Church of Ireland of favouring him: four bishops sat in the Jacobite Parliament of 1689. King William made clear his resentment towards those who had held office under James, but showed favour towards the Presbyterians, doubling Charles II's annual grant to their clergy. Recriminations about the wars added to the mutual hostility between the largest Protestant denominations in Ireland.

Scepticism and Heterodoxy

Thus far we have dealt with divisions within Protestantism stemming from common theological assumptions understood differently. But Christians of all kinds also faced challenges to revealed religion: the belief that God's purposes could be discovered through Scripture. In the later seventeenth century scholars questioned the authenticity of Biblical texts and applied the test of human reason to long-established beliefs. Few denied the existence of God but their questioning led them to a God who intervened less in everyday life than traditionally believed. Some claimed that the clergy wilfully misinterpreted Scripture to enhance their power and profit. These developments were international; discussed in print they generated wide interest but also anger and alarm.

Scriptural Criticism

During the Reformation Protestants claimed that the Catholic Church mistranslated the original Hebrew and Greek texts of the Bible; now the texts themselves were subjected to scrutiny, by scholars ranging from Samuel Fisher, an Oxford academic turned Quaker, to Richard Simon, a French Jesuit. If some books of the Bible accepted as canonical were of questionable authenticity, should they be excluded and should others, traditionally regarded as uncanonical, be included? Freethinkers and **deists** argued that Christianity should be compatible with reason and whatever was incompatible with reason could not be true. Newton's discoveries encouraged expectations that the workings of the world and the universe could be explained by physical or mathematical laws. This left little place for mysteries, such as the Trinity. Not a doctrine of the Early Church, it became the Church's official teaching in the fourth century. Intellectuals like Locke and Newton found it difficult to accept. Newton, as a Cambridge professor, had had to subscribe the Thirty-Nine Articles, which included the Trinity. Reluctant to relinquish his professorship but unable to believe in the Trinity, he drew up detailed arguments against it, which he kept to himself.

BOX 15.3: **The Evangelical Revival**

George Whitefield describes how he first preached in the open, buoyed by the fact that Christ 'had a mountain for his pulpit and the heavens for his sounding board' and had 'sent his servants into the highways and hedges' when the Jews rejected his Gospel. Whitefield started preaching to about a hundred Kingswood colliers, described by his biographer as 'very rude and very numerous; so uncultivated that nobody cared to go among them, neither had they any place of worship; and often, when provoked, they were a terror to the whole city of Bristol'.

They were glad to hear of a Jesus who was a friend to publicans and came not to call the righteous but sinners to repentance. The first discovery of their being affected was to see the white gutters made by their tears, which plentifully fell down their black cheeks, as they came out of their coal pits. Hundreds and hundreds of them were soon brought under deep convictions, which (as the event proved) happily ended in a sound and thorough conversion. The change was visible to all … As the scene was quite new, and I had just begun to be an extempore preacher, it often occasioned many inward conflicts. Sometimes, when twenty thousand people were before, I had not, in my own apprehension, a word to say, either to God or them. But I was never totally deserted and frequently … so assisted that I knew by happy experience what our Lord meant by saying 'out of his belly shall flow rivers of living water'. The open firmament above me, the prospect of the adjacent fields, with the sight of thousands and thousands, some in coaches, some on horseback, and some in the trees, and at times all affected and drenched in tears together, to which sometimes was added the solemnity of the approaching evening, … quite overcame me.

J. Gillies, *Memoirs of the Life of the Reverend George Whitefield* (1772), pp. 37–8. (This passage is based on a manuscript in Whitefield's own words.)

Priestcraft and Anticlericalism

Alongside intellectual giants like Locke and Newton many were interested in these new ideas out of intellectual curiosity or because they were fashionable. Others claimed that any intelligent layman could interpret the Bible and attacked the pretensions of clergymen, from Catholic priests to Presbyterians, who were accused of keeping Christianity 'mysterious', in order to maintain their profit and power.

Clergy responses to accusations of priestcraft were generally of two kinds. First, there were calls to restore the power of the Church, reduced by the Toleration Act, occasional conformity and the spread of Dissenting schools (not mentioned in the Act). They also wished to revive **Convocation**, which had not met since 1664. William reluctantly reconvened it in 1689; it met sporadically under William and Anne but never achieved the permanence or power that High Churchmen hoped for.

The second response was the evangelical revival which became apparent in the later 1730s and was identified with, but not confined to, the Methodists. There were signs of revival in Wales in the 1710s and the Methodists followed preachers like George Whitefield in organising massive open-air meetings. (See Box 15.3, The Evangelical

Revival.) Whereas High Churchmen hoped to suppress debate and punish 'blasphemy' and 'atheism', the evangelicals accepted that debates about the authenticity of texts and the compatibility of Christianity and reason could not be resolved either way. They reverted to a religion of the heart rather than the head and concentrated on bringing to their hearers the experience of conversion and their certainty of saving faith. 'Is not this the sum', wrote John Wesley, '"One thing I know: I was blind, but now I see"? An argument so plain that a peasant, a woman, a child may feel its force.' In highlighting justification by faith alone they returned to an often forgotten item in the Thirty-Nine Articles: 'that we are justified by Faith only is a most wholesome doctrine and very full of comfort'. Faith, however, could be elusive or demanding. It often required a struggle with man's sinful nature, far removed from the undemanding moral teachings of many Anglican clergymen, summed up by the text 'for His [God's] commandments are not grievous'.

Divisions among Protestants 1690–1750: England

High Church and Low Church

Despite the expulsion of the Presbyterians at the Restoration the Church of England remained broader than many of its members would have wished. High Churchmen were Tory in politics, upheld kingly and priestly authority and believed that the best way to counter immorality and scepticism was to re-establish the lost authority of the Church and its courts; restored at the Restoration, these had proved far less effective than before. Between 1711 and 1714, when Tories dominated the Commons, occasional conformity and Dissenting schools were declared illegal, but the sacramental test was fitfully enforced; those who failed to take it were protected from prosecution by acts of indemnity. Low Churchmen were generally Whigs, sympathised with Dissenters and were open to new ideas. Some expressed doubts about the Trinity. Benjamin Hoadly saw no need for churches, confessions of faith, clergy or liturgies. He argued that all that God required was that people should be sincere in their beliefs. He became the pet hate of High Churchmen, which led Whig politicians to praise his 'moderation'. He held a series of bishoprics, ending his days at Winchester. (See Figure 15.3, Low Church Attack on the High Church and Figure 15.4, High Church Attack on the Low Church.)

The most spectacular clash between High and Low Church was the trial of Dr Henry Sacheverell in 1710. He preached on the text 'In peril among false brethren', castigating clerics like Hoadly and the Whig ministers who patronised them. He was impeached on a charge of seditious libel, convicted and banned from preaching for three years. His trial provoked riots in London and his journey to the Welsh Marches after the

Figures 15.3 & 15.4 These neatly sum up the polemic between Low and High Church. In the first, Sacheverell rides on the leading horse. The horses trample liberty, property and toleration underfoot. The passenger in the coach is 'Perkin' (the Pretender) and on the back of the coach a pair of wooden shoes (symbolising French absolutism) hang on a gibbet. In the second the lead rider is Hoadly, the horses' names include 'moderation' (a pejorative term for Tories), occasional conformity and

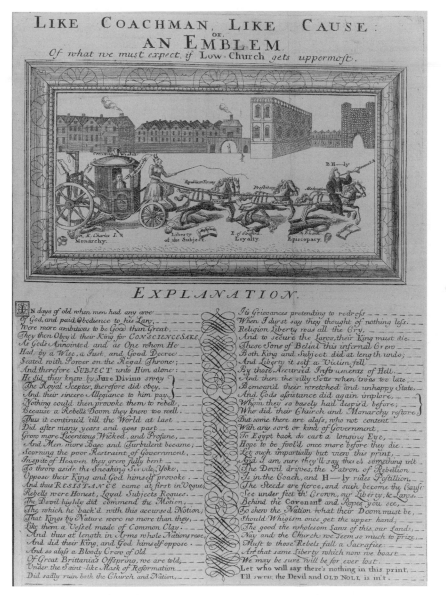

Figures 15.3 & 15.4 (Cont.)
Presbytery, the figure in the coach is crying 'no monarchy' and the Covenant hangs on the gibbet. Those trampled underfoot are Laud, Strafford and Charles I.

trial became a triumphal progress. The huge groundswell of support for Sacheverell emboldened Anne to replace her Whig ministers with Tories and a general election produced a Tory landslide. Low Churchmen may seem tolerant and 'modern' but High Churchmen enjoyed greater popular support. Their influence diminished because the

Figure 15.5 A fine new church built by public subscription showed the Church of England's strength in this thriving industrial town.

Hanoverian succession and the Whig supremacy ensured that Low Churchmen came to control the episcopate, reducing the level of conflict within the Church.

Church and Dissent

Many Anglican clergymen believed that the Church was in decline. The Toleration Act stated that everyone should attend either their parish church or a licensed meeting house, which proved unenforceable. But alongside dwindling congregations, especially in rural areas, were signs of vigour. Many churches were rebuilt, fitted with organs or 'beautified'; choral music was popular. Fine new churches were built in growing industrial cities like Birmingham and Liverpool. (See Figure 15.5, St Philip's Church, Birmingham, 1732.) Many churchgoers found a 'High Church' (or 'Anglican') style of worship, with its appeal to the senses, spiritually edifying. Many also shared the High Church ideal of divine right hereditary monarchy until the Hanoverian succession rendered it irrelevant. In 1715 angry crowds took out their frustration on Dissenting meeting houses; later they were reduced to provocative but futile Jacobite gestures; Anglican sermons gained the reputation of sending congregations to sleep. The parish system could not respond easily to shifting patterns of population. Some older towns, like Norwich or Winchester, had far more parishes than they needed but often growing towns had far too few: Hull had two parishes, Portsmouth only one. Areas of rural industry were even worse provided for.

After the explosion of puritan radicalism in the 1640s and 1650s, Dissenting denominations consolidated, trying to ensure that members conformed to their rules of doctrine and behaviour: mavericks were expelled. This led to small schisms or secessions which left the core membership little diminished. The only serious attempt at co-operation between two denominations, Presbyterians and Congregationalists, ended in 1719 when the latter refused to approve a Presbyterian ordinand with doubts about the Trinity. As the Presbyterians became less orthodox and more theological they lost much of their support; the Congregationalists clung to traditional Calvinism. Their evangelical impetus faded and pastors preached to the converted. Congregations were governed by the pastor and a few leading male members. Quaker meetings were increasingly directed by 'weighty friends' and the role of women, once so prominent, became narrowly circumscribed. Eventually they ceased to seek converts. This is not to suggest that Dissent withered away. Often parents had large families and their children remained within the flock. Although Old Dissent was slow to respond to the challenge of Methodism, by the 1750s the Congregationalists and Baptists were expanding rapidly. Dissenters' growing wealth and numbers were reflected in their meeting houses. At first these were small, often tucked away in side streets for fear of High Church crowds. By the 1730s such fears had abated and substantial meeting houses, like the Octagon at Norwich, were built by wealthy congregations. (See Figure 15.6, Octagon Chapel, Norwich.)

Dissenters wielded significant economic and social influence, but how numerous were they? In 1676 a census of the greater part of England and Wales was designed to show that Nonconformists were a small minority. The parish clergy were asked how many people never came to church; those who came occasionally were counted as conformists. The figure for Nonconformists came out at 4.4 per cent. The second source was the 'Evans list', compiled between 1715 and 1718 at the instigation of a group of Presbyterian, Congregationalist and Baptist ministers. They aimed to demonstrate to the new Whig regime the Dissenters' numbers, wealth and electoral influence, with a view to repealing the laws against them. Material about the Quakers can be gathered from their voluminous records. The figures, as compiled by Michael Watts, suggest that Dissenters made up 6.2 per cent of the population of England and 5 7 per cent in Wales. Presbyterians comprised more than half the Dissenters in England. They were strongest in areas where Puritanism had been prevalent under Elizabeth, such as Lancashire and Devon. In Wales, Independents and Baptists together outnumbered Presbyterians by almost two to one.

Figure 15.6 Initially a Presbyterian and later a Unitarian chapel, the Octagon was described by John Wesley as 'the most elegant meeting house in Europe'.

Methodism

By the 1730s religious conflict in England seemed to have ended. 'Enthusiasm' and spiritual anxiety were seen as unfashionable and uncouth. Both Dissenters and Anglicans largely ignored the increasing numbers, in industrial towns and villages, who lacked regular religious provision. Their working and living conditions were harsh; sickness, drunkenness and violence were endemic. Few preachers carried the Gospel to these people, but those who did were influenced by revivalist movements in America and Wales. Others formed 'religious societies', for mutual instruction and edification; many of their members underwent conversion experiences, including John and Charles Wesley, of the 'Holy Club' at Oxford. Like many early evangelicals their background was High Church, not Puritan. Charles became famous for writing hymns, while John's preaching sought to bring to others the faith he had found: 'not barely a speculative rational thing, a cold lifeless assent, a train of ideas in the head; but also … a sure confidence which a man hath in God that … *his* sins are forgiven and *he* reconciled to the favour of God'. Wesley's stress on the spiritual equality of rich and poor was denounced as socially subversive. He preferred preaching to the poor: 'Oh how hard it is to be shallow enough for a polite audience.' Clergymen and gentlemen incited mobs to attack Methodist meetings, echoing the response to the early Quakers.

Methodists had much in common with Puritans, but they were less intellectual – itinerant lay preachers with limited professional training played a key role in the movement – and not much interested in Church government: initially they saw themselves as revitalising the Church, not starting a new denomination, so they did not seek licences under the Toleration Act. Each 'society' (congregation) was divided into 'bands' for exhortation and discipline and all were part of a hierarchical organisation, headed by John Wesley. Many Methodists, especially those influenced by Calvinism, urged him to separate from the Church, but Wesley regarded himself as an Anglican. He took communion regularly and urged his followers to meet outside Anglican service times. Many could not understand his attitude, but it made some sense. He directed the thrust of the movement away from the South East, where the Church was comparatively strong, towards the industrial areas of the North and West, where it was weak. Methodism might seem a throwback to times of enthusiasm and superstition, but it was very effective – a reminder, perhaps, that people cannot live by reason alone.

Divisions among Protestants 1690–1750: Scotland

The General Assembly hoped that the re-establishment of Presbyterianism would bring a return to the Covenanter regime of the early 1640s, but it was to be disappointed. The civil authorities refused to punish excommunicates; a Kincardineshire man told his kirk session that the Pope excommunicated them every year and they were none the worse for it. Scotland north of the Tay was effectively unrepresented in the Assembly and its orders were largely ignored. Hardline Presbyterians felt increasingly beleaguered. One spoke of the threat from 'atheism, deism, Socinianism, irreligion, profaneness, scepticism, formality, hatred of godliness and a bitter persecuting spirit'; he called, with no sense of irony, for the harsh punishment of deviants. In 1696, an Edinburgh divinity student was executed for allegedly denying the divinity of Christ. John Simson, Professor of Theology at Glasgow, was investigated for alleged Arminian beliefs and later accused of Arianism and suspended. But although the hardliners' mindset did not change, that of the wider society did. Despite Simson's difficulties, the universities, where the clergy were trained, were an important catalyst. New professors at Glasgow, 'in the western provinces of Scotland where the clergy till that period were narrow and bigoted … opened and enlarged the minds of the students which soon gave them a turn for free enquiry, the result of which was candour and liberality of sentiment'.

Additional impetus for the spread of more liberal ideas came from the newly established British Parliament in London, which in 1712 granted Episcopalians freedom of worship. As the Presbyterians had taken over the parish churches the Episcopalians opened meeting houses. The clergy were required to take the oath of allegiance and abjure the **Pretender**, which created division between Jurors and Non-jurors. Parliament also replaced election by heritors and elders with **lay patronage** (again). Congregations were often deeply resentful, but many landowners wanted a moderate, urbane minister in the manse. By the 1750s 'Moderates' formed an identifiable movement within the Kirk.

In the first half of the eighteenth century the unity of the Kirk came under strain from two opposed approaches to the binding authority of the Covenants and the Westminster Confession. On one hand 'New Light' theology argued that human reason could not resolve fundamental questions, so it was wrong to force people to accept as true interpretations laid down in man-made documents like the Confession. On the other, traditionalists deplored the compromises forced on them by the Union and resented swearing allegiance to a monarch required by law to conform to the Church of England. Some seceded from the Kirk, but they disagreed among themselves on the lawfulness of taking oaths to the civil authorities and the extent to which historic covenants were still binding. These secessions differed from the divisions within English Dissent based on the duty of the godly to separate from the ungodly. The seceders continued to believe in the national Church and hoped that in due course it would return to what they saw as its essential principles; in the meantime they kept their faith pure and the reaction against the Moderates added to their numbers.

Divisions among Protestants 1690–1750: Ireland

In the 1690s Church of Ireland members felt increasingly threatened. Harvest failures drove as many as 50,000 Scots to migrate to Ireland, leading to fears that they would be outnumbered by Presbyterians. Their anxieties were increased by the re-establishment of Presbyterianism and persecution of Episcopalians in Scotland. From 1690 the Synod of Ulster legislated for Presbyterians: 'They are a people embodied under their lay elders, presbyteries and synods', wrote the Archbishop of Dublin in 1716, 'and will be just so far the king's subjects as their lay elders and presbyteries will allow them.' They extended their influence outside Ulster; some called their church 'the Church of Ireland'. The government had connived at their building meeting houses so long as the number of congregations did not increase, but it grew by nearly half between 1689 and 1707 and by another third between 1707 and 1716. (See Box 15.4, The Fears of the Church of Ireland.) The Ulster bishops and clergy tried to counter this perceived threat. No Toleration Act had been passed in Ireland so Presbyterians were legally vulnerable.

BOX 15.4: The Fears of the Church of Ireland

An anonymous pamphlet (ascribed by a contemporary to the bishop of Meath) expresses the fear that the Presbyterians will become the dominant Protestant denomination in Ireland and sets out the case for a sacramental test.

'Tis well known that the British [Scots] are already possessed of near one fourth part of the kingdom, that they have spread themselves into other provinces and that there are frequent colonies coming out of Scotland to carry on the plantation of the party; that the commons are generally fond of the Solemn League and Covenant and retain an affection for it (though the nobility and gentry are otherwise affected); that by the second article of the Covenant they are bound to endeavour, without respect of persons, the extirpation of prelacy as well as popery; that the Assembly in their Catechism have declared that a false worship is not to be tolerated,

that they judge ours to be such; that the Kirk of Scotland hath acted in pursuance of these doctrines since His Majesty's happy accession to the crown and would allow no toleration to the Church party in Scotland, though they received several messages from His Majesty in favour of their persecuted brethren; so that by these doctrines and practices 'tis easy to infer what sort of usage we are to expect from them if they had the power in their own hands; and they cannot think it unreasonable that some stop should be put to that power which, when once grasped, will put them upon the execution of their principles ... No state did ever yet put its subjects into places of trust and power that thought themselves obliged in conscience to overturn its constitutions ...

[Anthony Dopping?], *The Case of the Dissenters of Ireland Consider'd in Reference to the Sacramental Test* (Dublin, 1695), pp. 2–3.

The clergy denied the validity of their marriages and required them to bury their dead according to the Church's rites. Presbyterian schoolmasters were forbidden to teach and Presbyterians were forced to pay tithes and serve as churchwardens. **Convocation** was briefly recalled late in Anne's reign, leading to attempts to enforce the 1560 Act of Uniformity and attacks on Dissenting meeting houses. More often, however, the clergy were outnumbered and magistrates sided with the Presbyterians. Presbyterian crowds harassed Church of Ireland clergy and disrupted burial services. Criticised for building meeting houses, they opened schools as well.

The Sacramental Test

Faced with the Presbyterian threat, some Churchmen advocated a sacramental test. Following a proposal to extend the Toleration Act to Ireland, the Lords called for the extension of the Test and Corporation Acts as well. In 1704 an English Tory ministry added to a new Irish Act against popery a clause requiring all those holding civil, military and municipal offices to take communion according to the rites of the Church. With Catholics already excluded from offices this was clearly designed against Presbyterians, but the English ministers reasoned (correctly) that Irish Whigs would not vote against a popery bill. In 1715, with the Whigs again in power, Presbyterians were given commissions in the militia and army and used their positions to harass Churchmen and Tories. When the emergency was over the English Whigs tried repeatedly to use their alleged good service as a pretext to repeal the Test, but the Irish Parliament was immoveable. Many peers and MPs were Whigs in politics and Tories in religion, or resented English interference in Irish affairs. When Parliament delivered yet another rebuff in 1733 the English ministers gave up.

It is a moot point how many Presbyterians were excluded from office as a result of the Test. Fewer and fewer were of sufficient status to serve as magistrates, army officers or MPs, 'so when their disabilities shall be taken off their want of fortune and interest will always hinder them from coming into the militia in any invidious or dangerous numbers'. The sons of Presbyterian landowners conformed to the established Church, partly, no doubt, to qualify for office. Probably the most significant impact of the Test was the exclusion of Presbyterians from municipal corporations; in the 1690s they had been able to control Belfast and Derry.

The Waning of Conflict

By the 1730s the relationship of Church and Presbyterians had lost much of its animus. Immigration from Scotland was offset by emigration to America. Some Presbyterians clung to Covenanting principles: the Seceders, who had broken with the Scottish Kirk on the issue of lay patronage, began to organise in Ulster. But more liberal ideas also reached Ireland. As in Scotland, some ministers questioned the authority of the Covenants and the Westminster Confession; their colleagues often agreed to differ, in order to maintain unity. Some members of the Church of Ireland developed similar ideas about reasonableness and politeness: there was no longer an unbridgeable gulf between Churchman and Presbyterian. As the Church left Presbyterians' churches alone, their hostility diminished; Presbyterian communion assemblies were now smaller – usually only a single parish – so seemed less threatening than under Charles II. Shortage of labour meant that both Churchmen and Presbyterians, eager to attract workers, could not be too fussy about their religious views. After the failed rebellion of 1715 Catholics posed less of a threat to Protestant Ireland, so neither group needed to pose as the main defence against popery.

Conclusion

By 1750 Protestantism had fragmented in all three kingdoms, but did this seriously weaken it? Clergymen might bicker, denominations might abuse one another, and there was occasional violence against meeting houses, but this rarely led to serious casualties.

Protestants fought for and against the Jacobite rebellions of 1715 and 1745, but the key issue was the succession and the main religious division was between Protestant and Catholic. This division was most blurred in Scotland, thanks to continuing Episcopalian support for the House of Stuart. In England, Tory support for Hanover was often lukewarm but in the final analysis most reluctantly preferred Hanover to Stuart. The legal recognition of most Protestant denominations under the Toleration Act made them part of the establishment in a way that Catholics or Non-jurors were not. Church of Ireland and Irish Presbyterians abused one another but joined to maintain and extend the penal laws against the Catholic majority. In all three kingdoms the religious ethos of the ruling elite was Protestant. Protestants might have Catholic friends (or, in Ireland, Catholic servants and tenants), but Protestant dominance did not seem seriously challenged: banditry and agrarian violence were sporadic and localised. Throughout the wars of the eighteenth century anti-Catholicism gave a focus and coherence to anti-French feeling which disputes between Protestants lacked; common Protestantism went deeper than Protestant differences.

SUGGESTIONS FOR FURTHER READING

Most works relating to this topic have a 'one-country' rather than a 'British' approach. The major exceptions are two fine books by T. Harris: *Restoration: Charles II and his Kingdoms 1660–85* (London, 2005) and *Revolution: the Great Crisis of the British Monarchy 1685–1720* (London, 2006). See also Macinnes, *The British Revolution*, J. Smyth, *The Making of the United Kingdom 1660–1800* (Harlow, 2001) and D. Hirst, *Dominion: England and its Island Neighbours 1500–1707* (Oxford, 2012).

ENGLAND

Most of the works that follow are comparatively specialised. None matches the broad sweep of M.R. Watts, *The Dissenters from the Reformation to the French Revolution* (Oxford, 1978). • The best account of the Church in the 1640s is J.S. Morrill, 'The Church of England 1642–9', in Morrill, *The Nature of the English Revolution*. • For the gathered churches, see G.F. Nuttall, *Visible Saints: the Congregational Way 1640–60* (Oxford, 1957), M. Tolmie, *The Triumph of the Saints: the Separate Churches of London 1616–49* (Cambridge, 1977) and C. Durston and J. Maltby (eds.), *Religion in Revolutionary England* (Manchester, 2006). • The literature on Quakerism is vast but, for a thoughtful introduction, see A. Davies, *The Quakers in English Society 1655–1725* (Oxford, 2000). • For Wales see S.K. Roberts, 'Religion, Politics and Welshness, 1649–60', in I. Roots (ed.), *'Into Another Mould': Aspects of the Interregnum* (Exeter, 1998). • Understanding of the Restoration Church settlement is inhibited by the dearth of sources: for attempts to make sense of it, see I.M. Green, *The Re-Establishment of the Church of England, 1660–3* (Oxford, 1978), P. Seaward, *The Cavalier Parliament and the Reconstruction of the Old Regime, 1661–7* (Cambridge, 1989) and J. Miller, *After the Civil Wars: English Government and Politics in the Reign of Charles II* (Harlow, 2000). • The best study of the Church is J. Spurr, *The Restoration Church of England* (New Haven, 1991). See also T. Harris, P. Seaward and M. Goldie (eds.), *The Politics of Religion in Restoration England* (Oxford, 1990), especially Goldie's 'Danby, the Bishops and the Whigs'. • See also two other important essays by Goldie: 'The Theory of Intolerance in Restoration England', in O.P. Grell, J.I. Israel and N. Tyacke (eds.), *From Persecution to Toleration* (Oxford, 1991), and M. Goldie, 'The Political Thought of the Anglican Revolution', in R. Beddard (ed.), *The Revolutions of 1688* (Oxford, 1991). On persecution, see Harris, *Restoration* and J. Miller, '"A Suffering People": English Quakers and their Neighbours, c. 1650–1700', *Past and Present*, 188 (2005). • On the Revolution of 1688–9 and the Toleration Act, see J. Spurr, 'The Church of England, Comprehension and the Toleration Act of 1689', *English Historical Review*, 104 (1989), Harris, *Revolution* and Watts, *Dissenters*. • For the impact of the Revolution on the Church see G.V. Bennett, *The Tory Crisis in Church and State 1688–1730* (Oxford, 1975) and G. Holmes, *The Trial of Dr Sacheverell* (London, 1973), a first-class piece of scholarship which is also highly readable: Chapter 2 gives an excellent brief analysis of divisions in the Church. See also D.A. Spaeth, *The Church in an Age of Danger: Parsons and Parishioners 1660–1740* (Cambridge, 2000). • For the Presbyterians, see C.G. Bolam, J.J. Goring, H.L. Short and R. Thomas, *The English Presbyterians* (London, 1968). • For the Methodists, see R.E. Davies and E.G. Rupp (eds.), *History of the Methodist Church in Great Britain: I. The Eighteenth Century* (London, 1965). J.D. Walsh, 'Origins of the Evangelical Revival', in G.V. Bennett and J.D. Walsh (eds.), *Essays in Modern Church History* (London, 1966), is old but perceptive and wide-ranging. • See also the thoughtful discussion in P. Langford, *A Polite and Commercial People: England 1727–83* (Oxford, 1989), Chapter 6.

SCOTLAND

For 1640–60 see Macinnes, *British Revolution* and Brown, *Kingdom or Province?* • For 1660–90 see Harris, *Restoration* and *Revolution*; also J.M. Buckroyd, *Church and State in Scotland, 1660–81* (Edinburgh, 1980) and I.B. Cowan, *The Scottish Covenanters, 1660–88* (1976). A. Raffe, 'The Restoration, the Revolution and the Failure of Episcopacy in Scotland', in T. Harris and S. Taylor (eds.), *The Final Crisis of the Stuart Monarchy: the Revolutions of 1689–91* (Woodbridge, 2013), is a thoughtful recent study. • For the eighteenth century, see C.G. Brown, *A Social History of Religion in Scotland since 1730* (1987) and D. Allan, *Scotland in the Eighteenth Century* (Harlow, 2002).

IRELAND

Gillespie, *Seventeenth-Century Ireland* and S.J. Connolly, *Divided Kingdom: Ireland 1630–1800* (Oxford, 2008) are excellent starting points, as is the *New History of Ireland*, volume III. See also S.J. Connolly, *Religion, Law and Power: the Making of Protestant Ireland 1660–1760* (Oxford, 1992). • For Dissent, see P. Kilroy, *Protestant Dissent and Controversy in Ireland 1660–1714* (Cork, 1994), R. Gillespie, 'Dissenters and Nonconformists, 1661–1700', in K. Herlihy (ed.), *The Irish Dissenting Tradition 1650–1750* (Dublin, 1995), and D. Hayton, 'The Impact of the Irish Sacramental Test on Irish Dissenting Politics', in K. Herlihy (ed.), *The Politics of Irish Dissent, 1650–1800* (Dublin, 1997), reprinted in Hayton, *Ruling Ireland*.

SUMMARY

- There are two major themes in this period. The first is the multiplication of gathered churches between 1640 and 1660. This happened mainly in England and Wales with the collapse of effective authority in the established Church, and extensive debate and experimentation, strongly influenced by millenarianism. The result was the emergence of Independents, Baptists, Quakers and a multiplicity of small and often ephemeral sects. The Presbyterians were not part of this process: instead they offered an alternative Puritan vision for the established Church. They became a separate denomination after they were effectively expelled from the Church of England in 1662.
- The second theme is division within the established churches. The gathered churches had their schisms too, but these were generally small-scale because the churches maintained a degree of discipline and cohesion. The re-introduction of bishops in Scotland split the established Church but the gulf between Presbyterian and Episcopalian was too large for a single Church to accommodate them. The Presbyterians emerged triumphant in 1690 but the Episcopalians remained a substantial dissenting minority. In the eighteenth and nineteenth centuries Scottish Presbyterians showed an increased susceptibility to schism about niceties of theology and the extent to which the Covenants were still binding.
- In Ireland any common ground between the Church of Ireland and Presbyterianism disappeared with the full establishment of Presbyterianism in the 1640s and the exclusion of Presbyterians from the Church of Ireland in the 1660s. The two churches remained mutually hostile; in addition the Presbyterians shared the Scots' propensity to schism.
- In Wales, the impetus given to Nonconformity in the 1640s and 1650s was maintained and the Church of England steadily lost ground, especially with the growth of industrial towns in the nineteenth century.

QUESTIONS FOR STUDENTS

1. Why did gathered churches flourish in England in the 1640s and 1650s?

2. Why was episcopacy established in Scotland in the 1660s and abolished in 1690?

3. Why were Presbyterians not included in the Church of Ireland under Charles II?

4. Assess the significance of the English Toleration Act of 1689.

5. Account for the increasing divisions in Presbyterianism in all three kingdoms after 1690.

16 Popular Politics 1640–1750

TIMELINE

1661	Act against Tumultuous Petitioning
1662	Licensing Act
1679–81	Exclusion Crisis: three contested elections; petitions and addresses; Whigs and Tories
1681–5	Tory reaction: persecution of Dissenters, confiscation of borough charters; Killing Times in Scotland
1688–9	Attacks on Catholics and (in Scotland) Episcopalians
1694	Triennial Act, leading to ten general elections in twenty years
1696	Association
1706–7	Riots against Union (Scotland)
1710	Sacheverell riots
1714	Celebration of George I's coronation disrupted by Tories
1715	Attacks on meeting houses; Riot Act
1716	Septennial Act
1724–5	Furore over Wood's Halfpence (Ireland)
1725	Glasgow Malt Tax riots

Introduction

For a long time historians assumed that history was the story of great men (and occasionally women) and that ordinary people played no part in government and had no say in the way they were governed. Increasingly research into town and village communities has revealed the extent of participation in government, not just by the 'better sort' but also by relatively humble people. Meanwhile left-wing historians argued that the popular radicalism which became apparent in the later eighteenth century could be traced back into earlier centuries. They detected a largely underground tradition running from the Peasants' Revolt ('When Adam delved and Eve span/Who was then the gentleman?') through the Levellers and their Agreements of the People to Tom Paine. Here was a view of 'popular politics' as radical politics, created by people who thought for themselves, unlike the unthinking masses programmed by the Church to accept their subordination as part of the natural order. However, as historians looked more closely at the civil wars or the street politics of Georgian England it became clear that popular politics embraced a wide spectrum of opinion, conservative as well as radical, Royalist as well as Parliamentarian, Tory as well as Whig. Those who held such opinions might be influenced by the propaganda of the government or the clergy, but that does not mean that they could not make up their own minds. While many peasants followed their landlords to war in the 1640s, many others refused to do so; and landlords, in large numbers, fought on both sides. There had been divisions of opinion before the 1640s, but they were rarely as deep and persistent as those left by the civil wars. Issues such as the nature of the monarchy, or the relationship between Church and Dissent, persisted long after 1660. So did memories of the wars themselves: election-day crowds chanted 'down with the Roundheads, down with the Rump' in George I's reign and beyond.

This chapter falls into five main sections. The first three deal with the issues which shaped popular politics: most, but not all, were legacies of the civil wars. The fourth looks at the spread of news (information) and ideas. While it deals at some length with print, it shows that the importance of print varied and that news and ideas could be disseminated in other ways. The fifth looks at modes of popular political action – petitions, elections and riot.

Issues: 1. 'Corruption' and the Misuse of Law

Complaints about the abuse of power by royal servants are found in the Peasants' Revolt and Cade's rebellion. Usually this 'corruption' was blamed on 'evil counsellors' rather than the King himself – plausibly enough when the King was a child or a nonentity. At times, however, it became clear that the problem did lie with the King: critics of Charles

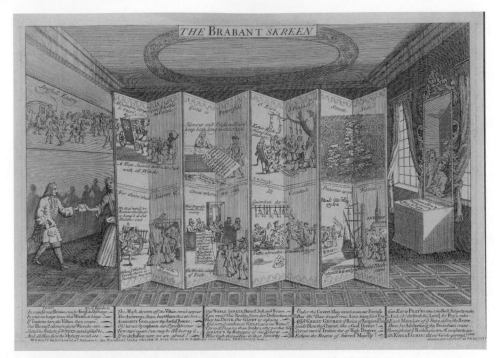

Figure 16.1 *The Brabant Skreen*, 1721. Walpole's success in protecting the King's ministers and courtiers from prosecution for their involvement in the South Sea Bubble earned him the nickname of 'the skreen' or 'skreen-master'. In this print the Company's cashier, Robert Knight, has fled to Antwerp, where the authorities refuse to extradite him. Although the print praises George I, his mistress is shown handing Knight a safe conduct (left) while on the right a mirror reveals three figures behind the screen (none of them explicitly identified as Walpole). The paper below the mirror reads 'patience, time and money set everything to rights'.

I might not say openly that he was the source of their grievances, but he clearly was. This was equally true of James II, but the Whigs in the Convention allowed the issue to be fudged to avoid alienating the Tories.

As the effective direction of government passed from monarchs to ministers, allegations of 'corruption' and misgovernment focused on politicians. 'Corruption' was emotive but vague: it included methods of management which politicians justified when in office and condemned when in opposition. It was also used to describe the ability of institutions outside the formal political process, like the Bank and the big trading companies, to influence government. The electoral techniques and methods of parliamentary management used by Whig oligarchs differed little from those used by Tories, but after 1715 the Whigs had the advantage of being in power and controlling the government's patronage. Moreover, Walpole's skill in giving backbenchers the policies they wanted – notably keeping the land tax low – meant that his critics had few arguments to use against him other than accusations of 'corruption'. Walpole's association with 'corruption' at times made him bitterly unpopular, notably when he managed

BOX 16.1: The King's Evil and the Royal Touch

Scrofula, a form of tuberculosis, was a common, unpleasant and sometimes fatal disease. Its major symptoms were fevers and, more visibly, swellings of the lymph nodes in the neck and unsightly sores on the face. The belief that it could be cured by the King's touch originated in England and France in the eleventh century and remained strong in the seventeenth: thousands tried to come to London to be cured. They had first to secure certificates that they had not been touched before, and from physicians or surgeons, locally and in London, that they were indeed suffering from the disease. There were numerous testimonies that people had been cured: the severity of the symptoms tended to vary, so it may have seemed that they had been.

The touching ceremonies were large and sometimes unruly. In theory they were limited to 200 people but sometimes there were as many as 600, not counting spectators. Officials of the royal court tried to maintain a degree of order; the sick were led up one at a time and the King stroked each one under the chin with both hands. The staging of the ceremonies was designed to inspire awe and wonder in those present. When the King was at Whitehall he normally touched in the Banqueting House, where the ceiling showed Charles's grandfather, James I, being carried up into heaven. At Windsor he touched in the Chapel Royal, in front of a large mural showing Christ healing the sick, a less than subtle claim to miraculous powers.

See especially Anna Keay, *The Magnificent Monarch*, pp. 112–19, 193, 211. Also www.sciencemuseum.org.uk/broughttolife/techniques/kingsevil.aspx (accessed 25/11/2014).

the 'cover-up' after the South Sea Bubble, a financial scam which bankrupted many investors. Walpole partly satisfied the public's demands for vengeance by agreeing that the real and personal property of the South Sea Company's directors should be confiscated, but he resisted demands for an enquiry into the involvement of ministers for which he was vilified in the press, depicted as a 'screen', or 'screen-master', covering up all kinds of misdeeds. (See Figure 16.1, *The Brabant Skreen*, 1721.)

Accusations of 'corruption' did not end with Walpole. They continued in various forms – attacks on 'the **influence of the Crown**' and misconduct in elections, not to mention criticism of the allegedly excessive influence of big business or organised labour. They cannot be said to have been created or perpetuated by the civil wars, but other issues can, and we shall now consider them.

Issues: 2. Monarchy and the Constitution

This links two distinct topics, each with implications for the other. The divine right of kings originated in the realms of political theory and the Church's endorsement of monarchy. The coronation ceremony, with the anointing of the King, emphasised the sacred and helped to create a mystical view of monarchy, expressed most visibly through the belief that the **royal touch** could cure scrofula. (See Box 16.1, The King's Evil and the Royal Touch.) Far from becoming outmoded, belief in the royal touch remained strong after the Restoration. Hard-headed aldermen from Norwich and Bristol paid for sick people to go to London to be 'touched' by the King. Charles II, widely seen as a cynical monarch, took his healing duties seriously. Between 1660 and 1685 he may have touched as many as 100,000 people. James II (and briefly Monmouth) continued the tradition, as did Anne. William III dismissed it as superstition and the Georges quietly laid it aside.

The royal touch could be seen as a peripheral feature of monarchy: it showed a widely held veneration, but did not affect the way the King governed. Two other aspects were more contentious. The first was the hereditary succession to the Crown. The mystical attributes of monarchy were believed to be transmitted through the royal bloodline, but the emphasis on heredity was also practical. Among English landowners, **primogeniture** was the norm, with the estate passing to the eldest son, or the eldest daughter in the absence of sons. Primogeniture had the advantage of certainty, but there was a danger that the rightful heir would prove unsuitable. If he was mad, as Henry VI sometimes was, a regency could be established, but James II's conversion, while politically foolish, did not amount to insanity. It led first to the Exclusion Crisis, then to his expulsion from England and finally to the Act of Settlement of 1701. Most Tories put their Protestantism before their attachment to the hereditary principle and the House of Stuart, but showed their dislike of the Hanoverians by Jacobite gestures, wearing white roses on the Pretender's birthday, drinking toasts to 'the king over the water', and singing songs like 'The king shall enjoy his own again'. Their behaviour convinced the Georges that the Whigs alone were loyal to Hanover, which encouraged further gestures of defiance from the Tories.

Belief in the divine right of kings could also influence the way monarchs governed. The Tudors and Stuarts claimed to rule by divine right, and developed the claim that active resistance to royal authority was, in effect, resistance against God. But if subjects were denied a right to resist misgovernment, what remedy did they have? Supporters of divine right argued that they could petition with prayers and tears and stressed that the King would be constrained to rule justly by his need to answer to God for his stewardship. Traditionally English and Scottish nobles had not found such arguments convincing and resorted to force to bring recalcitrant kings to heel. James I told the English Parliament that a king who failed to rule according to law degenerated into a tyrant, but his subjects found that James's (and Charles I's) understanding of the law differed profoundly from theirs. Charles II generally kept within the law, at least as understood by the Tories; James II emphatically did not. At the Restoration Parliament was content to leave the royal prerogative as it traditionally had been and if anything was inclined to strengthen it, because the main threat to the re-established order seemed to come from below. By the late 1670s issues which had seemed uncontentious had become the focus of bitter partisan debate.

The most fundamental was the hereditary succession. This had not been an issue in 1640–2 or the early 1660s because there seemed no reason to challenge it, but the prospect of a popish successor raised fears of 'popery and arbitrary government'. To be effective, James's exclusion from the succession had to be by Act of Parliament. The general elections of 1679 twice returned a House of Commons with a majority in favour of exclusion, but Charles dissolved the first before the exclusion bill could pass through both Houses and delayed meeting the second for more than a year. The Whigs responded with petitions demanding that Charles should summon a Parliament and keep it in being until all grievances had been redressed. This challenged the King's prerogative of summoning and dismissing Parliament and went further than the Long Parliament in 1641, which had passed the Triennial Act and an Act against dissolving that Parliament without its consent. The Whigs also revived two demands of the Long Parliament which Charles I had refused to concede. They blamed evil counsellors for the King's more unpopular decisions but treated any advice which impeded exclusion as evil counsel. When the Commons assembled late in 1680 the Whigs launched a series of impeachments designed to deter ministers from giving advice unpalatable to the Whigs, thus in effect claiming a veto on the King's choice of ministers, like the Long Parliament in 1641–2. (They did not proceed with their impeachments because they were based on little or no evidence.) They also demanded that James's 'creatures' should be removed from all civil and military offices, raising echoes of the Militia Ordinance of 1642.

Although some Whigs believed in principle that the royal prerogative should be curbed, for many these demands arose from the practical obstacles to exclusion. As in 1641–2, concern for self-preservation led to demands that would have reduced the King to a figurehead. The Tories saw this clearly and talked of 'Forty-one' and the danger of revolution from below. Although the Whigs dismissed such talk as scare-mongering, the Tories were genuinely frightened and angry. They urged the King to crush the Whigs and Dissenters and the King increasingly complied, especially after the Rye House Plot. By 1688, however, they realised that the Whigs' warnings had been well founded and joined in the bipartisan replacement of James by William. The financial settlement of 1689–90 gave the Commons the financial power to enforce their interpretation of the constitution and the Act of Settlement of 1701 limited the power of a future foreign king. With rare exceptions the royal prerogative ceased to be a major political issue.

Issues: 3. Religion

The most basic religious division was between Protestant and Catholic and anti-popery was a central feature of English Protestant identity, despite the fact that Catholics made up only about 1 per cent of England's population. But anti-popery was not confined to anti-Catholic polemic. More radical Protestants used anti-popish rhetoric to attack 'popish' survivals in the Church of England's liturgy and government including ceremonies, homilies and bishops. Anglicans responded by claiming that, by undermining the Church, the Puritans were aiding the Catholics. Knowing that the Catholic

BOX 16.2: **Whig and Tory Writings on Anti-popery, 1679**

The first extract is from a typical Exclusionist pamphlet, more forcefully written than most. The second is by Roger L'Estrange, the most effective Tory polemicist of the Exclusion Crisis who, while not challenging familiar Protestant views of Catholicism, argued that anti-popery was being misused in order to undermine the government.

Whig

… imagine you see the whole town in a flame, occasioned this second time by the same popish malice which set it on fire before. At the same instant, fancy that amongst the distracted crowd you behold troops of papists ravishing your wives and daughters, dashing your little children's brains out against the walls, plundering your houses and cutting your own throats by the name of heretic dogs. Then represent to yourself the Tower playing off its cannon and battering down your houses about your ears. Also, casting your eye towards Smithfield, imagine you see your father or your mother … tied to a stake in the midst of flames, when with hands and eyes lifted up to heaven they scream and cry out to that God for whose cause they die, which was a frequent spectacle the last time popery reigned amongst us …

> C. Blount, *An Appeal from the Country to the City* (1679) reprinted in *State Tracts* (2 vols., London, 1689–92), I, pp. 401–2.

Tory

A legal and effectual provision against the danger of Romish practices and errors will never serve their turn, whose quarrel is barely to the name of popery, without understanding the thing itself. And if there were not a Roman Catholic left in the three kingdoms they would be never the better satisfied, for where they cannot find popery they will make it, nay, and be troubled too that they could not find it. It is no new thing for a popular outcry in the matter of religion to have a state faction in the belly of it. The first late clamour was against downright popery and then came on popishly affected (that sweeps all). The order of bishops and the discipline of the Church took their turns next; and the next blow was at the crown itself; when every man was made a papist that would not play the knave and the fool, for company, with the common people.

> R. L'Estrange, *History of the Plot* (London, 1679), Preface.

Church had justified the killing of heretical princes, some blamed the regicide on the Jesuits, or claimed that the radical sects and even the Presbyterians had been created by the Catholics in order to undermine the Anglican Church. Anti-popish rhetoric could also be used against Anglicans and Tories, especially given the perceived link between 'popery' and 'arbitrary government'. The Catholic Church shared with absolute monarchy an emphasis on top-down authority and (Protestants believed) a commitment to keeping the people in subjection and ignorance, while the demands of kings, soldiers and priests kept them poor. In this context Tory commitment to strong divine-right monarchy could be seen as evidence of popery. Anti-popery broadened out to include 'favourers of popery' or those who were 'popishly affected' – in effect Tories rather than Catholics. In response Tories argued that the Whigs were using anti-popery to overthrow Church and monarchy. (See Box 16.2, Whig and Tory Writings on Anti-popery, 1679, and Figure 16.2, *The Committee, or Popery in Masquerade*, 1680.)

Figure 16.2 In this Tory satire the various types of Dissenters, including Anabaptists and Quakers, conspire together, headed by the Presbyterians, to overthrow the monarchy and the Church. A bust of Charles I, together with his orb and sceptre, lie on the floor together with Magna Carta and the works of Richard Hooker, while the Solemn League and Covenant hangs on the wall, together with a banner reading 'we are a covenanting people'; a dog cries out 'no bishops'.

James II's reign gave a renewed force to anti-popery, which was maintained by the Jacobite threat. Whig ministers took the threat seriously and Whig polemic and demonstrations continually emphasised the danger from Jacobitism and popery. However, the major religious conflicts were now between Protestants. They had their roots, first in Elizabethan and Jacobean clashes between puritans and anti-puritans and then in the suppression of the Church of England and the fragmentation of Puritanism in the 1640s and 1650s (see Chapter 15). At the Restoration, Anglicans blamed the Independents and Baptists for the regicide, to which the Presbyterians had contributed by rebelling against the King. The Quakers had not existed in 1649 but they were denounced for overturning revealed and organised religion. The sects showed their hostility to lawful authority by separating from the Church, while the Presbyterians were accused of schism – dividing the Church by their wilful refusal to comply with its liturgy and government. Under Charles II Dissenters were depicted as subversive trouble-makers and laws were passed forbidding **conventicles**. Other Acts excluded them from public offices and municipal corporations. Although the laws against Dissent were potentially draconian, before the 1680s they were enforced sporadically. James II's offer of toleration drove the Church's leaders to make a rival offer. The Toleration Act of 1689 was the least the Anglicans and Tories could do to deliver on the bishops' assurances. Dissenters remained excluded from municipal and other offices, although many got round the restrictions by taking communion annually in an Anglican church to meet the requirements of the Test Act. Many Anglicans claimed that this demeaned communion, but the Churchmen themselves became divided as they struggled to adapt to the fact that the Church could no longer claim to be the Church of all English Protestants. The invective of High and Low Churchmen towards one another matched that between Churchmen and Dissenters, which led to the sacking of meeting houses.

News and Polemic

For political views to lead to political action, people needed to be aware of events and to gain a sense of the significance of that news through discussion. The most effective means of disseminating news and ideas was through print, but print had its limitations, partly from state controls on the press, partly through limited levels of literacy. This section will consider first other forms of transmission, word of mouth and scribal (handwritten) letters; then the extent of literacy; and finally print.

Word of Mouth and Handwritten Letters

Word of mouth was the simplest form of communication and within a community it could be quick and effective, if prone to distortion as stories were passed from one person to another. Most towns and villages were relatively small and news could spread quickly even in London. In December 1688, as James II's Irish soldiers headed home after his flight, rumours spread rapidly that they had burned several towns and slaughtered men, women and children. (These rumours were untrue: the soldiers had 'barely a knife to cut their victuals'.) On less fraught occasions, news could be transmitted by letters, either private correspondence or newsletters to paying subscribers. These newsletters were viewed with suspicion by the government and often intercepted at the post office, so most newsletter writers were careful what they wrote. Few were as reckless as Edward Coleman, whose newsletters were peppered with his own opinions, but John Dyer gained a reputation in Anne's reign for including material which others omitted; more remarkably his news was fresher than that found in the printed newspapers. Apart from the risk of interception, scribal newsletters had their drawbacks: they were expensive, but this could be offset by spreading the cost. Town corporations subscribed for one copy, which circulated among the aldermen. Taverns and coffee-houses purchased both scribal and printed news, which attracted customers. In the 1660s there was little printed news, but Samuel Pepys picked up information from the royal court, the Royal Exchange and various taverns; he seldom visited coffee-houses, which later became notorious as centres for the discussion of news.

Literacy

It is often assumed that levels of literacy (the ability to read and write) remained low until the provision of state elementary education in the nineteenth century. There was a rapid expansion of grammar schools in the sixteenth and early seventeenth centuries but this went into reverse during the eighteenth century and some all but disappeared. Grammar schools catered for the sons of gentlemen, professionals (especially the clergy), yeomen and wealthier tradesmen. Even supposedly 'free' schools cost money and poor families needed their children to start earning from about 7 years old. However, focusing on grammar schools, which left written records, gives an incomplete picture. There were also many village schools, with a single master, who taught basic reading, writing and arithmetic for a relatively modest salary. Many such schools left few or no records, but some had a more continuous existence. In the wealthy village of Willingham, Cambridgeshire, a hundred villagers clubbed together, paying £1 a year each (a substantial salary) to hire a schoolmaster. In Cambridgeshire between 1574 and 1628, 23 villages had continuous schools or teachers, 55 had teachers some of the time and in only 23 is there no record of a teacher. In the later seventeenth century there are fewer references to teachers, but the records are less full. Cambridgeshire, thanks to the university, would have had an unusually high concentration of graduates in need of employment. In general, England lagged well behind Scotland, where a parish-based school system was well established by the second half of the seventeenth century and literacy rates were substantially higher (except in the Highlands).

Evidence for the provision of schooling is too scattered and unreliable to give an overall picture of literacy and, as we shall see, not everyone learned literacy skills in a school. It is impossible to measure the ability to read but it is possible to measure the ability to write, through signatures (as distinct from marks) on wills, inventories and depositions (statements in court). These suggest that between the 1520s and 1714 writing literacy increased from about 10 per cent to 45 per cent among men and from 1 per cent to 25 per cent among women. Whereas today children learn reading and writing together, in the seventeenth century reading was taught before writing. Moreover, while some people – professionals and those trading over distance, for example – had a functional need to write, many others did not: labourers and village craftsmen could negotiate face to face with employers and had no need of written agreements. But they might want to read for other reasons: access to the Bible or simple curiosity about the world or the desire to be entertained. It seems very probable that many people learned to read who did not go on to learn to write. We cannot know how many, and the evidence is anecdotal, but many women, even very poor women, learned to read (and sometimes write) despite the scarcity of formal schooling for girls. (See Box 16.3, Literacy Among the Poor.)

BOX 16.3: Literacy Among the Poor

Thomas Tryon

The son of a poor tiler, Thomas ended his life as a merchant in London. He began his schooling at five but soon quit to work in the cloth industry, spinning and carding [combing] wool. After some years he began to earn a few pence helping shepherds look after their flocks and persuaded his father to buy him a few sheep. At thirteen he could not read and set out to acquire an education.

… Thinking of the vast usefulness of reading I bought me a primer and got now one, now another [of the shepherds] to teach me to spell, and so learned to read imperfectly, my teachers themselves being not ready readers. But in a little while having learned to read competently well, I was desirous to learn to write, but was at a great loss for a master, none of my fellow-shepherds being able to teach me. At last I bethought myself of a lame young man who taught some poor people's children to read and write; and having by this time got some two sheep of my own I applied myself to him, and agreed with him to give him one of my sheep to teach me to make the letters and join them together. But I was as much of a loss for time, being forced to get my fellow shepherds now and then to look after my sheep whilst I went to learn, and thus [in?] some time I attained to write well enough for common use, improving my hand by frequent practice.

> *Some Memoirs of the Life of Mr Tho. Tryon …*
> *Written by Himself* (London, 1705), pp. 13–16.

Elizabeth Bowler

While Tryon left a fairly full account of his education, we do not know how Bowler, a deaf mute in her twenties, learned to write (and presumably read). The document does not state explicitly that she was deaf and dumb from birth, but nor does it say she was not. The fact that the clerk of the court wrote Kingman's name in capitals suggests that he was very surprised that she could write.

Buckinghamshire Quarter Sessions, Aylesbury, 23 July 1721 John Kingman junior … adjudged to be the putative father of a male bastard born to Elizabeth Bowler, spinster, who was both deaf and dumb. The said Elizabeth Bowler was able to answer by signs and demonstrations all questions put to her by persons in court who were well acquainted with her in household and other work.

[Sarah Clarke and Mary Topping] stated that they had been well acquainted with Elizabeth Bowler for the past twenty years. By signs in court she said she was with child by Jack Kingham. It was begotten in her father's shop in Princes Risborough last harvest home, although usually he had no carnal knowledge of her body … When asked to write the name of the man she printed in block capitals JOHN KINGMAN.

> W. le Hardy (ed.), *Calendar of Quarter Sessions*
> *Records* (Aylesbury, 1958), V, p. 110.

Print

The growth of literacy was accompanied by a great increase in the volume of print: the number of surviving titles increased exponentially between the sixteenth and seventeenth century (especially after 1640) and again between the seventeenth and eighteenth century. These titles were of all kinds: single-sheet ballads, traditional tales like Dick Whittington, religious tracts and sermons, works of science and geography, natural history and astrology: 400,000 almanacs a year were printed in the late seventeenth

BOX 16.4: **The Public Sphere**

Historians often discuss the spread of political information and debate in terms of a widening 'public sphere'. The term was coined by Jürgen Habermas in 1962, to describe the emergence of arenas, such as coffee houses or salons, where a limited group of men, educated and 'bourgeois', could rationally debate the issues of the day and, through debate, reach a level of consensus. Habermas contrasted this active, thinking public with later 'consumers' of news, manipulated by the mass media. When he wrote, historians generally saw politics under George I and II as the preserve of a small aristocratic elite: the people at large played no part and Grub Street writers and the denizens of coffee houses and salons little more. However, as historians became aware of the vigour of popular politics Habermas's analysis seemed to have little to offer.

In the late twentieth century, 'public sphere' began to be used of a different sort of politics. In their efforts to persuade Elizabeth to agree to measures deemed essential for the survival of the Protestant nation, ministers, clergymen and MPs appealed to a wider public, through leaked government documents, printed and manuscript papers, sermons, rumour and innuendo. They accepted in principle that it was dangerous to extend political debate, but argued that it was justified by the extreme dangers facing the kingdom. Puritans and Catholics used similar tactics to promote their interpretation of the dangers and possible remedies for them. Under James I and Charles I the leaking and polemic became more extensive, reaching a climax in the civil war. Both sides sought to win 'the people' over to their interpretation of the issues at stake, while deploring the populist tactics of their opponents. At the Restoration Charles II accepted that it was no longer feasible to treat government as a private matter for king and council: something had to be said to the people.

In the literature on the growth of the 'public sphere' from Elizabeth's reign, Habermas rarely appears, until after the Glorious Revolution, when Steven Pincus claimed that 'political economy' (or economic policy) became the dominant theme of public debate. He suggested that this was prefigured in Habermas, who argued that manufacturing rather than land was now the dominant element in the economy. In this he followed Marx, but begged the question of *when* industry became pre-eminent: most economic historians place the Industrial Revolution in the nineteenth century. Rather oddly, Habermas and Pincus saw the burgeoning financial and commercial sectors as impeding the growth of manufacturing, with which they competed for resources. However, the economic pre-eminence of the Dutch was built not on Dutch agriculture or manufactures, but on buying, selling and carrying goods produced by other people.

In recent years two very different 'public spheres' have developed: the 'post-Reformation' public sphere, developed particularly by Peter Lake, and Pincus's 'post-Revolution' 'bourgeois public sphere'. The former has met with substantially more acceptance among historians than the latter.

The most convenient way in to this question is P. Lake and S. Pincus (eds.), *The Politics of the Public Sphere in Early Modern England* (Manchester, 2007). The introduction, by the two editors, yokes together their differing points of view, which becomes clear on reading their individual chapters (3 and 9). See also J.G. Finlayson, *Habermas: a Very Short Introduction* (Oxford, 2005).

century, enough for 40 per cent of households. In the sixteenth century much knowledge was accessible only to the small minority who could read Latin. By the eighteenth century ordinary readers had access to a vast quantity of knowledge (and entertainment) in English through cheap print or subscription libraries. What one might call the 'knowledge gap' between the few and the many had greatly diminished, especially in London and the larger towns, where people gathered in clubs and societies to socialise and to improve their knowledge. At a humbler level the inability to read did not necessarily exclude people from the world of print. There were strong traditions of ballad-singing and reading aloud, which extended to scribal or printed newsletters. These developments substantially extended the political 'public'. In the fifteenth century a significant number of yeomen, tradesmen and professionals were aware of events and had definite views about how government should, and should not, function. By the eighteenth century the informed public was substantially wider.

But how much of this print dealt with public events? The Tudors and early Stuarts tried to control the press through pre-publication censorship. The printing industry was confined to London and the two universities. Works could be published only if licensed by a designated clergyman or secretary of state. Those who published unlicensed works could be seriously punished: Prynne had his ears cropped twice. Crown censorship collapsed from 1640 and the decade saw an explosion of political publishing. Printing presses sprang up all over the country and travelled with the armies. One-off news reports gave way to newspapers in their hundreds. While deploring the common people's presumption in discussing politics, MPs printed speeches which they had given – or wished that they had given – in the Commons. By the mid 1640s political journalists showed a sophistication and a depth of inside knowledge and analysis which was not matched until the twentieth century. They explained how parties were organised, how committees functioned and how measures were pushed through the Commons. It was not to last. Censorship was reimposed in the 1650s and continued, with a brief hiatus in 1679–81, until the lapsing of the Licensing Act in 1695. The Act had once more banned printing presses outside London, but after 1695 they began to appear in provincial towns; provincial newspapers soon followed. Most contained mainly national news, lifted from the London papers, thus disseminating news – and opinions – more widely. In Scotland the press developed more slowly and works were also imported from England and the Continent, but in the eighteenth century the Scottish publishing industry flourished. (See Box 16.4, The Public Sphere).

Censorship was never fully effective. Under Charles II some politically contentious works were published, such as Andrew Marvell's *An Account of the Growth of Popery and Arbitrary Government* (1678). James II was undermined by works smuggled in from Holland, notably *A Letter from Mijnheer Fagel,* which stated authoritatively that William and Mary were willing to allow Catholics to worship freely but not to hold offices. Newspapers, which had disappeared for much of Charles II's reign, reappeared in 1679–81, briefly in 1688–9, and then in increasing numbers from 1695. The first regular Scottish newspaper, the *Edinburgh Gazette*, appeared from 1699. But the press was not free, any more than Dyer was free to say what he liked in his newsletters. Parliament regarded its debates as confidential and those, like Dyer, who publicised them could be punished for breach of privilege. Editors and printers who overstepped the mark could be prosecuted for seditious libel, imprisoned on trumped-up charges, or otherwise harassed. Under George I even the boldest, Nathaniel Mist, acknowledged that there were limits to what he could publish. When a reader complained of army tyranny Mist replied that he could not print generalised accusations and needed hard evidence. He did report the conviction at Gloucester assizes of dragoons who beat up three alleged Jacobites, adding that getting soldiers used to blood and action by attacking unarmed tradesmen was good for discipline. However, cases of alleged violence by soldiers which did not lead to convictions rarely, if ever, appeared in the newspapers. Gossip and personal criticism of leading politicians was common; criticism of the government and the army was not.

Modes of Political Action

The middling and poorer sorts who made up the great majority of the population lacked political influence but greatly outnumbered the political elite. If they felt sufficiently angry they could rise up and make their numbers tell, as in the Peasants' Revolt and Cade's rebellion. Rebellion was risky, however. If it failed, as it usually did, the government ordered extensive reprisals to discourage others from rebelling in future. Moreover, rebellion against the monarch was treason, even if it was ostensibly aimed at 'evil counsellors'. As a consequence, popular political action generally took forms which stopped short of outright rebellion. They could be peaceful or violent, but even when they were peaceful there was often an implicit threat of force if a reasonable request was denied. We shall consider three forms of action: petitions, voting in elections and riots.

Petitions and Associations

Petitioning was ostensibly the most peaceful and deferential form of political action. Petitions were presented by inferiors to superiors (such as a landlord, Parliament or the monarch) and as such explicitly acknowledged the superior's authority. However, submissive language could cloak an element of threat. In appealing to the superior's obligation to behave justly there was a clear hint that to respond negatively would be unjust: deference and obedience could be conditional on fair treatment. When subordinate authorities petitioned the King or the Privy Council they could warn that failure to heed their advice could lead to disorder. Thus the magistrates at Maldon in 1629

wrote that if grain exports through the town continued they feared that the townspeople would riot – as indeed they did. A rather different twist came in the 1640s with the
use of mass petitions accompanied by large and often threatening crowds. In 1640–2
the Commons did not discourage these crowds because they put pressure on the King
to comply with their demands. By 1648, with public opinion increasingly hostile, the
Commons saw these crowds as threatening and passed an ordinance against tumultuous petitioning, which was superseded by a similar Act in 1661. Petitions could still
prove threatening, however. The Whig petitions of 1679–81 were presented by no more
than ten people, as the law prescribed, but they were backed up by demonstrations
and rowdy, sometimes violent, street politics designed to intimidate the Tories and the
King.

A rather different form of document was the **association**. In the first, in 1584, members of the political elite banded together to defend Elizabeth and, if anything happened
to her, to exact vengeance on Mary Queen of Scots and the papists. The Protestation,
drawn up by the Commons in 1641, stressed the threat posed by papists and army plotters to Parliament and Protestantism. Initially it was to be subscribed by office holders,
later by all adult male Protestants. Another association was mooted in Parliament in
1680. It was abandoned because it was no substitute for exclusion, but the King, understandably, saw it as a threat. In 1696, after a plot to assassinate William III, the Whigs in
Parliament promoted an association which was, like the Protestation, to be subscribed
by all adult male Protestants. Although ostensibly designed to protect the King, this
was a partisan measure, because it described William as the 'rightful and lawful' King,
which some Tories were reluctant to do: the Whigs always claimed that the Tories were
loyal to James II rather than William. In Norwich there were two rival petitions, one
more acceptable to the Tories than the other, which between them were subscribed
by a substantial majority of adult males. The Associations of 1696 show that, like the
petitions of 1640–2, even if they did not lead to direct political action, they brought
political issues to even the humblest members of society.

Elections

The most direct way that some outside the political elite could influence events was
through elections. It is easy to dismiss eighteenth-century elections as manipulated by
landowners, who marched their tenants to the polls, watched them vote and marched
them home again; threats of eviction, beer and bribes counted for more than political
principles. All of these features can be found and they became increasingly common
after 1714. Earlier, particularly between 1640 and 1713, the electorate grew in size and
electors were offered substantially more choice than under the Tudors. We need to
consider who could vote and the choices offered to them, and then the extent to which
those who could not vote could influence elections.

Under the Stuarts the Commons committee of elections and privileges tended to decide disputes about borough franchises in favour of the wider option, to reduce the possibility of royal interference. It has been estimated that, under Anne, about one third of adult males had the right to vote. But could electors use their vote? A vote in Buckingham counted for more than a vote in Yorkshire. In large constituencies it was hard for electors to get to the polls, especially as polling could last for days. Moreover, for voters to influence the outcome of elections they needed to have a choice. Under the Tudors electoral contests were rare. Normally local landed families agreed among themselves who should be elected: two-member constituencies made this easier. Once two candidates had been chosen, others would refrain from standing rather than risk the dishonour of defeat. Contests on issues of political principle were extremely rare. There were one or two in Elizabeth's last years and a few in the 1620s, but significant numbers first occurred in the general elections (for the Short and Long Parliaments) in 1640. Under Charles II there was no general election between 1661 and 1679, when there were two, in which political issues featured prominently. Who candidates were became less important than what they stood for. Voting was a public act, recorded in poll books, which in the eighteenth century were often printed. It was one of the acts – subscribing petitions or loyal addresses were others – by which a man became identified as a Whig or a Tory. The successes of the Whigs in 1679–81 and the Tories in 1685 can both be seen as reflecting shifts in public opinion and the same can be said of the elections held under the Triennial Act, between 1695 and 1715. Many seats were not contested, but enough were for elections to influence the shape of the House of Commons.

It was not only electors who influenced the outcome of elections. Although elections were generally a male preserve, women could influence the process, as electoral patrons, electors' wives or spectators. An election was a spectacle, with strong elements of theatre, and the audience, crowded around the hustings, tried to influence, or intimidate, electors. In small towns electors came under strong pressure: one candidate tried to hide, but was discovered in a nettle patch and dragged off to vote. However, the most powerful influence of the unenfranchised was in larger towns, where candidates or their landowner backers recruited large numbers of men, often armed with cudgels, plied them with beer and marched them in to intimidate the opposition. (See Figure 16.3, 'The Humours of an Election: an Election Entertainment', by William Hogarth, 1755.) At Coventry in 1722 Lord Craven recruited several thousand countrymen, journeymen and apprentices in support of the Tory candidates. When they marched into the town they were beaten back by a Whig force which included past and serving soldiers. At Bristol the colliers from nearby Kingswood also supported the Tories. In 1713 the Whigs were given a hall to assemble their voters some way from the hustings. They soon found that if they wanted to vote they would have to run the gauntlet of the colliers, wielding cudgels. They soon gave up, the poll was closed and the Tory candidates declared elected. Only 189 Whigs had managed to vote.

Figure 16.3 Eighteenth-century elections were notorious for sharp practice, drunkenness and violence, portrayed here by William Hogarth, the greatest painter of the age, with his usual savage wit.

Riots and Demonstrations

Only a small minority of elections were decided by violence, and such results were often overturned on petition, but violence played an important role in popular politics. At times this reflected genuine anger and fear. In 1640 an angry crowd besieged Lambeth Palace, looking to seize Laud. At Colchester popular anger focused on Sir John Lucas, an unpopular landlord, a courtier and a Laudian. Crowds sacked his house and then marched to the Stour valley where they plundered and burned Catholics' houses. At times, fear predominated, especially when Charles moved artillery into the Tower during Strafford's trial or when his 'cavaliers' clashed with citizens at the end of 1641. In 1688 Protestants wreaked revenge on Catholics, especially priests and their chapels. Many feared being slaughtered by the Irish, as did those who rioted in the North West on hearing of the Irish rising. The rioting in England in 1640–2 was unique in its geographical extent, its duration and its violence. The nearest equivalents in the following century occurred in Scotland. The most substantial, long-running and violent riots were in Edinburgh in 1706–7, driven by opposition to the Union with England (see Chapter 14). The Glasgow Malt Tax riots of 1725 met with a savage military response.

Figure 16.4 A detailed representation of what was probably the largest pope-burning of the Exclusion Crisis.

Some crowd activity was more for show than genuinely dangerous. Pope-burnings were designed to make a polemical point, but they were often semi-festive. They started in 1673, after York's second marriage, and reached a peak in 1679–81 when huge processions were held in London on 17 November, Elizabeth's accession day. The processions featured characters from the Popish Plot, a variety of popish stereotypes, including Jesuits with bloody daggers and nuns bearing a banner 'Courtesans in ordinary'. There were also Tories ('We Protestants in masquerade bring in popery'). The procession made its way slowly across the City, finishing at Temple Bar, where on one occasion the effigy of the Pope was forced to bow down before a great statue of Elizabeth before being burned; a little devil who had been whispering in his ear escaped. (See Figure 16.4, *The Solemn Mock Procession of the Pope, Cardinals, Jesuits, Friars etc.*, 1680.) It was designed to be offensive to Catholics and to suggest that there was massive popular support for exclusion, but it was also highly entertaining; one observer called it a 'play'. The French ambassador watched it incognito. He found it all very extraordinary, but especially that, when it was over, everyone went peacefully home to bed. It would not have been like that in Paris, he said.

The political contests of the Exclusion Crisis and after gave rise to relatively limited violence. In 1681–2, when York and Monmouth were seen as rivals for the succession, Monmouth's supporters ordered passers-by to drink his health; if they refused they were made to drink water from the gutter instead. There were skirmishes, particularly at the bitterly contested elections for London's sheriffs, but no pitched battles, and in general the violence was confined to London. James II was sensitive to insults to his religion. He banned bonfires on 5 November, so people put candles in their windows instead. This became the norm in the following decades on most days of public celebration. Unlike contributing to a bonfire, setting out candles was an individual act which could be seen as evidence of party affiliation: Quakers, who did not observe 'days' on principle, were likely to be attacked by both sides for not illuminating their windows. As partisan divisions grew stronger the festive calendar became politicised. In Norwich, guild day, when the new mayor was installed, was a longstanding day of celebration in which citizens of differing political and religious views joined together. However, on guild day in 1710 the new mayor hung out a picture of Dr Sacheverell, the Whigs' favourite hate figure. The list of contested days of celebration multiplied. The law required observance of only three: 29 May (Charles II's birthday and the anniversary of his entering London in 1660) was to be celebrated, as was 5 November, the anniversary of the Gunpowder Plot; 30 January, the anniversary of Charles I's execution, was to be a day of fasting and humiliation. Under Charles II the Whigs added 17 November, suggesting that Elizabeth was a model Protestant monarch, unlike Charles II. Under George I the Tories celebrated Queen Anne's birthday – Anne had stressed that her heart was wholly English – while the Whigs added not only George I's birthday but those of the Prince and Princess of Wales, together with the anniversary of George's coronation. Jacobites and some Tories celebrated the Pretender's birthday on 10 June.

In terms of celebration George's reign got off to a bad start, with Tories disrupting Whig celebrations of the coronation, setting up maypoles and depicting George as a cuckold or with turnips around his neck: he was said to have grown turnips in Hanover. The Whigs revived pope-burnings in which they also burned the Pretender and Ormond. (See Figure 16.5, A Pope-burning of 1717.) In London the Whig processions were organised at the Roebuck tavern and the Tories gathered in strength to try to prevent them taking place. This led to street battles in which many were injured and several killed. The Tories held their own in the fighting, but the Whigs controlled the magistracy, so Tories were convicted and imprisoned and Whigs were acquitted. The Tories found revenge attacking Dissenting meeting houses; many were damaged or burned in the North, the West Midlands and Oxford between May and August 1715. The riots began on the King's birthday, 28 May, the day before Charles II's. The Tories naturally tried to outdo their rivals in their celebrations, breaking the windows of those

(a)

Times with one Voice in general Applause.   **HUZZA.**

(b)

L. *A Cardinal, Jesuit, and Fryer Cordelier:* M. *Three other Fryers and Confessors.* N. *A Royal Bearer carried by Four Men.*

(c)

F. *The Warming pan,* &c. G. *The Champion in Armour.* H. *The Sans-Bell.* I. *Two Men sprinkling Holy Water.* K. *The Pope, the Devil, and the Pretender.*

(d)

A. B. *Generals* Mar *and* Forster.   C. *The* Pretender's *Standard.* D. *A Drum Muffled.* E. *Six* Scots *Rebels in their* Highland *Dress as they* enter'd London.

Figure 16.5 A more cheaply produced representation of a pope-burning after the 1715 rebellion. One of the riders is carrying a **warming pan**, symbol of the Pretender's alleged illegitimacy, and six Scots are depicted in Highland dress. Both the pope and the Pretender are consigned to the flames.

who celebrated the King's birthday for good measure. At Wrexham the crowd destroyed a Baptist chapel amid chants of 'Down with the Rump and the German', while at Oxford the Quaker meeting house was destroyed, to cries of 'an Ormond, an Ormond': the Duke had been chancellor of the university, and extremely popular. In general, however, the rioters concentrated on Presbyterian meeting houses. At Shrewsbury the self-styled 'loyal mob' issued a 'proclamation' warning other denominations to have nothing to do with the Presbyterians or else their meeting houses would be targeted as well.

The meeting house riots, followed by the Jacobite rising, made the government determined that popular celebrations should pose no threat, so they were taken over by the army, abetted in some towns by artillery companies. These might be largely for show, but at Norwich the company was established by Townshend, one of the King's leading ministers, and became his personal paramilitary force, which had the advantage of not being subject to military discipline. (Mist remarked that describing the company as 'honourable', like its London namesake, would be totally inappropriate.) Elsewhere the pattern of celebration was usually similar. The corporation, or at least the 'loyal' part, would feast in the town hall or a convenient inn, with army officers and guests. Before the feast a detachment of soldiers escorted them to and from church. They then drilled for a while, usually in the market square, and fired volleys. After the feast the corporation and guests came out to a bonfire where they drank loyal healths to the King, members of the royal family and leading Whigs; each health would be followed by a volley from the soldiers. It was spectacular in its way, but the role of the townspeople changed, from participants to spectators, and the whole occasion became a display of loyalty to King and government and military force. Moreover, in garrison towns the army saw its role as suppressing disaffection, as seen at Bridgwater in 1721, when several townspeople were injured. (See Box 12.3.) The King blamed the townspeople and exonerated the soldiers. This is not to suggest that George I's was a military regime. There was no English equivalent to the shooting of the Glasgow Malt Tax rioters. The army disliked being used against rioters, but both officers and men felt profound contempt for Jacobites and welcomed the chance to beat up unarmed men and molest women without fear of retribution. The army confined itself to low-level disaffection. The more serious disorders in London were dealt with by the civic authorities, with the help of the City militia.

Riots (Scotland and Ireland)

Popular involvement was equally important in Scotland. The Covenanting revolution was driven by popular support and the Whig and Presbyterian triumph in the Scottish elections of 1689 owed much to popular intervention. After the Union, riots sometimes seriously threatened public order. The Shawfield riots in Glasgow in 1725 began as a protest against the Act imposing a Malt Tax, but escalated into the violent demolition of the house of a local MP, Daniel Campbell, who had allegedly supported it. A local detachment of soldiers was called in: an officer ordered his men to open fire on the crowd and several were killed. The lord advocate, in Edinburgh, called upon General Wade, with a substantial force, to restore order and punish those involved, but many questioned his authority to do so and pressure had to be put on the judges before they would take action against the rioters. The London government ordered the burgh to compensate Campbell: several rioters were transported. This firm action probably prevented a widespread refusal to pay the Malt Tax in Edinburgh and other towns.

The passing of the Riot Act (which applied in Scotland as well as England) made it possible to use the army to suppress disorders, but this seldom happened. The Mutiny Act and the army estimates were granted annually by Parliament and the Commons were likely to react angrily to the use of the military to coerce civilians: cudgels and the flats of swords might be acceptable, but firing on civilians was not. The government tried to put pressure on judges to deal firmly with rioters, but jurors often sympathised with the accused. Tax evasion was widespread: smugglers enjoyed much public support and were prepared to use firearms against the taxman. Much the same applied in Ireland: violent disorder was common in Dublin, sometimes involving soldiers, but the authorities' greatest problems came from mass civil disobedience. This could be supplemented by occasional violence, as in the case of Wood's Halfpence (see Chapter 15).

Conclusion

In the century after the civil wars political and religious divisions bit deep into English society. Party differences became part of everyday life: there were Whig and Tory clubs, newspapers, race meetings and even doctors. Churchmen and Dissenters and High and Low Churchmen denounced one another venomously, joining only to condemn the Methodists. Whereas earlier society had tended to be divided horizontally – subjects against royal officials, peasants against landlords – now divisions ran vertically through all social strata. This change had happened rapidly, in the 1640s, when the civil wars stimulated widespread debate on political issues and people were forced to choose between incompatible opposites. Not everybody did choose – many stayed neutral, or tried to – but it was difficult: both sides tended to treat neutrals as hostile. With the revival of clear-cut divisions in the Exclusion Crisis neutrality again became difficult, especially for the gentry, as they were pressed to declare themselves by voting in elections and subscribing petitions or loyal addresses.

Political divisions bred political violence. Tudor rebellions were less bloody than the Peasants' Revolt or Cade's rebellion, when unpopular officials were beheaded as if they were outlaws. In the century before the civil wars, food and enclosure riots were often peaceful and rarely involved serious violence. The rioters appealed to ideals of fair dealing or respect for customary rights which were widely shared among their social superiors. Violence was most likely if, as in the draining of the fens, the King was clearly implicated in attacks on customary rights. This pattern changed abruptly with the riots of 1640–2, which were unprecedented in scale and violence. In the civil war or in the times when politics was dominated by 'the rage of party' there was no shared common ground to which to appeal. On the contrary, there were occasions which encouraged conflict. Elections were the most obvious, especially when they were frequent, but partisanship also distorted national or civic celebrations. Normally these were affirmations of unity, but adversary politics bred conflict and the habit of illuminating windows made it hard for people to avoid committing themselves: the fact that George I's and Charles II's birthdays fell on successive days encouraged gangs of soldiers to smash the windows of those who illuminated, or failed to illuminate. Processions can be fun, but they can also be triumphalist and threatening, as can still be seen during the 'marching season' in Northern Ireland. They became especially threatening when effigies of living people were burned alongside that of the Pope. As the magistracy was controlled by the Whigs, the Tories resorted to violence because they could not hope for fair dealing in the courts. The Whigs responded in kind. On days of celebration like 5 and 17 November, both sides seem to have looked forward to a good fight: 'I love a mob,' declared the Duke of Newcastle. 'I have led a mob myself.' As on election days, their enthusiasm was fuelled by alcohol: they gathered in taverns before the processions started. In the mid eighteenth century, food rioters generally behaved peaceably and still invoked traditional regulations for the marketing of grain, as set out in Charles I's books of orders, but violence was now a regular feature of the political landscape.

SUGGESTIONS FOR FURTHER READING

The conservatism which evolved into Toryism had its origins during or even before the civil wars: see D. Underdown, *Revel, Riot and Rebellion: Popular Politics and Culture in England 1603–60* (Oxford, 1985) and M. Stoyle, *Loyalty and Locality: Popular Allegiance in Devon in the English Civil War* (Exeter, 1994). (Chapter 12 gives an overview of allegiance in other counties.) • On the royal touch see A. Keay, *The Magnificent Monarch: Charles II and the Ceremonies of Power* (London, 2008). • On Tories and Jacobites, K.G. Feiling, *History of the Tory Party, 1640–1714* (Oxford, 1924) is old but still very useful, especially for Anne's reign. See also Colley, *In Defiance of Oligarchy* and Monod, *Jacobitism and English Politics*. • J. Black (ed.), *Britain in the Age of Walpole* (Basingstoke, 1984) and Langford, *The Excise Crisis* offer useful introductions to Walpole's regime. • The most incisive introduction to anti-popery is P. Lake, 'Anti-Popery: the Structure of a Prejudice', in R. Cust and A. Hughes (eds.), *Conflict in Early Stuart England: Studies in Religion and Politics, 1603–42* (Harlow, 1989). See also J. Miller, *Popery and Politics in England, 1660–88*

(Cambridge, 1973). • On news, see R. Cust, 'News and Politics in Early Seventeenth-Century England', *Past and Present*, 112 (1986) and J. Miller, 'Public Opinion in Charles II's England', *History*, 80 (1995). • On literacy, D. Cressy, *Literacy and the Social Order: Reading and Writing in Tudor and Stuart England* (Cambridge, 1980) is essential reading. On the reading experience of humbler people, see two works by M. Spufford: *Small Books and Pleasant Histories: Popular Fiction and its Readership in Seventeenth-Century England* (London, 1981) and *Figures in the Landscape: Rural Society in England 1500–1700* (Aldershot, 2000), chapters 10–11. • On the newspaper press, see J. Peacey, 'The Revolution in Print', in M. Braddick (ed.), *The Oxford Handbook of the English Revolution* (Oxford, 2015), and G.A. Cranfield, *The Development of the Provincial Newspaper 1700–60* (Oxford, 1962). • M. Knights, *Representation and Misrepresentation in Later Stuart Britain: Partisanship and Political Culture* (Oxford, 2005) has much to say on many aspects of popular politics, including petitions and associations. • The study of early modern elections has been reshaped by M. Kishlansky, *Parliamentary Selection: Social and Political Choice in Early Modern England* (Cambridge, 1986). W.A. Speck, *Tory and Whig: the Struggle in the Constituencies 1701–15* (London, 1970) played a significant role in re-establishing the importance of party, as opposed to kinship, patronage and clientage, in the politics of Anne's reign. See also Holmes, *British Politics in the Age of Anne. The History of Parliament: the Commons 1690–1715*. Vol. II contains a rich variety of electoral case studies. • There are two fine studies of popular violence in 1640–2: D. Cressy, *England on Edge: Crisis and Revolution 1640–2* (Oxford, 2006) and J. Walter, *Understanding Popular Violence in the English Revolution: the Colchester Plunderers* (Cambridge, 1999). Together they supersede B. Manning, *The English People and the English Revolution* (London, 1976) which showed the significance of the people's role in events, but insisted on constructing an analysis based on class conflict, despite much evidence to the contrary. • On popular politics in the early eighteenth century, see Wilson, *The Sense of the People*, N. Rogers, *Whigs and Cities* (Oxford, 1989) and Miller, *Cities Divided*. • Finally, the classic analysis of eighteenth-century food riots is E.P. Thompson, 'The Moral Economy of the English Crowd in the Eighteenth Century', *Past and Present*, 50 (1971).

SUMMARY

- Some of the content of eighteenth-century popular politics dated back to the fifteenth century and earlier, but the sixteenth and seventeenth centuries added new sources of division, such as religion, and divisions became fiercer and permeated far more deeply into society, reaching even the poorest. Illiteracy was no barrier to participation in politics: news often circulated by word of mouth and the lack of political rights did not prevent many people from participating in politics and especially in elections.

- Although there were signs of greater popular interest and participation before 1640, during the civil wars political information and opinions affected far more of the people than ever before. Both sides were eager to influence hearts and minds and printed matter grew greatly in volume and circulated far more widely. Moreover, the scale of the wars meant that soldiers and the issues of war spread throughout the country.

- Although many historians have assumed that it was mainly Parliament which appealed to the people, this was not the case. Many people supported the King out of principle; many more turned against Parliament because of the means it used to win the war and the increasing demands of the army. The regicide was greeted not with joy but with horror; Charles II was restored amid huge popular acclaim.
- In the half century after 1660 the conservative forces in religion and politics grew stronger. High Church Anglicanism, weak in the 1660s, grew stronger and more militant, as shown in the smashing of Dissenting meeting houses in 1715. In Anne's reign, when the electorate was at its largest, the Tories performed notably more strongly than the Whigs, winning crushing victories in 1710 and 1713, leading the Whigs to reduce the size of the electorate and the frequency of elections.

QUESTIONS FOR STUDENTS

1. Why did Walpole's enemies repeatedly accuse him of corruption?
2. How far did the English press become free after the lapsing of the Licensing Act?
3. How democratic was the English electoral system in the first half of the eighteenth century?

4. Account for the prevalence of ideas of divine-right monarchy in the reign of Anne.
5. Why was there such extensive political violence in the 1710s?

Conclusion

From Warlords to Royal Armies

In 1450 much, but not all, military power was in the hands of clan chiefs or feudal nobles: royal armies were usually agglomerations of private armies. Over time, service in royal armies had come to be governed less by feudal obligations than by commercial contracts. In Scotland military service was a general duty, organised through the **host**. In Tudor England the state widened military obligations to include service in the militia and sought to gain a monopoly of armed force, but in a crisis the monarch still relied on the nobility to serve with their own military followings and in the civil wars many lords recruited regiments, often from among their servants and tenants. The first professional standing army in Britain or Ireland was the New Model; after the Restoration its ethos was preserved in the new royal standing armies, supported by militias, which might perform useful auxiliary functions, but were no match for properly trained regulars. The Scottish army under Charles II was small and had to be reinforced by the militia and (controversially) the 'Highland Host'.

The English standing army was adequate for peacetime, but too small for war, for which additional forces were raised. These became larger and larger during the wars against France from 1689. Parliament viewed these additional forces with deep suspicion, identifying standing armies with Cromwell and the 'tyranny' of Louis XIV; at the coming of peace in 1697 and 1713 the English army was drastically reduced. As there was also a standing army in Ireland, to maintain the ascendancy of the Protestant minority, monarchs from Charles II onwards stationed additional regiments in Ireland, to provide a reservoir of military power for England. The Union with Scotland led to the creation of a British army, with English, Scottish and (Protestant) Irish units rotated between the three kingdoms and imperial garrisons like Gibraltar and Jamaica. From George I's reign the Jacobite threat and the growth of empire meant that the peacetime army became larger and its training and regulations were standardised.

The growth of the British army reduced autonomous noble power in two ways. First, within the army a noble now derived his power to command men from a commission from the king, his commander in chief. He might also buy a commission to provide a younger son with an honourable career. Second, the government set out to break the power of those seen as dangerous or disaffected. Most Irish Catholics lost their land, and the power over men that went with it, and were denied the right to bear arms. Scottish clan chiefs were also seen as disaffected. Cromwell had shown that a military conquest of Scotland was possible, but it had been slow and expensive and the Hanoverian regime preferred to rely on the 'loyal' clans to police their neighbours and its intervention was limited to building a few military roads and Highland forts. After Culloden it relied less on military force than on undermining the Highland way of life, which was made easier as chiefs put profit before traditional loyalties.

Kings, Parliaments and People

Despite widespread suspicion of standing armies, the growth of the royal army did not lead to absolute monarchy. From the 1690s the English, and later British, Parliament accepted the need for a substantial professional army to guard against French aggression and the Jacobite challenge and to secure the growing empire. It guarded against the threat of military rule by retaining control over the army's funding, granting the military budget for a year at a time. It also retained control over military discipline by scrutinising the Articles of War, under which the army was governed, and passing annual mutiny acts. (There was no Irish mutiny act before 1780, but as the army was a major instrument of the Protestant ascendancy, Protestants did not see this as a problem.) The growth of a royal standing army did not lead to a concentration of power in the King's hands. The army was occasionally used to suppress disorder, particularly smuggling; but, despite the Riot Act, soldiers were rarely used to suppress riots. Officers preferred to leave such matters to the civil authorities.

In both Britain and Ireland Parliament had the financial power to constrain the King, but Parliament became increasingly susceptible to pressure from the wider public. This was particularly apparent between 1640 and 1714, when a distinctive and sophisticated popular politics developed. Whig ministers did their best to reverse this process, but did not fully succeed. From the 1760s, with the government's growing difficulties with the American colonies, extra-parliamentary politics became more vigorous and sometimes violent. Since the Restoration there had been few calls for parliamentary reform, but now criticism of the electoral system became widespread and vociferous. The old system staggered through to 1832 but thereafter successive reform acts widened the electorate to include a larger and larger proportion of adult males, and eventually women.

One reason for the growth of popular politics was the growing range of information available, particularly to the growing proportion of the population who could read. The volume of cheap print continued to increase, bringing knowledge of faraway and exotic places in which Britain increasingly had an interest. The thirst for knowledge encouraged the multiplication of clubs and societies. Movement from the countryside to new industrial cities led (for some) to a sense of alienation, but also a wider range of contacts and issues, new forms of entertainment and new solidarities of factory and class, church and trade union.

The Age of Reason

The period from about 1680 has often been seen as one of major intellectual change in Europe, a time when traditional beliefs, long taken on trust or imposed by Church and state, were subjected to analysis based on reason and found wanting. In older works in particular, this was often treated as inevitable and inexorable: once the fallacies behind the old beliefs were exposed, they were abandoned as indefensible. Challenges undoubtedly occurred in this period, but we have seen already that the challengers did not sweep all before them and the old ideas often proved tenacious. Moreover, a growing emphasis on 'politeness' meant that often conversation was kept away from sensitive topics and personal beliefs.

Religion

In the first half of the eighteenth century many conventional Christians, ministers and laypeople felt threatened from all sides by scepticism, heterodoxy, deism and atheism. John Toland and others cast doubt on the authenticity of many texts in the Bible. Locke questioned the concept of original sin, arguing (in *An Essay Concerning Human Understanding*) that children were born neither good nor evil and derived their values and morality from their upbringing. The initial reaction of the clergy to these ideas was to punish those who advanced them and burn their books. Others, however, argued that there might be mistranslations in the Bible but this did not invalidate Scripture as a whole; many points were too difficult for human reason to grasp, or not suscep-tible to the sort of definitive proofs found in the natural sciences. Others, faced with evidence that seemed incompatible with Scripture, passed over it quietly or talked of God's inscrutability or omnipotence. Geology was a popular hobby in the eighteenth century, particularly among clergymen; most managed to reconcile their geological findings with the book of Genesis: either they understood the seven-day creation figuratively or said simply that God worked in mysterious ways. Others responded to challenges by proclaiming their faith even more forthrightly: experience of conversion provided all the 'proof' they needed. Evangelical enthusiasm became stronger in the eighteenth and nineteenth centuries. Radical critics of traditional religion generally moved warily. Locke published anonymously and Newton kept his doubts about the Trinity to himself. For a while in the early eighteenth century it became fashionable to flirt with heterodox opinions and denounce priestcraft, but many thought Toland had gone too far. David Hume, now seen as the greatest philosopher of the eighteenth century, denied that certain knowledge was possible, dismissed the immortality of the soul as ridiculous and could not accept that people possessed an innate sense of morality. He had few followers.

Political Ideas

The seventeenth century saw a flowering of English political thought. Hobbes is now seen as a towering figure, but the politics of *Leviathan* were generally condemned at the time and took second place, in Hobbes's view, to the larger and bitterly anti-clerical section on religion. Locke, by contrast, became a mainstream figure, often credited with explaining and justifying the Glorious Revolution in his *Second Treatise of Government*. (Most of the key points in his analysis had in fact been anticipated by Leveller writers, whose writings had only a limited impact at the time.) Locke argued power was entrusted to kings by their people. Like any trust, it was revocable if the person entrusted failed to use it for the purposes for which it had been granted. If this happened the people were absolved from their allegiance and could legitimately rise up, overthrow their ruler and appoint another in his stead. This model of authority and government was the polar opposite of the divine right of kings, in which regal power came from God, not the people, and the king was answerable only to God for his conduct. If the people were dissatisfied they could respond with prayers and tears, but they could not actively resist the king, the Lord's anointed. Under Charles II political polemic tended to be dominated by the divine right of kings: those who rejected it found it hard to argue, in the prevailing political climate, that resistance to Charles I had been justified. This began to change under William III, as works by radicals of the 1640s and 1650s were printed. When the succession after Anne became a deeply fraught political issue, the rights and wrongs of the civil wars were fought out in print. Political thought based on the divine right of kings was largely abandoned, not because it was wrong, but because James II (and the House of Stuart) converted to Catholicism, totally changing the context of the debate. Most Tories put their Protestantism before their loyalty to the Stuarts.

Magic and Superstition

'The triumph of reason' seemed most self-evident where scientific knowledge swept away belief in the spirit world and magic: as the poet Alexander Pope put it, 'God said "let Newton be" and there was light.' It was not as simple as that. Few would have understood Newton's *Principia Mathematica* (1685) in its original Latin: it needed to be translated and explained. From Newton's point of view it answered a number of specific questions about the workings of the cosmos but did not thereby discredit magical beliefs: he himself was fascinated by alchemy. Like Newton, many educated people were able to combine an interest in the new science with older beliefs such as folk remedies and the use of magic to find stolen goods. Prominent members of the Royal Society brought scientific methods to the study of magical phenomena. Dr Joseph Glanvill argued that witchcraft must exist because women confessed in open court to being witches. Attitudes to witchcraft had always varied. Some argued that it must exist because it was mentioned in the Bible and drew on the voluminous demonologies of medieval witch-hunters; others expressed scepticism or demanded a reasonable level of proof, and these demands became more stringent in the later seventeenth century. Nevertheless, witch beliefs remained widespread and sometimes sceptical judges could not prevent a conviction: one wrote in 1682 of accused women describing 'sucking devils with saucer eyes' so realistically that the jury convicted them. He added that they seemed 'weary of their lives'. By the time of the last witchcraft conviction in 1712 scepticism had grown about the possibility of proving in court that someone had harmed others by occult means. The Witchcraft Act of 1736 removed the possibility of prosecuting a person for witchcraft, leaving those who believed that they were victims only unofficial methods of seeking redress. It was believed that a witch could not drown because the devil enabled her to float, so crowds would 'swim' a suspected witch or, if all else failed, lynch her. Witch beliefs continued amidst other magical beliefs among the poor and uneducated. The better-off dismissed them as ignorant superstitions or recorded them as 'curious' relics of a bygone age.

Conclusion

In looking at a wide range of changes over three centuries it is easy to think in terms of modernisation and to fall into the 'Whig' fallacy of assuming that those groups and ideas who triumphed did so because they were inherently superior – the survival of the historically fittest. Those who lost out were the 'bad guys' of English Protestant history:

absolute monarchy, Catholics, the Stuarts, Jacobite Scots and Gaelic Irish. From the struggles between the forces of progress and reaction emerged the nineteenth-century British (in other words English) constitution, based on liberal democracy, limited monarchy and religious toleration – and, of course, the Industrial Revolution and a world-wide empire. After the experience of decolonisation, the decline of traditional industries and the emergence of new super-powers it is difficult to share the confidence of the High Victorian era and it is worth remembering that things could have turned out differently.

Glossary

Abjuration, Oath of: In 1702 the English Parliament passed an Act requiring office holders to swear that James II's heirs had no claim to the throne. It was extended to Ireland where it could also be tendered to voters in parliamentary elections and secular priests registered under an Act of 1704.

Absolute monarchy: Used generally as a pejorative term to describe monarchies like that of France, in which the king claimed the power to legislate and impose taxes without consent and to override the law when the interest of the state required it.

Adiaphora: An ecclesiastical term meaning 'things indifferent' which were to be used because required by the church authorities.

Advowson: The right to nominate the priest or minister of an ecclesiastical benefice, this was a piece of property which could be bought and sold.

Affinity: The following of a powerful landowner, which could include tenants, household men and retainers.

Alien: A foreigner who did not enjoy the full rights of a citizen, in terms of trading and property ownership. Aliens could gain full rights through naturalisation or partial rights by becoming a denizen.

Allegiance, Oath of: Designed to identify Catholics, it involved a statement of allegiance to the monarch and an explicit renunciation of the Pope's claim that he could depose monarchs and absolve their subjects from their allegiance.

Anabaptists: Radical Protestants who in the 1520s and 1530s claimed direct inspiration from God and, following a conversion experience, were re-baptised. Their extreme behaviour (especially their regime at Münster) made them notorious.

Antinomian: The belief that the **elect** were incapable of sin whatever they did, a deviant offshoot of **predestination**.

Arminian: Literally followers of the Dutch theologian Arminius, who undermined the theology of predestination by insisting that people could accept or reject God's grace. In England the term was used of followers of Laud; see **Laudian**.

Articles, Lords of the: A committee of the Scottish Parliament used to prepare legislation. Under James VI its membership was increasingly controlled by the King (through the nobles and bishops) and it effectively determined which bills were brought before Parliament.

Articles of War: Military code of discipline.

Assessment: A weekly, later monthly, tax on land, established by Parliament in 1643. It became the model of the later land tax.

Association: Faced with threats of the life of Elizabeth (in 1584) and William III (in 1696) large numbers of their Protestant subjects joined to protect them against the Catholics and undertook to avenge their deaths if they were assassinated. The 1696 Association was subscribed by a much higher proportion of adult males than that of 1584.

Attainder: An Act of Parliament declaring that a person is guilty of treason and should suffer the consequences, including execution, forfeiture of all property and (in the case of a nobleman) the loss of their titles and their family's claim to noble blood.

Baptists: Similar to **Anabaptists** in their claim to direct divine inspiration and commitment to adult baptism, but without the extremism and violence. They became divided into Calvinist Particular Baptists, who believed in predestination, and General Baptists, who did not.

Bard: A poet, often living in the chief's household in Celtic societies.

Bawn: An enclosure, lightly fortified to protect people and cattle, found particularly in Ireland. Bawns were a significant feature of the Ulster Plantation.

Bede-roll: A document recording pious donations to the parish.

Bill: A piece of draft legislation which has to be approved by both Houses of Parliament and the monarch before it can become an Act or statute.

Black rent: Protection money (Scotland).

Bloodfeud: Could literally mean a feud to the death but in Scotland came to mean a method of resolving disputes whereby a lord or chief arbitrated between disputants and enforced his ruling. Often quicker and cheaper than taking a case to the king's courts.

Bond of manrent; see manrent, bond of

Bonds and recognisances: Binding a person over to keep the peace and to appear in court was a basic part of the criminal law, but it could be used by the king (especially Henry VII) to keep a powerful subject at his mercy or extort money from him.

Boots: A form of torture, used in Scotland, whereby the victim's feet were encased in some sort of frame and wedges were hammered in, damaging the feet and shins.

Brehon, brehon law: Gaelic Irish form of law, often transmitted orally, in which the emphasis was on restitution rather than punishment.

Burgage: A piece of real property in an English or Irish parliamentary borough which gave its owner the right to vote. Burgages could be bought and sold; in small boroughs they could be accumulated by the landlord, to reduce the electorate.

Burghs: Scottish boroughs, of two kinds. Royal burghs enjoyed a range of economic privileges, including the right to trade overseas. Their constitutions and charters were broadly similar and they sent 'commissioners' (members) to Parliament. They also had their own assembly, the convention of royal burghs, which continued to meet long after the Union. Burghs by barony were generally controlled by a lord and could not trade abroad.

Cameronians: A group of extreme Covenanters who emerged in the early 1680s, they rejected the authority of Charles II and recognised only Christ as the ruler of the Church. Also known as the Society People, they played an important role in the armed resistance to the Crown and the bishops during the 'Killing Times'. Their inflexible commitment to the Covenant kept them out of the restored Presbyterian kirk after 1690 and they remained prone to schisms.

Canon, canon law: A canon was a law of the Catholic Church (and later of the Church of England); canon law was the system of law based on these canons. A canon was also a clergyman involved in the running of a cathedral.

Castle Chamber: The Irish equivalent of Star Chamber.

Cateran: A masterless man: often a mercenary soldier or a brigand (Scotland).

Chancery: The court of the lord chancellor, which was not tied to the complex and cumbersome procedures of the common law and so could base its rulings on common sense and natural justice. Over time, however, it built up its own rules and conventions and became notorious for slowness and expense.

Chantry: A side chapel in a church, often dedicated to a particular saint, in which chantry priests, funded by the gifts of the faithful, said masses for the souls of the dead. Their wealth was confiscated by Edward VI's government.

Chieftain: Generally used of the head of a subaltern clan or sept in Gaelic societies.

Church ale: The practice of selling ale and other refreshments to raise funds for the parish. Condemned by Puritans for encouraging drunkenness.

Churchwarden: A parish official, elected by the parishioners, initially responsible for the upkeep of the church and the management of parish funds. Later churchwardens acquired other responsibilities, including the upkeep of highways and bridges and the relief of the poor.

Classis: In Presbyterianism an assembly formed of pastors and elders from several parishes, similar to a presbytery. Under Elizabeth the 'classical movement' was an attempt to construct a Presbyterian system from the bottom up.

Clothier: A merchant and entrepreneur who organised the process of cloth production, usually employing workers in their own homes.

Clubmen: Peasants and artisans who took up arms against the armies in the 1640s.

Coign; see livery

Combinations: Forerunners of trade unions, in which workers combined to defend their interests.

Common council (London): Whereas the aldermen served for life and (with the lord mayor) played a key role in governing the City, the common council was elected annually and had limited functions, which included the election of sheriffs and other City officials. The common council elections in December 1641 led to a radical transfer of power within the City.

Compound: To pay a reduced amount (for example of a fine) in order to be let off the rest. Royalists after the civil wars often compounded for their estates, paying less than their full value.

Comprehension: Attempts to broaden the Church of England by changing its liturgy and government in order to accommodate Presbyterians.

Conventicle: A Nonconformist religious meeting. The English and Scottish parliaments passed a series of laws against conventicles: the first in England was in 1593, following the appearance of the first separatists. The Acts remained in being after the Toleration Act, but almost all Protestants (apart from Socinians and Non-jurors) were exempt from their penalties. In Scotland there were particularly severe measures against open-air meetings ('field conventicles').

Convention: An elected assembly not summoned by a king, in Ireland in 1659, in England in 1660 and in England and Scotland in 1689.

Convocation: The representative body of the clergy in England and Ireland, with bishops forming the upper house and representatives of the lesser clergy the lower. It could pass laws for the Church (canons) and tax the clergy. After the English Convocation gave up its right to tax the clergy separately it met only sporadically.

Copyhold: A form of lease in which the terms of tenure were recorded on the manor court roll and the tenant was given a copy. Copyhold tenures came to be recognised as legal by the courts.

Corporation: A body which can act as a legal person, using powers vested in it by an authority, such as a royal charter. A municipal corporation can hold courts, manage property and sue or be sued, according to the terms of the charter.

Corporation Act (1661): This was designed, by the Cavalier Parliament, to exclude Nonconformists and former Parliamentarians from municipal office by imposing a range of religious and political tests, including the renunciation of the Covenant. These were extended by the 1673 Test Act, which required office-holders to receive communion in an Anglican church. The Acts were repealed in 1828.

Corporations of the poor: Created around the 1690s by Act of Parliament, these aimed to reduce the cost of poor relief by moving many of the poor into workhouses.

Correction, House of (or Bridewell): Places where the disorderly poor could be incarcerated and subjected to punishment and discipline.

Counsellors: Ministers or advisers.

County committee: Set up by Parliament during the first civil war to run the war effort, they became notorious for their alleged tyranny and corruption.

Court leet: Local courts dealing with disputes, breaches of the peace and minor crimes.

Court martial; see also martial law: The army's code of discipline was set out in the **Articles of War**, which were enforced in courts martial. In Ireland, Scotland and occasionally England courts martial also exercised jurisdiction over civilians: much of the subjugation of Ireland depended on martial law.

Covenant: The Covenant of 1638 was the founding document of Scottish Presbyterianism. The Solemn League and Covenant of 1643 attempted to extend it to England and for another century and more Presbyterians argued about the extent to which their leaders were upholding Covenant principles.

Cucking stool: Used as a shame punishment, ducking scolds (usually women but sometimes men) in water.

Curia: The papal court.

Deacon: In Presbyterian churches deacons assisted the pastor with secular affairs and especially the relief of the poor.

Deist: Someone who believes in some sort of divine power, but not necessarily a deity and certainly not the God of the established churches or revealed religion.

Demesne: The land reserved by a landlord for his own use, either to feed his household or to produce crops for sale. In feudal times it was normally cultivated by serfs, for whom work on the demesne was part of their rent.

Denizen: Someone admitted to citizenship by royal letters patent, but with less extensive rights than those who are naturalised; one who is free to live in England.

Directory: Scottish service book, without set forms of service, leaving the minister free to determine the form of worship. Introduced into England in 1645.

Distraint of knighthood: One of Charles I's fiscal scams, this exploited an old law whereby gentlemen of sufficient wealth should present themselves to be knighted, or pay a fine.

Ejectors: Following an ordinance of 1654, those who examined the parish clergy and removed those whose learning or morals were deemed unsatisfactory.

Elders: The senior lay members of Presbyterian congregations who assisted the pastor, particularly with moral discipline.

Elect: According to predestination, those whom God had foreordained to be saved.

Enfeoffment to uses: The practice of vesting land in trustees in order to avoid wardship and other feudal incidents.

Engagement: The agreement between Charles I and some Scottish lords in 1647 which led to the Scots' invasion of England in 1648.

Entail: A legal device to prevent someone who had inherited an estate from selling part or all of it.

Erastian: Usually understood to mean undue interference by secular authorities in religious life.

Escheat: To be forfeit to the Crown.

Estates: Used of the various elements in the Scottish Parliament (sometimes summoned as a convention of estates): nobles, clergy, representatives of royal burghs and shires. In England sometimes used of lords spiritual, lords temporal and the Commons.

Eucharist: Holy communion.

Evangelical: Those (usually Protestants) who place more emphasis on the Bible and on preaching the Word than on worship.

Excise: A system (originated by the Dutch) for taxing goods produced and consumed within the realm, it became the mainstay of the eighteenth-century revenue.

Excommunication: Excluding a person from communion and so (in the Catholic Church and Church of England) depriving them of access to the means of salvation and cutting them off from the community.

Felony: A more serious crime, such as murder or robbery, often carrying the death penalty. Lesser crimes were misdemeanours.

Feoffees: Usually used of trustees.

Feu, feu farm: Practice in Scotland whereby the Crown, Church and other landowners granted land in perpetuity to tenants at enhanced rents. The landlords gained a large short-term increase in income, which was soon eroded by inflation and rents became worth less and less in real terms.

Fifteenth and tenth: A form of taxation introduced in England in the fourteenth century which was superseded under Henry VIII by the subsidy.

Fine: The landlords in Scottish Gaeldom: chiefs and leading gentry.

Forced loan: An exaction in which the king demands that his leading subjects lend him money and the details of repayments are often left vague.

Fosterage: The practice among Gaelic chiefs of sending their children to be raised in other families, in the hope of establishing good relations between them.

Franchise: An area where a person enjoys some exemption from the king's laws and the jurisdiction of his courts. The extent of liberties and franchises was curtailed by legislation in 1536. (Franchise can also mean the right to vote in elections.)

Freeholder: Someone who owns his land outright and is free to dispose of it as he chooses.

Free quarter: In which soldiers are quartered on civilians without any payment, other than promises.

Fundamental laws: In early seventeenth-century England, when the Crown's lawyers manipulated the letter of the law, a term coined to describe its underlying principles.

Galloglass: Foot soldiers with heavy swords or axes. (Ireland.)

Gathered church: A congregation formed through the voluntary association of true believers or 'visible saints'.

General Assembly: The governing body of the Scottish Kirk, it claimed authority over all of Scotland, although it often contained few or no members from North of the Tay. Suppressed by James VI and later Charles II, it was restored in 1638 and again in 1690.

General band: A device whereby Scottish nobles were made financially answerable for the misdeeds of their followers.

General Council of the Army: Established in June 1647 as the army organised in response to Parliament's attempts to disband it, this consisted of representatives of the officers, the rank and file and the general staff. It remained the army's major decision-making body until it was disbanded early in 1648.

Gentry: The more substantial landowners, wealthy enough not to need to work their land, and inferior in status to the nobility.

Gleaning: The traditional 'right' of the poor to pick up grains of corn for their own use after the harvest was finished.

Grandees: Pejorative term used by the Levellers and some soldiers of the army leadership in 1647–8.

Grand jury: A jury, supposedly consisting of freeholders, which made **presentments** to the quarter sessions of matters that needed to be rectified and considered, in criminal cases, whether the accused had a case to answer.

Heritable jurisdictions: In Scotland, rights of jurisdiction which were the property of landed families and could be passed on from father to son. Abolished temporarily in the 1650s and permanently after the 1745 rebellion.

Heritors: The better-off Scottish landowners.

Homily: Short sermons printed in the English Prayer Book for use by clergymen with limited talent for preaching. Favoured by Elizabeth and others who wished to control what was said in the pulpit.

Host: This could mean an armed force in which all Scottish adult males could be obliged to serve, or a consecrated wafer used in the Catholic mass.

Huguenot: A French Protestant.

Impeachment: A procedure whereby the Commons prosecuted a person accused of a criminal offence before the Lords, sitting as a court. In theory a means by which the Commons could remove unpopular ministers.

Impositions: Additional customs duties not voted by Parliament.

Impropriations: Tithes or other property belonging to the Church which have passed into the hands of laymen, often as a result of the dissolution of the monasteries.

Incidents: Feudal rights of the Crown used to raise money.

Indenture: A legally binding agreement between individuals, often (as in the case of masters and apprentices) setting out the obligations on both sides. Used by powerful men to bind members of their **affinity** to them.

Indentured servants: Poor men bound themselves by indentures to work for a master for a period of years in one of the plantations in America or the Caribbean. Also imposed on convicted felons as an alternative to the death penalty.

Influence of the Crown: The way in which kings, or rather their ministers, used the Crown's patronage to win support in elections and in Parliament.

Interlopers: Merchants who traded with English colonies in defiance of the Navigation Acts.

Isles, Lord of: An ancient title, abolished in the late fifteenth century, when it was held by the head of the Macdonalds.

Jacobite: A supporter of the exiled James II, his son or grandson.

Journeyman: A craftsman working for a master (literally paid by the day).

Jury: Used for a wide variety of purposes: in criminal trials, to enquire into rights of way and titles to land and in a wide range of investigations, including cases of sudden death.

Justice of the peace (JP):   The workhorse of local government and the criminal justice system, he was usually a member of the gentry and was unpaid: service in local government was a concomitant of status.

Keelmen: Workers in the rivers Tyne and Wear who carried coals in small boats to larger ships which carried them to London and elsewhere.

Kerne: Lightly armed horsemen, very effective in Irish warfare.

King's Evil; see also royal touch: The monarch was believed to be able to cure scrofula by touching or stroking the victim.

Kirk: Can mean either an individual parish church or the Church of Scotland.

Kirk session: The body, consisting of pastor, elders and deacons, responsible for parish government in Scotland.

Lairds: The equivalent of the gentry in England: lesser untitled landowners.

Lamb's war: The Quakers' use of shock tactics and confrontation to attract attention in the 1650s.

Laudian: A follower of Laud, emphasising worship rather than preaching and promoting 'the beauty of holiness'.

Lay patronage: The norm in the established churches in England and Ireland, but contentious in Scotland where the Covenanters claimed that ministers should be 'called' by their congregations, or by its senior members and the local heritors. Abolished in Scotland in 1638, restored at the Restoration, abolished again in 1689 but restored in 1712.

Lecturer: Similar to a 'reader' in the early Kirk: someone who read from the Bible (or, in England, read homilies) but did not preach.

Legate: An agent sent to act on the Pope's behalf.

Liberty: A place exempt from the jurisdiction of the Crown or other authority: similar to a franchise.

Reivers, reiving: From the Anglo-Scottish borders, used of those who stole livestock and goods.

Resumption, Acts of: Acts of Parliament to claw back royal grants, particularly of land, to make it easier for the king to 'live of his own'.

Retainers: Members of a powerful man's affinity (or retinue), often linked to him by an indenture and the payment of a fee (also known as a retainer).

Rood screen: Placed in a church between nave and chancel, this depicted Christ's crucifixion and the Day of Judgment, as a constant reminder to the congregation.

Royal touch: It was widely believed that kings could cure people suffering from scrofula (or the 'King's Evil') by touching them.

Sacramentary: Someone who denied transubstantiation.

Seculars: Opposite of regulars: clergy who were not members of a religious order.

Seekers: Term coined in the 1640s to describe those who could not find certainty in any of the gathered churches and moved from one to another; many eventually became Quakers.

Sept: A division or subaltern branch of a clan.

Serf: An unfree peasant, whose rent included labour services on his lord's demesne and who was unable to marry or leave his village without his lord's permission.

Servitors: English soldiers, lawyers and administrators, who sought to make their fortune and bring English 'civility' to Ireland.

Sheriff: Important figure in medieval English county government, responsible for serving writs, arresting suspects, selecting jurors and collecting moneys due to the Crown.

Ship Money: Well established in coastal areas as a way of procuring ships for defence against pirates, it was extended to inland areas under Charles I and became, in effect, a tax on land not granted by Parliament.

Shire: The usual Scottish term for county: the two terms were used more or less interchangeably in England.

Society People; see Cameronians

Socinians: Denied the divinity of Christ and therefore the Trinity. Later often known as Unitarians.

Sole right: In 1692 the Irish Parliament claimed (in defiance of Poynings' Law) that it had the sole right to introduce money bills, which the London government, in effect, conceded.

Star Chamber: A court consisting of the English Privy Council and several judges, it was used to deal with powerful men who might overawe local juries. It initially delivered quick, impartial and inexpensive justice to poorer litigants, but later it was used to uphold the king's interests and prerogatives, for example in promoting the draining of the fens and upholding the Crown's claim to control the press. Its simplified procedures and lack of juries now made it seem biased in the Crown's favour and it was abolished in 1641. (See also **Castle Chamber**.)

Livery: Basically means badge or uniform showing that the wearer is of a certain status or else in the service of a more powerful person: used in that sense in 'livery and maintenance'. Also used in cases of wardship, where the heir sues out his livery, and in guilds where the liverymen are the senior members. In Ireland 'coign and livery' meant the claim by chiefs that their peasants were obliged to give hospitality to their household and soldiers.

Lordship (of Ireland): After the twelfth century conquest English kings took the title Lord of Ireland. The first to claim to be King of Ireland was Henry VIII in 1541, in order to counter any challenge to his authority from the Pope.

Lords justices: In the absence of the lord lieutenant of Ireland, responsibility for government fell to a small group of senior officials, usually including the Lord Chancellor and Archbishop of Armagh. In the eighteenth century, as lords lieutenant normally came over to Ireland only every two years, for Parliament, the role of the lords justices became more important.

Lords of the Articles; see under Articles

Maleficium: The ability to cause physical harm by occult or magical means. Under the Witchcraft Act of 1563 this became a criminal offence.

Manor: A unit of land under the authority of a lord who usually owned part or all of the land and exercised jurisdiction over the inhabitants through a manorial court, over and above the obligations of those who were his tenants; the court also regulated open fields, common pasture, highways and ditches. Details of the various obligations were recorded on manorial rolls.

Manrent, Bond of: Formal agreements, between equals or between lord and man, based on service and payment in return for justice and protection; played an important part in bringing order to Scottish society in the fifteenth and sixteenth centuries.

March: Frontier or border area.

Martial law: The laws governing the army (set out in Articles of War). The English Petition of Right (1628) declared that it was illegal to use martial law against civilians, but this frequently happened in Ireland.

Militia: A civilian force, officered by members of the gentry headed by the lord lieutenant, usually a peer. Its training and military equipment were generally said to be of poor quality.

Millenarian: The belief, of which there were several versions, based on the book of Revelation, that after a thousand years those who had suffered for their faith would be brought back to life or their souls would be saved. It encouraged some radicals to seek to establish Christ's rule on earth.

Misdemeanour: A lesser criminal offence which could not carry the death penalty. See also **felony**.

Nave: The part of the church furthest from the altar, in which the people sat.

Navigation Acts: A series of Acts, starting in 1651, designed to exclude the Dutch from carrying goods to and from English ports and to give English traders a monopoly of trade with English colonies.

Nightwalker: A person (particularly a young woman) found in the streets at night without a good reason.

Obit: Records of those who have died so that their souls can be prayed for.

Occasional Conformity: Occasional attendance at public worship, used particularly of Dissenters who took communion in an Anglican church in order to qualify for office under the 1673 **Test Act**.

Old English: Catholics of English descent in Ireland.

Old Protestants: Used in Ireland from the 1650s of Protestants whose families had settled there before 1641.

Orangist: A supporter of the Princes of Orange in their struggle to increase their power within the Dutch Republic.

Orders, Books of: Detailed instructions to Justices of the Peace on the proper enforcement of a range of social and economic legislation, particularly relating to the poor.

Ordinary and extraordinary revenue: Ordinary revenue was enjoyed by the Crown as of right or granted to a monarch for life. Extraordinary revenue was granted for a limited period for a specific purpose, often war.

Overseers of the poor: Parish officials concerned with the collection and management of the poor rate.

Own (king living of his own):   The belief, found in both England and Scotland, that the king should normally subsist on his own resources, such as lands and feudal rights, plus some grants from Parliament, such as customs duties; he should seek other grants from Parliament only in an emergency.

Oyer and terminer: A commission to an individual or group to hear and determine certain cases, often issued after riots or rebellions.

Palatinate: A particularly extensive liberty or franchise, such as County Durham.

Pale: The area of Ireland under more or less effective English control.

Patent: A document conferring authority to perform a particular task or service and sometimes to levy money to pay for it. Monopolies were usually granted by patent.

Patronymic: A surname meaning 'son of'.

Peers: Noblemen with the right to be summoned to the House of Lords; more generally 'equals', as in a jury of one's peers.

Petition of Right: A document approved by Parliament in 1628 which claimed, not entirely accurately, to re-state the law on a number of points on which Charles I was seen as exceeding his lawful authority. Charles agreed to the Petition, but with the fixed intention of not being bound by it.

Petty sessions: Meetings of the Justices of the Peace for a division of a county to deal with lesser business; developed when the county quarter sessions, which dealt with more serious business, became over-burdened.

Plantation: A colony established in an area seen by the colonisers as backward and in need of improvement (and a potential source of profit).

Popular: Used pejoratively, particularly by James I and Charles I, of people who tried to win support among the people in order to undermine duly constituted authority.

Poynings' Law: Passed by the English Parliament in 1494, this stated that only bills approved by the English Privy Council could be considered by the Irish Parliament. Substantially weakened by the Irish Parliament's claim to the 'sole right'.

Praemunire: A fourteenth-century statute, which forbade Church courts to encroach on the jurisdiction of the King's courts.

Predestination: The belief, at the heart of Calvinist theology, that God had determined since the beginning of time who should be saved and who damned.

Prelates, prelacy: Bishops and government of the Church by bishops.

Prerogative: The reserve power which the king possessed over and above his specific powers, to be invoked in an emergency if the national interest required it. As some of the king's acknowledged powers came to be challenged (such as his power to call and dismiss Parliament at will), 'prerogative' was used of the specific powers as well.

Presbytery: A meeting of pastors and elders from several parishes, similar to a classis.

Presentment: A list of grievances or matters that needed to be rectified, drawn up by a jury, particularly a grand jury.

Pretender: Literally a claimant, particularly a (false) claimant to the throne. After James II's death (1701) it was used of his son and grandson.

Primitive Church: The early Church as recorded in the New Testament.

Primogeniture: Inheritance by the oldest son.

Privateer: A licensed pirate.

Proprietary [colonies]:   Those where the Crown granted the right to found a colony to a particular individual or individuals.

Provost marshal: An officer in the militia or army charged with training and particularly discipline; at times, used to police or discipline civilians, particularly the unruly and vagrant poor (and, in Ireland, the Irish).

Purgatory: An intermediate state between heaven and hell in which the souls of the dead were cleansed.

Puritan: Impossible to define precisely, this was used as a term of abuse against zealous Protestants who valued the preaching of the Word above worship and were intolerant of frivolous, rowdy or promiscuous pastimes; particularly concerned to keep the Sabbath undefiled by work, games or self-indulgence.

Rapparees: Catholic Irish bandits; see also **Tories**.

Recusant, recusancy: Literally a refuser: used of Catholics who refused to attend Protestant parish churches.

Regulars: Catholic priests who belonged to a religious order; these included monks and friars, but also the Jesuits.

Strangers: The usual word for foreigners ('foreigner' meant someone from another town or region).

Subsidy: A new land tax introduced under Henry VIII to replace the outmoded assessments of the fourteenth century (see **fifteenth and tenth**).

Surnames: The nearest English approximation to clans, found in a few dales on the Anglo-Scottish border. Notorious for reiving, they were subjugated under Elizabeth.

Surplice: A white gown which Church of England clergymen were required to wear; much disliked by Puritans.

Surrender and regrant: A device designed to bring Gaelic Irish lords under royal control. They would surrender their lands to the king, who would grant them back with proper English legal title but also certain restrictions on their behaviour. The device ultimately failed because neither party was fully committed to making it work.

Tanist, tanistry: In an effort to avoid a disputed succession to the head of an Irish clan the chief sometimes designated a successor (tanist) in his lifetime, but his wishes were not necessarily followed on his death.

Teinds: Tithes in Scotland.

Tenant in chief: In feudalism someone who held land directly from the king.

Tenant right: In the North of England, the practice whereby a son would normally inherit his father's tenancy; this made for a continuity of mutual loyalty between lord and tenant.

Tenure: The terms under which one person held land of another.

Test Acts: In England, the Act of 1673 required all office-holders to make a declaration against transubstantiation and take communion in an Anglican church: the former excluded Catholics, the latter could exclude conscientious Dissenters. The 1678 Act excluded Catholics from Parliament, which in practice meant the House of Lords. The Scottish Test Act of 1681 imposed a series of requirements which restricted access to office, voting in parliamentary elections, etc., to strong monarchists and Episcopalians. In Ireland, an Act of 1704 aimed mainly at Catholics imposed a sacramental test on all office holders, which excluded Presbyterians.

Tithe: A levy of one tenth of the produce of farmers to pay the stipend of the parish priest or minister.

Tories: Irish Catholic bandits. The term was extended in England, as a term of abuse, to strong Anglicans who opposed the exclusion from the throne of James, Duke of York.

Transportation.   In the late seventeenth and early eighteenth centuries more and more convicted felons were transported, usually as indentured servants, to America and the Caribbean, as an alternative to the death penalty.

Transubstantiation: The Catholic belief that, in the Mass, the bread and wine were physically transformed into the body and blood of Christ.

Triennial Act: The original Scottish Act, requiring the king to call a Parliament at least once every three years, was largely replicated in England in 1641. This Act had received the royal assent, so remained in force at the Restoration, but was undermined by a similar Act of 1664 which lacked effective means for its implementation. A very different Act was passed in 1694, by which time parliaments were meeting annually; this required the king to dissolve each Parliament within three years, to ensure regular general elections.

Triers: Appointed by an ordinance of 1654 to check the qualifications of parish ministers: see also **ejectors**.

Uses: Trusts designed to avoid liability to feudal incidents such as wardship.

Vestry: A form of parish council, sometimes elected by a wide spectrum of parishioners, sometimes selected by co-option.

Vicegerent: Someone appointed to act on behalf of the king or another person in authority.

Villein: Similar to serf.

Wampum: Cowrie shells much valued by Amerindians and used as a medium of exchange.

Wardship: A device whereby the king was obliged to act as a guardian for the sons of tenants in chief whose fathers had died before they came of age. Usually the king sold the guardianship to the young man's family.

Warming pan: It was widely claimed that James II's son, born in 1688, was not his son at all, but a 'suppositious' child smuggled into the Queen's bedchamber in a warming pan, which was filled with coals and used to warm the bed. This seems improbable: many courtiers, including some Protestants, were present to observe the birth and one wonders why a warming pan would be needed in June. It was later used as a symbol of the Old Pretender and the Jacobite cause.

Westminster Confession: Confession of faith drawn up by the Westminster Assembly of Divines (which met from 1642). It became the approved Confession of the Covenanters.

Whiggamore: A radical Covenanter, like those who seized power through the Whiggamore raid of 1648. The word derives from 'Whiggam', a cry used by carters to gee up their horses. The shorter form, Whig, was coined, as an insult, in 1679–80, to describe the supporters of exclusion.

Yeoman: A substantial working farmer, producing a significant marketable surplus: noticeably better off than a husbandman. The wealthiest accumulated land by purchase or renting and eventually became minor gentry.

Index

(S) indicates Scotland, (I) indicates Ireland